f 37·So

ESSAYS ON THE ECONOMIC HISTORY
OF THE ARGENTINE REPUBLIC

ESSAYS ON THE
ECONOMIC HISTORY
OF THE ARGENTINE REPUBLIC

BY CARLOS F. DÍAZ ALEJANDRO

New Haven and London, Yale University Press, 1970

218727

Designed by Sally Sullivan,
set in Linotype Times Roman type,
and printed in the United States of America by
The Colonial Press Inc., Clinton, Mass.

Distributed in Great Britain, Europe, and Africa by
Yale University Press, Ltd., London; in Canada by
McGill-Queen's University Press, Montreal; in Mexico
by Centro Interamericano de Libros Académicos,
Mexico City; in Australasia by Australia and New
Zealand Book Co., Pty., Ltd., Artarmon, New South
Wales; in India by UBS Publishers' Distributors Pvt.,
Ltd., Delhi; in Japan by John Weatherhill, Inc., Tokyo.

Para Mongui

¡Tierras son ésas de donde salieron, a la voz de San Martín, unos puñados de hombres, a cruzar los Andes, postrar a ejército cuantioso y redimir a Chile; y los cruzaron, los postraron y lo redimieron en veinticuatro días!

¡Campañas haga iguales en la industria Buenos Aires, dignas de aquellas maravillosas y centáuricas que dieron apariencia de dioses a los hombres!

Todo lo alcanzará Buenos Aires, que a tiempo supo exponerse a morir, por ser dueña de sí, y ahora sabe vivir cuerdamente, rica en ardientes corazones y en mentes fértiles.

José Martí, writing in *La América*,
New York, June 1883.

Contents

Foreword

This volume is one in a series of studies supported by the Economic Growth Center, an activity of the Yale Department of Economics since 1961. The Center is a research organization with worldwide activities and interests. Its research interests are defined in terms of both method of approach and subject matter. In terms of method, the Center sponsors studies which are designed to test significant general hypotheses concerning the problem of economic growth and which draw on quantitative information from national economic accounts and other sources. In terms of subject matter, the Center's research interests include theoretical analysis of economic structure and growth, quantitative analysis of a national economy as an integral whole, comparative cross-sectional studies using data from a number of countries, and efforts to improve the techniques of national economic measurement. The research program includes field investigation of recent economic growth in twenty-five developing countries of Asia, Africa, and Latin America.

The Center administers, jointly with the Department of Economics, the Yale training program in International and Foreign Economic Administration. It presents a regular series of seminar and workshop meetings and includes among its publications both book-length studies and journal reprints by staff members, the latter circulated as Center Papers.

Gustav Ranis, Director

Preface

This book reflects my vacillations between an early intention to write a survey of Argentine economic history and later doubts about the sanity of such a project, which eventually led me to concentrate on a few topics. The title of the volume is meant to caution the reader against expecting a complete and unified discussion of the many complexities and puzzles that have characterized economic life on the Río de la Plata since the sixteenth century. These essays, in fact, say little about the period before 1862 and give only scanty, and somewhat superficial, attention to several interesting post-1862 developments. Perhaps the most glaring omission is the lack of a thorough exploration of the public sector labyrinth and of a description of its historical expansion. Public enterprises, the armed forces, health, education, and other public and private services are treated only cursorily.

Even to an economist untrained in other social sciences, the influence of political, social, and psychological factors on the evolution of the Argentine economy is striking. I have tried to take some of those noneconomic forces into account, but my respect for the principle of comparative advantage has limited these excursions to the extent that some may find them too few and timid. The interplay between economic and noneconomic factors and their joint influence on Argentine development has been viewed in the following light. The major goals of most politically active elements in Argentina, as in other Latin American countries, are rapid and efficient economic growth, greater political and economic autonomy, and a more even distribution of income, wealth, and political power among families and regions of the country. These goals have strong roots, and although some of the historical circumstances that influenced their adoption are discussed in the essays, no effort is made to analyze them in depth. Whether, for example, nationalism is or is not a "good thing" is not discussed; but, because nationalism has often motivated the adoption of certain economic policies, its presence has to be recognized and the trade-offs between nationalistic and other targets have to be mentioned. The failure to reach a national consensus on priorities regarding the different goals has been at the root of the political turmoil that has plagued Argentina since 1930. Typically (exaggerated partisan claims notwithstanding), policies aimed at obtaining one goal hamper the efforts to reach others. For example, policies aimed at decreasing regional concentration may reduce economic growth, which may also suffer from measures aimed at increasing national autonomy. The difficult task of striking an acceptable balance among those goals and designing policies which efficiently obtain the desired mix requires not only a government backed by competent technicians, but also one that has the respect and confidence of the majority of the population.

It has been assumed that social and political factors and anticipated relative costs determined the importance given to different goals in each period. The decision as to importance, in turn, influenced economic variables operating through public policy. In other words, noneconomic factors are taken into account, albeit scantily, not because they are supposed somehow to make the behavior of Argentine economic agents very different from the rest of the world's, but because they have influenced decisions on public economic policy. In short, the essays follow economic methodology and emphasize quantifiable economic variables and their relationships.

The first two essays summarize the main trends in the Argentine economy since about 1860. The two following look in greater detail at the rural and manufacturing sectors. Finally, the last three discuss more specific topics that I found interesting: the pre-1940 tariff, the evolution of relative prices for capital goods, and postwar inflation and stop-go cycles. Although the essays share some common themes, they are not completely integrated. For example, in organizing presentation I have used different time periods, depending on the subject matter. The systematic study of Latin American economic history is a relatively new discipline, and this book mainly represents a survey of researchable areas rather than definitive economic history. More detailed future investigations no doubt will modify many generalizations and assertions put forth here.

Friends looking at early drafts of this study have complained that it makes pre-Perón Argentina look much too rosy, while being unduly critical of Perón's performance. The book seems "reactionary." Perhaps that impression arises from my attempt to heed the warning of historians that the past should not be judged by the criteria of the present. Furthermore, while it may be comforting to blame postwar difficulties either on the machinations of foreigners or on old oligarchs, I doubt that lasting social reforms can be promoted while spreading incomplete or distorted notions of the past or that such reforms need be accompanied by inefficient economic policies. Bizarre (and slightly paranoid) notions about economic history have helped to generate many exotic policies that have neither accelerated growth nor brought Argentina closer to realizing her social and political goals. Admiration for the pre-Perón Argentine economic mechanism does not mean that I do not share with my friendly critics a distaste for many aspects of the social and political climate found then in Argentina. But it would be silly to deny on those grounds the many economic and social achievements realized during those years. Greater emphasis on social reform, especially during the prosperous pre-1930 years, and more attention to the needs of the rural masses would have reduced postwar Argentine economic and political difficulties. However, postwar public policy still had many choices open to it, and its mistakes also should be blamed for worsening Argentine performance. Note the case of Uruguay, a country in many ways similar to Argentina, where, in spite of early social reforms, postwar economic and political developments have been on the whole unfavorable. Social reform, at least in mixed societies, unless accompanied by efficient economic policies, is extremely fragile. On the other hand, blaming all recent troubles on a regime deposed back in 1955 seems as sensible as blaming foreigners and oligarchs for those difficulties.

Argentines do not need foreign scholars to tell them about their past. Yet if this book, written mainly to satisfy my curiosity about the economy of their country, helps to give Argentine youth an outsider's view of their nation's economic history which they find stimulating, I would be very pleased. Other great Latin nations have gone through long periods of stagnation and social conflict; it is to be hoped that, like them, Argentina, led by its youth and forgetting past sterile feuds, will resume a leading role not only in an increasingly united Latin America but also in world affairs. In spite of its many troubles, Argentine society shows signs of great creativity and vitality, perhaps best exemplified by its dazzling array of internationally famous writers. At a time when many despair of the long-run feasibility of an autonomous and prosperous Latin America, what happens in traditionally independent and relatively wealthy Argentina is of critical importance for all the nations south of the Río Grande.

Three institutions have been especially helpful throughout the preparation of the essays. Yale University's Economic Growth Center has sponsored the work patiently and gracefully. The Centro de Investigaciones Económicas of the Di Tella Institute in Buenos Aires has overwhelmed me with kindness since September 1963. And the University of Minnesota provided me with a stimulating and enjoyable haven where this work was completed.

I have worked, off and on, for so many years on this project that I cannot hope to give adequate credit to all the individuals who have helped me with their ideas and comments. Simon Kuznets and Alberto Fracchia have been especially helpful. I am also indebted to the following for lengthy written comments on all or part of earlier drafts of this book: A. Berry, N. Butlin, M. Corden, J. M. Dagnino-Pastore, A. Diz, A. Domike, D. Felix, T. Halperín, L. Jarvis, C. P. Kindleberger, N. Leff, R. Mallon, G. Ranis, L. Reca, T. Scitovsky, H. Schwartz, and V. Tokman.

My work has greatly benefited from the published and unpublished research done at the United Nations Economic Commission for Latin America, and I am grateful to this organization for its help during my trips to Santiago. Mr. L. Rojas, in particular, made available to me much unpublished material on the Argentine economy.

For many useful conversations I am especially grateful to O. Altimir, A. Ferrer, C. Furtado, B. Hopenhayn, E. Malaccorto, F. Pazos, R. Ruggles, J. Sourrouille, and J. Villanueva. Comments from M. Brodersohn, H. Diéguez, G. Helleiner, M. Mamalakis, L. Reynolds, and V. Ruttan are also gratefully acknowledged. Miss Lola Frederickson went gracefully beyond the call of duty in typing and editing many drafts of this book, with the aid of Miss Donna Brand.

Final revisions of the essays were accomplished while I held grants from the John Simon Guggenheim Memorial Foundation and the Social Science Research Council. The last major revision was completed in August 1968. Since then, only stylistic changes have been incorporated in the manuscript.

During the long and painful process of going through galleys and page proofs, as well as indexing, Miss Mary Downey provided invaluable and cheerful help. The jacket illustration and frontispiece are the work of my brother, José Ramón Díaz Alejandro; to him, *Stupor Mundi,* this volume is dedicated.

New Haven, Connecticut   C. F. D. A.
July 1970

Abbreviations

BCRA   Banco Central de la República Argentina. When used alone as a source citation, this refers to BCRA's *Origen del Producto y Composición del Gasto Nacional, Suplemento del Boletín Estadístico* no. 6 (Buenos Aires, June 1966).

CONADE   Consejo Nacional de Desarrollo. When used alone as a source citation, this refers to Presidencia de la Nación, CONADE, *Cuentas Nacionales de la República Argentina* (Resumen de los resultados provisionales de la primera parte del Programa de Investigación CONADE-CEPAL sobre Distribución del Ingreso en la República Argentina) (Buenos Aires, April 1964).

ECLA   United Nations Economic Commission for Latin America. When used alone as a source citation, this refers to the mimeographed Statistical Appendix to the ECLA study published as *El Desarrollo Económico de la Argentina,* 3 vols. (Mexico, 1959). The mimeographed appendix bears the identification E/CN.12/429/Add.4.

GDP   Gross Domestic Product

GNP   Gross National Product

O.S.   Poder Ejecutivo Nacional, Secretaría de Asuntos Económicos, *Producto e Ingreso del la República Argentina en el Período 1935–54* (Buenos Aires, 1955).

1

The Argentine Economy before 1930

It is common nowadays to lump the Argentine economy in the same category with the economies of other Latin American nations. Some opinion even puts it among such less developed nations as India and Nigeria. Yet, most economists writing during the first three decades of this century would have placed Argentina among the most advanced countries—with Western Europe, the United States, Canada, and Australia.[1] To have called Argentina "underdeveloped" in the sense that word has today would have been considered laughable. Not only was per capita income high, but its growth was also one of the highest in the world.

Melancholy as it may be to dwell on old splendors when the present is uninspiring, the task of examining the past for clues about recent difficulties is indispensable in the Argentine case. This essay will review the main features of the pre-1930 economy not only because of its intrinsic interest, but also with this end in mind. It will be important to see whether Argentina had begun to slip and lose its relative position vis-á-vis the most advanced nations before 1930, or whether that came later. The essay will conclude with a

1. As early as 1895, according to Michael G. Mulhall, the Argentine per capita income was about the same as those of Germany, Holland, and Belgium, and higher than those of Austria, Spain, Italy, Switzerland, Sweden, and Norway. On the other hand, Argentina's per capita figure (£24) was below those for Canada (£36), the United States (£44), and Australia (£51). Michael G. Mulhall, *Industries and Wealth of Nations* (London, New York, and Bombay: Longmans, Green, and Co., 1896), p. 391. I am grateful to Simon Kuznets for calling my attention to this reference. By 1860, Canada, the United States, and Australia had accumulated a larger stock of human and physical capital than Argentina (in per capita terms). During 1810–60 Argentine growth was hampered not only by political unrest and a declining market for leather, but also by the policies of the Rosas regime, overthrown in 1852, which frowned on foreign influences on Argentine life. Per capita GNP in 1860 may be placed at around $200 (at 1964 prices).

review of the main strengths and weaknesses of the economy as it stood in 1929.

It is a difficult and arbitrary task to break into the flow of economic history. I shall take as my starting point the period around 1860 when, after more than fifty years of political turmoil and civil wars following the May Revolution of 1810 against Spain, the Argentine ruling classes responded vigorously to the growth opportunities created by European industrialization and technological advances in transportation.

THE QUANTITATIVE RECORD OF GROWTH

From 1860 to 1930 Argentina grew at a rate that has few parallels in economic history, perhaps comparable only to the performance during the same years of other countries of recent settlement. The expansion was most remarkable up until the outbreak of World

Table 1.1: Indicators of Economic Growth in Argentina before 1930

| | | | | Annual growth rates (percentages) | |
| | Annual averages | | | 1865–69/ 1910–14 | 1910–14/ 1925–29 |
	1865–69	1910–14	1925–29		
Length of railroad tracks (kilometers)	503	31,104	38,435	15.4	1.4
Population (thousands)	1,709	7,271	10,970	3.3	2.8
Merchandise exports (million gold pesos)	29.6	431.1	–	6.1	–
Merchandise imports (million gold pesos)	38.0	410.0	–	5.4	–
Area sown with crops (million hectares)	0.58[a]	20.62	25.18	8.3	1.3
Index of quantum of merchandise exports	–	100.0	176.6	–	3.9
Index of quantum of merchandise imports	–	100.0	143.6	–	2.4

Note: Preliminary revisions of official export statistics, carried out by a group of Argentine economic historians, yield a growth rate in the gold value of exports of 5.6 percent per annum between 1865–67 and 1910–14.
[a] Refers to 1872.

Sources: Ernesto Tornquist and Co., *The Economic Development of the Argentine Republic in the Last Fifty Years* (Buenos Aires, 1919), pp. 26, 116–17, 139–40. U.N., *Análisis y Proyecciones del Desarrollo Económico: V, El Desarrollo Económico de la Argentina* (México, 1959), 1:110.

War I; the fifty years before 1914 in Argentina witnessed one of the
highest growth rates in the world for such a prolonged period of
time. Unfortunately, no aggregate measures of economic activity are
available before 1900; Table 1.1 summarizes data that can be taken
only as indicators of growth.

Rural output and exports expanded *pari passu* with the railroad
network, while the immigration of labor and capital provided other
required inputs. It may be guessed that real GDP grew at an average
annual rate of at least 5 percent during the fifty years preceding the
outbreak of World War I. Between 1869 and 1914, population grew
at an average annual rate of 3.4 percent.

A key element in this growth was the export of rural goods. The
data of Table 1.1, which present the goods' value in gold pesos, do
not shed light on the evolution of the export quantum.[2] Estimates of
that quantum are presented in Table 1.2, which includes items that,
during 1910–14, accounted for 88 percent of the value of merchandise
exports. The method used was to take time series on the weight of
different exports and to multiply them by their unit value during
1910–14. The total of the items listed yields a growth rate of 5.2
percent from 1875–79 until 1910–14; the actual value of exports
during the same years grew by 6.6 percent. The method and data
are too rough to warrant detailed discussion; it is enough to conclude
that both the quantum and the value of exports expanded between
1875 and 1914 at a high rate of at least 5 percent per annum.[3] The

2. The value of the gold peso with respect to the pound sterling and the
gold dollar was, with minor changes, steady during most of the period under
study. The gold peso was roughly at par with the gold dollar and exchanged at
five gold pesos per pound sterling.

3. Taken at face value, the estimate for the export quantum implies an
increase in the average unit value for Argentine exports, in terms of gold,
between 1875–79 and 1910–14 of about 57 percent, which is not in harmony
with other evidence regarding world price movements during those years.
Indices for unit values of British imports from "areas of recent settlement"
show a 30 percent drop from 1872 to 1900 and an increase of only 13 percent
between 1900 and 1913. Indices of import unit value for industrial Europe
(from "areas of recent settlement") show a fall of 33 percent between 1872
and 1900, and an increase of only 16 percent for 1900 to 1913. See Charles
P. Kindleberger, *The Terms of Trade: A European Case Study* (Cambridge:
M.I.T. Press, 1965), pp. 34 and 50. Changes in freight rates could account
for part of the differences in the estimates. The presumption that Table 1.2
underestimates the growth in the export quantum is strengthened by the fact
that the physical weight used as the basis for calculation does not take into
account increases in the value added to rural produce by export industries
during 1875–1914.

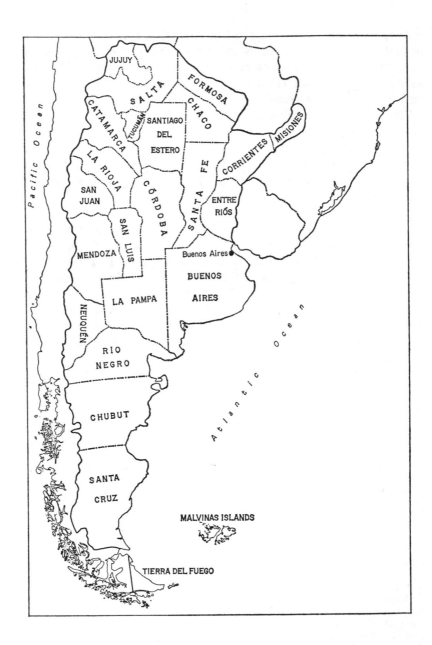

Provinces of Argentina

Table 1.2: Estimates of Quantum of Exports, 1875–1914
(Annual averages, in million gold pesos at 1910–14 prices)

	1875–79	1880–84	1890–94	1900–04	1910–14
Wool	34.1	41.3	52.7	66.7	51.9
All hides	24.6	22.5	35.6	35.6	44.0
Salted and jerked meat	5.3	3.6	6.6	2.8	1.1
Chilled and frozen					
mutton and lamb	0	0	3.5	9.7	8.9
Frozen beef	0	0	0.1	10.6	49.7
Chilled beef	0	0	0	0	4.3
Canned meat	0	0	0.6	0.5	3.0
Wheat	0.2	1.2	28.1	55.1	78.1
Corn	0.3	1.3	6.0	34.4	72.4
Linseed	0	1.2	3.6	32.2	41.0
Oats, barley, and rye	0	a	a	0.5	14.6
Quebracho extract	0	0	a	0.7	4.9
Quebracho logs	0	0	0.7	3.3	5.0
Total of items listed	64.5	71.1	137.5	252.1	378.9

a Values less than 0.1 million.

Sources: Data on the weight of the different export items from Tornquist, *Economic Development*, pp. 30–31, 167–72; Comité Nacional de Geografía, *Anuario Geográfico Argentino* (Buenos Aires, 1941), pp. 267, 273–74, 312.

economy was propelled throughout the nineteenth century by the introduction and vigorous expansion of new exports; as the growth rate of old lines slackened, new products with high growth rates entered the export list. After 1840, wool exports gave a stimulus that hides, jerked meat, and tallow could no longer provide.[4] Between 1880 and 1900, grain exports rose from practically nothing to several millions of tons; after 1900, chilled and frozen beef exports became significant and rose very rapidly.

Data on aggregate and sectorial output, starting in 1900, show rapid growth until World War I and slower growth between 1914 and 1929, as shown in Table 1.3. The sectorial growth rates indicate that the dynamism arising from exports of rural origin and the capital inflow associated with it, spread out to other sectors of the economy. In particular, meat-packing plants and other industrial establishments using rural goods as their main inputs gave an important boost to

4. See Comité Nacional de Geografía, *Anuario Geográfico Argentino* (Buenos Aires, 1941), p. 274. Exports of jerked meat were destined primarily for slave consumption in Brazil and the West Indies. (Some authors have claimed that the seeds of the tango were brought to the Río de la Plata by ships returning from delivering jerked beef to Cuba.)

Table 1.3: Real Rates of Growth of Global and Sectorial Value Added
in Argentina, 1900–04/1925–29
(Annual averages in percentages)

	1900–04/1910–14	*1910–14/1925–29*
GDP, at factor cost	6.3	3.5
Agriculture, livestock, and fisheries	3.4	3.6
Mining	11.5	5.7
Manufacturing	7.7	4.4
Construction	11.6	0
Services	6.8	3.7

Note: Basic data are expressed at 1950 prices. The source gives the following annual growth rates between 1900–04 and 1925–29: GDP, 4.6 percent; gross domestic income (taking into account terms of trade effects), 4.7 percent.

Source: ECLA, p. 4.

manufacturing. It may be conjectured that the pattern of sectorial growth before 1900 was not very different from that of 1900–14, perhaps the main difference being a slightly higher growth rate for the rural sector.[5]

Capital stock data confirm the rapid growth of the economy during the first fourteen years of this century, and its slower growth between 1914 and 1929. These data, summarized in Table 1.4, also dramatize the degree to which the economy was oriented in 1900 toward the export of rural produce. The capital stock of railroads, built primarily to facilitate exports, and of the rural sector accounted for nearly one-half of the total. A substantial part of capital in industry and services, furthermore, represented activities involved with the export sector. Even without much information for 1865–1900, it is clear that net investment resulted in a fast increase in capital and was concentrated in the rural sector, including improvements of land and cattle stocks, in social overhead capital surrounding export activities (railroads, harbors, etc.), and in housing and other urban facilities (streets, municipal services, etc.) required to accommodate the inflow of immigrants.

5. As suggested before, it is almost certain that the growth of the export quantum during 1865–1914 was higher than the growth in rural exportable output. The difference would be explained by increases in the proportion of value added to exportable products by manufacturing (for example, meat-packing plants, flour mills, wool washing, etc.). Changes in the share of domestic consumption of exportable goods were not very important during these years. Regarding the growth of the rural sector, it should be borne in mind that while new activities witnessed phenomenal growth, other established lines, such as wool, grew slowly and actually declined after 1900.

Table 1.4: Allocation and Growth of the Capital Stock in Argentina, 1900–29

I. *Allocation* (percentages of the total)

	Allocation in 1900	Allocation of the net increase between 1900 and 1914	Allocation of the net increase between 1914 and 1929	Allocation in 1929
Agriculture, livestock, and fisheries	28.3	13.2	24.6	20.3
Industry (manufacturing, mining, and construction)	8.4	13.2	14.4	12.3
Electricity, communications, and other public utilities	0.9	2.1	4.8	2.6
Railroads	17.5	16.4	−5.9	10.4
Other transportation	0.3	0.8	11.1	3.6
Housing	33.5	37.8	30.6	34.7
Government services	8.6	13.7	9.7	11.2
Other services	2.5	2.8	10.7	4.9
Total	100.0	100.0	100.0	100.0

II. *Growth Rates* (annual averages in percentages)

	1900/1914	*1914/1929*
Total capital stock	7.6	2.2
Agriculture, livestock, and fisheries	4.4	2.8
Industry	10.0	2.7
Services	8.3	2.0

Source: ECLA, pp. 91–107.

Although the social overhead capital built before 1930 was not without some large gaps, as in paved roads and storage for grain in the countryside, it created facilities available to all types of activities, whether or not directly connected with foreign trade. The pre-1930 export-led growth built the bases on which a gradual diversification of production could take place.

Estimated labor supply data for 1900–29, which are rough, are shown in Table 1.5. (Between 1914 and 1947 there was not a single general population census.) A high proportion of the labor force was engaged in manufacturing activities, a fact partly explained by the inclusion under manufacturing of railroad repair shops and satellite construction industries. In other respects, the pattern of labor allocation during 1900–04 was what could be expected from the orientation of the economy toward rural exports and from its income level. As

Table 1.5: Allocation and Growth of the Labor Supply in Argentina, 1900–29

I. *Allocation* (percentages of the total)

	Allocation in 1900–04	Allocation of the net increase between 1900–04/1910–14	Allocation of the net increase between 1910–14/1925–29	Allocation in 1925–29
Agriculture, livestock, and fisheries	39.2	25.0	40.0	35.9
Manufacturing	19.8	22.1	21.1	20.8
Mining	0.2	0.3	0.2	0.2
Construction	4.5	11.9	−1.3	4.7
Electricity and communications	0.8	1.1	2.1	1.2
Transport	4.6	7.3	3.9	5.1
Government services	3.6	5.3	7.5	5.2
Other services	27.3	27.0	26.4	27.0
Total	100.0	100.0	100.0	100.0

II. *Growth Rates* (annual averages in percentages)

	1900–04/1910–14	1910–14/1925–29
Population	4.3	2.8
Total labor supply	4.4	2.2
Agriculture, livestock, and fisheries	3.0	2.6
Industry	5.8	1.7
Services	4.8	2.4

Source: ECLA, p. 400. Figures for labor supply between census dates were obtained by interpolation.

with physical capital, the expansion of the labor force under export-led growth established the basis for a future expansion of other activities by creating, especially in urban centers, a large pool of skilled and semiskilled employees and workers that could be tapped easily by industrial newcomers.

Information on the quantity and quality of inputs does not warrant a detailed "anatomy" of pre-1930 growth, but it may be noted that the two classic inputs, physical capital and unadjusted labor, "explain" most of the 1900–29 growth taken as a whole. Total output grew at 4.6 percent per annum, while physical capital and labor grew at 4.8 percent and 3.1 percent, respectively. If the contribution of capital is given a weight between one-half and one-third, and that of labor between one-half and two-thirds, the unexplained "residual" would be limited to between 14 and 20 percent of the growth rate. This "residual" could be explained by the expansion of education and economies of scale.[6]

The expansion of 1862–1930 was interrupted from time to time by depressions; major setbacks occurred in 1875–76, 1890–91 (the Baring Crisis), and 1914–17. These cycles were initiated by factors exogenous to the domestic economy, such as droughts, changes in world commodity markets, and fluctuations in foreign investment. At the same time, in a manner typical of export economies, exogenous shocks were aggravated by induced changes in domestic investment and liquidity. The government sector, following the ideas of those years, did little deliberately to control the cycles.

Pre-1930 Argentine experience fits the broad outlines of the staple theory of trade and growth.[7] Although national accounts data for the nineteenth century are lacking, it appears that growth then was related closely to successive booms in the exports of land-intensive commodities, with land having a very low opportunity cost. The economic usefulness of pampean land was not discovered overnight, as in the case of an oil deposit, but arose as a result of a combination of growing European needs for primary goods, technological progress in transport, and an increasing interest by Argentine policy makers in promoting exports, foreign investment, and immigration. By the beginning of the twentieth century, however, the Argentine growth rate had become less dependent on the discovery of new resource-

6. Land under cultivation grew at an annual rate of 4.4 percent between 1900–04 and 1925–29, so that the residual could not be expected to be much greater if land is introduced as a third classical input. Simon Kuznets has pointed out to me that Canadian and United States experience also suggests that rapid quantum growth of labor and capital will not be accompanied by large residuals. If Argentine data on capital and labor are divided into subperiods during 1900–29, a less clear situation emerges. According to the source used for Tables 1.4 and 1.5, the aggregate capital-labor ratio during 1920–29, although higher than that for 1900–09, was lower than the one reached during 1910–19. Heavy investments in social overhead capital before World War I partly explains this curious peaking. Note also that total manhours worked grew less than the labor force during 1900–29.

7. See Melville H. Watkins, "A Staple Theory of Economic Growth," *Canadian Journal of Economics and Political Science* 29 (May, 1963): 141–58; and Richard E. Caves, "Vent for Surplus Models of Trade and Growth," in *Trade, Growth and the Balance of Payments; Essays in Honor of Gottfried Haberler* (Chicago: Rand McNally and Co., 1965), pp. 95–115. However, the gap between average labor productivity in the resource-based industry and the rest of the economy were not as wide in Argentina as in countries relying on mineral exports, facilitating a faster approach to a neoclassical economy.

based export commodities and on the performance of any one export. It still relied heavily on steady expansion of exports, resulting from the growth of the world economy and from completion of the process of adjustment by which primary production was being transferred from Europe to countries of recent settlement. By 1900–30, however,

Table 1.6: Structure of the GDP of Argentina, 1900–29
(in percentage of total)

	At 1950 prices			At 1937 prices		
	1900–04	*1910–14*	*1925–29*	*1900–04*	*1910–14*	*1925–29*
Agriculture	15.8	14.8	14.9	19.6	18.8	19.1
Livestock	17.2	10.2	10.6	18.4	13.6	11.7
Fisheries	0.2	0.2	0.2	0.1	0.1	0.1
Subtotal:						
Rural	*33.3*	*25.2*	*25.7*	*38.1*	*32.5*	*30.9*
Mining	0.2	0.3	0.4	0.3	0.4	0.6
Manufacturing	13.8	15.6	17.7	9.9	11.5	13.2
Construction	6.6	10.8	6.5	2.7	4.6	2.8
Subtotal:						
Industry	*20.6*	*26.7*	*24.6*	*12.9*	*16.5*	*16.5*
Commerce	19.0	21.7	21.3	13.9	16.4	16.1
Transport	3.7	5.6	7.2	4.0	6.2	8.1
Communications	0.3	0.5	0.7	0.4	0.6	1.0
Other public utilities	0.2	0.4	0.7	0.4	0.8	1.3
Housing	6.8	5.6	4.8	13.1	11.2	9.5
Finance	1.5	1.7	2.0	1.4	1.6	2.0
Personal services	9.1	7.4	7.5	9.0	7.5	7.7
Government services	5.5	5.3	5.5	6.7	6.6	7.0
Subtotal:						
Services	*46.1*	*48.1*	*49.7*	*49.0*	*51.0*	*52.6*

Sources and method: Data in 1950 prices from ECLA, p. 4. Indices of output from the same source were converted to 1937 prices by using data on the national accounts for 1937, at current prices, found in O.S., pp. 112–13. Data for the transport and housing sectors from ECLA worksheets. Data on the national accounts before 1935 are rough.

export-based growth was beginning to account for variations in the overall growth rate more than for its average level.[8]

8. See regressions 2.1 and 2.2 in essay 2. In the equation for 1905–40, percentage changes in the export quantum explain half of the variance in annual growth rates of domestic product. However, the constant term in the equation is 2.1 percent, or about two-thirds of the annual growth rate for

Pre-1930 growth can be said to have been "export-led," not because exports and their associated capital inflows provided growing aggregate demand (in a Keynesian fashion), but because, more fundamentally, exports and capital inflows led to an allocation of resources far more efficient than the one which would have resulted from autarkic policies. In particular, the domestic cost of capital goods, which would have been astronomical under autarky, say, in 1880, was reduced to a low level by exports of commodities produced by the generous use of an input—land—whose economic value under autarky would have been quite small. As the Argentine economy expanded and diversified, wide disparities in opportunity costs under different foreign trade policies began to decrease, but remained— and will continue to remain—substantial so long as world trade is relatively free and transport costs low.

THE STRUCTURE OF THE ECONOMY BEFORE 1930

Table 1.6 presents the contribution of various sectors to gross domestic product. Available time series are expressed at 1950 prices, which, because of the drastic changes occurring in Argentine relative prices since 1930, give a misleading impression of the pre-1930 structure of production. Unfortunately, the earliest year for which "implicit" sectorial prices are available is 1935. The prices for 1937 have been chosen as an alternative base to 1950, as they come closest to the price structure that existed before 1930.[9]

The crude correction for changes in relative prices shown in Table 1.6 and other fragmentary information on prices indicate that if the share of the rural sector in total value added could have been measured at current prices during 1900–29, it would have moved from around 40 percent at the beginning of the century to slightly more than 30 percent in 1925–29. Industry, including construction, would probably have fluctuated within the 10–15 percent range,

those years (3.2 percent). See also Caves, "Vent for Surplus Models," p. 102, where he proposes a model combining neoclassical and export-based growth processes that provides a more accurate view of 1900–30 Argentina than either process in isolation.

9. Between 1929 and 1935 the index of the ratio of rural to nonrural wholesale prices fell from 149.1 to 95.7 (with 1939 = 100). In 1937 this index stood at 126.1, the highest level for 1935–39. These figures suggest that national accounts expressed in 1929 prices would give an even larger share to the rural sector, and a smaller share to industry, than those expressed in 1937 prices.

leaving the service sector to account for half of the GDP.[10] These figures, incidentally, illustrate the importance of taking into account differences in relative prices when making either inter-country or inter-temporal comparisons.

Further insight into the pre-1930 economy may be gained by considering the average labor productivity in various sectors and the gaps existing among them. A relative scale of those productivities, measured using 1937 prices, is given in Table 1.7. The range is not

Table 1.7: Average Labor Productivity in Argentina, by Sectors, 1910–29
(Relative to overall average labor productivity)

	1910–14	1925–29
Total (excluding value added in housing)	100	100
Rural sector (agriculture, livestock, and fisheries)	107	95
Nonrural sector	96	103
Manufacturing	63	70
Mining	212	280
Construction	72	65
Transport	127	175
Communications and other public utilities	175	210
Commerce and finance	146	145
Personal services	63	65
Government services	178	149

Sources: Productivity data measured at 1937 prices. Data on GDP implicit 1937 prices obtained as in Table 1.6. Data on labor force from ECLA, p. 400. Value added in housing is excluded from total value added, as no data on the labor force in providing housing services are available. It should be recalled that data on labor are deemed to be rough.

unusually high. In contrast with typical dualistic underdeveloped countries, the Argentine rural sector showed a higher average productivity than did manufacturing; if the nonrural sector is taken as a whole, insignificant differences in productivities appear between rural and nonrural activities. Nonrural workers may have had a higher

10. When value added for each sector is estimated at 1937 prices, the GDP growth rate resulting from their summation is lower than that estimated at 1950 prices. The contrast is as follows: 1900–04/1910–14: 6.0 percent (at 1937 prices) and 6.3 percent (at 1950 prices); 1910–14/1925–29: 3.4 percent (at 1937 prices) and 3.5 percent (at 1950 prices). If one continues measuring in 1937 prices, the *net increase* in GDP between 1900–04 and 1925–29 was generated in the following manner—27 percent from increases in rural output, 15 percent from manufacturing, 4 percent from mining and construction, and the rest from services.

capital stock to work with, but rural workers had the fertile pampean land as a complementary factor.[11] Although these figures do not necessarily prove much about the integration of the domestic market, or whether factors of production received similar marginal returns in different sectors, they suggest an absence of the duality that characterizes most underdeveloped countries.

A better understanding of the integration of the economy before 1930 may be gained by a sketch of the main intersectorial flows and relationships. Four main sectors may be distinguished—the rural sector (agriculture and livestock), industry, which could be stretched to include not only mining, manufacturing, and construction, but also electricity, communications, and other public utilities, "modern services" such as transport, finance, and commerce, and other services, including government and personal services. The rural sector was the "mother industry" in the terminology of those days. Its producers handed their marketable output mainly to railroads which took their products to coastal cities, either for direct shipment abroad or for further processing by industry. The latter in turn would ship part of their output abroad or would sell it for domestic consumption. Of the total value of rural production, it may be estimated that one-fourth was exported after substantial further processing by domestic industry (meat, flour, etc.), another fourth was exported with negligible processing (corn, oats, etc.), and one-half was consumed domestically, either in situ or after being transported to, and processed in, consuming centers within Argentina. Although exports represented almost exclusively goods of rural origin, they embodied value added by industry and modern services.[12] Subsistence agriculture

11. Manufacturing then included not only handicrafts but also activities not usually associated with modern industry. On the other hand, rural activities included non-pampean agriculture, some of which was relatively backward. The low average productivity figures for manufacturing suggest that the relative weight of the backward subgroups was smaller in rural activities than in manufacturing. Estimates made by ECLA show that while the capital-labor ratio in the rural sector was lower than the average for the whole economy, it was higher than that for industry throughout 1900–30. These estimates are given in 1950 prices. See ECLA, pp. 393 and 400.

12. According to the 1953 input-output table, when exports were still mainly goods of rural origin, the total value of exports was made up as follows— value added by the rural sector, 31 percent; value added by food processing manufacturing, 25 percent; value added by transport, commerce and communications, 33 percent; value added by other sectors, 11 percent. See BCRA, *Transacciones Intersectoriales de la Economía Argentina* (Buenos Aires, April 1964), p. 35. The composition of the value of exports before 1930 was

declined rapidly, especially after the middle of the nineteenth century; by 1925–29 only a few pockets remained, principally in the north-western region. Rural activities in the pampean zone, which accounted for more than three-fourths of the value of rural production in 1925–29, were as market-oriented as those in the United States or Canada.[13]

The ships and railroads taking rural products abroad or to Argentine urban centers returned to the rural sector a flow of intermediate and final manufactured goods and services produced abroad and domestically. These return flows are likely to have had two characteristics: (1) they used up less foreign exchange (including factor payments abroad) than that generated by rural output, and (2) they had a smaller value than the outgoing flow. The first characteristic resulted in a pool of exchange used by the urban sector to finance its imports from abroad, while the second implied that at least part of those imports were financed by a capital inflow into the urban sector from the rural sector.

These comments are highly speculative, as little information exists on intersectorial real or financial flows, even for recent years. Furthermore, the high degree of modernization achieved by the economy even in the nineteenth century suggests that these flows were quite complex.

Information on pre-1930 international trade is helpful in obtaining a more accurate picture of the economy. Table 1.8 presents the

Table 1.8: Ratio of Merchandise Imports C.I.F. to GDP at Factor Cost
(Expressed as percentages; variables at 1937 prices)

1900–04	23.1
1910–14	26.2
1925–29	22.6

Sources and method: Quantum series obtained from *Análisis y Proyecciones*, 1:110. Method used to estimate coefficients at 1937 prices as in Table 1.6.

average merchandise import coefficient, measured at 1937 prices.

---

probably similar, although the greater weight of grain exports then may have reduced the share of value added by food processing. The great importance of forward linkages in rural production is evident from these figures.

13. As a first approximation, the pampean zone may be identified with the provinces of Buenos Aires, Santa Fe, La Pampa, Córdoba, and Entre Ríos. See U.N., *Análisis y Proyecciones del Desarrollo Económico: V, El Desarrollo Económico de la Argentina* (México, 1959), 2:46 for a more precise definition of this zone.

For 1900–29 imports amounted to about one-fourth of the GDP. Toward the end of this period, the import coefficient was not very different from what it had been at the start.

The structure of merchandise imports is given by Table 1.9.

Table 1.9: Structure of Merchandise Imports according to Uses
(Percentages of all merchandise imports)

	1900–04	1910–14	1925–29
Consumer goods	38.7	36.7	37.1
Nondurable	36.6	31.8	26.0
Durable	2.1	4.9	11.1
(Automobiles)	(–)	(1.1)	(6.3)
(Other)	(2.1)	(3.8)	(4.8)
Intermediate products and raw materials	37.2	32.6	30.8
Fuel and lubricants	3.1	5.1	4.7
Metallic products	7.6	6.2	5.9
Other	26.5	21.3	20.2
Capital goods	21.0	29.9	31.8
Construction materials	6.6	10.8	10.2
Rural machinery and equipment	1.6	2.3	4.9
Industrial machinery and equipment	12.1	14.2	13.3
Transport and communications machinery and equipment	0.7	2.6	3.4
Miscellaneous	3.1	0.6	0.4

Sources: Data from ECLA, p. 110. Basic data are expressed in pesos at 1950 prices.

Finished consumer goods represented nearly two-fifths of all imports throughout 1900–29; the arrival of the automobile offset the shrinkage shown by the share of nondurable consumer goods. Besides automobiles, other important items under this category were tropical foodstuffs and textiles. In general, high quality items for private consumption, except beef and a few other foodstuffs, were imported. Nevertheless, a substantial share of consumption of goods such as nontropical foodstuffs, wine, beer, and low quality textiles were produced locally. In contrast, practically all machinery and equipment were imported; as shown in Table 1.9, they accounted for between 14 and 21 percent of the import bill during 1900–29 and showed a tendency to rise. Including construction materials, imports of capital goods represented 22 percent of all gross fixed investment in 1900–04, 20 percent in 1910–14, and 24 percent in 1925–29. Imports of intermediate products and raw materials, whose share showed a tendency to decline, included items primarily destined for consumption and construction such as textiles, wood, unprocessed agricultural products (coffee, cocoa beans, and similar products), paper, and cardboard.

The structure of imports according to industrial origins during 1928–29 is presented in Table 1.10. Comparable data for earlier

Table 1.10: Structure of Merchandise Imports according
to Industrial Origins, 1928–29
(Percentages of all merchandise imports)

Foodstuffs	10.5
Tobacco and its manufactures	1.6
Beverages	1.3
Textiles and its manufactures	25.4
Chemicals, pharmaceutical products, and paints	4.6
Paper, cardboard and its manufactures	2.6
Wood and its manufactures	5.2
Iron and its manufactures	9.1
Machinery and vehicles	16.2
Other metals and its manufactures	3.3
Stone, earth, glass, and ceramics	3.8
Fuels and lubricants	9.2
Rubber and its products	1.4
Other	5.8

Source: Dirección General de Estadística de la Nación, *Anuario del Comercio Exterior de la República Argentina, Correspondiente a 1940* (Buenos Aires, 1941), p. 44. Percentages obtained from data in current prices.

years are not available, but the pattern shown, in which textiles and iron and steel dominate, is typical of the whole pre-1930 period. These two items, in different stages of processing, accounted for roughly one-half to two-thirds of the import bill. Other important items were goods that with the resource endowment of Argentina could hardly be produced domestically. These include tropical products, coal, and even wood and sand for construction.[14]

The high propensity to import manufactures no doubt decreased potential backward linkages arising from the export sector and the investment in social overhead capital. The Argentine farm machinery and other metallurgical industries, for example, did not profit from export expansion and railroad building as much as those in the United States, Australia, and Canada. Yet for the whole period

14. The pampean zone was devoid of hardwood trees when the Spanish arrived. As in the Great Plains of the United States, this created serious difficulties for settlers. Lack of stones made matters worse.

1860–1930 the Argentine growth rate did not suffer noticeably from this relative weakness of backward linkages. It may even have benefited from greater specialization along lines of comparative advantage, in contrast with Australia during that period. In pre-1930 Argentina it is doubtful that maximization of backward linkages from the export sector was the most efficient economic policy. (See essays 4 and 5 for further discussion.)

The characterization of exports as composed mainly of goods originating in the rural sector may be misleading. It suggests that Argentina can be lumped with countries depending on the export of a few commodities of unstable value. Argentine exports before 1930 were quite diversified, as may be seen in Table 1.11. That practically all of the commodities originated in the rural sector and often were sent abroad with slight domestic processing is less important than the fact that the variety of exported goods helped to decrease fluctuations in foreign exchange earnings.[15] Furthermore, the export picture during 1860–1930 was a highly dynamic one, not only because the overall value was expanding fast, but also because important changes took place in its structure, responding to changing European needs and technological advances. Before 1860, exports were primarily made up of hides and skins, tallow, jerked beef, and wool. In 1837, two-thirds of the value of exports from the harbor of Buenos Aires were made up of hides, 9 percent of jerked beef, and 7 percent of wool.[16] Wool exports expanded rapidly beginning in 1840 when less than 2,000 tons were exported, reaching 66,000 tons in 1870, and 237,000 tons in 1899.[17] By 1875–79, wool accounted for about half

15. Among other things the stability advantage of diversifying exports will be greater the greater the *negative* correlation between the prices of each pair of commodities. This point is made and elaborated in W. C. Brainard and R. N. Cooper, "Uncertainty in International Trade: A Guide to Diversification for Primary Producing Countries," mimeographed (New Haven: Yale University, 1965), pp. 21–22. In the same paper the following correlation coefficients between world prices are given (for 1951–63)—beef and wheat, −0.53; beef and wool, −0.86; beef and butter, −0.15; corn and wheat, +0.48; wheat and wool, +0.54; beef and hides, −0.04. These figures suggest that Argentine diversification, for 1951–63 at least, has been helpful in decreasing one source of instability in exchange earnings.

16. Horacio C. E. Giberti, *El Desarrollo Agrario Argentino* (Eudeba, Editorial Universitaria de Buenos Aires, 1964), pp. 16–17.

17. Ibid., pp. 18–19. Wool was one of the first commodities to become prominent in European imports from countries of recent settlement. Regarding wool, Australia had a definite advantage over Argentina. I am grateful to Noel G. Butlin for calling my attention to these and other points regarding Europe's demand for primary goods, and supply responses outside Argentina.

Table 1.11: Structure of Argentine Merchandise Exports before 1930
(Percentages of total)

	1893–94	*1900–04*	*1910–14*	*1925–29*
Live animals	5.8	2.3	2.0	0.9
Meat: chilled beef	0	0	0.6	7.5
frozen beef	0.1	3.9	7.6	3.3
frozen mutton	2.0	2.7	1.3	1.6
jerked beef	4.5	1.1	0.3	0.2
other	—[a]	–	–	2.8
Hides and skins	16.9	11.2	11.0	8.1
Wool	27.7	22.0	12.9	8.2
Dairy products: butter	nil	0.7	0.3	1.7
other	–	–	–	0.4
Cattle by-products: tallow	2.7	2.1	2.5	1.6
other	–	–	–	1.1
Wheat	25.9	20.7	19.4	22.2
Corn	1.3	14.4	17.9	18.5
Linseed	3.3	9.5	10.2	12.2
Other cereals	–	–	–	3.0
Wheat flour and its by-products	1.5	2.5	2.6	2.1
Oilseeds and their oils (excluding linseed)	–	–	–	0.3
Fresh fruits	nil	nil	nil	0.1
Cotton	0	nil	nil	0.5
Quebracho and its products	0.8	1.8	2.4	2.2
Sugar	nil	1.0	0.3	0.2
Products from mining, fishing, and hunting	0.9	0.5	0.5	0.1
All others	–	–	–	1.2

[a] Dash indicates data not available in the precise categories used for 1925–29.

Sources: Basic data (all expressed at current prices) from the following: *Anuario de la Dirección General de Estadística, Correspondiente a 1894* (Buenos Aires, 1895), pp. 136–71; República Argentina, *Anuario de la Dirección General de Estadístiea, 1905* (Buenos Aires, 1906): 289–336; *Anuario de la Dirección General de Estadística, Correspondiente al Año 1914* (Buenos Aires, 1915), pp. 750–59; República Argentina, *Anuario del Comercio Exterior, Año 1927* (Buenos Aires, 1929), pp. 501–74; República Argentina, *Anuario del Comercio Exterior, Años 1928 y 1929* (Buenos Aires, 1931), pp. 568–640.

the value of exports. Europe's growing food needs, plus the expansion of Argentina's railroad network, resulted in a rapid rise in grain exports after 1880. During that year crops represented less than 2 percent of all exports (Argentina being an importer of wheat and flour before 1870). During 1880–84 annual averages of 34,000 tons of wheat and 56,000 tons of corn were exported, and by 1895–

99 exports of wheat and corn reached annual averages of 801,000 and 910,000 tons, respectively. As shown in Table 1.11, wheat, flour, corn, and linseed represented about one-third of all exports during 1893–94. By 1900–04 they reached nearly one-half. Argentine landowners, whose interests were mainly pastoral, showed more flexibility than those of Australia in taking advantage, with the help of immigrant tenants, of favorable circumstances in world grain markets.

As rising per capita incomes in Europe induced mass consumption of meat, new opportunities appeared. The arrival of the refrigerated ship allowed Argentina to service this expanding market. Frozen mutton began to be shipped to England in the 1880s; small amounts of frozen beef were sent abroad during the early 1890s; and chilled beef began to be exported shortly before World War I. Exports of other types of meat lost ground and by 1925–29 frozen and chilled beef, which in 1893–94 represented an insignificant fraction of all exports, accounted for more than 10 percent. By this time, the commodities that had dominated exports in 1870 (wool, hides, tallow, and jerked beef) accounted for only 18 percent. The outlook was clouded in 1925–29 by the growth of rural protectionism in industrialized countries and by economic difficulties in Europe. But new export lines showed promise (cotton, butter, fruits) and there was hope new markets would appear for beef (especially the United States). For several decades Argentina had shown a remarkable capacity and flexibility in responding favorably to new trade opportunities, many of which could not have been predicted ex ante. So long as the industrialized countries were able to maintain their growth rates and their commitment to relatively free trade, export prospects were far from gloomy, even if pre-World War I halcyon days could not have been expected to return. The bursts of new exports that occurred in the nineteenth century were not likely to be repeated but steady export gains, arising from growth in the world economy and completion of the transfer of primary production from the exhausted European soils to countries of recent settlement, could have been expected, assuming European and North American statesmen behaved sensibly.

The geographical pattern of trade before 1930, shown in Table 1.12, indicates that Argentina took full advantage of free convertibility. Unfortunately, before 1927, about one-fourth of exports were shipped abroad "for orders," the final destination of which cannot be established easily. The data shown, however, are sufficient to

Table 1.12: Geographical Pattern of Trade of Argentina before 1930
(Percentages)

Merchandise Imports	1910–14	1925–29
	100.0	100.0
United Kingdom	31.2	19.6
Germany	16.8	11.5
United States	14.4	24.6
France	9.4	6.9
Italy	8.5	8.7
Belgium	5.2	4.8
Spain	3.1	2.5
Brazil	2.5	4.4
Peru	0.1	2.1
Netherlands	0.9	1.3
Other	7.9	13.6

Merchandise Exports	1927–29
	100.0
United Kingdom	29.6
Germany	13.5
Netherlands	10.6
Belgium	9.9
United States	8.8
France	6.6
Italy	6.4
Brazil	3.8
Other	10.8

Sources and method: As in Table 1.11.

demonstrate the high degree of geographical diversification of Argentine trade. The information for the late 1920s also shows a trade pattern, which, although of little interest in a world of convertibility, became a source of difficulty during the following three decades. This pattern consisted of a surplus with Western Europe and a growing deficit with the United States. The rise of the United States as the leading industrial country, while remaining a major producer of temperate-zone foodstuffs and fibers, coupled with the growth of bilateralism, has presented Argentina with serious headaches since 1930.

In the case of some important exports there was a marked dependence on one or a few markets. In 1929 the United Kingdom absorbed more than 99 percent of all exports of chilled beef, 91 percent of frozen mutton, 85 percent of butter, and 54 percent of frozen beef. Other products showed a more diversified pattern; the two main markets for hides and skins were the United States (44 percent of Argentine exports) and Germany (21 percent). For wool, wheat, corn, and linseed the diversification was even greater; the three top markets for each of these products and their share in Argentine exports in 1929 were as follows:

Wool.—Germany (23 percent), United Kingdom (18 percent), and Belgium (17 percent).

Wheat.—United Kingdom (34 percent), Belgium (14 percent), and Netherlands (11 percent).

Corn.—Belgium (16 percent), Italy (11 percent), and France (10 percent).

Linseed.—United States (35 percent), Netherlands (23 percent), and United Kingdom (10 percent).

On the side of imports, Argentina benefited from the keen competition among industrial countries for a share in its prosperous market.[18]

FACTOR MARKETS

Argentine markets, for most goods as well as factors, may be considered as part of the well-integrated, pre-1930 world markets. The free flow in most goods and factors existing then between Argentina and the rest of the world, in fact, often makes it difficult to separate the Argentine from rest-of-the-world markets.

The labor market

Before 1930 Argentina could be said to have faced a labor supply schedule made up of two segments: the first one, consisting of most of the labor force already in the country, was probably fairly inelastic with respect to the real wage rate; the second one, applicable for needs slightly below and beyond the labor force already in the country, was more elastic and, as a simplification, could be said to have been perfectly elastic at the going real wage rate (plus some differential) in the industrial centers of Italy and Spain, the main

---

18. Data on 1929 geographical distribution of exports and imports obtained from República Argentina, *Anuario del Comercio Exterior, Años 1928 y 1929* (Buenos Aires, 1931), pp. 567–640. The popularity of U.S. automobiles explains a good part of the increase in the U.S. share in the Argentine import bill between 1910–14 and 1925–29. Agricultural machinery also loomed large in Argentine imports from the U.S.

sources of emigration to Argentina. During most years, the economy operated in the elastic range as immigrants poured into the country.

Although this description of the labor market is an idealized simplification neglecting expectations, cultural factors, etc., its basic accuracy is supported by migration data. Labor flows were very sensitive to changing business conditions in Argentina and reversed themselves quickly. For example, during the "Barings" downturn of 1889–91 a *net immigration* of 220,000 persons in 1889 dropped to 30,000 in 1890 and turned into a *net emigration* of 30,000 in 1891. In spite of European hostilities, the depression of 1914–17 was accompanied by a change from net immigration of 145,000 in 1913 to an average yearly net emigration of 19,000 during 1914–19.[19] Furthermore, the integration of the Argentine labor market with those of Europe, especially of Italy and Spain, was so tight that European workers would cross the Atlantic just to participate in Argentine harvests, returning abroad after completing the task. This fact may help to explain the high figures for gross emigration even in years with high net immigration.[20] During 1910–13, while gross entry of immigrants coming in second and third class (excluding those from Uruguay) reached 1.14 million, gross emigration via second and third class (excluding those going to Uruguay), was nearly half a million. It has been estimated that during 1900–10, a yearly average of 100,000 seasonal workers entered and left Argentina within a year; in the previous decade the average had been half that amount.[21]

19. Data obtained from Ernesto Tornquist and Co., *The Economic Development of the Argentine Republic in the Last Fifty Years* (Buenos Aires, 1919), p. 15; and República Argentina, Dirección Nacional de Estadística y Censos (hereafter DNEC), *Informe Demográfico de la República Argentina, 1944–1954* (Buenos Aires, 1956), p. 28. The former source excludes first-class passengers; the latter includes all passengers. Some of the emigration during 1914–19 resulted from the drafting by Italy of some of her residents in Argentina.

20. This statement has to be worded weakly because in the United States, where seasonal migration does not seem to have been very important, gross emigration also reached high levels. During 1908–15, gross emigration amounted to 30 percent of gross immigration into the United States. See "Immigration and the Foreign Born," by Simon Kuznets and Ernest Rubin, Occasional Paper 46, National Bureau of Economic Research, Inc., 1954, p. 28.

21. See James R. Scobie, *Revolution on the Pampas: A Social History of Argentine Wheat, 1860–1910* (Austin: University of Texas Press, 1964), pp. 60–61. Argentine official immigration statistics show an average yearly gross emigration of 55,200 during 1890–1899, 94,600 during 1900–09, and 188,900 during 1910–14. These figures refer to all second- and third-class overseas passengers, including those going to Montevideo. Referring to these migrant

With this fluidity, it is not unreasonable to suppose that the labor supply was highly elastic to changes in real wages during most years.

The importance of immigration in the expansion of the labor supply can hardly be exaggerated. As shown in Table 1.13, between 1857

Table 1.13: Net Immigration into Argentina from Overseas 1857–1930
(Thousand persons for the period indicated)

	Non-Argentines using second and third class overseas transport	*All persons using overseas transportation in all classes*
1857–60	11.1	12.7
1861–70	76.6	80.5
1871–80	85.1	90.7
1881–90	637.7	648.7
1891–1900	319.9	337.8
1901–10	1,120.2	1,134.3
1911–20	269.1	280.0
1921–30	856.0	905.8
Total 1857–1930	*3,375.7*	*3,490.5*

Source: Anuario Geográfico, p. 186.

and 1930 there was a net immigration of about 3.5 million into a country whose total population was 1.7 million in 1869.[22] With no immigration, and an assumed growth of 2 percent per year, population would have grown from 1.7 million in 1869 to 5.7 million in 1929; instead the population in 1929 was 11.6 million, or nearly 10 million more than in 1869. According to this rough calculation, 60 percent of the population growth during 1869–1929 can be credited to the decision to allow net immigration.[23]

---

workers, Scobie states: "Four to five months' labor in the wheat-corn harvest could bring him from forty to fifty pounds sterling—five to ten times what he could earn in his homeland—and this represented a net profit to take back to Italy or Spain in May" (pp. 60–61). The harvest in the pampean zone also attracted migrant workers from the less developed parts of Argentina (mainly from the northwest).

22. These figures include only the net immigration arising from overseas transportation; it therefore excludes overland migration between Argentina and neighboring countries. According to the 1914 census, there were 207,000 persons born in Bolivia, Brazil, Chile, Paraguay, and Uruguay living in Argentina; for 1895 the corresponding figure was 116,000 and for 1869, 41,000. Data obtained from DNEC, *Informe Demográfico*, p. 37.

23. For 1910–13 the Argentine birth rate was 38.2 (per thousand) and the death rate was 17.5; for 1925–29 the corresponding figures were 29.9 for the birth rate and 13.0 for the death rate. Data obtained from Sociedad Rural

Table 1.14 shows the link which existed between the Argentine labor market and those of Italy and Spain. Of the 6.3 million overseas

Table 1.14: Structure of Gross Overseas Immigration by Nationality
(Including only second and third class passengers; percentages of total)

	1857–80	1881–1900	1901–10	1911–30	1857–1930
Italians	63.1	61.7	45.1	33.9	45.7
Spaniards	16.0	19.5	37.0	38.0	31.8
French	9.6	8.0	1.9	1.5	3.7
Germans	1.2	1.5	1.1	3.2	2.1
Poles	0	0	0	5.0	2.1
Russians	0.2	1.5	4.8	2.6	2.8
Other	9.9	7.8	10.1	15.8	11.8
Total	100.0	100.0	100.0	100.0	100.0
Total in thousand persons	440.5	1,489.0	1,764.1	2,602.3	6,296.3

Source: Anuario Geográfico, p. 185.

immigrants who came to Argentina during 1857–1930,[24] 46 percent were Italians and 32 percent were Spaniards; the Italian share tended to decline during these years, while that for Spain and Eastern Europe tended to increase.[25] The Argentine share in the migratory flows of non-Latin peoples was small, compared with those of the United States, Australia, and Canada.[26]

The influence of immigration on Argentine life, of course, goes beyond its effect on the labor market. Culturally and socially, the immigration of 1857–1930 practically created a different country.

Argentina, *Anuario de la Sociedad Rural Argentina* (Buenos Aires, 1928), p. 62; and DNEC, *Informe Demográfico*, p. 14. The Argentine birth rate has shown a declining secular trend since 1869.

24. The figures refer to *gross* immigration.

25. A slight majority of Italian immigrants before 1914 came from the north of Italy. From 1876 to 1900, 63 percent of Italian immigrants came from that region; the share fell to 49 percent during 1901–13. This contrasts with Italian migration to the United States, in which the southern Italian share was larger. See Scobie, *Revolution on the Pampas*, pp. 29–30. Scobie obtained these figures from official Italian sources.

26. The cultural differentiation of migratory flows was probably accompanied by some real wage differentials. But the existence of people, such as the Italians, who migrated to both the United States and Argentina suggests that, at the margin, the real wage received by new immigrants was approximately the same in New York City and Buenos Aires in 1900–14. It may be of some interest to construct a model for these years explaining the choice of new homeland by European immigrants.

Table 1.15 presents the weight of the foreign born in several classifications of total population. The high point of foreign participation was

Table 1.15: Foreign Born as Percentages of Total Population
and of Other Categories

Foreign born in:	*1869*	*1895*	*1914*	*1930*
Total population	12.1	25.4	30.3	23.4[b]
All males	16.9	30.5	35.7	–
All females	7.1	19.8	24.2	–
Federal district	49.2	52.0	50.5	–
Males of Federal district	–[a]	–	55.7	–
Pampean provinces	–	–	30.3	–
Non-pampean provinces	–	–	14.4	–
Ages 14 and younger	–	8.0	7.1	–
Ages 15 to 64	–	37.5	42.6	–
Ages 65 and older	–	33.4	51.1	–

[a] Dash indicates data not available.
[b] Estimate by Gino Germani (see below).

Sources: República Argentina, *Censo de la Nación*, for 1869, 1895, 1914, 1947, and 1960. Also Gino Germani, *Estructura Social de la Argentina* (Buenos Aires: Editorial Raigal, 1955), pp. 23, 81, and 84; *Anuario Geográfico*, p. 162; Tornquist, *Economic Development*, p. 9; Dirección Nacional de Estadística y Censos, *Informe Demográfico de la República Argentina, 1944–1954* (Buenos Aires, 1956), pp. 29–37.

probably 1914, when native Argentines outnumbered foreign-born residents by only little more than two to one. In the Federal District the foreign born were as numerous as native Argentines, and among males in that city the foreign born were in the majority.[27]

Table 1.15 indicates that the foreign born made up a greater percentage of the permanent Argentinian labor force than of the total population of the nation. The percentage of males between the ages

27. For a detailed study of population and migration statistics, and the impact of immigration on the social fabric of Argentina see Gino Germani, *Estructura Social de la Argentina* (Buenos Aires: Editorial Raigal, 1955), and Gino Germani, *Política y Sociedad en una Epoca de Transición* (Buenos Aires: Editorial Paidós, 1962). Germani estimates that among adult males (twenty years and older) in the Federal District, a fantastic 80 percent were foreign born as early as 1869; 81 percent were foreign born in 1895 and 77 percent were foreign born in 1914. See *Política y Sociedad,* pp. 187–88, 199. Germani's thesis is that in Argentina massive immigration implied the virtual disappearance in the urban centers and in the pampean zone of the preimmigration native social type and native social structure. The *relative* importance of immigration was far greater for Argentina than for the United States, where the highest ratio of foreign born to total population reached only 14.4 percent (in 1890 and 1910).

of 20 and 60 in the total population rose from 22.5 percent in 1869 to 25.3 percent in 1895 and to 26.5 percent in 1914. As shown in Table 1.16, the participation of persons aged between 15 and 60

Table 1.16: Distribution of Population in Argentina by Ages
(Percentages of total)

	1869	1895	1914
Less than 5 years	18.1	17.9	17.4
5 to 14 years	25.9	24.4	23.0
Under 15 years	44.0	42.3	40.4
15 to 19 years	10.9	10.0	11.0
20 to 29 years	18.6	18.3	20.0
30 to 39 years	11.9	13.8	12.6
15 to 39 years	41.4	42.1	43.6
40 to 49 years	7.1	8.3	7.8
50 to 59 years	3.8	4.2	4.8
40 to 59 years	10.9	12.5	12.6
15 to 59 years	52.3	54.6	56.2
Over 59 years	2.5	2.5	3.3
Unknown	–	0.5	0.1

Source: Adapted from data found in *Anuario Geográfico*, p. 161.

in the total population rose from 52.3 percent in 1869 to 54.6 percent in 1895 and to 56.2 percent in 1914.[28]

Immigration was accompanied by a drastic change in the population distribution over the Argentine territory. Urban centers (those having a population of at least 2,000 inhabitants), which in 1869 accounted for only 28 percent of the population, saw their share increase to 37 percent in 1895 and to 53 percent in 1914.[29] By 1914, nearly 30 percent of the population lived in three cities of at least

28. In 1914, 87 percent of the foreign born living in Argentina were between the ages of 15 and 65; and for every foreign-born female there were 1.71 foreign-born males. See Germani, *Política y Sociedad,* pp. 188–89. In the provinces of Buenos Aires, Entre Ríos, and Santa Fe, there were 122 males to 100 females around 1896, according to Mulhall—a fact that helps explain some of the lamentations of the tango. The foreign born, according to Germani, accounted for 47 percent of the labor force in 1914. Their participation was 37 percent of labor in primary production, 53 percent of labor in secondary activities, and half of the labor in tertiary activities.

29. In the five pampean provinces plus the Federal District, 62 percent of the population lived in urban centers during 1914. Argentine urbanization was lower than that of Australia, but higher than that of Canada at that time, and comparable to that of several industrialized regions of Western Europe.

100,000 inhabitants (Greater Buenos Aires, Córdoba, and Rosario). Greater Buenos Aires plus the four large pampean provinces (Buenos Aires, Santa Fe, Entre Ríos, and Córdoba) included 54 percent of the population in 1869, 67 percent in 1895, and 73 percent in 1914. Just the province of Buenos Aires plus the Federal District, which in 1869 accounted for 29 percent of the population, included by 1914 46 percent of the total population. The provinces of the northwest, which during Spanish rule were the richest and most populated regions of Argentina (Catamarca, Tucumán, Santiago del Estero, La Rioja, Salta, and Jujuy), saw their share drop from 29 percent in 1869 to less than 13 percent in 1914.

During the second half of last century, then, most of the Argentine labor market quickly became integrated and capitalistic, in the sense that workers were hired and fired primarily on economic grounds, and labor was able to move freely within and in and out of the country.[30] Furthermore, in spite of some cyclical unemployment, for 1860–1930 as a whole Argentina can be characterized as a full-employment economy in which temporary unemployment had a relatively simple cure: going back to the home country or to other labor-poor countries such as the United States. (When Argentine depressions coincided with those in the rest of the world, however, solutions were not that simple.) Another difference between the Argentine labor market and those of typical underdeveloped countries may be noted. While in the latter labor is supposed to flow secularly from the rural areas into cities, in Argentina the opposite was the case before 1930. Immigrants landed mainly in the city of Buenos Aires, from where some went, by railroad, to the rural areas. The two-way flow of labor between urban and rural areas was a further factor strengthening the flexibility of the labor market. How real wages evolved in this environment will be discussed later.

Pre-1930 public policy was concerned not only with increasing the labor quantum but also with improving its quality. Of population aged between six and thirteen years, only 20 percent attended school

---

30. It is possible that due to social and cultural factors, labor mobility was greater between Italy and the pampean zone than between the northwest provinces and the pampean zone. While the provinces of the northwest maintained some characteristics similar to those of the labor surplus economies, these pockets of disguised unemployment had small quantitative importance. Although individual European immigrants occasionally were not able to buy a return ticket, it is doubtful that during any pre-1930 year there was a large pool of trapped immigrants.

in 1869. This percentage rose to 31 by 1895 and to 48 in 1914. It may
be estimated that in 1929 it reached 60 percent (the figure for 1947
was 74 percent). Students attending second-level educational institutions and universities rose from 20,000 and 5,000, respectively,
in 1910 to 73,000 and 22,000 in 1930.[31]

The capital market

Although not much is known about the pre-1930 capital market, it
seems that it was also closely bound to world markets, especially
those of Great Britain and, after World War I, the United States.
Real savings generated both abroad and domestically were transferred
into railroads, land improvements, houses, factories, etc., which grew
at remarkable rates during 1860–1930. The real transfer of foreign
savings into Argentina presented no serious difficulties, while the
relaxed balance-of-payments situation of most years also facilitated
the transformation of domestic savings into imported capital goods.

Available figures on gross fixed capital formation before 1930 expressed as percentages of GDP are extraordinary; for 1905–09 this
percentage is placed at 48, and for 1925–29 at 33. These data would
imply not only a remarkable capital inflow but also a tremendous level
of domestic savings; but they are misleading, being expressed at 1950
prices, which reflect the steep increase in the relative prices of
capital goods that has taken place in Argentina since 1935–39. Table
1.17 makes a correction to take into account those changes in the
price structure. The results are striking; the gross investment coefficient

31. In the Federal District alone, the percentages of children aged between
6 to 13 years attending school evolved as follows:

	Male	Female
1869	49	51
1895	64	60
1914	73	71
1947	87	85

The trend in the poorer provinces of the northwest is illustrated by the figures
for Jujuy:

	Male	Female
1869	17	10
1895	27	18
1914	46	40
1947	70	65

See DNEC, *Informe Demográfico,* pp. 52–53; and Organisation for Economic
Cooperation and Development, *Education, Human Resources and Development in Argentina* (Paris, 1967), p. 38.

is about halved. Although the procedure used is admittedly rough, the coefficients expressed at 1937 prices give a more realistic picture of real capital formation, as well as of the effort involved in that accumulation. If we had national accounts expressed at current prices

Table 1.17: Gross Fixed Capital Formation as a Percentage of GDP
at Market Prices in Argentina, 1900–37

	1950 prices	*1937 prices*
1900–09	39.2	17.2
1910–14	42.2	18.7
1915–19	13.0	6.0
1920–24	26.4	12.0
1925–29	33.3	15.3
1937	25.9	12.0

Sources and method: Data in 1950 prices from ECLA, pp. 3, 82. Data for 1937 obtained from O.S., pp. 122–23, 110–11. Fixed capital formation was subdivided into two categories: construction and improvements, on the one hand, and machinery and equipment, on the other. Quantum indices for each of these categories, as well as for the GDP, were derived from data at 1950 prices. These indices (1937 = 100) were then multiplied by the 1937 figures at current prices.

for 1900–30 they would probably show an even lower rate of gross fixed capital formation, as relative prices had already changed between 1929 and 1937 so as to increase those of manufactured goods in general, and of imported goods in particular, among which were most of the machinery and equipment used in Argentina at that time.

Whether expressed at 1937 or current prices, gross fixed capital formation was nevertheless a high fraction of GDP during 1900–30; before the war it moved around 18 percent, falling after the war to between 12 and 15 percent. Although no comparable figures exist for 1860–1900, it is likely that, especially for 1880–1900, the rate of capital formation was similar to that of 1900–14. Whose real savings financed this accumulation? No precise answer is feasible, although several observations can be made.

Foreign capital financed a large share of the capital formation, especially before World War I. As shown in Table 1.18, the stock of long-term private foreign investment reached roughly one-half of the value of the total fixed capital stock in 1913. The immediate pre-World War I years marked the high point of foreign influence in Argentina, with foreigners amounting to around two-fifths of the labor force and owning, directly or indirectly, a large share of fixed capital

Table 1.18: Stock of Foreign Capital in Argentina, 1900–27
(Million dollars at current prices)

	1900	1909	1913	1923	1927
I. *Stock of long-term private*					
foreign investment	*1,120*	*2,176*	*3,136*	*3,088*	*3,474*
United Kingdom	912	1,423	1,860	1,906	2,002
United States	–ª	19	39	193	487
Other	–	733	1,237	989	984
Railroads	–	776	1,037	1,134	1,187
Government bonds	–	668	–	–	–
Companies engaged in commerce	–	193	–	–	–
Land and mortgage companies	–	146	–	–	–
Building companies (*immobiliarias*)	–	145	–	–	–
Tramways	–	88	–	–	–
Gas, electricity, and water works	–	56	–	–	–
Banks	–	36	–	–	–
Harbors	–	21	–	–	–
Meat-packing plants	–	8	–	–	–
Other	–	40	–	–	–
II. *Stock of total fixed capital owned*					
directly and indirectly by foreigners					
as a percentage of fixed capital					
stock of Argentina	32	41	48	37	34

ª Dash indicates data not available.

Sources: Análisis y Proyecciones, 1:28, and ECLA, pp. 251–57. The figures for investment in railroads include those for 1909 French-owned assets; figures for 1913–27 include only British owned railroads. See also Naciones Unidas, *El Financiamiento Externo de América Latina* (New York, 1964), especially pp. 13–17.

stock.[32] One-third of foreign investments were in railroads, and 60 percent of foreign capital was British. The stock of long-term foreign investments in Argentina in 1913 was only 18 percent lower than the equivalent figures for Canada in 1914.[33]

32. The comparison of foreign direct investments (which include land and other assets not included in the capital stock) with fixed capital is taken from the source shown in Table 1.18. No solid data are available on the total wealth of the country nor on foreign participation in such wealth.

33. Data obtained from ECLA, p. 254. Canada benefited from her proximity to the United States and her special association with Great Britain. In December 1930, Argentina accounted for 12 percent of all British long-term investments overseas, while Canada accounted for 14 percent, Australia for 13 percent, and India and Ceylon for 15 percent. See *The Problem of International Investment, 1937*, A Report by a Study Group of Members of the Royal Institute of International Affairs (Reprints of Economic Classics, A. M. Kelley, New York, 1965), p. 142. Between World War I and the Great De-

Data on the financing of investment during 1901–15 yield results similar to those already shown; for those years, 47 percent of gross fixed investment was foreign-financed.[34] Especially after the 1880s, external sources were of critical importance in the financing of social overhead capital and other activities required to integrate Argentina with world markets. This was accomplished both directly by investment in railroads, urban public utilities, etc., and indirectly by the purchase of government bonds.[35]

Although it may be ventured that during 1880–1914 foreign savings financed between one-third and one-half of net physical investment, after 1914 their relative contribution dropped and changes took place in their sources, as shown in Table 1.18. During World War I Argentina, a nonbelligerent, lent $250 million to the Allies, while beginning to shift its main links from the London to the New York capital market. Most of the increase in the stock of foreign capital between 1913 and 1927 came from United States investments, although this flow was not enough to yield as vigorous an expansion of foreign capital as during 1900–13. Less than one-fifth of gross fixed investment was financed by foreign capital during 1921–29.[36]

---

pression, the flow of capital into Canada was much larger than that into Argentina. See A. Bunge, "Paralelo Económico Argentino—Canadiense 1908–1926," *Revista de Economía Argentina* 22, no. 128 (Feb. 1929). I am grateful to Carmen Hrubisko for calling my attention to this reference.

34. ECLA, p. 90. It is not clear how these data were obtained, or what is the precise definition of foreign capital that is being used (the deficit in the current account?). Balance of payments data are weak for these years, making it difficult to check on this point.

35. Several authors have suggested that the funds placed by foreigners in the hands of the federal and local governments yielded to Argentina a lower rate of return than the funds invested directly by those foreigners in the country. See *Problem of International Investment, 1937*, p. 269: "In Argentina, as in most Latin American countries, a very large part of the external debt was contracted for unproductive purposes." Wasteful use of foreign loans seems to have taken place especially during the 1920s.

36. Same source, and same reservations, as in footnote 34. Some Argentine economic historians have argued recently that official export series for pre-1930 years (especially before 1900) may have underestimated substantially the value of exports. If so, the net contribution of foreign capital would have to be reduced. It is further argued that London often acted simply as an intermediary between Argentine rural exporters and borrowers. For example, an unknown amount of stocks of railroad companies operating in Argentina were purchased by Argentines in the London market. Such behavior may be explained on the grounds of differences in liquidity preferences between Argentine and British investors. Behind those differences toward liquidity and risk, of course, often lay unequal degrees of political power and sophistication.

By 1930–31 United States investments in Argentina had reached, according to what source is used, either one-third or two-fifths of the amount of British investments in that nation. Table 1.19 compares

Table 1.19: British and United States Investment in Argentina, 1930–31
(Million current dollars)

	RIIA 1930	ECLA 1931
United States investments	*808*	*654*
Government bonds	449	—[a]
Direct investments	359	–
British investments	*1,850*	*2,026*
Railways	1,055	1,312
Government bonds	296	–
Other	499	–

[a] Dash indicates data not available.

Sources: ECLA, pp. 251–54, and RIIA (Royal Institute of International Affairs, *The Problem of International Investment, 1937*), pp. 270–71.

data on British and United States investments for 1930–31 from two different sources; if consideration is made for estimating difficulties the discrepancy is small. North American capital in many cases bought out existing British enterprises; its direct investments went mainly into power, transport, communications, banking, meat packing, and oil companies.[37] Some United States capital went into new manufacturing activities, such as automobile assembling, which led some Argentine groups to distinguish between "good" foreign capital (mainly North American, going into import-substituting manufacturing) and "bad" foreign capital (mainly British, associated with exports and railroads).

The domestic contribution to financing pre-1930 capital accumulation was large and tended to grow. Argentina generated substantial domestic savings, not only in its prosperous rural sector, but also in manufacturing, commerce, and other services sectors. Domestic gross savings seem to have amounted to around 10 percent of the GDP in most years before 1930. A capital market made up of some modern financial intermediaries channeled part of those savings toward

---

For a revision of export series see R. Cortés Conde, T. Halperín Doughi, and H. G. de Torres, "Evolución del Comercio Exterior Argentino; Exportaciones, 1864–1964" (mimeographed).

37. *Problem of International Investment, 1937*, p. 270.

Table 1.20: Financial Data of Pre-1930 Argentina
(Yearly averages in million paper pesos at current prices)

	1913–14	1915–19	1920–24	1925–27	1928–29
Money supply	–ᵃ	–	–	–	2,109
Money plus quasi money	1,732	2,564	3,847	4,171	4,797
Savings accounts	319	573	1,157	1,501	1,875
Assets of commercial banks	1,894	2,495	3,800	3,868	4,266
Mortgage debt	–	2,989ᵇ	–	3,541ᶜ	–
Short- and long-term domestic public debt	644ᵈ	1,063	1,393	1,398	1,999
GDP, at market prices	3,781	5,169	7,001	7,969	8,718

Note: All stock figures are taken at the end of the year. Money supply includes currency in the hands of the public plus demand deposits. Quasi money includes savings accounts in commercial banks, deposits with fixed time limits (*plazo fijo*), plus other deposits in commercial banks. Savings accounts (*depósitos en caja de ahorros*) include accounts outside commercial banks (such as the National Postal Savings Institution, the National Mortgage Bank, etc.). Assets of commercial banks include those of the Banco de la Nación Argentina. Mortgage debt includes that in the hands of individuals as well as in mortgage institutions.

ᵃ Dash indicates data not available.
ᵇ Refers to 1915 only.
ᶜ Refers to end of 1925 only.
ᵈ Refers to 1914 only.

Sources and method: Data on all of the above obtained from *Anuario Geográfico*, pp. 425, 428, 429, and 436, and from Tornquist, *Economic Development*, pp. 235–38. Data on the public debt from U.N., *Public Debt 1914–1946* (Lake Success, New York: Department of Economic Affairs, 1948), p. 11. GDP at current market prices obtained using the following wholesale indices:

1913–14 = 67.5	1925–27 = 91.5
1915–19 = 96.7	1928–29 = 86.5
1920–24 = 98.3	1937 = 100.0

Quantum series for the GDP with 1937 = 100, and the value of the GDP in 1937 at current prices obtained as in Table 1.17. Wholesale price indices from the *Anuario Geográfico*, p. 368.

housing, commerce, rural activities, and manufacturing. Table 1.20 presents information on the degree to which Argentina had become a monetized economy and on the state of its capital market between 1913 and 1930. Although the data are fragmentary and are not always easy to interpret,[38] they reveal a highly monetized economy with

38. For example, it is likely that part of the domestic public debt shown in Table 1.20 was held by foreigners; it has not been possible to obtain data on the holding of these instruments. Part of the mortgage debt was also held by foreigners.

an expanding capital market. The ratio of money and quasi money to the GDP moved from 0.46 in 1913–14 to 0.55 in 1928–29; savings accounts, which were held primarily by Argentine residents, amounted to 8 percent of the gross domestic product in 1913–14, rising to 22 percent in 1928–29. It is a sad commentary on the post-World War II Argentine inflation that in 1960–64 the ratio of money and quasi money to the GDP was only 0.24.[39]

A large market for mortgage debt existed before 1930, which was of special importance in channeling funds to rural entrepreneurs and urban home-building. Between 1915 and 1925, outstanding mortgage debt had a value of around half of the GDP, although this proportion showed a declining trend.[40] Of the total mortgage debt in 1915 and 1925, half involved the National Mortgage Bank and other mortgage companies and associations. The share of the National Mortgage Bank rose at the expense of other institutions between 1915 and 1925 (from 20 to 37 percent of the total debt).[41] Private creditors accounted for 43 percent of the whole debt in 1915, but only 32 percent in 1925; the rest of the mortgage debt involved commercial banks, insurance, and other institutions. Data on the nationality or residency of creditors of the mortgage debt are scarce and apparently speculative; an estimate for 1915 places two-thirds of it in the hands of creditors domiciled in Argentina.[42]

The market was well supplied with debt instruments expressed in fixed money terms, but there was an almost total lack of widely traded equity instruments. Commercial and industrial companies relied primarily on bank credit for short-term financing and on retained earnings and ad hoc arrangements for long-term financing. Of the value of all transactions in the Buenos Aires Bourse during

39. The figures for 1960–64 have been obtained from BCRA *Boletín Estadístico* (Oct. 1965), pp. 2 and 42. The time series for money and quasi money before 1940 are less reliable than those for after 1940; however, the difference between the old and new series for 1940–42, when they overlap, is less than 3 percent. Increases in savings accounts amounted to more than 1.5 percent of the GDP, on the average, during 1915–29. Whether current savings or portfolio changes generated those increases is not known.

40. The value of outstanding mortgages had a rapid expansion between 1905 and 1915; in the earlier year their value was about 1,000 million paper pesos (m$n). This estimate is found in Tornquist, *Economic Development*, p. 235.

41. The National Mortgage Bank obtained its funds both from time deposits and the sale of paper to the public. This paper (*cédulas hipotecarias*) was popular; it continued to flourish during the 1930s but was a victim of the financial policies of the Perón regime.

42. See Tornquist, *Economic Development*, p. 237.

1926–29, 64 percent represented trading of mortgage paper; 25 percent, trading of bonds of the national and local governments; and only 11 percent, trading of stocks and debentures of corporations.[43] This shortcoming led to discussions during the 1930s about ways to improve long-term industrial financing, and eventually to the creation of an industrial bank during the 1940s.

One last feature of the pre-1930 capital market worth noting is the large participation of domestic institutions. The substantial share of the National Mortgage Bank, created by public law in 1886, in the mortgage market has already been noted. The official Banco de la Nación Argentina, founded in 1891, accounted for more than two-fifths of the assets of the commercial banking system; foreign banks, on the other hand, held a relatively small share.[44]

Much of domestic savings was invested directly by the savers themselves, but robust data on these transactions are lacking. It would not be surprising, however, if they were less important before 1930 than after World War II and the institutionalization of inflation.

The land market

Much discussion has taken place on whether the land tenure system that developed during the second half of the nineteenth century was (1) equitable and socially healthy, (2) conducive to the most economically efficient methods of rural production, or (3) conducive to rapid rural capital accumulation and technological change. This issue and land distribution data will be examined in greater detail in essay 3; this section will just sketch the origins of the pre-1930 land holding patterns and the flexibility it allowed for land buying and leasing.

The most fertile Argentine lands are those relatively close to the seaboard and the urban center of Buenos Aires; as one moves west and south, humidity and fertility as a rule decrease.[45] This simple

43. See *Anuario Geográfico Argentino*, p. 366. By far the most popular debt instrument was the *cédula hipotecaria* of the National Mortgage Bank, which by itself accounted for 57 percent of the value of all Bourse transactions during 1926–29. During these years annual transactions in the Bourse averaged 640 million paper pesos.

44. See Table 100 in the Statistical Appendix.

45. The humid pampean zone, comprising the best lands in the country, has an area of 37.5 million hectares; it includes three-fourths of the province of Buenos Aires (north, center and southeast), almost all of the province of Entre Ríos, the south and center of the province of Santa Fe and a small eastern part of the province of Córdoba. See ECLA 2:132.

fact, plus the additional advantage enjoyed by these lands from their proximity to harbors and main urban centers, had an important implication for Argentine economic, and perhaps political, history. Although during the nineteenth century it appeared that the country had an unlimited supply of raw land, the additional land that came under cultivation as a result of the railways and the elimination of the Indian menace on the frontiers was on the whole of lower economic quality than that closer to the metropolitan zones on the banks of the rivers flowing into the Río de la Plata estuary. Therefore, from the start of the economic expansion of 1860–1930, the latter lands, which had been occupied early by a relatively small number of families, enjoyed considerable rents. As increases in world demand for rural goods induced the expansion of the frontier into marginal lands, those rents increased. The economic superiority of littoral lands also insured their owners against the possiblity that the autonomous opening up of new lands by bold pioneers and military conquests could lead to very severe drops in rents. This situation may be contrasted with that for the United States during the early nineteenth century, when the opening up of the North American middle west brought ruin, or at least lower relative rents, to eastern landlords whose lands were inferior to the Great Plains.[46] While the expanding frontier meant near elimination of the eastern landlord in the United States as a significant economic and political agent, it was accompanied by the opposite effect in Argentina.[47]

46. The different economic, social, and political repercussions of an expansion which proceeds from poorer to better lands, compared with another that goes from better to poorer lands, may be summarized in the following conjecture: expanding societies of the former type will be more progressive and dynamic than the latter type. Before such a conjecture can be tested, however, more precise and quantifiable dependent variables must be formed. The continued influence of the landlord class, not only in Argentina but also in the whole of South America, in contrast with the United States, may be explained to a large extent by the geographical fact that in many regions the economic quality of the land sharply decreases as one moves toward the heart of the continent. In this sense, South America is by nature more Ricardian than the United States, as the best lands were appropriated first. In this respect Canada is more like the United States than South America. In an unpublished paper, Roberto Cortés Conde asserts that politically powerful landowners kept the frontier closed in western and southern Argentina during the nineteenth century to avoid lower land values and higher wages. It is doubtful, however, that the implied control over outlying areas could have been maintained in the face of massive immigration and expanding rural output.

47. For a poignant description of the impact on Virginia's aristocracy of the opening up of western lands in the United States, see Frederick J.

Table 1.21 shows that land values in the province of Buenos Aires held their privileged position in spite of the expansion of the frontier;

Table 1.21: Relative Land Values in Provinces
of the Pampean Zones, 1888–1935
(Value of one hectare in Buenos Aires Province = 100)

	1888	1911	1935
Buenos Aires	100	100	100
Entre Ríos	67	51	56
Santa Fe	26	49	105
Córdoba	22	41	55
La Pampa	9	22	21

Sources: Data on land values found in Scobie, *Revolution on the Pampas*, p. 171, and Gastón H. Lestard, *Reseña y Ritmo de la Economía Argentina* (Buenos Aires, 1937), p. 62.

although the railroad appears to have narrowed value differentials, the gap was maintained (with the exception of the province of Santa Fe). More disaggregated data, if available, would probably show more clearly the continued preeminence of real estate located in districts closest to the littoral.

As frontier lands (such as those in southern La Pampa and Buenos Aires provinces) were less suitable to intensive cultivation than those closer to the Río de la Plata, viable rural establishments had to be larger than, say, those in fertile areas of the Santa Fe Province (also nearer major harbors and markets). This necessary size helped to strengthen the predominance of larger estates, especially for cattle raising, and hampered colonization of new lands by small farmers.

The Spanish government ruling over what is now Argentina distributed public domain lands in a manner similar to that employed in other parts of Hispanic America: large tracts were turned over to private owners as compensation for military, political, or financial services to the Crown. What is now known as the pampean zone was one of the most underdeveloped parts of Hispanic America. Its land

---

Turner, *Rise of the New West, 1819–1829* (New York: Collier Books), chapter 4. In contrast, land values around the city of Buenos Aires and other littoral regions soared at the start of the 1862–1930 boom. According to H. S. Ferns: "There is much evidence to suggest that land values appreciated by something like 1,000 percent between 1883 and 1887 in Buenos Aires Province; 420 percent in Santa Fe, 750 percent in Córdoba, and 370 percent in Entre Ríos." *Britain and Argentina in the Nineteenth Century* (Oxford: Clarendon Press, 1960), p. 424.

was worth little before Argentine independence, thus increasing the
tendency toward disposing of it in large chunks. With independence
came the possibility of freely shipping such commodities as hides,
wool, tallow, and jerked and salted beef. Land began to increase
in value, and rents became significant, but the predominance of
pastoral activities and the relative scarcity of labor maintained
the pattern of large landholdings. The period of 1810–60 was
one of acute political turmoil, and land ownership was often the
reward to victorious political and military leaders, although many
older landowners still managed to hold onto their property (and
their political influence). Several distinguished Argentine families of
today trace the origins of their wealth to the land rewards obtained by
victorious Unitarian generals after 1852. By 1860 the pattern of land
ownership in the pacified regions of the pampean zone (pacified from
both Indians and civil wars) was still characterized by vast private
estates. With abundance of land relative to labor and capital, the
estates had to be large to yield an income that military and political
chieftains considered adequate. The government, however, still had
at its disposal enormous land tracts, often populated by nomadic
Indian tribes. The disturbance caused by these tribes was finally
eliminated by a military expedition in 1879–80.[48]

Public lands were quickly turned over to private owners in large
chunks, mainly as a result of pressing government financial needs.
The 1879–80 campaign was partly financed by the sale of bonds
redeemable in public lands, and the victorious military were rewarded
with real estate. At the time bondholders exchanged their funds for a
promise of land, or even when they in fact obtained the property, the
land was not worth much, being marginal in a geographical as well
as in an economic sense. The state further disposed of lands by
auctioning them off; generous limits were set for any single buyer, but
even those seem to have been circumvented. Furthermore, before
1879 the government began granting railway companies land along the
new tracks (as in the United States) to encourage their expansion.

Although in retrospect these policies appear as a gigantic giveaway,
the lands had little value when the transactions took place. Furthermore, there were no legal barriers, say in 1880, to keep anyone with

48. This military expedition, led by General Roca, tremendously expanded
the effective domain of Argentina; the pacified area of the province of Buenos
Aires was about doubled, while the vast Patagonian territories (also claimed
by Chile at that time) located south of the Río Negro, were also incorporated
into Argentina.

the required foresight and funds from buying land at low prices. Nevertheless, with a lack of information for this type of transaction, plus imperfections in the capital market, making borrowing difficult for small investors, the manner in which public lands were disposed of during the second half of the nineteenth century was less than socially optimal, giving insiders (including political friends) considerable advantage. While buyers showed fine foresight and were quick to spot a good bargain, the state, in practice very much influenced by large landlords, showed a remarkable lack of social and business sense in dumping land on the market at a precipitous rate. Funds needed for either waging war or subsidizing certain activities like railway building could have been obtained with some effort from other sources, at least in part.

The United States Homestead Act was known and admired in Argentina, but only pale imitations were enacted. Besides some colonization schemes in Sante Fe Province, little of substance was done to encourage small-scale land ownership. By the time of the large immigrations (1880–1914), which coincided with the expansion of grain production, the best lands had been taken up by a relatively small number of owners. Immigrants interested in rural activities had to begin either as agricultural tenants or as employees in livestock establishments. More on this in essay 3.

Yet there was nothing rigid about the market for land. Once good lands had been appropriated, most landowners had no interest in interfering with liberal rules of the game which yielded handsome rents and capital gains. There were no significant noneconomic barriers to buying and selling nor to leasing under different types of arrangements, and the land market was on the whole competitive. Potential buyers or leasers (often newly arrived immigrants) were mobile; if a given landowner tried to charge noncompetitive rents they could seek other deals quite easily. At no point was the concentration of land ownership high enough to give landowners a country-wide oligopolistic power. Land turnover was high.[49] The main

49. "In Argentina, there is a market in land, as in other countries there is a market in portable securities. . . . If we exclude . . . sales in the National Territories . . . we see that [during 1901–18] of a total area of 176.5 million hectares, 64 percent of that part of the territory . . . has changed ownership." From a report by the Director of Rural Economy and Statistics, quoted in Tornquist, *Economic Development,* pp. 240–1. A British publication observed in 1916: "the Argentine landowner has no feudatory traditions to live up to, neither is he troubled with questions of entail, primogeniture, and other inheritances of a classic past; he regards his property from a business

barriers preventing the newly arrived immigrant from buying land were two: lack of long term credit at interest rates he could afford, and the sharp increase in land values that had been taking place since the arrival of the railroad and the expansion of exports. Capital market imperfections for transactions involving small borrowers was the more important of these two barriers.[50] The concentration of land ownership (measured in economic values, not in hectares) was in all likelihood not much different from the concentration of the ownership of other forms of wealth around 1930.

TRENDS IN FACTOR PRICES AND INCOME DISTRIBUTION BEFORE 1930

The reason for examining factor prices and income distribution before 1930 is based on a desire not only to understand how the economy worked but also to see whether in those facts one may find an explanation for the emergence of social turbulence at a later period.

Real wages

Nineteenth-century wage data are hard to come by; the only warranted conclusion is that real wages in the short run fluctuated considerably. The bulk of wage earners' budgets was made up of exportable rural commodities such as wheat, meat, etc. If there is a tendency for money wages to be less flexible than exchange rates and export prices, it follows that foreign trade fluctuations will have a direct impact on real wages. The years from 1880 to 1900 were known for unstable monetary conditions and a fluctuating exchange rate for the paper peso; from this experience the link between exchange rates and real wages first gained attention.[51]

standpoint." *The Argentine Year Book 1915–1916* (Buenos Aires: Robert Grant and Co., 1916), p. 229.

50. In spite of these difficulties many immigrants, after several years of hard work and good luck in leased lands, were able to accumulate enough funds to buy their own land. On the other hand, some Argentines who had benefited from the military campaigns of 1879–80 by receiving small- and medium-sized plots of land from the government, sold them to speculators or large landowners. See Giberti, *El Desarrollo Agrario Argentino*, p. 23.

51. See for example the classic study of J. H. Williams, *Argentine International Trade under Inconvertible Paper Money, 1880–1900* (Cambridge: Harvard University Press, 1920), and A. G. Ford, *The Gold Standard, 1880–1914, Britain and Argentina* (Oxford: Clarendon Press, 1962). Ford states: "For in Argentina the economic and political structure was such that a depreciating paper currency (in terms of gold) moved the distribution of a

Data on wages for 1900–30 are more abundant. Pampean real wages seemed higher than in some European cities. A comparison of hourly wage rates in 1911–14 between Buenos Aires and Paris and Marseilles for seven different categories showed the Buenos Aires wage rates higher than those in Marseilles in all categories (by about 80 percent), and higher than most corresponding Parisian wage rates (on average by about 25 percent).[52] A 1921 report of the British Department of Overseas Trade stated that Argentine wages before World War I were higher than in European countries, although they had not been increasing in the same proportion.[53] The relative cheapness of foodstuffs in Argentina was an important factor in this comparison. Yet it is not very surprising that in 1910–14, a time when the worldwide terms of trade between foodstuffs and manufacturers were favorable to the former, the value of the marginal product of unskilled labor in the land-rich pampean zone was higher than in the exhausted lands of Europe, and also higher than in many relatively labor-abundant cities of the old continent, especially those of Italy and Spain. Whether in fact Argentine real wages exceeded those paid in Paris and London for very long cannot be settled readily with available evidence.

Estimates of the evolution of Argentine real wages between 1904 and 1935–40 are brought together in Tables 1.22 and 1.23. These fragmentary data indicate that, following the outbreak of hostilities in Europe, real wages fluctuated considerably, dropping in 1915–19 and recovering in 1920–24. Real wages continued to expand during 1925–29, remaining at the level of those years during the 1930s. As in Great Britain, the blow of the Great Depression to the working

given real income in favor of these interests [the landowning and exporting interests] and against wage earners" (pp. 90–91). Such an effect continues to exist today; see my *Exchange Rate Devaluation in a Semi-Industrialized Country: The Experience of Argentina 1955–1961* (Cambridge: M.I.T. Press, 1966), chapter 2. Even without a wage lag one can establish a similar link between foreign trade conditions and real wages, assuming that the production of exportables is less labor intensive than production of home goods, as indeed seems to be the case.

52. Data obtained from the *Boletín del Departamento Nacional del Trabajo*, no. 19 (Dec. 31, 1911), pp. 807–12 (for Argentina) and p. 830 (for France). French data appear to have been converted into pesos at the going exchange rate.

53. Great Britain, Department of Overseas Trade, *Report on the Financial, Commercial and Economic Conditions of the Argentine Republic* (London, Sept. 1921), p. 55.

Table 1.22: Summary of Evidence on Wage Rates in Argentina, 1904–40
(Money data in paper pesos; annual averages)

	1904	1909–14[a]	1920–21	1935–40
Skilled workers (per hour)	0.40	0.55	0.74	0.97
Unskilled workers ("peones," per hour)	0.24	0.35	0.49	0.54
Minors (per hour)	–[b]	0.13[c]	–	0.32[d]
Adult male workers in manufacturing, transport and construction (per hour)	–	0.45[c]	–	0.78[d]
Railroad employees (per year)	903	1,081	1,642	2,033[d]
Estimate of index of cost of living	75	100	180	122
Estimated indices of real wages for:				
Skilled workers	99	100	75	145
Unskilled workers	90	100	78	125
Minors	–	100[c]	–	227[d]
Adult male workers in manufacturing, transport and construction	–	100[c]	–	159[c]
Railroad employees	111	100	84	170[d]
"Workers in the Federal Capital"	–	100[c]	97	143
Per capita real GDP	91	100	92	107

[a] Made up of yearly figures for 1909, 1910, 1911, and 1914.
[b] Dash indicates data not available.
[c] Refers only to 1914.
[d] Refers only to 1935.

Sources and method: All data on wages refer to Federal Capital, except those for railroad employees, which include the whole country. Hourly wages for skilled workers from the following publications: A. E. Bunge, *Estadística del Trabajo* (*Informe*) (Buenos Aires, 1914); Departamento Nacional del Trabajo, División Estadística, *Anuario Estadístico del Trabajo*, pp. 123–47; *Boletín del Departamento Nacional del Trabajo*, no. 18 (Sept. 30, 1911), pp. 575–86; *Anuario Geográfico*, pp. 554–61; Department of Overseas Trade, Great Britain, *Report on the Financial, Commercial and Economic Conditions of the Argentine Republic* (London, 1921), p. 55. The average for skilled workers was obtained by using series for four to eleven categories (for example, carpenters, painters, plumbers, etc.). Series on wages for "peones," minors, and adult male workers obtained in a similar fashion from the same sources. Data on railway wages from *Revista de Economía Argentina* (Nov. 1936), p. 171. Cost of living index for after 1914 from *Anuario Geográfico*, p. 557; figures for earlier years from unpublished estimates found in ECLA files. GDP series obtained as in Table 1.20. Real wage series for "workers in the Federal Capital" from *Anuario Geográfico*, p. 555.

class was ameliorated by a drop in the relative prices of foodstuffs. Real wages, including leisure gains from shorter work hours, during 1925–39 were above those for prewar years.[54] Comparison of indices

54. Consumption data of some wage-goods support this inference. Apparent consumption of beer grew at an annual rate of 5.2 percent between 1910–14

for real wages and per capita real domestic product imply (assuming a constant relation between labor force and population, and that the real wages shown can be used as approximations for those of the whole labor force) a rising wage share in the domestic product from

Table 1.23: Wages, Hours Worked, and National Income, 1914–39

	Index of real wage in the Federal Capital (1914 = 100)	Average number of hours worked during a week in the Federal Capital	Index of per capita real GDP (1914 = 100)
1914	100	53.6	100
1915–19	78	53.4	95
1920–24	113	49.5	113
1925–29	140	49.3	126
1930–34	144	47.5	114
1935–39	143	45.3	122

Sources and method: Anuario Geográfico, p. 555 and p. 559; per capita real GDP from ECLA, *El Desarrollo Económico de la Argentina*, 1:15, and its mimeographed statistical appendix.

1915–19 to 1930–34 and a higher share in 1935–39 than before World War I.

To attract immigrants, Argentine real wages had to be higher, at least at the margin, than those in Italy and Spain, and had to be competitive with those of other immigrant-receiving countries, even if cultural factors gave Argentina an edge in the case of Latin migrants. Wages, together with leisure and working conditions, also had a tendency to improve, apparently at a greater pace than the growth of per capita domestic product. In comparison with other relatively advanced countries, however, the position of Argentine real wages was less favorable during the 1930s than before World War I. A report showed that an Argentine unskilled urban laborer in 1937–39 received wages about two-thirds as high as those in Germany, one-half as high as in Great Britain, and one-third as high as in the United States. The same report indicated that, measuring wages only with respect to their purchasing power over food, these percentages would be higher: "The absolute buying power of the agricultural

and 1925–29; that for edible oils at 4.6 percent, and for coffee at 3.9 percent. Population during this period grew at 2.8 percent. The expansion of apparent consumption for wheat flour, sugar, and wine, however, was smaller. Data obtained from *Revista de Economía Argentina* (Jan., 1942), pp. 158–60, 188–90.

laborer in Argentina is higher than in the United States when expressed in terms of bread, meat, milk, cheese or oranges." [55]

The abundance of cheap foodstuffs was widely credited for the lack of labor disputes, with the role played by European immigration in giving great elasticity to the labor market being neglected. The following statement, typical of this attitude, was published in 1943, and must have been written, ironically, shortly before a social storm broke over Argentina:

> Argentina . . . has not suffered the great social upheavals which took place in the old industrial countries. . . . The cost of living, relatively reasonable because of the abundance and cheapness of foodstuffs, explains why an almost absolute tranquility has reigned during the last 25 years in the field of industrial labor.[56]

If the Argentine worker had lived by bread and meat alone, it would be difficult to explain post-1940 social and political events.

The returns to capital and entrepreneurship

Foreign investors who contributed to expanding the capital stock before 1930 naturally expected a rate of return higher than what they could have obtained in their own countries. On the whole their expectations were fulfilled, at least before 1930. Railroads, meat-packing plants, public utilities, and land companies yielded steady profits; foreign bond holders were paid punctually during 1900–30. Debate raged even then as to whether those profits were normal or were inflated as the result of market power of foreign companies. It is difficult to settle this matter quantitatively; however, competition among foreign capitalists, if only between British and North American capitalists, was a force tending to keep down the

55. Armour Research Foundation, *Technological and Economic Survey of Argentine Industries with Industrial Research Recommendations* (Lithoprinted in Ann Arbor, Michigan, 1943), p. 76. The information on wages in Argentina, Germany, Great Britain, and the United States is found on page 70.

56. *Anuario Geográfico Argentino; Suplemento 1942* (Buenos Aires, 1943), p. 298. On the same page, however, it is pointed out that Argentine social legislation was far from having achieved "justice in the relations of workers with management and with society." The last serious labor unrest had occurred during 1919, when a conflict which started as a metallurgical strike spread rapidly and was repressed harshly by the government. Private gangs aided the government in a climate of xenophobia directed against foreign-born workers; the similarity with contemporary events in the United States is striking.

profit rate. Especially since the start of this century, British investors in Argentina have lived in fear of those from North America. It remains true that much foreign capital was placed in activities which, for technological reasons, came close to being natural oligopolies and oligopsonies. Railroads and public utilities are obvious examples; less clear-cut is the meat packing and meat shipping business (linked to meat marketing in the United Kingdom). The Argentine government, especially Congress, kept an eye on these interests, but difficulties in defining normal profits gave rise to considerable ill will between government officials (and public opinion behind them) and companies subject to investigations. The attitude of most foreign investors toward the legitimate curiosity of local authorities was far from enlightened and thus aggravated frictions. During the 1930s, in particular, the cavalier attitude of some foreign investors in meat packing and public utilities resulted in major scandals.

Investments in what is now called social overhead capital were largely private. In some cases the government provided special concessions, such as land grants and profit guarantees for railroads. In retrospect, however, it seems that the profits of these enterprises would have been sufficient to attract private entrepreneurs without additional stimuli.[57]

Even less is known about profit rates earned by Argentine entrepreneurs in commerce, manufacturing and rural activities. From the ratio of land rents to land values, and from interest rates in the Buenos Aires money market, it appears that in the expanding capital-poor Argentina of 1900–30, those profit rates, although mostly competitive, were substantial.[58] Some commercial interests in the export-import trade, especially in the export of grains, were often accused of obtaining extraordinary profits thanks to their market power; as in the case of the meat exporters and the railroads, more heat than

57. High profits in railroads appear to have reflected high social rates of return. In Argentina, in contrast with the United States, canals were never a serious alternative to railroads for moving exportable surpluses from the interior of the pampean zone to the main harbors (Buenos Aires, Rosario, Bahía Blanca). It may be noted that during the early stage of railroad building in Argentina, the state directly built several lines.

58. Average discount rates (on commercial paper) in private commercial banks were as follows (in percentages, annual averages): 1901–04 = 5.8; 1905–09 = 6.0; 1910–14 = 7.3; 1915–19 = 7.0; 1920–24 = 7.2; 1925–29 = 6.9. The price level rose sharply between 1914 and 1919, but declined between that date and 1929; in 1929 the price level was only 28 percent above the 1913 level. Data on interest rates obtained from *Anuario Geográfico Argentino,* p. 430.

light has been shed so far by the persistent dispute surrounding these activities.[59]

Land rents

Land values and rents rose with only temporary setbacks during 1860 to 1930;[60] lands which were marginal during the early years became rent earners as growing European demand for food pushed

Table 1.24: Data on Land Prices of Rural Properties in Argentina
(Paper pesos per hectare)

	Average of all rural property bought and sold	*Buenos Aires Province*	*Santa Fe Province*	*Córdoba Province*	*Entre Ríos Province*	*La Pampa Province*
1888	—[a]	29	7	6	19	3
1901–05	14.1	–	–	–	–	–
1906–10	25.5	–	–	–	–	–
1911–15	40.1	–	–	–	–	–
1916–18	49.8	–	–	–	–	–
1931	–	361	403	188	247	102
1935	–	225	237	123	127	48

[a] Dash indicates data not available.

Sources and method: Tornquist, *Economic Development*, pp. 240–41; Gastón H. Lestard, *Reseña y Ritmo de la Economía Argentina* (Buenos Aires, 1937), p. 62; Scobie, *Revolution on the Pampas*, p. 171. Figures in gold pesos for 1888 have been translated into paper pesos using the rate of 1.48 paper per gold peso; see *Anuario Geográfico*, p. 423. The land values for the provinces refer to cereal growing properties.

the railroads further into the interior. Increases in land values were especially sharp between 1890 and 1914. Data on land values, shown

59. After 1900 the grain export market was dominated by the Big Four, which had a considerable degree of oligopsonistic power. But these firms also brought to grain exports a uniformity of standards in bagging and grading not known previously. See Scobie, *Revolution on the Pampas,* pp. 93, 103, 110. The Big Four represented both domestic and foreign capital. A Buenos Aires grains future market began to operate around 1910, increasing the flexibility of farmers. This market continued operating until the present, except during 1947–57 and some wartime years.

60. During the period under study fluctuations in "the" rate of interest were relatively small; therefore fluctuations in land values can be taken as a good indication of changes in (expected) land rents.

in Table 1.24, are fragmentary and their lack of homogeneity makes interpretation difficult. But they are enough to indicate the pre-1930 land boom.

While between 1888 and 1929 the price of gold in paper pesos less than doubled, land values in the province of Buenos Aires expressed in paper pesos rose by more than ten times; in other provinces the increase was also spectacular.[61] Those who had acquired land one way or another during the early years of the 1860–1930 expansion and had held on to it had their foresight (or indolence) amply rewarded during the following decades. But the fall in values during the 1930s proved that land was not always the best asset to have in one's portfolio.

In a closed static economy increases in land values in one region of the country take place generally at the expense of a decreased value for other lands and/or other assets. The increase in the value of pampean lands during 1860–1930 was not of this nature. The only property values that may have suffered as those in the pampean zone soared were those of assets located outside Argentina's borders, mainly in Europe's agricultural regions.

Income distribution

There are few data on income distribution in Argentina before 1930. Starting in 1935, national accounts split up total income into that going to wages and salaries (wage income) and that going to profits, rents and interests (including in the latter category income of unincorporated enterprises and the self-employed, which no doubt contain elements of wage income). Table 1.25 presents this classification for 1937 which is probably close to that for 1925–29. On this assumption, it may be estimated that during those years about one-fourth of GDP went to rents and gross profits of the rural sector, while one-third went to gross nonwage income of urban sectors; the rest, about two-fifths of GDP, went to wages and salaries. In 1937, net–factor payments abroad represented about 5 percent of GDP at factor cost; if this percentage is taken as representative of 1925–29,

61. In 1888 one gold peso was worth 1.48 paper pesos; the rate in 1929 was around the 2.27 paper per gold peso rate set by the Conversion Law of 1899. Throughout this period, the gold peso was worth 1,451.61 milligrams fine gold, equal at mint par to $0.965 U.S. dollars. See Virgil Salera, *Exchange Control and the Argentine Market* (New York: Columbia University Press, 1941), p. 15.

it would imply that nearly one-tenth of all nonwage income was remitted abroad.[62]

The special price structure of Argentina should be borne in mind when considering these figures. Relative prices for foodstuffs were low, while those of most manufactured goods were high. Assuming that the expenditure basket of wage earners included a higher pro-

Table 1.25: Distribution of the GDP at Factor Cost
in Argentina in 1937
(Percentages of GDP)

Wage income (excluding social security contributions of employers)	*40.2*
Rural sector (agriculture, livestock, and fisheries)	5.4
Manufacturing	7.7
Construction and mining	2.3
Commerce	7.0
Transport and communication	4.9
Other private services	5.5
Government	7.4
Non-wage income (including social security contributions of employers)	*59.8*
Rural sector	23.3
Manufacturing	7.3
Construction and mining	1.5
Commerce	7.1
Transport and communications	4.2
Other private services and housing	16.0
Government (social security contributions)	0.5

Sources: ECLA worksheets, and O.S., pp. 112–13.

portion of foodstuffs than that of nonwage earners, it follows that a direct comparison of Table 1.25 with similar ones for other countries

62. These somewhat bold assertions receive modest support from the pioneering research of Alejandro E. Bunge, who estimated the national wealth and income in Argentina for 1916. Those estimates show that labor income of workmen and domestic and other servants accounted for about 42 percent of the national income for that year. But the methods employed by Bunge are not clear; his estimated total income seems best to correspond to the gross domestic income. Bunge also estimates the share of income going to nonresident foreigners at about 4 percent of the national income. Bunge's results are given in Tornquist, *Economic Development,* pp. 258–59; they originally appeared in the first number of his *Revista de Economía Argentina.* Unfortunately, available estimates of factor payments abroad for the whole 1900–29 period are shaky. They suggest, however, that they rarely exceeded 6 percent of GDP.

will yield a misleading impression regarding relative income inequality.[63] Yet considerable inequality existed in income distribution
by families, although it is doubtful that it was much worse than in
the United States of those years. If the spending habits of some Argentines in the Paris of the 1920s was spectacular, so were the antics
of American millionaires of pre-New Deal days.[64] One difference was
that while the latter had derived most of their wealth from industrial
and commercial ventures, a majority of the former were recruited
from the landowning class. From the lack of data, however, little
more can be said about the pattern of income distribution among
families.[65]

In spite of the high degree of integration achieved in the pre-1930
domestic economy, considerable regional income inequality remained.

63. At least two other points should be borne in mind in any such
comparison; (1) the distinction between earners of wage and nonwage incomes
is arbitrary and is likely to differ between countries with different institutional
structures (with different proportions of self-employed); (2) a country with
a large rural sector will tend to have a relatively large rent share in its national
income; any judgement regarding the inequality of income distribution must
take into account not only the categories of wage and nonwage income, but
also the pattern of land distribution.

64. Bunge provides an estimate of the distribution of (pretax) income by
families for 1916. His estimate, subject to the reservations discussed in footnote 62, is as follows:

	Percent of population	Percent of total income
Families earning less than 1,000 paper pesos a year	55.0	29.8
Families earning between 1,000 and 2,500 paper pesos	27.5	24.3
Families earning between 2,500 and 3,000 paper pesos	11.1	17.6
Families earning between 3,000 and 6,000 paper pesos	4.4	10.2
Families earning more than 6,000 paper pesos a year	2.1	18.1

See Tornquist, *Economic Development,* p. 259. One United States dollar was
worth in the exchange market 2.36 paper pesos in 1916. The plight of the
rural poor in Argentina at that time was probably not worse than that of
rural blacks in the United States South.

65. Victoria Ocampo, the distinguished "first lady of the Spanish American
literary scene" (according to the *New York Times*), recently gave this candid
recollection of living habits of her upper-class family: "in Europe we were
exiles from Argentina, and in Argentina we were exiles from Europe. My
parents kept trying to bridge the gap by traveling, and traveling before the
wars was much more than putting clothes into a suitcase and taking a plane.
. . . The first time I remember going, it was like a Biblical exodus. We
traveled as if in caravan—my father and mother, my sisters, our nurses, a
cook, a chauffeur and a farmhand. Why all that? So we could have the kind
of food and service we were used to. For fresh eggs and milk, we took
hens and one of our cows on board. It sounds strange now, but that's the
way it was." *New York Times Book Review* (Oct. 2, 1966), p. 38.

In lieu of direct information, Table 1.26 presents some indicators. Northwestern provinces (Jujuy, Salta, Tucumán, Santiago del Estero, Catamarca, La Rioja, San Juan) generally had much higher death and illiteracy rates than the pampean zone. The northern, western,

Table 1.26: Mortality and Illiteracy Rates in Major Argentine
Provinces and Territories

	Mortality rate in 1925–30 (per thousand inhabitants)	Infant mortality rate in 1925–29 (per thousand live births)[a]	Illiteracy rate among registered voters in 1930 (per hundred registered voters)	Percentage of total Argentine population in 1914
Federal Capital	13.2	77.9	2.5	20.0
Buenos Aires	11.2	98.6	17.3	13.5
Santa Fe	11.8	114.1	19.2	11.4
Córdoba	16.1	134.7	28.1	9.3
Entre Ríos	13.2	117.1	35.4	5.4
Tucumán	22.5	169.9	37.1	4.2
Corrientes	10.8	101.7	42.0	4.4
Mendoza	16.7	156.9	37.4	3.5
Sgo. del Estero	12.0	–	44.0	3.3
San Juan	21.6	229.1	34.9	1.5
Salta	26.8	197.7	33.7	1.8
San Luis	13.2	123.8	29.8	1.5
Catamarca	10.5	113.2	34.2	1.3
La Rioja	10.7	–	35.3	1.0
Jujuy	30.1	219.8	27.3	1.0
Chaco	–[b]	–	37.1	0.6
Misiones	–	–	42.4	0.7

[a] Infant mortality rates refer to deaths of children less than one year old.
[b] Dash indicates data not available.

Source: Anuario Geográfico, pp. 162, 168, 173, 512. Discrepancies between rankings according to mortality and illiteracy rates may arise from faulty reporting in individual provinces.

and southwestern regions also lagged, although less dramatically, behind the pampean provinces. The income differentials implied by Table 1.26 had a straightforward explanation: the pampean zone had a higher per capita endowment of capital, physical and human, as well as of fertile land, plus a better location in comparison with the rest of the country. The large gap between literacy rates in the Federal Capital and other regions indicates differences in the endowment of human capital, but it also points out governmental negligence in narrowing regional inequalities.

On the whole, the great expansion of 1860–1930 benefited in a smaller or larger extent all major groups connected with the Argentine economy—native and immigrant workers, urban capitalists, landowners, foreign investors, and, as H. S. Ferns has pointed out, even the British working class (a major consumer of cheap Argentine foodstuffs).[66] The growth of output was so large that it would have been surprising if this had not been the case. It is difficult to say who benefited most, although, as Ferns also suggests, many pampean landowners did even better than most foreign capitalists. Still, the northwestern provinces and rural workers obtained relatively few benefits from the great expansion.

The deceleration of growth during 1914–29: "A Great Delay"?

Two Argentine economists have suggested that the deceleration of growth observed between 1914 and 1929 resulted from the failure of economic authorities to give greater encouragement to manufacturing. It is their opinion that the type of expansion registered before 1914 could not be expected to continue. Introducing a new stage into the Rostovian scheme, they claim that the period 1914–33 constitutes a "Great Delay," which is sandwiched between the "Preconditions" (1880–1914) and "The Takeoff" (1933–52).[67]

Without analyzing at this point the fruitfulness of the Rostow scheme in the Argentine case, it will be useful to discuss the notion that 1914–29 constituted a wasted opportunity for economic policy, caused by the failure of the authorities to realize that an era was coming to an end.

A first step must be to examine more closely the evolution of the economy during these years. A glance at available macroeconomic data, summarized in Table 1.27, indicates that between 1914 and

66. The overall gains to the United Kingdom from its investments in Argentina were made up not only by the rate of return on the capital invested, but also by the improvement in the British terms of trade which those investments in Argentine export activities made possible.

67. See Guido di Tella and Manuel Zymelman, "Etapas del Desarrollo Económico Argentino," *Revista de Economía Latinoamericana*, no. 2, Year I (Caracas, April–June 1961), pp. 30–50. The article is based on Ph.D. theses of the authors at the Massachusetts Institute of Technology, a revised version of which has also been published as *Las Etapas del Desarrollo Económico Argentino* (EUDEBA, Buenos Aires, 1967).

Table 1.27: Evolution of the Argentine Economy between 1913 and 1929

	Total percentage changes		Percentage annual growth rates	
	1913–17	1917–29	1913–29	1917–29
Real GDP	−19.6	116.7	3.5	6.7
Rural sector	−13.5	91.1	3.2	5.5
Manufacturing and mining	−16.9	146.7	4.6	7.8
Construction	−82.4	749.8	2.6	19.5
Government services	14.7	52.7	3.6	3.6
Other services	−15.0	104.0	3.5	6.1

Source: ECLA, p. 4.

1929 two clear-cut subperiods can be distinguished: one of depression, which in fact started before the outbreak of World War I, and another of rapid recovery and expansion lasting from 1917 to 1929. A slowdown in the capital inflow during the second half of 1913, due to European monetary tightness, was followed by crop failures in 1914 and finally by the outbreak of war, which decreased for several years exports and the inflow of foreign capital. The export quantum fell by 27 percent between 1912–13 and 1916–17; as was to be the case during World War II, bulky grains suffered most, due to shipping shortages while meat exports were able to expand. The dramatic drop in construction activity shown in Table 1.27 for 1913–17 reflected the cessation of foreign borrowing and investment; building of railroads and other social overhead capital came to a standstill.[68] Machinery and equipment imports by 1917 were only one-third of 1913 levels.

From 1917 on, exports and foreign capital recovered; as shown in Table 1.27 the 1917–29 expansion was brisk. As was to be expected, GDP growth was highest in the early recovery years, but there was no clear-cut tendency for the expansion to halt. The average annual growth rates for the real GDP were as follows:

> 1918–19–20: 9.8 percent per annum
> 1921–22–23: 7.2 percent per annum

68. It is interesting to observe that the drop in the GDP during 1913–17 (19.6 percent) was larger by far than the drop between 1929 and 1933 (9.7 percent). In fact, the depression of 1913–17 seems to be the severest one on record for this century, not excluding the recent 1962–63 recession. Population, which during 1900–13 had grown at an annual rate of 4.1 percent, grew at a rate of 2.3 percent per year during 1913–17, and of 2.7 percent between 1917 and 1929.

> 1924–25–26: 4.1 percent per annum
> 1927–28–29: 6.0 percent per annum

The export quantum, which expanded at an average annual rate of 6.6 percent between 1916–17 and 1928–29, did not show a tendency to stagnate, as may be seen from the following figures on their average growth rate:[69]

> 1918–19–20: 8.9 percent per annum
> 1921–22–23: 2.3 percent per annum
> 1924–25–26: 6.3 percent per annum
> 1927–28–29: 6.9 percent per annum

The international net terms of trade remained during 1925–29 roughly at the same favorable levels reached during 1910–19, although they had deteriorated during 1920–24.

Given this picture for 1917–29, it is not surprising that economic authorities during the 1920s saw no need to make dramatic innovations in policy. Railroads were not expanding as fast as before, the pampean zone had been fully occupied, and fresh British investments in Argentina were meager; but North American capital continued to flow in, even if not as fast as it was going into Canada. Immigrants were still pouring in. Agricultural protectionism was raising its ugly head even then, yet hope was often expressed that the United States would soon become an important market for Argentine beef, giving an impetus which stagnating England was unable to provide. Furthermore, as Table 1.27 indicates, manufacturing showed a respectable growth rate.[70]

Low British economic growth and low European population expansion between 1913 and 1929 negatively influenced not only Argentine development but also the development of Australia and Canada. As shown in Table 1.28, Australian growth between 1913–14 and 1929–

69. These annual growth rates have been obtained by comparing successive three-year averages of the (highly variable) annual export quantum. Data for GDP and export quantum obtained from ECLA, and from unpublished material of that institution.

70. To some observers this rate was not high enough. Alejandro E. Bunge, from his *Revista de Economía Argentina,* throughout the 1920s advocated further protection for industry and became the first economist to suggest that, since 1914, the Argentine economy had been stagnating. Bunge attached great importance to the slowdown in railroad construction. In his eagerness for industrial development, he chastised the modest social legislation of the Radical governments and their attempts to regulate foreign investments. See his *La Economía Argentina,* vol. 3 (Buenos Aires, 1928), p. 146.

Table 1.28: Evolution of the Australian Economy
between 1913–14 and 1929–30

	Percentage average annual growth rate
Real GDP	*1.1*
Pastoral, agricultural and dairy	1.5
Mining and manufacturing	0.8
Construction	−1.5
Public undertakings	0.2
Other services	1.7

Source: N. G. Butlin, *Australian Domestic Product, Investment and Foreign Borrowing, 1861–1938/39* (Cambridge: University Press, 1962), pp. 460–61.

30 was inferior to that of Argentina, in spite of the alleged progressiveness of the leadership of the former country relative to the latter.[71] Per capita real GNP grew in Canada at only 0.7 percent per annum during 1913–29. This slowdown in Australian and Canadian growth, furthermore, did not have any obvious damaging effects on their ability to grow faster in later years. Indeed, several important countries saw their growth rates sag during 1913–29.[72] The Argentine response to these exogenous circumstances does not appear either especially farsighted or unusually stupid. A sustained lag in Argentina's growth rate behind most of Western Europe and countries of recent settlement is difficult to find before 1930.

Even admitting that the export growth rate registered during the early part of the century could not be expected to continue (because of limitations imposed by either foreign demand or domestic supply), the case for greater tariff protection during 1918–29 was not compelling on purely economic grounds. Essay 5 will explore this issue

71. Australia is generally credited with a greater interest than Argentina in the development of manufacturing during those years. Both countries no doubt suffered from the stagnation of the British economy after World War I. Between 1910 and 1930 Australian population grew at slightly less than 2 percent per annum.

72. Even in the United States, where per capita growth during that period was higher than in Argentina, Australia, and Canada, it was lower during 1913–29 than it had been during 1870–1913. Germany's per capita GNP in 1929 was no higher than in 1913, and that of the United Kingdom grew at an annual rate of 0.3 percent between those years. See U.S. Department of Commerce, *Long Term Economic Growth, 1860–1965* (Washington, D.C.: Bureau of the Census, ES4-No. 1), p. 101. Canadian data were also obtained from this source. The per capita Argentine real GDP grew at an annual rate of 0.9 percent during 1913–29.

in greater detail. Here it will be enough to notice that a gradual slowdown in export growth would have produced, given the liberal policies of those years, a tendency for the exchange rate to devalue, which would have set up automatic forces favoring import substitution. Similarly, gradual changes in factor endowments, and especially in the capital/land and labor/land ratios, could have been expected to induce changes in the productive structure of the country working through the price mechanism. In fact, during the 1930s the economy was to prove that it could respond quickly to that type of stimulus. Given this flexibility, it would have taken great faith in industrial externalities to have favored, say in 1925, a deliberate effort to re-allocate resources by special government policies from at-the-moment-prosperous rural activities toward protected industries. Unless it is claimed that Argentine authorities should have foreseen the Great Depression, or that they should have hit upon Keynesian policies during 1914–17, the "Great Delay" thesis is weak.

THE POSITION OF ARGENTINA IN 1929

By 1929 Argentina had reached a GNP per capita of around 700 U.S. dollars (at 1964 prices, and with purchasing power equivalents).[73] Although this figure was below that for the United States ($1,800 at 1964 prices), and even those for Australia and Canada (around $1,000 and $1,300 at equivalent 1964 prices), the per capita growth rate of Argentine national income during the previous seventy years was probably higher than in those countries. The wide gap existing in 1860 that separated Argentina from other countries of recent settlement had been narrowed by 1929. Population expansion, which in these resource-rich, labor-poor countries could be taken as an index of progress, was larger in Argentina than in Canada and Australia between 1869 and 1929. Population in 1929 was 5.2

73. The translation of GNP figures in pesos into dollars can be done in a number of ways. Two methods were tried: (1) using the United Nations figures expressed in 1950 pesos, translating them into 1950 dollars at the "purchasing parity exchange rate," estimated by the United Nations at 6.3 pesos per dollar, and then translating 1950 dollars into 1964 dollars using the implicit price deflator for the United States GNP; and (2) beginning from 1937 data at current prices for the GNP, using quantum and wholesale price indices to estimate the 1929 GNP, and then using the market exchange rate for that year for an estimate in 1929 dollars, from which figures in 1964 dollars were obtained as in (1). Both methods yield similar results.

times what it had been in 1869 in Argentina, while for Canada and Australia the corresponding figures were 2.8 and 4.0, respectively.[74] Between 1895 and 1929, while Argentine population grew at an annual rate of 3.2 percent, that of Canada grew at 2.1 percent and that for Australia expanded at only 1.8 percent. The Australian real GDP grew at an annual rate of 2.5 percent between 1900 and 1929, while the corresponding Argentine figure was 4.8 percent. While in both Australia and Canada the non-European native population was insignificant, in Argentina this was not the case; especially in the western and northwestern zones, there were large groups of citizens of Indian background, often with educational levels and attitudes less favorable to growth than those of European immigrants. It is likely that in 1929 the per capita income of the residents of the pampean zone only was very close to the Australian and Canadian levels.

In 1928–29, Argentina ranked eleventh among the major trading nations. Its per capita exports were $90 a year in terms of 1928–29 U.S. dollars, while those of Australia and Canada were $105 and $125, respectively. With twenty-six inhabitants per automotive vehicle, it ranked ahead of the United Kingdom in per capita number of these vehicles in 1930, in spite of the relative lack of roads in the country.[75] The illiteracy rate (calculated as a percentage of the population of 14 years of age and older), which had dropped from 77 percent in

74. The following sources have been used for income and population data for the United States, Canada, and Australia: M. C. Urquhart, ed., *Historical Statistics of Canada* (Toronto: The Macmillan Company of Canada, 1965), pp. 14, 130; Bureau of Census and Statistics, *Official Year Book of the Commonwealth of Australia,* no. 23, 1930 (Melbourne: Government Printer, 1930), pp. 662–64; N. G. Butlin, *Australian Domestic Product,* p. 7; and Council of Economic Advisers, *Economic Report of the President* (Washington, D.C., January, 1965), pp. 190, 213. In the United States, population in 1929 was 3.1 times that of 1869. See U.S. Department of Commerce, *Historical Statistics of the United States* (Washington, D.C.: U.S. Government Printing Office), p. 7. For other comparisons between Australia, Canada, and Argentina see Arthur Smithies, "Argentina and Australia," *American Economic Review 55,* no. 2 (May 1965): 17–22, and the comments by M. C. Urquhart in the same issue, pp. 45–49. Colin Clark placed Argentina, together with the United States, Canada, Australia, New Zealand, Great Britain, and Switzerland, among the countries with the highest living standards during 1925–1934. See Colin Clark, *The Conditions of Economic Progress* (London: Macmillan and Co., 1940), p. 2.

75. See *Anuario Geográfico Argentino,* p. 466. The United States led with 5 inhabitants per automotive vehicle; Canada and Australia had 8 and 11, respectively. Other sources put the number of inhabitants per automotive vehicle in Argentina during 1930 at 28.

the 1869 Census to 36 percent in the 1914 Census, was around 25 percent in 1929 (and reached 14 percent in the 1947 Census). By 1929 Buenos Aires had become one of the great cultural centers of the Spanish-speaking world; its newspapers and publishers often were the first to print the work of leading cultural figures. Several important essays of Miguel de Unamuno, for example, first appeared in *La Nación*. The Argentine death rate in 1929, 13.1 per thousand inhabitants, was not far from that in Canada (11.4 per thousand inhabitants).[76]

Domestic rural entrepreneurs showed little interest in industry, but foreign capital and domestic urban capitalists (most of them immigrants) were active in that field, so that although a reasonable 1929 forecast was a continuation of a species of export-led growth, it looked as if it would be increasingly sustained by import-competing industrial expansion. This gradual change in leading sectors could have been expected to occur as a normal result of both the changing Argentine factor endowment and the expansion of the domestic market, which brought more decreasing cost industries to the borderline of profitability in competition with imports. So long as foreign demand for traditional exports continued to grow at rates not too far below those registered since 1900, net import substitution in that full employment society would remain relatively modest. But a slowdown in foreign demand, or any difficulty in increasing the domestic supply of these exports, was bound to produce, even without any special government action (so long as the exchange rate was allowed to move), an expansion of the import substituting sector and of nontraditional exports. This second line of defense was very important during the 1930s.

Not the least of the favorable legacies left by pre-1930 prosperity was a high level of official gold reserves which helped Argentina weather the shock of the Great Depression. These reserves, which at the end of 1899 were less than 2 million gold pesos, rose to 224 million gold pesos at the end of 1914 and to 471 million gold pesos in 1920. By the end of 1928 they stood at 490 million, of which

76. *Historical Statistics of Canada*, p. 39 and DNEC, *Informe Demográfico*, p. 14. In the provinces of Buenos Aires and Santa Fe the death rate was near 11 per thousand inhabitants; in the same provinces the rate of illiteracy had fallen to 10 percent and 13 percent, respectively, in 1947. The number of telephones installed in Argentina rose from 61,000 in 1912, to 281,000 in 1930, and to 461,000 in 1940.

247 million gold pesos remained in 1935, when the BCRA was created.[77]

Although political tensions were rising during 1929, the person wishing to take an optimistic long-run view had some powerful arguments. Looking back over the previous twenty years, it appeared as if Argentina had witnessed a peaceful and irreversible surrender of political power from the traditional (landholding) ruling groups that dominated government during 1860–1916 to the rising urban middle classes, represented by the Radical Civil Union. Under a conservative president, Roque Sáenz Peña, a new electoral system providing for universal, secret, and obligatory vote for citizens registered on the national military rolls was approved (in 1912). In the 1916 election, Hipólito Yrigoyen was elected president, opening an era of control of the government by the Radicals, which was to last until the onset of the Great Depression (1930).[78]

By 1929, the struggle between the province of Buenos Aires and the rest of the country, a source of unrest during the nineteenth century, had become less acute. The concentration of wealth and population in the pampean zone, and especially around the metropolitan center of greater Buenos Aires, was still resented, but this political and economic dominance could not be challenged easily, being rooted in superior natural resources and geographical position. Although the concentration of population in the pampean zone and its higher than average real income may be deplored on equity or geopolitical grounds, it is difficult to make a good case against it on the basis of economic efficiency. Perhaps the fact that immigrants came into the country via the city of Buenos Aires led to its greater than optimal growth, and a correspondingly lower than optimal expansion in other zones, but any such distortions (presumably due to lack of information

77. A gold peso was worth nearly one (0.965) of the pre-1933 gold dollars. Therefore, taking into account the 69 percent increase in the dollar price of gold, the new Argentine Central Bank had gold reserves worth 403 million new dollars in 1935.

78. An English author observed in 1929: "Argentina today is one of the more stable and better ordered states, not only in America but also in the world; it is one of the few states where a revolution is as unlikely as it is in England." Quoted in Darío Cantón, *El Parlamento Argentino en Epocas de Cambio; 1890, 1916 y 1946* (Buenos Aires: Editorial del Instituto Di Tella, 1966), p. 13. The quote is from Cecil Jane, *Liberty and Despotism in Spanish America* (Oxford: Clarendon Press, 1929), p. 173. I have retranslated from Spanish. Pre-1930 growth had generated a diversified social structure; by 1914 urban workers, rural peons and domestic servants represented only 50 percent of the active population. See Germani, *Política y Sociedad,* p. 196.

and market imperfections) had an insignificant direct effect on economic growth either before or after 1930.[79] Nevertheless, resentment against pampean and Buenos Aires domination remained a source of potential political trouble.

Argentina in 1929 had a worldwide reputation as a country with a prosperous future and was expected to play an increasingly important role not only in inter-American but also in intercontinental political affairs. Indeed, many influential Argentine leaders regarded their country as the logical counterpoise to the United States in the Americas, and dreamed of increasing Argentine influence in neighboring countries. With the wisdom of hindsight, several negative elements in the socio-economic fabric of the nation may now be examined. They are elements which, under the combined pressures of the conservative political reaction during the Great Depression, World War II, and rapid industrialization, led to the Perón regime in later years.

A fundamental source of tension in pre-1930 Argentina was this:

> Anglo-Argentine intercourse . . . depended upon the strictest mutual respect and independence on the plane of politics, while on the plane of economics it involved a complex and delicate interdependence. Like the United States, Canada, and Australia, Argentina was one of the significant frontiers of British business enterprise during the century before World War I.[80]

79. The 1914 census had shown that the pampean zone (Federal District, Buenos Aires, Santa Fe, Entre Ríos, Córdoba and La Pampa), containing 30 percent of the national territory, accounted for 74 percent of the population. The metropolitan zone known as the greater Buenos Aires had nearly 26 percent. According to the censuses, the population of the Federal District alone (i.e., excluding suburban centers located in the province of Buenos Aires), grew from 187,000 in 1869 to 663,000 in 1895 and to 1,576,000 in 1914. These figures represented 10.8 percent, 16.8 percent, and 20.0 percent of the total population, respectively. Often used to prove Argentine regional unbalance, they say little about the efficiency or inefficiency of population distribution. Population concentration in the pampean zone does not seem very different from that along the United States' eastern seaboard, especially if it is borne in mind that Argentina lacks geographical sites such as the Pacific coast, the Great Lakes and the Gulf of Mexico, which in the United States act as counterpoises to the eastern seaboard. The concentration of Australian population in the southeastern corner of that country represents a more unbalanced pattern than that of Argentina.

80. Ferns, *Britain and Argentina,* pp. 1–2. Common roots have not kept Canadians and Australians from resenting United States investments in their countries. It is not, then, very surprising that Latin Argentina led the way in economic nationalism when even Canada now has potential Anglo-Saxon Peróns.

Unlike Canada and Australia, Argentina had not only a different language and culture from that of its Anglo-Saxon investors, but also a tradition of political independence born, in fact, when the citizens of Buenos Aires defeated a British attempt to wrest the Río de la Plata from Spanish control in 1807. Southern European immigrants shared with native Argentines a mistrust of Anglo-Saxon ways and manners.

An atmosphere of resentment against foreign investors and the liberal system created since 1862 developed shortly after external capital began to flow into the country. Criticisms were levied first against specific features of that system, but gradually spread to a general condemnation of British-Argentine ties. Some nationalists began to glorify the Rosas regime (1829–52), which was characterized by cool and erratic relations with foreign powers, restrictions upon trade, and heavy reliance on traditionalist and religious elements. Railroads, meat-packing plants, and public utilities were accused of making exorbitant profits by taking advantage of oligopolist and oligopsonist power. As early as the 1890s, railroad companies were attacked in newspapers and by public officials for not providing enough freight cars during the grain harvest season; "repeatedly it was pointed out that despite their high freight rates, the railroads were derelict in providing sufficient rolling stock." [81] Foreign-owned meat-packing plants and owners of the refrigerated ships which transported their output abroad were suspected of exercising oligopsonist power to drive down the price at which they purchased live animals; agitation

81. Scobie, *Revolution on the Pampas,* pp. 96–97. This author claims that the real problem was the inefficient port facilities that tied up freight cars for days awaiting unloading. The same author quotes a study that appeared in the *Journal of Political Economy* 10, no. 3 (June 1902): 333–60, by R. R. Kuczynski, in which it was concluded that short-haul (under 100 miles) charges for wheat in Argentine railroads were far lower than in the United States, although those over 200 miles were more expensive. On the other hand, a British author has written the following regarding the early years of railroad investment in Argentina: "Argentina rapidly became a railway inferno where no fewer than 21 private railway companies and three state railways were struggling for the business of approximately 4 million people. The struggle might have had some beneficent consequences if the railway companies had seriously fought for the right to provide service, but too often they neglected investment in such elementary essentials as locomotives and goods wagons in favor of miles of line laid down either to keep out a rival company or to get a guaranteed profit from a government anxious to please its friends by promoting railways into areas where those friends had land." Ferns, *Britain and Argentina,* p. 410. The proliferation of railroad companies foreshadowed a similar proliferation of automobile companies that occurred nearly one hundred years later. The charge that railroad companies often duplicated their competitors' tracks, however, appears exaggerated.

for congressional investigation of these concerns became acute every time the meat trade became depressed and gained momentum after the reformist and nationalistic Radical party gained power in 1916. (Some elements of the Radical party came from families that had supported the Rosas regime, defeated by the liberals who built the economic system prevailing after the mid-nineteenth century.) In the case of the oil-extracting industry, the Radical governments succeeded in forcing foreign companies to discontinue attempts to exploit deposits and in general engaged in minor hostilities with foreign investors, especially over public utility rates.

Although some of the accusations against foreign investors were based more on emotional first-generation xenophobic nationalism than on facts and economic reasoning, the cavalier contempt with which most investors treated even sensible inquiries about their activities accentuated the bitterness of Argentine resentment. As late as 1934, a British meat-packing company attempted to smuggle out of the country (under the marking of corned beef!) records of its Argentine activities which had been subpoenaed by the Senate under a law upheld by the Argentine Supreme Court.[82]

Friction between foreign investors and Argentines, including as Argentines the newly arrived poor immigrants, was perhaps the most potentially explosive issue kept under control by the prosperity of the 1920s. Prosperity also dampened the rise of rural populism among cereal tenant farmers, who since the late nineteenth century had complained about high rents and oligopsonist commercial interests in the grain export trade.[83] The interests of the beef raising, land-

82. Dudley M. Phelps, *Migration of Industry to South America* (New York: McGraw-Hill Book Co., 1936), pp. 186–87. Although this author is on the whole sympathetic to the foreign investor, he states: "Undoubtedly, the whole incident was uncalled for, and the Anglo company brought discomfiture upon itself by its unwillingness to conform with the decision of the Court" (p. 187). The Argentine government in 1934 was conservative but sensitive to the interests of beef-raising landowners. One may speculate that the clash between the beef-raising "oligarchy" and British meat packers and importers, which was accentuated by the Great Depression and the creation of commonwealth preferences, was one of the reasons why pro-Fascist sentiment spread so rapidly among Argentine upper classes after 1930. Another major scandal during the 1930s involved a foreign-owned public utility that supplied the city of Buenos Aires with electricity and was charged with bribing public officials to obtain a renewal of its concession under favorable terms.

83. Rural restlessness had broken into open violence during 1912 in the zone of Alcorta, in the province of Santa Fe. The clash of Latin and Anglo-Saxon cultures created frictions in areas other than those related to direct foreign investment. It apparently also explains the failure to attract more

owning "oligarchy" were not identical to those of foreigners in the
export business, but there grew in Argentina the belief that a corrupt
alliance of foreigners and domestic "oligarchs" in import and export
activities ran the country only for their own profit.

The real wages of most Argentine urban and rural workers before 1930 were not very different from those of many western European workers. Their social and political position, however, was less
satisfactory. In the rural zones a system of more or less benevolent
paternalism was the rule, especially on the large estates devoted to
beef and sheep raising. Health and education facilities catering to
peons of the livestock ranches and to cereal tenant farmers were few
and of low quality. In the cities, trade unions were few; as late as
1936 there were only 370,000 union members in the whole country
(the labor force could be estimated at around 4 million for that year),
and they were concentrated in a few organizations such as the trade
union for railroad workers.[84] The reformist Radicals paid only
limited attention to social issues related to the working class; indeed,
early in their administration (1919) the government bloodily sup-
pressed a rash of strikes. The fact that the leadership of the workers
was often in the hands of European immigrants, many of anarchistic
beliefs, did not help to generate sympathy among nationalistic
elements.[85] Social legislation before 1930 was scanty; there was none
concerning trade unions, and no general system of social security
existed. As late as 1942, only 647,000 persons contributed to a few
scattered retirement and pension funds, mainly for civil servants and

immigrants from northern Europe and the difficulties experienced by rural
colonies of northern Europeans in Argentina. See Ferns, *Britain and Argentina,*
pp. 78 and 140.

84. *Anuario Geográfico Argentino,* p. 545. By 1940, the number of trade
union members had risen to 473,000. Other sources give slightly different
estimates.

85. See José L. Romero, *A History of Argentine Political Thought* (Stanford:
University Press, 1963), pp. 223–25. It will be recalled that Table 1.23 showed
a sharp drop in real wages during 1915–19. During these years, European-style
socialist parties expanded rapidly among urban masses; however, these parties
failed to attract either the rural workers or the nationalistic children of urban
immigrants. The conditions of the working class in Argentina between World
War I and the Great Depression bear some resemblance to that of the working
class of the United States; in both countries, there were Bolshevik or anarchist
scares immediately after the war, followed by a period when prosperity
smoothed social tensions. Modest social legislation introduced by the first
Radical administration does not appear to have had much impact among
workers.

employees of public services and banks; in the same year, only 8,000 females received benefits from maternity funds.[86]

The high proportion of foreigners in the labor force (nearly half in 1914) slowed down the growth of working-class solidarity and political power. It was easy to rally native middle class public opinion against labor leaders or rebellious tenants who often hardly spoke Spanish and who advocated European ideologies. Peons on livestock ranches and farms, who usually came from older Argentine racial stock with considerable Indian background, were not easily reached by reformist urban immigrants; they remained passive. These descendants of the nineteenth-century gauchos were to become a potent political force during the 1940s and 1950s, after they had migrated to urban centers,[87] and were to become also a favorite target of insulting epithets from their previous employers.

Heavy preponderance of the foreign-born among rising urban entrepreneurs similarly robbed this group of much of its potential influence in political life. Even to this day, it is common to hear complaints about the timidity of urban entrepreneurs and their willingness to allow traditional, land-based families to retain social and political leadership.

The generosity of Argentine law, which granted resident aliens nearly equal rights with citizens while imposing fewer duties, may be partly to blame for the slow incorporation of immigrants into political life. Many of them saw little point in becoming citizens and, in contrast with immigrants into the United States, withheld a total commitment to their new land for as long as they could. Indifference and alienation flourished. To many, the ideal was to become rich in Argentina and then return to their native land. Those who felt this way but failed to become rich, often turned bitter toward the establishment and passed that attitude on to their children.

The counterpart to the slow "nationalization" of immigrants was the retention of considerable power in the hands of long-resident groups, especially the families of those who emerged victorious in 1852. The economic basis for this power, so long as world trade was prosperous and Argentina chose to participate in it, was secured by those factors

86. See *Anuario Geográfico Argentino,* Supplement 1942, pp. 295–303.
87. David Felix has pointed out to me the parallel existing between the role played by the southern rural black migrants in the United States urban crisis and that of the "little blackheads" in the Peronist movement.

outlined in the section on the land market.[88] The first generation of this class had little in common with the caricature of the indolent landlord. The land was won mainly by fighting either Indians or political enemies, and nineteenth-century liberal ideas filled their minds. Their leadership generated the remarkable post-1860 growth which transformed Argentina from one of the most backward countries in Latin America into the most prosperous and cultured one. It is of course true that liberal policies regarding trade and immigration directly benefited owners of the relatively abundant factor of production, i.e., land, but there is little doubt that at that time those policies also encouraged economic growth. Leaders such as Domingo F. Sarmiento (president during 1868–74) clearly saw the link between education and development and embarked on ambitious programs which today could grace the best development plans.

The descendants of this elite received an inheritance of lands whose values seemed destined to grow forever automatically. Few thought worthwhile the additional efforts necessary to become industrial entrepreneurs. Although the refinement and culture of these groups continued to increase, they began to lose the political talents and energy displayed by their ancestors. The industrial elite can be renewed by the emergence of new products, processes, and entrepreneurs, but renewal of the rural elite is more difficult; at least in the case of Argentina, renewal appears to have been slight.

Nevertheless, the slow digestion of foreign capital and labor, the social and economic gap between the rural masses and the urban middle class, regional frictions, and the decline in the quality of political leadership were not of a nature to make a revolutionary explosion inevitable. Pre-1930 Argentine society remained on the whole flexible, and social mobility was about as high as in other countries of recent settlement. The majority of the elite, although wealthy and powerful, remained attached to a liberal ideology until at least the 1920s, as witnessed by the educational system.[89] It is

88. According to Gino Germani, in 1914 the foreign born accounted for only 10 percent of owners of real estate, 18 percent of civil servants, and 22 percent of owners of livestock establishments. On the other hand, 74 percent of owners of commercial establishments and 66 percent of industrial owners were foreign born. See his *Política y Sociedad,* p. 195.

89. In 1929, out of a population of 11.59 million, there were 1.41 million pupils in primary schools with 53,600 teachers. In the same year, 10 percent of the budget of the national government was spent on primary education. in 1934 there were 90,300 pupils in secondary schools registered with the

not inconceivable that a few more decades of an expanding world economy would have induced an acceleration in the growth of urban leadership which could have reconciled the aspirations of urban workers, entrepreneurs, and rural masses with a gradual decline in the influence of landowners, without damaging the production of rural exportable commodities. Yet such a balancing act, even under prosperous conditions, is difficult in Argentina. The main problem arises in that policies which are best from the viewpoint of economic efficiency (e.g. free, or nearly free, trade) generate an income distribution favorable to the owners of the relatively most abundant factor of production (e.g. land) and therefore strengthen the position of the traditional elite. The same issue can be viewed in another way. A policy that artificially diverted exports of meat and grains toward domestic consumption could be expected to be popular with urban masses who spend a high share of their budgets on these commodities and with urban entrepreneurs concerned with the size of their wage bill. Long run efficiency and a popular income distribution could only be reconciled by a sophisticated fiscal system, not an easy thing to achieve.

It has been said that in the United Kingdom "agriculture provided a strange story, in which emotion played as much part as economics. Antagonism to the landed interest had always been at the heart of the Free Trade movement; enthusiasm for it inspired the Protectionists." [90]

Exactly the same statement can be applied to Argentina, if we substitute Protectionist for Free Trade and Free Traders for Protectionists. While in Great Britain what was popular was economically efficient, in Argentina these two goals were in apparent conflict. In the days of Spanish domination and under the Rosas regime, restrictions on exports had been used to maintain low domestic prices of wage goods.[91] These policies were important factors in the

---

Ministry of Education and 22,300 pupils registered in national universities. See *Anuario Geográfico Argentino*, pp. 497–524.

90. A. J. P. Taylor, *English History, 1914–1945* (Oxford: Oxford University Press, 1965), p. 341.

91. As pointed out to me by Charles P. Kindleberger, export interests in the United States checked this danger by constitutionally prohibiting export taxes. Changes in rural relative prices have not only a powerful influence on the distribution of current Argentine income, but also on wealth distribution, as most land values are closely tied to those prices.

eventual overthrow of those regimes by movements spearheaded by pampean landowners.

It will be seen in the next essay that economically Argentina was able to adjust to the Great Depression rather well; but the depression hardly created a climate conducive to continuation of the gradual emergence of a new urban elite. Traditional elements grabbed back the political power so gracefully relinquished in 1916 and proceeded to grope for a new order that could substitute for the now-discredited liberal system. The frictions and tensions generated during the 1860–1930 expansion became aggravated in the 1930s by political reaction, the stagnation of exports and rural output, and the pressures of further industrialization and urbanization. Urban growth, previously fed by foreign immigration, came to depend mainly on an inflow from the stagnant countryside. While under the shadow of World War II pro-Fascist and pro-Allied groups within the traditional groups jockeyed for positions, the conditions were being prepared for an explosion of nationalistic and populist sentiment averse to the foreign trade and foreign capital in which so much faith had been placed before 1930, but which provided many disappointments and humiliations to Argentina during the Great Depression.

2

The Argentine Economy since 1930

Between 1930 and 1965 the world economy continued to give Argentina shocks and stimuli. First came the Great Depression, then World War II, and finally a long period of expanding world trade. How Argentina reacted to these exogenous forces is the subject of this essay.

The Argentine growth rate during this period seriously slipped behind those of other countries of recent settlement. Whether this was a result of domestic policies or unfavorable exogenous circumstances will be discussed.

This essay will examine only the broad outlines of Argentine growth since 1930; other essays will look into the rural and manufacturing sectors in greater detail. Three key features of growth will be presented first, treating the period as a whole. This will be followed by a discussion of the forces that resulted in the observed rate and pattern of growth. Three major periods will be isolated in post-1930 policy-making; this will allow a more precise discussion regarding the timing of Argentina's slippage behind other countries of recent settlement.

THE QUANTITATIVE RECORD: THREE KEY FEATURES

The three key features of Argentine development since 1930 have been (1) a low and irregular growth rate in per capita income, (2) a marked disparity in sectorial growth rates, and (3) an absolute decline in the export quantum.

Table 2.1 presents post-1930 annual growth rates for the economy as a whole and for major sectors. Data from two different official sources are presented because, for some periods, fairly important and unexplained discrepancies exist. The overall growth rate has

Table 2.1: Rates of Growth of Global and Sectorial
Real Value Added in Argentina, 1925–29/1961–65
(Annual averages in percentages)

	1925–29/1957–61		*1925–29/1961–65*
	CONADE	BCRA	BCRA
GDP at factor cost	2.8	2.7	2.7
Agriculture, livestock, and fisheries	0.9	1.2	1.2
Oil and mining	7.2	7.1	7.8
Manufacturing	4.1	3.7	3.6
Construction	2.9	3.0	2.6
Electricity and other public utilities	5.7	5.7	6.2
Transport	3.6	3.3	3.2
Communications	3.7	3.5	3.1
Commerce	2.0	1.7	1.8
Financial services	3.8	3.8	3.8
Housing services	2.5	2.5	2.3
Government services	4.3	4.3	3.8
Other services	3.1	3.2	3.0

Sources and method: Data for 1925–39 from ECLA, p. 4; for 1935–65 from CONADE, *Cuentas Nacionales de la República Argentina*, worksheets of CONADE, and from BCRA. Data were linked using the average value for each series from each source during 1935–39. Data for 1925–29 are expressed in 1950 prices; data for 1935–65 are expressed at 1960 prices. Rates of growth are obtained by comparing the average values for 1925–29 with those for 1957–61 or 1961–65 (i.e. the figures for in-between years are ignored). The same procedure will be followed in other tables, unless otherwise specified. Unfortunately, it is not possible to subdivide construction into industrial, commercial, and residential.

been around 2.7 percent per annum, while population has been expanding at an annual rate of about 1.9 percent.[1] The 0.8 per capita

1. Average population evolved as follows: 1925–29 = 10,970,000; 1935–39 = 13,493,000; 1957–61 = 20,314,000; 1961–65 = 21,685,000. Data obtained from U.N., *Statistical Bulletin for Latin America* vol. 3, no. 2, pp. 8–11. Long term growth rates are only slightly changed if, instead of GDP, either the Gross Domestic Income (taking into account changes in terms of trade) or the GNP (which also takes into account factor payments abroad) are used. For Domestic Income (taking into account changes in terms of trade) or the different aggregates, between 1935–39 and 1961–65: GDP, at factor cost, 3.0 percent; GDP, at market prices, 3.0 percent; GDI, 2.7 percent; GNP or GNI, 2.8 percent. Between those two periods, the GDP rose by 114 percent, the GNP by 107 percent, and the GDI by 100 percent, according to BCRA. Net factor payments abroad represented 4.0 percent of the GDP (expressed at 1960 prices) during 1935–39, and only 0.6 percent of GDP during 1961–65. When annual growth rates are estimated fitting a trend line to the logarithms of all BCRA yearly estimates during 1935–66, the following results are obtained: GDP, at market prices, 2.93 percent; GDI, 2.73 percent; GNP or GNI, 2.86 percent; Population, 1.86 percent.

growth rate is below the corresponding figure for 1862–1930 and below post-1930 growth rates in countries similar to Argentina.

To those familiar with Argentine writings and commentary even this meager expansion may seem an exaggeration. The years before the Great Depression are commonly pictured as a golden age; one may wonder whether the gains in per capita product are not just a statistical illusion. Other time series, however, confirm that per capita gains have been made since 1930, at least using conventional income measures.[2]

Since 1930, however, the growth has been so small, the cyclical fluctuations so violent, and the swings in income distribution so pronounced that it is easy to believe that during some years several groups have been worse off than they, or their parents, were during 1925–29. Furthermore, in some public services (e.g. telephones, railroads, the post office, and statistical services) and in some import-substituting manufactures, quality has deteriorated so that a quality-corrected growth rate would be even smaller. The figures presented in Table 2.1 have not been corrected for changes in the external terms of trade either. Although time series for the Argentine terms of trade are of doubtful reliability, it is likely that they declined between 1925–29 and recent years; correcting the growth rate for this decline would further shave it (although slightly).

As one would expect in a country where high levels of food and clothing consumption had been reached by 1929, increases in per capita consumption since then have taken mainly in durable goods and products that did not exist at that time. This, plus changes in taste (e.g. the switch from yerba mate to soft drinks), further complicate the welfare comparison of recent years with 1925–29.

Other less tangible considerations also have to be taken into account when comparing the welfare of the average Argentine citizen today with that of 1925–29. Political instability now intrudes more into daily life than it did before, making planning of personal matters more difficult. Inflation also contributes to increased anxiety and un-

2. Disaggregated time series that can be used as a rough check on Table 2.1 are presented in Table 85 of the Statistical Appendix. The most disturbing indicator shown there is that for steel and iron absorption. Its very low growth rate seems to be due, however, to unusually high investments in social overhead capital during 1925–29 and to supply difficulties during 1957–61. Another check on Table 2.1, which has not been attempted, would be to see what growth rate emerges when both 1925–29 and recent outputs are valued at world prices. A lower growth rate would probably result from that exercise.

Table 2.2: Rates of Growth of Global and Sectorial Real Value Added
by Major Subperiods, 1927–29/1963–65 (ECLA/BCRA)
(Annual averages in percentages)

	ECLA/BCRA *1927–29/1941–43*	BCRA *1941–43/1953–55*	BCRA *1953–55/1963–65*
GDP at factor cost	*1.8*	*2.9*	*3.1*
Agriculture, livestock, and fisheries	1.5	1.1	0.9
Oil and mining	9.8	2.6	11.1
Manufacturing	3.4	2.9	4.6
Construction	0	5.3	1.2
Electricity and other public utilities	5.2	6.0	8.2
Transport	1.9	4.4	2.9
Communications	3.5	3.8	0.7
Commerce	−0.3	2.2	3.7
Financial services	1.8	6.3	2.4
Housing services	2.3	2.9	2.8
Government services	3.6	5.9	1.3
Other services	2.6	3.7	2.5

Sources and method: As in Table 2.1.

certainty. Finally, the decline in Argentina's relative world position and its failure to fulfill great pre-1930 hopes have created an unhealthy atmosphere of frustration. It is therefore understandable that, in spite of the growth shown in Table 2.1, many Argentines feel that welfare or the quality of life has declined since 1925–29.

The growth rate has been far from uniform during the post-1930 years. Tables 2.2 and 2.3 subdivide this era into three periods whose special characteristics will be examined subsequently. The first period, encompassing the Great Depression, witnessed the least growth, while more recently the average rate of expansion has been around 3 percent. Annual growth rates have fluctuated a great deal. Rapid growth has been achieved during short spans, usually associated with recoveries from recessions; the highest annual growth rates achieved during periods of five consecutive years have been as follows (using real GDP as the basic series):

> 1932–37: 5.0 percent (ECLA)
> 1943–48: 5.4 percent (BCRA)
> 1953–58: 5.0 percent (BCRA)

Negative growth in real GDP was registered during 1930–32,

Table 2.3: Rates of Growth of Global and Sectorial Real Value Added
by Major Subperiods, 1927–29/1953–55 (ECLA/CONADE)

	ECLA/CONADE 1927–29/1941–43	CONADE 1941–43/1953–55
GDP at factor cost	1.8	3.3
Agriculture, livestock, and fisheries	1.5	0.2
Oil and mining	9.5	3.1
Manufacturing	3.2	4.5
Construction	0	4.9
Electricity and other public utilities	5.2	5.6
Transport	2.0	5.1
Communications	3.5	4.2
Commerce	−0.6	3.3
Financial services	1.8	6.4
Housing services	2.3	2.9
Government services	3.5	6.0
Other services	2.6	3.9

Sources and method: As in Table 2.1.

1940, 1945, 1949, 1952, 1959, and 1962–63; between 1929 and
1932 aggregate output fell by nearly 14 percent, while between 1961
and 1963 as well as during 1952 and 1959 it fell by more than 5
percent (BCRA, ECLA). Clearly, the economy has been characterized before and after 1930 by sharp fluctuations in aggregate output.

A second key feature is also shown in Tables 2.1, 2.2, and 2.3: the
main sectors grew at very different rates (which were also variable
from period to period) to an extent not explainable simply by differences in income elasticities of demand. In particular, one major sector
grew at a rate significantly below that of population. The rural sector,
which during the first three decades of this century expanded at an
annual rate of 3.5 percent, grew at slightly more than 1 percent per
year after 1930. Its expansion was larger during the Great Depression
than in the more prosperous years following.

As a result, the structure of the economy in 1963–65 was substantially different from that in 1927–29. Table 2.4 shows the gross
domestic product structure during these two periods, measured both
at 1937 and at 1960 prices. A glance at the table shows the usefulness
of even a rough calculation in presenting national accounts using
alternative base years for prices.[3] Although at 1960 prices, distorted

3. Changes in relative prices since 1929 will be discussed in greater detail
in essay 6. The method used to compute value added at 1937 prices is outlined
in essay 1, Table 1.6. The reader is reminded that the results can be accepted
only as crude estimates.

Table 2.4: Structure of the GDP of Argentina, 1927–65
(Percentages of total)

	At 1960 prices		At 1937 prices	
	1927–29	*1963–65*	*1927–29*	*1963–65*
GDP at factor cost	*100.0*	*100.0*	*100.0*	*100.0*
Agriculture, livestock, and fisheries	27.4	17.1	30.5	18.4
Oil and mining	0.3	1.5	0.6	3.5
Manufacturing	23.6	33.7	13.4	18.6
Subtotal	51.3	52.3	44.5	40.5
Construction	4.2	3.6	3.1	2.6
Electricity and other public utilities	0.5	1.8	1.3	4.7
Transport	5.5	6.5	8.4	9.6
Communications	0.8	0.9	1.0	1.1
Commerce	23.5	16.9	16.1	11.2
Financial services	1.4	2.0	1.9	2.6
Subtotal	35.9	31.7	31.8	31.8
Housing services	2.1	2.2	9.3	9.4
Government services	4.5	6.8	6.9	10.0
Other services	6.2	7.1	7.5	8.4
Subtotal	12.8	16.1	23.7	27.8

Sources and method: See Table 2.1 (ECLA and BCRA only). Method as in Table 1.6.

by greater postwar protection, the share of manufacturing value added is nearly twice that of the rural sector for 1963–65, when measured at 1937 prices both are roughly equal. Expressed at 1960 prices, the Argentine manufacturing share in GDP is higher than that of the United States for 1963–65! A group of services (public utilities, transport, communications, finance, housing, government, and other private services) whose relative prices have been eroded by inflation, show a share of 27.3 percent of GDP for 1963–65 when measured at 1960 prices, and a share of 45.8 percent, when measured at 1937 prices. But however measured, declines are observed for the share of the rural sector and, to a lesser extent, for those of commerce and construction, sectors which before 1930 received special encouragement from the growth of foreign trade and the expansion of social overhead capital.[4]

The lopsided nature of recent growth may also be illustrated by comparing the 1927–29 structure, shown in Table 2.4, with the allocation of the net increase in GDP between 1927–29 and 1963–65,

4. Commercial activities related to foreign trade accounted for 36 percent of all gross commercialization margins during 1935–37, for 21 percent during 1953–55 and 23 percent in 1963–65. See BCRA, p. 34 (data in 1960 prices).

shown in Table 2.5. The rural sector, with 30.5 percent of the GDP in 1927–29 (at 1937 prices), contributed only 10.6 percent of the increase in GDP. The corresponding figures for the sum of mining, oil, and manufacturing are 14.0 percent and 27.3 percent. Services that

Table 2.5: Allocation of Net Increase in GDP (at factor cost)
between 1927–29 and 1963–65 among Main Sectors
(Percentages of total increase in GDP)

	At 1960 prices	At 1937 prices
Total increase in GDP at factor cost	*100.0*	*100.0*
Agriculture, livestock and fisheries	10.0	10.6
Oil and mining	2.3	5.4
Manufacturing	40.6	21.9
Subtotal	52.9	37.9
Construction	3.1	2.2
Electricity and other public utilities	2.7	6.9
Transport	7.2	10.3
Communications	0.9	1.1
Commerce	12.4	8.0
Financial services	2.3	3.0
Subtotal	28.6	31.5
Housing services	2.3	9.4
Government services	8.3	12.1
Other services	7.8	9.0
Subtotal	18.4	30.5

Sources and method: See Table 2.1 (BCRA, CONADE).

could be said to be complementary to the production of commodities —construction, public utilities, transport, communications, commerce, and finance—kept their joint 1927–29 share when measured at 1937 prices. But services least directly related to the production of commodities (housing services, government, and other private services), which in 1927–29 represented 23.7 percent of GDP, accounted for 30.5 percent of the increase in aggregate output. Government services by themselves contributed 12.1 percent of the increase in GDP, when in 1927–29 they represented only 6.9 percent of total output.

As in other countries, the contribution of most services to Argentine output is measured by quantifying their *inputs* (e.g., government services essentially measure employment), without looking too closely at changes in the quality of these services. The high proportion in the increase of GDP between 1927–29 and 1963–65 accounted by all services (62 percent at 1937 prices and 47 percent at 1960 prices), plus the generalized impression that the quality of many services has deteriorated, strengthens doubts as to the extent of real growth during the last thirty-six years.

The allocation of increases in the labor force, shown in Table 2.6, confirms the trends outlined previously. It is to be expected that marginal increases in the labor force will be allocated differently from the average employment structure as development proceeds. Some of the contrasts shown in Table 2.6, however, cannot be explained

Table 2.6: Allocation of the Labor Supply in Argentina, 1925–61
(Percentages of the total)

	Allocation in 1925–29	*Allocation of the net increase between 1925–29 and 1960–61*	*Allocation in 1960–61*
Total	*100.0*	*100.0*	*100.0*
Rural sector	35.7	3.9	21 7
Oil and mining	0.3	1.0	0.6
Manufacturing	22.0	31.0	26.0
Construction	5.5	6.5	6.0
Public utilities	0.5	1.2	0.8
Transport	4.6	7.0	5.7
Communications	0.5	1.7	1.0
Commerce, finance, and housing services	13.6	15.2	14.3
Government services	4.6	17.7	10.4
Other services	12.6	14.9	13.6

Sources and method: Data on the labor force, 1925–50 (active population), from ECLA, p. 400; for 1947–61 from unpublished research of CONADE. Both series were linked using 1950–54 as their common point. The CONADE data was then extended backwards using the indices derived with 1950–54 as the base. The figures obtained in this fashion for 1925–29 differ slightly from those presented in Chapter 1.

on such grounds alone; witness the figures for the rural sector and for government services. The three major commodity-producing sectors (rural, mining, and manufacturing activities), which in 1925–29 employed 58.0 percent of the labor force, by 1960–61 employed only 48.3 percent. Of the decrease in the rural share of the labor force (14.0 percentage points), less than a third (4.3 percentage points) were picked up by mining and manufacturing, the rest going to services (government services picking up 5.8 percentage points by themselves). Growing urbanization did not necessarily mean faster industrialization.

Even more striking are the changes in capital allocation, shown in Table 2.7. Unfortunately, there are no data available on the

Table 2.7: Allocation of the Capital Stock in Argentina, 1929–55
(Percentages of the total)

	Allocation in 1929	*Allocation of the net increase between 1929 and 1955*
I. *By sectors of the economy*		
Rural sector	20.3	1.0
Manufacturing, mining, and construction	12.3	21.3
Transport, electricity and communications	16.6	4.9
Government services	11.2	36.1
Other services	39.6	36.7
II. *By types of capital goods*		
All machinery and equipment	30.4	19.5
Construction and improvements	57.0	70.2
Cattle stocks	12.6	10.3

Sources and method: Part I calculated on the basis of data presented in ECLA, pp. 91–101. These estimates of capital stock are measured at 1950 Argentine prices. Part II from preliminary and unpublished CONADE data.

sectorial structure of capital stock after 1955. The rural sector, plus transport, electricity, and communications, obtained only 6 percent of the increase in the net capital stock between 1929 and 1955. The relative loss of these sectors, as in the case of labor, was offset only to a small extent by an industry gain (defined as manufacturing, mining, and construction). Government services are the major gainer, accounting for more than a third of the increase in capital according to these data.

The unbalanced nature of post-1930 growth is also reflected in the allocation of net capital formation by types of goods; construction and improvements took up a disproportionate share, while that corresponding to machinery and equipment was less than 20 percent. The reasons for such phenomena will be discussed below.[5]

A third feature of post-1930 growth may be seen in Table 2.8; on

5. It will also be seen that part of these imbalances have been corrected during recent years, not shown in Table 2.7.

Table 2.8: Quantum Indices of Argentine Merchandise Exports
and Imports, 1925–64
(1951–54 = 100)

	1925–29	1930–39	1940–44	1945–49	1950–54	1955–59	1960–64
Merchandise exports	*179*	*167*	*135*	*133*	*106*	*124*	*160*
Livestock products	152	136	162	163	109	140	157
Agricultural products	212	206	90	96	103	113	149
Merchandise imports	*180*	*119*	*65*	*123*	*101*	*119*	*137*

Sources and method: Quantum indices for 1925–54 were obtained from *Análisis y Proyecciones del Desarrollo Económico*, V, *El Desarrollo Económico de la Argentina*, 1:110–15. For post-1950 years, the sources were: *Boletín Mensual de Estadística*, several issues, and *Comercio Exterior*, Informe C. 48 (April 1958), both issued by the Dirección Nacional de Estadística y Censos (hereafter, DNEC). Indices were linked using their overlap during 1951–54. The overall quantum for merchandise exports includes items other than livestock and agricultural products.

the average, export quantum for the postwar period (1945–64) was 27 percent below that of 1925–29 and about 22 percent below the Great Depression levels of 1930–39. During the postwar era the import quantum remained at the level of the 1930s, equivalent to only two-thirds of the 1925–29 volume. The reduction has been particularly striking for agricultural exports (especially cereals and linseed). Few countries in the world can show such poor export performance during the same period; several can show a decline in the per capita export quantum, but few can join Argentina in the sad category of countries whose export quantum declined absolutely.[6]

This performance contrasts with the role of exports before 1929 when, together with capital inflows, they provided the major push toward expansion. The contrast is often presented as export-led growth vs. inward growth. It may be of interest to examine during both periods evidence on the relation between year-to-year changes in the export quantum, and similar changes in the growth rate of real GDP. For this purpose the 1930s may be regarded as part of the first period, as it is commonly asserted that the economy was then still

6. Other major factors influenced the balance of payments during the period under study; unfortunately, only sketchy information is available for several of them. On the one hand, the postwar years witnessed a decline in net service payments as a result of the nationalization of railroads and several public utilities and the expansion of the Argentine merchant marine and Argentine insurance companies. However, nationalistic policies resulted in a net outflow of capital, at least for the immediate postwar period. An apparent decline in the terms of trade from the 1925–29 levels will be discussed below.

highly vulnerable to external shocks. If one compares percentage changes in the quantum of exports, x, with percentage changes in real gross domestic product, y, the following results are obtained:[7] for 1905–40,

$$y_t = 2.10 + 0.25\,x_t + 0.19\,x_{t-1} + 0.24\,x_{t-2/3} \quad R^2 = 0.48; \quad (2.1)$$
$$ (0.05) \quad\;\; (0.05) \quad\quad\;\; (0.08)$$

for 1941–63,

$$y_t = 2.59 + 0.05\,x_t + 0.08\,x_{t-1} + 0.06\,x_{t-2/3} \quad R^2 = 0.05. \quad (2.2)$$
$$ (0.07) \quad\;\; (0.08) \quad\quad\;\; (0.14)$$

The subscripts t denote a given year; for example, the subscript $t - \tfrac{2}{3}$ refers to the average rate of growth of the export quantum for the two years before the last one. The figures in parentheses represent the standard errors of the corresponding coefficients; R^2 refers to the squared multiple correlation coefficient. Equations (2.1) and (2.2) reflect the changed role of exports before and after 1940; the R^2 is much larger in the first equation, while the individual coefficients for the x's are also higher. Similar results are obtained if the capacity to import is used as the independent variable instead of the quantum of exports.[8]

The apparent independence of the GDP growth rate from that of exports shown by equation (2.2) is, of course, devoid of much long-run economic significance; it merely states that the links between these two variables became more subtle and less easily quantifiable, due mainly to flexible lags. While during the first period exports (as well as capital inflows) influenced *short-run* fluctuations in the growth rate primarily via the aggregate demand side, during the second exchange earnings affected growth via the supply of imports of capital goods and raw materials, which they made feasible. The short-run independence of the domestic product from export fluctuations during 1941–63 improved the stability of the growth rate only

7. Percentage changes were computed dividing the anual change by the *larger* of the two compared figures. Data on export quantum and national product were obtained from the sources listed in Table 2.1, plus ECLA (see citation in Abbreviations) and worksheets of ECLA.

8. The capacity to import is defined as the value of exports in foreign currencies deflated by a price index for imports. When this concept is used as the independent variable, the R^2 for 1941–63 rises to 0.12. Capital movements have not been taken into account due to the shaky nature of available data. For 1905–40 the average annual rate of growth of output is 3.2 percent; for 1941–63 it is 2.5 percent (practically equal to the value of the constant term in equation 2.2).

to a limited extent: the standard deviation of the growth rates for the product during 1905–40 was 5.40 percent, while that for 1941–63 was 4.95 percent. Indeed, the ratio of the standard deviation to the mean product growth rate rose in the second period.[9]

The three key features of growth since 1925–29 are of course not independent. In particular, it is tempting to link the slow expansion of the rural sector (coupled with the growth in domestic demand for exportables) with the decline in exports and to blame the disappointing performance of the economy on too much industry at the expense of the rural sector. This diagnosis has become popular during the last few years; but it is misleading. Neither the absolute nor the relative (with respect to overall growth) manufacturing growth rate has been especially high. Although the observed rates are of an ex-post nature, they fail to show too much industry. The relatively low shares of net capital formation and of the increases in the labor force going into industry after 1929 have also been noted. The problem has not been one of too much industry, but one of too few exports, whether of rural, mineral or manufactured goods or even of services. Exports are not the whole story, however. What would have happened if the strategy of import substitution had been different? In particular, what would have happened if activities such as steel, oil-extraction, and petrochemicals had received priority over the expansion of light consumer goods industries? These questions suggest that, besides analyzing recent Argentine economic history in terms of industry vs. agriculture, it should also be discussed in terms of exportable and importable goods vs. home goods such as construction activities and government services. In other words, the failure to put more resources into export and truly import-competing industries and the allocation of too many resources to home goods have given rise to the main problem of the last four decades: a persistent foreign exchange shortage leading to low rates of real capital formation and of productivity gains.

The terms *exportable, importable,* and *home* goods will often be

9. The standard deviation in the annual growth rate of the export quantum was quite high and very similar in both periods: 17.3 percent for 1905–40 and 16.4 percent for 1941–63. For the capacity to import the corresponding figures were 19.5 percent for 1905–40 and 21.4 for 1941–63. These figures illustrate the important role that fluctuations in the export quantum have had in determining variability in the value of export earnings. Cf. A. I. Macbean, *Export Instability and Economic Development* (Cambridge: Harvard University Press, 1966), especially chapters 1–5.

used in this and other essays. They are defined as in standard international trade theory. An importable good is one that is used domestically, but can be either imported or produced at home. Its long-run domestic price is equal to the world price, translated into domestic currency at the going exchange rate, plus transport and commercialization costs, plus tariffs. Its domestic price will move, *ceteris paribus,* with foreign prices and the exchange rate. An exportable good is one that is produced domestically but may be either exported or consumed or invested at home. Its long-run domestic price is equal to the world price, translated at the going exchange rate, minus transport and commercialization costs, and minus export taxes. As with the price of importables, the price of exportables will respond directly to changes in world prices and the exchange rate, *ceteris paribus.* Exportable and importable goods together may be referred to as tradeable goods. Home goods, or nontradeable goods, are those whose domestic prices are not directly linked to world prices, nor to exchange rates. This may come as a result of prohibitive transport and commercialization costs, as for most services, or as a result of prohibitive tariffs or quotas, which break the link between domestic and foreign prices. In the latter case, the term quasi-home goods may be used. Many manufactured goods in Argentina passed from the category of importable to that of quasi-home goods due to the nature of the system of protection. For example, many types of textiles, which were importables during the 1930s, became quasi-home goods during the 1950s.

This classification involves a drastic but useful simplification. In practice, the borderline among these categories will shift depending on government policies and the values of several economic variables such as tariffs and exchange rates. Under many circumstances it may be better to talk about activities which add value to intermediate goods rather than finished goods. The reader should also be warned that just as not all manufacturing activities could be said to produce importable goods (some even process primary goods before they are exported), not all rural goods can be labeled exportable.

THE FOREIGN EXCHANGE SHORTAGE

A foreign exchange shortage or a low capacity to import can only be defined relative to a constellation of desired targets in economic performance.[10] Here we can assert that the single most important feature of the economic history of Argentina since 1930 has been a persistent shortage of foreign exchange because, with the exception of the war and immediate postwar years, the capacity to import has been lower than that required to achieve a sustainable growth rate of 5 percent per year. If it is further stated that all other requirements for that growth rate were present or would have been present as soon as growth reached those higher levels, and that no substantial possibilities existed to substitute other inputs for the needed foreign exchange, we can talk about an exchange bottleneck limiting economic expansion. The bottleneck may arise either because of unfavorable external circumstances, to which the economy cannot adjust rapidly, or because of domestic policies (e.g. an exchange policy keeping the price of foreign exchange below its equilibrium level).

This approach simplifies considerably the analysis of growth. For any country, growth usually will be constrained by several factors— savings capacity, labor force, organizational difficulties, etc.; but a shortage of one may be made up by increasing the availability of others, so that the maximum rate of growth possible is not limited by any one ingredient, but by a general shortage of growth-generating inputs. Thus, a complete analysis should include a discussion of the availability of each of those ingredients, as well as trade-offs among them. But for post-1930 Argentina we shall not discuss the reasons why the economy did not grow at 7 or 8 percent per annum; to answer the question of why the economy did not grow at 5 percent, the concept of a foreign exchange shortage is a useful simplification.

The two classical inputs, labor and capital, provide another way of looking at the exchange bottleneck. Between 1929 and 1955 the

10. Discussion of the concept of a foreign exchange shortage was pioneered in Latin America by ECLA in several publications; it was given special importance in *El Desarrollo Económico de la Argentina*. See also H. B. Chenery and M. Bruno, "Development Alternatives in an Open Economy: The Case of Israel," *Economic Journal* 57 (March 1962); Ronald I. McKinnon, "Foreign Exchange Constraints in Economic Development and Efficient Aid Allocation," *Economic Journal* 64 (June 1964); and H. B. Chenery and A. M. Strout, "Foreign Assistance and Economic Development," *American Economic Review* 56, no. 4, part I, pp. 679–733. For applications of the concept to Argentina see Javier Villanueva, "Industrialization Problems with Restrictions in the Foreign Sector: A Geometrical Note," *Oxford Economic Papers* 18, no. 2 (July 1966); F. Masson and J. Theberge, "Necesidades de Capital Externo y Desarrollo Económico: El Caso de Argentina," *El Trimestre Económico* 34 (4), no. 136 (Oct.–Dec. 1967); and Aldo Ferrer, *La Economía Argentina* (México: Fondo de Cultura Económica, 1963).

labor force grew at 1.8 percent per annum, while total physical capital grew at around the same rate. Preliminary figures on the capital stock for recent years show an average growth rate of 2.3 percent per annum between 1929 and 1962. Physical capital is quite a heterogeneous aggregate; it includes livestock, construction and improvements, and machinery and equipment. Looking just at machinery and equipment, one observes that while they grew at an annual rate of more than 9 percent between 1900 and 1929, their 1929–55 growth was only 1.3 percent; preliminary estimates put the 1929–62 rate of expansion at 3.3 percent.[11]

The growth of the Argentine labor force should not be taken as a rigid and exogenously given parameter, but, because of the possibility of immigration, as a highly elastic endogenous one. This leaves us with the growth of capital, and with the growth of machinery and equipment in particular (and possibly with a residual), as the determinants of growth. Why was the growth of the capital stock in the form of machinery and equipment so much greater before 1930 than after that date? Although foreign savings made an important contribution to capital formation before 1929, by then GNP had reached levels that could sustain large national savings. Indeed, at current prices gross national savings during the post-World War II period have fluctuated around 20 percent of GNP. The capacity to save, therefore, is not a serious barrier to achieving a sustained 5 percent growth rate. Imports during 1925–29 represented 35 percent of the total value of gross capital formation in machinery and equipment.[12] As the export sector produced a rising amount of foreign exchange to finance these imports, it could have been said to be the major (nonconstruction) capital goods industry of the country. This indirect fashion of obtaining machinery and equipment was more efficient than setting up plants to produce directly in Argentina most types of

11. Data sources as in Tables 2.6 and 2.7. Capital in machinery and equipment grew at nearly 14 percent per annum between 1900 and 1914 and at more than 5 percent annually during 1914–29. These data on capital stock are shaky and should be taken only to indicate broad movements. Labor force data are better, but none are available for total manhours. It may be assumed, however, that total manhours worked grew less than the labor force.

12. See ECLA, 1:27. Note that gross capital formation includes costs of installation, internal transport, etc. When imports are taken as a percentage of the value of domestic manufacture plus imports for selected branches of industry, the following results are obtained for 1925–29: metals, 61 percent; machinery, vehicles and equipment, excluding electrical, 70 percent; electrical machinery and appliances, 98 percent. (See essay 4.)

machinery and equipment, so long as foreign demand for exports remained elastic.[13] Ex post, the slow growth of capital in machinery and equipment can be blamed on a relatively slow growth in the domestic production of these goods, and/or a slow growth in the amount of foreign exchange allocated to import them. So a situation in which foreign exchange difficulties are allowed to slow down the expansion of the stock of machinery and equipment can be blamed either on a failure to expand exchange earnings or on a failure to follow the right strategy of import substitution. A third possibility, that of increasing the share devoted to imports of machinery and equipment out of stagnant or falling exchange earnings, can be ruled out as a long-run solution, not only because sooner or later an upper barrier would be hit (at 100 percent), but also because industrialization sets off demands for foreign exchange for current uses that are difficult to compress. Because import substitution is in the short run an import-intensive activity, and because there is a presumption that export activities present more efficient ways to employ additional resources, the major blame for the exchange shortage and the resulting slowdown in capital accumulation should be placed on the failure to expand exchange earnings.[14]

13. If foreign demand for exports is assumed to be perfectly elastic at (dollar) price Px, and the foreign supply of machinery and equipment is assumed to be perfectly elastic at (dollar) price Pk, the usual neoclassical marginal conditions for efficiency would indicate that labor and other inputs should be allocated between export industries and import-substituting domestic industries of machinery and equipment in such a way that, for the case of labor:

$$\frac{\partial K}{\partial Lk} = \frac{Px}{Pk} \cdot \frac{\partial X}{\partial Lx} \tag{2.3}$$

where $\frac{\partial K}{\partial Lk}$ denotes the marginal product of labor in the machinery and equipment industry; $\frac{\partial X}{\partial Lx}$ the marginal product of labor in the export industry; and $\frac{Px}{Pk}$ refers to the exogenously given terms of trade between exports and these capital goods. For most of the period under study, given Argentina's factor endowments, this condition called for a predominance of the *indirect* way of obtaining machinery and equipment. Compare with Ronald Findlay, "Optimal Investment Allocation between Consumer Goods and Capital Goods," *Economic Journal* 76, no. 301 (March 1966): 75–76.

14. Markos J. Mamalakis, considering other Latin American experiences, has stressed the link between exchange shortages and machinery and equipment availability. See for example his "Forced Savings in Underdeveloped Countries: a Rediscovery or a Misapplication of a Concept?", *Economía Internazionale* 27, no. 2 (May 1964) and "El Sector Exportador, Etapas de Desarrollo

This discussion appears to put excessive weight on capital formation of a specific type as a source of growth. The greater durability of structures such as housing and social overhead capital embodying construction services, however, and their more indirect effect on output, partly justify such emphasis. Several authors have also indicated that a good part of the residual arises from not fully taking into account quality changes in machinery and equipment.[15] Not all technological change is embodied in these goods, but it seems reasonable to suppose that most of it is. Even when technological improvements are not embodied in capital, as in the case of better seeds and agricultural practices, taking full advantage of this new knowledge often involves the purchase of new machinery and equipment, while access to these capital goods will stimulate technical education and the use of better practices. Low availabilities of new machinery and equipment, therefore, will not only reduce the growth of physical capital, but will also hamper technological change.

An exchange bottleneck limits the expansion of internal demand at times when there is excess capacity of most other growth-generating inputs. The limitations on demand may be applied continuously or sporadically; in the latter case one observes the stop-go cycles that

Económico, y El Proceso Ahorro-Inversión en América Latina," *El Trimestre Económico* (México) 34 (April–June 1967): 319–41. For an earlier discussion of the relation between the saving constraint and that given by capacity in the capital goods industry see Evsey D. Domar, *Essays in the Theory of Economic Growth* (New York: Oxford University Press, 1957), chapter 9 ("A Soviet Model of Growth"), p. 236. Several economists at ECLA during the 1950s, including Osvaldo Sunkel, Celso Furtado, and Aníbal Pinto, also emphasized this point in publications of that organization. See also Osvaldo Sunkel, "Política Nacional de Desarrollo y Dependencia Externa," *Estudios Internacionales* (Chile), Year I, no. 1 (April 1967), esp. pp. 62–63.

15. Growth rates for capital, labor, and land of around 2.3 percent, 1.8 percent, and 0.5 percent respectively during the last 35 years, compared with a rate of output expansion of 2.7 percent, imply some residual. But basic data are too crude and aggregated to attempt a thorough anatomy of growth. It may be conjectured that changes in the sectorial composition of output, plus a failure to take into account all quality changes in new machinery and equipment, account for most of the residual. Improvements in education after 1929 appear to have played a smaller economic role than during the earlier period. T. P. Hill has reported on the basis of postwar North American and Western European experience that no connection whatever could be observed between growth and gross investment in construction, so that in so far as any general association existed between growth and investment it was entirely attributable to machinery and equipment. See T. P. Hill, "Growth and Investment According to International Comparisons," *Economic Journal* 74, no. 294 (June 1964). Possibilities for substituting construction for machinery and equipment in production processes seem limited.

have characterized recent Argentine economic history. A better allocation between home and tradeable (either exportable or importable)
goods could have raised the growth rate with the same domestic resources at hand. Within realistic limits (set by foreign demand), the
growth rate would have been higher the greater share of resources
devoted to producing exportable goods.

It is often difficult to draw the line between home goods and
tradeables. Some services are close complements to exportable production (e.g. railroad services taking crops to harbors), while others
(e.g. housing services for residents) may be said to be pure home
goods. Although national income categories do not lend themselves
to subdivisions among home and other goods, a crude attempt is
made in Table 2.9 to distinguish at least different degrees of tradeable-

Table 2.9: Growth Rates of Commodity-Producing Sectors and Services,
1927–29/1963–65
(Annual averages in percentages)

	Commodity- producing sectors[a]	Services associated directly with commodity production[b]	Other services[c]
ECLA/BCRA			
1927–29/1963–65	2.6	2.2	3.2
1927–29/1941–43	2.5	0.4	2.9
1941–43/1953–55	2.1	3.4	4.5
1953–55/1963–65	3.4	3.2	2.0
ECLA/CONADE			
1927–29/1941–43	2.3	1.2	
1941–43/1953–55	2.5	4.3	

[a] Include agriculture, livestock, fisheries, oil, mining, and manufacturing.
[b] Include construction, public utilities, transport, communications, commerce, and
finance.
[c] Include housing, government, and other services.

Sources: ECLA, BCRA, CONADE.

ness, assuming commodity production has the highest degree. Other
services, closest to pure home goods, grew at a higher rate than
either of the other two categories, when the whole post-1930 period
is examined. During 1941–43/1953–55 these services grew at a
rate more than twice that of commodity-producing sectors, but since
1953–55 this trend has been reversed.

Why the relative neglect of tradeable goods and the resulting exchange bottleneck? In particular, were foreign or domestic policies

and circumstances responsible? It is risky in economic history to allocate responsibility and to decide on cause and effect; after all, regardless of how bad external circumstances were, some domestic policy could have been devised to provide the required exchange, although perhaps at a very high social cost. It will be argued that, on the whole, external circumstances were responsible for the exchange shortage between 1929 and the war, but that domestic policies must bear the brunt of blame for postwar years. The expansion of home goods and import-substituting activities during the 1930s was for all practical purposes forced upon Argentina by the rest of the world; but the same cannot be said for 1945–65. During this latter period Argentine shares in world markets fell drastically and her interest in attracting foreign capital waned (especially during 1943–55). Note that for the postwar era, domestic policies can be blamed for (1) a failure to expand exports, whether of rural or manufactured goods, in spite of expanding world trade, and (2) a failure to follow an import-substitution strategy consistent with the decision not to expand exports. Because Argentine exports include goods widely consumed domestically, the blame for the failure to expand exports could be subdivided into criticisms of too low a rate of output expansion of exportables, and of too high an expansion of domestic absorption of these exportables. In the long run, however, export growth could hardly be based on a stagnant production of exportables and an ever decreasing share of domestic absorption, so that the major blame goes to the failure to expand output. Only for shorter periods then is this subdivision valid.

The remaining sections of this essay will elaborate the general thesis regarding the causes and effects of exchange difficulties.

TERMS OF TRADE: INTERNAL AND EXTERNAL

Previous discussion indicates the importance of examining the evolution of two major types of relative prices: (1) those between home and tradeable goods and (2) those between rural and industrial commodities. The latter may refer to world prices for Argentine exports relative to her imports, or to domestic prices of rural goods relative to the domestic prices of manufactures. Both types will be examined.

Data on the Argentine simple external terms of trade (dollar prices of exports divided by dollar prices of imports) are a bit puzzling; a closer look at the component series is warranted. Table 2.10 presents data on export dollar unit values from two different publications of ECLA, as well as from the National Statistical Office after 1951; for the sake of comparison, similar data for Canada and Australia are

Table 2.10: Export Dollar Unit Values and Price Indices, 1925–64
(1935–39 = 100)

	Argentina, ECLA I/DNEC	Argentina, ECLA II	Australia	Canada
1925–29	154	249[a]	–	145
1930–34	77	115	88	94
1935–39	100	100	100	100
1940–44	119	131	94	122
1945–46	191	212	123	183
1947–49	344	336	249	209
1950–52	303	346	327	251
1953–55	264	306	293	249
1956–58	226	258	259	258
1959–61	221	–[b]	226[c]	262[c]
1962–64	216	–	–	–

[a] Refers only to 1928–29.
[b] Dash indicates data not available.
[c] Refers only to 1959–60.

Sources and method: Column marked Argentina, ECLA I/DNEC is based on data shown in *El Desarrollo Económico*, 1:110 (1925–49); Ruth Kelly, "Foreign Trade of Argentina and Australia, 1930 to 1960," *Economic Bulletin for Latin America* (March 1965): 50 (1950–54); DNEC, *Boletín de Estadística*, several issues (1951–65). These series were linked using their overlap during 1951–54. Column marked Argentina, ECLA II obtained from ECLA, *Inflation and Growth*, vol. 3, Statistical Appendix, Table X-VIII. Data for Australia obtained from Ruth Kelly, "Foreign Trade," p. 50; those for Canada were obtained from M. C. Urquhart, ed., *Historical Statistics of Canada* (Cambridge: University Press, 1965), p. 301.

included. Although exports from the three countries are not identical, they are made up mainly by primary products. There are differences between columns 1 and 2 before 1935–39, presumably due to different methods of accounting for the dollar devaluation of the early 1930s. After 1935–39, however, the evolution of the indices does not appear peculiar. The same cannot be said for import unit values, shown in Table 2.11. Unit dollar values appear to have increased for Argentina much more than for Canada and Australia between 1935–39 and the 1950s. Argentine imports throughout this period were made up mostly of manufactured goods, not so different from imports into

Table 2.11: Import Dollar Unit Values and Price Indices, 1925–64
(1935–39 = 100)

	Argentina, ECLA I/ DNEC	Argentina, ECLA II	All Latin America, ECLA II	Australia	Canada	U.S. wholesale prices excluding food and farm products
1925–29	131	243[a]	135[a]	–	139	119
1930–34	99	147	104	–	98	94
1935–39	100	100	100	100	100	100
1940–44	152	131	128	133	134	114
1945–46	196	198	175	165	158	129
1947–49	276	261	232	219	204	172
1950–52	352	304	251	221	244	192
1953–55	326	304	257	228	231	199
1956–58	326	299	263	239	243	215
1959–61	289	–[b]	–	245[c]	243[c]	221
1962–64	286	–	–	–	–	221

[a] Refers only to 1928–29.
[b] Dash indicates data not available.
[c] Refers only to 1959–60.

Sources and method: As in Table 2.10, plus U.S. Department of Commerce, *Statistical Abstract of the United States, 1965* (Washington, D.C.: U.S. Government Printing Office, 1965), p. 356.

Latin America, Canada, and Australia, or from items making up the United States wholesale index of nonfood, nonfarm products, also shown in Table 2.11. Furthermore, according to Charles P. Kindleberger, the export dollar unit value indices of industrial Europe increased between 1928 and 1952 by 107 percent; between the same years the import dollar unit value for Canada increased by 74 percent; that for the whole of Latin America, according to ECLA, increased by 100 percent; and the U.S. wholesale price index for nonfood, nonfarm products increased by 71 percent.[16] Yet the first column of Table 2.11 indicates that between 1925–29 and 1952 the dollar unit value of Argentine imports rose by 207 percent! [17]

16. See Charles P. Kindleberger, *The Terms of Trade: A European Case Study* (Cambridge: M.I.T. Press, 1956), p. 49. Data for the U.S., Canada, and all Latin America obtained from the sources listed in Table 2.10.

17. According to Kindleberger, the increase in the index for dollar unit value of European exports was 116 percent between 1938 and 1952. The data of columns 1 and 2 of Table 2.11 indicate increases in the unit value of Argentine imports of 284 percent (between 1935–39 and 1952) and of 234 percent (between 1938 and 1952) respectively. Between 1938 and 1952 the U.S. wholesale price index for nonfarm, nonfood commodities rose by 94 percent.

It is extremely doubtful that columns 1 and 2 of Table 2.11 accurately reflect dollar import prices for Argentina.

It is necessary then to include an alternative, though rough, to the external terms of trade that can be obtained from the first two columns of Tables 2.10 and 2.11. This is done in Table 2.12, using

Table 2.12: External Terms of Trade of Argentina, 1925–64
(1935–39 = 100)

	Argentina, ECLA I/DNEC	Argentina, ECLA II	Export indices ECLA I/DNEC; Import indices Canada and U.S. wholesale
1925–29	117	102ᵃ	111
1930–34	78	78	79
1935–39	100	100	100
1940–44	78	100	89
1945–46	97	107	120
1947–49	124	129	169
1950–52	86	114	124
1953–55	81	100	114
1956–58	69	86	93
1959–61	76	–ᵇ	91
1962–64	75	–	89

ᵃ Refers only to 1928–29.
ᵇ Dash indicates data not available.

Sources and method: From Tables 2.10 and 2.11. For the third column it was assumed that after 1960 the Canadian import price indices moved in the same proportions as the U.S. wholesale index for nonfood, nonfarm products.

the Canadian import prices (supplemented for 1960–64 with U.S. data), to deflate the first column of Table 2.10. These terms of trade show a more favorable picture for Argentina than those of the first two columns, although the directions of change are similar. For 1940–46 this estimate gives too rosy a picture of the Argentine trade position. Imports were either more expensive or less available to neutral Argentina than to allied Canada, but for later years they show a more realistic picture than the other two columns.

The internal terms of trade may be defined as the ratio of domestic prices of rural goods to those of nonrural commodities. Two alternative series may be considered—one using wholesale price indices, and another using the implicit prices for rural activities and the manufacturing sector, according to the national accounts. Both are presented in Table 2.13. Broad movements are similar in both series,

Table 2.13: Internal Terms of Trade in Argentina, 1926–64
(1935–39 = 100)

	Wholesale prices	Implicit prices
1926–29	132	—ᵃ
1930–34	87	–
1935–39	100	100
1940–44	62	72
1945–46	74	83
1947–49	80	72
1950–52	68	82
1953–55	68	85
1956–58	78	93
1959–61	85	96
1962–64	93	103

ᵃ Dash indicates data not available.

Sources and method: The first column represents an index of the ratio of wholesale prices of all rural products to wholesale prices of nonrural goods. Data obtained from Comité Nacional de Geografía, *Anuario Geográfico Argentino* (Buenos Aires, 1941), p. 369; BCRA, *Boletín Estadístico* (Buenos Aires, Sept. 1962), pp. 51–62; and DNEC, *Boletín Mensual de Estadística,* several recent issues. The second column represents an index of the ratio of implicit prices for the rural sector to the implicit prices for the manufacturing sector. Data obtained from O.S., pp. 112–13, 132–33; and BCRA, pp. 2, 18.

but they show substantial differences for several periods; of the two, the index based on wholesale prices appears more reliable.[18]

During the period under study there were several occasions in which Argentina exerted substantial market power in world trade

18. It has been pointed out that the wholesale price index for nonrural goods underestimates the degree of price increase that has taken place in these goods since 1935–39, as it underrepresents machinery and equipment whose prices have led the increase (more on this in essay 6), while it is heavily loaded with intermediate goods and raw materials whose prices have increased less. Note, however, that column 1 of Table 2.13 based on wholesale prices, gives on the whole a more favorable price trend for manufactured goods than column 2, which is based on net, or implicit, prices to manufacturing activities. Furthermore, for 1950–61 the evolution of the wholesale price index for nonrural goods has been very similar to the implicit prices for total manufacturing gross output, as shown by the following indices (1960 = 100):

	1950–52	*1953–55*	*1956–58*	*1959–61*
Nonrural wholesale prices	11.6	17.9	30.0	98.3
Implicit prices for gross output of manufacturing	12.1	17.6	30.7	98.0

(Implicit prices for gross output of manufacturing obtained from CONADE worksheets.)

of some commodities, especially in the short run, but on the whole
the external terms of trade may be taken to be exogenously given
by world markets. The Argentine government, however, may influence
the domestic terms of trade between rural and manufactured goods in
a number of ways—using export and import taxes, import controls,
exchange rate policy, etc. Assuming that the rural and manufactured
goods used to obtain the internal terms of trade correspond, even
roughly, with those appearing in the external terms of trade, we may
obtain an index summarizing the net impact of all government
policies which modify the price signals received from world markets.[19]

Table 2.14: Indices of Ratios of Internal to External Terms of Trade, 1925–64
(1935–39 = 100)

	A	B	C	D
1925–29	113	119	—a	–
1930–34	112	110	–	–
1935–39	100	100	100	100
1940–44	79	70	92	81
1945–46	76	62	86	69
1947–49	65	47	58	43
1950–52	79	55	95	66
1953–55	84	60	105	75
1956–58	113	84	135	100
1959–61	112	93	126	105
1962–64	124	104	137	116

a Dash indicates data not available.

Sources and method: As in 2.12, 2.13. Column *A* represents the ratio of the first
column in Table 2.13 to the first column of Table 2.12 (multiplied by 100). It has
been assumed that the average for 1926–29 could be taken to represent the average
for 1925–29 of the internal terms of trade. Column *B* represents the ratio of the
first column in Table 2.13 to the third column in Table 2.12 (multiplied by 100).
Column *C* represents the ratio of the second column of Table 2.13 to the first column
of Table 2.12 (multiplied by 100). Column *C* represents the ratio of the second
column of Table 2.13 to the third column of Table 2.12 (multiplied by 100).

This new index is presented in Table 2.14; the one under column *B*
is, according to previous discussions, the most reliable. It also yields

19. It is also assumed that all price indices utilized neglect quality changes
in the same proportions, so that even if secular quality changes preclude a clear
statement regarding the evolution of the true terms of trade, statements can still
be made regarding biases in public policy. The reader should hardly need to be
warned again that only gross tendencies should be read from these data. It
may be noted that the comparison of internal and external terms of trade is
a technique of analysis widely used by ECLA.

results most in accordance with a priori expectations. It shows that, because of domestic policies, from 1925–29 through 1947–49 the internal terms of trade moved against rural goods to a greater extent than the external terms of trade, but that after 1947–49 the opposite has been the case. The war years indices have little significance as the link between world and Argentine markets was broken by reasons other than public policy. The index was by 1962–64 roughly at the levels of 1935–39, but remained lower (i.e. showing greater discrimination against rural goods) than for 1925–29. In view of the protectionist system which gained momentum during the 1930s and was strengthened during the 1950s and 1960s, it is not plausible that the index could have been higher (i.e. implying less discrimination) in 1962–64 than in 1925–29 (as shown in column *A*).

With war years set aside, three distinct periods emerge from index *B* of Table 2.14. The first, 1930–39, when its average was 105; the Perón years, 1945–55, when the index stood on average at 55 (although showing a tendency to rise after 1947–49); and the post-1955 period, when the average has been 94, while showing an upward trend (although yearly figures would show occasional setbacks). This index neatly summarizes the point that since 1929 economic policy has been biased against the rural sector with different degrees of intensity.

Table 2.15 presents, in columns *D* and *E*, indices partly reflecting preferences in public policy between home and tradeable goods. These indices relate the price of foreign exchange in domestic currency to the domestic price level, relative to the world price level. It is worth emphasizing that these indices can be taken only as rough approximations of what ideally we wish to measure; the limitations of the purchasing-power parity theory are too well known to be repeated here. The trends shown are sufficiently violent, however, to give us assurance that the following comments are relevant.[20]

The period 1945–55 clearly witnessed exchange policies that, by themselves, discouraged the production of tradeable goods. The average of column *E* for those years was 64, compared with 102 for 1956–64, and 98 for 1926–29 (1935–39 = 100). Between 1935–39 and 1953–55 there was a gradual increase of the overvaluation of the average exchange rate applied to exports and imports, but this trend was reversed beginning in 1956–58.

20. If the wholesale price index for domestically produced manufactured goods is used for the calculations, results very similar to those shown are obtained.

Table 2.15: Indices of Average Exchange Rates and Price Levels,
Argentina and the United States, 1926–64
(1935–39 = 100)

	A *Average exchange rate for merchandise imports (index of pesos per U.S. dollar)*	B *Average exchange rate for merchandise exports (index of pesos per U.S. dollar)*	C *Argentine overall wholesale price index relative to the U.S. wholesale price index*	D *Index of (A) divided by (C)*	E *Index of (B) divided by (C)*
1926–29	69	76	78	88	98
1935–39	100	100	100	100	100
1940–44	114	114	125	91	92
1945–46	113	110	151	75	72
1947–49	114	110	147	77	75
1950–52	184	178	285	65	62
1953–55	211	221	439	48	50
1956–58	653	747	719	91	104
1959–61	2,287	2,581	2,360	97	109
1962–64	3,756	4,137	4,423	85	94

Sources and method: Exchange rates obtained from data in *Anuario Geográfico*,
pp. 431–32; DNEC, *Comercio Exterior 1955–57* (Buenos Aires, 1960); and *International Financial Statistics* (Supplement to 1966/67 issues), pp. 2–3. Wholesale
prices as in Table 2.13.

Exchange rate policy was of great importance for the long run
evolution of the production of exportables, but other factors besides
the exchange rate played a key role with regard to importables, e.g.
the protectionist system. Yet the overvaluation of the import exchange
rate shown in column *D* for 1945–55, coupled with a haphazard
protectionist system, resulted in a bewildering variety of effective
rates of protection to different branches of industry. This system, by
severing links between world and domestic prices for several manufactured goods (through import and exchange controls), turned some
importables into home goods.

A devaluation larger than increases in the domestic price level
raises the relative price, in a small country, of *both* importables and
exportables. Some policy combinations (i.e. devaluation plus an
increase in import tariffs) can then yield both (1) an improvement in
the price ratio of tradeables to home goods, and (2) a deterioration
in the price ratio of rural to manufactured goods. These conditions
appear to have occurred between 1926–29 and 1935–39, as can be
seen by comparing Tables 2.14 and 2.15.

One more bit of information may be squeezed out of Tables 2.14 and 2.15, under certain assumptions, regarding the combined impact of protection and the import exchange rate, on the domestic prices of manufactured goods. Assume that the domestic price of exportable goods (Px) is equal to the export exchange rate (Kx), times the dollar price of exports (Rx). For simplicity, export taxes and restrictions are ignored. The domestic price of manufactured goods (Pm) may be regarded as equal to the dollar price of imports (Rm), times an unknown factor which reflects both the import exchange rate and the protectionist system (T). Expressing both Kx and T in real terms (i.e. deflated by the domestic wholesale price index), we can then obtain an index for $(1/T)$ by taking the ratio of column B of Table 2.14 to column E of Table 2.15. This procedure yields the following index for $(1/T)$:

$$1926–29 = 121$$
$$1935–39 = 100$$
$$1945–55 = 86$$
$$1956–64 = 92$$

The combined effect of the exchange rate for imports and the protectionist system may be broken down by using column D of Table 2.15, as we can write:

$$\frac{1}{T} = \frac{1}{1+w} \cdot \frac{1}{Km} \tag{2.4}$$

where w reflects protection (expressed in terms of equivalent ad valorem import rates) and Km is the *real* exchange rate applied to imports. Then an index for $(1/1 + w)$ emerges, as follows:

$$1926–29 = 106$$
$$1935–39 = 100$$
$$1945–55 = 56$$
$$1956–64 = 84$$

These results conform roughly with what is known about the evolution of the protectionist system—a moderate increase in tariffs and restrictions during the 1930s, followed by severe restrictions during the Perón years, and some relaxation after 1955, but leaving it more restrictive than it was during 1935–39.[21] From the point

21. As export taxes and export controls have, during several years, violated the assumption that $Px = Kx \cdot Rx$, the index for $(1/1 + w)$ may be more exactly interpreted as representing an index for $1–Z/1+w$, where Z reflects ad valorem export taxes and export restrictions as ad valorem equivalents.

of view of manufactured goods' prices, relaxation of protection was partially offset by the return to more realistic import exchange rates.

The tables presented have suggested the usefulness of dividing the post-1930 years into three periods, during which different economic policies were followed. These three periods also correspond to different political regimes. In September 1930 the Radical government was overthrown by civilian and military conservative elements in a coup that appeared popular at the time. Several conservative regimes, sometimes with fascist leanings although also influenced by traditionally pro-British rural interests, remained in power until June 1943, when a pro-Nazi coup eventually led to the political domination of General Juan Domingo Perón. Perón's hegemony lasted until September 1955; from that date until June 1966 there was a gradual but far from smooth return to a more liberal political system. For other purposes (i.e. the analysis of the stages of industrialization), different subdivisions may be more useful. But in the rest of this essay, the economic policies followed during 1930–43, 1943–55, and 1956–66 will be examined separately.

THE SHOCK OF THE GREAT DEPRESSION AND THE IMMEDIATE RESPONSE (1930–43)

Between 1925–29 and 1930–34 the international terms of trade of Argentina deteriorated sharply. At the same time, the export quantum fell by more than 6 percent, and the net capital inflow decreased. The quantum of merchandise imports dropped by nearly 40 percent. Throughout the 1930s, furthermore, agricultural protectionism (hidden sometimes in sanitary regulations) and preferential blocs (such as that of the British Commonwealth) continued to threaten Argentine external markets.[22] For Argentina, a net debtor with a ratio of exports to GDP of nearly 30 percent, the drop in the world price level, in its international terms of trade, and in its exports, were disasters of the first magnitude. It is then remarkable that between

22. Data on exports and imports obtained from *Análisis y Proyecciones,* 1: 110–15. A. J. P. Taylor, evaluating the growth of protectionist feeling in England during the Great Depression, has written: "The whole process was a dramatic reversal of the secular trend by which Great Britain had become predominantly industrial, while drawing food from the rest of the world. The reversal was peculiarly perverse at this time." (See A. J. P. Taylor, *English History, 1914–1945* [Oxford: Oxford University Press, 1965], p. 341.) Argentina was perhaps the main victim of such peculiar perversity.

1927–29 and 1941–43, real GDP and the hard pressed rural sector managed to grow at an annual rate of 1.8 percent and 1.5 percent, respectively, while manufacturing expanded at 3.4 percent. After dropping by nearly 14 percent between 1929 and 1932, GDP expanded every year until 1940. This growth did not depend on the arrival of war; by 1939 real Argentine GDP was nearly 15 percent above that of 1929 and 33 percent above 1932, while in the United States a similar comparison yields an increase of only 4 percent between 1929 and 1939. Australia's performance is similar to that of Argentina between 1929 and 1939 in absolute amounts, although better in per capita terms, while the Canadian one resembles that of the United States. Value added in manufacturing in Argentina expanded between 1932 and 1939 by an impressive 62 percent.

Although few data are available, it is generally believed that no serious open urban unemployment existed after 1934. Indeed, although net immigration fell from the 1920s' levels, after 1934 it showed a tendency to increase, as may be seen from the following figures on average yearly net immigration:[23]

$$
\begin{array}{ll}
1925\text{–}29 & = 91{,}000 \\
1930\text{–}31 & = 45{,}800 \\
1932\text{–}34 & = 4{,}400 \\
1935 & = 21{,}100 \\
1936 & = 27{,}200 \\
1937 & = 43{,}900 \\
1938 & = 40{,}300
\end{array}
$$

A relative reallocation of resources toward manufacturing and away from the rural sector could have been expected solely on the

23. Dirección Nacional de Estadística y Censos (hereafter DNEC), *Informe Demográfico de la República Argentina, 1944–1954* (Buenos Aires, 1956), p. 28. The push of unemployment and the threat of war in Europe were no doubt as powerful as the pull of recovery of Argentina in determining the level of net migration. While during 1925–29 only 37 percent of the net immigration was made up of women, during 1934–38 women made up 70 percent of that total. These figures may also reflect a more reluctant attitude of the Argentine government toward permitting increases in the labor force. Yet the fact remains that some immigration of males was permitted during 1934–38, and at an increasing rate. No data are available on the age breakdown of these immigrants. As in North America, immigrants during those years included many distinguished persons fleeing political and racial persecution. In July 1938, however, tougher immigration regulations were decreed. It may be noted that, perhaps reflecting greater trade union pressure, Australian population grew during the 1930s at less than half the Argentine rate.

basis of changes in the international terms of trade and the expectations generated by the Great Depression regarding future export markets for most rural goods. As can be noted in column *B* of Table 2.14, however, the government also took measures that on balance reinforced the improvement in the manufacturing terms of trade. They included increases in import duties and the creation of a system of multiple exchange rates, where the buying rates applied to traditional exports were lower than the selling rates offered importers. The exchange controls established in 1933 also increased transaction costs for importers. These policies, which began to be applied in a systematic fashion in November 1933, not only reinforced the gap opened by the depression between profit rates in manufacturing as compared with those in the rural sector producing exportables, but also raised the absolute level of profits in import-substituting activities. As shown in Table 2.9, during this period the commodity-producing sectors expanded faster than services taken as a whole.

Besides influencing relative prices, the government during some of those years attempted to sustain a high level of aggregate demand. The 1933 devaluation of the peso helped to maintain purchasing power, not only via its favorable impact on export and import competing activities, but also by reversing the falling trend in the domestic price level which, during 1930–1933, had transferred income away from entrepreneurs with net debtor positions. By 1934, the devaluation had placed domestic wholesale prices slightly above their 1929 level. In the United States the wholesale price index for all commodities in 1934 was more than 21 percent below the level of 1929. Fiscal policy during the early years of the Great Depression (1930–31) was on the whole expansionary, but by pressure of circumstances rather than by design. The authorities who took power in 1930 tried to cut down the fiscal deficit inherited from the previous administration, and the otherwise remarkable set of expansionary measures adopted during November and December 1933 still stressed the importance of bringing the budget into balance.[24] Table 2.16

24. See Ministerios de Hacienda y Agricultura de la Nación (hereafter MHAN), *El Plan de Acción Económica Nacional* (Buenos Aires, 1934), where the Minister of the Treasury calls for: "a vigorous reduction in expenditures, and a decided application of taxes," (p. 77). For 1929 it can be estimated that expenditures of the national government amounted to around 12 percent of the GDP. In both Great Britain and the United States, governments were also trying to balance their budgets in the midst of the crisis.

Table 2.16: Indicators of the Fiscal Policy of the Argentine
Federal Government, 1928–39

	Current revenues[a] as percentage of total expenditure	Total expenditure[b] excluding servicing of the national debt (million pesos at 1929 prices)
1928–1929	78.1	768
1930	60.8	934
1931	75.5	764
1932	87.4	648
1933	91.2	711
1934	96.2	702
1935	99.7	775
1936	94.1	825
1937	90.4	878
1938	86.5	997
1939	80.5	1,102

[a] Include profits accruing to the government because of the exchange differential between buying and selling rates, all taxes and other minor revenues from fees, fines, etc.
[b] Deflated by the wholesale prices index.

Source: Basic data from *Revista de Economía Argentina* (July, 1944), pp. 190–91.

presents data on the finances of the national government. From 1933 until 1937 current revenues covered at least 90 percent of all expenditures. But the rising level of real expenditure no doubt resulted in a net expansionary stimulus to the economy; real federal expenditures (excluding servicing of the public debt) were, in 1937, 27 percent above the level of 1932, and 7 percent above the 1928–29 level. Beginning in 1935, when the BCRA was created, the share of expenditure covered by current revenues dropped steadily while real expenditures continued to increase, to a large extent due to a massive road-building program; the 1939 level of expenditure was 34 percent above the level of 1936. Fiscal policy between 1935 and 1940, then, was an important stimulus to economic recovery, although its performance during 1932–35 is ambiguous.

Until 1935 Argentina did not have a central bank and lacked refined tools to control monetary developments. The abandonment of peso gold convertibility in December 1929, however, severed the close dependence of the money supply on the balance of payments, although government payments on the external debt continued to drain reserves from the banking system. The drop in the money

supply was limited to less than 14 percent between 1928–29 and
1932–33. But monetary authorities were either unwilling or unable
to stop a rise in interest rates during the worst years of the depression; effective yields on government-backed mortgage paper (*cédulas
hipotecarias*) rose from an average of 6.1 percent for December
1928 and December 1929 to 7.0 percent in December 1932, while
yields on government bonds rose from 6.2 percent to 7.5 percent
between the same two periods.[25] From their peak in 1932, interest
rates declined; the average yield on government bonds and mortgage
paper during 1937–39 was 5.0 percent. From its creation, the BCRA
maintained steady interest rates and at a level significantly lower
than those of 1928–32. The money supply in 1939 was 29 percent
above that of 1935; the management of the new BCRA followed, on
balance, policies that accommodated and reinforced the expansionary
fiscal policies of the federal government.[26]

The remarkable 1933–39 recovery was due mainly to domestic
policies, but it was also aided by the improvement of the external
terms of trade which began in 1934.

In spite of import substitution efforts, exports were not neglected.
As can be seen in column *E* of Table 2.15, the real exchange rate
applied to merchandise exports remained roughly constant between
1925–29 and 1935–39. Furthermore, Argentina fought in bilateral
negotiations to maintain her traditional markets (while making modest
progress in creating new export lines). The best-known effort is the
Roca-Runciman treaty of 1933 with the United Kingdom, which
to this day remains a source of bitter debate. The United Kingdom,
holding the threat of Commonwealth preferences over Argentine meat
exports, was able to obtain substantial concessions regarding British
exports and investments in exchange for merely a promise not to
cut imports of Argentine meat, especially chilled beef, below certain
levels.[27]

25. Data on interest rates obtained from BCRA, *Suplemento Estadístico de
la Revista Económica* (several issues; Aug. 1937–April 1947). Table 101 in
the Statistical Appendix presents monetary statistics during the Great Depression.

26. Between 1935 and 1939 the wholesale price index rose by 12 percent.
At several points during these years the BCRA undertook operations designed
to soak up liquidity that it considered excessive. A special source of concern was
the inflow of hot money coming from a Europe threatened by war.

27. Many Argentines considered the concessions excessive and unnecessary
to achieve Argentina's export goals, and blame cattle-owning interests and their
prejudices against industry for the concessions given to imports from the

Table 2.17: Export Quantum Indices in Argentina, 1925–29/1935–39
(1925–29 = 100)

	Level in 1935–39	Share in total exports in 1925–29
Overall index	*93.5*	*100.0*
Losing items		
Meat	87.3	13.6
Hides	89.3	7.8
Dairy products	49.8	3.2
Other cattle products	92.5	3.2
Cereals and linseed	91.1	54.4
Forest products	90.1	3.4
Gaining items		
Wool	111.5	11.0
Fresh fruits and vegetables	176.6	0.8
Other agricultural products	189.3	0.9
Other manufactured products	122.7	1.6

Sources and method: Data obtained from *Análisis y Proyecciones*, 1:115. Share of exports computed from data expressed in 1950 prices.

Table 2.17 presents a summary of how Argentine exports fared during the depression. With the exception of dairy products, the fall in the quantum of traditional exports was small. Although 1935–39 exports were aided by droughts in the United States and Canada,

---

United Kingdom. But British gains were achieved at the expense of United States, Japanese and Italian exporters, rather than Argentine manufacturers, as can be seen by the very fast rate of growth of import-substituting industries, especially cotton textiles, during these years. More than 50 percent of Argentine imports from the United Kingdom were made up of textiles and carbon coke. Yet, between 1925–29 and 1937–39, output of textiles increased at an annual rate of nearly 11 percent, while oil production grew at an average annual rate of more than 7 percent. As a matter of fact, the textile industry could be called the main leading sector of growth for those years. The collapse of free convertibility during the 1930s placed Argentina in a difficult position, as her normal trade pattern involved surpluses with Western Europe and deficits with North America. Therefore, Argentine commercial policy endeavored to divert purchases from the United States toward Western Europe, especially Great Britain, under the slogan of "buy from those who buy from us." By 1938 about 60 percent of Argentine imports were made through barter or compensation agreements. See Ruth Kelly, "Foreign Trade of Argentina and Australia, 1930 to 1960," Part II, *Economic Bulletin for Latin America* 10, no. 2 (Oct. 1965): 191. The Roca-Runciman treaty was foreshadowed by the Argentine-British commercial accord of November 1929, when threats of imperial preferences already were used to obtain essentially unilateral Argentine concessions to the United Kingdom. See Virgil Salera, *Exchange Control and the Argentine Market* (New York: Columbia University Press, 1941), pp. 64–65.

the data suggest that efforts were made to maintain exports in spite of adverse world conditions. On the whole, the country kept its share in world commerce for most of its traditional exports.[28]

The 1930s and early 1940s provide a few examples of activities that began the decade as protected infant industries and in a few years moved into the export field. They are found primarily in non-traditional agriculture and closely allied activities, such as those producing apples, pears, grapes, cotton, edible oils, and tomato preserves. Table 2.17 shows that exports of minor agricultural goods, as well as of manufactured products, expanded. Manufacturing was beginning to seek new markets abroad, which the war expanded rapidly. During 1941, a Trade Promotion Corporation was organized under the supervision of the BCRA with the aim of encouraging exports of nontraditional products, especially to North American and Latin American countries.[29] Ironically, this corporation was transformed under the Perón regime into a supermarketing board (I.A.P.I.) whose price policies discouraged the production of exportable goods.

In summary, Argentine authorities responded to the shock of the depression in such a manner that, in spite of a drop in the import quantum by more than 28 percent between 1925–29 and 1935–39, the real GDP expanded by 20 percent.[30] This performance was made

28. In the case of wheat, the Argentine share of world exports was 21 percent during 1920–26 and 19 percent during 1934–38; for corn, her share was 52 percent during 1920–26 and 64 percent during 1934–38; for linseed, the share was 73 percent during 1920–26 and 68 percent during 1934–38. Data obtained from *Anuario de la Sociedad Rural Argentina,* Sociedad Rural Argentina, No. 1, pp. 138–56, 174–83, and 202; and from *Análisis y Proyecciones* 2:48. The Argentine share in the British meat market dropped in spite of her efforts: "Between 1932 and 1938, Argentine shipments of chilled and frozen beef to the United Kingdom fell 10.6 percent. . . . During the same period, Argentina's share of beef imports into the United Kingdom declined from 75 to 62 percent of the total, while that of Australia rose from 8 to 19 percent. . . . It would appear . . . that the contraction of Argentine shipments of beef to the United Kingdom was a result of the Ottawa and subsequent restrictive agreements . . . ." R. Duncan, "Imperial Preference: The Case of Australian Beef in the 1930's," *Economic Record* 39, no. 86 (June 1963): 161.

29. Leather shoes, cotton and wool textiles are among the manufactured items exported during the war. The Trade Promotion Corporation also encouraged exports of cheese, eggs, wine, fruits and livestock by-products. See U.S. Tariff Commission, *Economic Controls and Commercial Policy in Argentina* (Washington, 1948), p. 33.

30. *Análisis y Proyecciones* 1: 110, 115. The latter page shows the main items in the balance of payments. Servicing the external debt became quite burdensome to Argentina during the 1930s due to the increase in the real value of such obligations as a result of the drop in international prices. Argen-

possible by a change in demand structure and by vigorous import substitution in manufacturing as well as the rural sector. The change
in the structure of demand shifted expenditure from fixed investment
(with a high import component) to consumption (with a lower import component). Between 1925–29 and 1935–39 real fixed investment fell by 16 percent, while real consumption grew by 28 percent.[31]
The fall in investment was greatest in sectors associated with the
pre-1930 pattern of trade and immigration of both capital and
people (including important segments of social overhead capital)
while investments in import-substituting activities expanded. The
change in the structure of production and a more intensive use of
capacity, especially in manufacturing, yielded an increase in the marginal output-capital ratio, which became more marked during the
1940s—especially during the war years.

The rapidity with which advantage was taken of import-substitution
opportunities was due not only to the incentives provided by price
changes and public policy, but also to the relative simplicity of the
new activities and to favorable conditions for industry in Argentina
(relative to other Latin American countries). Before 1930, exports
and capital inflows had allowed large imports of items for which
domestic production was on the borderline of becoming competitive.
The change in world prices, nudged by public policy, shifted the line
of Argentine comparative advantage to cover such items as textiles,
cement, and several industrial crops. Adequate urban social overhead
facilities, some industrial experience, a literate urban labor force, and
large urban markets facilitated the fast growth of industry.[32]

---

tina, however, was one of the few countries in the world that did not default
on its debt servicing during these years.

31. See *Análisis y Proyecciones* 1: 114.

32. There is evidence that so close was Argentina to being able to compete
with imports in several activities during the late 1920s, that some entrepreneurs
had placed orders for machinery to set up new import-competing lines before
the Great Depression hit. Earlier attempts that failed had also left unutilized
capacity which was used during the 1930s. There is one case where an
important manufacturing firm had machinery to install a cotton textile plant
in customs in 1929, and claimed that it was waiting for greater tariff protection
before clearing these capital goods through customs. See speech of June 12,
1929, by Deputy J. C. Raffo de la Reta in *Diario de Sesiones de la Cámara de
Diputados, Año 1929*, vol. 1 (Buenos Aires: Congreso Nacional, 1929), p. 251.
In the case of cement, domestic output expanded at the remarkable annual
rate of 17.9 percent between 1928 and 1938; while in 1928 domestic output
represented 34 percent of total domestic consumption of cement, by 1938 this
percentage reached 94.

Given world trade conditions, Argentine industrial development during the 1930s appears to have been an efficient use of resources. Protection could be justified for those years on "infant industry," as well as on employment and terms-of-trade, grounds.[33] The mixture of devaluation cum import duties (as well as the differential exchange rates) could be defended on the ground that Argentina at that time had some influence on her export prices; attempts to expand substantially the quantum of traditional exports in the face of depressed and protectionist world conditions could have had an unfavorable effect on her terms of trade. Of course, it cannot be argued that her policies were optimal; the point is that with such world conditions there is a strong presumption that those policies led to a fairly efficient use of resources. In contrast with later years, the policies of the 1930s did not shut out foreign competition completely; the competitive nature of the pre-1930 economy was to a large extent preserved, in spite of the stricter nature of the exchange constraint.[34] The decrease in the capacity to transform of the economy, especially in the capacity to transform domestic savings into machinery and equipment, can be blamed almost wholly on world conditions, which suddenly turned against an economy built on the premise that world trade would in the long run continue to expand.

33. Argentine policies were to some extent of the beggar-thy-neighbor type. But Argentina could argue, with good reason, that at that time her level of imports was really determined by what the rest of the world bought from her, and that the measures she adopted simply allowed a greater level of national output for the given capacity to import. (One of the key economic policy makers during these years was Raúl Prebisch; these experiences no doubt markedly influenced his thinking as reflected in his postwar publications). The balance of payments effects of import tariffs were not limited to the merchandise account; they also attracted direct foreign investment (mainly from the United States) which flowed into import-substituting activities.

34. Discussing exchange policies of less developed countries (LDC's) during the Great Depression, a Deputy Managing Director of the International Monetary Fund has remarked: "Some other LDC's turned to what we may call a dual exchange rate system, sometimes coupled with exchange taxes. Argentina is an interesting example. In essence, the system involved an official market and a free market; and, ordinarily, prior permits were required for the official market but not for the free market. The authorities could use the free market as a kind of safety valve and could control the spread between the official and free rates in several ways. . . . On the whole, considering all of the difficulties faced by Argentina as an exporter of food and raw materials during a world depression, this system worked fairly smoothly." See Frank A. Southard, Jr., "International Financial Policy, 1920–44," *Finance and Development* 2 (Sept. 1965): 141–42.

It is commonly believed that the war provided a strong stimulus to Argentine industrialization and economic expansion. It is true that the war granted manufacturing something close to absolute protection and opened up new export markets for its goods. Meat producers were also able to expand output. On the other hand, imports of capital and intermediate goods became difficult to obtain, at a time when Argentina could only produce most of these goods at very high real costs. Exports of bulky rural products, like wheat and corn, suffered from the shortage of ships. The neutral status of Argentina (maintained until near the end of the war) made the acquisition of critical imports even more difficult. While during the six-year period 1933–39, manufacturing output rose by 43 percent (source: ECLA), during the next six-year period, 1939–45, it rose by only 23 percent (source: BCRA). Real GDP rose by 27 percent during 1933–39 (ECLA) and by only 13 percent from 1939 to 1945 (BCRA). Real capital formation fell as a percentage of GDP, while real investment in new machinery and equipment fell in absolute amounts. Indeed, the *net* capital stock in the form of machinery and equipment (including that of transportation) fell, according to rough estimates, about 30 percent between 1938 and 1945. This was due partly to the deterioration of the railroad system, which may have taken place even without the war, but most of that fall is explained by the war-induced leftward shift in the supply of machinery and equipment to Argentina. On balance, then, the war had the effect of slowing down economic growth. This situation offers a sharp contrast to what happened in the United States, Canada, and Australia during the same years.

Some readers may be puzzled by the description offered of the economic policies of 1930–43. Argentine industrialization is commonly associated with the name of General Perón and with the war; the 1930s are often referred to in Argentine political and social history as the infamous decade. There is little doubt that during 1930–43 governments maintained themselves in power by electoral frauds and other undemocratic practices. Corruption was widespread. Yet the fact remains that those governments relied on a team of competent technicians who were able to influence economic policy to a substantial degree. Especially since 1933, this team generated policies that were more enlightened than those followed in more advanced countries. They were also responsible for the creation of new institutions (such as the BCRA and the regulatory agencies for

the marketing of rural products) and new tools of policy (such as
the income tax), which could be used to guide and encourage growth
and to reconcile economic efficiency goals with a desired distribution
of income. As one looks at official announcements of those years,
there is little doubt that the authorities knew well the implications of
their policies for industrialization. The following remarks are from a
speech made by the Minister of Agriculture, Luis Duhau, in December 1933:

> The historic stage of our prodigious growth under the direct
> stimulus of the European economy has finished. . . . After
> writing off the external stimulus, due to the confused and dis-
> turbing state of the world economy and policy, the country
> should look in itself, with its own resources, for the relief for its
> present difficulties. The plan proposes to stimulate efficiently
> industrial output using two different means; the construction of
> reproductive public works and by adjusting imports to the
> country's real capacity to pay.[35]

In November 1933 the Minister of the Treasury, Federico Pinedo,
referring to the new measures planned said:

> The execution of a vast program of public works will result in
> an immediate increase in the demand for a great quantity and
> variety of goods which Argentina produces, or could produce.
> And here we reach a point which must be noted: the preventive

35. MHAN, *El Plan de Acción,* pp. 163–67. (Translation by the author.) It
is somewhat ironic that the income tax was introduced by the conservative
regime of the 1930s rather than the populist Radical regimes of the 1920s.
Raúl Prebisch and Ernesto Malaccorto played a key role in the creation of the
income tax; to the argument that an income tax could not work in a predominantly rural economy, Prebisch offered the counter example of Australia, whose
income tax he had studied during the 1920s. Comparing economic policies
during the 1930s, Ruth Kelly argues that on the whole the burden of the
depression was less evenly spread in Argentina than in Australia, suggesting
that in the latter country the industrial sector fared relatively worse than in
Argentina. See Kelly, "Foreign Trade of Argentina and Australia, 1930 to
1960," p. 190. But the same author also points out many similarities in
Australian and Argentine domestic policies during those years. Thanks to
imperial preferences, a relatively prosperous wool market and an aggressive
trade policy, Australian exports performed better than those of Argentina during
the depression. The preponderance of foreign firms in the marketing of exports
may have reduced Argentine flexibility and aggressiveness in dealing with
foreign customers, especially the United Kingdom, during the depression.

control of imports will enable us to avoid such a demand stimulating imports, so that it will be used to promote domestic economic activities.[36]

The comment that the 1930s industrialization was a lucky outcome of policies aimed at helping only the rural sector and improving the balance of payments does not appear justified. It is true that, as in Australia and the United States, measures were taken to assist rural producers. Nevertheless, industry was also explicitly aided by public policy. Economic authorities were not committed to industrialization per se, as the Perón regime would claim to be in later years, and lacked a clearly articulated industrialization plan (which few countries had at that time). On purely economic grounds, however, their pragmatic approach to industrialization is preferable to one which a priori favors any project labelled industry over any other labelled agriculture and livestock. Infant industry and terms of trade argument would have to be stretched unduly to argue that protection then granted to industry was insufficient. It should nevertheless be noted that throughout 1930–43, dogmatic enemies of industrialization and die-hard rural proponents of free trade, inside and outside the government, opposed and slowed down reforms introduced by the economic team.[37]

36. MHAN, *El Plan de Acción*, p. 89. The proposed public works program was to be financed by foreign and domestic loans; but it was not until 1936 that such a program had the net effect of allowing the federal government to run a modest budget deficit.

37. As late as 1940, the Minister of the Treasury had to argue that the measures promoting industrialization did not lead to a reduction in exports, as these were exogenously determined by world conditions, and there existed excess capacity in export activities. See Ministerio de Hacienda de la Nación, *El Plan de Reactivación Económica ante el Honorable Senado* (Buenos Aires, Nov. 1940). This remarkable document was motivated by the outbreak of World War II; it was feared that such an event would cause a severe recession in Argentina by reducing the demand for exports (due to shipping difficulties). The plan proposed further measures to stimulate industrialization and to maintain domestic purchasing power. The style of Raúl Prebisch is unmistakably present in this document. Congress failed to act on most provisions of this plan, in part due to the fact that the impact of the war was not as unfavorable on exports as expected. Among other proposals, the plan suggested: (1) a free trade zone with other Latin American countries; (2) an expansion of long-term industrial loans; (3) measures to stimulate industrial exports; and (4) a housing program for low-income families. There are few countries in the world where the industry vs. agriculture debate has been more violent and longer lived, and more sterile, than in Argentina. Typically, the debators quickly begin searching for Machiavellian plots and conspiracies with little

DELAYED RESPONSES TO THE GREAT DEPRESSION (1943–55)

World market conditions were more favorable to Argentina during 1943–55 than in 1929–43. After the war, public policy had an option not present during the Great Depression—to guide economic growth on the basis of expanding exports of both rural and manufactured products. To some extent, this option implied a return to pre-1930 export-led growth, but it could have differed significantly from that earlier era by a greater reliance on the export of manufactures, as well as by more import substitution, in the same way that postwar Australian and Canadian growth differed from their pre-1930 expansion.

In retrospect, one may ask how a growth rate of 5 percent per annum could have been achieved during 1943–55. Several policies could have obtained this goal, given world conditions, although with different degrees of efficiency and real effort. Two major strategies could be distinguished: (1) reliance on export expansion, using import substitution only to the extent that exports, traditional or new, met with inelastic world demands that would not allow the target growth rate to be met, or (2) letting exports remain at existing levels (or even reducing them) and putting the whole burden on import substitution. Although the second course can be presumed to be less efficient than the first and would imply a higher level of real effort and/or a lower level of per capita consumption, it is conceivable that coherent policies could have led to the realization of the desired growth rate without running into an exchange bottleneck. Planning would have had to be careful, especially regarding the ways in which capital goods were to be obtained and the means by which minimum efficiency could be maintained in the new industries, in view

---

regard for establishing what is actually going on in the economy. The following annual percentage growth rates for the production of key industrial commodities may be noted in defense of 1930s industrialization:

	1928–29/ *1938–39*	*1938–39/* *1948–49*	*1948–49/* *1958–59*
Portland cement	15.0	1.5	5.9
Crude oil	6.8	2.5	5.8
Electricity (from public utilities)	6.7	5.4	6.1

Basic data obtained from sources listed in Tables 42 and 85 of the Statistical Appendix. Pre-1940 electricity growth rate refers to 1929–39. (See also U.N., *Energy Development in Latin America* [New York, 1957]).

of the protectionist policies accompanying this option. During the war and immediately after, Argentina accumulated substantial foreign exchange reserves, allowing for some flexibility in planning.[38]

The path chosen was closer to strategy (2) than to (1), although it is doubtful that the economic authorities of the early postwar period were fully conscious of what their economic goals were and of what decisions were needed to implement them. At least for some policy makers, the growth rate was not an important objective. They were more interested in generating urban employment and providing some social services, so that a third strategy (3), stimulating the growth of home goods, appealed to them. This third strategy is hardly compatible with achieving a 5 percent growth rate simultaneously with balance of payments equilibrium, especially when a policy of hostility toward foreign capital was also followed until 1953. Either strategy (2) or (3), or a combination of both, naturally induces a closing of the economy.

These choices were made under a regime dominated by the charismatic figure of General Juan Domingo Perón, who first gained recognition as one of the leaders of the June 1943 coup. Why did Argentina under his leadership turn her back on foreign trade and foreign capital? Had not pre-1930 experience shown the advantages of relatively free trade and free factor movements?

The last pages of Essay 1 indicated that the great expansion of 1860–1930 had generated social frictions, which, however, had remained largely beneath the surface. Until 1929 the system, on the whole, had worked, and prosperity smoothed tensions. But the depression discredited the liberal system and brought to the surface latent frictions. The manner in which Argentina was treated by her trade partners, especially the United Kingdom, increased nationalistic feelings and reduced the influence of Argentines who advocated encouragement of foreign trade and investment. The climate of corruption and repression dominating the political life of the 1930s extended, in the mind of the public, to the dealings between the government and foreign investors and traders; major scandals involving foreign investors reinforced this feeling.

The conservative regimes of the 1930s, in spite of their flirtations with fascist reformism, brought to a halt the modest momentum for political and social reform started by the Radical governments. Their

38. At the end of 1946 net reserves of gold and foreign exchange were estimated at $1,687 million. See BCRA, *Memoria Annual, 1958*, p. 3.

failure to buttress the relatively healthy economic structure with
social and political arrangements allowing for growing security and
political participation for rural and urban masses contributed to
the creation of revolutionary possibilities.

The expansion of manufacturing, coupled with rural stagnation,
stimulated internal migration toward the urban centers, especially
Greater Buenos Aires.[39] The growing urban labor force appeared to
be a passive mass without leadership or organization; it will be
recalled that members of labor unions amounted to 473,000 in 1940,
at a time when the total urban labor force was about 3.5 million. The
traditional parties, including Radicals and Socialists, showed a curious
sluggishness in providing leadership for this group. By 1943 most of
the urban workers were either children of immigrants or had come
from rural and small urban communities of the interior and were
of older Argentine stock. The Socialist Party leadership, on the other
hand, came from immigrants or was closely identified with foreign
ideologies, which often did not fit popular nationalistic feelings.
Finally, the wage share in national income declined between 1935–
36 and 1940–42 (under mildly inflationary conditions) while the
social security system remained grossly underdeveloped.

Under these circumstances, and also taking advantage of new
pressures created by the war, a gifted leader, General Perón, was able
to build up massive support for himself and for a program of higher
wages and social reform, accompanied by extreme nationalism. Favoring domestic consumption over exports pleased the urban masses,
and strengthening import restrictions pleased urban entrepreneurs.
All who would lose, it appeared, were foreigners who had to do
without Argentine wheat and beef and could not sell manufactures to
Argentina, and the oligarchs who had previously profited from the

39. According to the census for 1947, Greater Buenos Aires had a population of 4.72 million persons, or 29.7 percent of the population of the whole
country. In 1914, this urban conglomeration had 2.03 million inhabitants, or
25.8 percent of total population. Greater Buenos Aires is here defined as in
the 1960 census, i.e. including the Federal District plus 18 departments of the
province of Buenos Aires. The census for 1947 revealed that by that date
62.5 percent of the population lived in urban centers of at least 2,000 inhabitants. It has been estimated that, just between 1943 and 1947, 20 percent of the
1943 rural population moved to urban areas. See U.N., *Report on the World
Social Situation* (New York, 1957), p. 175, quoting Gino Germani. While this
migration kept alive the ancient regional resentment against Buenos Aires
(skillfully exploited by the Perón regime), it should be recalled that several
regions of the non-pampean interior benefited from the post-1930 expansion of
import-substituting rural activities.

export-import trade and their association with foreign investors. Favorable foreign prices and demand conditions, which lasted until 1949, plus the foreign exchange accumulated during the war, temporarily hid the balance of payments consequences of these policies. These conditions also permitted not only the launching of expensive programs favoring the urban masses, but also the purchase of several major foreign-owned assets such as railroads, thus pleasing nationalists without requiring radical alteration of property rights.

Policies against foreign trade and investment were motivated not only by frictions generated during earlier periods, and by the frustrations and humiliations of the 1930s, but also by the outlook for world commerce in 1945.[40] A person making decisions in 1945 could not be at all sure about the future of international trade. The previous fifteen years had been disastrous and many were forecasting a major postwar depression or another war between the United States and the USSR. (When Korean hostilities broke out, some thought this expectation was being realized.) Traditional markets for Argentine exports in Western Europe were under the gun of the Red Army and faced enormous tasks of reconstruction, which precluded an early return to free trade and convertibility. Inconvertibility caused Argentina real losses, not only during the 1930s but also during the war, when sterling balances piled up while increases in the British and world price levels reduced their value. As Virgil Salera has pointed out, during World War I Argentina formally extended loans to the Allies, but during World War II, Britain achieved a better result by blocking Argentine sterling balances unilaterally.

The decision to neglect foreign trade and shun foreign investors had, therefore, deep roots in history and, in particular, can be viewed as a delayed response to the Great Depression.

In spite of relatively favorable external conditions provided by a world economy that after all did not experience a major postwar depression nor a third world war, the average annual growth rate in real GDP between 1941–43 and 1953–55 was around 3 percent. Commodity-producing sectors grew substantially less than services

40. At the time of Argentine complaints over Commonwealth preferences during the Great Depression, a tactless British ex-undersecretary for Foreign Affairs suggested that Argentina join the British Commonwealth to avoid the discriminatory trade barriers. The ex-undersecretary no doubt considered his idea generous, but to proud Argentines, independent since 1810, the suggestion added insult to injury. See Virgil Salera, *Exchange Control and the Argentine Market* (New York: Columbia University Press, 1941), pp. 78–79.

(see Table 2.9). While government services (or more accurately, government employment) expanded at about 6 percent per year, the rural sector grew at a rate variously estimated at 1.1 and 0.2 percent per annum. The growth of government services, as well as of transport and financial services, was also higher than the highest estimate for the manufacturing growth rate (see Table 2.3). The ratio of the manufacturing growth rate to that for the whole economy was smaller during the period under discussion than during 1927–29/1941–43 (using either source).

Most of the expansion taking place between 1941–43 and 1953–55 was packed into a three-year interval between 1945 and 1948 when GDP expanded by nearly 29 percent (CONADE), or by 25 percent (BCRA). From 1948 to 1955 aggregate output expanded only by an additional 16 percent (CONADE), or by an additional 12 percent (BCRA). Between 1948 and 1955 population grew by a total of 16 percent; the peak reached in per capita product during 1948 was not surpassed during the rest of the Perón years. Once the favorable external conditions of 1945–48 and the reserves accumulated until 1946 had disappeared, and in spite of the brief Korean commodity boom, the economy was not capable of sustaining a growth rate superior to that of population.[41]

The Argentine growth lag behind other countries of recent settlement became pronounced during the war, reappearing and remaining after 1948, as indicated by the following indices for per capita gross output (or expenditure):

	Argentina	Australia	Canada
1928–29	100	100	100
1938–39	96	111	90
1945–46	102	132	139
1959–60	117	184	159

Although Australia, benefiting from Commonwealth preferences and a relatively prosperous wool market, surpassed Argentina during the 1930s, the latter performed better than Canada (and the United

41. An additional word of caution is required regarding data for 1946–50. Recent data revisions for 1950–61 have corrected most or all of the downward biases of old industrial indices for those years; it is not clear that they have done the same for 1946–50. But any underestimation that may remain is likely to be small. See, however, Hugh H. Schwartz, "The Argentine Experience with Industrial Credit and Protection Incentives, 1943–1958" (Ph.D. thesis, Yale University, 1967).

States). Furthermore, during 1913–39, and also during 1900–39, Argentine per capita output growth slightly exceeded that of Australia. Starting during the war, however, Argentina steadily lost ground except during the brief 1946–48 boom.[42]

As shown in Tables 2.14 and 2.15, the net effect of public policy was to twist further the domestic terms of trade against the rural sector and to discriminate in favor of nontraded goods. These policies were implemented using a variety of tools—overvalued and multiple exchange rates, government controls over marketing of rural produce, a policy of absolute protection for many, but not all, manufactured products, etc. The discrimination against rural expansion was worse than that implied by relative prices; this sector found it very difficult to obtain, either domestically or abroad, certain inputs (fertilizers, tractors, etc.) that could conceivably have allowed it to react to the

42. Annual average growth rates (expressed as percentages) before 1940 are as follows for Argentina and Australia:

	1913–14 to 1938–39	*1900–01 to 1938–39*
Real GDP at factor cost		
Argentina	2.9	3.9
Australia	1.4	2.4
Population		
Argentina	2.3	2.9
Australia	1.5	1.6

Indices for population and gross output (or expenditure) are as follows for 1928–60:

	1928–29	*1938–39*	*1945–46*	*1959–60*
Population				
Argentina	100	120	135	178
Australia	100	110	118	162
Canada	100	113	123	178
Gross output (or expenditure)				
Argentina	100	115	138	208
Australia	100	122	156	298
Canada	100	102	170	282

Argentine per capita output, which in 1928–29 was about 70 percent that of Australia and 55 percent that of Canada, by 1959–60 had become only about one-half and two-fifths of corresponding Australian and Canadian figures, respectively. Canadian and Australian data obtained from Kelly, "Foreign Trade of Argentina and Australia, 1930 to 1960," p. 52; A. Ferrer and E. L. Wheelwright, "Industrialization in Argentina and Australia: A Comparative Study" (mimeographed), p. 18; M. C. Urquhart, ed., *Historical Statistics of Canada* (Toronto: The Macmillan Company of Canada, 1965), pp. 14 and 132 (Canadian data refer to real gross expenditure); and N. G. Butlin, *Australian Domestic Product, Investment and Foreign Borrowing* (Cambridge, England: At the University Press, 1962), pp. 33–34.

price decline by increasing productivity. This lack of modern inputs, not fully reflected in price data, was also accompanied by weak public efforts in agricultural research and extension services, and labor shortages in the countryside.

As shown in Table 2.8, the export quantum declined sharply during 1945–54; by 1950–54 it was 37 percent below the levels for the depression years of 1930–39. Lack of foreign demand could hardly be blamed for this shrinkage; the Argentine share in world trade of her traditional export commodities fell substantially, and in 1952 the country even had to import wheat.[43] The main explanation for the export performance was that rural output increased between 1935–39 and 1950–54 by only 14 percent (and output of the traditional exportable goods *declined* by 10 percent), while domestic absorption of rural goods increased by more than 40 percent.[44] Part of the stagnation in rural output may be blamed on poor weather, especially during 1950–54, but government policy toward rural exportables (of which price policy was only a part) must bear the principal blame. Vulnerability to bad breaks was greatly increased by public policies. Exports of manufactured goods, which had expanded during the war and the immediate postwar period, shrank to insignificant levels after 1946. Argentina turned her back on the worldwide expansion of trade, while Canada and Australia profited from it.

Although the sharp fall in the export quantum may not have been foreseen by the authorities, part of their overall strategy was not to bother much with exports. Their main interest centered on some aspects of import-substituting industrialization, and on the provision of health, education, recreation, and other mass services. Besides pleasing nationalistic and reformist sentiment, this policy had the

43. The following percentages give Argentina's share in world exports of selected products

	1934–38	*1945–49*	*1950–54*
Corn	64	43	21
Wheat and flour	19	9	9
Linseed and its oil	68	31	44
Wool	12	14	10
All meat	40	35	19

Data obtained from ECLA, *El Desarrollo Económico de la Argentina,* 2:48. All Argentine exports, which in 1928 accounted for 3.1 percent of total world exports, by 1965 represented only 0.8 percent of that total. See *Techint Boletín Informativo,* no. 155 (Nov. 1966), p. 6.

44. See essay 3. Between 1935–39 and 1950–54 population increased by 32 percent.

additional advantage of generating employment and security for the urban working class, a political pillar of the regime. Light manufacturing, construction, government, and the nationalized railroads came to be viewed more as sources of jobs than as activities producing goods and services. The migration from rural to urban areas which had been taking place since the 1930s was accelerated by this policy, even though it was extremely doubtful that the social value of the marginal product of labor in, say, the nationalized railroads, was higher than in rural activities producing exportables.[45]

The policy of import substituting for some industrial products was not an integrated and thought-out plan. Rather, it proceeded from one improvisation to another, reacting to short-run economic and political pressures. Toward the end of the war and during the early postwar years, the main preoccupation was defending industries that had arisen and expanded during the war, regardless of their efficiency. This attitude had an important implication; as the protection granted existing activities included not only the shutting out of foreign competition (using primarily exchange and import controls rather than tariffs), but also the importation of their inputs at an increasingly overvalued exchange rate, some branches of industry (the potential producers of imported inputs) often suffered, not only relative to the favored activities, but also in comparison with a situation of free trade and equilibrium exchange rates. Oil extraction is one example of an activity discriminated against by that system of protection. Some types of machinery and equipment were also relatively neglected.[46] The policy of stimulating light industries rather than more

45. These policies would have have been less harmful in an underdeveloped country with rural surplus labor and a perfectly elastic (for a range) supply schedule of labor to the urban centers. But the Argentine rural sector (especially that in the pampean zone) was fully commercialized, in the Ranis-Fei sense, since the latter part of the nineteenth century. Withdrawals of labor from the rural sector under such circumstances lead *ceteris paribus* to a drop in rural output. See Gustav Ranis and John C. Fei, "A Theory of Economic Development," *American Economic Review* (Sept. 1961). It may also be conjectured that the per capita real costs of providing social overhead facilities rose as a result of the rural-urban migrations.

46. As a first approximation, degrees of import substitution achieved in different branches of industry may be measured by the ratio of imports to the total value of apparent consumption (imports plus the value of domestic production) of several industrial products. For textiles and clothing this ratio fell from 0.31 in 1935–39 to 0.10 in 1945–49; for wood products the ratio fell from 0.30 in 1935–39 to 0.17 in 1945–49. In contrast, the ratio for vehicles and machinery fell only from 0.48 in 1935–39 to 0.40 in 1945–49, and in the case of petroleum derivatives there was an increase in the imported share

capital-intensive ones could conceivably be defended on efficiency grounds, but this would imply that either (1) exports were expanded to finance the importation of goods produced by the lagging heavy industries, or (2) the foreign exchange saved by the expansion of light industries was sufficient to finance the required imports. A combination of (1) and (2) could, of course, be sufficient. During the euphoria of 1945–48 little thought was given to these matters and when exports contracted in 1949 the country faced an exchange bottleneck, because import substitution had not released enough exchange to finance imports required by a 5 percent growth rate. First priority was given then to raw materials and intermediate goods imports needed to maintain existing capacity in operation.[47] Machinery and equipment for new capacity could neither be imported nor produced domestically (at least in the short run). A sharp decrease in the rate of real capital formation in new machinery and equipment followed.[48]

The impact of the exchange bottleneck on nonconstruction capital formation worsened the economy's capacity to transform, which in turn made the bottleneck more intractable. Expansion of import-substituting activities, or even export activities, required investments in new machinery and equipment with high import components. Hostility toward foreign capital, which could have provided a way out of this difficulty, aggravated the 1948–53 crisis.

Protection and credit policies gave rise to a constellation of costs and prices that increased the profitability of investment in some branches of manufacturing, while decreasing it not only for the rural sector producing exportables, but also in several potentially import-competing industrial branches. Even when prices reflected, on average,

---

from 0.16 in 1935–39 to 0.20 in 1945–49. Measures of import substitution are discussed in greater detail in essay 4. Services rendered by Argentines also replaced those previously rendered by foreigners; the Peronist regime encouraged the merchant marine (influenced by World War II shipping shortages) and local insurance. Profit and interest remittances were also nearly eliminated by the nationalization of foreign assets and debts.

47. The *share* of capital goods in total merchandise imports dropped as the real *level* of imports fell; imports of capital goods represented 37 percent of all imports in 1947–48 and only 30 percent during 1949–51. By 1952–55 the share had fallen to 27 percent. These imports include parts for equipment and machinery already in operation.

48. Purchases of new machinery and equipment, both imported and domestically produced, as a percentage of GNP (both expressed at constant 1935–38 prices), fell from 6.0 percent in 1946–48 to 3.3 percent in 1949–51 and 3.6 percent in 1952–55. In 1935–38 this percentage had been 4.9. See essay 6.

social opportunity costs, their erratic movements induced by policy changes and by inflationary conditions increased uncertainty and deprived such signals of a great deal of their usefulness.[49] A situation developed where neither coherent planning nor the price mechanism were used to allocate resources rationally. Minor disequilibria were allowed to turn into major structural imbalances for lack of an adjustment mechanism.

In summary, it may be useful to distinguish between the different types of economic inefficiencies that government policies created. One major type, which could be called "macro" inefficiencies, includes (1) those arising from the unnecessary closing of the economy (discouragement of exports) and (2) once the closing of the economy is granted, those arising from the failure to have a balanced expansion of industry that would create a productive structure capable of meeting demands generated by a 5 percent growth. But even taking these "macro" inefficiencies as given, the tools used by the government to promote its aims (import prohibitions for some goods, credit rationing with negative or very low real rates of interest, etc.), by curtailing competitive pressures and creating quasi-monopolistic conditions in the domestic market, led to further "micro" inefficiencies as the favored industries were not pressed to improve efficiency and minimize costs in their operations.[50] Micro-inefficiencies arose within

49. Table 89 in the Statistical Appendix presents a measure of the variability of real wholesale prices during 1945–55. The high values shown in its last column arose to some extent from world price movements (as in the case of wool and rubber). But in most cases the high variability was a result of erratic policies, including selective and unsteady price controls applied in the midst of an inflationary situation.

50. A once-and-for-all inefficient use of resources resulted from the way in which the government embarked on a buying spree during 1945–48, not only of foreign assets located in Argentina, but also of imports, using for these purposes the exchange accumulated during the war. During the early postwar period severe shortages of many industrial goods persisted in the United States and Western Europe; it is said that Argentine officials, acting as buying agents, bought these scarce goods without paying much attention to price tags and even used extralegal means to persuade foreign authorities to grant the necessary export permits. Such eagerness to buy may have been due to an expectation of a new world war; with fresh memories of blocked exchange reserves during 1940–45 (as well as of unexportable surpluses of grain), the main interest centered on spending foreign exchange as quickly as possible, before shipping difficulties developed again. The increase of foreign exchange reserves and the decrease in net capital stock in many sectors of the economy during the war may be viewed as a war-imposed switch in Argentine wealth holdings. It was to be expected that after the war more real capital and less foreign exchange would be held. But this return to equilibrium was handled in a rather improvised fashion.

Table 2.18: Changes in the Capital Stock of Argentina, 1929–55
(Percentages)

	Percentage change in capital stock			Allocation of total change in capital stock		
	1929–39	1939–45	1945–55	1929–39	1945–55	1939–55
I. ECLA data						
Total	11	2	31	100	100	100
Sectorial distribution						
Rural	2	−4	5	3	3	1
Industry	18	0	60	19	24	23
Public utilities, communications	39	4	22	9	2	3
Railroads	−22	−25	−16	−20	−3	−8
Other transport	142	−8	19	45	4	2
Housing	6	7	28	17	31	36
Government	30	25	61	30	32	39
Other services	−5	−7	50	−2	6	5
Distribution by type of capital good						
Machinery and equipment	14	−12	42	33	30	19
Construction and improvements	11	7	31	69	68	78
Cattle stocks	−4	10	10	−2	2	3
II. CONADE data						
Total	−ᵃ	0	45	–	100	100
Machinery and equipment	–	−29	81	–	38	19
Construction and improvements	–	11	39	–	56	70
Cattle stocks	–	17	19	–	6	11

ᵃ Dash indicates data not available.

Sources and method: ECLA, pp. 91–107. ECLA data are expressed in 1950 prices. Those for CONADE, obtained from unpublished preliminary estimates of that organization, are expressed at 1960 prices.

most sectors also as a result of deficiencies in public services and changes in labor legislation and work-rules.[51]

The policies followed during 1943–55 were, in many ways, more extreme forms of those followed during 1930–43. They continued trends in allocation of resources which, although justifiable during the

51. These micro-inefficiencies had become so widespread by the time of Perón's overthrow in 1955 that Raúl Prebisch estimated that average labor productivity in industry could increase by 10 percent during 1956 simply as a result of changes in work-rules. See his "Sound Money or Uncontrolled Inflation" and "Final Report and Economic Recovery Programme," *Review of the River Plate* (Nov. 11, 1955, and Jan. 20, 1956).

depression, were out of line with the more favorable world conditions of 1943–55. Table 2.18 compares trends in capital formation before and after the war, according to two different sources. The capital stock increase of 1945–55 was larger than that of 1929–39; postwar capital formation benefited from accumulated reserves and the favorable international terms of trade of 1946–48. However, during both periods the share of net investment taking the form of construction and improvements was similar and quite high (for 1945–55 it was 68 percent according to ECLA, and 56 percent according to CONADE). In both periods, capital stock of the rural sector remained practically constant; in railroads it decreased.

According to ECLA, housing, government, and other services obtained a huge chunk of capital formation during 1945–55—nearly 70 percent. Some may wish to argue that this channeling of resources toward home goods was not the cause but the effect of exchange difficulties. Their argument could run as follows: faced with unfavorable foreign markets, the government's only choice was to allocate resources toward either import-substituting industries or home goods. The former, however, is import intensive in its early stages, so that to avoid further exchange difficulties and to generate employment, emphasis had to be given to home goods. This argument could be used to justify the faster growth of some services during the 1930s, but hardly during 1945–55. It was precisely at the time when foreign markets were most favorable that the greatest impulse was given to home goods. Between 1945 and 1949, value added in construction increased by a total of 61 percent (BCRA), while that in the rural sector remained practically constant. While a great shortage of manpower developed in the countryside, even to the extent that some crops went unharvested, labor flocked to the urban centers, in part to work in import-substituting manufacturing, but mostly to participate in home good activities such as urban construction.[52]

52. According to Alexander Ganz, the real gross investment of the national government during 1945–55 was distributed in the following way (percentages of total):

	1945–46	1947–51	1952–55
National defense	51	24	10
Housing, health, and other serial investments	15	18	13
Transport	26	27	29
Energy and communications	3	17	24
Agriculture	1	1	2
Industry	1	2	6
Other	3	11	16

Condensed from Alexander Ganz, "Problems and Uses of National Wealth

Table 2.19 presents the allocation of increases of the active population; of the two sources presented, CONADE data are more reliable, as they are based on the 1960 census as well as on that for 1947 (but this source does not provide pre-1947 data). Either source indicates

Table 2.19: Allocation of Changes in the Active Population, 1940–55
(Percentages of total)

	ECLA *1940–44/1955*	CONADE *1947/1955*
Total	*100*	*100*
Rural sector	4	−15
Oil and mining	0	1
Manufacturing	19	29
Construction	10	15
Public utilities	1	2
Transport	10	11
Communications	₁2	2
Commerce, finance, and housing services	19	17
Government services	21	17
Other services	13	21

Sources and method: As in Table 2.6.

that the three commodity-producing sectors (rural, manufacturing, oil, and mining) obtained less than one-fourth of the increase in the active population. Either source also shows that government services plus other private services *by themselves* absorbed more labor than manufacturing plus oil and mining.

It may still be true that, after 1949, shortages of exchange and of machinery and equipment led to construction expenditures as a way of maintaining urban employment without putting too much pressure on imports. The alternative of devoting more resources to exportables, whether rural or manufactured goods, was not tried until around 1953, and then the effort was feeble.

It is interesting to compare the make-work investments of 1929–39 with those of 1943–55. In the former years, these were concentrated primarily in road building, which more than offset the railroad deterioration; in the latter period, these investments took more of a

Estimates in Latin America," in R. Goldsmith and C. Saunders, eds., *Income and Wealth Series VIII*, International Association for Research in Income and Wealth (London: Bowes and Bowes, 1959), pp. 217–73. Besides trade unions, the Perón regime rested heavily on the support of the armed forces; this explains the high shares of investment allocated to national defense.

social character with the construction of low-cost housing, hospitals, and recreation facilities. It also appears that national defense was more generously handled during 1943–55 than in the earlier period.

Tables 2.18 and 2.19 indicate that the main macro missallocation of resources during 1945–55 was that between home goods (services) and exportables (mainly the rural sector). However, a closer examination of the allocation pattern within industry will also show too many resources going into quasi-home goods, such as clothing and textiles, and too few into activities at the frontier of import substitution, namely, oil extraction and refining, steel, chemicals, machinery, and equipment.

The attention given to social overhead capital closely linked with the production of commodities was different in 1929–39 and 1945–55. This applies not only to nonrailroad transport, but also to electricity and communications. Remarkably, the capital stock in electricity and communications increased by a larger percentage during the depression years 1929–39 than during 1945–55, when a government that boasted of encouraging industrialization was in power.[53]

Another bit of evidence supports the interpretation of 1943–55 policies as delayed and out of place responses to the shock of the Great Depression. Industrial and rural activities receiving greatest attention from the government, at least until 1953, were mainly those that had developed rapidly during 1930–43 and could have been expected to be nearing maturity. At that stage in their development, light import-substituting industries, as well as regional import-substituting crops, needed an increasingly competitive climate to insure their efficiency and to push them to seek export markets. Instead, they were surrounded by extremely protective policies which would have been hard to justify even during the 1930s. In spite of having access to some cheap imported inputs at overvalued exchange rates, they failed to develop large export markets.

The continuity of pre- and post-1943 economic policies, with the latter becoming crude caricatures of the former, is also shown by the nationalization of foreign-owned assets and the repatriation of the external debt. Since early in the war, Argentina had been building up

53. A further contrast is that dealing with the state-owned oil company, Yacimientos Petrolíferos Fiscales. Between 1929 and 1943, the company increased output at an annual rate of 8.2 percent; from 1943 to 1955 (the period of a nationalistic government), the company increased its output at a rate of 3.7 percent per annum.

blocked sterling balances, earning little interest, while the world price level was rising. At the same time, she continued to pay interest on her external debt and dividends to foreign owners of assets. To modify this situation, Argentina began paying off debt held in the United Kingdom, using blocked balances. Proposals for buying part of the railroads and other British-held assets, also using blocked sterling, began to be studied. As is well known, the authorities who rose to power after 1943 purchased not only all of the railroads, but other foreign assets as well, while completing the repatriation of the foreign debt. Once again we have the Perón regime applying policies that had low opportunity costs during earlier depression and war years, but which had become less desirable on economic grounds as a result of postwar changes in external conditions. Unfortunately for Argentina, her government went for extreme nationalism when its price was highest.[54]

An important difference between the industrialization policies of 1930–43 and 1943–55 should be noted. During the former period, policies were followed which in general improved the economic environment for industry, without much intervention in individual markets. During the latter, the government followed more discriminatory policies within the industrial sector, including price controls and selective credit, exchange and protective policies.

Another important feature of the 1943–55 period was the emergence of a significant degree of price inflation. In *relative* terms,

---

54. Argentina settled old accounts with the United Kingdom and the system of Imperial Preferences in 1945, when she repudiated the Roca-Runciman treaties of 1933 and 1936 and called for new negotiations at a time when the United Kingdom was in great need of food. On September 1946 a new treaty was signed. At the time, it was expected that Argentina would buy only part of the British-owned railroads. In February 1947, however, agreement was reached between private British interests and the Argentine government for the complete sale of the railroads, which took place in 1948. The Argentine government may have been influenced in this decision by its expectation of a new world war between the USSR and the U.S.A., weakness in the pound sterling during 1945–49, and world shortages of the goods it wanted to buy. See BCRA, *Memoria Anual 1946,* esp. pp. 2–3 and *Memoria Anual 1947,* p. 1. Of the total of foreign exchange reserves which Argentina had at the end of 1946 ($1,687 million), only $569 million were in inconvertible currencies, including pound sterling. A detailed calculation of the social rate of return earned by Argentina in these asset-buying and debt-repatriation transactions would be of some interest. As early as 1939, Argentina tried to use blocked sterling balances to purchase British-owned Buenos Aires tramways; London refused the proposal, however. See Salera, *Exchange Control and the Argentine Market,* p. 220, n. 10.

Argentina began to follow inflationary policies in 1933. Between 1929 and 1939, while wholesale prices in the United States fell by 19 percent, the corresponding index in Argentina rose by 12 percent. The main reasons for this divergence were the devaluation of the peso and other measures adopted to handle the exchange shortage caused by the depression. The same basic problem—exchange shortage—would accompany inflation in later years, especially beginning in 1949.

As in most of the world, inflation accelerated during 1939–48. The wholesale price index rose at an annual rate of 11.4 percent, a figure not much greater than the corresponding 8.5 percent in the United States. Thus, most of the Argentine price increases until 1948 could be said to have been a result of worldwide price trends, communicated via the trade mechanism.[55] During 1946–48, however, expansionary fiscal, monetary, and wage policies accentuated inflationary pressures that would have become very severe had not Argentina been blessed with favorable terms of trade and large exchange reserves.[56]

Since 1949 the sources of inflationary pressure have centered, as during the 1930s, upon the exchange shortage and the policies adopted to cope with it. The mechanism of adjustment for deficits in the balance of payments calls for changes in relative prices, which also generate changes in income distribution. In an economy where downward price flexibility is limited, attempts to change relative prices will lead to an upward movement in the price level. The price structure may be changed, but only in the context of a rising price level. Furthermore, as these changes give additional real income to entrepreneurs in export and truly import-competing activities (at the short-run expense of the rest of society), they will provoke claims for higher income by losing sectors of the economy. If granted, these claims will not only offset the initial change in relative prices but will

55. An appreciation of the peso to offset world price trends was never considered as a serious possibility.

56. Before 1900 Argentina indulged in substantial autonomous inflation. A British observer noted in 1899: "the Argentines alter their currency almost as frequently as they change their presidents. . . . No people in the world take a keener interest in currency experiments than the Argentines." Quoted in A. G. Ford, *The Gold Standard, 1880–1914* (Oxford: Clarendon Press, 1962), p. 90. The Conversion Law of 1899, however, ushered in a long period of negligible autonomous inflation that coincided with favorable external circumstances. The financial disorder which existed previous to 1899 coexisted with vigorous economic growth (but was also accompanied by violent cycles).

also give a new push to the price level. An inflationary spiral can be generated easily by these forces, coupled with a passive monetary policy.[57] More will be said about this in essay 7. Here it will be enough to note that, between 1948 and 1955, wholesale prices rose at an average annual rate of 20 percent, while in the United States the annual increase was less than 1 percent. This inflation took place while real output expanded at very low rates. It could be viewed as resulting from the struggle among urban workers, urban entrepreneurs, the public sector, and the rural sector to maintain the gains or re-cover the losses in real income sustained during the 1946–48 boom. The disruptions caused by inflation and unstable relative prices made it more difficult to reach an allocation of resources that could produce a sustained 5 percent growth rate.

Wage policy encouraged an impressive rise of the wage share in

Table 2.20: Participation in the GNP at Market Prices of Wages and Salaries, Social Security Contributions and Factor Payments Abroad, 1935–1955
(Percentages)

	Net wages and salaries	Employers' social security contributions	Employees' social security contributions	Net factor payments abroad
I. *Old series*				
1935–36	38.3	0.8	0.8	5.2
1937–39	37.5	0.8	0.8	4.3
1940–42	36.5	0.8	0.8	3.6
1943–44	36.8	0.8	0.8	3.0
1945–46	37.0	1.6	1.4	2.2
1947–49	40.6	2.6	2.2	0.4
1950–52	43.7	3.3	2.5	0.2
1953–55	43.7	4.1	3.0	0.1
II. *New CONADE series*				
1950–52	39.4	3.2	2.5	0.2
1953–55	38.8	3.8	2.8	0.2

Sources and method: Obtained from national accounts data expressed at current prices. Basic sources as in Table 2.1; social security contributions for Old Series from ECLA worksheets.

national income. Table 2.20 presents data on three income components that were particularly affected by Perón's policies—wages and salaries,

57. See Julio H. G. Olivera, "La Teoría No Monetaria de la Inflación," *El Trimestre Económico* (México) (Oct.–Dec. 1960); and "On Structural Inflation and Latin-American Structuralism," *Oxford Economic Papers* 16, no. 3 (Oct. 1964).

social security contributions, and net factor payments abroad. The share of net wages and salaries showed a marked increase beginning in 1948, while the shares for social security contributions nearly doubled between 1944 and 1945 and continued to rise thereafter. The decline in net factor payments abroad during the postwar era continued a trend already visible in earlier years.

When looking at figures on the wage share, the comments made in essay 1 regarding the Argentine price structure and sectorial composition of production should be borne in mind. Furthermore, as in all countries, the line between wages and salaries and other income is difficult to draw for the self-employed. At the same time, changes in their proportion within the economy affect the observed wage income share, which excludes imputed wages for the self-employed. Even if the undesirability of directly comparing Table 2.20 data with those of countries with different price and productive structures is granted, it may be asked whether the increase in the overall wage share is not simply the result of faster growth in sectors with high wage shares. Table 2.21 helps to clarify this question by showing that

Table 2.21: Participation in Sectorial Gross Value Added (at Factor Cost), of Wages and Salaries (including Employees' Social Security Contributions), 1935–55 (Percentages)

	Agricultural and livestock	Mining, manufacturing, and construction	Other sectors
1935–36	19.0	54.2	48.8
1937–39	19.0	52.4	47.4
1947–49	20.8	54.6	48.6
1950–52	20.3	59.0	52.9
1953–55	23.3	57.3	54.4

Sources: Old series, as in Table 2.20.

in the three major sectors of the economy the wage share rose.[58] Yet the relative decline in value added (at current prices) by the rural sector also contributed to the increase in the aggregate wage share.

Real wage rates for most types of employment increased after 1945–46. Their improvement was on the whole larger than increases

58. It has not been possible to obtain employees' social security contributions disaggregated by sectors. These are included under wages and salaries in Table 2.21, but not in Table 2.20. The same applies to indirect taxes, included in Table 2.20 in the GNP, but not in Table 2.21.

in per capita product taking place during the same years. Table 2.22 presents data supporting these statements; it also indicates that wage rates for unskilled workers rose faster than those of skilled ones.

Table 2.22: Indices of Real Wages and Output per Capita, 1935–55
(1935–39 = 100)

	Index of net total real wages per member of active population	Index of average real industrial wages per industrial worker		Index of hourly real wage rates according to wage contracts		Index of real gross domestic product per capita
		Index A	Index B	Skilled workers	Unskilled workers	
1935–36	97	102	102	99	98	96
1937–39	102	99	99	101	101	103
1940–42	107	96	96	100	103	103
1943–44	117	104	100	106	113	109
1945–46	120	101	97	98	105	110
1947–49	162	148	134	120	135	123
1950–52	162	141	122	102	123	114
1953–55	157	145	122	94	130	116

Sources and methods: First column: An index of all wage income *net* of *both* employers' and employees' social security contributions and at current prices, was first obtained from CONADE, pp. 34–37, and from unpublished ECLA worksheets based on O.S. Both series were linked using 1950 = 100. This index was then deflated by the implicit price deflator for private consumption, obtained from O.S., p. 156 (for 1935–50) and from BCRA, p. 57 (for 1950 on). Finally, it was assumed that active population has remained a constant percentage of total population during 1935–55; data on population were obtained from O.S., p. 164 and from U.N., *Statistical Bulletin for Latin America*, 3:5–6.

Second and third columns: Data from Oficina de Estudios para la Colaboración Económica Internacional, *Síntesis Económica y Financiera No. 1, Argentina*, pp. 68–69. Index *A* was deflated by the Buenos Aires cost of living index including housing rents. Index *B* was deflated by the same index *excluding* housing rents, which have been under official control since 1943. Wages exclude social security contributions.

Fourth and fifth columns: As the second and third columns; both were deflated by the *total* cost of living index (i.e. as Index *A*). These indices are based on hourly wage rates for each kind of worker, according to collective contracts.

Sixth column: Involves the GDP at factor cost, according to BCRA, p. 18.

It may be conjectured that the wage share would have risen somewhat after 1945–46, even without the help of government policy. An industrial expansion that was faster than rural growth tended to increase the aggregate wage share; but even within industry the share could have been expected to increase. Before 1930 Argentina had an elastic supply of labor, thanks to European immigration, and wage rates could not rise much above what was needed to bring an inflow of immigrants. After 1930 the doors to immigration, although partly closed, were not completely shut. During 1930–33, however, the depression created urban unemployment. This unemployment, plus normal population growth and continued rural stagnation, provided nearly all the manpower required by the predominantly urban recovery of 1933–43. Real wage rates showed little change between 1935 and 1945–46, and the overall wage share showed even a slight falling tendency. The 1946–48 boom, however, put pressure on the labor supply, and the remaining labor pool created by rural stagnation and population increase was quickly dried up. Indeed, this demand for labor induced massive immigration once again; during the five years between 1947 and 1951, net immigration of about 460,000 persons took place. Under these circumstances and with alternative migrating opportunities in other countries (such as Australia), real wage rates could have been expected to increase.[59]

The fact remains that other Peronist policies contributed to the increase in real wage rates after 1945–46. The twisting of the price structure in favor of relatively labor-intensive activities, a credit policy favoring these activities and small establishments, as well as direct government intervention in wage negotiations led to wage increases greater than increments in the value of the social marginal product of labor. Besides higher wages, the urban masses also benefited from government actions granting greater employment security; a comprehensive social security system; new recreational, educational, and health facilities; and, in particular, a feeling of self-respect and of political power. Few trade union leaders were aware that these gains were often obtained at the expense not only of other social classes, but also of economic efficiency and future growth. Perón was repaid with fierce loyalty.[60] Non-Peronist labor leaders, whether communist or center-left, have had an uphill battle since 1955 in trying to chip away at that loyalty, especially when the

59. Substantial unregistered immigration from neighboring countries (Chile, Bolivia, and Paraguay) also took place during and after these years.

60. Direct taxation, a relatively efficient tool for redistributing income, was also used, but not very dramatically. The share of direct taxes (excluding social security contributions) in GNP, which was 3.4 percent during 1940–44, rose to more than 5 percent during 1950–54. (See ECLA, 1:84.) Although property rights were curtailed under Perón, no significant attempts were made to redistribute wealth. The redistribution of income toward wage earners tended to increase the domestic demand for exportable goods,

correction of economically inefficient policies led to decreases in labor's share.

Peronist policies present a picture of a government interested not so much in industrialization as in a nationalistic and populist policy of increasing the real consumption, employment, and economic security of the masses—and of the new entrepreneurs. It chose these goals even at the expense of capital formation and of the economy's capacity to transform. The favorable external conditions of 1946–48 helped to mask the conflict between nationalist and populist goals and long-run economic development, a conflict that became clearer after 1948.

A final irony is that greater attention to exportables during 1943–55 would have resulted in more, rather than less, industrialization, as the examples of Canada and Australia suggest. Modestly expanding exports, by making feasible a higher overall growth rate, could have resulted in manufacturing expansion greater than that observed. Also, a different attitude toward foreign investment would have encouraged industrialization, especially in key sectors, in the same way as such investment encouraged manufacturing during the 1930s. Bitter memories of the Great Depression, as well as dimmer memories of the years immediately after World War I, led economic authorities to neglect the long-run economics of growth for the sake of short-run economic security.[61]

61. The Peronist regime was in many ways a pioneer and as such did not have the benefit of previous experiences. For example, its fumbling efforts at economic planning in a mixed developing society came before such policies became widely followed in other countries. The same applies to its foreign policy, which tried a neutralistic line. On the other hand, some of its policies that appear unwise in retrospect were not so different from what mature countries were doing at the time. For example, Argentina nationalized her railroads only a few years after the Labor government of the United Kingdom and the De Gaulle regime in France had nationalized important segments of their respective economies. The first plan of the Perón regime was mainly a collection of social and political intentions, with little discussion of priorities, specific projects or export targets. The second five-year plan reflected the sobering post-1948 exchange crisis and stressed economic goals. Noteworthy was the new emphasis on rural activities and those on the frontier of import substitution. Thanks to the 1947 census and the new national accounts estimated under public sponsorship, the second plan contained better global data than the first. Unfortunately, investment planning improved only when investable funds had dwindled. See Bruce Herrick, "Planificación Económica en Argentina bajo Perón," in *Ensayos sobre Planificación,* E. García and K. Griffin, eds. (Santiago: Universidad de Chile, 1967), pp. 351–75.

TOWARD THE ELIMINATION OF THE FOREIGN EXCHANGE
BOTTLENECK, 1955 TO THE PRESENT

Toward the end of the Perón regime, it became clear that little
further growth could be expected from additional investments in home
goods, either in services and construction, or in activities that had
passed to a quasi-home goods category, after exhausting their possibilities of import substitution, such as clothing and textiles. Droughts
in 1951–52 dramatized both the need to solve the exchange bottleneck
and the futility of pushing ahead in other activities until the exchange
situation became more relaxed. As early as 1951, measures were
taken to give better incentives to the production of rural exportables.
Later on, the cooperation of foreign capital was sought to develop
new import competing activities in more difficult industrial branches
such as the tractor industry. The Perón regime even began to discuss
allowing foreign capital into the oil industry, a bitter pill to its nationalistic wing. The external debt, which had a reasonable interest
and maturity structure when it was extinguished during 1946–48, once
again began to grow, but now taking the form of short- and medium-
term obligations with unfavorable conditions. But the policy switch
was too little and too late.

The overthrow of the Perón regime in September 1955 led to economic policies that can be characterized as efforts to reorient the
structure of production so that steady growth would not be detained
by periodic exchange crises. Exchange rate devaluations and the
gradual elimination of price controls were used to allow relative
prices to reflect opportunity costs. The result was a pattern more
favorable to producers of tradeable goods, especially in the rural
sector, as can be seen in Tables 2.14 and 2.15. Sporadic attempts,
like those of the Perón regime in 1952, were made to stop or slow
down inflation and to attract foreign capital. The results of these
policies, which extend to the present, have been generally disappointing.

From 1953–55 to 1963–65 the overall growth rate was 3.1 percent
per annum, with the rural sector showing a yearly average expansion
of less than 1 percent, and manufacturing growing at 4.6 percent per
annum. Only since 1962 have exports shown a marked upward trend,
beyond recovery from the 1951–52 droughts. Meanwhile exchange

difficulties gave rise during 1959 and 1962–63 to severe recessions. What accounts for this weak performance?

It will be useful to review some important features of the economy as they appeared toward the end of 1955. The corporate-state mentality of the Perón regime had resulted in an economy with a low capacity to transform, where producers, workers, and consumers expected the government to shield them from undesirable trends arising from the market. The price mechanism became a tool to redistribute income rather than to allocate resources. The structure of production showed some glaring imbalances after years of neglecting marginal adjustments. Severe bottlenecks had been allowed to develop in transportation, electricity, the supply of machinery and equipment, oil, and rural goods; in most cases, the government had neither allowed the price mechanism to reflect these imbalances in a steady fashion nor taken effective measures to remedy them by public investment. The system of protection not only created quasi-monopolistic positions but also hampered new exports of manufacturers. Efficient activities that had export potential were often forced to buy costly inputs from inefficient domestic sources.

In spite of the creation of new institutions such as the Industrial Bank, capital markets at the end of 1955 were in worse shape than they had been before 1943. Detailed goverment controls over the allocation and terms of credit, plus inflation, gave rise to a distribution of loanable funds that bore few links to either the entrepreneurial capabilities of borrowers or the social profitability of projects. In the mortgage market the government-owned Mortgage Bank supplanted completely the *cédulas hipotecarias* (mortgage paper), which had been a popular debt instrument before 1943.

These are some of the unfavorable initial conditions of the post-1955 period. The authorities had to induce a reallocation of resources in a society that had come to expect that any existing economic activity had a government-guaranteed right to prosper. It was also necessary to correct in a few years the structural imbalances accumulated since the outbreak of the war. The mechanism used for these purposes—the price system—was hampered by quasi-monopolistic markets and by rigid and arbitrary work rules. Furthermore, the bureaucratic establishment of the public sector was less than enthusiastic about implementing policies reducing the power it had gained before 1955.

The return to prices that more closely reflected social opportunity costs had an important impact on income distribution; in particular, it redistributed income and wealth in favor of producers of exportable and true import-competing goods, and away from those producing home and quasi-home goods. Urban workers bore the brunt of this redistribution. Because the year-to-year fluctuations have been violent, it is not clear whether real wage *rates* rose or fell after 1955. It is apparent, however, that the share of wages and salaries, net of social security contributions, dropped after 1955. Table 2.23 presents rele-

Table 2.23: Indicators of Income Distribution and Real Wages
in Argentina, 1950–61

	1950–52	1953–55	1956–58	1959–61
Net wages and salaries as a percentage of GNP at market prices	39.4	38.8	37.0	33.8
Employers' social security contributions as a percentage of GNP at market prices	3.2	3.8	3.3	2.6
Employees' social security contributions as a percentage of GNP at market prices	2.5	2.8	2.6	2.0
Index of real average hourly wage rates of industrial workers (1958 = 100)	86	87	95	84
Index of real average hourly wage rate, according to collective bargaining contracts (1958 = 100)	96	96	98	82

Sources and method: As in Tables 2.20–2.22, and Table 133 of the Statistical Appendix. Indices of money wage rates were deflated by the Buenos Aires cost of living index (including housing). Index of hourly wage rates according to collective contracts obtained from unpublished CONADE material. The index of average hourly wage rates of industrial workers is given in Table 133 of the Appendix for each year during 1939–65.

vant data. The decline in the wage share and, for many workers, real wages, plus attempts to revise work rules, led to acute social and political difficulties.

The conflict between economic efficiency and a fair income distribution has never been sharper in Argentina than during 1955–66. Unfortunately, even as the need for reconciling efficiency and equity became more acute, the main instrument that could be used in that task, the tax and expenditure system of the central government, became weaker. Table 2.23 provides some evidence on the weakness of the revenue machinery: social security contributions declined as percentages of GNP, not because of any changes in the structure of the system, but mainly as a result of an increase in tax evasion.[62]

A recent study confirms that post-1955 income distribution has been more unequal than that for pre-1955 years. Some of the data of this study is summarized in Table 2.24. Even if one grants that 1959

Table 2.24: Family Income Distribution in Argentina, 1953, 1959, and 1961
(Percentages of total income)

Percentages of families, starting with those of lowest incomes:	1953	1959	1961
0–20	7.4	6.8	7.0
21–40	10.7	9.5	10.3
41–60	13.6	12.3	12.9
subtotal 0–60	31.7	28.6	30.2
61–80	18.1	16.9	18.0
81–90	13.1	12.2	12.7
subtotal 61–90	31.2	29.1	30.7
91–95	9.5	10.8	9.8
96–100	27.6	31.3	29.3
subtotal 91–100	37.1	42.1	39.1

Source: Adapted from Alberto Fracchia and Oscar Altimir, "Income Distribution in Argentina," *Economic Bulletin for Latin America* 11 (April 1966): 114. The authors point out that these results are preliminary; they also discuss methodology and data limitations (pp. 106–21).

was an exceptional year (during which a sharp devaluation produced a drop in real wages and an increase in rural income), the figures for 1961 indicate a slightly greater inequality than in 1953. The study, which also takes into account distribution of personal and principal income, concludes that "from the early 1950's to the beginning of the 1960's a significant deterioration occurred in the distribution of income in Argentina. The lowest 60 percent of all income recipients decreased their share in total income. The next higher groups lost, but their loss was small. The top 10 percent achieved a substantial increase in its share of the total, and this gain was largely concentrated

62. Tax revenues of the national government expressed as a percentage of GDP fell from 13.2 in 1956 to 11.9 in 1960–61 and to 10.9 in 1965. The revenues of the social security system, also expressed as percentages of the GDP, fell from 5.0 in 1956 to 3.5 in 1960–61, but rose to 4.8 in 1965. See CONADE, *Plan Nacional de Desarrollo, 1965–1969* (Buenos Aires, 1965), p. 171 (Table 93).

in the upper half of that group." [63] Data on income distribution for 1961–66 are not yet available, but it appears that no major changes have taken place from the 1959–61 pattern. While between 1961 and 1965 real GDP rose by about 10 percent, real hourly wage rates, according to collective agreements, rose by 12 percent for unskilled workers and by 9 percent for skilled workers.[64]

Since 1959, substantial open urban unemployment has reappeared for the first time since the depression; it may have reached from 6 to 10 percent of the urban labor force during 1962–64.[65] The switch from home toward tradeable goods had, at least in the short run, an unfavorable impact on urban employment.

The unsettled economic and political conditions of post-1955 Argentina did not encourage large-scale immigration; in fact, a tendency appeared for large numbers of professionals and technicians to leave the country permanently. Enrique Oteiza has prepared the following estimates of some categories of Argentine immigrants admitted to the United States since July 1950:[66]

	Professionals and technicians	Top level administrators	Skilled workers
July 1950–June 1956	1,129	450	793
July 1956–June 1961	2,817	927	2,399
July 1961–June 1966	4,143	1,054	3,629

In addition many professionals have migrated to other Latin American countries and to Western Europe.

63. "Income Distribution in Argentina," *Economic Bulletin for Latin America* 11 (April 1966): 117. This study also makes some additional interesting observations: (1) The lowest income groups in Argentina receive a larger share of income than is often the case (especially in Latin America); there is not an important segment of the population living at the margin of the economy (p. 117); (2) large incomes result only to a small extent from returns on property; the influence of the rentier group is small, and the upper income groups are dominated by the independent entrepreneur (pp. 118–19).

64. See Instituto de Desarrollo Económico y Social, *Situación Actual y Perspectivas de la Economía Argentina*, no. 5 (Buenos Aires, April 1966), p. 59.

65. Unemployment data are shaky. The economic difficulties of the 1950s did not stop the expansion of the share of Greater Buenos Aires in total population. While in 1947 the share was 29.7 percent, it reached 33.8 percent in 1960. In 1947 the Federal District plus the provinces of Buenos Aires, Córdoba, Entre Ríos, and Santa Fe accounted for 70.7 percent of the total population; in 1960 their share was the same.

66. See Enrique Oteiza, "Emigration of Highly Qualified Personnel from Argentina," Research paper of the Centro de Investigaciones Económicas del Instituto Torcuato Di Tella (Aug. 1967), p. 40.

The continuation of an exchange shortage and a low growth rate after 1955 requires explanations beyond emphasizing the magnitude of the task to be accomplished.[67] In particular, the manner in which the return to a freer price system was managed is open to criticism. It was noted earlier that during 1943–55 relative prices not only failed to reflect opportunity costs accurately, but also showed violent fluctuations. These gyrations continued after 1955, primarily as a result of the sporadic and jerky fashion in which the exchange rate and other government controlled prices (such as public utility rates) were adjusted. While, on the average, prices came closer to reflecting opportunity costs, their fluctuations decreased the usefulness of their signalling role. Table 2.25 presents a measure of their variability; the figures for most items are above 10 percent. It is difficult to imagine how entrepreneurs in need of precise cost accounting projections could operate efficiently in such an environment. The orders of magnitude of the figures in Table 2.25 are similar to those corresponding to 1945–55. Some prices, such as interest rates and rents, remained under state control, and at levels giving rise to haphazard rationing.

Political instability has had an important influence on the fluctuations of relative prices as well as on expectations regarding their future level. Each regime has had to define anew its own policies toward the exchange rate, public utility rates, protection, interest rates, and taxation. Post-Perón politics have been conducted in a climate poisoned by deep distrust among social classes and institutions. Urban workers have on the whole remained faithful to Perón or neo-Peronist leaders. The middle and upper classes, as well as the armed forces, have been divided between those favoring a soft and a hard approach toward Peronist groups; but the division has favored those who, to avoid real or imagined threats of Peronist comebacks, have been willing to take extraconstitutional measures. This state of latent civil war has threatened to burst into the open when factions within the armed forces (certainly not an oligarchic monolith) have confronted each other with heavy military equipment, as during 1962–63. Because economic policies on the exchange rate, taxation and labor law have an immediate political impact, and because more often than not the "right" economic policies are the "wrong" ones for political

67. Another unfavorable exogenous factor which *in part* accounts for the post 1955 performance is the further deterioration of the external terms of trade.

Table 2.25: Indices of Variation of Real Wholesale Prices
for Selected Commodities in Argentina, 1956–64

	Standard deviation divided by mean, 1956–64
Domestic products	
Cereals and linseed	0.13
Industrial crops	0.10
Fruits	0.22
Vegetables and garden crops	0.20
Cattle	0.19
Wool	0.21
Dairy products	0.06
Fish	0.11
Manufactured foodstuffs and beverages	0.07
Tobacco	0.20
Textiles	0.11
Clothing	0.10
Wood and wood products	0.14
Paper and cardboard	0.12
Chemical products	0.08
Fuels and lubricants	0.13
Rubber	0.07
Leather	0.06
Glass, stone, and earth	0.06
Metals, excluding machinery	0.09
Nonelectric machinery and equipment	0.11
Electrical machinery and equipment	0.21
Products of extractive industry	0.17
Imported goods	
Foodstuffs and beverages	0.16
Wood	0.13
Paper and cardboard	0.29
Chemical products	0.12
Rubber	0.18
Metals excluding machinery	0.10
Products of extractive industry	0.09

Sources and methods: As in Table 89 of the Statistical Appendix. Wholesale price indices for recent years obtained from DNEC, *Boletín de Estadística.* For most commodities no clear trend could be noticed in their real prices during 1956–64.

and social harmony, it is not surprising that since 1955 there have been frequent hesitations, policy reversals, and government changes.[68]

68. Between September 1955 and the present, at least five major political regimes may be distinguished: (1) the Provisional Government of September 1955–May 1958; (2) the constitutional regime of President Arturo Frondizi

Due to downward rigidities, the post-1955 readjustment of the price structure could not have been accomplished without strong pressures on the price level. Additional pressures could have been expected from the efforts of workers and producers of home and quasi-home goods to maintain their real income. Nevertheless, these factors can hardly justify the average rate of annual price increases of 33 percent taking place during 1955–64, which contrasts unfavorably with an annual inflation of 16 percent during 1943–55. A large share of the responsibility for the acceleration of inflation rests on the large public sector deficits financed by borrowing from the BCRA. Relative to GNP, these deficits were generally larger during 1956–64 than during 1950–55.[69] At the root of these deficits was the deterioration of the taxing machinery of the government; real public expenditures on goods and services fell as a percentage of GDP, from 14.0 during 1950–55 to 12.7 during 1956–63.[70] It is startling that in the three-year period 1961–63, total real revenues of the public sector, excluding those of public enterprises, were hardly 9 percent above 1953–55.[71] The failure of revenues of some public enterprises, such as

---

from May 1958 to March 1962; (3) the Provisional Government of March 1962 to October 1963; (4) the constitutional regime of President Arturo Illia, from October 1963 until June 1966; and (5) the military regime headed by General Juan Carlos Onganía, from June 1966 until present. Each of these regimes produced major changes in economic policy and in the cabinet within their tenure of power. Often these changes of government were greeted with a sickly euphoria; unfortunately the Argentine patient seems to demand ever more frequent doses of this palliative. Much time and effort are wasted by public and government officials waiting to see who the next president or minister of the economy is going to be. The time horizons of policy-making officials have become extremely short, as survival takes precedence over other considerations. Public opinion, on the other hand, expects new ministers to perform economic miracles in a few months; grumbling begins punctually two or three months after a new minister is installed.

69. The averages of the annual ratios of net public sector borrowing from the banking system to the gross national product are as follows: 1950–52, 0.6 percent; 1953–55, 2.2 percent; 1956–58, 2.3 percent; 1959–61, 1.6 percent; 1962–64, 3.3 percent. Net public borrowing is defined as the increase in public sector liabilities in the hands of the banking sector minus the increase in public sector deposits with the banking sector. Monetary data obtained from BCRA, *Estadísticas Monetarias y Bancarias, Años 1940–1960,* Supplement of the *Boletín Estadístico,* no. 6 (June 1962), and later issues of the *Boletín Estadístico.*

70. Data obtained from CONADE, *Plan Nacional de Desarrollo,* Table 9.

71. Real revenues include current income of national and local governments as well as the revenues of the social security system. The latter actually show a sharp decrease between 1953–55 and 1961–63. See CONADE, *Plan Nacional de Desarrollo,* Table 10.

railroads, to cover even their operating expenses, often inflated by considerable overstaffing and inefficiency, also contributed to the deficits. Coupled with a policy of adjusting the exchange rate only by sporadic and massive devaluations, those deficits led to an inflation characterized by erratic fluctuations in relative prices. Under these conditions, the reconstruction of an efficient capital market became impossible, and the resource allocating function of the price system continued to be curtailed.

The failure of post-1955 regimes to improve the efficiency of railroads and harbors has been a negative influence on commodity-producing sectors, especially agriculture and livestock. It has in turn put pressure on other social overhead facilities. Before 1943, a reasonable level of efficiency in railroads assured a predictable flow of rural produce to the harbors where it was quickly shipped abroad, reducing the need for storage facilities. Postwar difficulties in railroad and harbor operations gave rise to the need for additional storage, often improvised to the detriment of an efficient use of capital and labor. The low rates charged to users of the railroads in all likelihood did not compensate for the inconvenience and losses which they suffered.

The decline of average labor productivity in railroads, harbors and several other service sectors is often excused on the grounds that no other employment is available, and overstaffing is to be preferred to open unemployment.[72] It is true that the exchange bottleneck was allowed to become so serious that the reallocation of resources needed to correct it also became increasingly painful. It was tempting to adopt policies that made the best of a bad situation, rather than tackling the exchange difficulties head on. Only in this limited short-run sense can it be said that overstaffing was a result of stagnation brought about by the exchange bottleneck.

At a time of expanding world trade, it is very doubtful that the long-run social marginal productivity of labor was higher in home

72. Between 1943 and 1954 the number of persons employed in the railroads rose by 58 percent; indices of employment per unit of freight carried, and per unit of distance covered by the railroads, rose by around 25 percent between 1944 and 1956. See ECLA, *El Desarrollo Económico de la Argentina,* 3: 106–07. Since 1956 both the quantum of services rendered by the railroads and their employment have declined; while no reliable figure exists for recent years, it is likely that labor productivity has declined further. The decline has been due to a great extent to the reduction of the net capital stock in railroads. The exchange shortage plus the weak financial position of the government have made re-equipment a difficult task. Indices of labor productivity by sectors are presented in Tables 86 and 87 of the Statistical Appendix.

goods than in export activities. The reallocation required after 1955 had to be handled delicately to avoid social dislocation and undue hardships, but the pace at which it proceeded was disappointingly slow. Public policy often fitted demand to the existing structure of installed capacity and employment rather than inducing new capacity and labor skills that could make high growth compatible with balance of payments equilibrium.

Although the need to rationalize the system of protection has been recognized since 1955, not much was done about it during 1955–67. The level of protection, one of the highest in Latin America, continued to isolate most manufacturing from foreign competition, and its incidence continued to be haphazard.[73] Potential new export activities, as well as true import competition, have had their costs increased by the obligation to buy inputs from inefficient domestic firms. Input-output interrelationships give new meaning to the old jingle, "For want of a nail a shoe was lost. . . ."[74]

Although a greater inflow of foreign funds contributed to faster accumulation of capital, especially in machinery and equipment, and to technological change, their repayment conditions and allocation have been far from optimal for Argentina. This led to excess capacity in several import competing activities and a debt structure greatly burdening the balance of payments during recent years.

Such weaknesses in public policy slowed down the formidable task of correcting distortions developed in earlier years, and Argentina dropped further behind other countries of recent settlement. With a per capita gross national product of about $850 (at 1964 prices) during 1960–64, it became more understandable to place her at the head of Latin American countries rather than at the tail of countries of recent settlement.

In spite of these criticisms, the record for 1955–65 is better than that implied by output growth rates. Capacity expanded faster than output, and thanks to the efforts of these years, future growth rates

73. See the document E/CN.12/554 of ECLA, *Derechos Aduaneros y Otros Gravámenes y Restricciones a la Importación en Países Latinoamericanos, y sus Niveles Promedios de Incidencia,* pp. 21–22. During 1967 steps were taken to lower and rationalize import duties.

74. Examples of possible new Argentine exports frustrated by the high cost of domestic inputs are given by Bela Balassa, "Integration and Resource Allocation in Latin America" (mimeographed). Essays 4 and 5 give details of the protective system.

may increase above the historical 3 percent. The level and composition of capital formation improved. Investments in electricity and communications remedied most of the severe deficiencies that existed in 1955; for the first time in nearly twenty years there are no restrictions on the use of electricity. Rural capital stock rose sharply. Until recently it appeared that most of this investment simply replaced a labor force that had few alternative employment opportunities. Now, however, there are indications that those efforts are beginning to be reflected also in higher rural output. With the help of foreign capital, investment in critical manufacturing activities such as petrochemicals, motor vehicles, and steel boosted productive capacity that has not been fully utilized. These investments did not have as high a rate of social return as those in export activities, but they were preferable to further investment in home goods. The share of gross investment going to purchase new machinery and equipment rose from 37.5 percent during 1950–55 to 50.7 percent during 1956–63.[75]

Other efforts carried out since 1955 have had even longer gestation periods. The creation in 1957 of an autonomous research and extension service for agriculture and livestock is likely soon to yield a handsome payoff, helping to bring about a technological revolution in the countryside which should have taken place in the late 1940s.

During 1955–64, bases were also laid for a more abundant flow of machinery and equipment, so that future ex ante saving decisions will be easier to transform into capital goods than was possible in the past. The increased productive capacity of import-competing capital goods industries and the rural sector, plus a more flexible attitude toward foreign investment, have contributed to increasing the potential future rate of investment in machinery and equipment.

75. See CONADE, pp. 188–89. These figures are obtained from gross investment at 1960 prices. A great spurt of investment took place in 1960–62, during President Frondizi's administration. Frondizi hoped fast economic growth would solve the conflict between efficiency and equity. The fact that large chunks of postwar investments have been undertaken in sudden spurts (1946–48 and 1960–62, for example) probably led to their less than optimal allocation. The widespread feeling among observers of the Argentine economy that aggregate post-1955 output figures do not give the full flavor of Argentine progress during these years also comes from larger post-1955 availability of durable consumer goods, especially automobiles, and greater contacts with foreign cultural and technological trends. Argentina's forced or voluntary isolationism during 1939–55 influenced negatively its quality of life, especially that of the middle classes, in both obvious and subtle ways.

CONCLUDING REMARKS

The economic history of Argentina since 1930, but especially since 1943, should be required reading for planners of countries beginning their industrialization. It is a dramatic example of the dangers arising in the development process when a balance between the production of exportables, importables, and home goods is neglected. In an economy with a severe exchange bottleneck, not even a gross savings rate of 20 percent will bring rapid growth, as the Argentine experience shows.[76] Under such conditions, the transformation of saving intentions into tangible machinery and equipment becomes a difficult task. It appears that for most small and medium-sized countries the capacity to transform smoothly ex ante saving propensities into nonconstruction capital goods requires either expansion of foreign exchange earnings or a balanced "blood, sweat, and tears" program of industrialization. The pressures and stresses brought about by unbalanced growth did not meet with quick and healthy responses in Argentina; rather, they led to near stagnation and social difficulties.

The most ironic lesson of postwar Argentine experience is that if there had been less discrimination against exports, manufacturing expansion would have been greater. Indeed, the annual growth rate of manufacturing during 1900–29 (5.6 percent) was higher than during 1929–65 (3.7 percent, BCRA/ECLA). The ratio of imported to total consumption of manufactured goods probably would have been higher, but there is little to be said on economic grounds for minimizing this ratio.

What has been the cost to Argentina of mistaken economic policies? Without attempting a precise quantification, Table 2.26 presents some key macroeconomic magnitudes which suggest what could have been.[77] Essay 3 shows that if Argentina's major export staples had

76. At current prices, gross savings were 13 percent of GNP during 1935–38 and 20 percent during 1950–52. Real capital formation, however, was about the same in both periods. The increase in the relative prices of capital goods resulted primarily from the exchange bottleneck. More on this in essay 6.

77. When growth has been braked by a major bottleneck, it is better to measure the cost of resource misallocation in this fashion, rather than following a more neoclassical approach. The hypothesized relaxation of the exchange constraint supposes that it would have been accompanied by a fuller and more efficient utilization of all growth-promoting inputs. Although most of that gain may be of a once-and-for-all nature, its effects spread through a large number of years. Better resource allocation would also, in all likelihood, result in a faster rate of technological progress.

Table 2.26: Actual and Possible Profiles of the Argentine Economy,
1935–39 and 1960–64

	Actual		Possible 1960–64	
	1935–39	*1960–64*	*Target 4%*	*Target 5%*
I. *Billion 1960 pesos*				
Exports of goods and services	589	578	1,092	1,092
Imports of goods and services	562	599	1,041	1,041
GDP at factor cost	2,229	4,612	5,941	7,547
Rural value added	585	783	1,085	1,085
Manufacturing and mining	614	1,570	2,004	2,839
Construction and services	1,029	2,258	2,852	3,623
II. *Percentages of the GDP*				
Exports of goods and services	26.4	12.5	18.4	14.5
Imports of goods and services	25.2	13.0	17.5	13.8
Rural value added	26.3	17.0	18.3	14.4
Manufacturing and mining	27.6	34.0	33.7	37.6
Construction and services	46.2	49.0	48.0	48.0

Sources and method: Actual data obtained from BCRA (see Table 2.1). Possible 1960–64 obtained as is explained in the text.

been able to maintain their 1934–38 share in world trade, her quantum index for those exports would have grown at an annual rate of 2.2 percent between 1934–38 and 1959–63. Thus it is not farfetched to suppose that all exports could have grown at an annual rate of 2.5 percent between 1935–39 and 1960–64,[78] even without specially strong incentives given to nontraditional exports. Table 2.26 projects imports and exports from their 1935–39 base using that rate. Real GDP is then projected using two alternative growth rates—4 and 5 percent. If it is assumed that rural value added could have grown at the same rate as exports, and that construction and services could have seen their share in GDP recover somewhat from the depressed level of 1935–39, the required expansion of manufacturing and mining (primarily arising from import substitution) is obtained as a residual. The profiles emerging from these rough but not unreasonable assumptions for 1960–64 indicate that an overall growth rate of between 4 and 5 percent, yielding a per capita growth more than twice that actually achieved, was not at all beyond the reach of

78. Between 1937 and 1960 the quantum of Australian exports rose at an annual rate of 2.5 percent; that for Canada rose at 3.7 percent per annum. See Kelly, "Foreign Trade of Argentina and Australia, 1930 to 1960," p. 50, and *Historical Statistics of Canada,* p. 179. These two countries enjoyed Commonwealth preferences, but it is doubtful that by the 1960s they had a large impact on export growth.

Argentina. With these assumptions and a target of 4 percent, the mining and manufacturing share for 1960–64 is in fact lower than that actually achieved. To those eager to see the share of rural value added decline, it may be sobering to note that the target 5 percent profile shows a lower rural share than that actually registered in 1960–64, even though exports were assumed to grow faster than they really did. If more favorable policies had been followed toward the export sector during the postwar, the GDP during 1960–64 would have been at least 29 percent higher than that actually observed.

The Argentine experience also suggests that, whatever the desired degree of import substitution, it is of critical importance to choose industrial and protective policies that minimize the costs of that substitution. The inefficiency of many Argentine manufacturing activities arises not so much because, according to optimal resource allocation, they should never have been set up; rather, it often results from a system of protection that failed to encourage the quick maturing of infant activities and failed to promote what Harvey Leibenstein has called "X-efficiency." [79]

Finally, looking over the whole period of 1870–1966, one is struck by the difficulty, at least for Argentina, of differentiating rapid self-sustained growth from that which is not. Most economists of 1929 probably would have asserted that Argentine growth had become self-sustained. If one looks at the same economy in 1967, it is best to regard the question of whether or not Argentina is on the path of self-sustained growth as too imprecise to merit an answer.

79. An example of micro-inefficiency arising from industrial policy is the automobile industry. Given the decision to promote this industry (which may have involved a lower social rate of return than putting those resources into export expansion), several further policy decisions affecting the efficiency of the auto industry remained to be made. Allowing more than ten firms in a protected market that could absorb at most 200,000 vehicles a year does not appear, prima facie, as the optimal decision.

3

The Rural Sector

The rural sector in a developing economy is expected to carry out several important tasks—to provide a growing volume of wage goods and raw materials for industry and urban conglomerations and gradually to release labor to be absorbed by urban occupations, while remaining a net supplier of foreign exchange and investable funds. Until 1930 the Argentine rural sector was a net importer of labor, so that it differs from typical underdeveloped countries in this important respect. When after 1930 labor flowed out of the rural sector, it became clear to all that agriculture and livestock activity, especially in the pampean zone, had harbored little or no surplus labor. As early as the beginning of this century, labor engaged in rural activities accounted for no more than 40 percent of the whole labor force; by 1925–29 this share had fallen to 36 percent, and by 1960–61 it reached 22 percent.

Most Argentine rural output can either be consumed domestically or, in most years, be placed easily in world markets. Commodities of rural origin have accounted for nearly all exports since the early days of the Spanish conquest. Their share in total exports has hardly changed even though the share of rural value added in GDP has been halved between 1900 and 1965. Rural production has been blessed with favorable natural resources. The pampean zone is unique in the world for its combination of fertility, compactness, and closeness to ocean transport centers. Other regions, although less gifted, respond readily to irrigation and the intensive use of labor and capital.

Long-term trends in rural output, inputs, and productivity, especially since 1900, will be reviewed first. A description of the growth and structural characteristics of the pre-1930 rural economy, including patterns of landholding, will follow. The rest of the essay will deal with the post-1930 stagnation of rural output and its possible causes.

Low private rural rates of return, an inadequate land tenure system, a technological lag, and characteristics of foreign demand will be discussed as possible explanations for rural stagnation. Tentative conclusions on this issue will close the essay.

LONG-TERM TRENDS IN THE RURAL SECTOR

Two clear-cut eras may be seen since 1862. The first was one of rapid rural expansion, lasting until around 1930; the second, lasting until at least 1962, is one of stagnation and even decline in important branches of production.

Output data are scarce before 1900, but to judge from export quantum figures presented in Table 1.2 it may be guessed that, between 1862 and 1900, rural output, including dynamic products such as cereals and linseed and vegetative ones such as jerked beef, expanded at an annual rate of no less than 4 percent. The expansion continued, with only temporary setbacks, throughout the first three decades of this century. The rate of expansion, shown in Table 3.1,

Table 3.1: Annual Growth Rates of Rural Output, 1900–65
(Percentages)

	1900/04 to 1925/29	1925/29 to 1960/64
Total rural value added	3.5	1.2
Total rural gross output	3.8	1.1
Agriculture, gross output	4.4	1.3
Livestock, gross output	2.6	0.9

Note: Throughout this chapter "agriculture" will refer only to crop raising; "rural" will refer to both agriculture and livestock. CONADE data for rural output show smaller growth rates since 1930. See Tables 2.1, 2.2, and 2.3. BCRA rural data include some crops left out of CONADE's calculations; they therefore seem more reliable.

Sources: ECLA, pp. 2–9; BCRA, pp. 18, 36.

was probably smaller during this latter period than in the last decades of the nineteenth century, primarily due to the decline of activities such as sheep raising. Until the end of the nineteenth century all rural production could expand simultaneously, thanks to plentiful lands plus a growing railroad network and labor force, but the beginning of the twentieth century began to witness the squeezing out of the less profitable activities from the land.

Rural expansion dropped sharply after 1930. Its growth pattern also changed drastically. Between 1900 and 1929, more than 50 percent of the increase in gross output came from increments in the production of cereals and linseed and another 25 percent from increments in cattle production. Cattle, cereals, and linseed can be unambiguously labeled exportable goods. Between 1929 and 1963, the output increase, meager as it was, was supported primarily by commodities with a smaller degree of exportableness, e.g. industrial crops and vegetables consumed almost wholly within the country. Although some of these expanding activities originally replaced imports, many quickly began resembling nontraded goods, e.g. yerba mate.

Before examining the two major phases in rural growth, output expansion will be contrasted with that of inputs. Although output and value-added data are of reasonable quality, those for inputs are considerably shakier. Furthermore, regional data are not always available. Because during different periods activities and regions grew at unequal rates, aggregates hide a serious adding-up problem. It would be of special interest to separate the pampean zone from other regions; lack of complete input data makes this impossible. Therefore, only broad tendencies should be extracted from Table 3.2.

Column E has been obtained by dividing column A by input indices made up of columns B, C, and D. Subcolumn 1 results from an input index giving the same weights to capital, land, and labor, while subcolumn 2 is obtained by using an input index which gives weights of 0.25 to labor and 0.375 to capital and land.[1] Both yield similar trends. These crude indices of total factor productivity show a slight decreasing tendency between 1900–04 and 1915–19, and a small but unsteady tendency to increase thereafter.

It may at first seem surprising that, while between 1900–04 and 1925–29 the productivity index showed little change, it rose by around 30 percent between 1925–29 and 1955–59. A first point to note is that part of this gain may be due solely to the aggregation of pampean and non-pampean activities that have different land/output, capital/output and labor/output coefficients. Non-pampean rural activities

1. Lack of detailed data on factor shares in the rural sector is the main justification for these somewhat arbitrary weights. During 1955–59 the share of wages and salaries in value added by the rural sector was 24.4 percent. See CONADE, p. 109.

Table 3.2: Indices of Rural Output and Inputs, 1900–59
(1935–39 = 100)

	A	B	C	D	E	
	Index of overall output (value added)	*Index of physical capital stock in rural activities*	*Index of land used in rural activities*	*Index of labor used in rural activities*	*Index of total factor productivity*	
					1	*2*
1900–04	37.0	41.7	28.4	47.7	94	97
1905–09	45.8	53.3	50.8	54.3	87	87
1910–14	51.8	62.5	69.4	64.0	79	79
1915–19	61.4	71.3	79.2	71.8	83	83
1920–24	74.6	81.4	79.3	79.2	93	93
1925–29	88.1	93.5	87.7	86.5	99	98
1930–34	87.9	100.6	95.8	93.9	91	90
1935–39	100.0	100.0	100.0	100.0	100	100
1940–44	112.9	99.2	103.3	98.3	113	112
1945–49	111.9	101.0	101.4	94.5	113	112
1950–54	114.1	105.6	92.0	85.5	121	120
1955–59	128.4	114.3	107.5	75.7	129	126
1960–64	133.8	—[a]	–	–	–	–

[a] Dash indicates data not available.

Sources and method: Output data as in Table 3.1 (output here refers to value added). Physical capital data (which includes cattle stocks) obtained from ECLA, p. 93, and from A. Ferrer and A. Fracchia, *La Producción, Ingresos y Capitalización*, statistical appendix (Buenos Aires, n.d.). Data on land from CONADE, which includes all land under cultivation but excludes *natural* pasture land. It should also be noted that hectares under cultivation (crops and pastures) have been used to make up the index, without correcting for land quality. Labor data for 1914, 1937, 1947, and 1960 obtained from G. Gallo Mendoza and N. Silvia Tadeo, *La Mano de Obra en el Sector Agropecuario* (Buenos Aires: CONADE, Oct. 1964), pp. 24, 35, and 51. The following weights were used to obtain an overall estimate in man-equivalent units: men (year-round), 1; women (year-round), 1/2; children (year-round), 1/3; seasonal workers, 1/4. Labor data for 1900–14 were obtained from the sources listed in ECLA, Table 1, p. 400. A simple interpolation provided data for the rest of the years. See text for an explanation of column *E*.

have gained in relative importance since 1930. Yet even if disaggregation showed greater productivity gains after 1930 than before, that comparison would have limited relevance. More significant is the comparison of Argentine and United States total rural productivity indices shown below (with 1935–39 = 100):[2]

2. Data for the United States obtained from John W. Kendrick, *Productivity Trends in the United States* (Princeton University Press, 1961), pp. 362–64. The

	Argentina	*U.S.A.*
1900–09	91	85
1910–19	81	85
1920–29	96	86
1930–39	96	96
1940–49	113	120
1950–54	121	148
1955–59	129	177

Only a small part of the spectacular advances made in rural technology in North Atlantic countries since the 1930s found their way to the Río de la Plata.[3]

Average land productivity implicit in Table 3.2 shows a falling tendency during the first two decades of the century; until 1914 there was a sharp expansion of area under cultivation as the railroads continued to penetrate the hinterland. As noted in essay 1, the best Argentine lands are located near thte coastal zones, so that a decreasing marginal productivity of land (measured in hectares) could have been expected, *ceteris paribus*.[4] In ten-year averages, the land-productivity index has evolved as follows:

1900–09 = 110	1930–39 = 96
1910–19 = 76	1940–49 = 110
1920–29 = 97	1950–59 = 122

In spite of apparent post-1920 increases in average land produc-

Argentine index is that shown in column *E*-1 of Table 3.2. The U.S. index for 1955–59 refers to 1955, 1956, and 1957. The impressive rise in rural productivity registered in North American and Western European countries has not been properly digested by those who argue in favor of special government support to industry on the ground that industry generates greater productivity gains than agriculture.

3. In a pioneering study Marto A. Ballesteros found a sharper rise in the index of output per unit of input between 1908 and 1940, and a decrease in the index between 1940 and 1952. His index of output per unit of input is as follows: 1908 = 68;   1914 = 73;   1920 = 75;   1930 = 98;   1937 = 100; 1940 = 104; 1947 = 99; 1952 = 98. See Marto A. Ballesteros, "Argentine Agriculture, 1908–1954: A Study in Growth and Decline" (Ph.D. diss. University of Chicago, 1958), p. 47. The key difference between his results and mine is the index for labor inputs; Ballesteros' index rises by only 3 percent between 1908 and 1940. Ballasteros' labor data are based on the censuses for 1914 and 1937; I have been unable to find a good explanation for the discrepancy between these data and those of ECLA and CONADE.

4. The fast expansion of social overhead capital servicing rural activities, not reflected in the input indices of Table 3.2, was not enough to offset these diminishing returns.

tivity, the 1950–59 index was only 11 percent above that for 1900–09. Even this modest increase is mostly an illusion created by aggregation, as will be seen later. It is an exaggeration to say that all suitable land is already within going rural establishments; the supply of land has not yet become perfectly inelastic. Nevertheless, while in 1900–09 large increases in rural output could be expected from extensions of the area under cultivation (in spite of diminishing returns), since the 1930s further expansions in output have had to rely mainly on increases of average land productivity. To say that land productivity has risen slowly since 1920–29 is just another way of presenting the poor performance of the rural sector during the last three and a half decades.

Land is the only input that may be reliably disaggregated, but only for post-1935 years. The Consejo Nacional de Desarrollo (CONADE) has estimated the following indices for cultivated land:

	Pampean	*Non-pampean*
1935–39	100	100
1940–44	103	111
1945–49	100	137
1950–54	89	167
1955–59	104	194
1960–63	94	191

CONADE has also estimated output indices for pampean and non-pampean rural activities. The CONADE overall output and value-added indices, however, do not coincide with those of the Central Bank, used in Table 3.2. The Central Bank, in turn, has not disaggregated rural output into pampean and non-pampean. The various output indices are as follows:[5]

	CONADE *Pampean*	CONADE *Non-pampean*	CONADE *Total*	BCRA *Total*
1935–39	100	100	100	100
1940–44	108	120	114	113
1945–49	92	129	107	112
1950–54	84	139	103	114
1955–59	100	159	116	128
1960–63	96	161	115	132

5. See CONADE, *Plan Nacional de Desarrollo, 1965–69* (Buenos Aires, 1965), p. 46, Tables 12 and 13. Both overall CONADE and BCRA indices refer to value added; overall gross output indices show a similar evolution. The CONADE overall index was obtained from unpublished sources.

Even if aggregate average land productivity is computed using CONADE's total index, it shows an *increase* of 8 percent between 1935–39 and 1955–59, even though *decreases* in land productivity are obtained when the pampean and non-pampean sectors are taken separately. The explanation for this apparent paradox is that the sector with the higher output/land ratio—the non-pampean zone—grew fastest. This result confirms the suspicion that part of the apparent increase in total factor productivity after 1930, observed in Table 3.2, is simply a result of aggregation.

On the whole, Table 3.2 suggests that the evolution of the rural sector was remarkably balanced until 1940–44, in the sense that few changes were registered in the capital/labor and land/labor ratios. So long as substantial additional land was available, land, labor, and capital grew more or less proportionally. Beginning in 1945–49, noticeable increases were registered in the capital/labor ratio, not so much because of increases in the capital stock, but because of decreases in labor. This unhealthy reason also accounts for the increase in the land/labor ratio. Shortages since the war of rural machinery and equipment, as well as lack of incentives, are reflected in the meager advances of the capital/land ratio. Even as workers migrated to urban centers during 1940–55, rural entrepreneurs had difficulties in finding tractors and other machinery.

The land-input index presented in Table 3.2 excluded natural pastures. Therefore, in all likelihood it overestimates the growth of land in use before 1935–39 and underestimates it after 1935–39.[6] If, in view of this difficulty and also on the grounds that land may have a near zero opportunity cost for the rural sector taken as a whole, another index is computed using only labor and capital inputs with equal weight, then a total productivity index is obtained that differs substantially with those of Table 3.2 only for 1900–04 and 1955–59.

At first sight, some comfort may be taken from the index of average labor productivity implicit in Table 3.2, which evolved as follows:

1900–09 = 81	1940–49 = 117
1910–19 = 84	1950–54 = 133
1920–29 = 98	1955–59 = 170
1930–39 = 97	

6. Before 1935–39 the trend was for a switch from natural pastures toward either crops or pastures such as alfalfa. Since 1935–39 a reverse trend took place.

However, the rapid rise in labor productivity after the 1930s, especially during the 1950s, took place in the context of a declining labor/land ratio, which by itself could be expected to result in an increase of labor productivity.[7] Furthermore, during the 1950s the capital/labor ratio rose, increasing labor productivity. Under these circumstances, such an increase does not lend much comfort, especially when it is recalled that at a time of severe exchange difficulties, labor withdrawn from exportables was being channeled mostly to urban nontradeable activities.

THE GREAT EXPANSION 1862–1930: OUTPUT

In colonial days the Río de la Plata region depended heavily on the export, to overseas regions as well as to what is now the Argentine Northwest and Bolivia, of livestock products. Descendants of cattle brought by Spanish settlers reproduced freely on the treeless pampas; before 1750 practically all exported hides came from hunting expeditions of wild bovine cattle.[8] Crops and sheep raising were much more limited. A systematic exploitation of bovine livestock began around 1750 when more animals became attached to ranches. Efforts were made to take advantage of tallow, but meat remained almost a free good. The population of the Buenos Aires area, including both city and countryside, is estimated to have risen from 16,000 persons in 1744 to 105,000 in 1810. By 1810 the rest of Argentina had 300,000 inhabitants.[9] With independence and freer international trade, the exploitation of livestock grew in sophistication; urban salting establishments appeared and specialization took place among different stages of cattle raising. Military raids were organized into zones dominated by Indian tribes to gain control of salt deposits, a key input of salting plants. After 1810 sheep raising

7. This fact may also account for part of the increase observed in the *total* productivity index. Agricultural output per man-hour in the United States evolved as follows (1935–39 = 100): 1900–09 = 80; 1910–19 = 82; 1920–29 = 84; 1930–39 = 95; 1940–49 = 127; 1950–54 = 180; 1955–59 = 226; 1960–64 = 289. Since the 1930s the Argentine index has lagged behind that for the United States. U.S. data obtained from U.S. Department of Commerce, *Long Term Economic Growth, 1860–1965* (Washington, D.C.: Government Printing Office, 1966), p. 190.

8. For information regarding the rural sector before 1862 I have relied primarily on Horacio C. E. Giberti, *El Desarrollo Agrario Argentino* (Buenos Aires: Eudeba, 1964); and Carl C. Taylor, *Rural Life in Argentina* (Baton Rouge: Louisiana State University Press, 1948).

9. Giberti, *El Desarrollo,* pp. 13 and 17.

and crops made modest gains, but flour was still imported and hides made up about three-fourths of the value of exports shipped in the harbor of Buenos Aires during the 1820s.[10] Sheep-raising gathered momentum during the 1830s, but the acceleration of wool exports came between 1850 and 1870. Scottish and Irish settlers played an important role in the remarkable expansion of sheep during those years. By 1870 Argentina had about the same number of sheep as the United States (41 million) and by 1895–1900, it was second only to Australia in the size of the stock of sheep.[11]

The year 1862 inaugurated a period of relative political stability during which the government became committed to close coopera-

Table 3.3: Output and Export Quantum of Selected Rural Goods
(Thousand metric tons; annual averages)

	1860–69	1875–79	1885–89	1895–99	1900–04	1910–14	1925–29
Output							
Wool	–[a]	–	–	–	187	151	147
Wheat	–	–	–	1,621	2,538	4,003	6,770
Linseed	–	–	–	226	526	790	1,839
Maize	–	–	–	1,970	2,858	4,869	7,076
Exports							
All hides	–	70	85	100	100	125	181
Wool	45	90	129	211	178	137	130
Wheat	0	6	111	801	1,591	2,277	4,448
Linseed	0	0	51	209	475	679	1,618
Maize	0	13	277	910	1,518	3,194	5,521
All meat	–	34	45	95	161	437	805

Note: Wool production and exports are measured on the basis of unwashed wool. Exports refer to calendar, not commercial, years. Hides include those of bovine, ovine, and other cattle. Wheat exports include flour exports expressed in terms of wheat. Wheat output during 1891–94 amounted to 1,414 thousand tons.

[a] Dash indicates data not available.

Sources: As in Table 1.2, plus *The Argentine Year Book, 1914* (Buenos Aires: R. Grant and Co., 1914).

tion with foreign capital and markets. Table 3.3 reveals the spectacular rural expansion that took place until 1929. Around 1880 agri-

10. Giberti, *El Desarrollo,* p. 16. Jerked beef accounted for about 10 percent of exports.
11. See Federico Pinedo, "La Argentina en Proceso Ascendente," in *Economic Survey* (Buenos Aires, July 26, 1966), pp. 649–50. Australian wool was of higher quality than that of Argentine sheep.

cultural activities gained, for the first time in Argentine history, a significant place in rural output and exports.

The 1862–1929 expansion was so remarkable that little conflict arose over the division of rural production between exports and domestic consumption. For many goods, such as wool, linseed, and maize, domestic consumption even in 1929 represented a small fraction of output. For wheat and beef the share of domestic absorption was higher, oscillating between 40 and 50 percent of output. During 1920–29, 49 percent of all rural output went to domestic consumption and 51 percent to exports.[12] No aggregate figures are available for earlier years, but it is doubtful that such proportions changed significantly during 1880–1920.

Regional "belts" for different products became established during 1862–1930, as the growth of railroads and internal communications encouraged greater specialization within the rural sector. Wheat- and corn-growing, cattle-breeding and cattle-feeding, sugar cane cultivation, etc. clustered in suitable zones, leading to contrasts in social and economic life among different communities. For example, while rural life on the cattle ranches of Buenos Aires province and the sheep ranches of Patagonia had feudalistic overtones, some communities in the mixed farming and dairy zones of Santa Fe, where colonization by small farmers had been most active, and in the vineyard belt of Mendoza came close to being Jeffersonian havens. Whatever the pattern of specialization, pampean rural regions became thoroughly commercialized, and rural activities not aimed for the market declined.[13]

The success of the refrigerated ships toward the end of the nineteenth century set the stage for a dramatic case of forward linkage; modern meat-packing plants were set up in Argentina to prepare mutton and beef for transatlantic voyages. Before and during World War I most meat was frozen for this purpose; after 1920 chilling became more popular as this more delicate process better preserved flavor. These developments also induced a greater degree of specialization and technification in cattle raising.[14] No forward linkages of

---

12. ECLA, 2:45.
13. A detailed description of different rural zones is found in Taylor, *Rural Life,* chapters 1 and 2. Although livestock was associated with a system of land tenure with feudalistic overtones, it also led to considerable forward linkage.
14. The first refrigerated ship arrived in Buenos Aires in 1877 and the first meat-packing plant was set up in 1883. These early efforts usually

comparable importance took place among agricultural commodities. Although exports of wheat flour expanded rapidly, reaching a peak during 1915–19, they remained a small fraction of all wheat exports.

INPUTS DURING THE GREAT EXPANSION: SPECIAL CHARACTERISTICS

The rapid growth in the application of land, labor, and capital to rural activities that took place *pari passu* with output expansion has already been indicated. This section will discuss some features of this process in greater detail.

Patterns of landholding

The quantitative expansion of land under cultivation from about 0.58 million hectares in 1872, to 2.46 million in 1888, to 4.89 million in 1895, and finally to 27.20 million hectares in 1930, has been stressed previously. The census of 1914 is the best single source available to determine what patterns of landholding accompanied this expansion.

Table 3.4 presents a classification of rural holdings in 1914, according to size. A holding is a unit of operation, whether the operator owns the land or not; as a given person may own more than one holding (or, although less likely, as several persons may jointly own a holding), these figures do not give an accurate picture of land ownership. In all likelihood it was more concentrated than what is suggested by Table 3.4. The distinction made between pampean provinces and the rest of the country is useful because the former include the most fertile lands where most of the exportable crops are grown, while the latter include vast arid zones such as the Patagonia region.[15]

---

involved lamb rather than beef. The first exports of frozen beef took place in 1885. Until around 1900 the volume of frozen and chilled meat was relatively small; during 1890–98 an annual average of 2,800 tons of beef and 38,500 tons of lamb and mutton were exported. In 1900 the United Kingdom banned imports of live cattle, stimulating the construction of meat-packing plants. By 1905–09, an annual average of 167.3 thousand tons of frozen and chilled beef were exported, as well as 72.2 thousand tons of lamb and mutton. In spite of these developments, the share of livestock products in exports continued to decline (except during the decade of World War I); from 94 percent in 1871–79 that share declined to 65 percent in 1890–99 and 37 percent during 1920–29. See Giberti, *El Desarrollo*, pp. 26–31 and *Anuario Geográfico Argentino*, p. 376.

15. The production of exportable-type rural goods has been concentrated in the pampean provinces. According to the 1914 census, these provinces ac-

Table 3.4: Rural Holdings Classified According to Size, 1914
(Area in thousands of hectares)

	Pampean provinces		Rest of the country	
	Number of holdings	Total area	Number of holdings	Total area
25 hectares and less	43,582	480	57,254	484
26 to 50 hectares	22,096	849	12,566	489
51 to 100 hectares	33,844	2,580	11,520	900
101 to 500 hectares	70,626	15,886	16,059	3,963
501 to 1,000 hectares	8,997	6,232	4,828	3,414
1,001 to 5,000 hectares	8,139	18,464	11,859	29,489
5,001 to 10,000 hectares	1,343	10,439	1,818	14,816
10,001 to 25,000 hectares	477	7,247	1,089	18,150
25,001 hectares and more	107	5,067	399	23,893
Total	*189,211*	*67,243*	*117,392*	*95,598*

Note: One hectare is equivalent to 2.471 acres.

Source: R. Argentina, *Tercer Censo Nacional* 5 (June 1, 1914): 3–7. Pampean provinces include Buenos Aires, Santa Fe, Entre Ríos, Córdoba, and La Pampa.

Table 3.4 indicates the prevalence of large estates (or strictly speaking, large units of operation) in 1914; in the pampean provinces slightly more than ten thousand holdings, of more than one thousand hectares each, accounted for 61 percent of the rural area, while in the rest of the country holdings of more than one thousand hectares covered 90 percent of the rural area. In the rich pampean zone, the largest 584 holdings, owned at most by that many families, covered nearly one-fifth of this region.

Tables 3.5 and 3.6 show that the largest holdings were primarily dedicated to livestock, mainly cattle and sheep raising. As shown in Table 3.5, while less than 1 percent of the holdings dedicated mainly to the production of cereals, linseed, and other crop-raising activities had more than one thousand hectares, more than 20 percent of the holdings devoted mainly to livestock fell into that size category. And of all holdings of one thousand hectares and more, 96 percent were

counted for 99 percent of the area under wheat cultivation, 93 percent of the area under maize and 99 percent of the area under linseed. The same census showed that 68 percent of bovine cattle stocks and 63 percent of all sheep were located in the five pampean provinces. The pampean zone proper (i.e., excluding arid and semiarid lands within the pampean provinces) in 1959 accounted for 92 percent of grains and oil-bearing crops, 77 percent of meat output and 73 percent of wool and milk output. Around 60 percent of all rural output is produced in the pampean zone.

Table 3.5: Classification of Rural Holdings According to Size and
Principal Activity, 1914 (all Argentina)
(Percentages of total holdings in each line of activity)

	Mainly livestock	Mainly cereals and linseed	Mainly other activities
Total number of holdings (thousands)	112.32	112.13	51.01
25 hectares and less	15.2	24.8	80.0
26 to 50 hectares	10.7	12.2	9.2
51 to 100 hectares	13.8	20.3	5.7
101 to 500 hectares	30.9	39.6	4.3
501 to 1,000 hectares	9.0	2.4	0.3
1,001 to 5,000 hectares	16.1	0.6	0.3
5,001 hectares and more	4.3	0.1	0.1

Source: Tercer Censo Nacional 5:73.

mainly devoted to livestock (Table 3.6). In contrast, the production
of cereals and linseed was concentrated in holdings of between 50
and 500 hectares; 60 percent of holdings growing them had that
size, while more than 50 percent of all holdings of that size were

Table 3.6: Classification of Rural Holdings According to Size and
Principal Activity, 1914 (all Argentina)
(Percentages of total holdings in each size category)

	Mainly livestock	Mainly cereals and linseed	Mainly other activities
Holdings of 25 hectares and less	20.0	32.4	47.6
Holdings of 26 to 100 hectares	38.4	51.0	10.6
Holdings of 101 to 500 hectares	42.7	54.6	2.7
Holdings of 501 to 1,000 hectares	77.6	21.1	1.3
Holdings of 1,001 hectares and more	96.3	2.9	0.8

Source: Tercer Censo Nacional 5:73.

mainly used for growing those crops. Although no data are available
on total production by holdings of different sizes, it is a safe guess
that at least 80 percent of the output of cereals and linseed came
from these middle-sized holdings. Finally, other rural activities (mainly
crops such as fruits, vegetables, cotton, yerba mate, grapes, and
tobacco), primarily located outside the pampean provinces and often
using irrigation, were carried out in small holdings; 89 percent of
those holdings had less than 50 hectares, while nearly 50 percent
of all holdings of less than 25 hectares were devoted to these crops.

Sugar cane, found in the northwestern provinces, was a notable exception to the typical pattern among industrial crops, because often it was cultivated in large estates.

If attention is focused exclusively on the pampean provinces, the contrast between the size of holdings in agricultural versus livestock activities is maintained. In these provinces agricultural holdings of more than 1,250 hectares covered only 2.6 percent of the area devoted to rural activities; however, livestock holdings larger than 1,250 hectares covered more than 56 percent of rural areas. A total of 1,761 of the largest livestock holdings, with an average size of about twelve thousand hectares each, covered one-third of the rural areas of the fertile pampean provinces.[16]

It is tempting to divide the pampean rural sector into large landowners producing cattle and small tenants producing cereals. Although in some circumstances this simplification is useful, often a given rural holding was devoted to several activities. Mixed farming has been fairly common in some pampean regions for a long time, e.g., around the Esperanza zone in Santa Fe.[17] Rotation between cereals and livestock has been even more common.

Besides the link between size of holdings and rural activities, the 1914 census revealed other interesting patterns. Table 3.7 classifies directors of rural holdings according to nationality and main line of activity; a director was the person actually managing the holding. A contrast emerges between the nationality of directors of livestock holdings, and that of directors of cereals and linseed holdings. The former were predominantly Argentine, while the latter were mainly immigrants, especially Italians. A standard business practice for large cattle ranchers during 1880–1914 was to "sow" their previously uncultivated fields with "gringos" (the Argentine nickname for Italians) who were typically given three-year tenure contracts to grow

16. See Table 110 in the Statistical Appendix. In Buenos Aires, the most fertile province, livestock holdings of more than 5,000 hectares covered nearly 30 percent of the rural area of the province (26.5 million hectares). There were 716 holdings in this category, according to the 1914 census, covering 7.8 million hectares. In the province of Santa Fe, in spite of its relative abundance of colonization projects aimed at providing immigrants with family farms, 226 livestock holdings covered 3.7 million hectares, or about 37 percent of the rural area of the province.

17. Sometimes tenure contracts forbade tenants to diversify. See Taylor, *Rural Life,* p. 11. It may be noted that what for Argentine standards is regarded as a small farm is rather large when compared to other Latin American countries.

Table 3.7: Classification of Directors of Rural Holdings
According to Nationality, 1914
(Percentages of total)

	Mainly cattle and livestock	Mainly cereals and linseed	Mainly other activities
Total of the country	*100.0*	*100.0*	*100.0*
Argentine	74.2	36.3	58.5
Spanish	7.1	9.5	11.6
Italian	6.7	39.0	20.9
Other	12.0	15.2	9.1
Pampean provinces	*100.0*	*100.0*	*100.0*
Argentine	63.0	28.0	37.9
Spanish	12.0	10.7	15.8
Italian	12.0	46.1	37.9
Other	13.1	15.2	8.4
Rest of the country	*100.0*	*100.0*	*100.0*
Argentine	84.4	77.7	72.1
Spanish	2.7	3.7	8.9
Italian	1.9	3.7	9.5
Other	11.1	14.9	9.5

Note: "Directors of Rural Holdings" refers to the persons managing the rural unit.

Source: Tercer Censo Nacional 5:309–19.

cereals, at the end of which the tenant left the land sown with alfalfa. The participation of immigrant directors in pampean rural activities other than livestock and cereals was above immigrant participation in the total labor force. Argentine rural entrepreneurs were mainly concentrated in livestock and in non-pampean zones.

The census provided data on whether directors were owners, tenants, or employees; data for agricultural holdings are summarized in Table 3.8. Only 44 percent of the agricultural holdings were directed by their owners; in the pampean provinces the proportion of owner-operated holdings was even smaller—33 percent.[18] One may

18. The percentage of pampean holdings devoted to fine cereals (wheat, linseed, oats, barley, and rye) that were cultivated by their owners declined from 42 percent in 1899 to 31 percent in 1916 according to Giberti, *El Desarrollo,* p. 34. Writing in 1896, M. G. Mulhall noted: "the tillage farms [are] in the hands of 300,000 Italians, Swiss, and German settlers. It is not uncommon to see a wheat-field of 5,000 acres, the owner of which probably landed at Buenos Aires without a dollar, not more than twenty years ago. Most of the grain-farms, however, are 60-acre lots taken up since 1885 by settlers who had no capital, on condition of giving the owner of the land half the crop during ten years, after which the land becomes the settler's property." *Industries and Wealth of Nations* (London, New York, and Bombay: Longmans, Green and Co., 1896), p. 363,

Table 3.8: Classification of Directors of Mainly Agricultural Holdings
According to Nationality and Ownership of Holdings, 1914
(Thousands)

		Holdings directed by:		
	Owners	Tenants	Employees	Total
Total of the country	*72.4*	*75.5*	*15.2*	*163.1*
Argentine	43.0	20.9	6.6	70.5
Spanish	4.6	9.9	2.1	16.7
Italian	15.2	34.5	4.6	54.3
Other	9.6	10.2	1.9	21.6
Pampean provinces	*37.1*	*65.8*	*10.8*	*113.7*
Argentine	15.7	14.2	3.8	33.7
Spanish	2.7	8.7	1.5	13.2
Italian	12.9	33.7	4.2	50.6
Other	5.8	9.2	11.3	16.2
Rest of the country	*35.3*	*9.7*	*4.4*	*49.4*
Argentine	27.3	6.7	2.8	36.8
Spanish	1.9	1.2	0.6	3.5
Italian	2.3	0.8	0.4	3.7
Other	3.8	1.0	0.6	5.4

Source: Tercer Censo Nacional 5:837–41.

guess that the percentage of agricultural land cultivated by owners was smaller than these figures indicate. Of all owner-operated agricultural holdings in the country, 59 percent belonged to Argentines. The corresponding figure for just the pampean provinces was 42 percent. Of all Argentine directors of agricultural holdings in the country, 61 percent owned the holding they cultivated. (In the pampean provinces the figure was 47 percent.) In contrast, only 32 percent of foreign-born directors owned the land they cultivated. Again the percentage is lower in the pampean provinces—27 percent. These data reflect Argentine colonization and land policies, which made only feeble attempts to facilitate the eventual ownership by immigrants of the lands they cultivated. Table 3.9 presents corresponding figures for livestock holdings; 59 percent of all these holdings were directed by their owners (57 percent in the pampean provinces), proportions which are higher than those for agricultural holdings. Argentines owned 78 percent of all owner-operated livestock holdings (and 69 percent in the pampean provinces alone), while of all Argentine directors in both the pampean provinces and in the whole country, 62 percent owned the holding they cultivated. These figures, contrasted with those of Table 3.8, reflect the greater Argentineness of the livestock sector; if data were available on the size of holdings, they would probably reinforce this conclusion. In the pampean zone, then, Argentines occupied the top and bottom social positions as landowners and peons in livestock, while the middle rural classes were made up largely of immigrant agriculturalists.

Table 3.9: Classification of Directors of Mainly Livestock Holdings
According to Nationality and Ownership of Holdings, 1914
(Thousands)

		Holdings directed by:		
	Owners	*Tenants*	*Employees*	*Total*
Total of the country	*66.6*	*30.4*	*15.4*	*112.3*
Argentine	51.8	20.1	11.4	83.3
Spanish	3.1	3.8	1.0	8.0
Italian	4.3	2.2	1.0	7.5
Other	7.3	4.2	2.1	13.6
Pampean provinces	*30.5*	*15.9*	*7.1*	*53.5*
Argentine	20.9	8.0	4.9	33.9
Spanish	2.3	3.4	0.6	6.3
Italian	3.7	2.0	0.8	6.5
Other	3.6	2.5	0.8	6.8
Rest of the country	*36.1*	*14.5*	*8.3*	*58.8*
Argentine	30.8	12.1	6.5	49.4
Spanish	0.8	0.4	0.4	1.6
Italian	0.6	0.2	0.2	1.0
Other	33.8	1.7	1.3	6.8

Source: Tercer Censo Nacional 6:679–82.

This survey of pre-1930 land tenure and use, as reflected in the 1914 census, has brought out two features that are generally considered to be detrimental to rural growth: very large estates and holdings cultivated by persons other than their owners. Furthermore, a substantial share of output, especially of cereals and linseed, was produced by the foreign born who often did not regard their Argentine residency or that of their children as permanent, and therefore made few efforts to integrate into the local community. Yet these circumstances were not inconsistent with rapid output expansion during 1862–1930. Whether land tenure became an obstacle to improvements in rural technology after 1930 is an issue that will be discussed below.

Land tenure, however, had an obvious influence on income distribution as well as on social and political status. The owners of the 1,761 livestock holdings covering one-third of the pampean rural area enjoyed considerable wealth and political influence. They had more than a passing interest in issues such as railroad building and exchange rate policy. In most matters there was no direct conflict between the interests of landowners and economic growth; but the fact that many growth-promoting policies conspicuously benefited a small and wealthy group contributed in no small amount to sour popular commitment to those policies (e.g., the promotion of rural exportables either by price policies, or by government support to rural research and extension services).

Tenancy contracts were typically for three years and were often used by landowners to turn uncultivated fields into pastures able to support fine livestock. A class of migrant tenants arose in the pampean zone without incentives to build permanent homes or improvements in their rented land. Tenant interest in local community affairs was low, and rural health, educational, and other social facilities suffered. Livestock ranches included magnificent mansions, where the smallest details spoke of the culture and sophistication of the rarely present landowners. On these same ranches, however, there was an appalling lack of health and educational facilities for the farm-hands who, though well-fed, remained typically at a cultural level not much above that of their gaucho forebears.

Thus, although the land tenure system created between 1860 and 1914 proved compatible with rapid output expansion, it failed elsewhere. By hampering the development of a strong and assertive rural middle class such as in the United States, it planted the seeds of future political instability and therefore, indirectly, of future economic difficulties. James R. Scobie has characterized the role of the agriculturalist before World War I as follows:

> the agriculturist in Argentina rarely possessed political power or influence. . . . For many years, the small agriculturalist was apolitical. Isolation, illiteracy, and transiency made political organization or action difficult, if not impossible. The agricultural immigrant tended to cling to his original nationality and to avoid entanglement in the treacherous and incomprehensible field of local politics. . . . He had come to Argentina to attain a material objective—to make enough money to buy a farm, to establish himself in a town or city, or to return to his homeland with a profit—not to reform or change the political structure. As a

result the farmer was remarkably unsuccessful in making his needs felt or in assuming any civic role in Argentina.[19]

The political role of ranch peons and migrant workers was even smaller, while rural conditions in the northern provinces were generally worse than in the pampean zone. Unequal land distribution set the stage for a conflict between economically efficient policies and what most Argentines regarded as a fair distribution of income and wealth. If land tenure had been such that the term *agropecuario* had been associated with visions of Jeffersonian farmers rather than of cattle barons, it is doubtful that Perón could have got away with his rural policies. Instead, the many who left rural zones after 1930 and migrated to cities received his philippics against rural oligarchs enthusiastically.

Capital formation

According to the Economic Commission for Latin America, the capital stock devoted directly to rural activities grew at an annual rate of 3.6 percent between 1900 and 1929 (source of data as in Table 3.10). It is difficult to estimate capital growth before 1900, especially because a good share came from improvements in the quality of livestock and not in its quantitative expansion.[20] Fences and water systems also supported rural expansion, especially in the livestock sector. In 1848 wire fencing was introduced and spread rapidly; the use of windmills expanded greatly during the last two decades of the nineteenth century and during the twentieth century as well. As in some areas of the Great Plains of the United States, fences and windmills became the two pillars of advancing civilization;[21] but as late as 1888, only 818 threshing machines were recorded in the country.[22]

19. James R. Scobie, *Revolution on the Pampas: A Social History of Argentine Wheat, 1860–1910* (Austin: University of Texas Press, 1964), p. 153. That the land tenure system proved compatible with the 1860–1930 growth does not prove, of course, that it was either the only or the best system to achieve high growth.

20. Bovine cattle was estimated at 21.96 million head in 1888 and 25.87 million head in 1914; between the same dates the quantity of sheep declined. See *Anuario Geográfico Argentino*, p. 257.

21. President Sarmiento (1868–74) urged the cattle ranchers: "Don't be a barbarian: fence!" While in the United States the demand for fencing provided a potent stimulus to the Chicago steel industry, in Argentina most of such demand was met by imports.

22. Taylor, *Rural Life*, pp. 143–45.

Around 1900 a change began to take place in the composition of rural capital. Livestock, housing, fencing, and land improvements constituted the largest share of capital but, beginning with the turn of the century, rural machinery and equipment came into increasing

Table 3.10: Structure of the Capital Stock Directly
Devoted to Rural Activities
(Percentages of the total)

	1900	1914	1929
Total	*100.0*	*100.0*	*100.0*
Machinery	3.5	9.3	17.8
Vehicles	4.3	3.7	8.5
Other durable goods	–	11.3	13.3
Permanent cultivations	5.1	9.7	7.0
Irrigation and drainage works; deforestation and other land improvements	13.8	10.0	9.1
Housing	9.9	19.3	13.7
Livestock	63.3	36.6	30.6

Source: ECLA, p. 93. The figures from which these percentages have been taken are expressed in 1950 prices.

use. According to Table 3.10, machinery, vehicles, and other durable goods accounted for only 8 percent of the rural capital stock in 1900, but their participation rose to 24 percent in 1914, and to 40 percent in 1929. The real value of these three items, letting 1900 = 100, rose to 571 in 1914 and to 1,400 in 1929. The upsurge of mechaniza-

Table 3.11: Stock of Selected Rural Machinery and Equipment in Argentina

	Number of combines[a]	Number of threshers[a]	Number of tractors[b]
1907–08	520	5,740	?[c]
1914–15	1,760	5,437	?[c]
1925	–[d]	–	6,000
1929–30	32,831	10,219	16,300

[a] Refers to those registered with the Ministry of Agriculture.
[b] Refers to those imported up to the date shown.
[c] Data not available, perhaps nil.
[d] Dash indicates data not available.

Source: Marto A. Ballesteros, "Argentine Agriculture, 1908–1954: A Study in Growth and Decline," Appendix C (Ph.D. diss. University of Chicago, 1958), pp. 98–100.

tion is confirmed by Table 3.11. By 1929–30 Argentina had more than one-half the number of combines that existed in the more numerous farms of the United States.[23] Domestic manufacturers of some types of rural machinery also sprang up; according to ECLA, around 1910 one-third of domestic requirements for rural equipment was supplied locally. But mechanization was slow in corn harvesting; not until 1951 was corn-picking machinery used in Argentina.[24]

On the whole, during the first three decades of this century the rural sector was sufficiently flexible to introduce new techniques involving mechanization and capital formation; land tenure was not an insurmountable barrier to technological change. Even large cattle ranchers had a somewhat capitalistic outlook; Carl C. Taylor expressed his opinion, in 1942–43, that "the cattle area of Argentina is probably the best-fenced agricultural area in the world, suggesting elements of pride and social status as well as utility and efficiency." He also remarked on the quality of the animals on the large ranches and the care lavished on them.[25] It is true that census figures for 1914 indicate that there was a marked negative correlation between average real capital stock per hectare (excluding livestock and, of course, the value of land) and the size of rural holding. But because these figures are not homogeneous regarding land quality and rural activities, it is difficult to interpret this result.[26]

23. In 1930 there were 61,000 grain combines on the farms of the United States. On the other hand, the number of tractors in the United States (920,000 in 1930) was, even in per capita terms, far greater than that in Argentina. The cheapness of horses was generally given as the reason for the small number of tractors in Argentina. Data obtained from U.S. Department of Commerce, *Historical Statistics of the United States*, pp. 284–85. As early as 1896, M. G. Mulhall wrote about Argentina: "All the most improved agricultural machinery from United States and England is in use . . ." (*Industries and Wealth of Nations*, p. 363).

24. Ballesteros, "Argentine Agriculture," Part 3, p. 97. Ballesteros suggests that the failure to substitute hybrid for ordinary corn varieties hampered the introduction of such machinery. This conjecture is supported by the fact that in recent years the use of corn-picking machinery has spread *pari passu* with the use of hybrid corn. ECLA's estimate of the importance of domestic production of rural machinery and equipment is found in U.N., *El Proceso de Industrialización en América Latina* (New York, 1965), p. 15.

25. Taylor, *Rural Life*, pp. 4–5 and p. 143. But these fine animals were often used primarily as status symbols and cattle shows gave prizes based more on looks than on the efficiency of animals as producers of meat and milk.

26. See R. Argentina, *Tercer Censo Nacional* 5 (June 1, 1914): 453–56. If one makes a few assumptions regarding average values for categories in-

The capitalistic nature of the rural sector was also reflected in the development of a lively market for the rental of rural machinery, which allowed small and medium-sized farmers to use this equipment without tying up capital in their purchase.

Research and development, the quality of labor, and
inputs of intermediate products

The rural index of total factor productivity—including as inputs unadjusted land, labor, and physical capital—indicated that these three inputs explain nearly all of the expansion of output that took place between 1900 and 1929. Although one may grant that in the rural sector the distinction between increases in physical capital and technological change is especially difficult, most written commentaries concur with the implication of Table 3.2. For example, writing as late as 1942–43, Carl C. Taylor said: "Farming operations are, on the whole, so extensive that there has been little necessity of refining knowledge and using precise techniques. All farm products are produced at such low costs that to know the very best scientific methods and to use the most careful management are not prime requisites of success in farming." [27]

The same author, referring to how farmers obtained new knowledge indicates that "they did not learn from the common schools and they learned very little from agricultural experiment stations and the agricultural extension service because neither was in existence until relatively recently." [28]

---

cluded in ranges for size and investments, the following results are obtained for the five pampean provinces:

Size of rural holding	Estimated average real capital stock, excluding livestock, per hectare
25 hectares and less	306 paper pesos
26 to 50 hectares	102 paper pesos
51 to 100 hectares	50 paper pesos
101 to 500 hectares	19 paper pesos
501 to 1,000 hectares	17 paper pesos
1,001 to 5,000 hectares	8 paper pesos
5,001 to 10,000 hectares	7 paper pesos
10,001 to 25,000 hectares	5 paper pesos
25,001 and more hectares	4 paper pesos

In 1914 one U.S. dollar was worth 2.36 paper pesos.

27. Taylor, *Rural Life,* p. 373. Few gains in total factor productivity were registered in rural United States during these years.

28. Ibid., p. 372.

New methods were picked up in a number of ways: large livestock producers purchased animals from the finest found abroad and often employed experienced foreign farm managers whose knowledge and improved herds then spread to other producers; meat-packing plants, with a demand for high quality animals, induced producers to shift to new techniques appropriate to such livestock; foreign seeds and types of plants best suited to Argentina were borrowed; salesmen of farm machinery induced farmers to improve cultivation methods so that the purchase of the machinery would make sense; and some magazines and newspapers regularly carried items regarding best rural practices.[29] Rural research, education, and extension services were not commensurate with the importance of this sector for the economy. Large landowners, who during these years had considerable influence on the public sector, must share with the latter the blame for this neglect. As Taylor pointed out, many agricultural scientists did not know farm practices, while few farmers knew scientific practices. Practically no fertilizers were used in the pampean provinces. High prices and ignorance regarding their results under pampean conditions contributed to a negative attitude toward fertilizers. Among sheep raisers, however, the use of sheep dip was almost universal.

On the whole, rural practices, especially in the pampean provinces, were not very different during 1920–29 from those employed in other countries of recent settlement. At least, yields per unit of land were similar in Argentina and the United States, as may be seen in the following figures for 1920–29, giving average annual kilograms per hectare harvested:[30]

	United States	*Argentina*
Corn	1,684	1,878
Wheat	939	878
Oats	1,064	1,127
Barley	1,221	1,052

29. The role of new machinery, as viewed by Taylor, provides support for the Hirschman thesis regarding the desirability of capital intensive techniques in less developed countries; "In the cultivation of . . . crops the use of the most scientifically constructed farm machinery has induced, if not forced, modern methods. These machines are constructed of rigid iron and steel, built to operate in a given way, and farmers automatically learn to practice the methods of planting, cultivating, and harvesting which these machines dictate. Most of the machines were built in response to what scientific agriculture required and those who use them have come to practice a degree of scientific method without knowing science." Ibid., pp. 373–74.

30. Data obtained from ECLA, volume 1, pp. 55–56, 116.

Table 3.12: Indices of Rural Gross Output, 1925–64
(1935–39 = 100)

	1925–29	1930–34	1935–39	1940–44	1945–49	1950–54	1955–59	1960–64
Total rural[a]	90.0	91.7	100.0	113.0	111.8	114.0	128.3	133.9
Total agriculture	90.3	93.9	100.0	109.7	102.3	107.3	126.2	139.7
Cereals and linseed	97.9	99.6	100.0	97.0	67.7	60.0	74.5	74.9
Fodder[b]	–[c]	–	100.0	110.1	131.9	86.2	111.0	131.0
Oilseeds	–	–	100.0	249.6	348.0	286.6	329.3	393.1
Industrial crops	75.7	76.7	100.0	116.9	131.4	171.8	191.8	221.1
Fruits and flowers	–	–	100.0	161.1	161.8	268.9	321.8	378.8
Garden vegetables	75.8	86.3	100.0	145.8	162.7	352.2	367.9	412.0
Total livestock	89.1	87.1	100.0	116.7	122.9	118.9	127.1	122.7
Cattle	89.6	87.1	100.0	110.7	119.0	116.0	128.1	121.0
Wool	95.1	104.6	100.0	133.3	130.8	115.2	110.1	116.2
Milk	81.1	90.7	100.0	129.6	142.1	153.6	158.5	153.4
Poultry, eggs, etc.	–	–	100.0	120.8	108.7	95.0	99.4	100.6
Rural construction	–	–	100.0	112.9	111.9	135.1	155.2	148.5
Forestry, fishing, hunting	80.2	89.2	100.0	126.8	161.0	207.6	220.0	251.5

[a] The index for total rural gross output includes considerable double-counting. For example, according to Lucio Reca, a considerable part of the increase in gross output between 1935–39 and 1940–44 was due to the greater use of corn for feeding hogs. It should also be noted that the growth of the several rural activities has been so dissimilar that different weighting schemes could yield quite different overall growth rates.

[b] During recent years fodder crops have been increasingly substituted for natural pastures.

[c] Dash indicates data not available for pre-1935, in the same categories used for post-1935 years. However, pre-1935 "cereals and linseed" include some fodder crops; pre-1935 "industrial crops" include some oilseeds; and pre-1935 "garden vegetables" include fruits.

Sources: For 1925–39, as in Table 3.1. Post-1935 data obtained from BCRA, p. 36. Data were linked using 1935–39 = 100 for both.

Although these average yields hide differences in fertility, capital, and labor intensities, their closeness suggests that no large rural technological gap existed at that time between the two countries.

STAGNATION IN THE RURAL SECTOR 1930–63: OUTPUT

Rural output has grown since 1930 at an annual rate of around 1 percent, well below population expansion. The performance of different rural activities has offered sharp contrasts; these can be seen in Table 3.12. Garden vegetables, oilseeds, fruits, flowers, and industrial crops (goods with small degree of exportableness), showed high growth rates, while the main exportable commodities such as cereals, linseed, cattle, and wool, either grew very slowly or actually fell. Table 3.13 shows even more clearly the extent to which output

Table 3.13: Contributions of Rural Activities to the Increase
in Gross Rural Output between 1935–39 and 1960–64
(Percentages of total)

	Share of each activity in total gross rural output, 1935–39	Increase in gross output of each activity as percentage of the increase in total gross rural output between 1935–39 and 1960–64
Industrial crops	9.1	32.5
Garden vegetables	2.6	24.1
Cattle	29.0	18.0
Fruits and flowers	1.3	10.5
Oilseeds	1.1	9.8
Fodder	9.2	8.4
Milk	4.7	7.3
Rural construction	3.1	4.4
Forestry, fishing, hunting	0.9	4.2
Wool	6.6	3.1
Poultry, eggs, etc.	2.1	0.0
Cereals and linseed	30.3	−22.5
Total	*100*	*100*

Source: BCRA, p. 22.

expansion since 1935–39 has depended on non-traditional activities. Industrial crops, garden vegetables, oilseeds, fruits, and flowers, which represented only 14 percent of gross output in 1935–39, account for 77 percent of the total output increase between those years and 1960–64. The expansion in cattle and wool has not been enough to offset the decline of cereals and linseed.

Table 3.12 indicates that in the post-1930 period three phases may be distinguished: (1) 1930–44, when the output of traditional exportable commodities grew slowly or stagnated while new rural activities expanded rapidly; (2) 1945–54, when output of traditional exportables fell while new activities continued to expand; and (3) 1955 until the present, characterized by a recovery of traditional exportables and a slowdown in the growth of new rural activities.[31]

Measured at 1960 prices, the structure of rural value added (at factor cost) evolved as follows between 1935–39 and 1960–64 (in percentages of total rural value added):[32]

	1935–39	1950–54	1960–64
Cereals and linseed	30	15	17
Fodder	9	7	9
Oilseeds	1	3	3
Industrial crops	9	14	15
Fruits and flowers	1	3	4
Garden vegetables	3	8	8
Cattle	29	30	26
Wool	7	7	6
Milk	5	6	5
Poultry, eggs, etc.	2	2	2
Rural construction	3	4	3
Forestry, fishing, hunting	1	2	2

Two additional points emerge from output data. The Great Depression failed to cut the output of traditional exportables, but the misguided agricultural policies (and unfavorable weather) of 1945–54 succeeded in depressing it. The behavior of new activities is remarkably similar to that of import-substituting light manufacturing—rapid growth during the 1930s, 1940s, and early 1950s, and, once most of the opportunities for import replacement were exhausted, an expansion close to that for population.

31. Although the bulk of new rural output was absorbed domestically and its growth was based primarily on import substitution, some activities were also important exporters. Apples, tea, tung, by-products of oilseeds, sugar, etc., are examples. Cultivation of some of these crops had begun in Argentina many years before the 1930s as in the case of sugar cane and grapes. On the other hand, the category of cereals and linseed include some crops such as rice that were never traditional exportables. See also Table 111 in the Statistical Appendix.

32. Data obtained from the same source listed in Table 3.12.

Data for individual rural commodities dramatically show the collapse of key exportable goods and the expansion of several import-competing crops.[33] On the side of exportables, the drop of around two-thirds in corn and linseed output between 1940–44 and 1950–54 is noteworthy. Even during 1960–64 the corn and linseed crops were 32 percent and 59 percent below their 1925–29 levels. While between 1935–39 and 1960–64 Argentine wheat output rose by less than 5 percent, those of Australia and Canada rose by more than 90 and 110 percent respectively. An interesting exception to the gloomy pampean picture has been the rapid growth of grain sorghum; only 15,000 tons were produced in 1951, but by 1962–64 its average annual output had reached 1.2 million tons. The post-1930 expansion of sunflower, cotton, rice, tobacco, yerba mate, tomatoes, and tung has been spectacular. The development of several northern provinces closely followed the expansion of some of these crops.[34] Inputs going into non-pampean expansion were as a rule not taken away from traditional rural production; better policies could have resulted in growth for both importable and exportable rural goods, although at the expense of urban home goods and services.

CAUSES OF RURAL STAGNATION DURING 1930–63

An answer for the stagnation of rural output may be sought in Table 3.2. Between 1935–39 and 1955–59, land used in rural activities remained practically constant while labor inputs dropped by nearly 25 percent. Increases in physical capital and apparent technological progress were able to offset labor withdrawal but left only a modest margin for an increase in output. This simple answer is, of course, not very illuminating. Why were not more land, labor, and capital applied to the rural sector? And why was technological change so slow relative to that taking place in other countries? This section will review possible answers. They will be grouped into three categories: (1) those attributing the stagnation primarily to a decline in private

33. See Table 112 in the Statistical Appendix.
34. The traditional clash between the pampean and other provinces over tariff policy was strengthened by this fact. Some of the non-pampean provinces depend heavily on just one or two of these crops. During recent years, several regions have been adversely affected by the inability of the domestic market to absorb large increases in the output of these commodities. Examples are the Cuyo zone (grapes and wine), Chaco (cotton), Tucumán (sugar), and Misiones (yerba mate). Exports have been unable to eliminate production surpluses.

rates of return; (2) those emphasizing land tenure as the main barrier to growth; and (3) those pointing to a lag in rural technology as the major culprit. These categories are interrelated; few argue that any one of them fully explains the stagnation, but together they provide a useful framework for discussion. After each is examined, the influence of foreign demand on rural growth will also be discussed.

The relative prices of rural goods

A first hypothesis to consider is that rural stagnation has been caused by unattractive private rates of return for fresh investments. Lacking data on potential rates of return, an alternative hypothesis regarding relative prices for rural goods may be discussed. Table 3.14 presents three indices measuring relative prices for all rural products.

Table 3.14: Indices of Relative Prices for Rural Products, 1926–65
(1935–39 = 100)

	A	B	C
1926–29	132.2	—[a]	–
1930–34	86.5	–	–
1935–39	100.0	100.0	100.0
1940–44	62.4	73.1	67.6
1945–46	74.4	82.3	79.4
1947–49	80.2	69.3	75.1
1950–52	68.4	76.3	68.2
1953–55	67.7	81.8	69.8
1956–58	77.7	88.2	80.1
1959–61	84.8	94.5	83.5
1962–64	92.9	97.9	87.9[b]
1965	81.1	96.4	–

[a] Dash indicates data not available.
[b] Refers to 1962–63 only.

Sources and methods: Column *A.*—Index of ratio of wholesale prices of all *rural* products to wholesale prices of *nonrural* goods. Comité Nacional de Geografía, *Anuario Geográfico Argentino* (Buenos Aires, 1941), p. 369; BCRA, *Boletín Estadístico* (Buenos Aires, September 1962), pp. 51–62; Dirección Nacional de Estadística y Censos (hereafter, DNEC), *Boletín Mensual de Estadística*, recent issues.

Column *B.*—Index of ratio of implicit prices for the rural sector and implicit prices for "industry" (defined as mining, manufacturing, and construction). O.S., pp. 112–13, 132–33; BCRA, pp. 2, 18.

Column *C.*—Index of ratio of wholesale price of all *rural* products to estimated prices paid by rural producers (general index). The latter were obtained from Asociación Argentina de Productores Agrícolas, *Precios de Paridad para Productos Agrícolas en la Argentina* (Buenos Aires, 1958) and subsequent estimates by the same organization.

In view of the difficulties of weighing price series covering long periods, three series are provided for 1935–65. Although their correspondence is far from perfect, they tell essentially the same story— a sharp drop of real rural prices during World War II, a weak recovery during 1945–55, and a stronger upward swing since 1956. By 1962– 65 real rural prices were about 10 percent below their 1935–39 level. As shown by column *A*, however, the 1935–39 level was substantially below pre-depression prices.

The drop in these rural terms of trade, as shown in essay 2, was sharper than that experienced by the external terms of trade during 1926–52; since 1950–52, however, rural terms of trade improved in spite of an apparent further deterioration in the external price ratio. Thus, from 1926–29 until 1950–52 the rural sector faced not only on the whole unfavorable foreign price trends, but also the erosion of its real prices caused by domestic policies. These policies included overvalued exchange rates, export taxes, protection of manufacturing, and controls over rural prices enforced by a monopsonist state trading agency.

It is common to blame price policies for the stagnation of rural activities, especially those of an exportable nature. Indeed, it may be observed that the output of such key crops as cereals and linseed reached their lowest points around 1950–54, when real prices also touched bottom. Yet the correlation between aggregate rural output and the overall rural terms of trade is not a close one, and the apparent price elasticities that emerge are generally low and/or statistically insignificant. A comparison of Tables 3.14 and 3.12 suggests this result; output variance is notably smaller than that of real prices. Sharp price drops during 1930–34 and 1940–44 were not accompanied by contractions in output, and real price increases since 1950–52 have been much larger than output expansion. The failure of output to expand more vigorously between 1950–52 and 1962–64, in spite of improving real prices and steady or falling real wage rates, has been especially disappointing. After using relevant data for the thirty-seven years included between 1929 through 1965, the following result is obtained for an overall naive supply function of the rural sector:

$$q_t = 2.183 - 0.010\, p_t + 0.029\, p_{t-1} - 0.111\, p_{t-2/3} + 0.462\, Y_t$$
$$(0.109) \qquad (0.131) \qquad (0.091) \qquad (0.043)$$
$$+ 0.146\, r_{t-1} + 0.016\, r_{t-2} \quad R^2 = 0.87; \quad (3.1)$$
$$(0.067) \qquad (0.066)$$

where

q is the index of rural output;

p is the index of the ratio of domestic wholesale prices for rural goods to domestic wholesale prices for nonrural goods;

Y is the index of the growth of productive capacity in the whole economy (this index was made to grow at 2.7 percent per annum —the average growth rate during the years in the regression);

r is the index of rainfall in the pampean region.

All variables were transformed to logarithms; the t subscripts denote years—$p_{t-2/3}$ refers to the average of relative prices two and three years before the output observation. The standard errors of the coefficients are given in parentheses under the corresponding co-efficients. All price coefficients are less than twice their standard errors; a trend variable plus rainfall monopolize explanation.[35]

The *apparent* price inelasticity of total output may result from several factors. Rural producers may form their expectations of future prices and profits differently from what is implied in the lagged prices of the equation; we may thus observe them off their curves. Bad experiences during the Great Depression and the war may have induced producers to take a dim view of the long-run prospects for farming, regardless of price behavior over a four-year period. Whole-sale prices for rural products may not reflect accurately prices received by producers and, more importantly, wholesale prices of nonrural products are not an exact measure of production costs at the farm.[36] In particular, it is doubtful that available indices fully reflect the post-war labor scarcity in the pampean rural zone resulting from migration to the cities. Indices cannot capture intangibles such as the atmosphere surrounding government rural policy, confidence in the future of property rights, and labor relations in the countryside (which changed drastically after Perón came to power). Prices of modern inputs such

35. The use of simple least squares to estimate the overall supply schedule may be defended on two grounds: (1) all price variables except p_t are lagged, and q_t could not be expected to influence p_{t-1} and $p_{t-2/3}$; and (2) a large share of rural output may be said to have faced during this period a perfectly elastic demand either from the world market or from the price setting government monopsony. The trend variable is justified on the ground that, even when relative prices are constant, the normal result of growth in all inputs of an economy is an increase in all outputs. The coefficient of Y_t may then be taken as an approximation to the growth-elasticity of the rural sector for a given set of relative prices.

36. But note that in Table 3.14 columns *A* and *B* are similar for the years they overlap.

as fertilizers and pesticides are also underrepresented. Furthermore, the instability of relative prices suggests that no one could take very seriously one year's prices as the basis on which to plan future production.[37] Finally, for beef the link between prices and output is complex, as will be later shown. Thus, the historical evidence on the link between overall rural output and relative prices remains ambiguous. Although prices no doubt influenced producers by affecting their expectations about future rates of return in farming, they cannot provide the whole answer to the question of rural stagnation.

The failure of naive attempts to explain long-term output changes by using only observed prices is not surprising. *Ceteris paribus*, changes in relative prices explain movements along a given production possibility frontier, but outward shifts of that frontier will be due to more complex long-run forces, and relative output prices will be only one of them. Even the link between prices and movements along a given frontier may be tenuous when relative prices fluctuate violently.

Although the aggregate supply schedule is difficult to pin down, there is evidence that rural entrepreneurs react quickly to changes in relative prices *and costs* within the sector, as pampean land and weather permit a wide choice of rural activities in a given location.

Several major changes have taken place during the last thirty years in relative prices between cereals and cattle, as is shown in Table 3.15. This table lumps consecutive years during which the grain/cattle price index was either below or above the 1926–65 average. With the exception of 1930–31, prewar years were favorable

37. Two extreme examples can be given. In 1946 *real* rural price rose 56 percent above the average for the previous five years; between 1958 and 1959 *real* cattle prices rose by 44 percent. Even with most dynamic entrepreneurs one could hardly expect percentage increases in output anywhere close to those of price increases. (In these examples real prices are defined relative to wholesale prices of nonrural goods.) Similar examples could be given for other commodities. It may also be noted that one could expect asymmetries in the rural response to changes in policies and terms of trade; discouraging terms of trade and policies leading to a labor outflow may result in a quick fall in output, but encouraging terms of trade and policies may not lead so readily to increases in production, due to the difficulty of getting workers now in cities to move back to the farms. One may also wonder to what extent farmers reacted negatively, not so much to the level of real domestic rural prices, but to the difference they could observe (especially during the immediate postwar period) between world and domestic prices for their products. Finally, during the postwar years many social overhead activities servicing the rural sector, such as railroads, harbors, and storage facilities, suffered declines in quality not reflected in price indices.

Table 3.15: Indices of Wholesale Prices for Cereals and Linseed
Relative to Wholesale Cattle Prices, 1926–65
(Yearly averages, 1939 = 100)

	(Index of cereal and linseed prices ÷ index of cattle prices) × 100[a]	Area planted to major cereal (and linseed) crops[b] (million hectares)	Area planted to wheat, corn, and linseed (million hectares)
1926–29	113.7	18.39	16.06
1930–31	83.5	19.46	17.24
1932–39	108.0	20.28	17.11
1940–45	71.1	17.83	13.65
1946–49	115.3	14.63	10.32
1950–55	80.5	14.42	9.55
1956–58	99.5	15.95	9.80
1959–60	71.0	14.56	8.85
1961–63	103.8	15.20	10.26
1964–65	61.0	15.06	10.86

[a] The average for this column is 93.2.
[b] Includes wheat, corn, linseed, oats, barley, and rye.

Sources: Price data as in Table 3.14. Data on area planted found in various publications of DNEC.

to grains. Shipping shortages resulted in mounting surpluses of bulky grains during the war; meat, on the other hand, was not only easier to transport (and store alive) but also could be more readily absorbed by the domestic market.[38] The first four postwar years witnessed a relative improvement of cereal prices (especially during 1946, when the index reached 147); the rest of the Perón years, however, showed relative prices favorable to cattle. Another irony of this regime is that although its rural policies were motivated by populism, albeit of the urban species, in relative terms they hurt cattle ranchers less than farmers producing wheat, corn, etc., on their own land. Since 1955 grain-cattle price swings again have become more frequent and larger in amplitude.[39]

A basic reason for the instability of grain-cattle prices is found in

38. Around 1935–39 only about one-third of beef output was exported, while the corresponding figures were 75 percent for corn, 90 percent for linseed, and 50 percent for wheat. Grain surpluses were burned as fuel during the war in Argentina.
39. According to CONADE, the ratio of the standard deviation to the mean of the time series for the relative price of cattle to grains was 0.31 during 1933–45, 0.06 for 1946–55, and 0.25 during 1956–64. See CONADE, *Diagnóstico Preliminar del Sector Agropecuario,* pp. 11–12.

the cattle production function. As cattle today can be used either for slaughter or to produce more cattle tomorrow, an increase in its price today, which is expected to persist, will induce ranchers to *reduce* slaughtering and to increase stocks. This response will in turn lead to even higher cattle prices so that, for a range, prices will spiral upwards. After a turning point is reached, similar forces will send cattle prices into a downward spiral, as lower prices lead to liquidation of stocks, leading to lower prices, etc. The nature of turning points may not always be the same; overstocking or excessive liquidation, limits set by export and import prices for beef, etc., are some of the plausible explanations for turning points.[40] Shocks provided by droughts and government actions (devaluation with differential export taxes and price controls, for example) also set off new cycles or aggravated existing ones. The swing from cattle into grains during 1956–58 was the result of official action, while the 1961–63 swing seems to have been started by a worsening of natural pastures due to lack of rain. The 1959–60 swing from grains into cattle was the outcome of a devaluation accompanied by differential export taxes and the lifting of controls over meat prices.

Table 3.15 also presents areas devoted to the production of major grains. There is no good fit between column 1 and either columns 2 or 3 for the whole period. A better correlation between these columns appears for 1950–65, although even here the fit is far from perfect. The figures show, however, the remarkable reallocation of pampean land that has taken place since the 1930s in favor of pastures and livestock and away from cereals and linseed (the opposite to the pre-1930s trend in land use).

Besides grain-cattle prices, two other major factors influenced rural entrepreneurs regarding land use. Emigration of rural labor, which gained momentum after 1945, and the resulting increases in rural wages and labor scarcity, harmed crops more than cattle. Mechanization of planting and harvesting advanced slowly until around 1955, so that these activities remained very labor intensive. On the other hand, labor requirements for livestock were lower and more evenly spread throughout the year, so that ranchers could more easily resist the labor demands that became irresistible at harvest time for farmers with matured crops. The Perón regime drove crop activities into a dif-

40. For a more complete discussion of the cattle cycle see my *Exchange Rate Devaluation,* chapter 4. However, a full explanation of the cattle cycle in Argentina, including its turning points, remains to be developed.

ficult corner: labor was withdrawn at the same time that other policies made rural mechanization difficult and costly. An index of rural wage rates relative to wholesale prices for cereals and linseed rose from a level of 100 during 1935–39, to 136 in 1947–49, and 173 for 1950–55.[41] It is significant that corn, one of the most labor-intensive activities, suffered one of the most violent decreases in output.[42] With prices for labor and rural machinery rising relative to that for land, rural producers turned to activities with high land/labor and land/capital ratios, while capital formation in the form of larger cattle herds was encouraged.

Government regulations over tenancy contracts, beginning during World War II, also stimulated the shift from grains into cattle. Controlled rents lagged behind general price increases. Tenants were given the right to renew their contracts under old conditions and guarantees against eviction. Landowners realized that once they allowed a tenant on their land, they lost control over that property or had to make side-payments to persuade tenants enjoying frozen rents to move. Under these circumstances, they preferred to devote their holdings to pastures and extensive cattle production year after year, rather than alternate between cattle and tenant-produced grains, as in the past.[43]

The sensitivity of cattle slaughtering to meat prices, relative to

41. Data on rural wage rates obtained from Asociación Argentina de Productores Agrícolas, *Precios de Paridad* (Buenos Aires, 1958). Domestic production of tractors did not reach significant levels until after 1955. The importation of tractors and rural machinery was first delayed by the war and postwar difficulties of supply; after 1947 exchange control authorities appear to have given low priorities to these imports, until the severe crisis of 1951–52. It has been estimated that the number of tractors in use during 1946–51 was about 40 percent *below* the corresponding number for 1937–39 (CONADE, *Diagnóstico Preliminar,* p. 18). ECLA has estimated that the stock of all rural machinery in 1949 was about 20 percent below 1939; even by 1955 that stock was 8 percent below the 1939 level (ECLA, p. 93).

42. The rural labor shortage became so acute during 1951–52 (and the exchange crisis so severe) that the army was sent to harvest crops in some regions. A minimum of foresight could have avoided the need for such dramatic gestures. Substantial improvement in urban wages and living conditions was perhaps the main force accounting for massive migration to cities during the immediate postwar years.

43. See Comité Interamericano de Desarrollo Agrícola (hereafter CIDA), *Tenencia de la Tierra y Desarrollo Socio-Económico del Sector Agrícola, Argentina* (Washington, D.C.: Union Panamericana, 1966), chapter 10. Arthur L. Domike, who directed this study, considers tenancy regulation at least as important as wage policy in explaining the shift from grains to cattle.

those of other rural products such as grains, is illustrated by the following regressions. For 1923–42:

$$b_t = 1.645 - 0.151\, pb_t - 0.254\, pb_{t-1} - 0.197\, pb_{t-2} \quad R^2 = 0.50, \quad (3.2)$$
$$ (0.097) \quad\quad (0.088) \quad\quad\quad (0.088)$$

where

b_t = slaughter of beef in year t divided by slaughter of beef in year $t - 1$. The slaughter is measured in tons of beef;

pb_t = index of beef prices relative to wholesale rural prices in year t, divided by the same index for year $t - 1$; similar interpretation applies to pb_{t-1} and pb_{t-2}.

These results confirm the discussion regarding the short-run response of cattle ranchers to changes in beef prices relative to other rural prices. For 1943–62 the following equation is obtained:

$$b_t = 1.517 - 0.203\, pb_t - 0.359\, pb_{t-1} + 0.062\, pb_{t-2} \quad R^2 = 0.48. \quad (3.3)$$
$$ (0.118) \quad\quad (0.114) \quad\quad\quad (0.120)$$

The main conclusion warranted by these somewhat rough equations is that there is indeed significant response to relative prices within the rural sector.[44] Better data and more sophisticated models would presumably show a positive link between beef prices and desired cattle stock.

Attempts to explain area planted to linseed, corn, and wheat during 1935–65 as a function not only of the prices of these goods, but also of other relevant variables, are presented in Table 3.16.[45] The coefficients obtained for each independent variable in the three regressions have under them in parenthesis their standard errors. All variables were transformed into logarithms, so the coefficients may be interpreted as elasticities. The real prices used in the regressions are rather artificial; for a given year (t) they were formed by arbitrarily selecting a lag structure giving weights of 0.5, 0.3, and 0.2 to the real prices ruling during years (t), $(t - 1)$, and $(t - 2)$, respectively. Year (t) refers to the year of planting. Real prices were

44. If instead of using beef prices relative to rural wholesale prices, beef prices relative to *non*rural prices are used in the regressions, poorer results are obtained. Data on beef prices and slaughter obtained from Junta Nacional de Carnes, *Estadísticas Básicas,* pp. 6 and 13.

45. See footnote 35 for a justification of the use of simple least squares in the estimation of rural supply responses. For the three commodities at hand those considerations apply *a fortiori.* These and earlier regressions are presented as evidence of considerable supply response to prices for individual activities; they clearly do not represent an econometric model of the rural sector.

Table 3.16: Coefficients of Regressions Attempting to Explain
Area Planted to Selected Crops, 1935–65

| | *Area planted to:* | | |
	Linseed	*Corn*	*Wheat*
Linseed price	1.45	0.20	−0.11
	(0.34)	(0.28)	(0.17)
Corn price	−0.92	0.09	−0.20
	(0.40)	(0.40)	(0.22)
Wheat price	0.17	0.43	0.55
	(0.40)	(0.37)	(0.28)
Cattle price	0.43	0.59	−0.01
	(0.42)	(0.39)	(0.23)
Urban wages	−1.42	−1.22	−0.22
	(0.24)	(0.26)	(0.16)
Relative yields	0.84	0.12	−0.67
	(0.57)	(0.67)	(0.40)
Rainfall	−0.02	0.10	0.35
	(0.25)	(0.25)	(0.14)
Price variability	−0.06	−0.10	−0.06
	(0.07)	(0.08)	(0.05)
R^2	0.86	0.72	0.64
Durbin-Watson statistic	1.96	1.13	1.68

Source: Author's calculations.

obtained deflating output price indices by the wholesale index for
nonrural prices.[46] This forced lag structure may be justified on the
ground that the complexity of interrelationships among pampean rural
activities is so great that attempts to allow for both this complexity
and unconstrained lags would leave few degrees of freedom.

The inclusion of the other independent variables shown in Table
3.16 can be explained straightforwardly. In the absence of homogeneous data on rural wages for the whole of 1935–65, an index of
urban wages was used as a proxy. Money wage rates, like rural prices,
were deflated using the wholesale index for non-rural prices. The
yields of linseed, corn, and wheat were used to form an aggregate

46. Prices for linseed, corn, and wheat were obtained from DNEC, *Boletín
de Estadística* (from 1956 on); and from tables of the ECLA ("Estadísticas
Agrícolas Básicas," 1957). Price data for pre-1950 years are of doubtful
reliability. In some cases, different prices can be obtained for a given year
from different sources. Price series for corn, linseed and wheat used in the
regressions are highly correlated; the R^2 between each pair never falls below
0.65. Price data could be refined to take into account only prices ruling
during planting months; it should be noted, however, that in many years official
minimum and support prices were announced after planting had started.

index; for each regression the average yield of a given crop relative to the aggregate index during the previous three years was used as an independent variable. The expected result is that, as technological change improves a crop yield relative to others, farmers will plant more of it, *ceteris paribus*.[47] The index of price variability for each crop was formed by taking the sum of absolute values of percentage changes in the real price of the crop during t, $t-1$, and $t-2$. The sign of this variable is expected to be negative.

The results show a respectable degree of supply response. The coefficients measuring the own price elasticity for linseed and wheat are substantially higher than their standard errors and, especially in the case of linseed, indicate a high elasticity. Cross-elasticities are less satisfactory, however. The damaging effects on rural output of the urban labor pull are indicated by the negative coefficients attached to urban wages, especially for corn and linseed. Coefficients for relative yields, rainfall, and price variability are on the whole disappointing, although those for relative yields in linseed, rainfall for wheat, and price variability for corn are noteworthy.

The estimations presented in Table 3.16 could stand a great deal of refinement. Experimentation with lags, improvement of the price and rainfall data (taking into account rainfall at planting time), models of price expectations, and geographical disaggregation are some possible improvements that will lead to a better understanding of the complexities of pampean rural activities. For our purposes, however, it is enough to have established that pampean farmers do respond rationally to economic and technological data in deciding their land allocation.[48]

Although within the rural sector relative prices quickly affect resource allocation, a proportional increase in all rural prices may,

47. The correlation between lagged yields and lagged prices was found to be very near zero. Lagged yields may be taken as the basis on which farmers form their expectations regarding future yields. See Jere R. Behrman, "The Relevance of Traditional Economic Theory for Understanding Peasant Behavior: A Case Study of Rice Supply Response in Thailand, 1940–1963" (mimeographed).

48. For 1948–64, Lucio Reca, Remy Freire, and Larry A. Sjaastad have also obtained results which imply significant (intended) supply responses to relative prices within the rural sector. See Larry A. Sjaastad, "Argentina y el Plan de Desarrollo" (mimeographed, 1966). Lucio Reca has obtained good fits for sunflower and wheat, showing "strong and clear" supply responses by farmers. His results for corn, however, are also poor. Freire obtained good results for flax (linseed) and wheat. See his "Price Incentives in Argentine Agriculture" (mimeographed, n.d.).

according to historical experience, leave rural output little changed for several years. The combination of short-run resource flexibility within the rural sector, and little of it between rural and nonrural activities, may be explained by the difference in entrepreneurial risk as between a switch from wheat into linseed, and a switch from producing textiles to growing wheat.[49]

If it is granted that there is some resource flexibility within the rural sector, have fluctuations in relative rural prices been desirable? An answer may be framed with reference to world prices for these commodities: on the assumption that Argentina is a price-taker in the international trade of these goods, changes in domestic rural prices reflecting changes in world prices would induce a pattern of rural output maximizing its dollar value as well as foreign exchange earnings.

Table 3.17: Coefficients of Determination between Relative World and Domestic Prices for Selected Rural Commodities, 1951–63

	Between levels of relative prices, world and domestic	*Between yearly percentage changes in relative prices*
Wheat	0.32	0.38
Corn	−0.02	0.16
Linseed oil (and linseed)	0.88	0.73
Wool	0.65	0.48
Meat	0.24	0.55
Hides	0.27	0.03

Sources: Basic foreign and domestic price data obtained from *International Financial Statistics*, several issues (for export dollar prices for wheat, corn, wool, and linseed oil), and from DNEC, *Boletín Mensual de Estadística*, several issues (for dollar unit values of exports of meat and hides and all domestic prices).

To test the correspondence of domestic and foreign price structures, the prices of six rural commodities (wheat, corn, linseed, wool, meat,

49. It is possible to read too much into results showing that farmers respond to relative prices in their choice of crops. Perhaps as a reaction against earlier beliefs regarding the alleged economic irrationality of peasants and farmers, economists have taken to beating this straw man with great gusto and at great length. No doubt that evidence on high supply elasticities for individual crops may keep government officials from unusually foolish policies. But for framing long-run growth policies for the rural sector this information is less useful. Few would argue that rising real rural prices provide the best way to generate rising rural output in the long run. Furthermore, while evidence showing significant responses of area planted to prices is plentiful, that regarding significant responses of yields per acre to prices is scarcer.

and hides) have been examined during 1951–63. An index was formed out of those six prices and then each price was deflated by that composite index. The procedure was carried out for both peso and dollar prices. Table 3.17 presents the coefficients of determination between both the *levels* and the yearly *changes* of those domestic and dollar relative prices. If markets and price indices were perfect, and there were neither differential transport costs nor export taxes nor other discriminatory levies on exports, one would expect a perfect correlation between these foreign and domestic relative prices. But the correlation is far from perfect. Even if one grants the existence of inexact data (although these are better than average in quality) and market frictions, the low coefficients of determination indicate that government policies have substantially interfered with *relative* price signals from world markets, so that for a given global discrimination against the rural sector, foreign exchange earnings have not been maximized.

To obtain a more precise measurement of rural price instability and discrimination arising from domestic policies, the following procedure has been followed. First, the domestic prices of five major commodities (wheat, meat, corn, wool, and linseed) were deflated by the wholesale prices of nonrural goods. Second, the export dollar prices of these goods were deflated by United States wholesale prices. The ratio formed by dividing the first index over the second may be taken as an index of the discrimination forthcoming from export taxes and quotas, exchange rate and price policy, the system of protection, etc. The lower the index, the greater the net discrimination against a given commodity. Naturally, this index can give only a rough idea of what we are after (a measure of the net impact of all domestic policies on the domestic real price of exportables) as neither indices nor markets are perfect.[50] Table 3.18 summarizes these indices for recent years; they reflect a gradual trade liberalization since the Perón regime until 1964–65, when some controls were reintroduced, and the relatively favored position meat enjoyed before 1956. The table also presents the ratio of the standard deviations of the yearly series over their mean. This measure of dispersion indicates erratic

50. In the discussion it is assumed that domestic policies can affect unit values in pesos, but not in dollars. For most exportables this is a reasonable assumption. For beef and linseed oil it is more doubtful, at least in the short run. Note that the index shows only the net effect of all domestic policies; for example, during some years high price supports served partially to offset overvaluation of the exchange rate.

Table 3.18: Indices of Discrimination against Selected Exportables, 1951–65
(1959–61 = 100)

| | Average of indices | | | | | Normalized standard deviations of annual indices | |
	1951–55	1956–58	1959–61	1962–63	1964–65	1955–65	1959–65
Wheat	47	70	100	94	80	0.19	0.11
Meat	77	83	100	109	105	0.15	0.08
Corn	46	80	100	126	86	0.24	0.16
Wool	47	84	100	102	89	0.19	0.14
Linseed	60	90	100	104	83	0.17	0.15

Sources: International Financial Statistics, for U.S. wholesale prices and dollar prices of wheat, corn, wool, and linseed oil; DNEC, *Boletín de Estadística*, several issues, for all other prices.

domestic policies, even during 1959–65, resulting in large fluctuations of real rural prices. The incentives provided by higher average rural real prices since 1955, have been eroded by these fluctuations. To usual rural concerns about weather, pests, world prices and such, uncertainty about abrupt changes in public policy has been added. Furthermore, erratic resource switches within the rural sector probably had a negative effect on technological change and productivity of activities requiring specific capital goods and long planning horizons. Had those reallocations been induced by world market conditions, such negative effects could have been justified by short-run exchange maximization, but that was seldom the case. Price fluctuations, as David Felix has noted, become more harmful to innovations as rural establishments modernize and increase their cash transactions. At that point illiquidity risks, which remain small when there are few cash input purchases, become larger.

A more aggregated though rougher measure of discrimination against the rural sector may be obtained by comparing the actual rural share in GDP, measured at current prices, with what that share would have been if Argentine relative prices had followed world price trends. We start with 1926–29 as the base. In this exercise, the realized rural output will be used for both shares, thus underestimating the incidence of the net tax on rural activities.[51] The

51. It will be recalled that, as early as 1926–29, the level of import duties was not insignificant. The price indices shown in Tables 2.10 and 2.11 have been used in these calculations, as well as domestic wholesale prices and the national accounts presented in the Statistical Appendix. I am grateful to Tibor Scitovsky for suggesting to me this exercise.

results, which should be taken only as indicators of orders of magnitude, are as follows (expressed as percentages of GDP at factor cost):

	At current prices	*At 1926–29 prices following world price trends*	*Difference*
1925–29	33	33	—
1935–39	26	28	2
1947–49	16	32	16
1950–52	15	25	10
1953–55	18	26	8
1956–58	17	20	3
1959–61	17	18	1
1962–64	17	18	1

This gross measure of the tax on rural activities was especially severe during the Perón years, particularly when the external terms of trade were very favorable to primary products. Even during 1947–49, however, while the "tax" sliced off at least half of the potential rural value added, that represented an addition of only 24 percent to the value added of the rest of the economy. What the rest of the economy can hope to squeeze from the rural sector has declined sharply, relative to value added in those other sectors, during recent years.

In summary, the discussion of the role of output prices in rural stagnation has provided some support for the thesis that mistaken price policies contributed to that stagnation, especially in grains. The evidence does not, however, support the proposition that low output prices were the only factor explaining stagnation. Indeed, a good part of the decline in real rural prices during the last 30 or 40 years was inevitable in the light of world market trends. In the United States, in spite of farm programs, the parity index for farmers has declined from a level of 92 in 1929 to 75 in 1964 (1910–14 = 100). In Canada, the index of the ratio of wholesale prices of farm products to the general wholesale index has declined from 115 in 1929 to 98 in 1960 (1935–39 = 100).[52]

The hypothesis blaming rural stagnation on the decline of the

52. Council of Economic Advisers, *Economic Report of the President* (Washington, D.C., 1965), p. 277; M. C. Urquhart, *Historical Statistics of Canada* (Cambridge: At the University Press, 1965), pp. 293, 298. In both Canada and the United States rural output and productivity have expanded substantially in spite of this price trend.

expected private rate of return may provide a better explanation, but this is difficult to document. Not only are data on many inputs lacking, but it is also difficult to know how rural entrepreneurs allowed the cumulative disasters of the Great Depression, World War II, and Perón to affect their view of the long-run future of farming and ranching. Nevertheless, the wage coefficients in Table 3.16 indicate that the rate of return hypothesis performs better than one which considers only output prices. While urban activities met higher wage bills with the help of generous public credit and protectionist policies, the postwar rural sector faced higher wage costs even as its real output prices declined. The combination of Peronist policies on rural prices, wage rates, and restrictions on the import of many rural inputs no doubt depressed actual and expected rural profit rates, inducing lower rural output. The rapid expansion of grain sorghum since 1950, of other crops since 1930 and the introduction of new livestock varieties also indicate that pampean producers can respond vigorously to new profitable opportunities.

Special attention has been paid to pampean activities; the price responsiveness of non-pampean crops has not been examined. It will be recalled that these crops expanded very rapidly during the 1930s and 1940s. Although few thorough studies are available on the causes of that rapid growth, it appears that it resulted from favorable domestic prices, arising from greater protection against foreign competition, as well as special credit programs. Output of these crops usually was expanded by incorporating more (non-pampean) land into cultivation; the issue of choosing among alternative crops did not arise as often as in the pampean zone. The expansion of these regional activities during 1930–50 recreated the nineteenth-century pampean growth style, except that now the stimulus came mainly from import substitution. During recent years several of these activities have run into problems of surplus output (e.g. sugar, yerba mate) and at least for short-run downward output adjustments, they have exhibited an apparent price inelasticity of supply. Their great importance in regional economies outside the pampean zone has induced government help in handling surplus production to avoid sharp decreases in their domestic prices.[53]

53. An index of the ratio of wholesale prices for industrial crops (available only since 1939) to nonrural wholesale prices has evolved in the following way (1939 = 100): 1940–44 = 70; 1945–46 = 83; 1947–49 = 98; 1950–52 = 80; 1953–55 = 68; 1956–58 = 99; 1959–61 = 102; 1962–64 = 101. Until 1952,

Land tenure as an obstacle to rural growth

A widespread opinion blames the structure of landholding for the rural stagnation since 1930. It is argued that, although large landholdings and tenancy contracts described earlier did not interfere with growth while new lands could still be incorporated into extensive production, once the pampean zone had been occupied, further output expansion had to come from a more intensive exploitation of the soil, for which the pattern of landholding was ill suited. Large landowners are alleged to have little interest in exerting the additional effort required by intensive techniques, because extensive cultivation is sufficient to yield satisfactory earnings, even without maximizing net earnings per hectare. Greater leisure, coupled with the social prestige attached to land ownership and some methods of cultivation, compensate for the foregone profits that could be obtained by intensive cultivation. Extensive cultivation also frees landowners from risks that additional inputs required by intensive techniques would entail, while sentimentality and the prestige attached to land ownership presumably keep them from selling part of their estates to "lean and hungry" entrepreneurs. The pampean *estancia*, it is said, operates with low cash needs, so that fluctuating profits present few risks of illiquidity. Thus, market penalties cannot put inefficient landowners out of business. Furthermore, it is argued that tenants not subject to these high level income effects lack incentive to invest in their rented lands, because they would obtain only part of the rewards forthcoming from such an investment. Finally, it is asserted that inflation has increased the value of land as a hedge against the erosion of real wealth, thus making landowners more reluctant to part with it even when they do not use it to full capacity. Low and falling land taxes, coupled with higher taxes elsewhere, have also reduced the opportunity cost of holding idle land.

Most arguments on this issue have brought forth little solid information. Until recently, no systematic study of the pattern of landholding was available, and discussion was based on inconclusive scraps of evidence.[54]

---

prices for industrial crops were in general relatively higher (using 1939 as the base) than for other rural products; since then the record is more mixed, but with a tendency toward the worsening of their relative prices.

54. The new study is that of CIDA, *Tenencia de la Tierra y Desarrollo Socio-Económico*. This pioneering and careful work was directed by Arthur L. Domike. This and earlier sections owe a great deal to this study, as well as

Table 3.19: Area Covered by Rural Holdings Classified According to Size;
Pampean Provinces, 1914 and 1960
(Percentages of total rural area)

Five pampean provinces	1914	1960
25 hectares and less	0.7	1.0
26 to 100 hectares	5.1	7.6
101 to 1,000 hectares	32.9	39.9
1,001 to 5,000 hectares	27.5	30.8
5,001 to 10,000 hectares	15.5	10.5
10,001 hectares and more	18.3	10.2
Pampean provinces excluding		
La Pampa Province		
25 hectares and less	0.8	1.1
26 to 100 hectares	5.8	9.0
101 to 1,000 hectares	35.6	44.4
1,001 to 5,000 hectares	27.0	29.3
5,001 to 10,000 hectares	12.8	8.3
10,001 hectares and more	18.0	7.9
Province of Buenos Aires		
25 hectares and less	0.8	1.1
26 to 100 hectares	4.7	6.8
101 to 1,000 hectares	34.3	43.8
1,001 to 5,000 hectares	30.4	33.8
5,001 to 10,000 hectares	14.4	9.0
10,001 hectares and more	15.4	5.5

Sources: Rural censuses for 1914 and for 1960.

Table 3.19 presents the distribution of rural land in pampean provinces according to the size of holdings in 1960 and 1914. Although the size categories directly comparable are rather gross, a trend toward smaller holdings between these years is apparent. Holdings of more than 5,000 hectares, which in 1914 accounted for 33.8 percent of all rural land in pampean provinces, covered only 20.7 percent in 1960. In the four main pampean provinces the figures are 30.8 percent and 16.2 percent, respectively; in Buenos Aires province they are 29.8 percent and 14.5 percent. Holdings of between 26 and 1,000 hectares show the largest gains; for all pampean provinces they increase from 38.0 to 47.5 percent of the area.

The CIDA study (see n. 43), based on the 1960 census, has analyzed landholding according to size and type of tenancy. Some of its results are presented in Table 3.20. For 1960, it finds that 38

---

to comments by Dr. Domike, even though some disagreements may remain as to interpretation of the data,

Table 3.20: Distribution of Rural Land in Argentina
According to Size and Ownership, 1960
(Percentages of all rural land)

	Less than family size[a]	Family size[b]	Size of holding Medium multifamily size[c]	Large multifamily size
All Argentina total	*3.4*	*44.6*	*33.9*	*18.1*
Exclusively owners	1.4	17.1	20.9	13.6
Sharecroppers and tenants	0.5	6.3	2.4	1.4
Mixed property	0.2	3.2	3.3	1.6
Fiscal lands	0.7	11.2	3.8	0.2
Other forms	0.6	6.8	3.5	1.3
Pampean zone[d] total	*3.2*	*40.7*	*36.0*	*20.1*
Exclusively owners	1.6	18.7	19.8	13.4
Sharecroppers and tenants	1.0	11.7	6.1	1.8
Mixed property	0.3	6.4	6.6	3.7
Fiscal lands	0.0	0.2	0.1	0.0
Other forms	0.4	3.7	3.4	1.2

[a] Holdings insufficient to satisfy the minimum needs of a family and not enough to fully utilize productively the labor of the family throughout the year.
[b] Holdings sufficient to maintain a family at a satisfactory standard of living using the labor of the family and the technical knowledge found in the area.
[c] Holdings requiring nonfamily labor for full use of the land, but not so much as to require a hierarchichal organization based on an administrator. In the pampean zone, for example, medium multifamily units are those using on the average from 4 to 12 workers. The minimum size of multifamily units in the pampean zone fluctuates between 200 and 1,000 hectares (see the source cited, pp. iv, v, and 33).
[d] A smaller area than the five pampean provinces used in other tables.

Source: Comité Interamericano de Desarrollo Agrícola, *Tenencia de la Tierra y Desarrollo Socio-Económico del Sector Agrícola: Argentina* (Washington, D.C.: Unión Panamericana, 1966), pp. 23 and 32.

percent of all rural land was in holdings directed exclusively by owners and was of family size or medium multifamily size (see notes to Table 3.20 for definitions of these terms). In the pampean zone. a subset of the five pampean provinces, this figure amounts to 38.5 percent. The study puts forth as a plausible hypothesis that half of the rural land is exploited inadequately due to land tenure considerations.[55] The study also notes a tendency toward the subdivision of large pampean estates although it asserts that the trend is relatively slow.[56]

55. Ibid., p. 21.
56. Ibid., p. 36.

Inadequate land tenure is made up of minifundia, too small to be efficiently operated (estimated at about 3 percent of all land); of holdings of appropriate size but with unsatisfactory and unstable tenancy arrangements (20 percent of all land); and of large estates, latifundia, in which land is not being fully exploited (25 percent of all land.)[57]

The study finds that multifamily farms have lower capital/land and labor/land ratios than family farms and, therefore, their output/land ratio is only about two-thirds that of family farms. On the assumption that fertility is the same for all size holdings in each agricultural zone considered in the study (seven within the pampean region), it is concluded that, on average, multifamily holdings are inadequately exploited and administered. Although this study understandably could not go into full detail on the issue of fertility differences between large and small farms within a given rural zone, it refers to evidence supporting the hypothesis that no significant fertility differences exist.[58]

Although doubts about land quality in different size holdings qualify these results, it appears that net output per acre is not maximized on land held in large estates. Just how much rural stagnation this alone can explain will be discussed subsequently.

Tenancy conditions are also blamed for low increases in output. Here, though, blame is not placed on historical favoritism plus laissez-faire, as in the case of size distribution, but on government control of the market for leasing land. Rent contracts were frozen "temporarily" during World War II, and, with sporadic adjustments,

57. Ibid., p. 21. The last group is said to have 35 percent of all land; this is presumably a misprint. Even the figure of 25 percent for latifundia seems large when compared with the 18/20 percent in large multifamily size holdings given in pp. 23 and 32 of the same work. On the other hand, Arthur L. Domike has pointed out to me that the use of permanent labor as the criterion for classification threw many large multifamily units into smaller size categories. Furthermore, the existence of multiple unit ownership and artificial subdivisions indicate that land ownership may be substantially more concentrated than what is indicated by data on holdings. Domike thinks that the real figure for large estates in which land is not being fully exploited could be anywhere between 25 and 35 percent of all rural land.

58. Other studies based on the 1960 census confirm that output per hectare declines as the size of the holding increases. See Table 113 in the Statistical Appendix. This table also shows that the concentration of cattle raising in large estates, and grains (especially maize) in small farms was maintained at least until 1960.

that custom has been continued until the present.[59] Inflation rapidly lowered the real value of frozen cash rents, inducing tenants to hold on to leased land from which they could not be removed except by mutual agreement. Before the war the usual practice was to rotate between grains (tenant), and alfalfa and cattle (owner). Afterwards monocultivation by tenants became widespread, especially in maize; this led to soil exhaustion. Fear of future freezes on new contracts kept many owners from renting to new tenants. The risk of losing control over their land weighed more heavily than foregone rents. Between the 1947 and 1960 censuses, the number of sharecroppers and tenants in the pampean zone decreased by 70,000, or 58 percent of those existing in 1947; the percentage of rural land in the pampean provinces owned by producers jumped from around 40 to more than 60 percent. A good share of land transferred from tenants to owners probably returned to large landowners, who often gave tenants favored with frozen contracts special payments inducing them to leave. As late as 1965, the Consejo Nacional de Desarrollo stated that "the market for long term tenancy contracts is practically non-existent and only short term contracts have prospered." [60]

The destruction of the market for long-term tenancy contracts represented a setback for rural growth-promoting arrangements. Soil exhaustion and reduced investments were two natural results of these misguided policies. The tendency of large landowners to favor land-intensive cattle and grassland over labor-intensive crops was reinforced. Pre-1943 arrangements, from the point of view of rural growth, were clearly preferable to those prevailing after 1943. Argentine stalemate politics are well illustrated by this issue; in an attempt to increase the income and security of tenants and share-croppers, partial measures were taken that did not give them full land ownership but were sufficient to induce economic inefficiency and to reduce rural investment by landowners. After more than twenty

59. This situation may be changed by the military regime that took power in 1966.

60. CONADE, *Plan Nacional de Desarrollo,* p. 441. The plan recommends tenancy contracts of a minimum of ten years, to encourage investments by tenants and as a hedge against unfavorable weather conditions. Since 1955 some tenants benefiting from frozen contracts purchased, with credit granted by public banks, the lands they tilled. Low limits on compensation to tenants for their permanent improvements have had, by themselves, a negative impact on capital formation and technical change.

years of these laws the only clear result is a decrease in rural efficiency
with no large permanent effects on land ownership.

In summary, landholding has been far from ideal for growth
during the last thirty-five years. This has been due only in small part
to classical Latin American latifundia. More importantly, public
land policies worsened rural flexibility and dynamism. Furthermore, it
is not warranted to blame only deficiencies in land tenure for rural
stagnation. This may be seen by the following calculation for pampean
production of traditional exportables, that remained almost constant
between 1935–39 and 1960–64. Even granting that half of pampean
land is affected by inadequate landholding yielding zero output
growth,[61] we could have expected, with reasonable policies, a 2
percent growth of traditional exportables, forthcoming from a 4
percent output growth in the pampean half held in good forms of
tenure. There must be other factors explaining why even the good
half of pampean land failed to increase its production.

Doubts also may be expressed about the assumption that once the
pampean zone had been fully brought under cultivation, all further
increases in the output of traditional exportables had to come from
yield increases. Recent evidence suggests that non-pampean lands
can contribute significantly to the output of those commodities. The
supply of land fit for traditional exportables is indeed upward sloping,
but not perfectly price inelastic.[62]

Output would benefit not only by a rebirth of a market for long-
term tenancy contracts, but also by the imposition of heavier taxes
on land. Ideally, these taxes would be levied on potential land

61. Output in the livestock sector, where large estates are more prevalent
than in crop raising, showed a larger rate of expansion than pampean exportable crops of cereals and linseed after 1935–39. In spite of postwar tenancy
regulations, it is doubtful that on balance all rural output produced in large
estates could have shown an absolute decline after 1935–39; cereal and
linseed no doubt declined, but their place was usually taken in those holdings
by livestock. Some nonpampean rural activities that have shown satisfactory
growth since 1925–29 are produced under systems of land tenure more
regressive than those of the pampean zone. It should be noted that the argument
asserting that large, but price-taking, landowners do not maximize profits (or
when land is fixed, sustainable net output or value added per acre), does not
by itself explain output stagnation if the gap between potential and actual
profits is a constant.

62. See CONADE, *Plan Nacional de Desarrollo,* p. 41. The north of Santa
Fe and Entre Ríos, and parts of Chaco, Formosa and Corrientes are considered
the natural frontier of the pampean zone, especially for wheat, corn, and
oilseeds. That land under cultivation had changed little since 1930 does not
say much about the shape of this supply schedule.

productivity so as to penalize failure to maximize net output per acre. During the last thirty years the real value of rural property taxes has decreased in many pampean areas. The rural sector has been taxed via export and import levies, or equivalent schemes, whose incidence on output has been more negative than what could have been expected from land, or even property, taxes. Not only are land taxes more efficient than those on rural commodities; they may also provide a formula for reconciling policies desirable for economic efficiency, such as export promotion, with what urban Argentine society considers a fair distribution of income and political power, i.e. minimizing the economic and political weight of traditional landowners.[63]

Technological change

Improvements in the quality of traditional rural inputs and the application of new ones account for a large part of rural output increases that have occurred in North America and Western Europe during the last thirty years. This technological advance gained momentum in the United States during the 1930s when rural prices were unfavorable; it continued even as real rural prices showed a downward trend.[64] The private rural rate of return, in other words, has been maintained close to those in other sectors of the economy, not so much by price policy, nor by keeping rural wages low, but by cutting unit costs thanks to technological progress. It is reasonable then to review Argentine efforts to stimulate technological change, given the price policy and landholding pattern that prevailed after 1930. Al-

63. The precise degree of economic and political influence wielded nowadays by rural landlords is far from clear. Rural value added during recent years has fluctuated around only 17 percent of GDP at factor cost. Furthermore, a recent study on income distribution observes: "In the upper income category no single wage and salary group is important, this income category being dominated by the self-employed. Several groups are individually important among the latter, but perhaps the most important point to note here is that, although there are substantial numbers of large-scale farmers and cattlemen in this highest income bracket, even in Argentina the most common source of high incomes is not the agricultural sector. As is shown in the table, most of the highest incomes are earned in commercial or industrial enterprises." See "Income Distribution in Argentina," *Economic Bulletin for Latin America* 11, no. 1 (April 1966): 121. The power of landowners seems to be based mainly on the rural contribution to exports and on social prestige from old glories. One cannot help but conclude that on this issue many social commentators and critics are fighting the battles of years gone by.

64. On the other hand, few productivity gains were made in the U.S. rural sector during the prosperous period of 1900–30.

though recognizing that both the aggregate demand and supply for technological improvements are not independent of price policy and land tenure, this section will regard public policy on research and extension services as exogenous and, in the light of experience in other countries, of critical importance for achieving rural productivity gains.

Data on public and private research and extension services and on rural education are scarce. There is a lack of studies on the Argentine rural sector, which is amazing in view of its importance in the economy.[65]

Before the 1956 creation of the Instituto Nacional de Tecnología Agropecuaria (INTA), public research and extension services were grossly inadequate. Five research stations were created in 1912, of which the one in Pergamino became leader for pampean products.[66] Research on wheat was conducted from 1912 on; late in the 1920s aspects of corn and linseed cultivation were also studied. Research was concentrated almost wholly on seed improvement, neglecting agricultural economics and other technical aspects of production. Public and private research on livestock was practically nil, in spite of the influence and wealth of cattle ranchers. Fresh impulse was given to the Pergamino station in 1937, at which time it had only one professional on its staff. Beginning in 1949, however, the Peronist neglect of agriculture was extended to rural research; the Pergamino station, which had 14 professionals in 1949 lost half of them shortly afterwards.[67] Little was done by the public sector to check and control such obvious problems as hoof-and-mouth disease. In contrast, by 1962 the Pergamino station, now part of INTA, had 40 research technicians, 47 extensionists, and 5 professionals in auxiliary services. The INTA regional group embracing the whole pampean zone, including the Pergamino station, had 106 researchers and 129 extensionists by June 1959. Of the research technicians, 68 had been incorporated since the creation of INTA; the corresponding figure for those in extension services is 111.[68] The early INTA years were de-

65. This deficiency is being remedied, however. A large number of Argentines are now being trained in agricultural economics, especially in the United States.

66. See INTA, *Estación Experimental Agropecuaria Pergamino, 1912–1962* (Buenos Aires, n.d.), pp. 1–10.

67. By 1947 an Argentine agricultural engineer, Antonio Marino, had developed two promising hybrid varieties of corn. His efforts were ignored by the public sector because of his political views.

68. Centro Regional Pampeano de Tecnología Agropecuaria, INTA, *Memoria Técnica 1955–1959*, vol. 7 (Buenos Aires, n.d.), pp. 4–7. In 1963 the

voted primarily to organization, so that only recently have its efforts begun to pay off in productivity gains. Nevertheless, it is already a widely respected institution.

Private research and extension services were very modest before 1956, especially during 1940–56. Few companies were established to supply modern rural inputs (tractors, improved seeds, fertilizers, pesticides, etc.) and high import duties and controls in most cases eliminated the possibility of buying them abroad. Under these conditions, there was little that private salesman, who in earlier years had acted as disseminators of new techniques, could do.[69] Since 1956, private efforts in this field have increased. Factories with a vested interest to promote new techniques have been set up and associations of producers have been created to disseminate new operation methods in both agriculture and livestock.

In rural education a similar picture emerges, as suggested by Table 3.21. Taking into account that the average length of studies before a

Table 3.21: University and High School Graduates in Rural Sciences
(Yearly averages)
Degrees Conferred by Universities in Argentina

	1910– 20	1921– 30	1931– 40	1941– 45	1946– 50	1951– 55	1956– 60
Agronomy	13.1	33.6	41.2	105.8	126.4	139.4	127.6
Veterinary medicine	26.5	28.4	30.7	76.6	58.2	62.0	58.2

Graduates from Secondary Schools

	1951–55	1956–60	1961–63
Total: *Bachillerato Agrotécnico*	34	45	152
Three-year course	–	4	50
Five-year course	–	3	68
Six-year course	34	38	34

Sources: Ministerio de Educación y Justicia, "Enseñanza Media, Años 1914–1963" mimeographed (Buenos Aires, n.d.), 1:203, 217–20; Jane Turns, "Agricultural Development in Argentina," mimeographed, Washington, D.C., n.d., p. 78.

degree is obtained in agronomy or veterinary medicine is about six years, it appears that, after long neglect, there was an upsurge of

whole of INTA was estimated to have a total of 536 persons engaged in research and 385 persons engaged only in extension services.

69. In the case of at least one company, import controls on seed treatment and other handling equipment delayed postwar private research. See *Cargill News* (April, 1966), p. 3.

interest during the late 1930s and early 1940s, which was later dissipated. New interest in these disciplines has arisen since 1955, best indicated by the numbers of graduates from secondary schools; but only recently has the number of secondary school graduates approached what could be considered reasonable levels.[70] Special programs to train agricultural economists, previously nonexistent, have been initiated.

In summary, public support for rural research, extension, and education was exiguous before 1956. Although difficult to quantify, this neglect explains a good part of the poor rural performance since 1930.

The contrast between Argentine and United States technology may be illustrated by current manufacturing inputs into rural activities expressed as a percentage of the value of rural gross output. In the United States this statistic was 12.0 percent during 1958; the corresponding Argentine figure was only 5.5 percent in 1950. In the United States, chemical inputs represented 4.9 percent of gross rural output, while the Argentine figure was 0.3 percent.[71]

The use of modern current and durable inputs has been in part held up by excessive prices not reflecting true opportunity costs. For example, imports of fertilizers and fungicides paid duties of 40–60 percent as of July 1962. The postwar protective system no doubt hindered the rapid spread of new current inputs, as well as of rural machinery and equipment; but lack of the research necessary to adapt foreign innovations to Argentine conditions, and poor extension facilities for the dissemination of new techniques, must also bear a good share of the blame. Fertilizers illustrate this point. Argentine fertilizer consumption is one of the lowest in the world; for 1960–61, in terms of kilograms per hectare cultivated, the figures

70. By 1963 the number of pupils registered in the *Bachillerato Agrotécnico* reached 2,352. See "Enseñanza Media, Años 1914–1963" (mimeographed Buenos Aires, n.d.), 1:217–20. INTA has devoted attention to the creation of 4-A Clubs for rural youth. According to INTA, there are 3,500 *Ingenieros Agrónomos* in Argentina, of whom 850 worked for INTA (in 1966). The Food and Agriculture Organization of the United Nations has estimated that Argentina needs 20,000 *Ingenieros Agrónomos* to meet current needs. See the *Review of the River Plate* 141, no. 3637 (April 29, 1967): 143.

71. Data obtained from input-output tables found in ECLA, 1:106, and U.S. Department of Commerce, *Survey of Current Business,* vol. 45, no. 9 (Sept. 1965): 34. Textiles (bags) and wood products account for about two-thirds of all manufactured current inputs into rural activities in Argentina during 1950. See also CONADE, *Plan Nacional de Desarrollo,* p. 190, for comparative figures in the use of plaguicides in Argentina and the U.S.A., during 1960–61.

were 39 for the United States, 21 for Australia, 8 for Canada, and 0.5 for Argentina (the same figure it had in 1949–50).[72] Their pampean use has been nil. Tests of the response of pampean crops to fertilizers have been undertaken only recently. With the present structure of rural industry and the externalities involved in this research, it is not surprising that private entrepreneurs have not filled up the research gap left by the public sector.[73] It is doubtful that reasonable fertilizer prices could *by themselves* substantially increase pampean productivity until extension agents (or salesmen) can show with a fair degree of certainty improved results from the application of fertilizers. Similar problems face the use of fungicides and other inputs.[74]

In spite of many years of public neglect, some of the technological advances made abroad managed to penetrate rural zones. Occasionally, domestic public and private enterprise also added to the fund of applicable knowledge.[75] Table 3.22 presents corn and wheat yields in Argentina and the United States during 1920–64 (as well as for Argentine linseed). Argentine wheat yields have generally kept up with those in the United States, but with corn this has not been the case. The explanation for this contrast may be that improved wheat seeds developed abroad could be used in Argentina without much additional research, while hybrid corn species developed in the United States could not be transferred directly.[76] At any rate, corn

72. See U.N., "El Uso de Fertilizantes en Argentina," E/CN.12/741 (mimeographed) (March 3, 1966), p. 3.

73. Ibid., pp. 24–25. Private entrepreneurs who produce fertilizers may be expected to contribute something to research and extension efforts, however. Early fertilizer tests by INTA have given mixed results.

74. The need in this field for enlightened government supervision, as well as support, has been illustrated by problems that arose when vaccines against hoof-and-mouth disease were first introduced. Some of these privately produced vaccines were defective and not only caused the loss of cattle but damaged the confidence of producers in health campaigns. It may also be noted that rural input prices are not always higher in Argentina than abroad. Richard Mallon has given the following examples of inputs cheaper in Argentina: windmills, spreaders, high-power sprayers, and benzene hexachloride.

75. New crops have also been introduced, improving the efficiency with which land and other inputs are used. This is the case, for example, of grain sorghum, which has shown extraordinary growth during the last 15 years. Attempts to measure technological change using data presented in Table 3.2 in regressions for rural production functions yield results that are not credible.

76. Other suggestions have been made to explain this contrast. Corn may be more sensitive to the application of fertilizer, an area where the Argentine lag has been great. Flint corn, grown in Argentina, may respond less satisfactorily to fertilizers. The unstable tenancy conditions existing in the corn

Table 3.22: Yields of Wheat, Corn, and Linseed in Argentina
and the United States, 1920–65
(Kilograms per hectare harvested)

	1920–29	*1930–39*	*1940–44*	*1945–49*	*1950–54*	*1955–59*	*1960–64*
Wheat							
Argentina	878	929	1,098	1,102	1,151	1,337	1,382
United States	939	844	1,098	1,061	1,123	1,475	1,592
Ratio	0.94	1.10	1.00	1.04	1.02	0.90	0.87
Corn							
Argentina	1,878	1,842	1,998	1,766	1,529	1,734	1,765
United States	1,684	1,572	2,077	2,322	2,523	3,213	3,896
Ratio	1.12	1.17	0.96	0.76	0.61	0.54	0.45
Linseed							
Argentina	710	668	654	645	692	597	660

Source: ECLA, *El Desarrollo Económico de la Argentina* (México, 1959), 2:20–26;
U.S. Department of Commerce, *Statistical Abstract of the United States, 1965*,
p. 651; DNEC, *Boletín Mensual de Estadística* (Washington, D.C., 1965), several
issues.

and linseed yields in 1960–64 were below those of 1920–39, while
those for wheat showed a 53 percent gain.[77]

There is evidence that the technological improvement led by INTA
is making progress, especially in the pampean zone. While in 1960
only 15 percent of pampean producers used herbicides, by 1965 the
proportion had increased to 54 percent.[78] Hybrid corn is spreading

---

belt of Argentina (as a result of the official freeze on rent contracts), and
the monocultivation that resulted, influenced the lag in yields. The higher
share of domestic consumption in wheat production may have induced Perón
and his successors to devote more attention to improving techniques of wheat
growing. Obviously, more research is needed to explain this contrast.

77. It is often pointed out that part of this yield increase may be due
simply to having a larger share of the wheat crop grown in higher quality
land, as area under wheat cultivation declined between those two dates.
Regional studies on wheat cultivation carried out in CONADE, however,
indicate that most of the apparent increase in the overall yields is indeed the
result of increases in yields of individual zones. Lucio Reca has estimated
that only about 7 percent of the increase in wheat yields can be credited
to changes in location. His research also confirms the decline in the yields
for corn and linseed, and indicates a lack of technical change in livestock
activities since the 1930s. See his "The Price and Production Duality within
Argentine Agriculture, 1923–1965" (Ph.D. diss., University of Chicago, 1967),
pp. 96–97. Corn yields suffered slightly from changes in location of output.
In spite of public neglect, average yields for the seven most important
pampean crops in 1962–64 were higher than in Australia, except for corn. See
D. F. Fienup, "Argentina: The Sleeping Giant" (mimeographed, n.d.), p. 64.

78. Estimates of Italconsult Argentina S.A., *Encuesta Entre Productores
Agropecuarios* (Buenos Aires, 1965), p. 19. Between 1956 and 1966 the consumption of fertilizers has more than doubled.

vigorously; while around 1956 the corn area using hybrid seeds was nil, by 1965 at least one-third of that area was employing hybrids. Hybrid corn has also encouraged mechanization by reducing losses involved in the use of harvesters.[79] Although the spread of hybrid varieties had not resulted, as of 1965, in sustained yield increases, it had offset yield drops arising from monocultivation and the loss of soil fertility. In some cases, however, faulty quality control over hybrid seeds may have reduced their effectiveness.

If 1935–40 yields are taken to equal 100, average yields for other important commodities have evolved as follows:[80]

	1941–46	1947–52	1953–58	1959–64
Sunflower	91	81	72	77
Barley	126	121	132	126
Oats	104	124	129	134
Rye	102	110	124	125
Cotton	116	110	106	111
Grapes	[no data]	100	94	95
Sugar cane	96	110	119	152

Advances may be noted in a few individual cases, especially during recent years (e.g. sugar cane). Not shown in the commodity list above are potatoes, whose yield has nearly doubled since 1960, thanks to INTA efforts.[81]

Large increases in rural capital have taken place since around 1955. For many of these investments, a neat separation between increases in physical capital and technological change is exceedingly difficult. Therefore, they will be considered in this section. Table 3.23 presents estimates for the most important items; even in the depressed years 1962–63, average gross investments in the selected items more than doubled those of 1950–52. Growth in the number of tractors has been spectacular; between 1952–54 and 1961–63 their number more than tripled.[82] To a large extent, that mechanization

---

79. Ears of hybrid corn line up in a more systematic fashion than those of nonhybrid varieties. According to one supplier of hybrid seeds, as much as 60 percent of Argentine maize was planted with high yield hybrid seed in 1966. See *Cargill News* (April 1966), p. 3.

80. Data obtained directly from Darrell F. Fienup, *Changes in Argentinian Agricultural Production and Productivity over the Past 25 Years* (Institute of Agriculture, University of Minnesota, n.d.), pp. 15–18.

81. Ibid., p. 16.

82. See CONADE, "Diagnóstico Preliminar del Sector Agropecuario" (mimeographed, Buenos Aires, 1965), p. 18. During 1937–39 there was an

Table 3.23: Gross Rural Investment in Selected Goods, 1950–63
(Yearly averages in million pesos at 1960 prices)

	1950–52	*1953–55*	*1956–58*	*1959–61*	*1962–63*
Fencing and watering systems	2,308	3,179	4,190	5,124	5,604
Domestically produced tractors	0	840	5,052	7,986	6,187
Other domestically produced equipment	5,951	7,902	12,144	20,053	20,023
Imported rural equipment	6,606	5,177	3,979	1,700	1,181
Total of items listed	*14,865*	*17,098*	*25,365*	*34,863*	*32,995*

Source: Unpublished CONADE worksheets.

has simply served to offset—but with a lag of about ten years—the impact on rural output of the drop in labor inputs that took place after the war. However, mechanization has been more than a substitute for labor; areas previously devoted to feeding horses have been freed for other uses, and tractors have increased the flexibility of planting and harvesting processes. Tractors and harvesters allow farmers to take full advantage of rains at planting time and to avoid losses due to unfavorable weather such as hail and rainstorms at harvest time. The use of tractors in plowing has also resulted in deeper penetration of the earth. Thus, it could be expected that higher and less variable yields will be forthcoming from greater mechanization. This mechanization has been accompanied by organizational changes improving efficiency in machine use. For example, an active market for renting agricultural machinery has reappeared in the pampean zone.

Some improvements have also taken place during recent years in the handling and storing of grains. Lack of storage facilities in farms and harbors has been a persistent problem for rural producers and exporters. In livestock management, larger investments in fencing and watering systems are being accompanied by more efficient operating methods.

---

average of 20,500 tractors in use; by 1946–48 there were only 10,400. The number recovered to 30,500 during 1952–54 and reached 102,600 during 1961–63. A guesstimate places the number of tractors in use in 1966 at around 140,000. On the other hand, the stock of horses has declined from 6.3 million in 1937 and 5.4 million in 1947 to 3.0 million in 1960. The stock of cars and trucks in the rural sector increased sharply during recent years. Generous tax incentives have stimulated the post-1955 expansion of rural capital. Heavily protected domestic producers of rural implements have enthusiastically supported this policy, whose cost to the Treasury has not been negligible.

All of these improvements, however, represent only a modest start in the task of catching up that faces the rural sector. Much remains to be done with fertilizers, hybrids, education, and rural credit. Progress should be made also in artificial pastures and livestock diet supplements, storage of livestock feed, artificial insemination (only 12 percent of pampean rural enterprises used it in 1965), sanitary controls and animal health, chemical inputs (plaguicides, etc.), and handling and storing of crops. Public rural policy is still made by several agencies coordinated only in the loosest fashion. Research and extension services, in spite of the remarkable record of INTA, as well as public market information services for farmers, are still far from ideal in number and quality.[83] Resources applied in these fields are likely to show high social rates of return.

The outlook for further technological change is promising.[84] A recent survey showed that 55 percent of interviewed pampean rural entrepreneurs indicated that their holding could be cultivated in a better way (higher yields could be obtained by greater use of machinery, permanent pastures, etc.); the same survey showed that 75 percent of the interviewed entrepreneurs are less than 54 years old and 43 percent, less than 44 years old.[85] The momentum and experience gathered by INTA, coupled with these characteristics of rural entrepreneurs, should produce substantial results in the near future.[86] Corn, one of the crops that suffered most since the war, is

83. Extension services, in particular, appear low relative to research. Government action could also help to damp the violent cattle cycles that have existed in the past. Better data on cattle stocks, improved information on market prospects and a flexible policy toward credit and domestic consumption of meat could help in this respect. Improved storage for cattle feed would also help to stem slaughtering triggered by lack of rain and deterioration of natural pastures. After surmounting initial difficulties, progress is being made in spreading the use of artificial pastures with the help of a large loan from the World Bank.

84. Average rural output during 1964–65–66 was 11 percent above the average for 1961–62–63. It is not yet certain what part of this increase was due to good weather and which could be due to capital deepening and technological change; the three factors seem to have played a part.

85. *Encuesta Entre Productores Agropecuarios,* pp. 28–29. Among non-pampean entrepreneurs 81 percent thought their methods of cultivation could be improved. The survey also shows that younger entrepreneurs use tractors, herbicides, and fertilizers to a greater degree than older producers. Even in the old-fashioned *estancias,* the risks involved in greater use of modern inputs (requiring larger working capital) may be taken, once research has reduced uncertainty regarding likely results from the use of these inputs.

86. It is sometimes argued that the production of temperate-zone foodstuffs has become one of the most capital-intensive activities and that, therefore, it

likely to witness yield increases similar to those registered in the
United States after the war. The rural technological lag which has
been evident since the 1930s may come to be considered, in a broad
historical view, a passing aberration.[87]

RURAL STAGNATION AND MERCHANDISE EXPORTS

Practically all exports before 1930 were of rural origin. Many were
processed domestically to an important extent, but there were few
other manufactured exports. One could expect, therefore, that slow
rural growth since 1930 had a negative influence on exports, especially because Argentina's exportables have a high and rather inflexible domestic per capita consumption. The close link between exports and rural output could have been broken by new manufactured
exports. But, as Table 3.24 indicates, the structure of exports has
remained remarkably steady since 1930, the main change being an
increase in the livestock share at the expense of those of cereals and
linseed, a change reflecting a similar switch in the structure of rural
output. It made the postwar structure of exports look more like that
of 1890–99, than that of the 1920s. In a more hopeful direction, the
share of other manufactured products shows signs of expansion in
recent years.

Table 3.25, showing export quantum indices since 1925–29, makes
even more melancholy reading than Table 3.24. In spite of a more than
50 percent increase from 1950–54 to 1960–64, the export quantum
in the latter period was not only below that for prosperous 1925–29,
but also below Great Depression levels. Cereals and linseed exports
during 1960–64 were about one-half what they had been in 1925–29.
During 1945–59, merchandise exports were, on the average, 32 percent below the 1925–29 level, and 28 percent below that of 1935–39.
Amidst this gloom, some positive developments may be noted: exports

should be left in the hands of countries such as Canada and the U.S.A. (see
The Economist of May 28, 1966, for an article expressing this point of view).
There is little doubt, however, that in spite of technological change, Argentina
maintains comparative advantage in the production of temperate-zone foodstuffs, thanks to her endowment of land.

87. The modernity of the pampean rural zone has never seemed greater
than in recent years. See, for example, Table 114 in the Statistical Appendix,
showing the small gap between the number of persons per automobile in urban
and nonurban regions of the pampean provinces. But in other fields, neglect
for the quality of rural life has not yet been remedied. Rural electrification,
for example, is still scanty.

of fruits and oilseeds (except linseed) and their products gained momentum during the 1930s and continued to expand throughout the postwar period. Some of these items began to be produced thanks to tariff protection and are examples of infant activities that did

Table 3.24: Structure of Merchandise Exports, 1928–64
(Percentages of the total)

	1928–29	*1935–39*	*1945–49*	*1955–59*	*1960–64*
All merchandise exports	*100.0*	*100.0*	*100.0*	*100.0*	*100.0*
Livestock products	*32.0*	*38.4*	*43.3*	*51.2*	*46.9*
Live animals	0.9	0.7	1.9	1.1	2.2
Meat	13.4	17.9	16.0	26.1	22.0
Hides	6.7	6.9	8.5	6.4	6.2
Wool	7.5	9.0	8.5	12.1	12.0
Dairy products	1.6	1.1	2.9	3.5	2.8
Livestock by-products	2.0	2.8	5.3	2.1	1.7
Agricultural products	*64.4*	*55.9*	*47.3*	*43.3*	*45.2*
Wheat	26.3	15.8	17.4	16.9	12.3
Corn	19.7	19.8	9.2	6.9	10.3
Linseed and other cereals	15.5	15.4	5.5	5.5	4.7
Flour and wheat by-products	1.8	1.9	1.4	1.6	2.0
Oilseeds and by-products	0.3	0.9	11.1	8.8	11.3
Fresh fruits and other agricultural products	0.9	2.1	2.8	3.5	4.6
Forestry products	*2.1*	*2.6*	*2.2*	*2.4*	*1.2*
Mineral products	*0.3*	*0.8*	*0.3*	*0.5*	*1.1*
Products from hunting and fishing	*0*	*0.4*	*0.4*	*0.2*	*0.4*
Other manufactured products	*1.3*	*1.8*	*6.5*	*2.4*	*5.2*

Sources and methods: Data obtained from several DNEC publications, mainly *Comercio Exterior*. For 1955–64, percentages were computed on the basis of dollar value; for earlier periods, peso values were used.

grow up. As another encouraging note, the export quantum for 1963–65 stood at 183 (1951–54 = 100), a level slightly above that for 1925–29, the first time an average for three consecutive years has yielded such result.

During the last few years, the geographical diversification of exports has been somewhat greater than before the war. While during 1927–29 the four top customers (United Kingdom, Germany, Holland, and Belgium) accounted for about two-thirds of all exports, in 1959–62 the four top customers (Italy now taking Belgium's place), took up only slightly more than half of all exports. But Western European integration threatens the gains from this diversification; "The Six" of

Table 3.25: Quantum Indices of Argentine Exports, 1925–64
(1951–54 = 100)

	1925–29	1930–34	1935–39	1940–44	1945–49	1950–54	1955–59	1960–64
Exports of goods and services	–[a]	–	161	130	128	105	126	158
Merchandise exports	179	167	167	135	133	106	124	160
Livestock products	152	132	140	162	163	109	140	157
Meat	201	158	175	241	186	105	183	183
Hides	130	107	117	215	120	114	132	144
Wool	123	124	137	127	174	108	104	133
Dairy products	144	125	72	142	136	101	135	140
Cattle by-products	210	167	104	223	191	121	134	148
Live animals	–	–	–	–	–	–	119	278
Agricultural products	212	211	200	90	96	103	113	149
Cereals and linseed	285	282	260	104	103	103	121	147
Fresh fruits and vegetables	25	22	45	41	61	94	–	–
Other agricultural products	23	34	43	63	91	112	–	–
Flour and by-products of wheat	–	–	–	–	–	–	125	194
Oilseeds and their by-products	–	–	–	–	–	–	102	152
Fresh fruits	–	–	–	–	–	–	145	228
Other agricultura products	–	–	–	–	–	–	47	78
Forestry products	127	119	114	78	98	104	64	60
Other products	122	74	150	622	382	102	180	705

[a] Homogeneous series are not available for the whole period. In most cases, however, very similar series are available for comparison.

Sources: Data for 1925–54 obtained from ECLA, *El Desarrollo Económico de la Argentina*, 1:115, and from unpublished ECLA work-sheets. Data for 1951–65 obtained from DNEC, *Comercio Exterior*, Informe C. 48 (April 1958), and the *Boletín de Estadística* of the same institution. Series were linked using 1951–54 = 100. Series for exports of goods and services obtained from BCRA, p. 14.

Table 3.26: Share of Argentine Exports in Total World Exports
of Selected Commodities
(As percentages of total world exports in physical quantities)

	1924–33	1934–38	1948–52	1959–63
001.1 bovine cattle (live)	—ᵃ	3.7	10.3	5.6
011 meat: fresh, chilled, or frozen	–	39.7	27.0	18.4
011.1 meat of bovine animals	57.6	56.0	38.2	31.2
011.2 meat of sheep and goats	24.7	14.1	13.7	7.4
011.3 meat of swine	1.2	10.2	14.2	4.5
011.4 poultry	–	–	{11.6	0.2
011.5–011.8 edible offal	–	–		19.5
012–013 meat: dried, salted, or smoked	–	12.7	14.6	8.6
023 butter	–	0.1	0.1	2.8
024 cheese and curd	–	0.5	2.1	0.8
041 wheat	17.7	23.1	9.3	5.8
043 barley	6.6	12.4	7.5	3.1
044 maize	64.9	64.0	23.5	16.8
045.1 rye	6.8	11.5	18.5	3.3
045.2 oats	34.4	41.3	13.1	16.2
046 wheat flour	–	3.6	0.4	0.4
051.4 apples	–	0.4	6.6	12.4
081.2 bran and milling by-products	–	–	–	33.5
EX081.3 sunflower seed, cake, meal	0	0	62.4	94.2
EX081.3 linseed, cake, meal	0	0	54.0	71.8
221.5 linseed	78.5	79.0	17.4	6.7
262.1 wool, greasy	{12.2	{11.8	{10.6	9.9
262.2 wool, degreased				11.4

ᵃ Dash indicates data not available.

Sources: Food and Agriculture Organization of the United Nations, *Trade Yearbook*, several issues; ECLA, *El Desarrollo Económico de la Argentina*, 2:48; Ruth Kelly, "Foreign Trade of Argentina and Australia, 1930 to 1960," *Economic Bulletin for Latin America* 10 (March 1965): 56. The numbers before each item refer to the United Nations Standard International Trade Classification.

the European Common Market still account for about 40 percent of Argentine exports. "The Six" plus the countries in the European Free Trade Area account for two-thirds of exports.[88]

Nothing said so far has been helpful in rejecting the hypothesis that lack of foreign demand led to a contraction of exports and thus

88. See Table 115 in the Statistical Appendix. A simple example of how increasing Western European integration may hurt Argentina is provided by beef consumption by tourists. French tourists now often consume Argentine beef in Italy and Spain, although they are not able to do so in their own country. As integration proceeds, this roundabout way of getting to the French consumer may disappear.

slowed rural growth. Indeed, for the 1930s and the first half of the 1940s, this hypothesis is more plausible than another blaming the slow growth of domestic production and a growing domestic demand for exportables for poor export performance. Table 3.26, presenting the Argentine share in world exports of key commodities, sheds light on this issue. Between 1924–33 and 1934–38, few changes took place in the most important Argentine shares; in some instances—wheat, barley, and oats, for example—the shares increased, in spite of protectionist and preferential schemes in North America and Europe. Trade-diverting Commonwealth arrangements, in particular, posed a severe threat to Argentine export shares. The postwar years witnessed a plummeting of major shares; only in a few cases were improvements recorded (e.g. apples, tea, tung, and sunflower products), while important items such as maize, wheat, and linseed suffered spectacular losses.[89] For commodities such as linseed and beef, losses in world trade shares underestimate Argentina's plight, as in those and similar goods, imports from Argentina were often substituted for domestic production rather than for imports from other countries. In view of these data, the main burden of responsibility for poor postwar export performance may be placed on domestic supply difficulties rather than on a lack of foreign demand.[90]

89. When linseed, its oil, and by-products are expressed in equivalent terms, Argentina's share of the combined product drops from 68 percent during 1934–38 to 56 percent in 1959–63. (It was reduced to 31 percent during 1945–49.) Misled by apparent market power in linseed world trade, the Argentine government attempted after the war to make all of its sales in terms of oil rather than linseed.

90. Immediately after the war, restrictions on the quantities exported were often defended on the grounds that such a policy would maximize exchange earnings by taking advantage of Argentina's market power. Experience has shown that, in spite of high shares in world trade, that market power was more apparent than real. In a given year, Argentine actions can no doubt raise world market prices for several commodities, but they will not be able to maintain such prices for very long. By 1959–63 the only major commodity in which Argentina could be said to have substantial long-run market power was beef. Even in this case, however, the delicate nature of the short-run market for chilled and frozen beef (which has led to private and public regulation of shipments) should not be interpreted as evidence of long-run market power. The ticklish nature of shipments of frozen and chilled beef has for many years soured relations between cattle raisers and Argentine public opinion, on the one hand, and meat-packing plants and exporters, on the other. Meat plants and exporters have been accused of exercising undue monopsony power, while taking monopoly profits at the level of British retail sales and at Argentina's loss. In spite of the figures shown in Table 2.26, pessimism regarding future market prospects for exports is distressingly prevalent among many influential Argentines. Often short-run marketing

What would have happened to the export quantum had Argentina maintained her prewar shares in world commerce? If Argentine export shares in six major commodities (wheat, corn, linseed, meat, wool, and wheat flour) during 1934–38 are applied to world exports during 1959–63, a quantum index is obtained (using 1934–38 weights), showing an average annual growth rate of 2.2 percent between 1934–38 and 1959–63, and a total increase of 73 percent. In reality, the export quantum *declined* between these two periods by about 9 percent. Recent Argentine economic history would have been quite different if export growth of between 2 and 3 percent per annum had been achieved since 1935–39.[91]

The supply of exports is simply the difference between the domestic supply of exportables and their domestic demand. Nearly half of rural output was consumed domestically during 1925–29; of agricultural output 44 percent went into domestic uses, while 56 percent of livestock goods were also absorbed internally. By 1955–59, 73 percent of rural output was consumed internally. To what extent has growth in domestic demand contributed to poor export performance? Table 3.27 presents data on apparent domestic absorption (production minus exports) of rural goods. Between 1920–29 and 1950–59, per capita absorption of agricultural goods grew, on the average, at about 0.7 percent per annum, while for livestock it grew at only 0.3 percent. The largest increases in domestic demand appear to have taken place for products with the least degree of exportableness, i.e. non-pampean crops. The expansion in domestic demand was far from uniform; the most rapid increases took place between 1935–39 and 1945–49, although for beef the expansion lasted until 1955–59. There was a tendency for domestic demand to flatten out and even decrease thereafter, especially for pampean crops.[92] Thus, although in

---

troubles (which could be handled by wise inventory and selling tactics) are used as an excuse for not seeking wider export markets. A product-by-product and country-by-country analysis of markets for Argentine exports will no doubt turn up foreign demand limitations (at reasonable prices). But the point is that throughout the postwar era such limitations have been far less important than supply limitations.

91. Although deterioration in the terms of trade played some role in postwar exchange crises, the collapse in the export quantum was the main villain.

92. The increase in apparent domestic absorption of pampean crops during 1940–44 is simply the result of shipping difficulties; it will be recalled that grains were used as fuel during those years in Argentina. As the propensity to spend on exportables is different for wage than for non-wage income, the

Table 3.27: Total and Per Capita Apparent Domestic Absorption
of Rural Goods, 1920–63
(Annual averages; 1945–49 average = 100)

	All agricultural goods			All livestock products	Beef	Wheat
	Total	Pampean	Non-pampean			
Total apparent						
absorption						
1920–24	46	–[a]	–	52	52	52
1925–29	51	–	–	60	67	78
1930–34	57	–	–	67	67	83
1935–39	71	73[b]	78[b]	77	78	111
1940–44	123	158	88	94	77	122
1945–49	100	100	100	100	100	100
1950–54	105	100	118	108	117	105
1955–59	127	121	135	116	131	128
1960–63	124	113	141	108	123[c]	109
Per capita						
absorption						
1920–29	77	–	–	87	93	103
1930–39	79	–	–	89	90	120
1940–49	117	135	98	101	92	116
1950–59	99	94	108	96	106	99
1960–63	93	85	106	81	93[c]	82

[a] Dash indicates data not available.
[b] Refers only to 1936–39.
[c] Refers only to 1960–62.

Sources and methods: ECLA, *El Desarrollo Económico de la Argentina*, 2:45–47;
data also from CONADE (and International Bank for Reconstruction and Development); Junta Nacional de Carnes (beef), and Junta Nacional de Granos
(wheat). "Apparent domestic absorption" is defined as domestic production minus
exports. It neglects changes in inventories and includes intermediate as well as
final uses of rural goods. Because part of non-pampean crops have replaced imports
during the period shown, the series may overestimate the expansion of domestic
demand.

individual years a failure to curb domestic demand for rural goods no
doubt aggravated the exchange situation, for the period as a whole
the growth in domestic demand is not excessive. Given the wage-good
nature of these commodities and their likely demand price elasticities,
it would have taken steep increases in their prices or severe contractions in wage incomes, or both, to keep domestic demand from rising

changes which have taken place in Argentine income distribution during the
last thirty years have influenced the demand for exportables.

at least as fast as population growth (2.5 percent per annum between 1925–29 and 1955–59). These policies can bring temporary balance of payments relief by depressing the domestic absorption of exportables (as during the last several years), but it is doubtful that they could be relied on to offset the balance of payments effect of rural output stagnation for very long. The social unrest of the last few years is closely linked to government attempts to depress domestic absorption of exportables. In the long run only a faster expansion in their production can provide a permanent solution to the exchange crisis.[93]

FINAL REMARKS

Domestic policies, including those on output and input prices and wages, a technological lag, and sluggish foreign markets—all had some influence on post-1930 rural stagnation. Quantification of these separate influences is a difficult task, and this essay has only scratched the surface of this problem. The task is important because, depending on the diagnosis of post-1930 performance, different policy conclusions may be reached. More research is clearly needed in several of the issues surveyed in this essay. Nevertheless, if one had to choose on the basis of available evidence the most important causes for the observed evolution of rural output, the best answer seems to be as follows.

During 1930–45, exogenous factors were the main cause for pampean rural stagnation. The slowdown in foreign demand and changes in relative prices, brought about first by the Great Depression and then by war, persuaded producers that the gains to be made from fresh investments in the production of exportable goods were exiguous. Non-pampean rural activities, however, responded to incentives for

93. The following indices present, in a highly summarized fashion, the evolution of total rural output and domestic absorption of rural goods:

	1920–29	*1930–39*	*1940–49*	*1950–59*	*1960–64*
Output	72	84	100	108	119
Absorption	50	65	100	109	111

Overall absorption of rural goods, as measured by this index, shows an average annual rate of growth of 2.6 percent between 1930–39 and 1950–59, hardly above population increase. Because of changes in the proportions of value added to exports by domestic processing, the correspondence among rural output, domestic absorption, and exports of goods of rural origin is not exact.

import replacement generated both by exogenous forces and government policy.

During 1945–55, domestic policies further depressed the outlook for rural activities producing exportables. Expected private rates of return were lowered not only because government policy kept their output prices low, but also because of increases in the rural wages necessary to keep labor away from large urban centers. Expectations and productivity were also unfavorably affected by disruption of established production patterns and property rights. These policies perhaps could have been overlooked, had the public sector encouraged rural research and extension services to keep up with advances taking place in the rest of the world, and had a flow of credit and reasonably priced modern inputs (including labor-saving machinery) been provided for the rural sector. A way would have been opened for producers to replace labor and maintain their profits by cutting unit costs; but little action of the sort was taken. Of all these unfortunate policies, the one having the most damaging long-run effect on the rural sector has been neglect of technological change. Price, wage, and other policies can be reversed fairly quickly, but years of neglect on the technological front are harder to make up. For this the public sector is mainly responsible, because, with the externalities involved in research and extension efforts and the nature of rural industry (large numbers of isolated entrepreneurs), private enterprise could not be expected to play, even under favorable conditions, more than a modest role, especially in the early stages of research.

Since 1955, rural prices have on the whole improved and so has the private rate of return in these activities. Availability of rural machinery has increased. Yet output expansion was small until 1964. In view of many years of unfavorable conditions, the technological lag, and erratic fluctuations in real prices and costs even after 1955, this disappointing result may not be very surprising. It suggests, however, the limits of output price policy in bringing, by itself, sustained rural growth.

The technological lag, in brief, may be taken as the most stubborn culprit for post-1945 rural stagnation. This diagnosis implies a hopeful outlook so long as INTA and similar organizations maintain their momentum of the last ten years. A sharp decline in rural relative prices, due either to domestic policies or to extremely protectionist Western European policies, could of course frustrate this favorable outlook by discouraging not only individual producers but also public efforts in rural research and extension services. In spite of threats arising from the European Common Market, foreign markets for Argentine rural goods look generally promising. Lack of demand at world prices similar to those prevailing during the early 1960s does not appear to be a barrier to rural output expansion at a rate of, say, 3 percent per annum during the 1970s. This relatively modest rate would be far superior to anything achieved since 1930; furthermore, the arithmetic implied by considering exports as the difference between production and domestic absorption, suggests that the likely growth rates of rural exports corresponding to that output expansion would also be highly satisfactory.[94]

94. It can be estimated that during 1960–65, 74 percent of the value of rural output was absorbed domestically. Thus, if domestic absorption is projected to grow at 2 percent per annum and domestic output at 3 percent, the quantum of rural exports would grow at 5.9 percent per annum. As mentioned previously, a high rate of growth in the export quantum has taken place since 1951–54, but such expansion appears to have relied heavily on a reduction in the per capita domestic absorption of rural goods as well as on recovery from unusually unfavorable weather.

4

Stages in the Industrialization
of Argentina

In the literature on developing countries, it is customary to point out that industrialization, especially when its main stimulus arises from import substitution, proceeds in several stages; easy manufacturing (light consumer good industries) is tackled first; in later stages increasingly complex activities are expanded. This process is supposed to receive impetus from the backward linkage effect of light industries and other activities that depend heavily on imported inputs at the start.[1]

This essay will examine the main features of Argentine industrialization to see whether it can be broken down into meaningful stages and to investigate causes for such a pattern.[2] Several dangers and snags present in the transitions from stage to stage will be stressed as a warning against excessive reliance on the automaticity of backward linkage. Discussion will be limited mostly to manufacturing;

1. See for example, Albert O. Hirschman, *The Strategy of Economic Development* (New Haven: Yale University Press, 1958), p. 112: "In fact, much of the recent economic history of some rapidly developing underdeveloped countries can be written in terms of industrialization working its way backward from the 'final touches' stage to domestic production of intermediate, and finally to that of basic, industrial materials." Professor Hirschman also warns against assuming automaticity in backward linkage and pointed out possible snags in the process.

2. The terms *stages, import substitution, light industry,* etc., are used in a purely descriptive way. It remains to be seen whether in the Argentine case one can talk about stages of industrialization in any other fashion than a purely descriptive one. Import substitution will be defined below. While the terms light, heavy, easy, complex, etc., are ambiguous when applied to industries, I doubt that labor-intensive, capital-intensive, etc., would be much better in a world with many kinds of labor and capital. It is difficult to capture the great variety of industrial products and activities, with their different cost conditions, with any of these labels, but some such attempt at classification appears unavoidable for descriptive purposes.

emphasis will be given to the structure of this sector, rather than its links with the rest of the economy.

Value added in manufacturing expressed as a share of GDP at factor cost has risen steadily, with only minor setbacks, throughout the twentieth century. During the first thirty years the advance was relatively slow: from 15 percent during 1900–04, it rose to 19 percent during 1925–29. The next thirty years witnessed an acceleration of this trend, and by 1957–61 this share had risen to 30 percent.[3] A first classification suggests itself—industrialization before and after 1930.

MANUFACTURING AND THE GROWTH OF THE ECONOMY
BEFORE 1930

During the first thirty years of this century, real GDP expanded at only a slightly higher rate than exports and imports; while from 1900–04 to 1925–29 real GDP grew at an annual rate of 4.6 percent, the export quantum grew by 4.1 percent, and the import quantum by 4.4 percent. If one bears in mind that between 1900–04 and 1925–29 the Argentine terms of trade seem to have improved, it may be stated that little change took place in the openness of the economy. Manufacturing, from which the bulk of any import substitution effort had to come, expanded at an annual rate of 5.4 percent, not enough to make a significant dent in the ratio of imports to GDP, given an income elasticity in the demand for manufactured products of more than one. It has been estimated that the ratio of imports to GDP was 26 percent in 1900–04 and 25 percent during 1925–29.[4] A somewhat greater degree of import substitution, defined with respect to changes in the aggregate ratio of imports to total production, appears if 1900–09 is

3. These percentages have been calculated on the basis of data expressed in 1960 prices. If quantum indices for manufacturing and GDP are evaluated at 1937 prices, the share of manufacturing in GDP would become 10 percent for 1900–04; 13 percent for 1925–29, and 20 percent for 1957–61. The 1937 relative prices were probably closer to present-day world relative prices than the 1960 price structure. Between predepression years and 1937 the relative prices of manufactured goods increased in Argentina, so that if it were possible to evaluate quantum indices at, say, 1929 prices, the manufacturing share in GDP would be further reduced. Basic data used to obtain these percentages come from CONADE, ECLA, and unpublished data for 1935–50 from CONADE.

4. See ECLA, Volume 1, p. 26. Data expressed in 1950 prices.

compared with 1920–29. A better idea of the nature of pre-1930 manufacturing may be obtained by disaggregating both imports and manufacturing and observing the importance of the former relative to domestic production, for different industrial branches. It should be noted that the sum of imports plus production (not value added), does not represent domestic absorption due to manufactured exports, which were important in the foodstuff and chemical industries, or due to inventory changes. Table 4.1 shows the great weight of manu-

Table 4.1: Merchandise Imports as a Percentage of the Value of Gross Domestic
Production Plus Imports
(Selected manufacturing branches)

	1900–04	1925–29
Foodstuffs, beverages, and tobacco	6	5
Textiles and clothing	55	45
Wood products	39	37
Paper and cardboard	25	31
Chemicals and pharmaceutical products	45	38
Petroleum refining	100	53
Rubber products	100	93
Stone, glass, and ceramics	15	27
Metals	87	65
Machinery, vehicles, and equipment, excluding electrical	92	79
Electrical machinery and appliances	100	98

Note: Data used in preparing this table are expressed in 1960 prices. The Industrial Census of 1914, p. 68, implied the following percentages of imported products in the total value of domestic consumption: foodstuffs, 9 percent; clothing and toiletries, 12 percent; construction, 20 percent; furniture, 30 percent; artistic and decorative objects, 37 percent; metallurgical and related products, 67 percent; chemical products, 62 percent; graphic arts, 14 percent; textiles, 77 percent.

Sources: As in Table 4.14.

factured imports, especially in the more sophisticated industrial branches, although even simple branches such as textiles show a high import coefficient.[5] Indeed, textiles, together with metals and metal

5. In ECLA, Volume 1, p. 27, it is estimated that consumer good imports represented 13 percent of total consumption in 1900–04 and the same percentage in 1925–29, while imported items amounted to 46 percent of total investment in machinery and equipment in 1900–04, and 35 percent in 1925–29. Imports of intermediate products relative to total final demand were 10 percent in 1900–04 and 8 percent in 1925–29.

products made up the main items in the import bill, as may be seen in Table 4.2.

Table 4.2: Structure of Merchandise Imports
(Percentages of total imports)

	1900–04	*1925–29*
Foodstuffs, beverages, and tobacco	5.0	5.3
Textiles and clothing	36.8	22.4
Wood products	10.5	7.4
Paper and cardboard	0.9	2.4
Chemical and pharmaceutical products	6.8	7.0
Rubber products	0.8	1.3
Metals	17.8	17.9
Machinery, vehicles, and equipment	10.6	20.6
Stone, glass, and ceramics	2.3	3.8
Petroleum products	0.7	3.5
Other manufactured products	3.4	3.3
Mining products	4.6	5.0

Sources and method: Estimated from import data found in ECLA, pp. 109–30. These data were reclassified into categories compatible with those used in later years, dividing imports according to industrial origin. Basic data are expressed at 1950 prices. Compare with data in Table 1.10.

A good part of pre-1930 manufacturing growth can be attributed to export expansion. Meat-packing plants, those processing dairy products, milling, wool-washing establishments, plants producing quebracho extract, etc., shipped a large part of their output abroad.[6] The construction and upkeep of the large railroad network, of other export-oriented social overhead facilities, and of housing and urban facilities for immigrants also stimulated manufacturing.[7] It may be estimated that before 1930, between 15 and 20 percent of the gross value of manufacturing production was directly exported. Even if the

6. In 1900, when the United Kingdom banned the importation of live cattle, there were only three major meat-packing plants. By 1914 their number had reached ten. On the other hand, the old salting plants declined. It may be estimated that expansion of meat-packing establishments accounted for 5 to 10 percent of net manufacturing investment between 1900 and 1929.

7. During their rapid expansion, however, railroads did not have as much of an impact on manufacturing as they did in other countries such as the United States. Most of the iron and steel products, and even wood products, required by the railroads were imported. Argentina, while rich in fertile land, has lacked easily accessible deposits of iron ore, coke, and other minerals. Lumber has been very scarce in the pampean zone since colonial days. Sources of hydroelectric power are also relatively few and far from urban centers.

value added by domestic industries to exported goods represented a smaller percentage of gross production value than in other sectors, it is reasonable to assume that at least 10 percent of pre-1930 manufacturing value added was directly linked to exports. In contrast with later periods, manufacturing expansion during 1900–29 may be explained mainly by the growth of exports and domestic demand, with a relatively small contribution by import substitution.

The light and export-oriented nature of manufacturing emerges from Table 4.3, which presents data from the 1914 census, expressed

Table 4.3: Structure of the Manufacturing Sector
According to the Industrial Census of 1914
(Percentages of total manufacturing)

	Value of gross output	*Employment*
Total manufacturing	*100.0*	*100.0*
Foodstuffs and beverages	53.3	34.5
Tobacco	3.2	1.8
Textiles	1.7	3.4
Clothing	7.9	10.5
Wood products	8.7	12.9
Paper and cardboard	0.6	0.8
Printing and publishing	2.0	3.1
Chemical products	3.2	2.3
Petroleum refining	0.1	0
Rubber products	0	0
Leather products	6.3	7.5
Stone, glass, and ceramics	3.8	7.5
Metals	6.3	9.9
Vehicles and machinery	1.4	2.6
Electrical machinery and appliances	0.4	0.8
Other manufacturing	1.0	2.3

Sources: Industrial Censuses for 1914, 1935, and 1946.

at current prices, and reclassified using modern groupings.[8] Food processing, clothing, wood and leather processing, stone, glass, and ceramics, and miscellaneous activities including a not very well defined

8. This reclassification, presented in the 1935 and 1946 censuses, is likely to be rough and ready. Table 102 in the Statistical Appendix also presents estimates of manufacturing structure obtained by projecting backwards value-added figures, expressed at 1960 prices, using gross output indices. The eleven most important activities listed in the Industrial Census of 1914, judging by number of employees, are also presented in Table 103 of the Statistical Appendix. Dairy products, bread making, and the making of suits and coats head the list.

number of handicrafts, dominated manufacturing. Within branches usually expected to provide the more technically complex plants (like the metallurgical industries), the bulk of production was carried out in small labor-intensive establishments (e.g. railroad repair shops). The most modern activities were found under food processing; examples include large meat-packing plants, breweries, flour and sugar mills. Match and cigarette making could also be placed in this group.

The structure of manufacturing was influenced by factor endowment, through backward and forward linkages. The prosperous rural sector induced an expansion of food processing, both for export and domestic consumption. Quebracho trees and oil extraction stimulated chemical and petroleum-refining industries—the former mainly for export and the latter for domestic use.[9] Plentiful and bulky supplies of hides and wool encouraged leather processing (also aided by domestic quebracho extract) and woolen textiles. The cultural preeminence of Buenos Aires, which together with Madrid and Barcelona constituted the most important cultural centers of the Spanish-speaking world, gave impetus to printing and publishing. Many books and magazines were exported; here we have a concrete payoff to post-1860 Argentine educational efforts. Lack of cheap coal, iron ore, and other minerals retarded the growth of metallurgical industries; even today Argentine steel output lags behind those of Mexico and Brazil.

The structure of aggregate demand also influenced that of manufacturing; in particular, the construction boom culminating in 1910–14 stimulated activities such as stone, clay and ceramics, and wood processing.

Table 4.4 indicates that light or traditional activities not only dominated manufacturing but also accounted for most of the *net increase* in manufacturing value added between 1900–04 and 1925–29. Metals, vehicles and machinery, and electrical machinery and equipment contributed less than 10 percent of the increase, while the contribution of textiles was also meager. It will be seen that 1925–29/

9. Processing of nonedible and edible oilseeds provide other examples of forward linkage from the rural sector to industry. According to ECLA, "around 1910 one-third of domestic needs of agricultural implements was supplied by the [Argentine] national industry. Later, around 1930, it was possible to install a petroleum refinery built almost wholly within the country." See Naciones Unidas, *El Proceso de Industrialización en América Latina* (New York, 1965), p. 15. I have translated from the original Spanish. Petroleum refining was begun in 1905; by 1928 there were 7 refineries, and by 1941 there were 19.

Table 4.4: Participation of Branches of Manufacturing in the Total Increase in Value
Added in Manufacturing, 1900–04 to 1925–29

(Percentages of the total increase in factor cost or value added in manufacturing)

	BCRA/ECLA	CONADE/ECLA
Total	*100.0*	*100.0*
Foodstuffs and beverages	34.3	27.5
Printing and publishing	12.2	12.2
Other manufacturing and handicrafts	9.8	13.1
Leather products	6.6	4.1
Chemical products	6.0	4.2
Clothing	5.8	7.5
Metals	5.5	6.4
Stone, glass, and ceramics	5.4	4.9
Vehicles and machinery	3.7	3.3
Textiles	3.0	3.8
Wood products	2.7	6.2
Paper and cardboard	2.2	2.7
Petroleum refining	2.2	3.4
Tobacco	0.6	0.7
Rubber products	nil	0.1
Electrical machinery and equipment	nil	nil

Sources and method: As in Tables 4.6 and 4.8.

1948–50 witnessed a dramatic expansion of the textile industry, while during 1948–50/1963–65 metallurgical activities provided the main impetus to manufacturing expansion.

A DIGRESSION: INDUSTRIAL ENTREPRENEURS BEFORE 1930

The 1914 census contained information regarding the nationality of owners of manufacturing establishments. To put this information in proper perspective it should be recalled that the same census showed that 30 percent of the population was composed of the foreign-born. In the greater Buenos Aires area, half of the population was foreign born.[10] Even in the light of these figures, Table 4.5 shows a surprisingly high percentage of foreign-born owners of industrial establishments.

10. See Gino Germani, *Política y Sociedad en una Epoca de Transición; de la Sociedad Tradicional a la Sociedad de Masas* (Buenos Aires: Editorial Paidós, 1962), pp. 185–88. In 1914, the foreign-born represented 43 percent of the total population between the ages of 15 and 65. See Table 1.15. Germani estimates that the foreign-born were 47 percent of the active population in 1914.

Table 4.5: Classification of Owners of Industrial Establishments
According to Nationality in the Census of 1914
(Percentages of total for each category)

	Argentine	Foreign-born	Mixed ownership
Processing of foodstuffs	38	58	4
Clothing, shoes, and toiletries	15	84	1
Construction and related industries	26	72	2
Furniture and related industries	24	74	2
Artistic and decorative objects	25	73	2
Metallurgical and related industries	20	77	3
Chemical products	24	66	10
Printing, publishing, and graphic arts	39	56	5
Textiles	91	8	1
Other	40	52	8
Total	*32*	*65*	*3*

Source: Obtained directly from the data of the Industrial Census of 1914, p. 242.

Most were individual immigrants, although an influential minority was made up of foreign companies with direct investments.

Although only 32 percent of all owners were Argentine, 51 percent of all industrial personnel had been born in the country. In contrast, according to the 1914 Rural Census, Argentines represented 74 percent of all administrators in cattle raising and 43 percent of all administrators in agriculture.[11]

The census of 1895 had shown a higher percentage of industrial establishments owned by foreigners; at that time only 19 percent of the establishments were owned by Argentines.[12] As late as 1935, native Argentines accounted for only 39 percent of all owners of industrial establishments.[13]

These figures lend some support to the thesis that pampean landowners, who were the most influential and wealthiest social group in the country, showed little interest in manufacturing. Even in industries closely linked to rural production and exports, such as meat packing, other food processing, and leather working, the direct participation of pampean rural interests was limited. Of the 231 establishments mak-

11. Rural Census of 1914 (Volume 5 of the General Census), pp. 309 and 837. In the category of agricultural establishments administered by their owners, 59 percent of the establishments belonged to Argentines. According to Germani, *Política y Sociedad,* pp. 193–95, 82 percent of all civil servants were native born.
12. Industrial Census of 1914, p. 37.
13. Industrial Census of 1935, p. 34. It has not been possible to examine the comparative size of establishments owned by foreigners and Argentines.

ing leather shoes in 1913, only 43 were owned by Argentines; of the 294 establishments making soap and candles, Argentines owned only 70; of the 18 meat-packing plants none was owned by Argentines; even in flour milling only 180 of the 401 establishments existing in 1913 were owned by Argentines while only 21 percent of the bread-making establishments were Argentine-owned. Immigrants, for whom the acquisition of land was not easy, provided the bulk of the early entrepreneurial talent in manufacturing and commerce. There are many examples of immigrant merchants, especially in the import business, gradually becoming manufacturing entrepreneurs using their commercial profits.

Argentine participation was highest in manufacturing activities that, because of their dependence on specific natural resources or a tradition of handicraft, were located far from Buenos Aires. This was the case in the sugar industry (centered in Tucumán, with 82 percent of Argentine-born owners), the wine industry (located primarily in Mendoza, San Juan, La Rioja, and Catamarca, with 48 percent of the establishments owned by Argentines), and wool spinning (primarily of a handicraft nature, practically an all-Argentine industry located in Salta).

From its earliest stages, however, manufacturing tended to concentrate around the main domestic market in the area of Greater Buenos Aires. The 1914 census showed that of all manufacturing personnel, nearly 61 percent was found in the Federal District and the province of Buenos Aires, while an additional 15 percent was found in the provinces of Santa Fe and Córdoba.

It has been suggested that the immigrant origin of industrial entrepreneurs and the slow integration of immigrants to political life retarded the formation of a strong industry party. Even to this day, these entrepreneurs are generally regarded as timid and unaggressive, not only in their business behavior, but in the political and social arena. They seem especially so when compared with rural entrepreneurs whose Argentine roots often go back to the early nineteenth and eighteenth centuries.[14]

14. See Oscar Cornblit, "Inmigrantes y Empresarios en la Política Argentina" (mimeographed, Di Tella Sociology Center), and Eduardo A. Zalduendo, "El Empresario Industrial en América Latina: Argentina" (mimeographed, U.N. document E/CN.12/642/Add.1). Cornblit suggests that the slow rate at which immigrants entered into political life was due to the open climate they found in Argentina; they saw no need to organize politically to defend their interests (as in the United States) because they were not usually threatened.

INDUSTRIALIZATION POLICIES BEFORE 1930

It is the nearly unanimous opinion of students of Argentine economic history that before 1930 public policy was either indifferent or hostile to the expansion of manufacturing, unless it was directly related to exports of goods of rural origin.[15] It is pointed out that landed interests producing for export took a dim view of import-substituting efforts, lest they hurt industries in foreign countries that were good customers of Argentina's grain and meat. Furthermore, it is argued that rural interests eyed with suspicion the creation of a new industrial class that could challenge their social position and compete as employers of labor. These attitudes gave rise to a low social status for industrial entrepreneurs not linked with exports.

Most authors assert that very little tariff protection was granted to manufacturing; indeed, some claim that the tariff structure was such that its net effect was one of discouraging domestic industries. Essay 5 shows that these assertions are not warranted by tariff history, at least during 1906–40. Although the average tariff height fluctuated considerably and its structure was far from rational, it was maintained on the whole at levels that afforded substantial protection to many activities. It remains true, however, that no comprehensive industrialization policy existed before 1930.

As in most countries before 1930, the Argentine government took few measures to favor manufacturing using special credit facilities, labor training in industrial skills, etc. Official banks centered their attention on short-term financing of commercial and rural enterprises. Yet the strong links between European and Argentine capital and labor markets provided facilities not available to most entrepreneurs of developing countries.[16]

15. Among the authors who take this position are Leopoldo Portnoy, *La Realidad Argentina en el Siglo XX: II, Análisis Crítico de la Economía* (México: Fondo de Cultura Económica, 1961); Aldo Ferrer, *La Economía Argentina* (México: Fondo de Cultura Económica, 1963); Tomás Roberto Fillol, *Social Factors in Economic Development: The Argentine Case* (Cambridge: M.I.T. Press, 1961); Guido J. M. Di Tella, "Economic History of Argentina: 1914–1933" (Ph.D. diss. M.I.T., 1960); Ricardo M. Ortiz, *Historia Económica de la Argentina*, 2 vols. (Buenos Aires: Editorial Raigal, 1955); Adolfo Dorfman, *Evolución Industrial Argentina* (Buenos Aires, 1942).

16. Many examples can be found of firms hiring skilled European workmen for the purpose of both training local labor and helping to run newly established industries. Heavy traffic between Europe and Argentina made these transactions relatively straightforward. See U.S. Department of Commerce, *The Textile*

Another important, though short-lived, influence on pre-1930 manufacturing may be mentioned, namely World War I. Although the removal of foreign sources of supply encouraged import substitution, the war hurt activities associated with exports and the construction of social overhead capital; exports, capital inflow, and labor immigration dropped. Furthermore, the war reduced substantially the external supply of some importables (e.g. coal and machinery), which could not be rapidly replaced by domestic inputs, and on which domestic activity vitally depended. On balance, the shaky data for this period show a drop in manufacturing output during 1914–17. The common opinion that the war boosted industrialization appears to be at best a very partial view.[17]

MANUFACTURING AND THE GROWTH OF THE ECONOMY
SINCE 1930

The role of manufacturing changed with the Great Depression. Before 1930, it was just one of the sectors participating in the expansion of the economy, but since 1930 the growth of the economy has depended heavily on the ability of import-competing manufacturing to expand. This dependence was thrust upon Argentina by exogenous factors during 1930–45, but in the postwar era it has resulted from domestic policies discriminating against exports.

While real GDP grew at an annual rate of 2.9 from 1925–29 to 1957–61, manufacturing expanded at an annual rate of 4.1 percent.[18]

Market of Argentina, Trade Promotion Series, no. 132 (Washington, D.C., 1932), for an example involving the importation of German workmen to train Argentine operators of full-fashioned hosiery machines. During its early years of rapid expansion, in the nineteenth century, the rural sector also relied on European farmers and ranchers for know-how.

17. Di Tella and Zymelman have suggested that during World War I the larger and more modern firms expanded and prospered, while handicrafts and small-scale firms suffered under the recession that developed early during the war and from the cessation of the capital inflow into construction activities that had benefited many small firms in metallurgy and stone, earth and ceramics. See Guido Di Tella and Manuel Zymelman, "El Desarrollo Industrial Argentino Durante la Primera Guerra Mundial," *Revista de Ciencias Económicas* (Buenos Aires, April–June 1959), pp. 222–24.

18. These figures are based on data of CONADE, for 1935–61. By using data available in BCRA, p. 18, lower growth rates are obtained, as follows:

	1925–29/1957–61	*1925–29/1961–65*
GDP at factor cost	2.7 percent	2.6 percent
Manufacturing	3.7 percent	3.6 percent

In this essay, 1957–61 will often be used as the terminal period because some of the CONADE series are not available for more recent years.

Since the export quantum showed a *decline* between these two periods of more than 25 percent, manufacturing producing solely for domestic absorption must have expanded at a faster rate, in a strenuous import substitution effort, reflected in a decrease in the import quantum between 1925–29 and 1957–61 of more than 23 percent. Merchandise imports, which during 1925–29 represented around 25 percent of GDP, amounted to only 8 percent in 1957–61.[19]

Of the increase in real GDP between 1927–29 and 1963–65, *measured at 1960 prices,* 41 percent came from the expansion of manufacturing value added and only 10 percent from rural growth. In contrast, of the increase in real product between 1900–04 and 1927–29, 24 percent originated in agriculture, livestock, and fisheries, and 26 percent in manufacturing. In relative terms, manufacturing was more important in raising output (valued at postwar prices) after 1930 than before. But it is sobering to examine what happens when output indices are valued, even roughly, at 1937 prices. For 1927–29 until 1963–65, the manufacturing share in the GDP increase falls to 22 percent, while that for the rural sector increases to 11 percent. For 1900–04 until 1925–29, the manufacturing share falls to 15 percent, and that for the rural sector goes up to 27 percent. Although a greater role is maintained for manufacturing after 1930, that gain measured at 1937 prices shrinks and becomes less than the loss in the rural share. Relative prices for manufactured goods, which had already risen between 1929 and 1937, rose much further during and after the war.

The manufacturing expansion beyond what would have taken place if it had grown only at the same rate as GDP, was caused primarily by import substitution. Although data do not warrant a precise calculation, it may be estimated that as much as 90 percent of the more than proportional manufacturing growth between 1925–29 and 1959–61 can be accounted for by the reduction in the import coefficient in the total supply of manufactured products, i.e. by import substitution.[20]

19. These percentages have been estimated on the basis of 1950 prices. At current prices, the corresponding figure for 1957–61 is 10 percent.

20. Thus, import substitution is defined as a (negative) change in an import coefficient. However, this definition is not unambiguous due to aggregation problems. For example, the ratio of imports of a good to the total supply of that good may *decrease* for all goods in the economy and yet the overall ratio of imports to total supply may *increase.* Changes in weights, of course, would account for this result. It will be seen below that in the Argentine case it is important to bear in mind this aggregation problem. It seems that the best definition of import substitution is that which starts with the most disaggregated data available. It obtains the total picture of import substitution

Demand factors accounted for more than the residual 10 percent, but this expansionary force was almost offset by the less than proportional growth (indeed, by the absolute decline) in the export of manufactured and processed goods (most of them of rural origin, such as meat).

The remarkable drop in the export quantum between 1925–29 and 1957–61 placed an excessive burden on import substitution, because it required not only a drop in the ratio of imports to GDP but also an absolute decline in imports. Although in the long run the expansion of much of manufacturing takes place at the expense of potential imports, in the short run attempts to expand the growth rate of manufacturing and the whole economy result in a greater demand for imported raw materials, intermediate products, and capital goods. If a certain level of exports is given, this demand is likely to lead to balance of payments difficulties and a slowdown of economic expansion. If, for simplicity, it is assumed that manufacturing can be identified with the import-competing sector, and that all imports are made up of manufactured products, the short and long run relationship between imports and domestic manufacturing may be expressed as follows:

$$m = By - f \qquad (4.1)$$

In this simplified equation, m stands for the real value of imports, B the short-run marginal (and average) propensity to purchase importable-type goods, y the real level of total expenditure, and f the value of the domestic production of import-competing goods. In the short run, the maximum value for f is limited by existing capacity and therefore the marginal propensity to import will be equal to B, which is likely to be a high number, causing severe exchange pressures. In the long run, however, the growth of f will reduce imports.[21]

STAGES IN THE INDUSTRIALIZATION SINCE 1930

An analysis of growth since 1930 has to examine not only the reasons

by summing up the individual results rather than relying on the aggregate coefficient.

21. For an elaboration of the short-run difficulties faced by a country attempting to increase the growth rate of its import-competing sector see my "On the Import Intensity of Import Substitution," *Kyklos* 18 (1965), Fasc. 3, 495–509. It is estimated that the (short-run) income elasticity of demand for imports in Argentina during 1947–62 was nearly three. See essay 7 of this book.

for the decisions to allocate resources among agriculture and livestock, manufacturing, and services but also those regarding resource allocation within manufacturing. Given the decisions regarding rural exportable goods, it becomes of critical importance to adopt a manufacturing structure making overall growth compatible with payments equilibrium. If one assumes a desired growth rate and a given level of exchange earnings, arising not only from exogenous factors such as world prices for exports but also from domestic policies toward exportables and foreign capital, the required expansion of manufacturing would follow from the income and price elasticities of demand for manufactured goods and the fraction of exchange earnings available to import those goods. As demand can be supplied either by imports or domestic production, it would appear that, while for the whole of manufacturing the growth rate compatible with the desired goals is inflexible, for each of its branches no such rigidity would exist. Slower expansion and resultant higher imports for some branches could be offset by faster growth and lower imports in others. In other words, although the exchange constraint calls for an overall import-substitution effort, it may be carried out in different ways. Different manufacturing branches may be given a greater or smaller role at different stages. Of course, the economic efficiency of each alternative will be different.

Branches growing at a faster rate than that indicated by the domestic income elasticity of demand will sooner or later succeed in eliminating from the import bill the goods they produce, and, unless export markets are found or internal demand shows high elasticity with respect to their relative prices, their future growth will be limited by the income elasticity of demand. Continued expansion will then depend on the ability of the economy to shift smoothly from one leading sector to another. Failure to do so will be reflected in exchange difficulties, forcing a reduction in the growth rate. The further industrialization proceeds and the more branches exhaust their import-substituting possibilities, the smaller will be the flexibility allowed to this type of policy and the greater the danger that lagging branches could give rise to excessive import demand.[22]

Tables 4.6 and 4.7 present annual growth rates in the gross output of the main manufacturing branches from 1925–29 to 1963–65. Be-

22. Other reasons contribute to a lack of flexibility: the growing technical complexity of new import-substituting industries, their high capital intensity, and the strategic importance of remaining imports, among others.

Table 4.6: Average Annual Growth Rates of Real Gross Output in Manufacturing,
1925–61 (ECLA and CONADE)
(Percentages)

	1925–29/ 1937–39[a]	1937–39/ 1948–50	1948–50/ 1959–61
Total manufacturing	3.4	5.0	3.7
Foodstuffs and beverages	2.1	2.6	1.1
Tobacco	0.5	4.9	1.5
Textiles	10.8	9.1	0.8
Clothing	−0.4	4.4	0.7
Wood products	−2.2	6.4	0.1
Paper and cardboard	−1.7	6.3	4.4
Printing and publishing	−2.2	2.3	−0.2
Chemical products	−0.4	7.7	6.5
Petroleum refining	12.6	5.0	6.7
Rubber products	39.0[b]	3.0	7.1
Leather products	−2.2	7.2	0.9
Stone, glass, and ceramics	−2.5	6.3	2.5
Metals	5.1	5.4	7.8
Vehicles and machinery, excluding electrical	8.3	8.3	10.6
Electrical machinery and appliances	40.5[b]	8.7	17.6
Other manufacturing	0.1	5.1	3.9
Handicrafts	–[c]	3.7	0.4

[a] Different weights would clearly yield very different total growth rates for
1925–29/1937–39.
[b] Production was negligible during 1925–29.
[c] Dash indicates data not available.

Source: Data from CONADE for 1937–61; as in Table 2.1 for 1925–37.

cause of the instability of the Argentine economy, growth rates have
been computed comparing averages for three- or five-year periods.
For post-1935 years two major data sources are available; substantial
differences exist between them for some periods (especially 1937–
39/1948–50) and for some branches. As there are no strong reasons
to choose one source over the other in all discussions, both are
presented.[23] The post-1930 years have been subdivided into four

23. The discrepancies arise more from differences in classifications and
methodology than from basic data. Both efforts to revise indices of industrial
production have been handicapped by lack of a recent census. The last reliable
census of manufacturers available is that taken in 1954; the census taken in
1963 was not completed by the time BCRA and CONADE prepared their new
industrial data. They relied on ad hoc sectorial information in lieu of more
systematic sources. The reader should not need to be reminded again about
data difficulties. It would have been desirable to calculate the structure of
manufacturing using different price bases. Detailed price data, however, are not

Table 4.7: Average Annual Growth Rates of Real Gross Output in Manufacturing,
1937–65 (BCRA)
(Percentages)

	1937–39/ 1948–50	*1948–50/ 1959–61*	*1959–61/ 1963–65*
Total manufacturing	3.9	3.6	3.3
Foodstuffs and beverages	0.4	1.0	2.6
Tobacco	4.3	1.6	3.4
Textiles	8.3	0.6	1.4
Clothing	4.7	−1.4	−1.0
Wood products	4.3	2.3	0.9
Paper and cardboard	5.9	4.4	4.0
Printing and publishing	−0.2	2.7	1.3
Chemical products	6.6	5.4	6.5
Petroleum refining	4.7	6.4	7.8
Rubber products	5.2	7.1	3.1
Leather products	5.1	2.3	−7.7
Stone, glass, and ceramics	5.7	2.5	1.8
Metals	4.1	6.5	6.9
Vehicles and machinery, excluding electrical	9.1	7.3	7.4
Electrical machinery and appliances	9.3	15.5	0.1
Other manufacturing and handicrafts	4.8	2.0	−1.2

Source: As in Table 4.8.

periods: 1925–29/1937–39; 1937–39/1948–50; 1948–50/1959–61, and 1959–61/1963–65. The last two are separated simply because one source lacks data for the more recent years; the other subdivisions are based on considerations regarding industrial policy and the overall evolution of the economy.

Tables 4.8 and 4.9 show that the growth pattern for the different branches has been irregular. This irregularity could have been expected

available. Hugh H. Schwartz has estimated that between 1945 and 1955 manufacturing grew at more than 7 percent a year, a rate far above those emerging from CONADE and BCRA data; see his Ph.D. thesis at Yale University, "The Argentine Experience with Industrial Credit and Protection Incentives, 1943–1958," Appendix M. His weights are different from those of BCRA and CONADE. See Table 136 in the Statistical Appendix for a comparison of indices of manufacturing output for the critical 1943–50 period. Data difficulties exist for earlier periods also; for example, although Table 4.6 indicates a negative growth rate for paper and cardboard, other sources refer to a rapid expansion of the paper industry between 1931 and 1939. See *Anuario Geográfico Argentino*, p. 345, where it is stated that the number of paper plants went from 11 in 1928 to 35 in 1939. Also puzzling is the case of stone, glass, and ceramics during 1925–29/1937–39, as cement production increased at the impressive annual rate of 17.9 percent during 1928–38.

Table 4.8: Structure of the GDP at Factor Cost in Manufacturing,
1925–65 (BCRA/ECLA)
(Percentages of total)

	1925–29	*1937–39*	*1948–50*	*1959–61*	*1963–65*
Total manufacturing	*100.0*	*100.0*	*100.0*	*100.0*	*100.0*
Foodstuffs and beverages	36.6	37.3	25.4	19.2	18.7
Tobacco	0.8	0.7	0.7	0.6	0.6
Textiles	2.9	7.4	11.7	8.4	7.8
Clothing	6.9	5.4	5.9	3.4	2.9
Wood products	3.2	2.1	2.1	1.9	1.7
Paper and cardboard	1.9	1.3	1.6	1.8	1.8
Printing and publishing	9.8	6.3	4.0	3.6	3.4
Chemical products	5.7	4.4	5.8	7.1	8.0
Petroleum refining	1.6	4.9	5.3	7.2	8.4
Rubber products	nil	0.8	1.0	1.4	1.4
Leather products	6.5	4.2	4.7	4.1	2.6
Stone, glass, and ceramics	6.9	4.3	5.1	4.6	4.3
Metals	4.5	6.4	6.5	8.8	10.1
Vehicles and machinery	2.9	5.6	9.6	14.1	16.5
Electrical machinery and appliances	nil	1.1	2.0	6.6	5.8
Other manufacturing and handicrafts	9.6	7.9	8.7	7.3	6.1

Sources and method: Data for 1937–65 from BCRA, pp. 26–27. Figures for 1925–29 were obtained projecting backward BCRA data for 1937–39 using ECLA indices, found in ECLA.

during 1925–29/1937–39, when the economy was adjusting to the decline in real exports and capital inflow, while pushing ahead with import substitution. Activities closely linked with processing rural goods for export either declined or grew slowly, while branches dominated by import-substituting activities, such as cotton textiles, rubber tires, petroleum and its refining, expanded vigorously.[24]

The industrial expansion from 1937–39 to 1948–50 was the fastest of the three eleven-year periods and also the least irregular, although even then the various branches showed substantially different growth rates. That spread became more marked during 1948–50/1959–61; while the metallurgical industries grew rapidly, the more traditional

24. Some activities in food processing also derived impetus from import substitution. Edible oils, rice milling, fruit and tomato canning, and processing are examples of import competing food industries, located mainly in non-pampean provinces, whose rapid expansion was accompanied by an equally impressive growth in corresponding crops. On the other hand, meat packing, flour milling, etc., declined or stagnated.

Table 4.9: Structure of the GDP at Factor Cost in Manufacturing,
1925–61 (CONADE/ECLA)
(Percentages of total)

	1925–29	1937–39	1948–50	1959–61
Total manufacturing	100.0	100.0	100.0	100.0
Foodstuffs and beverages	29.3	29.3	23.3	17.5
Tobacco	0.9	0.7	0.7	0.6
Textiles	3.7	9.1	14.2	10.3
Clothing	8.9	6.8	6.6	4.7
Wood products	7.4	4.7	5.5	3.7
Paper and cardboard	2.4	1.6	1.9	2.0
Printing and publishing	9.8	6.1	4.7	3.1
Chemical products	4.0	3.1	4.2	5.5
Petroleum refining	2.5	7.4	4.5	6.2
Rubber products	nil	1.4	1.2	1.7
Leather products	4.0	2.5	3.3	2.4
Stone, glass, and ceramics	6.2	3.8	4.4	3.9
Metals	5.3	7.3	7.8	11.9
Vehicles and machinery	2.6	4.9	7.1	14.4
Electrical machinery and appliances	nil	0.8	1.2	4.9
Other manufacturing	2.3	1.8	1.9	1.9
Handicrafts	10.6	8.5	7.6	5.3

Sources and method: Basic information as in Table 4.6. Data on value added (factor cost) for 1960 was projected backward using output indices, on the assumption that the relation between gross output and value added has remained constant. (This assumption seems to have been made in the preparation of BCRA data presented in Table 4.8.)

industries tended to stagnate. By the end of the period under study, the structure of manufacturing was quite different from that of 1925–29, as shown in Tables 4.8 and 4.9. The metallurgical industries, which in 1925–29 represented less than 10 percent of manufacturing value added, by 1959–61 had increased their share to about 30 percent. Chemical products and petroleum refining expanded theirs from about 7 to 13 percent, while textiles jumped from 3 or 4 percent to 8 or 10 percent. Rubber products went from practically nothing to nearly 2 percent. All other branches declined in relative importance between 1925–29 and 1959–61. This secular change in manufacturing structure did not always proceed in a smooth and continuous fashion; thus, the share of textiles peaked during 1948–50, while several activities whose share declined between 1925–29 and 1937–39, saw theirs rise between 1937–39 and 1948–50, and once again fall after 1948–50. Leather, stone, glass and ceramics, wood, and clothing are in

Table 4.10: Relative Growth Trends within the Manufacturing Sector

	Apparent income elasticity of domestic demand	Sectorial annual rate of growth divided by annual rate of growth of GDP	
		1937–39/ 1948–50	1948–50/ 1959–61
Foodstuffs and beverages	0.6	0.7	0.4
Tobacco	0.5	1.4	0.6
Textiles	0.5[b]	2.6	0.3
Clothing	0.6	1.3	0.3
Wood products	0.3[b]	1.8	[a]
Paper and cardboard	1.7	1.8	1.7
Printing and publishing	−0.2[b]	0.7	[a]
Chemical products	3.0	2.2	2.5
Petroleum refining	2.7	1.4	2.6
Rubber products	2.6	0.9	2.7
Leather products	1.2	2.1	0.3
Stone, glass, and ceramics	1.4	1.8	1.0
Metals	2.9	1.5	3.0
Vehicles and machinery, excluding electrical	4.1	2.4	4.1
Electrical machinery and appliances	5.8	2.5	6.8

Note: The income elasticity of apparent demand has been obtained by regressions that use per capita apparent domestic absorption for each branch (value of domestic production plus imports minus exports) as the dependent variable and per capita GDP as the only independent variable for the years 1937, 1939, and 1946–61. Due to difficulties in disaggregating the export data, only exports from the foodstuff and beverages and chemical categories were taken into account. These exports, however, make up the bulk of exports of processed and manufactured goods and include meat, hides, dairy products, flour, and livestock by-products (all included under food and beverages); linseed and sunflower oil and quebracho extract (chemical products).

[a] Less than ±0.1.
[b] These coefficients have *t* ratios of less than 2. The *t* ratio for the textile coefficient is 1.8 (with 16 degrees of freedom). All others have *t* ratios greater than 2.

Sources: Basic data sources are CONADE for manufacturing and overall output (listed in previous tables). Imports as in Table 4.14. Estimates of exports based on data of DNEC, *Comercio Exterior*, and *Boletín Mensual de Estadística*, several issues.

such a category according to at least one of the sources of data used.

The relative performance of different branches may also be viewed comparing their annual growth rates with that for the economy as a whole, and with the *apparent* ex post income elasticity of demand for different types of manufactured products. The income elasticity of demand is said to be apparent not only because of data roughness, but also because the estimated demand functions neglect relative prices, income distribution, and availability of some durable goods. Changes in tastes, biases due to introduction of new products, and similar factors are also neglected. With the use of CONADE data, this comparison is worked out in Table 4.10.[25] It covers the period 1937–39/1959–61, thereby avoiding the early adjustment of the economy to the depression.[26] The comparison of the apparent income elasticity of domestic demand (including final as well as intermediate demand) for the products of each of the branches, with their output-growth elasticities, indicates how fast import-substitution advanced in each sector during different periods.[27]

During 1937–39/1948–50 it was primarily the lighter branches of manufacturing that showed output-growth elasticities greater than the apparent income elasticities of demand. Such was the case for foodstuffs and beverages, tobacco, textiles, clothing, wood products, print-

25. For 1935–50, CONADE manufacturing data appear superior to those of BCRA. This comment, however, is based only on the apparent reasonableness of the estimates, plus casual checking against industrial censuses.

26. Data on industrial production and imports (the latter required to calculate apparent consumption) are also more reliable starting in 1935–39.

27. By following the notation of Equation 4.1, the precise relationship of these variables can be expressed as follows (assuming for simplicity no exports of manufactured products and that overall output and income grow at the same rate):

$$\hat{m}/\hat{y} = 1/x(E_d - E_s \cdot z) \tag{4.2}$$

The "hats" in Equation 4.2 indicate rates of growth; E_d and E_s represent the income elasticity of domestic demand for manufactured products and the output-growth elasticity, respectively; while x and z represent the original share of imports and domestic production in the total domestic absorption of manufactured products, so that $x + z = 1$. When $E_d = E_s$, the ex post long run income elasticity of demand for imports ($\hat{m}/\hat{y}$) will equal that common elasticity. The rate of growth of imports will be positive in this case so long as both $\hat{y}$ and the common elasticity are positive. If E (the common elasticity) is greater than one, the import coefficient will rise. Defining import substitution as a fall in the import coefficient, we obtain the following condition for it to take place:

$$E_s > \frac{E_d - x}{1 - x} \tag{4.3}$$

Equation 4.3 shows that for import substitution to take place E_s must be higher than E_d by a margin that becomes greater, the greater the original value of x (the imported component of domestic demand). If one is given the value of x, the greater E_d, the greater the required margin by which E_s must exceed it to result in import substitution.

ing and publishing, and leather products. On the other hand, such key branches as electrical machinery and appliances, vehicles and machinery, metals, petroleum refining, rubber products, and chemicals grew at relative rates lower than the income elasticity of demand for their products. A simple comparison of output growth rates would show that the latter group, on the whole, grew faster than the lighter industries; but the important comparison is the one dealing, for each branch, with the apparent income elasticity of demand and the output-growth elasticity. Although import-substitution advanced during this period in the lighter branches, it lagged in those producing mainly capital goods and heavy intermediate products.[28] Further disaggregation of the somewhat heterogeneous categories used would strengthen this conclusion.

The lag was not noticed during the immediate postwar years, when plentiful foreign exchange made possible the importation of these goods. But beginning around 1949, Argentina was faced with severe exchange difficulties. Machinery and equipment as well as some key intermediate products and processed raw materials became progressively scarcer. By that time, the light branches had nearly exhausted their import-substitution possibilities, thus eliminating a possible source of exchange savings. To obtain the capital and intermediate goods required for economic expansion, exportables had to be encouraged and/or the lagging industrial sectors had to be given greater stimulus. The gap between the output-growth elasticities and the income elasticities of demand was reduced or eliminated during 1948–50/1959–61 for metallurgical industries, as well as in other branches producing intermediate goods. Even then, high income elasticities of demand for the output of these activities and special needs for capital goods maintained great pressure on imports, generating periodic payments crises. On the other hand, industries that had expanded vigorously during 1937–39/1948–50 stagnated after 1950.[29]

Two well-defined stages may then be seen in post-1930 manufac-

28. In using Table 4.10 it should be remembered that part of the output of foodstuffs and beverages and of chemical products was exported. It should be clear, furthermore, that because of the nature of the data as well as the conceptual difficulties, the figures in Table 4.10 are not meant to be used as precise calculations of import trends. These comparisons can be viewed as contrasting two subperiods with a longer period that is the sum of them.

29. As will be discussed below, changes in income distribution also influenced the relative growth of different branches of manufacturing during 1935–61.

turing growth, cutting across political regimes. Those phases are brought out in Tables 4.11 and 4.12 presenting the *increase* in value added by manufacturing branches expressed as percentages of the total *increase* in manufacturing value added. During 1925–29/1948–

Table 4.11: Participation of Branches in the Total Increase in Value Added in Manufacturing, 1925–29 to 1948–50
(Percentages of the total increase in factor cost or value added in manufacturing)

	BCRA/ECLA	CONADE/ECLA
Total	*100.0*	*100.0*
Textiles	21.6	23.7
Vehicles and machinery	17.1	11.3
Foodstuffs and beverages	12.7	17.8
Petroleum refining	9.5	6.3
Metals	8.7	10.0
Other manufacturing and handicrafts	7.5	6.3
Chemicals	5.9	4.3
Clothing	4.6	4.4
Electrical machinery and appliances	4.2	2.3
Stone, glass, and ceramics	3.2	2.8
Leather products	2.6	2.6
Rubber products	2.0	2.2
Paper and cardboard	1.2	1.4
Wood products	0.9	3.8
Tobacco	0.6	0.6
Printing and publishing	−2.6	0.1

Sources and methods: Basic data as in Tables 4.6 and 4.8.

50, textiles, foodstuffs, and beverages accounted for between 34 and 42 percent of the total expansion; after 1948–50, the same branches represented between 11 and 9 percent of output growth. On the other hand, the metallurgical sector (metals, vehicles, all machinery, and electrical appliances), which during the first stage contributed only between 24 and 30 percent of the overall expansion, after 1948–50 provided between 53 and 62 percent of it. Other light branches whose relative contribution during 1925–29/1948–50 exceeded substantially their post 1948–50 participations include clothing, leather products, and other manufacturing and handicrafts.[30] The opposite was the case

30. This latter category is very heterogeneous; it is likely that some of the discrepancies between CONADE and BCRA are explained by different ways of classifying activities in the borderline between handicrafts and food processing, leather and wood products, clothing and textiles.

Table 4.12: Participation of Branches in the Total Increase in Value Added
in Manufacturing, after 1948–50
(Percentages of the total increase in factor cost or value added in manufacturing)

	1948–50/1963–65	1948–50/1959–61
	BCRA	CONADE
Total	*100.0*	*100.0*
Vehicles and machinery	26.6	29.1
Metals	15.4	20.1
Petroleum refining	13.1	9.4
Electrical machinery and appliances	11.4	12.3
Chemicals	11.2	8.3
Foodstuffs and beverages	8.8	5.8
Stone, glass, and ceramics	3.0	2.8
Printing and publishing	2.5	−2.0
Other manufacturing and handicrafts	2.3	2.6
Paper and cardboard	2.1	2.3
Textiles	2.1	2.7
Rubber products	2.0	2.7
Wood products	1.0	1.5
Tobacco	0.4	0.3
Leather products	−0.4	0.7
Clothing	−1.5	1.0

Sources and methods: As in Table 4.11.

with such relatively complex activities as chemicals and petroleum refining.[31]

Similar conclusions are reached if the sources of import substitution are examined for 1937–39/1948–50 and 1948–50/1959–61 (also using CONADE data). Denoting by m' the import component of the sum of domestic production plus imports for *each* manufacturing branch, net import substitution in that branch may be expressed as follows:

$$(m'_1 - m'_2)(m_2 + f_2) \tag{4.4}$$

The subscripts $_1$ and $_2$ denote different time periods; for example, they could refer to 1937–39 and 1948–50. As before, m and f denote imports and domestic production, respectively.[32] The sum of import

31. The two post-1930 phases of industrialization have also been noted and discussed by Aldo Ferrer in his *La Economía Argentina* (México: Fondo de Cultura Económica, 1963), especially in chapters 14 and 15 and pp. 239–58.

32. This approach was developed by Hollis B. Chenery, "Patterns of Industrial Growth," *American Economic Review* (1960), p. 640. This methodology yields misleading results in cases where the consumption of certain commodities is postponed (e.g., they are neither produced domestically nor im-

substitution in all branches may be taken as total manufacturing import substitution.[33] Table 4.13 presents the contributions of different

Table 4.13: Net Import Substitution of Branches of Manufacturing
(Percentages of total import substitution in manufacturing)

	1937–39/ 1948–50	*1948–50/ 1959–61*	*1937–39/ 1959–61*
Primarily traditional consumer goods industries	*60.0*	*15.1*	*31.0*
Foodstuffs and beverages	8.6	0.9	4.2
Tobacco	1.2	0.9	0.9
Textiles	40.4	9.9	20.1
Clothing	−0.1	1.5	0.6
Wood products	6.1	1.5	3.0
Printing and publishing	0.3	−0.1	0.1
Leather products	0.9	0.0	0.4
Other manufacturing	2.6	0.5	1.7
Primarily new and intermediate and capital goods industries	*40.0*	*84.9*	*69.0*
Paper and cardboard	3.1	3.0	3.0
Chemicals	13.7	2.3	11.4
Petroleum refining	−2.2	8.2	1.9
Rubber	0.2	−1.7	−0.6
Stone, glass, and ceramics	2.8	2.8	2.5
Metals	10.2	18.7	15.7
Vehicles and machinery	9.4	31.8	22.3
Electrical machinery and appliances	2.9	19.8	12.7

Sources and methods: As described in the text.

sectors to import substitution in manufacturing. These results are similar to those obtained earlier; the burden of import substitution before 1948–50 was carried by textiles and other light branches, while since 1948–50 more than two-thirds of manufacturing import substitution came from metallurgical industries. If one takes 1937–

---

ported, as in the case of automobiles in Argentina during 1939–58, neglecting relatively unimportant levels of imports and domestic production). A greater degree of disaggregation could help to isolate at least the most outstanding cases of postponement, which could then be treated separately to keep biases from creeping into the results via aggregation. It has not been possible to do that. These calculations of import substitution represent only a convenient descriptive device of past economic history; by themselves they say nothing about the efficiency of the process.

33. This procedure, of course, gives a different result than if total import substitution had been computed using the aggregate ratio of imports to total absorption.

Table 4.14: Merchandise Imports as a Percentage of the Value of Gross
Domestic Production plus Imports, 1925–61

	1925–29	*1937–39*	*1946–49*	*1950–54*	*1955–59*	*1960–61*
Mining plus manufacturing	*35*	*22*	*16*	*12*	*11*	*12*
Mining	*80*	*61*	*53*	*58*	*61*	*32*
Manufacturing	*34*	*22*	*15*	*10*	*9*	*11*
Foodstuffs and beverages	*5*	5	2	2	2	2
Tobacco		11	7	2	0	1
Textiles	*45*	44	15	8	5	4
Clothing		3	3	1	0	0
Wood products	37	32	18	16	16	17
Paper and cardboard	31	40	30	21	17	18
Printing and publishing	—ᵃ	1	1	0	1	1
Chemical products	38	40	19	14	14	15
Petroleum refining	53	16	22	16	14	10
Rubber products	93	12	22	12	14	18
Leather products	—ᵃ	3	1	0	0	0
Stone, glass, and ceramics	27	18	9	8	3	3
Metals	65	46	37	25	21	22
Vehicles and machinery	79	49	43	29	23	25
Electrical machinery and appliances	98	56	22	21	8	9
Other	49	41	31	17	18	20

Note: Nonmining imports include produce and raw materials some of which are not manufactured; due to difficulties involved in the precise classification of these items, they were placed together with manufactured imports, e.g. banana imports are under foodstuffs and beverages. The sum of imports plus gross domestic output will inevitably include some double counting, e.g. imports of chemical products used by the chemical industry appear twice in that sum.

ᵃ Data not available or of doubtful reliability.

Sources and method: Estimates of the value of gross domestic output by main branches of the manufacturing sector obtained as follows: for 1937–61 the indices of gross output (1960 = 100) have been multiplied by the 1960 values, expressed at 1960 market prices. Post-1937 data were obtained from CONADE: published for 1950–61, pp. 198–99; unpublished for 1937–50. Those indices were linked with those found in ECLA, p. 11, to obtain 1925–29 figures. (It should be noted that when this procedure is followed the sum of the individual branches does not add up to the total value obtained directly from indices.) Merchandise imports, in categories similar to those for manufacturing output, were obtained from data found in Oficina de Estudios para la Colaboración Económica Internacional, *Importaciones, Industrialización, Desarrollo Económico en la Argentina* (Buenos Aires, 1963) 2:308–11. Indices and shares in total imports were translated into 1960 prices using the value c.i.f. in pesos of merchandise imports in 1960, according to DNEC. For pre-1935 value of imports, these data were linked with those found in ECLA, pp. 109–30, after having reclassified them into the standard industrial categories.

39/1959–61 as a whole, vehicles and machinery have the largest contribution, being closely followed by textiles.

The advance of import substitution in different branches may be observed directly in Table 4.14. Between 1937–39 and 1946–49 the drop in the imported share of textiles is spectacular, while that for metals, vehicles, and machinery is more modest.[34] Under policies discouraging exports and foreign capital, the required evolution in import shares for payments equilibrium was not one of simple constancy or even modest decline, but one of sharp reduction. In terms of the notation of equation (4.2) for imports of a given category to remain *constant* (i.e. $\hat{m} = 0$), the following condition must be met:

$$E_d/E_s = z \qquad (4.5)$$

If, for example, the original share of domestic output in total domestic absorption (z) is very low, say 0.2, the output growth elasticity (E_s) will have to be five times the size of the income elasticity of demand (E_d), for imports to remain constant in absolute amount. At the end of a period characterized by these features, the import coefficient will have declined substantially, its decline being greater, the higher the output growth rate and the higher the original ratio of imports to domestic absorption.[35]

The use of import coefficients of the type shown in Table 4.14 calls for several words of caution in the Argentine case. The *overall* import coefficient is simply a weighted sum of individual coefficients; changes in weights may lead to peculiar results. Compare, for example, the coefficients for 1950–54 with those for 1960–61. Most branches show reductions in their coefficients and, with the exception of rubber products, those showing an increase do so weakly. Yet the overall manufacturing coefficient shows a rise between 1950–54 and 1960–61. The apparent paradox disappears when it is noticed that seven branches that had the lowest import components during 1950–54 (foodstuffs and beverages, tobacco, textiles, clothing, print-

34. The instability of imports, even more marked than that of output, makes it advisable to take 4- and 5-year averages whenever possible.
35. With the additional notation, $s = m + f$, we can write for the case when $\hat{m} = 0$:

$$\frac{d(m/s)}{dt} = -[m/s] \cdot \hat{s} = -\hat{f}(z - z^2) \qquad (4.6)$$

It will be recalled that z (the share of domestic output in total absorption) takes on values between 0 and 1.

ing and publishing, leather, and stone, glass, and ceramics) accounted for 54 percent of output plus imports during 1950–54, but only 42 percent during 1960–61. On the other hand, the four branches with the highest import component during 1950–54 (paper and cardboard, metals, vehicles and machinery, and electrical machinery and appliances) saw their share in total manufactured supplies rise from

Table 4.15: Gross Output Indices of Manufacturing Activities
Showing the Fastest Rates of Growth during 1946–64
(1960 = 100)

	1946–49	1950–54	1955–59	1960–64
Soft drinks (1.9)	28.9	36.9	68.2	112.6
Biscuits and crackers (0.1)	50.0	60.8	85.0	126.7
Fish processing (0.2)	42.4	69.1	73.9	112.9
Socks and stockings (1.1)	38.3	33.9	49.6	99.0
Spun artificial silk (1.2)	46.4	71.8	114.3	99.5
Soap, excluding toilet soaps (0.5)	49.6	66.2	94.5	101.0
Perfumes (0.9)	41.0	47.3	79.6	101.2
Pharmaceutical products (1.4)	34.0	51.5	79.0	92.5
Other chemical substances and products (0.8)	35.2	45.6	76.1	101.2
Plastic products (0.8)	24.3	33.3	69.0	125.5
Petroleum refining (6.3)	41.3	61.0	85.7	117.7
Rubber footwear (0.6)	33.8	61.6	91.9	89.2
Cement (1.3)	49.8	61.0	84.2	105.4
Machine-made bricks (0.2)	37.3	61.0	103.7	96.0
Iron wires (0.3)	28.7	47.0	88.7	98.7
Screws, bolts, etc. (0.4)	48.8	63.1	88.1	96.4
Iron pipes and tubes (0.8)	16.0	31.4	73.5	98.6
Products of copper and bronze (1.0)	41.2	51.3	88.2	93.6
Iron and steel (4.6)	24.3	42.4	89.5	145.7
Lead and tin products (0.8)	40.1	48.7	95.5	91.8
Bicycles and motorcycles (1.3)	5.0	7.3	52.2	66.4
Non-electrical machinery and engines (4.1)	23.4	39.4	74.6	89.1
Auto, truck and bus repair (3.3)	44.6	64.3	82.7	129.5
Manufacture of automotive vehicles (2.8)	0	2.0	16.2	143.2
Manufacture of tractors (1.0)	0	0.1	45.3	72.3
Batteries (0.2)	36.7	66.2	79.1	134.9
Lamps and electric bulbs and tubes (0.1)	33.4	47.9	82.0	106.4
Electrical motors (1.8)	9.2	34.2	76.6	112.9
Radio and television equipment (1.2)	9.9	14.4	44.5	89.4
Other electrical machines and products (1.6)	15.8	36.1	96.3	80.3

Sources: Unpublished CONADE worksheets. The activities listed represented about 43 percent of the value of total manufacturing output in 1960. Data for 1963 and 1964 are provisional.

22 percent in 1950–54 to 35 percent during 1960–61.[36] With this change in demand structure, it is conceivable that the overall import share could have risen even while every one of the individual shares declined. (Similar effects may have taken place *within* each of the branches listed in Table 4.14.)

What accounts for this modification in the structure of demand for manufactured goods? Changes in income distribution offer a partial explanation. The postponement of some demands, enforced by import control and industrial policies, also explains the stagnation and later upsurge of supplies of several goods, especially some durable consumer goods and machinery. The behavior of traditional exports as well as changes in tastes (in the sense of shifts in preference maps), contributed to the decline of several activities in food processing and beverages. Finally, pure income elasticities of demand, following universal patterns, tend to be highest for the products of branches with highest import components.[37]

CONADE data on manufacturing output are based on information about nearly one hundred activities (of differing weight and importance). Tables 4.15 and 4.16 present the thirty activities showing the smallest and largest rates of gross output expansion during 1946–64. The figures in parentheses after each activity indicate its weight in the index for overall manufacturing output, reflecting its contribution in 1960. Although some of the fastest growing activities come from the more traditional branches, such as food and beverages and textiles, more than half come from the metallurgical industries, and the rest are dominated by new products such as plastics and artificial silk. Of important weight are petroleum refining, iron and steel, non-electrical machinery and engines, establishments for repair of automotive vehicles, and the motor vehicle industry. In 1955 Argentina

36. See Table 104 in the Statistical Appendix.

37. Smuggling may have also depressed the observed import component of such branches as textiles and tobacco. But it is doubtful that even if smuggling could be taken into account, their import coefficients would rise to the levels of those for metallurgical branches.

Table 105 in the Statistical Appendix gives the share of imports in the supply of selected goods, including some rural products whose elaboration forms an important part of food processing, and which during 1930–50 gave an important boost to industrialization. The figures on cotton textiles support the emphasis given to this activity in the discussion of the first stage of post-1930 industrialization; also noteworthy was the progress of import substitution in cement during that stage, especially between 1928 and 1938. For crude oil and rolled steel products, the decline in the import coefficient was slower.

Table 4.16: Gross Output Indices of Manufacturing Activities
Showing the Smallest Growth Rates during 1946–64
(1960 = 100)

	1946–49	*1950–54*	*1955–59*	*1960–64*
Preserved and processed meats (5.6)	128.9	97.2	139.1	113.0
Breweries (0.7)	129.1	153.5	137.2	82.3
Candies, marmalades, and jams (0.1)	91.1	103.4	111.4	92.3
Noodles and spaghetti (0.3)	95.1	96.5	100.3	92.1
Yerba mate processing (0.3)	95.0	100.1	104.5	99.7
Wheat flour (1.1)	85.3	89.4	101.0	98.6
Spinning and weaving of cotton and wool (7.1)	84.2	96.3	99.6	84.7
Wool washing (0.1)	330.1	202.2	214.3	214.8
Needle work and knitting (1.0)	95.5	105.2	118.0	86.2
Cloth footwear (0.1)	150.9	131.9	131.3	114.2
Coffins and urns (0.05)	89.0	91.4	98.5	101.4
Wooden boxes for packing (0.3)	102.6	83.2	92.3	108.6
Charcoal (0.2)	93.8	97.7	125.5	85.9
Wood sawing (0.5)	107.3	104.5	102.6	95.6
Furniture (excluding wicker) (1.2)	102.0	99.9	88.5	75.3
Parquets (0.05)	104.8	105.8	114.0	101.8
Paper envelopes and bags (0.4)	103.2	89.6	100.5	97.2
Newspapers and magazines (1.7)	101.3	71.8	85.0	97.6
Printing (1.4)	96.4	86.2	100.4	100.9
Non-edible vegetable oils (0.2)	83.8	67.8	81.6	103.6
Paints and allied products (0.3)	85.6	96.8	129.4	105.7
Tanning products (0.07)	166.2	154.5	113.5	98.4
Matches (0.1)	96.4	107.8	111.0	101.2
Leather footwear (1.7)	91.0	87.7	96.4	81.0
Processing of hides and furs (0.8)	95.6	94.1	112.4	87.9
Cement manufactures (0.3)	89.8	87.2	85.0	100.4
Tiles and mosaics (0.4)	86.5	96.5	114.0	100.4
Glass and mirrors (0.8)	102.0	103.1	123.9	101.7
Construction and repair of bodies for vehicles (0.4)	136.0	21.8	34.2	113.4
Common bricks (0.4)	84.0	95.7	114.0	100.0

Sources: As in Table 4.15. The activities listed represented around 27 percent of total manufacturing output in 1960.

produced only 6,000 automotive vehicles, but by 1965 annual output reached nearly 200,000. Of these, 120,000 were automobiles manufactured by thirteen major firms, the largest producing less than 60,000 vehicles. Output of crude steel rose from around 200,000 tons in 1954, to 1.37 million tons in 1965, of which SOMISA, the state enterprise, produced 770,000 tons, while the rest was contributed by eleven other installations.[38]

The list of slowest growing activities, some showing negative growth rates, is dominated by traditional and light sectors.[39] Of special importance are the following: spinning and weaving of cotton and wool, preserved and processed meats (mainly meat-packing plants), newspapers and magazines, and leather footwear. The decline of some activities was due to changes in taste (e.g. compare the performance of breweries and processing of yerba mate with that of soft drinks), and in technology (e.g. compare the performance of charcoal with that of petroleum refining). Among the stagnant activities are those providing goods for mass consumption and those linked with housing construction; for these industries the decline becomes more marked after 1950–54. Export stagnation is also reflected by such items as meat-packing plants.

Wide disparity of growth rates within manufacturing emerges again from Tables 4.15 and 4.16. It is not hard to see how one could arrive at very different overall manufacturing growth rates simply by changing weights. David Felix has stressed that in import substituting industrialization output curves for individual activities tend to take "a parabolic shape with very pronounced retardation effect." [40] When the activity is first established, it will expand at very fast rates, but once it eliminates rival imports, it will grow much the same as overall real income, unless it exports or drastic changes occur in income distribution. At any point in time, within manufacturing there will be activities at different phases of this cycle, giving rise to the observed spread in subsectorial growth rates, while the overall manufacturing growth rate is maintained at high levels by the continuous introduction of new fast-growing, import-substituting activities. These considerations are helpful in understanding the dynamics of manufacturing expansion during 1930–64, but they should be complemented with an examination of other forces influencing the pattern of industrial growth. Note, for example, in Table 4.15 that for several

38. See Asociación de Fábricas de Automotores, *Un Millón de Automotores Argentinos* (Buenos Aires, 1966), pp. 12–14, and Centro de Industriales Siderúrgicos, *La Siderurgia Argentina en 1965* (Buenos Aires, 1965), pp. 13–14. Output of laminated steel products in 1965 reached 1.5 million tons.

39. The period 1960–64 was marked by a severe recession during 1962–63.

40. See David Felix, "Import Substituting Industrialization and Industrial Exporting in Argentina," (mimeographed, Sept. 1964), p. 14.

dynamic activities the growth rate between 1950–54 and 1955–59 was greater than between 1946–49 and 1950–54; i.e., before reaching saturation in 1960–64 their growth was accelerating, suggesting that at least for some activities the output curve looked more like a logistic curve than a parabola (see indices for lead and tin products, bicycles and motorcycles, machinery and engines, radio and television equipment).

The two industrial stages since 1930 had different employment effects. According to censuses, the manufacturing labor force grew at an annual rate of 5.9 percent between 1935 and 1950. As shown in Table 4.17, textiles, food, and beverages alone generated nearly

Table 4.17: Structure and Rates of Change of Employment in Manufacturing, 1935–50
(Percentages)

	Structure of employment 1935	1950	Annual growth rate of employment 1935–50	Contribution of each sector to the total increase in employment, 1935–50
Total manufacturing	100.0	100.0	5.9	100.0
Foodstuffs and beverages	25.4	20.4	4.4	16.7
Tobacco	2.1	1.0	1.1	0.3
Textiles	12.0	16.5	8.2	19.8
Clothing	7.1	5.3	4.0	4.1
Wood products	7.4	7.4	5.9	7.4
Paper and cardboard	1.6	1.8	6.7	2.0
Printing and publishing	5.9	3.7	2.4	1.9
Chemical products	3.5	5.3	8.9	6.7
Petroleum refining	1.0	0.7	3.3	0.5
Rubber products	0.8	1.0	7.6	1.2
Leather products	4.5	3.9	5.0	3.5
Stone, glass, and ceramics	4.2	6.3	8.8	7.9
Metals	9.6	10.4	6.5	11.0
Vehicles and machinery	10.7	10.2	5.6	9.9
Electrical machinery and appliances	0.9	2.8	14.3	4.2
Other	3.1	3.0	5.8	3.0

Sources: Industrial censuses of 1935 and 1950. The Industrial Census of 1935 was carried out on October 31, 1935, and obtained information for July 1934 through June 1935. The Industrial Census of 1950, performed on December 31, 1950, obtained information for January 1950 through December 1950.

37 percent of the employment increase between those two dates. It is noteworthy that for 1935–50 the employment growth rate exceeds that for output (CONADE, 5 percent; BCRA, 4 percent). Even if

data difficulties arising from changes in census coverage are granted, it is unlikely that average labor productivity in manufacturing increased much during 1935–50.[41] Preliminary CONADE data for the post-1950 period indicate that manufacturing employment grew at only 1.8 percent between 1948–50 and 1959–61 and at 1.4 percent between 1950 and 1961.[42]

It is tempting to explain observed differences in labor productivity growth during the two post-1930 industrialization stages only in terms of the technology of the leading sectors for each phase. Between 1948 and 1961 real wage rates tended to stagnate and even decline, presumably stimulating the use of more labor-intensive techniques. There appeared to be no general labor shortage in the economy after 1950; indeed, after 1959, open urban unemployment became a serious problem on several occasions. Nevertheless, no such simple link is warranted. Not all activities leading post-1950 industrialization could be said to be capital-intensive. If the share of wages and salaries in value added is taken as an approximation of labor intensity, vehicles and machinery exceed in labor use even textiles and clothing.[43]

Why, then, the observed trends in employment and productivity? No good answer can be given to that question at this point. As a beginning toward an answer, the pre-1950 period may be subdivided. After 1939 a sharp drop in average labor productivity took place, presumably because the war forced an increase in the labor-capital ratio. Between 1939 and 1943 productivity declined about 20 percent (as shown in the notes to Table 4.18); sharper drops occurred in such traditional activities as clothing, wood products, and printing and publishing, where substitution of labor for machinery may be easier than in other branches. As shown in Table 4.18, the recovery

41. For 1925–29 to 1945–49, data of ECLA, p. 400, yield an annual growth rate of manufacturing employment of 2.6 percent, and a rate of 3.0 percent for 1935–39 to 1945–49. On the other hand, in U.N., *Patterns of Industrial Growth, 1938–1958* (New York, 1960), p. 14, it is pointed out that for 1938–48 Argentina had the highest annual rate of increase of employment in mining and manufacturing among the 30 most industrialized countries in the world (excluding the Socialist bloc). The latter source estimates that during those years employment in mining and manufacturing grew at an annual rate of more than 6 percent in Argentina.

42. As in the case of industrial output, employment data should improve when the results of the industrial census taken during 1964 become available.

43. See Table 106 in the Statistical Appendix. Dynamic branches, however, may on the average hire more skilled workers who are better paid than those in vegetative branches.

Table 4.18: Indices of Gross Output per Employed Worker
in Traditional Branches of Manufacturing, 1939–62
(1943 = 100)

	Foodstuffs, beverages	*Tobacco*	*Textiles*	*Clothing*	*Wood products*	*Painting, publishing*	*Leather products*
1939	117	96	102	127	137	141	103
1941	103	98	100	116	112	139	104
1943	100	100	100	100	100	100	100
1946	92	105	107	102	111	107	87
1948–49	89	118	108	121	127	119	82
1950–52	94	115	101	96	136	114	82
1953–55	106	115	107	95	163	104	80
1956–58	119	160	116	89	177	136	83
1959–62	126	212	107	91	207	177	79

Note: The old industrial statistics of the DNEC have been justly criticized for their incomplete coverage; however, they provide a relatively accurate picture for older firms in traditional activities.

Sources: Industrial statistics and indices as published by DNEC, *Boletín de Estadística* several issues. If the same output indices are divided by indices of total employment (i.e. including all employees, workers and members of the family of the owner working in the establishment) obtained directly from the censuses, the following results are obtained:

	1937	*1939*	*1943*	*1946*	*1950*	*1957*
Foodstuffs and beverages	117	121	100	86	102	121
Tobacco	90	99	100	111	128	182
Textiles	99	103	100	108	92	86
Clothing	138	137	100	100	144	122
Wood products	161	140	100	109	145	170
Leather products	86	108	100	88	92	86
All manufacturing: (CONADE output index and census employment)	123	125	100	93	118	146

of productivity after the war was slow; as late as 1950 most productivity indices in traditional activities were below those of 1939. The proliferation of small establishments and new labor legislation introduced by the Perón regime made it difficult for the employer to dismiss excess or inefficient workers, or even to transfer them within his factory. Work rules became rigid, and trade unions, feeling their new power, were not easily induced to change them. Older firms were especially hard hit by this change in labor relations. These factors contributed to the decline of productivity. Toward the end of the Perón government this situation began to change as the regime became more productivity conscious. After its overthrow the power of trade unions, still considerable, declined. Severe recessions beginning in 1959 eliminated many small inefficient establishments that had provided a large amount of employment. Both of these factors, plus reequipment, allowed several traditional branches (in spite of their stagnant output) to obtain productivity increases observed in Table 4.18 after 1950–55. The establishment of new plants in chemicals, basic metals, etc., contributed to an increase in overall manufacturing labor productivity.[44] A desire to minimize risks of labor trouble has also restrained managers in their hiring practices.

OTHER STRUCTURAL FEATURES OF ARGENTINE MANUFACTURING

This section will present additional characteristics of manufacturing, primarily obtained from census data, which will be helpful in evaluating post-1930 industrial policies to be discussed later.

Historical myopia is widespread in discussions about Argentine manufacturing. To some, industrialization really started during World War II. Data already presented should be enough to dispel this myth, but it may still be useful to consider the information presented in Table 4.19, classifying gross output generated in each sector according to the year of founding of establishments. Although those data tell nothing regarding when the establishments witnessed their fastest growth nor when they began producing new products, they convincingly demolish the hypothesis regarding the "newness" of industry. The relatively newest activity was wood processing, with one-third of its 1948 gross output being accounted for by establishments founded during 1941–48. Other new activities were electrical machinery and appliances, other manufacturing, and leather products. The somewhat paradoxical presence in this group of traditional activities such as wood and leather processing may be explained by their being made up largely of small firms with high mortality rates, as well as

44. Jorge M. Katz has argued that the rate of technological change and benefits from economies of scale have increased since 1955, thanks to larger foreign investments in Argentine industry. Presumably, both labor and total factor productivity have benefited from this trend. See Jorge M. Katz, "Características estructurales del crecimiento industrial argentino," *Desarrollo Económico* 7, no. 26 (July–Sept. 1967): 59–76. These results, however, may be produced at least in part by excessive aggregation. A full explanation for the slow employment growth in post-1950 Argentina, as in so many other countries, requires further research and a finer data breakdown, especially regarding different types of labor.

Table 4.19: Classification of Industrial Establishments According to Year of Founding
(Percentages of gross output in 1948 of each time period for each category)

	Before 1901	1901–10	1911–20	1921–30	1931–40	1941–48
All industry	16.5	10.0	13.0	20.3	21.8	16.7
Mining	2.9	40.0	3.4	27.8	17.3	8.0
Food and beverages	22.8	13.9	16.6	18.5	16.3	9.7
Tobacco	11.6	3.0	40.6	41.9	1.1	1.8
Textiles	15.7	4.4	6.7	15.3	33.5	22.4
Clothing	12.9	9.7	13.5	17.4	25.0	19.7
Wood products	8.4	7.5	9.7	17.0	24.0	32.8
Paper and cardboard	25.9	4.2	8.6	21.2	26.9	13.2
Printing and publishing	34.0	13.3	15.8	12.1	14.8	9.9
Chemicals	8.4	8.6	13.7	26.2	19.1	23.8
Petroleum refining	0	0	17.5	56.1	23.0	3.2
Rubber products	3.6	1.7	6.9	23.2	54.6	10.0
Leather products	18.4	7.3	9.8	13.4	22.8	25.6
Stone, glass, and ceramics	15.0	4.5	9.8	16.9	28.2	24.0
Metals	12.0	13.5	12.8	19.1	20.1	20.7
Vehicles and machinery	12.9	9.3	15.6	22.0	19.1	15.2
Electrical machinery and appliances	1.0	21.5	12.4	17.2	18.6	28.8
Other manufacturing	8.1	7.2	8.4	21.6	26.3	28.1
Gas and electricity	62.3	10.6	5.9	5.9	13.4	1.9

Sources: Industrial Census of 1948, pp. 82–89. Horizontal lines do not add up to 100 because the census was unable to establish data of founding for all establishments. This "unknown" category is highest for vehicles and machinery (5.9 percent).

by the predominantly light nature of manufacturing growth during the 1940s. Table 4.19 confirms the fast development of textiles (mainly cotton textiles) and rubber (mainly tires and tubes) during the 1930s. On the other hand, 72 percent of gross output of food and beverages produced in 1948 was accounted for by establishments founded before 1931, while the corresponding figures were 97 percent for tobacco, 75 percent for printing and publishing, 74 percent for petroleum refining, and 85 percent for gas and electricity. For metals and vehicles-cum-machinery the figures are lower, but still substantial: 57 percent and 60 percent, respectively. As late as 1954, 40 percent of the industrial labor force worked in establishments founded before 1931, while another 17 percent worked in those founded during 1931–40. In 1946 the proportions had been 56 percent and 25 percent, respectively.[45]

Industrialization did not spring full grown and fully armored out of anyone's brow, but, especially after 1943, it gave rise to abnormally high numbers of small establishments of doubtful long-run efficiency, as shown in Table 134 of the Statistical Appendix. The figures for the 1954 and 1957 censuses in all likelihood had different coverage as compared with earlier censuses; but even granting this, a decline in the average number of employees per establishment may be noticed after 1943. This tendency was especially marked for textiles, clothing, wood and leather products, and other manufacturing, and suggests an overexpansion of these sectors especially after the war.[46]

The proliferation of small establishments appears to have continued at least until 1953, as indicated in Table 135 of the Statistical Appendix. The average size of new establishments for the three or four years preceding the censuses of 1935, 1939, and 1946 had been 5.9, 6.3, and 6.0 workers per establishment, respectively. The census of 1954 yielded much smaller figures even for establishments founded between four and eight years before that census was taken. Differences in census coverage are not likely to account for all of this difference.[47]

The war and early postwar years also witnessed a reversal of the capital deepening that was taking place during the late 1930s (presumably after the excess capacity of the earlier 1930s had been used

45. See Table 107 in the Statistical Appendix.

46. If only establishments of 11 and more workers are considered, the average size of industrial establishments that emerges is as follows: 1935 census = 61.2 workers; 1937 census = 63.4 workers; 1939 census = 61.7 workers; 1946 census = 59.8 workers; 1954 census = 60.3 workers; 1957 census = 66.8 workers.

For establishments of 10 and fewer workers the averages are as follows: 1935 census = 3.3 workers; 1937 census = 3.4 workers; 1939 census = 3.4 workers; 1946 census = 3.4 workers; 1954 census = 3.2 workers.

The number of establishments hiring 10 and fewer workers registered by the 1954 census was larger than those for earlier years. But note that the average for the larger establishments is lower for 1946 and 1954 than for 1935, 1937, and 1939.

47. Table 90 in the Statistical Appendix, showing the allocation of blue-collar workers according to size of establishment, also supports the assertions made on the proliferation of small firms. Between 1935 and 1939 there was a tendency toward an increase in the share of workers in larger establishments; after 1939 a curious polarization takes place, with establishments with 50 and fewer workers *and* those with more than 500 workers both increasing their share at the expense of the middle category.

up). Table 4.20 presents data on horsepower capacity per blue-collar worker, which may be taken as a proxy for capital per worker, at least for the purposes of this discussion. The shortages created by the war in the supply of equipment and machinery explain most of

Table 4.20: Installed Horsepower Capacity per Blue-Collar Worker
in Branches of Manufacturing
(Horsepower per blue-collar worker)

	1935 census	1939 census	1946 census	1950 census	1954 census
Total manufacturing	2.6	2.9	2.0	3.0	3.7
Foodstuffs and beverages	4.5	5.2	3.9	4.8	5.2
Tobacco	0.5	0.5	0.5	0.5	0.8
Textiles	1.4	1.6	1.4	2.0	2.5
Clothing	0.4	0.4	0.3	0.4	0.4
Wood products	2.1	2.0	1.4	2.7	2.9
Paper and cardboard	4.3	6.6	4.2	5.3	10.4
Printing and publishing	1.1	1.2	1.1	1.4	1.7
Chemical products	4.1	4.5	3.8	5.3	6.6
Petroleum refining	9.0	12.3	25.3	18.0	16.6
Rubber products	4.0	2.6	3.7	3.5	4.4
Leather products	1.2	1.2	0.9	1.3	1.7
Stone, glass, and ceramics	3.9	5.3	2.9	3.9	4.8
Metals	1.4	1.5	2.0	2.8	4.2
Vehicles and machinery	2.0	2.0	1.9	2.2	2.7
Electrical machinery and appliances	1.3	1.1	1.4	1.6	2.1
Other manufacturing	3.6	3.4	1.7	2.7	3.7

Sources: Industrial censuses of the years shown.

the decline observed between 1939 and 1946, although the slow recovery from 1946 to 1950 (which came up only to a level roughly similar to 1939) suggests that other factors were also present. The same policies stimulating the proliferation of small establishments also led to the slow expansion of capital deepening.

Tables 4.20 and 4.21 also help to clarify the nature of various manufacturing sectors. They indicate that foodstuffs, beverages, and textiles, on the average, employed as early as 1935 techniques far removed from those of handicrafts. On the other hand, in 1935 metals had characteristics not very different from those of clothing, printing and publishing, and wood and leather processing. By 1954, however, that was no longer the case.

The relatively slow expansion in the use of electricity per employee

Table 4.21: Use of Electricity in Manufacturing
(Thousands of KWH per employee per year)

	1935 census	1943 census	1946 census	1948 census	1954 census
All manufacturing	*1.37*	*1.57*	*1.51*	*1.67*	*2.05*
Food and beverages	{1.71}	{1.77}	1.78	1.88	2.48
Tobacco			0.24	0.31	0.27
Textiles	{0.97}	{1.39}	1.80	1.82	2.23
Clothing			0.27	0.24	0.37
Wood products	0.38	0.25	0.30	0.37	0.42
Paper and cardboard	5.04	4.87	5.65	7.39	7.27
Printing and publishing	0.59	0.58	0.75	0.71	0.80
Chemical products	2.38	3.32	3.53	3.57	5.04
Petroleum refining	5.70	12.60	11.84	10.68	9.50
Rubber products	3.48	3.24	4.40	3.53	3.83
Leather products	0.55	0.54	0.53	0.49	0.71
Stone, glass, and ceramics	2.84	3.97	2.87	3.59	4.15
Metals	0.75	0.89	1.18	1.19	1.94
Vehicles and machinery	{0.81}	{0.64}	0.59	0.66	0.77
Electrical machinery and appliances			0.99	0.92	1.11
Other manufacturing	3.19	2.38	1.52	1.64	2.60

Note: Employees include both white- and blue-collar workers plus members of the family of the owners working in the establishment. Electricity used includes that purchased from public utilities as well as that generated within the establishment.

Sources: Industrial censuses for the years shown.

after 1943 was influenced not only by the proliferation of small establishments and the retardation of capital deepening, but also by an acute shortage of generating capacity, which began to be felt around 1944. The capacity installed in electrical public utilities was 1.22 million kilowatts in 1939, 1.29 million in 1945, 1.35 million in 1950, and 1.62 million in 1955. A more intensive use of this capacity was not enough to satisfy demand, and rationing schemes had to be introduced. Entrepreneurs were forced toward a socially inefficient reliance on their own electricity generators.[48] A number of circum-

48. Data on electricity generating capacity obtained from U.N., *Energy Development in Latin America* (E/CN.12/384/Rev. 1), and Dirección Nacional de Energía y Combustibles. According to the 1948 census, of all electricity used in manufacturing, 33 percent had come from generators owned by manufacturing establishments; in the 1954 census this proportion rose to 41 percent. Of the net *increase* in total electricity used in manufacturing between those two dates, 59 percent came from electricity generated within the establishments and only 41 percent from public electrical utilities. However, it appears that a secular rise has been taking place in the share of "own electricity" since 1935;

stances explain the slow growth of generating capacity since the late 1930s. Planners failed to foresee wartime shortages in equipment and seemed pleased with the excess capacity existing around 1939. The war, and Argentina's neutrality, made the purchase of this equipment difficult until the late 1940s. After this point, electricity provides another example of the failure of the Perón regime either to allow private enterprise to supply urgent needs or to have the public sector, via investment planning, satisfy those needs.[49] A fast rate of industrial growth was dependent on the expansion of complex activities which tended to have above average electricity needs. Thus, electricity shortages contributed to a slowdown in industrialization during 1948–53 and made the transition between its two main post-1930 phases more difficult. It may be noted in passing that the Argentine experience with electricity casts doubts about the efficiency of deliberate unbalanced growth as a way to facilitate investment decision making.

Although no census data are yet available for recent years, it is almost certain that they will show an increase in the average size of establishment, as well as increases in the share of the labor force in larger establishments, and in horsepower and electricity available per worker. The recent fast development of automobile and steel industries, as well as petrochemicals, electrical machinery and appliances, etc., induces such results. Furthermore, the severe recessions of 1959 and 1962–63 witnessed the disappearance of many small establishments.

The 1954 census revealed that in several activities a relatively small number of plants, controlled by a smaller number of companies, generated large shares of sectorial output. For example, the six largest establishments in tobacco processing produced 82 percent of its output; in rubber products three establishments generated 43 percent of output; and in electrical machinery and appliances three establishments accounted for 31 percent of output.[50] At a more disaggregated

---

in the census for that year the share was 34 percent, rising to 37 percent in 1937 and to 42 percent in 1939. Perhaps due to war and accompanying difficulties in buying generators, the share fell to 37 percent in 1943 (the same figure registered in 1946).

49. The average annual growth rate in electricity generated by public utilities was hardly different during 1943–55 (6.2 percent) from the rate achieved during 1929–43 (5.8 percent). Public utilities in Argentina generated 1,292 million kilowatt hours during 1929, 2,860 million kilowatt hours during 1943, and 5,905 million kilowatt hours during 1955.

50. See Table 91 in the Statistical Appendix. It is widely believed that industrial concentration has increased since 1954, spurred by the expansion of activities characterized by economies of scale.

level, of course, higher degrees of concentration could be found. But these data by themselves say little about the market power exercised by the largest firms, and given the small size of the domestic market, some such pattern of output concentration is inevitable as well as desirable. The combination of output concentration and extreme protectionism is what has given large firms considerable market power. Furthermore, even in the less concentrated activities, on several occasions, especially under Perón, the public sector has encouraged corporate-state type of cartelization.

Although public policies have influenced industrialization patterns, the government has had a modest role in direct management and ownership of manufacturing ventures. After several years of the Perón regime, less than 10 percent of gross manufacturing output was generated by firms totally or in part publicly owned and managed.[51] Government participation has been highest in petroleum refining (as well as in oil extraction), where the state company (Y.P.F.) has played a major role since the 1920s. Since the late 1930s the armed forces showed interest in iron and steel, shipyards, other transport equipment, and explosives.[52] Using property confiscated late in the war from Axis nationals and with other support, the Perón regime encouraged these interests. Especially since 1959, the public sector has divested itself of manufacturing activities, although the major com-

51. See Table 92 in the Statistical Appendix.

52. The relatively late development of the basic iron and steel industry in Argentina, in spite of the strong interest shown in it by the powerful armed forces, suggests that either (1) this activity can only be carried out at very high costs or (2) that the power of industrial users of imported iron and steel was a good match to that of the armed forces. As early as 1937 private entrepreneurs got in touch with top military leaders to promote the iron and steel industry. These efforts led to the *Ley Savio* of June 1947, which committed the armed forces and the public sector to promoting this industry. Credits were sought abroad, but without quick success: SOMISA (Sociedad Mixta Siderurgia Argentina) began operations only in June 1960. An ECLA study, published in 1954, expressed the following opinion: "There have been many discussions as to whether the installation of an integrated steel industry in Argentina is justified. The adverse opinions have been based less on the disadvantage of investing large sums of capital and more on the assumption that a country devoid of coking coals would produce expensive steel. The figures in Chapter III . . . show that a plant with a capacity of 850,000 tons at San Nicolás would have almost identical delivered costs for finished steel and for imported steel . . ." See U.N., *A Study of the Iron and Steel Industry in Latin America* (New York, 1954), p. 17. Organizational and management difficulties have hampered the realization of this ex-ante calculation; domestically produced Argentine steel remains much more expensive than equivalent products in world markets.

pany in crude steel production, SOMISA, is still dominated by the public sector and the armed forces.

The 1914 census showed that nearly 61 percent of the manufacturing labor force was located in the Federal District and the province of Buenos Aires; by 1935 this share had risen to 72 percent, but after that date it declined steadily.[53] The provinces of the west and northwest, which during the eighteenth and early nineteenth century had most of Argentina's industry, have accounted for a small share of employment during the twentieth century, and for a generally lower percentage of industrial wages and salaries. Concentration in the Greater Buenos Aires zone (the Federal District plus surrounding districts of the province of Buenos Aires), declined between 1935 and 1954 when measured using industrial employment as a criterion, but not substantially when the share of wages and salaries is used. In recent years, the decline of industrial concentration in Greater Buenos Aires has accelerated: the auto industry has been located primarily around Córdoba, while new steel, petrochemicals, and machinery establishments have flocked to the west bank of the Paraná river in the province of Santa Fe, around the city of Rosario. Industrial expansion outside the major pampean provinces, however, may not have kept up with overall industrial growth in spite of special government incentives to locate in those areas.[54]

The structure of gross manufacturing output, viewed from the input side, reveals a decrease in the share of imported inputs. Table 4.22 presents that share (excluding fuels), for different manufacturing categories.[55] In 1937 domestic activity in such branches as rubber products and metals and machinery consisted of little more than providing finishing touches to imported inputs. Table 4.22 also shows that the 1960 share of imported inputs was for several

53. See Table 93 in the Statistical Appendix.

54. It has been estimated that 63 percent of manufacturing value added in 1958 was generated in Greater Buenos Aires, and 87 percent by Greater Buenos Aires plus other districts in the province of Buenos Aires, plus the provinces of Córdoba, Entre Ríos, and Santa Fe. The province of Mendoza contributed nearly 4 percent, and Tucumán more than 2 percent. See Alberto Fracchia, Norberto González, Héctor Grupe, and Felipe S. Tami, *Relevamiento de la Estructura Regional de la Economía Argentina* (Buenos Aires: Editorial del Instituto Torcuato Di Tella, 1963), pp. 206–07.

55. Only *direct* import requirments are taken into account in the table— i.e., import requirements of domestic inputs to a given industry will appear only under the domestic industry providing those inputs, not under the activity using them.

Table 4.22: Imported Raw Materials and Intermediate Products (excluding Fuels) as Percentages of Final Value of Gross Output in Each Sector of Manufacturing

	1937 census	1939 census	1946 census	1950 census	1954 census	1960 CONADE
All manufacturing	18.8	18.6	8.0	6.0	6.9	—[a]
Food and beverages	{5.8}	{6.1}	1.9	1.3	1.8	1.5
Tobacco			13.3	4.9	0.8	1.2
Textiles	{27.6}	{24.6}	4.3	4.2	4.1	3.8
Clothing			11.6	6.4	7.8	5.3
Wood products	27.1	27.5	14.3	12.8	12.8	7.1
Paper and cardboard	28.8	27.0	17.0	{10.7}	11.5	8.8
Printing and publishing	19.4	20.5	19.8		10.6	14.5
Chemical products	21.4	20.8	8.7	5.6	7.7	14.8
Petroleum refining	31.5	29.2	18.6	14.7	21.3	–
Rubber products	49.3	46.3	24.0	11.8	14.7	22.4
Leather products	3.4	3.6	1.4	0.7	0.8	0.5
Stone, glass, and ceramics	11.8	13.4	5.0	3.0	3.2	5.0
Metals	41.5	39.6	16.6	13.1	13.6	23.6
Vehicles and machinery	{42.4}	{38.0}	14.1	8.4	9.0	17.0
Electrical machinery and appliances			14.3	11.4	14.0	13.9
Other manufacturing	11.6	12.4	7.5	5.7	7.0	5.2

[a] Dash indicates data not available.

Sources: Industrial censuses for years shown. The imported items are presumably valued at users' prices in the censuses. The 1960 figures have been estimated by CONADE; imports are expressed at users' prices. CONADE also gives the following data for the import component in 1960 of selected subsectors:

Meat processing	0.1 percent
Iron and steel	29.4 percent
Automobiles and tractors	14.7 percent
Other metals	19.7 percent
Other vehicles and machinery	17.8 percent

important sectors higher than in 1954, and in some cases even higher than in 1946. A major explanation is that for nearly twenty years covering the war and the postwar period, Argentina did without, or severely restricted, her absorption of automobiles, tractors, iron and steel, and complex machinery with high (direct or indirect) import components. The sharp drop in the share of imported inputs registered between 1939 and 1946–54 reflects in many cases not so much import substitution as postponement of absorption. Viewed in this light, the upsurge of import components for 1960 still fits in a secularly declining trend, in which the figures for 1946, 1950, and 1954 are abnormally low.[56]

The structure of gross output, viewed from the demand side, reveals that by 1950 manufacturing still provided mainly consumer goods, directly or indirectly, with less than 4 percent of its output going directly to capital formation. By 1961 this figure had risen to over 11 percent.[57] If all manufacturing branches are taken together, the increase in gross output between 1950 and 1961 breaks down as follows: 38 percent went to final consumption, 37 percent to intermediate demand, and 25 percent for investment. Expansion of exports absorbed only a fraction of 1 percent of the output increase. The share of investment goods is noteworthy and, although data for earlier years are lacking, it is probably much higher than that corresponding to 1929–50.

Inflation has led entrepreneurs to devote an inordinate part of their time to financial problems of their firms. Unfortunately, not much data exist on the financing structure of manufacturing, and even the available data may have become unrepresentative of the more recent situation. Data on sources of funds for 285 major manufacturing corporations during 1956–60, indicate that one-third of their sources of capital funds were internal (retained earnings, depreciation allowances, and reserves); 14 percent came from the issue of securities (mainly stocks), another 14 percent from bank loans, 21 percent from commercial and other loans, 16 percent from the postponement of tax and social security obligations, and 2 percent from miscellaneous external sources.[58] For more recent years, it is generally believed that funds obtained from internal sources and by postponing tax and social security payments, as well as by borrowing from abroad,

---

56. The secular decline in the share of imported inputs has led to an increase in the domestic employment multiplier of a peso spent on manufactures. But the share of wages and salaries in the value of gross output has tended to decline since 1935 in practically all branches of manufacturing, as shown in Tables 94 and 95 in the Statistical Appendix.

57. See Tables 96 and 97 in the Statistical Appendix.

58. Elaborated from data found in BCRA, *Boletín Estadístico* (Nov. 1961), p. 55. Hugh H. Schwartz has pointed out that the real value of banking loans to industry increased dramatically between 1945 and 1948. Loans outstanding to industry rose from less than 3 percent of GNP to 4.4 percent in 1948 and to more than 7 percent in 1952. This percentage has tended to fall since then. See Schwartz, "The Argentine Experience," pp. 77–82. Estimates by ECLA place the percentage for internal sources of capital funds in Argentina at 60 during 1952–55 and 40 in 1960–61. See the mimeographed Statistical Appendix of *El Proceso de Industrialización en América Latina*, p. 104.

have become of greater importance. The investment boom of 1960–61 was financed to a large extent by foreign funds, either directly or indirectly. On the other hand, after witnessing great activity during 1960–61, the stock market declined in importance; the role played

Table 4.23: Structure of Employment in Manufacturing
in Argentina and Other Countries
(Percentages)

	Argentina			Canada	U.S.A.	Australia
	1954 census	1957 census	1963 CONADE	1959	1963	1958–59
All manufacturing	100.0	100.0	100.0	100.0	100.0	100.0
Foodstuffs and beverages	19.0	18.7	15.8	14.7	10.0	{11.8}
Tobacco	0.9	0.7	0.4	0.8	0.5	
Textiles	18.7	18.7	15.5	13.2	13.3	15.4
Wood products	8.8	5.3	7.2	9.5	6.0	7.6
Paper and cardboard	1.7	2.1	1.9	7.2	3.6	2.1
Printing and publishing	3.0	3.3	1.7	5.7	5.6	4.1
Chemical products	5.0	6.1	5.0	4.2	4.6	{4.9}
Petroleum refining	0.7	0.9	0.9	1.3	0.9	
Rubber products	1.3	1.4	0.9	1.6	2.6	1.7
Leather products	3.5	3.1	2.4	2.4	2.1	1.0
Stone, glass, and ceramics	6.0	6.1	3.8	3.3	3.6	4.1
Metals	11.0	11.7	12.7	{27.5}	13.5	{44.3}
Vehicles and machinery	14.0	14.4	25.7		21.0	
Electrical machinery and appliances	3.5	4.7	4.0	5.7	9.0	
Other manufacturing	2.9	2.9	2.1	2.9	3.7	3.0

Note: Australian data seem to place leather footwear under clothing, apparel, and textiles; for the rest of the countries this category is placed under leather products. Whenever possible, instruments and related products have been placed under machinery and equipment.

Sources: For Argentina: Industrial Censuses for years shown and CONADE unpublished estimates. For Canada: *Historical Statistics of Canada*, ed. M. C. Urquhart (Cambridge University Press, 1965), pp. 463–74. For the United States: U.S. Bureau of the Census, *Statistical Abstract of the United States, 1965* (Washington, D.C., 1965), pp. 776–81. For Australia: United Nations, *The Growth of World Industry 1938–1961* (New York, 1963), pp. 32–33.

by the Banco Industrial and commercial banks has also suffered a relative decline as a result of changes in monetary policy.[59]

Data summarized in this and earlier sections induce international

59. During 1956–58 the total stock of banking credit to the private sector amounted to about 30 percent of the yearly GNP; during 1959–63 this proportion was reduced to 18 percent, and during 1964–65 it reached only 15 percent. Data from BCRA, *Boletín Estadístico*, several issues.

comparisons as a way of checking on the uniqueness of the Argentine path to industrialization. Unfortunately data are seldom in ready shape for those comparisons; besides differences in classification schemes, one runs against differences in price structures between Argentina and the rest of the world. In spite of these difficulties, a few tentative comparisons will now be presented.

Table 4.23 shows the structure of manufacturing employment in Argentina, Canada, the United States, and Australia. Although minor differences in classification may exist, on the whole these data are robust. The most striking fact emerging from this table is that the 1963 Argentine share of employment in metallurgical branches (metals, vehicles and machinery, plus electrical machinery and appliances) was very close to that for the United States and Australia, and superior to that of Canada (Argentina, 42.4 percent; Canada, 33.2

Table 4.24: Structure of Value Added in Manufacturing
in Argentina and Other Countries
(Percentages)

	Argentina 1963 CONADE	Argentina 1963 BCRA	Canada 1958	U.S.A. 1963	Australia 1958–59
All manufacturing	100.0	100.0	100.0	100.0	100.0
Foodstuffs and beverages	23.2	21.9	15.7	11.2	{13.3}
Tobacco	3.6	0.6	1.0	0.9	
Textiles and clothing	11.4	10.1	7.8	7.3	11.2
Wood products	2.7	1.7	6.2	3.8	6.6
Paper and cardboard	2.1	1.8	9.3	3.8	3.0
Printing and publishing	2.5	3.6	5.2	5.5	4.1
Chemical products	6.3	7.5	6.8	9.2	{9.4}
Petroleum refining	10.2	8.9	5.3	1.9	
Rubber products	1.9	1.2	1.8	2.4	1.8
Leather products	1.8	2.8	1.2	1.1	0.8
Stone, glass, and ceramics	3.5	4.3	3.8	3.8	4.7
Metals	12.2	8.9	{28.2}	14.1	
Vehicles and machinery	13.0	14.0		23.3	{42.0}
Electrical machinery and appliances	3.8	5.4	5.4	8.6	
Other manufacturing	1.8	{6.5}	2.3	3.1	3.1
Handicrafts	4.7		—ᵃ	—	—

ᵃ Dash indicates data not available.

Sources: As in Table 4.23 for Canada, U.S.A., and Australia. CONADE data for Argentina (first column) are based on figures of value added at market prices, i.e. including indirect taxes; those for BCRA (second column) are estimated at factor cost.

percent; United States, 43.5 percent; and Australia, 44.3 percent). The melancholy decline of Argentine printing and publishing is also highlighted. If differences in per capita incomes are borne in mind, the closeness of the employment structures is remarkable. If the last four columns of Table 4.23 had been presented without identification, most readers would have found it difficult to tell what column belonged to which country (perhaps with the exception of Canada, where the high shares of wood products and paper and cardboard provide a strong hint). Clearly, having an advanced employment structure does not necessarily yield advanced levels of productivity and per capita income.

When international comparisons involve value added data, reliability fades due to diverse price structures. Nevertheless, it is interesting to note in Table 4.24 that differences in structure between Argentina and other countries become more marked when value added is used. In the metallurgical industries, for example, the Argentine share (29 percent) is clearly inferior to those of Canada (34 percent), Australia (42 percent), and the United States (46 percent), even though relative prices and protection for this sector are higher in Argentina than in the other countries. The Argentine share for food and beverages is higher than those for the other countries in spite of lower relative prices.[60]

60. The structure of Argentine manufacturing may also be compared with the normal pattern, as presented in a United Nations study using cross-section data of several countries, covering postwar years. This is done and discussed in my "Etapas de la Industrialización Argentina," a paper presented to a conference on industrialization strategies held in September 1966 at the Di Tella Institute in Buenos Aires (forthcoming). Although Argentina's resource endowment is different from the normal for the rest of the world, its manufacturing structure during 1960–61 is close to normal. A comparison of per capita output for selected industrial activities in Argentina, Brazil and Mexico yields the following results (where Argentine per capita output is set equal to 100 in each activity):

	Brazil	*Mexico*
Pulp for paper and board (1965)	136	143
Sulphuric acid (1965)	49	152
Caustic soda (1964)	45	97
Cement (1965)	43	69
Pig iron (1965)	104	91
Steel ingots (1966)	80	112
Finished steel (1965)	38	69
Electricity (1965)	56	63
Gross domestic product (1960)	33	60

If differences in per capita income are considered, Argentina lags behind

A comparison of Tables 4.23 and 4.24 indicates that Argentine sectorial labor productivities, relative to that for manufacturing as a whole, diverge from those in other countries. An attempt has been made to test the following hypothesis using Argentine and United States data (for the years between 1953 and 1958): *ceteris paribus,* the greater the labor intensity of an Argentine industry, the greater will be its average labor productivity differential with respect to the corresponding United States industry. The results of this test, as well as some conceptual difficulties surrounding the hypothesis, have been discussed elsewhere.[61] The data provided modest support for this hypothesis. Average productivity of Argentine workers ranged from only 17 percent of that in the United States (in the case of elevators and moving stairways), to 105 percent (in petroleum refining). Other cases of high Argentine relative average labor productivity included cigarettes (83 percent of U.S. average labor productivity), tires and inner tubes (74 percent), and fish processing (79 percent). At the other extreme one found bread and bakery products (22 percent), musical instruments (24 percent), and tobacco processing, excluding cigarettes (28 percent). In spite of their labor-intensive character, the following activities emerged with high relative productivities: leather footwear (58 percent), apparel and related products (80 percent), and textiles (64 percent). On the average, Argentine labor productivity in manufacturing was about 40 percent of that in the United States. More disaggregated research, however, is required before these matters can be discussed with greater faith in the statistical results.

INDUSTRIALIZATION POLICIES AFTER 1930

The pattern and speed of industrialization has been influenced not only by more or less spontaneous market forces reflecting world trends (e.g. deterioration of the external terms of trade during the depression) and by domestic factor endowments and demand con-

---

Mexico and Brazil in several heavy industries such as steel and petrochemicals. (In 1964 Mexican petrochemical installed capacity per capita was 2.5 times that of Argentina.) Output and population data obtained from U.N., *Statistical Bulletin for Latin America,* vol. 4, no. 1.

61. See my "Industrialization and Labor Productivity Differentials," in *Review of Economics and Statistics* 47, no. 2 (May 1965): 207–14. For a similar study comparing Mexico and the United States see Edmar L. Bacha, "Comparación entre la Productividad Industrial de México y los Estados Unidos," *El Trimestre Económico* 33 (4), no. 132 (Oct.–Dec. 1966): 657–74.

ditions (e.g. low relative prices for leather inputs and high ones for steel inputs), but also by government policies, which sometimes reinforced and other times counteracted spontaneous market forces. The public sector has had at its disposal a vast arsenal of policy instruments since the last century, and its potential influence on the economy has steadily expanded. The state controls such traditional matters as taxes, tariffs, exchange rates, foreign investment, education, business and labor law. Since 1935, when the Central Bank was created, it has exerted a closer control on credit and the money supply. Public sector banks such as the Banco de la Nación (founded late last century), the Banco Industrial (founded in the early 1940s) and other national, provincial, and municipal banks account for about two-thirds of all loans and more than half of the deposits of the banking system.[62] Just the Banco de la Nación, the Banco Industrial, the Caja Nacional de Ahorro Postal, and the Banco Hipotecario (all controlled directly by the national government), account for 40 percent of all banking loans and most of the medium- and long-term banking loans. The public sector, furthermore, has major ownership and control of the following fields: railroads, electricity, air and ocean transport, primary gas and oil, telephones, pipelines, petroleum refining, and steel. Its power to set electricity, transport, and other public utility rates has been complete.[63]

This section will concentrate on how public policies influenced the structure of manufacturing, rather than on the link between overall manufacturing growth and such policies. Three types of policies had special influence on the pattern of industrialization since 1930: the protectionist system (buttressed by credit policy), the policy toward foreign capital, and the combined policies toward income distribution and employment.

Argentina lived from 1931 until 1959 under exchange control, which was often reinforced by import restrictions, duties, exchange surcharges, and prior deposits. There was a tendency to favor imports of raw materials, intermediate products, and some parts and machinery, while shutting out finished goods, especially durable and nondurable consumer goods. During most years, the exchange rate applied to the bulk of imports of raw materials and intermediate products was

62. These figures are taken from BCRA, *Boletín Estadístico* (Sept. 1966) p. 49. The figures refer to August 1966.

63. David Felix in "Some Notes on the Implementation of Argentine Industrialization Policy" (mimeographed), stresses that the power implied by this array of policy instruments is more formal than real.

overvalued, so that lucky holders of import licenses and exchange permits obtained these products cheaper, not only in comparison to importers of other products, but in all probability also cheaper than if a single free exchange rate had prevailed.[64] This subsidization of some imported inputs was especially marked during 1948–53 and was less important in earlier and later periods. In distributing foreign exchange, authorities gave first priority to raw materials, intermediate products, and spare parts because these inputs went to factories depending on them for their normal operations. Imports first to be cut after consumer goods were new machinery and equipment.

Prohibitions and high duties against some goods, coupled with implicit subsidies and a generous granting of import licenses for others, gave rise to a complex and discriminating structure of effective rates of protection for different activities. Existing or potential branches producing heavy intermediate products (basic metals, some chemicals, etc.), as well as other import-substituting activities not in manufacturing (such as oil extraction), were probably subject to *negative* effective protection during many postwar years until 1959, when currency overvaluation is taken into account. Activities producing finished consumer goods, on the other hand, received enormous protection.[65] Activities manufacturing machinery and equipment were in an intermediate position, as imports of these goods were regarded by authorities as the margin to be cut or expanded according to the exchange left after imports of raw materials and intermediate goods were taken care of. As a result, a more than usual uncertainty surrounded these activities.[66]

The protectionist system reinforced what could be considered the

64. Thus, part of the protectionist system compensated, but from the viewpoint of total import substitution only, for the overvaluation of the exchange rate.

65. These conjectures on effective protection receive support from rough estimates made by Bela Balassa in his "Integration and Resource Allocation in Latin America" (mimeographed). He finds that the highest effective tariffs in Argentina are those protecting textiles, clothing and shoes, foods and beverages, and lumber. For these four sectors the estimated effective protection is above 400 percent. While these figures apply to 1958, the general structure of protection in that year was typical of the postwar period. Although a general pattern of protection may be deduced, this does not imply that protection was granted in a systematic way. Little thought was given to framing a consistent overall system, with the result that no public official knew for certain the effective degree of protection granted to each activity.

66. Uncertainty about future government actions has plagued Argentine entrepreneurs of all types since the war. This has led many to hope more for stable rules of the game than for favorable ones.

normal industrialization pattern during the first stage of the post-1930 period. By the time this system reached its most extreme form (1946–53), the expansion of light branches had been going on for a long time and the need for great public concern with these flourishing industries may be questioned.[67] By 1948–50 most of the import-substitution that could be expected from these branches was

Table 4.25: Structure of Merchandise Imports, by Industrial Origin, 1928–65
(Percentages)

	1928–29	1930–34	1935–39	1945–49	1950–54	1955–59	1960–64
Total merchandise imports	100.0	100.0	100.0	100.0	100.0	100.0	100.0
Foodstuffs and tobacco	13.3	14.2	9.9	6.8	7.8	6.1	3.8
Textiles and their manufacture	25.3	30.6	25.6	15.6	9.5	3.4	3.4
Chemical and pharmaceutical products	4.7	6.5	6.2	6.8	7.3	7.1	6.9
Paper and cardboard	2.6	3.6	3.8	5.6	3.2	2.6	2.9
Wood and its manufactures	5.2	5.5	5.3	7.2	8.2	8.0	4.6
Stone, earth, glass, and ceramics	3.8	3.3	2.8	2.9	2.6	1.1	1.0
Iron, iron ore, and their manufactures	9.1	7.5	12.1	12.5	13.8	15.8	13.1
Machinery and vehicles (including parts)	16.1	8.1	11.9	18.8	20.3	25.1	44.8
Nonferrous metals	3.4	3.7	4.8	5.1	5.6	5.7	5.7
Fuels and lubricants	9.2	10.5	11.1	9.9	13.6	21.1	8.5
Rubber and its manufactures	1.5	1.3	1.0	1.7	1.8	2.0	2.7
Others	5.8	5.2	5.5	7.1	6.3	2.0	2.6

Note: Data for 1928–54 are expressed in pesos at current prices; for 1955–64 data are in dollars at current prices.

Source: Data obtained from DNEC, *Boletín de Estadística, Comercio Exterior,* and *Anuario del Comercio Exterior,* several issues.

exhausted; further growth based on import substitution had to come from the more rapid development of heavier industries.

67. During the war many of the industries that had been developing vigorously during the 1930s were able to export. The experience of the immediate post-World War I period haunted Argentines interested in industrialization. At that time, several activities which had developed under the special protection afforded by the war were allowed to contract or disappear under pressure of foreign competition once the war was over. It may be granted that it would have been a mistake to allow the unusually favorable, but short-lived, 1946–48 external conditions to result in widespread contraction of manufacturing. However, this certainly does not justify the extreme haphazard protectionist system created then. In fact, it could be argued that what was needed to consolidate the rapidly expanding industries and their export markets was a measured dose of foreign competition at home.

Tables 4.25 and 4.26 present the structure of merchandise imports, using various classifications and sources.[68] The most noticeable feature of these data is the decline in the share corresponding to light manufactured imports and of finished consumer goods, so that by

Table 4.26: Structure of Merchandise Imports,
According to Uses and Processing (ECLA), 1925–64
(Percentages)

	1925–29[a]	1930–34[a]	1935–39[a]	1945–49[a]	1950–54[a]	1950–54[b]	1955–59[b]	1960–64[b]
Total merchandise imports	100.0	100.0	100.0	100.0	100.0	100.0	100.0	100.0
Nondurable finished consumer goods	26.0	34.3	28.6	14.2	7.2	6.1	4.9	4.1
Durable finished consumer goods	11.1	5.5	5.1	9.7	5.4	3.7	4.2	4.7
Fuels and lubricants	4.7	6.5	5.9	6.8	14.1	18.4	21.5	9.7
Metallic intermediate products	5.9	6.5	7.8	10.3	13.6	14.0	17.6	13.8
Other intermediate products	20.2	27.4	27.3	29.1	32.8	32.9	26.7	24.8
Construction materials	10.2	6.8	6.2	5.6	5.6	5.3	3.3	4.0
Machinery and equipment for agriculture	4.9	1.4	1.7	2.2	3.5	3.3	3.1	2.6
Machinery and equipment for industry	13.3	9.3	11.3	12.7	11.4	9.7	10.4	20.6
Transport and communications equipment	3.4	2.3	6.0	9.4	6.0	6.3	7.9	14.7
Other	0.4	0.1	0.1	nil	0.4	0.3	0.4	1.0

[a] Computed using data in pesos at 1950 Argentine prices.
[b] Computed using data in dollars, at current dollar c.i.f. prices.

Sources: Data from ECLA, p. 109, and U.N., *Statistical Bulletin for Latin America,* several issues.

1950–54, foodstuffs, tobacco, textiles, and clothing, which before 1930 had accounted for about 40 percent of all imports, comprised only around 15 percent. Finished consumer goods, which before 1930 represented nearly two-fifths of all imports, by 1950–54 accounted only for around one-tenth. (It should be recalled that this reduction was achieved not only by replacing imports with domestic production, but in many cases by doing away with domestic consumption). By 1950–54 imports that could be substituted by light industries were few and included items that could not be produced in Argentina even with generous protection, and/or goods whose

68. See also Tables 108 and 109 in the Statistical Appendix.

importation was directly linked (via barter agreements) to Argentine exports.[69] On the other hand, the share of metals, vehicles, machinery and electrical equipment, either finished or as intermediate products, by 1950–54 represented around 40 percent of all imports, while the share of mining (mainly oil) and petroleum products stood at about 20 percent (when measured in dollar prices). Contrasts in the post-1930 evolution in the import quantum of different goods emerges most clearly from Table 4.27; a policy maker interested in the con-

Table 4.27: Quantum Indices of Merchandise Imports by Main Categories
According to Industrial Origin, 1925–61
(1937–39 = 100)

	1925–29	*1937–39*	*1946–49*	*1950–54*	*1955–59*	*1960–61*
Food, beverages, tobacco; textiles and clothing	113	100	57	34	28	27
Wood products; printing and publishing; leather products; paper and cardboard; chemical products; rubber products; stone, glass, and ceramics; and other manufacturing	126	100	93	72	87	110
Metals; vehicles and machinery; electrical machinery and appliances	135	100	139	100	125	200
Petroleum refining and mining products	108	100	130	168	236	158

Sources: As in Table 4.14.

tinuance of import substitution had to conclude as early as the late 1940s that greater impetus in metallurgical activities was required (see also Table 4.14).

The protectionist system developed before 1948–50 was not well suited to stimulate a smooth transition from one stage of industrialization to another. On the contrary, it created vested interests within manufacturing that took a dim view of new import substitution to provide, domestically, inputs that they imported with little difficulty at a favorable rate of exchange. Producers of light manufactured goods

69. Processed and unprocessed tropical foodstuffs, timber, and fibers used to manufacture bags (primarily employed to store and ship grains), are examples of this type of imports.

feared, with good reason, that domestic production of their previously imported inputs would result in an increase in their costs.[70]

Manufacturing stagnated during 1948–53. Although this period faced unfavorable exogenous factors like the drought of 1951–52, the failure of policy to recognize that future industrial growth had to come either from the expansion of manufactured exports or from the more complex import-substituting activities was an important cause of the stagnation. Protection and exchange rate policy were key elements hampering the required change in direction. As an indication of the subsidy given, *on the average,* to imports of raw materials, fuels, intermediate products and capital goods, the real average exchange rate (expressed as pesos per one U.S. dollar) applied to merchandise imports may be used.[71] With 1935–39 = 100, the index for the real import exchange rate fell to 79 in 1947–49, to 61 in 1950–52, and to 47 in 1953–55, rising after Perón's overthrow to 94 in 1956–58 and to 100 during 1959–61. During 1953–55, for example, an index of ad valorem import duties (1935–39 = 100) would have had to reach above 200 just to compensate, on the average and relative to 1935–39, for the overvaluation of the import peso. Some imports enjoyed even greater subsidization; for example, during 1951–55 the exchange rate applied to fuels and lubricants was five pesos per U.S. dollar, while the (overvalued) average import exchange rate moved in the range of 6.5 to 7.5 pesos. Prohibitions against finished consumer goods combined with subsidization of imported inputs gave already established light industry exorbitant effective rates of protection.[72]

Toward the end of the Perón regime, some of the implicit subsidies were reduced by reclassifying imports that could be purchased at different exchange rates. The exchange liberalization beginning in

70. Argentina lacked an instrument such as the Law of Similars, which stimulated backward linkage in Brazil. See Werner Baer, *Industrialization and Economic Development in Brazil* (Homewood, Illinois: R. D. Irwin, Inc., 1965), pp. 59–61. Stories are told of active lobbying by entrepreneurs of existing light industries against the establishment of potential domestic producers of their inputs. In spite of the cost advantage implied by the subsidization of some imported inputs, few light activities ventured into the export field after the immediate postwar period.

71. This real level is obtained by dividing an index of the average import exchange rate over the ratio of indices of Argentine overall wholesale prices to those of the United States.

72. The prohibitions allowed domestic producers to determine the price of finished goods only on the basis of the domestic market that, in most cases, was not large enough to generate vigorous competition.

October 1955 continued this process, culminating in a return to a single exchange rate in January 1959.[73] These policies encouraged the switch to a new stage of industrialization, helping branches at the frontier of import substitution, while hurting those that had slipped over the years into the category of home goods.

Other features of the protectionist system had an important influence on manufacturing. During the 1930s protection was granted through a combination of duties and exchange control, not wholly removing threats of foreign competition. But during the 1940s and 1950s (until 1959), emphasis was placed on quantitative restrictions severing all links between domestic and foreign markets, encouraging the creation of oligopolistic structures. During the Perón years, to justify applications for exchange permits, importers had to provide a detailed account of their import activity during the previous three to five years; this procedure hampered the entry of new entrepreneurs in many lines of activities. Often the output of a firm depended primarily on its luck and ability in obtaining permits to import raw materials. Cartelization was further encouraged in 1954 when the Central Bank resolved to grant import permits for industrial machinery on the basis of plans prepared jointly by the government and the Confederación General Económica, an association of industrial entrepreneurs closely linked at that time with the regime.[74]

73. But differential exchange surcharges were maintained favoring imports of raw materials and intermediate products. The changes that took place after 1953–55 in the relative price structure, primarily caused by a more flexible exchange rate policy, are illustrated by the following figures, showing indices of wholesale prices of imported products (in domestic currency) divided by the wholesale price index for all nonrural products, with 1959–61 = 100:

	1950–51	1956–57
Steel, iron, and other metals	74	86
Rubber	36	60

Basic price indices were obtained from BCRA, *Boletín Estadístico* (Sept. 1962), pp. 50–62, and DNEC, *Boletín Mensual de Estadística,* several issues. Similar experiences were registered in the relative price of oil which, as a result of a growing overvaluation of the peso, fell by nearly 50 percent between 1935–39 and 1950–51. See ECLA, 1:24.

74. See BCRA, *Memoria Anual,* 1954, p. 39. See also the Memorias for 1955 and 1956 for criticisms of the Perón exchange control system. It is repeatedly pointed out that often those who were lucky enough to obtain exchange permits, either by historical precedent or other means, sold them or the imported merchandise to third parties at fabulous profits. Little solid information exists on these shady matters and therefore the comments made earlier regarding the benefits accruing to light industry from the overvalued exchange rate should be qualified. Sometimes the windfall gains accrued, not

Under Perón, and even more recently, smuggling was the main market force disturbing the tranquility of many entrepreneurs. In recent years when, in spite of the removal of most quantitative restrictions, foreign competition has been kept out by prohibitive duties, smuggling has been credited by some observers for the modernization of the textile industry.

Public credit policy reinforced the influence of the protectionist system on the two phases of post-1930 industrialization. After its creation in 1944, the Banco Industrial rapidly became the main supplier of banking credit to industry.[75] Its loans and advances were channeled during 1944–53 primarily toward small establishments and handicrafts in food processing, beverages, tobacco, textiles, and clothing. After 1953 greater attention was given to larger establishments in new import-substituting activities.[76]

Most postwar public and private bank loans have been granted at negative real rates of interest and have been rationed among entrepreneurs using either ad hoc favoritism or historical records. These practices have strengthened established firms and delayed the entry of new entrepreneurs into either new or already existing activities, hampering both backward linkage and efficiency in old activities.[77]

During the war many manufacturing activities exported vigorously.

---

to the manufacturer processing the imported inputs, but to the commercial middleman selling them to the manufacturer. The larger manufacturing firms handling their import business directly avoided this difficulty.

75. Of all banking loans and advances to industry, the Banco Industrial share rose from 22 percent in 1946 to 78 percent in 1949. During 1951–55 this share was 53 percent, falling after Perón's overthrow and reaching little more than 10 percent during recent years. See O. Altimir, H. Santamaría, and J. Sourrouille, "Los Instrumentos de Promoción Industrial en la Postguerra," *Desarrollo Económico* 6, no. 24 (Jan.–March 1967): 723.

76. Altimir et al., "Los Instrumentos," *Desarrollo Económico* 7, no. 25 (April–June 1967): 894. See also David Felix, "Some Notes on the Implementation of Argentine Industrialization Policy" (mimeographed n.d.), pp. 13–14. Felix points out that medium- and long-term loans of the Banco Industrial fell from 45 percent of its total loans in 1947 to 28 percent in 1952. Loans for fixed investment financing fell from 29 percent to 14 percent between the same years.

77. During 1946–55 all bank deposits were nationalized, that is, commercial banks became branch offices for the BCRA, which in turn became one more instrument in the hands of central economic authorities. After 1955, the BCRA became somewhat more independent and controls over commercial banks were loosened. Their interest rates, however, remained under close public control and below the rate of inflation. During recent years the free money market has expanded vigorously, providing greater flexibility for entrepreneurs in need of credit.

Table 4.28 presents dollar values for goods under Title VI of export statistics, covering the main nontraditional manufactured exports from 1934 to 1959. Current dollar figures were corrected by the United States GNP implicit price deflator. According to these rough

Table 4.28: Merchandise Exports of Nontraditional Manufactured Goods
(Million U.S. dollars, annual averages)

	At current prices	At 1954 prices
1934–36	7.4	15.5
1937–39	10.5	21.5
1940–44	66.0	107.1
1945–46	113.8	158.9
1947–49	39.4	46.2
1950–54	21.2	37.2
1955–59	23.0	21.4

Note: "Merchandise Exports of Nontraditional Manufactured Goods" refers to items in Title VI of export statistics. Until 1951 basic data are expressed in current paper pesos, which were translated into dollars using the average exchange rate applied to exports. Due to the existence of multiple exchange rates during 1934–51, the figures should only be taken as rough estimations. The average export exchange rates used were the following:

1934 = 2.98	1939 = 3.39	1944 = 3.59	1949 = 3.56
1935 = 3.06	1940 = 3.49	1945 = 3.45	1950 = 4.61
1936 = 3.01	1941 = 3.55	1946 = 3.43	
1937 = 3.03	1942 = 3.64	1947 = 3.42	
1938 = 3.20	1943 = 3.65	1948 = 3.40	

Sources: DNEC, *Comercio Exterior*, several issues. Data on implicit GNP deflator for the United States from Council of Economic Advisors, *Economic Report of the President* (Jan. 1965), p. 196.

estimates, the real annual values of these exports during 1955–59 were about the same as they had been during 1937–39, when industry was much less developed. The war and immediate postwar expansion of manufactured exports was not continued and a sharp decline set in beginning in 1947. Although it was difficult to maintain new manufactured exports at 1940–47 levels, once the industrialized countries returned to peace, valuable export connections were allowed to wither.[78] The trade institute originally set up during the war to

78. The following quotes from official U.S. publications of the 1930s suggest that, even without the war, Argentina was poised at the brink of substantial increases in manufactured exports:
"Exports of leather from Argentina are expected to expand in the near future, as the local producers are keenly interested in creating a good foreign

stimulate manufactured exports to Latin America and the United States was transformed during 1946–55 into the Instituto Argentino de Promoción del Intercambio, concerned mainly with marketing domestic rural produce and bulk-buying foreign industrial goods.

Peso overvaluation is one key factor explaining the disappointing performance of manufactured exports after 1946, but the protectionist system is also responsible. Efficient activities were kept from exporting, especially during recent years when the exchange rate has been more favorable, by the fact that they had no choice but to purchase many of their inputs from inefficient domestic suppliers. For example, the high domestic cost of caustic soda has been blamed for low soap exports, and the poor quality and high cost of domestic thread has hampered exports of leather goods. Industrialization based on light activities could have been prolonged considerably if different policies had stimulated exports of textiles, leather goods, processed foodstuffs, etc.[79]

The protectionist system, including exchange rate and credit policy, was only one of the factors influencing the structure of

---

demand for their products. There are many existing conditions favoring the local tanning industry, which should be very helpful in increasing the exports of leather. The country is expected to become a more important factor in the international leather trade" (U.S. Department of Commerce, *International Trade in Leather,* Trade Promotion Series, No. 103, Washington, D.C., 1930, p. 43).

"Shoe manufacturers in Argentina believe that the prospects are favorable for a steady, fair-sized volume of export sales, since the quality of their products is better than that of most of the neighboring countries and since the Argentine quotations are lower than those generally offered by American and European suppliers" (U.S. Department of Commerce, *Leather Footwear: World Production and International Trade,* Washington, D.C., 1937, p. 40). This report also refers to shoe exports to Europe (especially Spain).

Table 98 in the Statistical Appendix shows a few specific exports that Argentina could have continued to promote abroad, apparently without great difficulty, after the end of the war.

79. Dairy products, not included under Title VI but covering such processed foodstuffs as cheese and butter, represented exports of about $50 million (at current dollars) as late as 1947–48; by 1951–52 they had dropped to around $16 million (at current dollars). Exports of textiles and clothing, which reached $54 million in their peak year of 1943, fell to less than $2 million by 1949 (both figures in current dollars). While in 1935 63,500 pairs of leather footwear were exported, in 1963 only 10,400 were sent abroad. In recent years, especially since 1962–63, some increment in the level of manufactured exports has been noticed. These exports have included new items such as machine tools as well as traditional items such as sugar. It is too early to tell whether this experience reflects a new trend or is simply the result of the depressed conditions of many industries during 1962–64.

manufacturing after 1930. For example, although favoring consumer good industries of the finishing touches species, it failed to induce by itself a significant motor vehicle industry. A second important element explaining changes in manufacturing structure is government policy toward foreign capital in general and toward foreign direct investment in particular.

Although after 1930 the capital inflow fell drastically, a modest stream of foreign direct investment was maintained, helping the 1933–43 industrialization. The expansion of rubber manufactures was almost wholly due to the establishment during the early 1930s of subsidiaries of well-known foreign tire firms.[80] Foreign manufacturing firms established in the 1920s, and even earlier, continued to expand. Ford and Chevrolet assembled automobiles in Argentina during the 1920s and continued their activities in the next decade.[81] By the late 1930s there was growing interest by many foreign firms in more complex manufacturing activities including iron and steel.

From 1943 until 1953 the government followed a policy of hostility or at least indifference toward foreign capital. Until 1948 plentiful exchange plus remaining possibilities of import substitution in branches where the cooperation of foreign know-how is not of critical importance were able to offset negative aspects of this policy. The 1948–54 stagnation induced its reconsideration. It became clear that the new industrialization stage required the cooperation, in one way or another, of foreign technology and experience in branches such as the tractor, motor vehicle, steel and other engineering industries.[82] This policy change which took place in 1953 became more marked after 1955, culminating in a massive inflow of direct foreign investment

80. Immigrants fleeing the deteriorating European scene, many of them taking along their capital (in some cases in the form of machines), played an important role in the expansion of the textile industry during these years. The U.S. depression and greater Argentine protection seem to have accelerated the inflow of North American branch plants into Argentina; D. M. Phelps lists six such plants during 1926–29 and eleven during 1930–33. See his *Migration of Industry to South America* (New York: McGraw-Hill Book Co., 1936), p. 13.

81. Ford began assembling automobiles in Argentina in 1917. By 1925 it had assembled 100,000 autos. Before 1947, 378,000 automotive vehicles had been assembled by all companies.

82. It is conceivable that these industries could be developed without the help of foreign technology and capital (which are often hard to separate), but for a country such as Argentina that effort would have a very high real cost. The government, in fact, launched several pilot projects during the late 1940s and early 1950s for the production of airplanes, motor vehicles, and other transport equipment. The Perón regime also dabbled with the idea of starting its own production of atomic weapons.

during 1960–61 into the more complex branches of manufacturing.[83] An upsurge of other contacts between Argentine and foreign firms, not necessarily involving credit, also took place after 1953. These contacts, important for the transmission of new techniques of production and management, had been hampered by the xenophobic and inward-looking climate of the earlier Perón years.

If a friendlier attitude toward foreign investment had prevailed during 1943–53, the transition between the two post-1930 industrialization stages would have been smoother. It is not unreasonable to suppose that under those circumstances the motor vehicle industry, for example, could have expanded immediately after the war, incorporating a greater share of domestically produced parts than it had done during the 1930s. Such a gradual process would have been more efficient than the haphazard post-1959 crash expansion of the automotive industry. Nationalistic policies cost Argentina the direct foreign investment that stimulated industrialization in Australia, Brazil, and Canada during the postwar period.[84]

When doors were again opened to foreign investment, special sweeteners were added to erase memories of earlier hostility. Ironically, the protectionist system built on nationalistic considerations has often

83. Foreign direct investment projects approved by the Ministry of Economy between May 1958 and December 1961, amounting to nearly 400 million U.S. dollars (excluding investments in oil extraction), were allocated in the following fashion: chemicals, 32 percent; automotive vehicles, 25 percent; basic nonferrous metals, 12 percent; petroleum refining, 8 percent; nonelectrical machinery, railroad and ocean transport equipment, and basic iron and steel, 13 percent; other, 10 percent.

About half of this investment came from the United States. Unfortunately, no comprehensive data on foreign ownership of Argentine industry are available for recent years. Table 99 in the Statistical Appendix gives data on the founding of United States-owned manufacturing plants in Argentina. They confirm that industrialization during the 1930s was supported by foreign investment, and that the 1945–54 efforts lacked such support. In contrast with pre-1930 foreign investments, little of the post-1930 capital inflow went into export activities. Areas where pre-1930 direct foreign investment had predominated (railroads, public services) have passed into the hands of the public sector, which, however, still relies on foreign funds for expansion plans. See Altimir et al., "Los Instrumentos," *Desarrollo Económico* 7, no. 27 (Oct.– Dec. 1967): 366–76.

84. Argentina's neutralism during most of the war also hindered its industrialization. While Brazil got Volta Redonda, Argentina was placed low on the list of receivers of scarce raw materials and industrial equipment from the U.S. In 1940, U.S. direct investments in Argentina were 60 percent higher than in Brazil; by 1955 they were only 40 percent of U.S. direct investment in Brazil. See ECLA, *El Proceso de Industrialización en América Latina,* Statistical Appendix, p. 170.

been used to shield powerful foreign companies, raising serious doubts whether this combination of high protection plus foreign investment leaves the country better or worse off than lower protection and lower import-substituting foreign investment. This argument is independent of noneconomic criteria regarding the optimum level of foreign investment. As with Canada, Australia, and Western Europe, Argentina will also have to reach its own political judgment as to where to draw the line in building an Argentine capitalism without Argentine capitalists.[85]

Table 4.10 presented estimates of the apparent income elasticity of demand for each of the major manufacturing branches. Per capita income is of course only one of the variables influencing demand; relative prices, the consumption-investment mix, changes in tastes due to urbanization, etc., are other possible explanatory variables. Of greater importance in Argentina is another omitted variable: income distribution. Since 1940 sharp changes in income distribution have taken place, and it could be expected that they had a significant influence on the structure of demand for manufactured products and, therefore, on the pattern of industrialization.

Taking four of the principal light manufactured goods, the following results are obtained when one attempts to explain their per capita apparent domestic consumption as a function of per capita gross domestic product (y), as well as of an index of the wage share in the national income (w), where all variables are expressed in logarithms:

$$C_1 = \quad 0.98 \mid 0.56\,y + 0.30\,w \qquad R^2 = 0.45 \qquad (4.6)$$
$$ (0.18) \quad (0.20)$$

$$C_2 = -3.62 + 0.43\,y + 0.80\,w \qquad R^2 = 0.72 \qquad (4.7)$$
$$ (0.15) \quad (0.16)$$

$$C_3 = -0.31 + 0.46\,y + 0.53\,w \qquad R^2 = 0.32 \qquad (4.8)$$
$$ (0.27) \quad (0.29)$$

$$C_4 = -1.87 + 0.57\,y + 0.49\,w \qquad R^2 = 0.52 \qquad (4.9)$$
$$ (0.19) \quad (0.20)$$

Variables C_1, C_2, C_3, and C_4, represent apparent per capita con-

85. Here I am paraphrasing Felipe Pazos. It is amazing that the infant industry argument is still used to justify tariff protection benefiting such infants as General Motors and Ford. A better argument can be made for using tariffs to protect budding domestic private entrepreneurs who, in dynamic industries, often appear on the verge of being squeezed out between foreign private firms and domestic public ones.

sumption of food and beverages, tobacco, textiles, and clothing, respectively. The figures in parentheses show the standard errors of the coefficients, while R stands for the multiple correlation coefficient. These estimates are based on data for 1937, 1939, and 1946–61.[86] The wage share coefficient is more than twice its standard error for tobacco and clothing; it does not fail this test by much for foodstuffs, beverages, and textiles. More refined and disaggregated data would probably improve the fit. But even as they stand, they support the thesis that income redistribution influenced the pattern of demand and thus affected the structure of manufacturing.[87] The post-1950 stagnation of traditional activities was caused not only by the exhaustion of their import-substituting possibilities and the low pure income elasticity of demand for their output, but also by the decline in the wage share, while their fast expansion during the 1940s was due not only to import substitution but also to gains made by the wage share.

The relationship between demand and the structure of productive capacity has not all been one way. Once capacity was created and workers were employed to put it into operation, governments were reluctant, especially until 1959, to take actions that could jeopardize employment security and the job-producing potential of these activities. Under these circumstances resource reallocation became difficult because any industry, simply by the fact that it was already operating, was given priority over other potential industries. The choice of existing versus potential industries is clear in decisions as to which exchange applications should be given priority—those for raw material imports for existing firms which could be inefficiently producing consumer goods, or those for machinery imports needed for new factories. During most of the period under study the former were favored. Similar considerations prevailed in rationing subsidized credit. Thus, existing plant and equipment, some of it set up under conditions no longer relevant, and the pattern of employment, exerted strong pressure on government to generate a demand structure making reallocation unnecessary. These factors were of special importance

---

86. See notes to Tables 4.10 and 4.14 for the sources of data.

87. The investment-consumption mix, not unrelated to income distribution, also influenced the pattern of industrialization. For example, the rapid growth of stone, clay, and ceramics from 1945 to 1950 and its much lower growth since 1950 followed the evolution of construction activity.

during 1948–55, when they exerted a negative influence on efficiency and nonconstruction capital formation.[88]

The Perón regime showed special concern with generating employment for rural workers streaming into urban centers. In a simple model with only labor and capital, this policy may at first sight seem warranted. Argentina, at least relative to the United States, is labor rich and capital poor. But even neglecting third factors such as skilled labor and land, it is obvious that other considerations (true prices for outputs and foreign exchange, for example) should have been taken into account when deciding which investments had the highest social rate of return. The preoccupation with employment reinforced the expansion of small-scale light manufacturing as well as construction. In its zeal to generate jobs, the government encouraged inefficient fragmentation in many industrial sectors which were sheltered from the consequences of their inefficiency by all-out protection against foreign competition and by corporate-state techniques on the internal front. Succeeding regimes have found the dismantling of this system, which has also retarded technological progress, politically difficult.

Throughout this section the phrase "industrial policies" and similar ones have been used freely, but the reader should not get the impression that a comprehensive plan existed in the minds of policy makers at all times. When it did, it was not implemented in a coordinated fashion by the many policy instruments at the disposal of the government. The patterns that have been detected resulted from attempts at reconciling diverse economic and social pressures converging on the public sector. Policy makers seldom took time out from day to day pressures to take an overall look at industrialization and to give it a definite direction. Political instability contributed to the lack of an integrated policy. As a result, the vast influence that the public sector exercises on industry through its many policy instruments and direct purchases is often capricious, inconsistent, and sometimes the prey of private interests that manipulate it for their own gain.

ARGENTINE INDUSTRY IN THE 1960s: CONCLUDING REMARKS

The study of Argentine industrialization suggests that, while it is

88. During those years domestic capacity for producing new machinery and equipment was limited, at the same time that imported input requirements of industries manufacturing consumer goods used up most of the available foreign exchange.

useful for descriptive purposes to divide this process into stages, this can be justified only as a preliminary step to analyzing policies and economic forces giving rise to those phases. The observed clear-cut stages were not inevitable, nor do they say much about what the optimal new stage should be. Backward linkage is far from automatic (and its optimality is questionable) since import-substituting industrialization generates forces within manufacturing opposing further import substitution.

In contrast with essay 2, this essay isolated industrialization stages independently of purely political events. In particular, post-1930 industrialization was divided in such a way that the years under the influence of General Perón (1943–55) were cut into two periods, each falling into a different stage. The name of Perón has become identified with industrialization, an unwarranted association when this process is analyzed with a long-run perspective. The early Peronist industrialization policies culminated and consolidated trends beginning early in the 1930s but had only limited success in encouraging the more complex manufacturing branches. Not until late in the Peronist regime was strong impetus given to heavier branches. It can be argued that, *given the decision not to promote exports of either rural or manufactured products,* the early postwar emphasis on light manufacturing was misplaced and that a forward-looking policy would have worried primarily about more complex industries, for which state support was of greater strategic importance, and about the expansion of oil extraction and key social overhead facilities.[89] This criticism of 1943–53 policies has to do with their internal inconsistency for achieving sustainable high growth rates. As new machinery and equipment must be either imported or produced domestically, a decision regarding export policy must imply a corresponding action on their domestic production, as foreign exchange savings that could have been expected from further expansion of light industries was limited. On the other hand, during that im-

89. Oil output, which expanded at an annual rate of 7.1 percent during 1935–43, grew at only 1.6 percent during 1943–55. Installed public service electricity generating capacity grew at less than 2 percent per annum during 1943–55. Also noteworthy was the neglect of higher education and the anti-intellectual climate (covering old-fashioned intellectuals as well as technicians and scientists), which permeated the Perón regime. It was during the late Perón years that the brain-drain from Argentina first gained momentum, although it grew worse after his overthrow.

mediate postwar period, authorities were concerned with avoiding a recurrence of events that immediately followed World War I and with generating urban employment. A type of Keynesian economics, rather than the economics of growth, guided public officials with fresh memories of the Great Depression well into the early 1950s. However, Argentine officials were not the only ones in the world with such an attitude during those years.

Post-1955 industrialization policies, in turn, continued trends initiated by the Peronist regime around 1953. Activities at the frontier of import substitution were developed with the help of foreign investors and generous protection. While correcting previous excessive emphasis on nontradeable goods, and although accompanied by other more favorable measures toward exports, the new industrialization policies induced fresh resource misallocations, best exemplified by the way in which the automotive industry was encouraged to expand.

It is difficult to quantify the costs of postwar policies. In essay 2 a possible macroeconomic guesstimate has been sketched. One difficulty in evaluating the cost of protection at a more micro level is that it cannot always be assumed that, because a given industry is not now competitive in world markets at true exchange rates, such a situation implies that no other policies could have obtained a different result. Excessive protection and oligopolistic tranquility may have kept some firms from searching for cost reductions and foreign markets. Thus, another ironic result of ultraprotectionist policies may have been to stunt the development of a dynamic class of industrial entrepreneurs and of the infant industries whose growth it was trying to foster.

If one acknowledges that a good share of these costs are sunk, the question may be raised as to what the next industrialization stage should be. More properly, it may be asked which industrial projects have the highest social rates of return and whether such a group of projects shows common characteristics. It may first be noted that, although the protectionist system existing during 1961–66 was less restrictive than that of earlier years (mainly in that quantitative restrictions played a smaller role), the level of duties (including exchange surcharges) remained at extraordinarily high levels and the tariff structure still resulted in a haphazard distribution of effective protection. Ad hoc tariff exemptions, several flat prohibitions, "Buy Argentine" regulations, previous deposit requirement, etc., add to the confusion.[90] It should also be observed that 1960–66 output data indicate that the post-1950 industrialization pattern has continued.[91] Finally, criteria for allocating bank credit did not change much during those years.

Discussion of the future of industrialization has been stimulated by the glaring inefficiencies reflected in high relative prices of many manufactured goods, as well as by the apparent inability of import

90. Regardless of how the average height of tariffs is calculated, 1959 Argentine import duties and charges were found to be higher than those of Brazil and Chile, and about eight times those of France. The average level of import duties and charges in Argentina, using the Brussels Tariff Nomenclature as the weighting system, reached 151 percent. See Santiago Macario, "Protectionism and Industrialization in Latin America," *Economic Bulletin for Latin America* 9, no. 1 (March 1964): 73. The great spread in effective rates of protection arising from the tariff structure may be seen in Bela Balassa, "Integration and Resource Allocation," Table 2. Its irrational nature is also discussed by Macario, pp. 68–83. A few examples of nominal ad valorem import duties (including exchange surcharges) in early 1965 are given below, in percentages:

Whiskey	173	Natural rubber	1	Fuel oil	20
Cotton yarn	115	Lumber	60	Spare parts for industrial	
Silk fabrics	68	Cotton	64	boilers	94
Paint	173	Sulphur	116	Internal combustion motors	174
Insecticides	52	Caustic soda	172	Harvesting machines	172
Light bulbs	275	Iron valves	174	Television sets	214
Ball bearings	138	Pig iron	25	Autos over 1,900 kgs.	609
Wood pulp	26	Steel plates	48		

On the other hand, during 1959–63, more than half of all merchandise imports have come in completely duty free, mostly as a result of special exemptions.

91. The total percentage increases in output between 1960–61 and 1965–66 have been as follows:

Total Manufacturing 23

Foodstuffs and beverages	18	Chemical products	39
Tobacco	12	Petroleum refining	48
Textiles	18	Rubber products	25
Clothing	1	Stone, glass, and	
Wood and its products	23	ceramics	25
Printing and publishing	15	Metals	39
Leather products	−12	Vehicles and machinery	33
Handicrafts and others	0	Electrical machinery	
Paper and cardboard	41	and appliances	6

The burden of industrialization continues to be carried by the import substituting efforts of several dynamic industries, although a recovery in the growth rate of a few vegetative branches is noteworthy. Recent data obtained from BCRA, *Boletín Estadístico* (Jan. 1968), p. 47. It would have been useful to separate "Electrical machinery and appliances" into its appliance and machinery components, which would probably show different developmental behavior over the last 40 years.

substitution to further contract the aggregate ratio of imports to GDP.

Relative prices of manufactured goods in Argentina traditionally have been higher than in North America and industrialized Western Europe, but this pattern (which will be discussed in essay 6) has been drastically accentuated by postwar policies. David Felix has found the following ratios of Argentine to United States prices for the period 1960–65, using a large sample of wholesale prices:[92]

Processed food and beverages	1.0
Textiles and clothing	1.4
Wood products	1.1
Leather goods	0.7
Paper and paper products	1.6
Chemical products	1.9
Rubber products	1.6
Stone, glass, and ceramics	0.8
Metals and metal products	1.5
Vehicles and machinery	2.2
Electrical equipment	1.6

Another recent study showed the following ratios of prices of Argentine products to similar foreign products (landed in Buenos Aires), for June 1965–June 1966:[93]

Cement	1.4
Ford automotive vehicles	3.3
Fiat automotive vehicles	2.8
Steel cables	3.8
Zinc	2.1
Seamless steel pipes	2.0
Steel plates	1.9

The Economic Commission for Latin America has compared the 1962 prices of a long list of Argentine manufactures with those found during the same year in Houston and Los Angeles. By computing the exchange rate (pesos per one dollar) required to equalize Argentine and United States prices for some of these products, the following

92. See David Felix, "Beyond Import Substitution: A Latin American Dilemma" (mimeographed), pp. 56–60.

93. See "Costos y Precios Industriales en la Argentina," *Techint, Boletín Informativo,* no. 155 (Nov. 1966), pp. 20–26.

results are obtained (the average merchandise exchange rate for that year was 113):

Beer	71	Washing soap	36	Vitamin C	383
Footwear	83	Refrigerators	213	Penicillin	109
Cotton fabrics	155	Washing machine	149	Aspirin	217
Rayon fabrics	180	Electric iron	165	Cement	131
Woolen fabrics	75	Sewing machine	137	Paint	106
Toilet paper	175	Radio	245	Trucks	269
Light bulbs	145	TV set	230	Diesel engine	306

These figures, besides indicating the high prices of most Argentine manufactured goods, also suggest the variety existing within that sector in costs and productivity.[94] In general, activities producing nondurable goods and relying on domestic raw materials tend to have low relative prices, while the opposite is the case for durable consumer goods and machinery and equipment.

According to the secretariat of the Latin American Free Trade Association, a sample of four major steel products showed that Argentine prices were between 1.5 and 2.5 times higher than those in Western European countries belonging to the coal and steel community, and were also higher than Brazilian and Mexican prices.[95]

Studies explaining the price differentials between Argentine and foreign manufactured products are scarce. A limited domestic market leading to small-scale operations, inefficient managers bemused by inflation and tranquilized by protection, and the high cost of iron, steel, and other inputs are often given as explanations. Only industrial studies at a microeconomic level can quantify the importance of each of these factors; some industries, for example, appear to be technologically very modern and yet have very high relative prices (e.g. the auto and electrical appliance industries), while others have relatively low prices but seem prima facie the refuge of old-fashioned entre-

94. Data obtained from ECLA, "The Process of Industrialization in Latin America," Statistical Appendix (mimeographed), p. 89, Table II–51. Given import duties, the rate of 113 pesos per dollar in 1962 was probably close to "equilibrium."

95. See *Economic Survey* (Oct. 11, 1966), p. 911. The study refers to 1965. When a correction is made for a likely overvaluation of the peso at the time the study was made, the range of the ratio of Argentine to Western European prices widens to between 1.3 and 2.8. Disaggregating within the metallurgical industry, Hugh Schwartz, in "The Argentine Experience," concludes that "individual Argentine metallurgical industries are marked by a wide range of cost positions, ranging from extreme comparative disadvantage to comparative advantage" (p. 180).

preneurs, ancient techniques, and thorough disregard for quality control (e.g. tanning and leather products).

The apparent inability of import substitution to further contract the aggregate ratio of imports of goods and services to gross domestic production has been even more disturbing to some than the high relative prices of manufactured goods. Expressed at 1960 prices, this coefficient moved from 23.1 percent in 1935–39 to 15.4 percent in 1945–49 and 11.6 percent in 1950–54. It has remained since then at roughly that level (11.2 percent in 1955–59 and 11.9 percent in 1960–64). The constancy in the aggregate ratio hides two conflicting tendencies: the growth in the share in aggregate demand of goods with a relatively high import component (a point stressed by David Felix), on the one hand, and net import substitution, measured *at the most disaggregated levels of activity,* on the other. In other words, if this import substitution had not taken place, and if the change in demand structure had been allowed to occur, the *ex ante* aggregate import coefficient would have been much higher than that actually registered.

Efficiency considerations make advisable a gradual rationalization of the tariff structure and a lowering of the average level of duties, accompanied by greater reliance on flexible exchange rates to avoid balance of payments difficulties. These policies will result in a domestic price structure closer to reflecting social costs and benefits than that of the postwar period. The upsurge in demand for goods of the importable type, which even accelerated import substitution may not be able to meet without a return to postponement and controls, could be satisfied in part by foreign exchange from additional exports made feasible by the proposed policies. These policies will also make new industrialization stages less predictable because the link between income elasticities of demand and output growth will be loosened. Some traditional branches as well as new activities may expand into foreign markets, and, although many import-substituting dynamic activities will still grow, others with higher costs may not need to do so with imports filling the gap.[96] The market, in short, is blind to the

96. The relative abundance of skilled and semiskilled labor in Argentina may lead to the development of exports of manufactured products using these inputs intensively and not characterized by sharp economies of scale. Recent experience with exports of machine tools is encouraging. Other metallic products requiring large doses of skilled labor, such as boilers, railroad wagons, etc., also show promise. During 1967 steps were taken to rationalize the protective system and encourage exports. Argentina, as other Latin American countries, may find a Latin American Common Market (with a moderate external common tariff) the least painful path toward liberalization of foreign trade.

labels we pin on different manufacturing activities, and so should be
the government officials who weigh social costs and benefits of alternative projects and policies. The new stage that could be opened by
the suggested policies will in all likelihood be more difficult to
characterize, even *ex post,* than those discussed in this essay. The
structure of manufacturing may become more specialized—although
 not necessarily along the lines of light versus heavy industry—and
less balanced, but more efficient.

5

The Tariff, 1906–1940

Few topics in Argentine economic history are as shrouded in confusion as the nature of the import tariff and commercial policy before World War II. Because of extreme protectionist policies followed since then, there is a tendency to regard the first forty years of the century as characterized by almost free trade. It has been suggested, furthermore, that tariffs and other policies were constructed in such a way as to discourage import-competing industries. Two quotes will illustrate this viewpoint:

> The group of cattle-raisers and exporters, which traditionally dominated Argentine politics, tended to favor the importation of manufactured products, rather than the raw materials necessary to manufacture them domestically. This gave rise to the peculiar policy, characteristic of Argentine tariff legislation, of hampering imports of raw materials by the use of tariffs, a policy which has been correctly labeled "protectionism in reverse." But it is even more interesting that even exchange control was used, to a certain extent, from its creation, to hamper rather than to encourage the industrial growth of the country.[1]

> Scrutiny of the tariff history as well as of the attitude of the authorities, which attitude has been accentuated, especially since 1933, reveals that it is as consistent as it is uncompromising in its emphasis on revenue. If a distinct trade policy is discernible at all, it is rather one of "protectionism in reverse". . . . The Argentine official attitude towards growing industry was remarkable in its outright hostility or, at least, "malevolent neutrality."

---

1. W. M. Beveraggi-Allende, *El Servicio del Capital Extranjero y El Control de Cambios* (México: Fondo de Cultura Económica, 1954), p. 214. I have translated the quote from the original in Spanish.

Though industrialization was not prohibited, it was, with few exceptions, discriminated against by the customs tariff. Once the exchange control was instituted in 1932, this discrimination often extended to foreign exchange matters also.[2]

Similar quotes could be multiplied.[3] Although the arguments are often contradictory and vague, most can be summarized in the following propositions.

1. Before World War II the level of Argentine tariffs was very low.

2. Tariffs were used primarily for revenue only.

3. The tariff structure was deliberately designed to discourage domestic industry.

4. The exchange control established during the 1930s was often used to discourage domestic industry.

5. All of these policies were suboptimal for Argentine growth and existed only because they benefited influential rural and exporting interests.

Propositions 1 and 2 appear plausible, not only because until the Great Depression free trade was accepted in most intellectual circles as the ideal commercial policy, but also on the basis of the Stolper-Samuelson and Heckscher-Ohlin theorems. The relatively abundant factor in Argentina was land, and native landowners had a powerful voice in government; moreover the relatively scarce factors, labor and capital, were provided to a large extent by immigrant foreigners, vulnerable to nationalistic feelings. These conditions called for a policy of free trade as well as for encouragement of immigration

2. Felix J. Weil, *Argentine Riddle* (New York: The John Day Company, 1944), pp. 134–35.

3. See, for example, T. R. Fillol, *Social Factors in Economic Development: The Argentine Case* (Cambridge: M.I.T. Press, 1961), pp. 43–44; Ricardo M. Ortiz, *Historia Económica de la Argentina* (Buenos Aires: Editorial Raigal, 1955), 2: 201–02. The most prolific Argentine protectionist during 1906–40 was without doubt Alejandro E. Bunge. This remarkable man, who as early as 1916 prepared estimates of the national wealth and national income of Argentina, was a forerunner of the Prebisch thesis and of the *Desarrollista* school; throughout the 1920s and 1930s he wrote about "aster" or "star" countries and "satellite" countries in international commerce, using these terms in the sense they were later to have under the labels of "center" and "periphery." Among his many writings, the following are most relevant on the tariff issue: *La Economía Argentina,* vol. 3 (Buenos Aires, 1928,) and *Una Nueva Argentina* (Buenos Aires, 1940). Besides higher tariffs he also advocated the banning of scrap iron and steel exports, to encourage their use by domestic manufacturers. The vast Argentine railroad network generated large quantities of scrap metal.

of labor and capital. Propositions 3 and 4 have a certain appeal arising from their cleverness in exposing a no less clever scheme. Proposition 5 is debatable, but those claiming that the Great Depression was inevitable and should have been obvious to any careful observer as early as 1915–20, can make some sort of a case for it.

For a student of Argentine history accustomed to these arguments, it comes as a surprise to read the following statements, referring to the pre-1940 period:

> Argentina is professedly a protectionist country. . . . Curiously enough, the vital industries of the country have not been favoured in any way by the fiscal system, which has been used to foster exotics and economic growths hardly suited to the conditions of the country. . . . With the exception of railway material, which for the most part, comes in duty free, all manufactured articles pay a very heavy duty indeed.[4]

> Argentina, prior to 1930, had not made one important tariff reduction prejudicial to the interest of manufacturers during the twentieth century.[5]

> These factories . . . that had begun to emerge during the rapid economic growth of the 1880's . . . had a very active interest in protection, for often tariffs provided the sole basis for their survival. There was, as a result, a concentration of lobbying pressure on congress which the vastly more important but unorganized agricultural interests of the country could not match. A case in point has already been noted: the bag industry, which gave employment to some two thousand workers stitching together imported, precut pieces of burlap with imported twine. . . . Almost identical was the case of the galvanized iron industry. Ordinary iron sheets were imported and then corrugated and galvanized in Argentina.[6]

Thus, the popular belief that little protection was granted domestic industry until the 1930's is not borne out by history.

4. N. L. Watson, *The Argentine as a Market* (Manchester: Manchester University Press, 1908), pp. 41–42.

5. D. M. Phelps, *Migration of Industry to South America* (New York: McGraw-Hill Book Co., 1936), p. 65.

6. James R. Scobie, *Revolution on the Pampas: A Social History of Argentine Wheat, 1860–1910* (Austin: University of Texas Press, 1964), pp. 130–31.

True, there was a lively disposition to reconcile "reasonable protection to national industries with the interests of commerce and
internal consumers," but some protection was granted as early
as 1876, and increasing emphasis was placed upon industrial
protection after World War I. Between 1913 and 1925, equivalent *ad valorem* tariff rates for a list of representative import
products ranged from 25 to 30 percent, and a League of Nations
study released in 1927 stated that effective tariff rates in Argentina were the third-highest among the 20 leading commercial nations in the world.[7]

More quotes can be found claiming that Argentina was a protectionist country all along.[8] Unfortunately, most opinions on either side
are given without factual support or, at best, present a few scattered
numbers. It seems more fruitful to explore available data on this issue.

This essay may then be interpreted as a long footnote to essays 1,
2, and 4, but its main contribution may be to suggest the need to re-
examine beliefs about Argentine and Latin American economic history, which are often based on little more than their frequent repeti-
tion.

THE LEVEL OF IMPORT DUTIES

In December 1905 a new tariff law was approved by the Argentine
Congress. The tariff went into effect in January 1906, and although it
was revised several times, principally in 1911, 1923, and 1931, the
basic law was still in force at the outbreak of World War II. Discussion will be limited to the period between 1906 and 1940, because

7. Arthur D. Little, Inc., *Some Aspects of Industrial Development in
Argentina* (Report to the Government of Argentina and the International Cooperation Administration, Aug. 25, 1961), pp. 22–23.

8. Even Felix Weil quotes, but rejects, opinions of several authors to this
effect. See his *Argentine Riddle,* pp. 133–35. According to Weil, "the prevailing
opinion among American students of the subject" was that Argentina was a
protectionist country (p. 133). United States official publications also shared
this point of view, as evidenced by the following quote from the U.S. Tariff
Commission written in 1945: "In recent decades the Argentine import tariff has
been one of the highest in Latin America, as well as in the world. . . . Form-
erly, the Argentine customs tariff was primarily a fiscal instrument, and rates of
duty were adjusted to obtain the revenue desired. In recent years, however,
particularly since the First World War, increasing emphasis has been placed
upon protection." See U.S. Tariff Commission, *Economic Controls and Commercial Policy in Argentina* (Washington, D.C., 1948), p. 9.

there is enough complexity here to keep us busy.[9] The 1906 law set an estimated unit value (*aforo*) on each imported item that could be changed only by law. Thus, although the law included duties expressed in both ad valorem and specific terms, so long as the aforo or tariff values were unchanged, all duties were in effect specific. Therefore their incidence depended, among other things, on world prices. The aforo and duties were expressed in gold pesos whose value was fixed in relation to other gold standard currencies until the beginning of the Great Depression. Variations in the exchange rate between paper and gold pesos, which took place during some of the years under study, do not affect the ratio of duties over the value of imports so long as both magnitudes are expressed either in gold or paper pesos. After the abandonment of the gold standard, both specific duties and aforo values were expressed in paper pesos.

The 1906 law contained few prohibitive duties, and quantitative import restrictions did not exist. This encourages the use of an admittedly crude measure of tariff height: the ratio of collected duties to the value of all merchandise imports. Table 5.1 presents, in column

9. Since independence was won in 1810, the Argentine (or Buenos Aires Province) tariff has had a lively history and was a cause of friction between Buenos Aires and the rest of the country. The provinces of the north and west, which had developed modest manufacturing activities under Spanish domination, were protectionist while Buenos Aires favored free trade. For discussion of the nineteenth century struggles over commercial policy and control of custom revenues among Argentine provinces see Aldo Ferrer, *La Economía Argentina* (México: Fondo de Cultura Económica, 1963), Chapters 5 through 8; H. S. Ferns, *Britain and Argentina in the Nineteenth Century* (Oxford: Clarendon Press, 1960), chapter 9; A. Dorfman, *Evolución Industrial Argentina* (Buenos Aires: Editorial Losada, 1942), pp. 318–20. Of special interest is chapter 5 in Juan Alvarez, *Las Guerras Civiles Argentinas* (Buenos Aires: Eudeba, 1966; first published by Roldán, 1912). This author takes for granted that the Argentine tariff was meant to be protectionist throughout most of the nineteenth century and early twentieth. In fact he seems to attribute the rapid growth of the city of Buenos Aires to the tariff. (See page 96 in Eudeba's edition.) Writing in 1896, Michael G. Mulhall observed: "There are millions of acres in the Pampas suitable for sheep-farming, which could carry 200 millions of sheep, were it not for a school of pseudo-economists at Buenos Ayres who decry pastoral industry, and endeavour to turn all the energies of the nation to tillage and manufactures" (*Industries and Wealth of Nations* [London, New York, and Bombay: Longmans, Green, and Co., 1896], p. 364). It is noteworthy that as early as 1804 residents of Buenos Aires were already debating the issues of Industry versus Agriculture and Protection versus Free Trade. See several 1804 issues of the *Semanario de Agricultura, Industria y Comercio,* as reprinted in Volume II of the Biblioteca de la Junta de Historia y Numismática Americana (Buenos Aires, 1937), especially pp. 77–109. The writer of that piece also complains of the excessive size of the city of Buenos Aires!

Table 5.1: Data on the Level of Import Duties in Argentina, 1906–1940

	A Total import duties as a percentage of the real value of merchandise imports	B Ratio of tariff value of imports to their real value	C Total import duties as a percentage of the tariff value of merchandise imports
1906	−a	−	19.8
1907	−	−	19.8
1908	−	−	22.0
1909	−	−	21.7
1910	20.1	0.927	21.6
1911	19.2	0.906	21.2
1912	18.5	0.861	21.5
1913	17.7	0.849	20.8
1914	16.2	0.843	19.2
1915	13.7	0.743	18.4
1916	12.6	0.594	21.2
1917	11.2	0.485	23.1
1918	7.8	0.331	23.5
1919	7.5	0.350	21.3
1920	7.5	0.349	21.6
1921	9.4	0.450	21.0
1922	11.7	0.541	21.6
1923	12.3	0.533	23.1
1924	13.6	0.714	19.1
1925	15.2	0.757	20.1
1926	15.3	0.840	18.2
1927	15.5	0.857	18.1
1928	17.4	1.014	17.1
1929	17.3	1.023	16.9
1930	16.7	1.020	16.4
1931	21.7	1.028	21.1
1932	28.6	1.040	27.5
1933	28.7	1.083	26.5
1934	22.4	0.923	24.2
1935	23.1	0.954	24.2
1936	23.3	1.046	22.3
1937	22.0	0.973	22.6
1938	21.9	0.972	22.6
1939	20.2	0.933	21.6
1940	15.4	0.720	21.4

a Dash indicates data not available.

Source: Data on receipts from import duties, real and "tariff" values of merchandise imports from Dirección General de Estadística de la Nación, Anuario del Comercio Exterior de la República Argentina, several issues for the period under study.

A, this ratio for 1910–40. By real value of imports is meant an estimate based on world prices ruling at the time imports were made; this is in contrast to tariff value, which measures imports according to aforo values (including the modifications introduced in such *aforos,* most of which took place in 1920, 1923, and the early 1930s. Changes in the yearly figures of column *A* could reflect, therefore, changes in aforo values, in tariff rates, in the relationship between aforo values and true world prices, or changes in the composition of imports (because different imports had different tariff treatment as well as different degrees of aforo realism).

Column *A* shows that substantial variation took place during 1910–40 in this measure of average tariff height. From around 20 percent during 1910–11, it fell to less than 8 percent in 1920–21, rising again to above 20 percent during the 1930s. These data suggest one possible source for conflicting views regarding the Argentine tariff; the 20 percent average import duty for 1910 hardly seems consistent with free trade, but the 7.5 percent duty of 1920 does not correspond to a protectionist policy.[10]

Column *B* in Table 5.1 presents the ratio of the tariff value of imports to their real value. It can serve as an index of how far the aforo values were, in a given year and on the average, from the real unit values in world markets. Although data are not available for 1906–09, it is generally accepted that for those years the divergence between aforo and real values was negligible.[11] The correlation between columns *A* and *B* is striking; for 1910–25, column *B* "explains" (in a statistical sense) 96 percent of the variation in column *A,* while for the whole period 1910–40, the corresponding figure is 80 percent. During the worldwide inflation that accompanied World War I, the aforo values of the 1906 law became smaller relative to actual world prices, resulting in a sharp decrease in ad valorem equivalent duties. In July 1920 and December 1923, across-the-board revisions were approved by Congress for aforo values. These revisions, plus the fall of world prices from peaks reached immediately after the end of the war (1919–20), put an end to

10. During 1914–19 the war removed foreign competition (as well as strategic inputs) from Argentine markets for many manufactured goods. After 1920 and until 1927 a depreciated paper peso also helped import competing activities. More on this below.

11. This view is found, for example, in Ernesto Tornquist and Co., *The Economic Development of the Argentine Republic in the Last Fifty Years* (Buenos Aires, 1919), p. 140, n. 1.

the downward trend observed in both columns A and B during 1906–20.[12] By 1928 aforo values were, *on the average,* in line with real values; this correspondence was maintained until 1940, as can be seen in Table 5.1.

The most important single influence on the incidence of import duties was then an exogenous variable—the world price level. When it rose the importance of import duties shrank; the opposite happened when it fell. Argentine reliance on de facto specific duties was, of course, responsible for such behavior. But changes in intended tariff rates (separate from changes in aforos) also played a role, albeit a small one, in explaining the behavior of column A. This can be seen in column C of Table 5.1, presenting collected duties expressed as a percentage of the tariff value of all imports; this column yields what the average import duty would have been if aforo values had not differed from actual prices. The values in column C are stable for 1906–25, all figures falling within 18.4 to 23.5 percent; fluctuations occurring during these years were mainly due to changes in import composition. During 1926–30 substantial reductions in tariff rates seem to have taken place, but they were reversed during the early 1930s. Indeed, 1932 and 1933 witnessed the highest average import duties (actual as well as intended) and, although a retreat took place in later years (as a result of commercial treaties, especially those with the United Kingdom), duties similar in intent and incidence to those of 1906–10 ruled during 1934–39.

In summary, although the incidence of duties was quite variable, during 1906–14 and 1925–40 it reached levels that can be presumed to have changed resource allocation from what it would have been under free trade coupled with a flexible exchange rate and different government revenue sources. In comparison with other countries, 1906–40 commercial policy cannot be called one of free trade. League of Nations tariff studies in 1927 concluded that, although the 1925 Argentine average tariff on a representative group of manufactured commodities was below that of the United States, it was above those of Canada, France, Germany, and Italy, among others, and at about the same level as that of Australia. The 1925 average for tariffs on manufactured articles was 35–40 percent for

12. Information on changes in the *aforo* value obtained from Dirección General de Estadística de la Nación, *Anuario del Comercio, 1940* (Buenos Aires, 1941), p. xxiii. Besides across-the-board increases in *aforos* during 1920 and 1923, many changes in individual *aforos* and in tariff rates took place in 1923 and during the 1930s.

the United States and 25–30 percent for Argentina and Australia. But it was also estimated that while the Argentine average tariff on manufactures had changed little between 1913 and 1925, that for Australia had risen.[13]

THE STRUCTURE OF IMPORT DUTIES

Arguments regarding the structure of import duties during 1906–40 and their alleged protectionism in reverse foreshadowed modern discussion of the measurement of effective protection.[14] Protectionism in reverse (in modern terminology negative effective protection) was

13. League of Nations, Economic and Financial Section, *Customs Nomenclature and Customs Classification* and *Tariff Level Indices,* both published at Geneva, May 1927. See especially pages 17–21 of *Tariff Level Indices.* This study also provides the ratio of *total revenues* to the *total value* of all merchandise imports for several countries, as follows:

	1913	*1925*
Australia	16.5 percent	18.5 percent
Canada	17.1	15.1
United States	17.7 (1912–13)	13.2
Argentina (from Table 5.1)	17.7	15.2

The Argentine customs tariff included a much larger number of tariff item numbers than the United States and the Australian tariff. See *Customs Nomenclature,* p. 23. The ratios of import duties to the actual value of total imports in Argentina, Canada, and the U.S.A. during 1910–40 were as follows (expressed in percentages):

	U.S.A.	*Argentina (Table 5.1)*	*Canada*
1910–14	18.5	18.3	17.5
1915–19	8.1	10.6	19.7
1920–24	12.5	10.9	13.4
1925–29	13.4	16.1	14.8
1930–34	18.1	23.6	15.4
1935–39	16.0	22.1	12.8

Data for the U.S.A. obtained from U.S. Bureau of the Census, *Historical Statistics of the United States, Colonial Times to 1957* (Washington, D.C., 1960), p. 539. Canadian data found in M. C. Urquhart, Ed., *Historical Statistics of Canada,* (Cambridge: University Press, 1965), pp. 197–98 and 178–80. Other observations for Australia's average tariff are (in percentages): 1906 = 17.6; 1920 = 14.1; 1928/29 = 21.2. Data obtained from *Official Year-Book of the Commonwealth of Australia,* Commonwealth Bureau of Census and Statistics (Canberra), no. 14 (1921), p. 533, and no. 23 (1930), p. 153.

14. For such analysis see Harry G. Johnson, "Tariff and Economic Development: Some Theoretical Issues," *Journal of Development Studies* 1, no. 1 (Oct. 1964); Bela Balassa, "Tariff Protection in Industrial Countries: An Evaluation," *Journal of Political Economy* 73, no. 6 (Dec. 1965); Santiago Macario, "Protectionism and Industrialization in Latin America," *Economic Bulletin for Latin America* 9, no. 1 (March 1964).

claimed to exist in several manufacturing activities where tariffs applied to imports of raw materials and intermediate products were higher than those for finished goods embodying those inputs. This issue, together with some other characteristics of the tariff, will now be discussed.

Duty-free imports

Protectionists often pointed to the large number of articles entering the country duty-free as evidence of the free trade nature of Argentine commercial policy. Column *A* in Table 5.2 indicates that be-

Table 5.2: Proportion of Imports Admitted Duty-free, 1906–40

	A Real value of duty-free imports as percentages of real value of all imports	*B* Total import duties as percentages of the real value of imports subject to duties
1906–09	29.9	29.7
1910–14	29.0	25.8
1915–19	28.0	14.9
1920–24	26.5	14.9
1925–29	29.8	23.0
1930–34	26.5	32.0
1935–39	27.2	31.1
1940	28.3	21.5

Note: For 1937–39 it was not possible to obtain data on the real value of duty-free imports. For these years data on tariff value have been employed. During the 1930s, differences between tariff and real values were small *on the average*. For the U.S.A. the figures corresponding to Column *B* were as follows during 1906–40 (in percentages):

$$1906–09 = 43.2$$
$$1910–14 = 40.1$$
$$1915–19 = 26.7$$
$$1920–24 = 31.3$$
$$1925–29 = 38.9$$
$$1930–34 = 51.5$$
$$1935–39 = 39.3$$

Corresponding Australian data are as follows (in percentages):

$$1906 \quad = 27.1$$
$$1913 \quad = 28.5$$
$$1920 \quad = 22.4$$
$$1928/29 = 25.0$$

U.S. and Australian data obtained as in footnote 13.

Source: As in Table 5.1.

tween 26 and 30 percent of imports entered duty-free. This implies that ad valorem equivalent duties on imports subject to tariffs were higher than those in column *A* of Table 5.1; this new average is given in column *B* of Table 5.2, but it can be observed that these two averages have a similar time profile.

The duty-free list established in the 1906 law remained in force, with few modifications, throughout the period under study. Thus 1910–14 data presented in Table 5.3 may be taken as typical for

Table 5.3: Tariff Values of Selected Imports Entering Duty-free during 1910–14
(Million gold pesos)

	Total value for 1910–14
Live animals	4.7
Fruits	4.1
Sheep dip	9.6
Burlap grain bags	3.8
Burlap and thread to make bags	38.6
Naphtha and lubricating oil	42.4
Wood as raw material or in semifinished form	6.0
Books and printed material	8.2
Iron, steel, and other metals in semifinished form	31.2
Agricultural machinery	17.2
Transport equipment and supplies (mainly for railroads and tramways)	122.0
Coal and coke	128.5
Electrical equipment and supplies	8.0
Construction materials	18.5
Seeds for sowing	15.2
Other manufactured goods from steel, iron, and other metals	28.5
Subtotal	*486.6*
Total imports entering duty-free	*513.5*

Source: Anuario de la Dirección General de Estadística, Correspondiente al Año 1914 (Buenos Aires, 1915), pp. 500–657.

the whole period. Transport equipment and supplies, and coal and coke accounted for nearly half of duty-free imports; in both cases railroads were the main customers. Preferential treatment to imports of railroad companies, aimed at stimulating railway construction, dated back to 1873 and was reaffirmed by the Mitre Law of 1907.[15]

15. The following sources have been used to obtain details of the Argentine tariff: *The Argentine Year Book, 1915–1916* (Buenos Aires: Robert Grant and Co., 1916), pp. 64–90, 261–62; U.S. Tariff Commission, *Economic Controls*

Intermediate and capital goods for the rural sector accounted for nearly one-fifth of duty-free imports. The more than fifty duty-free items can be characterized as "mainly consisting of essential industrial supplies, raw materials, agricultural machinery, and railway equipment." [16]

It would be unusual if, among duty-free imports, we could not find some harmful to some potential or actual infant industry. Besides importing locomotives, steel rails, and coal (which could have been produced domestically only at very high real costs), railroad companies no doubt purchased abroad *some* items that could have been produced in Argentina at slightly higher costs in the short run, but with the promise of lower costs after a few years. The close link between British-owned railroad companies and British suppliers also stimulated their purchase abroad.[17] In the case of other duty-free imports such as apples, later experience showed that Argentina could not only substitute them for domestic production, but also become their net exporter after a few years of protection. On the whole, however, it is hard to detect from the duty-free list any conspiracy against domestic manufacturers; in fact, the exemption of strategic capital goods and raw materials from import duties is a common practice among most protectionist countries of today.[18]

Structure of duties on different import categories

Data on real ad valorem equivalent duties for various import cate-

and Commercial Policy in Argentina (Washington, D.C., 1948), pp. 9–12; DNEC, *Anuario del Comercio Exterior Correspondiente a 1940,* (Buenos Aires, 1941), pp. 92–96.

16. U.S. Tariff Commission, *Economic Controls,* p. 10.

17. In 1913 and 1914, more than 60 percent of all duty-free imports came from the United Kingdom and British territories, while out of total imports subject to duties, only 20 percent came from those sources. See *Anuario de la Dirección General de Estadística, Correspondiente al Año 1914* (Buenos Aires, 1915), pp. 439, 657. The direct and indirect links between British investments and exports to Argentina date back to the nineteenth century. See Ferns, *Britain and Argentina,* p. 337. Referring to "core groups" of British capitalists in Argentina, Ferns states: "Their principal purpose in organizing railway enterprises seems to have been the sale of manufactures and of services."

18. Even A. Bunge estimated that: "Approximately 30 percent of what is imported today into Argentina should be absolutely free of any import duty" (*La Economía Argentina,* 3: 102). During 1959–63 more than half of Argentine imports entered the country free of surcharges as a result of special exemptions aimed at stimulating investment. These imports included machinery, raw materials, and intermediate products.

gories are unfortunately not easy to come by; the difficulty arises from differences between aforo and real values. One can obtain for a given year tariff rates based on aforo values, but it is not always possible to obtain a world unit value of imports that would allow estimation of the real duty.

Nevertheless, until 1927, trade statistics presented both the tariff revenues collected on all import categories and estimates of real values for a list of 32 to 34 different types of imports.[19] Table 5.4 presents, on the basis of these data, average ad valorem equivalent duties for the 32 to 34 categories for 1927 and 1909 (assuming that aforo values equaled real values in 1909). Although the categories are somewhat arbitrary and include within each group a wide spectrum of commodities, Table 5.4 casts light on the structure of duties, especially regarding the treatment given to imports with different degrees of processing.

Table 5.1 showed that the real average duty for all imports fell from 21.7 percent in 1909 to 15.5 percent in 1927 (again assuming that in 1909 no significant differences existed between aforo and real values). Table 5.4 shows that most categories participated in that decrease, not only because of a general increase in real above aforo values (indicated by the differences between the second and third columns), but also because of an apparent fall in basic rates (shown by the second column in comparison with the first).[20] The fall in rates is sharpest among foodstuffs and beverages. Besides this change, the rate *structure* does not show many substantial modifications, but where it does, it indicates a structure more favorable to industrialization in 1927 than in 1909. For wood, paper, iron and steel, other metals and stone, glass, etc., and their manufacturers, the 1927 tariff shows higher duties for the finished than for the semifinished products and raw materials. In 1909 this was the case for wood, other metals and stone, glass, etc., and their manufacturers, with little difference in the duties for finished and unfinished iron and steel products. Sundry paper manufacturers had a lower levy in 1909 than paper

19. Estimated tariff revenues are given for each tariff item number, but real import values are given only for the 32 to 34 types of imports. Tariff revenues have been added up to correspond to the categories for which real import values are available.

20. Categories making up three-fourths of the value of imports in 1909 show a drop in rates between column one and column two. It is possible that further disaggregation would indicate that such a fall is due only to changes in structure within each category. Taable 5.1, column *C,* also shows a fall in intended rates between 1909 and 1927 from 21.7 percent to 18.1 percent.

Table 5.4: Import Duties on Different Import Categories
(Percentages of the value of imports of each category)

| | | 1927 | | Percentage participation in the total real value of all imports | |
	1909	Percentage of tariff values	Percentage of real values	1909	1927
Live animals	0	0	0	0.5	0.6
Animal foodstuffs	40.2	17.2	14.1	1.5	1.3
Fruits	21.4	12.0	9.4	0.7	1.1
Spices and condiments	62.2	29.5	17.8	1.0	2.7
Vegetables and cereals	26.2	7.9	6.4	1.4	1.2
Substances for infusions and hot beverages	28.0	15.3	7.9	2.7	4.7
Flour, macaroni, fancy breads, etc.	32.5	30.9	24.7	0.3	0.2
Tobacco and its manufactures	33.4	52.0	39.9	2.0	1.5
Wines	65.7	46.3	27.9	3.2	0.6
Spirits and liquors	85.2	71.9	26.7	0.9	0.5
Sundry beverages	52.5	56.0	47.1	0.2	0.1
Silk, raw and manufactured	29.7	37.5	54.1	1.7	1.4
Wool, raw and manufactured	31.9	31.3	19.6	3.7	4.3
Cotton, raw and manufactured	26.4	22.9	17.9	11.2	9.3
Sundry textiles, raw and manufactured	22.1	10.5	7.2	3.2	7.5
Oils (vegetable, mineral) and lubricants	39.8	15.0	19.0	3.9	8.2
Chemical, medical, and pharmaceutical substances and products	27.6	21.5	20.8	3.4	3.5
Paints and dyes	23.8	25.5	22.9	0.7	0.7
Wood; as raw material and semifinished products	14.6	17.3	8.2	0.9	5.1
Manufactured wood products	32.9	31.4	29.0	1.7	0.9
Paper and pasteboard	30.3	14.9	17.4	1.3	2.3
Sundry paper manufactures	23.7	26.5	24.6	0.9	0.5
Leather and its manufactures	38.7	36.2	27.4	0.9	0.6
Iron and steel as raw material and semifinished products	15.5	11.2	13.1	6.7	4.4
Manufactures of iron and steel	15.2	18.5	16.3	5.4	13.0
Other metals as raw material and semifinished products	10.5	8.8	8.5	0.9	1.5
Manufactures of other metals	17.8	25.5	26.6	2.5	1.5
Agricultural inputs	1.8	1.0	0.7	5.5	2.9
Transportation equipment and supplies	2.6	a	a	10.5	a
Stone, glass, earthenware, etc.; raw materials	1.0	7.0	7.4	5.7	6.6
Manufactures of stone, glass, earthenware, etc.	26.8	33.4	18.1	1.5	1.7
Building materials	19.3	a	a	9.4	a
Electrical machinery and supplies	14.9	18.4	16.3	1.4	2.5
Sundry imports	20.8	21.5	18.4	2.7	7.2

a Category not used in 1927.

Sources: Anuario de la Dirección General de Estadística, Correspondiente al Año 1909, Tomo I (Buenos Aires, 1911), pp. 3–408; *Anuario del Comercio Exterior de la República Argentina, Año 1927* (Buenos Aires, 1929), pp. 53–569.

and pasteboard, but the former category includes books and other printed materials traditionally taxed at low or zero rates to encourage the flow of ideas and techniques. On the whole, and although the categories presented are still too aggregated, they fail to reveal systematic protectionism in reverse.

An attempt has been made to look at more disaggregated items in 1927; as only aforo values are given for these items, equivalent ad valorem duties will be calculated on those values. These rates will at least provide the tariff structure intended by the legislators. Table 5.5 presents data on cotton, wool, and silk imports (which made up

Table 5.5: Tariff Structure of Selected Imports in 1927
(Expressed as ad valorem equivalent percentage rates)

Cotton and its manufactures	*22.9*
Raw cotton	5.1
Spun cotton for weaving	5.1
Threads for sewing	7.9
Cotton cloth	23.2
Articles manufactured from cotton cloth	39.6
Wool and its manufactures	*31.3*
Spun wool for weaving	5.0
Spun wool for knitting and embroidering	13.6
Wool cloth	31.6
Washed wool	31.9
Articles manufactured from wool cloth	46.2
Silk and its manufactures	*37.5*
Spun silk for weaving	12.1
Silk cloth and thread	46.5
Articles manufactured from silk cloth and thread	45.2
Cocoa beans	5.0
Ground or powder chocolate or cocoa beans	46.1
Chocolate paste	34.3
Bonbons	46.1
Yerba Mate, not processed	10.2
Yerba Mate, processed	25.2
Unrefined sugar	59.1
Refined sugar	61.6
Tobacco leaf	54.3
Chopped tobacco leaf	52.2
Cigarettes	46.1
Cigars	42.7

Source: *Anuario del Comercio Exterior de la República Argentina, Año 1927*, pp. 55–205.

15 percent of the 1927 import bill), as well as on chocolate, yerba mate, sugar, and tobacco. Only in the case of silk cloth versus articles manufactured from silk, and of tobacco, we find a structure that could be said to damage domestic manufacturing interests. But even in these cases the rate differences are small, and with the high rates applied to finished products and the low rates applied to other possible imported inputs of these activities (fuels, some machinery, etc.) the net result may well have been positive effective protection.[21]

Cotton and wool products are of special interest, not only due to their quantitative importance, but also because they represented an even higher percentage of Argentine imports from her best customer, the United Kingdom, and because of the leading role textiles were to play in the industrialization of the 1930s. Table 5.5 shows that cotton spinning received very modest protection in 1927, but effective protection for weaving and the making of garments must have been substantial. Similar considerations apply to woolens; the high rate on washed wool is explained by the abundance of domestic wool and the desire to protect local wool-washing activities.[22]

The admittedly partial evidence presented suggests that cases of negative effective protection in the Argentine tariff have been grossly exaggerated. There were, no doubt, cases of this sort, and some branches of the metallurgical industry were especially handicapped by the tariff structure. Indeed, input-output interrelationships are so complex that it would be strange if one could not find some such cases in any country; a recent study of tariffs in industrial countries shows a sprinkling of negative effective protection for several activities in Western Europe, Japan, and the United States.[23] Furthermore,

21. Most machines came in at low rates of duty; but not all: "Prior to 1913 . . . partly from the pressures of the Unión Industrial . . . component elements and unfinished goods generally came in duty-free or at low rates, while complete machines competitive with those assembled in Argentina might pay 35 to 50 percent duty." T. A. Cochran and R. E. Reina, *Entrepreneurship in Argentine Culture: Torcuato Di Tella and S.I.A.M.* (Philadelphia: University of Pennsylvania Press, 1962), p. 95.

22. By 1932 duties on textiles had risen. According to a U.S. observer: "Duties on other wearing apparel may range from 25 to 300 percent of its real value. Cotton piece goods pay fairly low duties, averaging around 15 to 25 percent of their value." He also commented: "Import duties in Argentina are assessed both for revenue and for protection." See U.S. Department of Commerce, Bureau of Foreign and Domestic Commerce, *Textile Market of Argentina,* Trade Promotion Series No. 132 (Washington, D.C., 1932), pp. 9–10.

23. See Balassa, "Tariff Protection in Industrial Countries," p. 580: "Further instances of negative effective duty are agricultural machinery in the United States, pig iron in the EEC and Sweden, and paper in Sweden."

claims regarding protectionism in reverse compared duties on finished goods with higher duties on only one or two of their inputs. This does not prove negative effective protection since lower duties for other imported inputs could more than offset that negative influence.[24]

An example will illustrate the degree to which claims of "protectionism in reverse" have been exaggerated: "The hat industry complained as recently as 1940 that it was being victimized by the tariff: Felt made of rabbit skins is used in this industry . . . rabbit felt pays higher duty than hats made of it." [25]

Trade statistics for 1927 yield the following ad valorem equivalent tariff rates for felts and hats (computed on the basis of aforo values and expressed in percentages):

Felts, in pieces, woolen or mixed	32.0
Adherent felts, for hats	53.6
Nonadherent felts, for hats	53.9
Felts, in pieces, especially for hats	85.1
Hard felt hats, woolen	54.0
Hats of silk felt	53.9
Hard hats, other materials	54.0
Soft felt hats, woolen	144.4
Soft hats, other materials	100.7

These data confirm that *some* felts paid a higher duty than *some* hats;[26] however, an industry with import duties on competing products

24. Discussing increases in Argentine tariffs during the early 1930s, D. M. Phelps wrote: "It should be observed also that raw materials were mostly on the free list of Argentine imports and thus were not affected by the general increase in import duties. Therefore, an advantage was given to the local producer over the importer, even in those industries in which the raw materials were largely imported" (*Migration of Industry to South America*, p. 40). Tariff policy seems to have led to an early establishment in Argentina of assembly plants for automobiles, as suggested by the following quote: "The Argentine tariff provides for a 30 percent concession on unassembled automotive units, and a 15 percent reduction on semi-assembled units. As a consequence, practically all motor vehicles are partly, and the cheaper cars entirely, assembled in the country. The three leading American companies have completed assembly plants." George Wythe, *Industry in Latin America* (New York: Columbia University Press, 1945), p. 110.

25. Weil, *Argentine Riddle*, p. 140. Other examples of "protectionism in reverse," obtained from a periodical reflecting the views of some industrialists, are given in this book, pp. 138–42.

26. Obtained from DNEC *Anuario del Comercio Exterior, 1927*, pp. 132, 140, 200. Regarding the fur and hat industries, note also the following quote: "Argentina is a large producer and exporter of rabbit and nutria fur for hatters. . . . The bulk of the demand for men's felt hats is supplied by Argentine factories. . . ." U.S. Department of Commerce, *Textile Market of Argentina*, p. 38.

that ranged from 54 to 144 percent could hardly be said to have been victimized by the tariff. On the average, output tariffs clearly exceeded input tariffs.

Even a casual inspection of individual tariff rates also casts doubt on the argument that the tariff was for revenue only. If that motivation were predominant, one would expect high tariffs on goods that could not be produced domestically because of climate or geography. If the domestic demand for those goods is price inelastic, so much the better. Yet we find that in 1927, the ad valorem equivalent duty (calculated on the basis of aforo values) was 8.5 percent for tea, 12.0 percent for Brazilian and Paraguayan coconuts, 25.0 percent for coffee beans and 5.0 percent for cocoa beans, while bananas entered duty-free. These duties were considerably lower than those levied on other foodstuffs and beverages such as sugar, beer, and wine which competed with domestic production.[27]

Previous paragraphs should in no way be interpreted as a defense of the tariff structure during 1906–40. Their aim is to show that sweeping descriptions of the tariff as being aimed at protectionism in reverse or for revenue only are wrong. By the late 1930s it was widely recognized in government circles that there was a need to revise the tariff; modifications patched onto the 1906 law had not been enough to adjust for (1) divergences between aforo values and real values for many individual items and (2) the appearance of new products, unknown or unimportant when the 1906 tariff was approved.[28] In many cases, these factors gave rise to an irrational rate

27. That tariffs on sugar and wine had a protectionist design is admitted by critics of the tariff. In the case of the sugar industry, the tariff had a special item number for machinery for sugar mills, which entered the country duty free. The duty on beer in 1927 was 50.4 percent. Writing in 1896, M. G. Mulhall already observed: "Sugar was little cultivated before 1880, but the import duty of 100 percent *ad valorem* has favoured home production. . . ." He also noted: "there is also a large industry in the manufacture of artificial wines, of so deleterious a character that physicians consider the death-rate is much increased by this cause" (*Industries and Wealth of Nations*, p. 363). The good wines of Mendoza, however, took advantage mainly of new railway links to Buenos Aires to prosper.

28. See Ministerio de Hacienda de la Nación, *El Plan de Reactivación Económica Ante El Honorable Senado* (Buenos Aires, 1940), p. 22. As a *curiosum*, it may be notd that agricultural machinery, for which Bela Belassa found a negative rate of effective protection in the United States in 1962, was one of the most commonly given examples of negative protection in Argentina before World War II. For further criticisms of the tariff structure of Argentina see Phelps, *Migration of Industry to South America*, pp. 149–53. More research is needed on the issue as to whether the Australian and Canadian tariff structures were more or less favorable to industrialization than that of Argentina.

structure. But this irrationality, while detrimental to some domestic industries, benefited others. For example, in 1939 the aforo value of sulphuric acid was 65 percent *above* its estimated real value; this fact, coupled with a 42 percent duty computed on the aforo value resulted in burdensome costs for domestic manufacturers using this product. Domestic producers of sulphuric acid, however, benefited from this state of affairs and their output rose.[29]

Although many conflicting influences had shaped the tariff structure as it stood in 1940 and in earlier years, the following quotation presents a reasonable summary of its basic character: "Minimum duties of 5 to 20 percent ordinarily apply to goods not produced in Argentina, and duties of 30 to 50 percent are levied on products similar to those manufactured within the country." [30]

THE EXCHANGE RATE AND EXCHANGE CONTROLS

A protectionist tariff can be offset by an overvalued exchange rate, and exchange control may lead a country with zero tariffs to autarky. Therefore, we now turn to a brief examination of Argentine exchange rates and exchange control during 1906–40.

The exchange rate

It has been stated often that Argentine rural export interests traditionally favored a depreciated exchange rate over an overvalued one. The long-run rationale for this preference is straightforward; there is considerable evidence to support the conclusion that, for a number

29. Caustic soda, on the other hand, paid a much lower real duty. See Armour Research Foundation, *Technological and Economic Survey of Argentine Industries with Industrial Research Recommendations* (Chicago, 1943; lithoprinted), p. 64. This report strongly criticizes "the obsolete list of tariff valuations" (p. 64). An example of how obsolete values coupled with technological change affected an export industry and discouraged the use of new techniques is given in pp. 129–130: "For instance, we may consider the operation of dehairing hides. . . . The old method . . . is by applying a mixture of sodium sulphide and lime. Sodium sulphide is admitted under a rate of 42 percent on a tariff valuation of . . . 18 centavos paper. . . . However, recent prices have been 50 to 60 centavos paper, and consequently the tariff actually amounts to something like 12 or 15 percent of present value. . . . Many of the new preparations were not known at the time the tariff was made up. Consequently, they come under the heading of articles 'not enumerated in the tariff,' which classification pays a duty of 42 percent on the declared value at the present time." Throughout this report it is taken for granted that the Argentine tariff was proctectionist in intent. See especially p. 60.
30. U.S. Tariff Commission, *Economic Controls*, p. 10.

of different reasons, there was a bias in exchange rate policy before 1930 in favor of a relatively depreciated exchange rate.[31] However, it is seldom pointed out that in the absence of quantitative restrictions on trade, exchange depreciation has a stimulating effect not only on exports but also on import-competing activities. Rural interests could not help but stimulate import-competing activities whenever they urged a depreciated exchange rate, unless a policy were followed of using an exchange rate (dollars or pounds per one paper peso) that was higher for exports than for imports. In fact, when multiple exchange rates began to be used during the 1930s, import rates were higher than those for exports, giving (together with higher import duties) a powerful stimulus to industrialization.

A closer look at exchange rates and price levels during 1914–29 is presented in Table 5.6; indices for both dollar and pound rates are given. The second and fourth columns represent indices of the ratio of the Buenos Aires cost of living to those of the United States and the United Kingdom, respectively. A comparison of the first and second columns yields a rough idea regarding changes in the competitiveness of United States exports in Argentine markets vis-à-vis domestic products, arising from exchange rate and price level movements. A similar comparison can be made with the third and fourth columns for British goods. An index of the ratio of the first over

31. The bias was supposed to operate in the following way: if gold began to flow out of the country, the government was eager to declare peso inconvertibility, allowing a depreciation of the paper peso; on the other hand, appreciation tendencies of the paper peso were quickly checked by a return to gold convertibility. An appreciating tendency of the paper peso was stopped in 1899 by a return to convertibility, lasting until 1914. The paper peso, however, appreciated both in real terms and with respect to the gold peso at several points during the first World War (see Tables 5.6 and 5.7). In spite of impressive gold reserves amounting to 80 percent of paper pesos in circulation, convertibility was not resumed until 1927 (checking an appreciation tendency); during 1920–27 the paper peso depreciated with respect to its gold parity. Importers and those remitting interests and dividends abroad pressed without success for a quick return to full gold convertibility after World War I, even though European currencies remained inconvertible. See Virgil Salera, *Exchange Control and the Argentine Market* (New York: Columbia University Press, 1941), pp. 30–39. Fear of the deflationary impact of gold outflows was a powerful reason for abandoning convertibility in 1929 (and in earlier years), while wartime appreciation may have been used as a deflationary device. Lucio Geller, in a forthcoming study, stresses the role played by deflationary fears of the authorities in determining the abandonment of peso convertibility, while casting doubt on the size of benefits derived by large pampean landowners from devaluations. He points out the widespread use of land leasing contracts expressed in fixed peso terms.

Table 5.6: Exchange Rate and Price Indices, 1914–29
(1914 = 100)

	Paper pesos per one U.S. dollar	Buenos Aires cost of living relative to U.S.A. cost of living	Paper pesos per one U.K. pound	Buenos Aires cost of living relative to U.K. cost of living
1914	100	100	100	100
1915	101	107	99	88
1916	100	107	98	79
1917	96	106	94	77
1918	95	114	93	84
1919	97	93	88	75
1920	108	94	80	76
1921	133	94	105	74
1922	117	84	107	77
1923	123	81	115	79
1924	124	83	112	80
1925	105	78	104	78
1926	104	75	104	77
1927	100	76	100	79
1928	100	76	100	79
1929	101	77	101	80

Sources: Comité Nacional de Geografía, *Anuario Geográfico Argentino* (Buenos Aires, 1941), p. 431 (for dollar and pound rates); DNEC, *Costo del Nivel de Vida en la Capital Federal* (Buenos Aires, Feb. 1963), p. 44 (for Buenos Aires cost of living); B. R. Mitchell, *Abstract of British Historical Statistics* (Cambridge: University Press, 1962), p. 478; U.S. Bureau of the Census, *Historical Statistics of the United States, Colonial Times to 1957* (Washington, D.C., 1960), p. 126.

the second column (or the third over the fourth) may be called an index of real devaluation; figures over 100 would imply real devaluation with respect to the base year 1914. Such a measure is presented directly in Table 5.7, together with indices for the average height of the tariff. The combined effect of real devaluation (or appreciation) and tariff changes can then be obtained from both indices.

During 1915–21 the combined effect of real tariff reductions and changes in the real exchange rate exposed Argentine import-competing activities to greater competition. But during war years such a threat was not operational due to shipping shortages and other war-induced difficulties in industrialized nations. During 1920 and 1921, however, Argentine industries (some of which had successfully expanded during the war) were more exposed to foreign competition than during 1914. This painful period, which left bitter memories

Table 5.7: Indices for Average Tariff Height and Real Devaluation, 1914–29
(1914 = 100)

	Average height of tariff	Real devaluation toward U.S.A.	Real devaluation toward U.K.	Combined effect toward U.S.A.	Combined effect toward U.K.
1914	100	100	100	100	100
1915	85	95	113	81	96
1916	78	94	123	73	96
1917	69	91	122	63	84
1918	48	83	110	40	53
1919	46	105	118	48	54
1920	46	114	106	52	49
1921	58	142	141	82	82
1922	72	139	139	100	100
1923	76	151	145	115	110
1924	84	150	139	126	117
1925	94	134	134	126	126
1926	94	138	135	130	127
1927	96	131	127	126	122
1928	107	131	127	140	136
1929	107	132	126	141	135

Sources: Tables 5.1 and 5.6.

influencing post-World War II Peronist policies, did not last long. In fact, throughout 1922–29 import-substituting activities appear to have had a more favorable position than in 1914, in spite of lower average tariffs during 1922–27. So exchange policy, on the whole, complemented tariff inducement of import substitution although not always in a steady fashion. The inducement consisted not only of the substitution effect favoring domestic over foreign products arising from devaluation (and equivalent to across-the-board increases in ad valorem import duties), but also from income effects forthcoming from rural prosperity, which in the long run offset negative redistributive effects of devaluation. It is ironic that during 1946–55, when extreme protectionism became official policy, overvalued exchange rates discouraged some import-substituting activities such as oil extraction.

Exchange control

In October 1931 Argentina launched her system of exchange control which, although often altered, was to last uninterrupted until December 1958. There were several pressures resulting in its creation—

foreign debt payments (fixed in foreign values) becoming a high percentage of depressed exchange earnings; the triangular nature of Argentine merchandise trade (with dollar deficits and sterling surpluses) in a world moving away from multilateralism and free convertibility; fear that further devaluation would result in even more unfavorable terms of trade; and growing worldwide trade restrictions. At first sight, it appears self-evident that exchange control would reinforce the protectionist features of the tariff; if nothing else, it led to greater uncertainty and higher transaction costs for importers. Yet, it has been alleged that exchange control was used to a certain extent as a weapon against industrialization.

Besides exchange control, changes in demand composition and in terms of trade, higher tariff rates, etc., also influenced the Argentine economy and, therefore, the import structure during the 1930s. Although it is difficult to isolate the influence of each of these forces, a look at actual import figures may reveal at least to what extent demand was diverted toward imported finished goods that could easily be produced domestically.

Between 1925–29 and 1935–39, the quantum of merchandise imports fell by more than 28 percent. As shown in the second column

Table 5.8: Changes in the Level and Composition of Merchandise Imports,
1925–29/1935–39
(Percentages of total)

	Structure of imports, 1925–29	*Composition of the decrease in the level of imports, 1925–29/1935–39*	*Structure of imports, 1935–39*
Finished consumer goods	37.0	45.2	33.7
Machinery and equipment for agriculture	5.0	13.4	1.7
Other machinery and equipment	16.8	15.5	17.3
Intermediate products and raw materials	26.0	3.1	35.1
Fuels and lubricants	4.7	1.7	5.9
Materials for construction and public works	10.2	20.1	6.2
Other	0.3	1.1	nil
Total	*100.0*	*100.0*	*100.0*

Note: Totals do not add to 100.0 due to rounding errors. Original data are expressed at 1950 prices.

Source: ECLA, p. 109.

of Table 5.8, 45 percent of this drop resulted from a reduction in finished consumer goods imports. The drop in imports of agricultural machinery and materials for construction (reflecting both a shift and a decline in investment, as well as notable import substitution in cement) accounted for another third. Imports of intermediate products, raw materials, and fuels in 1935–39 remained near those of 1925–29; of the total import reduction, less than 5 percent arose from these goods.

Import structure was therefore different in 1935–39, under exchange control, than during 1925–29. Intermediate products and fuels increased their share in the import bill from 30.7 to 41.0 percent. The share of nonagricultural machinery also rose. The alleged machinations of the exchange authorities, if true, were quite a failure. In fact, during 1946–48 under a government pledged to extreme protectionism, intermediate products and fuels had an import share similar to that of 1935–39.[32]

PROTECTION: JUSTIFICATION AND LOBBIES

Two issues will now be explored: What justifications were given in favor of greater protection during 1906–40, and how legitimate were they? What sort of political pressures converged on the tariff?

Besides noneconomic considerations, the standard fallacious arguments appearing in protectionist writings included defense against "cheap Brazilian and Spanish labor" and undervalued foreign currencies.[33]

One of the best protectionist arguments was the need to diversify the Argentine productive structure. Perspicacious observers, especially Alejandro Bunge, voiced fears as early as 1923 regarding agricultural protectionism in the United States and British imperial preferences.[34]

32. This share was 42.6 percent. However, during 1946–48 the share of consumer goods was lower; that for machinery higher. Data obtained as in Table 5.8. It may be noted that most authors agree on the protectionist effect of exchange controls. See, for example, Ferrer, *La Economía Argentina,* chapters 13 and 14.

33. Dumping charges were also frequently made against foreign producers. Curiously, tariffs on manufactured imports are often justified on antidumping grounds by the same persons who argue that there is a secular tendency for prices of manufactured goods to increase relative to those of primary products in world markets. Note recent discussion in Latin America regarding steel.

34. In 1927 the United States banned imports of fresh meat from Argentina, allegedly on health grounds. The influential slogan "buy from those who buy from us" first gained prominence at that time in Argentina.

Although exports were made up of a relatively large number of products, most of them were of rural origin and therefore vulnerable. Should not Argentina take some insurance, asked Bunge, by following a more protectionist policy? This argument is respectable, but not compelling. The best insurance Argentina had against a decrease in foreign demand was a flexible internal economy; in fact, when the blow came in 1929–32, the country took it with relative grace and fared much better than most nations during the depression. While foreign demand was buoyant, Argentina took advantage of it; when it collapsed, resources were reallocated rather smoothly toward import-competing activities.[35]

Related to, but weaker than the diversification argument (and also buttressed by the misfortunes that befell Argentine rural exports due to exogenous forces during 1930–45) is the contention that greater protection should have been given to manufacturing before 1930 in view of an alleged inevitable secular decline in the growth-promoting capabilities of rural exportables. This decline, it is argued, was foreseeable before 1930 because either pampean land was becoming fully occupied or world demand for primary products was bound to have a lower growth rate in the future. Even if these debatable premises are fully accepted, the need for greater protection does not follow. There is little reason to doubt that under the relatively free market system then ruling in Argentina, *gradual* changes in demand and supply conditions for rural exportables would have been reflected in relative price changes (including exchange rate variations) inducing private entrepreneurs to move in the desired direction, without the need of additional protection. (If it is argued that the price system did not do this quickly enough at the onslaught of the Great Depression, then we are back to the argument that this catastrophe was foreseeable.) If the alleged secular tendencies were working gradually, it is not obvious that only public policy was able to foresee them; private entrepreneurs would have been just

35. The argument favoring import substitution on the ground of decreasing vulnerability to external shocks has proven to be a weak one in the light of recent experience of Argentina and other semi-industrialized countries. As new industries often require critical imported inputs in rigid proportions to their outputs, domestic activity remains vulnerable to exogenous fluctuations in foreign exchange earnings. It should be pointed out that A. Bunge also advocated the development of new lines of exports as a way to decrease fluctuations in exchange earnings (see Bunge, *La Economía Argentina*, 3:30). Among other things, he feared that a fall in exports would make the servicing of the Argentine foreign debt very burdensome, as indeed it became in the 1930s.

as able to detect the way the wind was blowing, reallocating their efforts accordingly in favor of industry, without greater official inducement than that justified on infant industry grounds.

Another argument could have followed this line: admittedly, Argentina was an almost fully employed society during most of 1906–40. But would not even higher tariffs have resulted, not in a withdrawal of resources from exports, but in greater immigration of foreign capital and labor and presumably in a higher per capita income (at least for Argentina)?

The assumptions necessary to make this argument valid appear farfetched. At any rate, between 1895 and 1929 Argentine population grew at a much faster rate than those of other immigrant-receiving countries; the annual rate of population expansion for those years was 3.2 percent for Argentina, 2.1 percent for Canada, and only 1.8 percent for Australia. It has even been suggested that immigration into Argentina went beyond the level maximizing per capita income, especially during the 1920s and 1930s. Furthermore, as recent experience has shown, direct foreign investment going into protected import-substituting activities will not necessarily raise a country's GNP valued at world prices.

The infant industry argument was often used to seek more protection; the example of wheat and flour was given in support of this position. Until the second half of the 1870s Argentina imported a large share of the wheat and flour required for her consumption, mainly from Chile and the United States. In 1875 a protective tariff was levied on these imports, and quickly thereafter Argentina not only replaced imports with domestic production but also became one of the world's leading exporters of wheat and flour. It was argued that similar developments would follow the imposition of higher tariffs on other products. Although the 1930s provided fresh examples of quickly maturing infant activities, these remained few and far between. Surely, the construction of railroads had a greater impact on wheat production than the 1875 tariff.[36]

36. An argument that could be labelled the "infant consumer" thesis blamed snobbism as a cause for the preference of many consumers for foreign over domestically produced goods. Before 1930 Argentine manufacturers frequently mislabelled their products to make it appear as if they were imported. (Even the tango had to triumph first in Paris before it was allowed to enter the homes and clubs of the Argentine middle and upper classes.) Presumably those who defended higher tariffs on these grounds could have argued that after a learning period, consumers would have realized the foolishness of their previous

One possible justification for high tariffs (or for a subsidy to import-competing activities) that could not have been used in the Argentine case, even in a rough qualitative way, is the Manoilescu-Hagen argument based on artificial differentials between rural and urban wages.[37] The flow of immigrants was channeled via the city of Buenos Aires, which also contained most of the Argentine industrial establishments. Immigrants wishing to work in the rural sector proceeded from Buenos Aires to the interior by train. Thus, import-competing activities located in Buenos Aires probably faced a looser labor market than pampean entrepreneurs producing exportable goods.

Noneconomic justifications for protection deserve attention because they are at the root of protectionist feeling. As stated by an Argentine economic historian, the argument is simply this: "The struggle for industrialization has been in Argentina the struggle for the democratic transformation of her style of life." [38]

Among many urban leaders, exports were linked automatically to oligarchical rural landlords allied with foreign interests and importers, while protection was linked with import substitution, industrialization, nationalism, and social democracy.[39] The argument sometimes took a regional character: free trade was the creature of the landlords of the province of Buenos Aires, while protection was a national policy benefiting not only manufacturing, but also rural activities in other provinces (sugar in Tucumán, yerba mate in Misiones, wine in Mendoza, apples and pears in Río Negro, rice and tobacco in

---

snobbism (assuming that in fact no quality differences existed between domestic and imported goods of the same price).

37. An analysis of this and other arguments for protection is found in Harry G. Johnson, "Optimal Trade Intervention in the Presence of Domestic Distortions," in *Trade, Growth, and the Balance of Payments: Essays in Honor of Gottfried Haberler* (Chicago: Rand McNally and Co., 1965).

38. Ortiz, *Historia Económica de la Argentina,* 2:201.

39. Differences in land tenure systems may explain why these associations were so different from those found in Denmark, New Zealand, and the U.S. midwest. In fact, the interests of producers of rural exportables, foreign investors, exporters, and importers were far from coincident. Writing in 1941 about 1920–29 exchange rate policy, Virgil Salera stated that: "the perennial conflict between the interests of Argentine exporters on the one hand and those of importing houses and foreign-owned utilities and manufacturing concerns on the other was manifesting itself in all of its varied forms" (*Exchange Control and the Argentine Market,* p. 33). The presence of powerful foreign firms in the import-competing sector casts doubts on the effectiveness of protection for achieving nationalistic goals by itself.

the northern provinces, etc.).[40] However expressed, this argument has met with a favorable emotional response in Argentina since at least the end of the last century.

In summary, respectable protectionist arguments do not appear powerful enough to support on purely economic grounds the thesis that the Argentine tariff should have been even higher during 1906–40. Fresh protectionist arguments arising from the Great Depression (employment and terms of trade effects) were taken into account by the tariff increases of the 1930s.[41] This is not to argue that the tariff was optimal every year during 1906–40; enough blemishes in it have already been pointed out.

Social pressures converging on the tariff were more complex than implied by the view that pre-1940 Argentina was managed by rural and foreign interests for their exclusive advantage. As one would expect, rural producers of exportable products took a dim view of the tariff; in particular they pressured, although not always successfully, to have their inputs exempted from import duties. The love of the Argentine cattleman or corn grower for the tariff was no greater than that of the Southern cotton planter in the United States during the nineteenth century.

Representatives of foreign countries, sometimes in the company of local importers and exporters, paid frequent visits to authorities requesting reductions of this or that rate, which often were granted after more or less veiled threats of commercial pressures had been voiced. Great Britain, which purchased most beef exports, was the champion in the use of these pressures especially during 1920–40, goaded by the depressed condition of her exports in the 1920s and by the bargaining strength of imperial preferences during the 1930s (when British pressures came close to blackmail in Argentine eyes).[42]

40. Therefore, especially for the period before 1940, it is a mistake to link protectionist feeling *exclusively* with bias in favor of manufacturing. In his writings for example, A. Bunge spent a good deal of his time arguing in favor of higher duties on fruits, tobacco, sugar, yerba mate, rice, tomatoes, and other vegetables.

41. The optimum-tariff or terms of trade argument attracted little interest in a pre-1930 Argentina keenly conscious of expanding rural output in Canada, Australia, and other regions.

42. One still hears in Argentina, and sometimes from respectable sources, the opinion that since the nineteenth century it has been British policy to hamper industrialization in the Río de la Plata region, while tolerating it for Brazil. The rationale for such a policy is not at all obvious, nor is it easy to reconcile with the brisk industrialization of such old British dominions as Canada and Australia, which like Argentina supplied England with foodstuffs and raw materials.

Brazil (a principal buyer of wheat and seller of yerba mate and rice), Spain, Italy, and nearly all exporters to the Argentine market also participated in the bargaining game, which Argentine representatives in foreign countries also played, no doubt.

Foreign-owned public utilities and transportation facilities had a keen and vocal interest in low tariffs for their inputs. Yet the growth of direct foreign investment in manufacturing during the 1920s and 1930s (mostly from the United States) created a countervailing protectionist foreign lobby. The violent protest raised by North American tire manufacturers when the government reduced duties on imported tires in the early 1930s showed how articulate their interests could become.[43]

The government itself, as an important buyer of manufactured products of all sorts, was torn between the desire to obtain its inputs from the cheapest source, even if foreign, and protectionist pressure to "buy Argentine." Steadily the latter force gained ground, especially during the 1930s.[44]

So far the cast of free traders contains no surprises; as expected, it is made up of rural exporters, foreign interests, and merchants in the import and export business. Perhaps more vocal in defense of free trade than those groups (at least in Congress) were the socialist and populist political parties. The reasons for their position are straightforward; items on the frontier of import substitution during 1906–40 were to a large extent wage goods. Furthermore, for many years during 1906–40, Argentina was a full-employment society, with a need to import labor. Immigrants remained attached to European products such as olive oil, and there was a general mistrust

43. This opposition to the tariff reductions collapsed when Michelin Tire Company declared that it was entirely satisfied with the tariff schedules as they stood. These companies prospered throughout the next decade. See Phelps, *Migration of Industry to South America,* pp. 139–46. Phelps points out that: "in all fairness we must admit that the motivation for a reduced tariff came in part from other North American companies, for the importers' association was composed of both North American and European companies" (p. 142). He also blamed nationalistic feeling against foreign companies for this action: "it should be pointed out that tariff changes were detrimental only to foreign concerns" (p. 137).

44. Portland cement, because of public construction, was one of the most important products in this debate. The share of domestic production in total apparent absorption of cement evolved as follows: 1915–19 = 7 percent; 1920–24 = 33 percent; 1925–29 = 36 percent; 1930–34 = 78 percent; 1935–39 = 95 percent. The first Portland cement factory started its operations during 1913. See OECEI, *Importaciones, Industrialización, Desarrollo Económico en la Argentina* (Buenos Aires, 1963), 1:172.

of domestic manufactures, shared by both the upper and lower classes. Examples of imported wage goods were cotton textiles, woolens, rice, yerba mate, fresh fruits and vegetables, edible oils and some consumer durables. Table 5.4 showed that the most important change in tariff structure between 1909 and 1927 was the decrease in levies applied to foodstuffs and beverages; this change, as well as the decrease in the overall level of intended rates taking place during 1925–30 (shown in column *C* of Table 5.1) appear to have resulted from campaigns by socialist and populist legislators.[45] It should be borne in mind that during 1916–30 the reformist and democratically elected Radical party controlled the government. This regime took nationalistic stands on such sensitive issues as oil (barring foreign firms from further investments) and the regulation of public utility rates. It also introduced modest advances in labor legislation. Still, protection, with its negative impact on the cost of living of masses of voters, could hardly be said to have been a popular issue. Some of the sharpest barbs of Alejandro Bunge's protectionist pen were aimed at socialist legislators who opposed further tariff increases, obtained reductions in specific items, and at all times complained loudly of existing rates.[46]

The defense of tariffs was left in the hands of (1) the domestic

45. The Socialist party platform explicitly advocated the removal of import duties. The distinguished Socialist leader, Juan B. Justo, was an eloquent defender of free trade, calling protectionism "an enormous lie." See Oscar Cornblit, "Inmigrantes y Empresarios en la Política Argentina," pp. 42–43, 46. The fact that Australian and British Socialists advocated protection during the 1920s while those in Argentina fought it, suggests that employment opportunities were much better in Argentina than in the former countries. The lowering of duties on imported olive oil in 1923 retarded the growth of the local edible oils industry, which boomed after 1930 thanks to greater protection. Domestic production supplied 39 percent of total consumption of edible oils in 1915–19, 33 percent in 1925–29 and 91 percent by 1939. Data from *Anuario Geográfico Argentino*, p. 342. Domestic oils were obtained primarily from sunflower and cotton seeds and peanuts. Low duties on rice also harmed domestic producers during the 1920s.

46. See especially Bunge, *La Economía Argentina*, 3: 81, 83, 97, 126–27. Dr. Bunge's polemics covered a wide variety of issues; besides his attacks on Argentine socialists, he also criticized the Radical party's efforts to create new social legislation and to regulate public utilities, that he feared would frighten away foreign capital (p. 138). He was a pioneer in advocating the creation of a customs union made up of Argentina, Chile, Bolivia, Uruguay, and Paraguay as early as 1909, with a high common tariff. See his *Una Nueva Argentina*, chapter 12. By 1940 he seemed fairly pleased with the levels reached by the tariff and claimed that the innovations introduced in economic policy by the Argentine governments during 1930–1940 were superior to those of the New Deal in the United States (*Una Nueva Argentina*, p. 271).

and foreign producers of either rural or manufactured goods who stood to gain directly from higher duties, acting either alone or as a pressure group (e.g. the Unión Industrial); (2) a few nationalistic and pro-industry writers; and, sometimes, (3) Treasury officials concerned with increasing public revenues. Revenue was one of the aims of tariffs; in 1905–09, duties accounted for 53 percent of national government revenues, the proportion falling to 44 percent in 1925–29, and 28 percent during 1935–39. Tariff rates maximizing revenue will not maximize their protective effect; the more price elastic the domestic supply of import-competing goods is, the lower will be the duty aimed at maximizing tariff revenues, but the higher should be the duty aimed at the expansion of import-competing firms. Yet unless there exists a large number of imported goods that cannot be produced domestically, even tariffs aimed only at generating revenue inevitably will have protectionist effects. More importantly, it has been shown that not only were many duties clearly protectionist in intention, but also that several possible candidates for tariffs for revenue only were neglected by the authorities. In recent years, import surcharges have provided a substantial share of government revenues, but few would argue that those surcharges are for revenue only.

The complexity of the social forces converging on the tariff explains in part the bewildering structure of duties and their fluctuations during the period under study. Although on balance protectionist and revenue considerations prevailed, the heterogeneous forces favoring freer trade prevented the adoption of a streamlined and ultraprotectionist tariff. However, a complete explanation for the confused state and the instability of the tariff before 1940 must include, besides the shifting balance among different social forces, the simple fact that the public sector, in spite of efforts by some outstanding civil servants, was not sufficiently efficient to tackle the complicated issue of tariff revision. During at least the last twenty years Argentina has been following an ultraprotectionist policy, and yet the protectionist system is in a sorry state. The last attempt to replace exchange surcharges and import restrictions (sprinkled with ad hoc exemptions) with a tariff was begun in 1958 and was completed in 1965; the result of those seven years of labor was simply a consolidation of existing import surcharges and levies; little was done to rationalize their structure.[47]

47. See Macario, "Protectionism and Industrialization in Latin America," pp. 61–103. In 1960, the simple average of import charges (expressed as ad

While the instability and peculiarities of the pre-1940 tariff decreased its protectionist impact, the complexities and arbitrariness of the post-World War II protectionist system (coupled with an often overvalued exchange rate) also damaged some import-competing activities and prevented the expansion of manufactured exports.

Finally, given complicated interindustry input-output relations and the rapidity of technical change, it is farfetched to argue that the elements of protectionism in reverse which existed during 1906–40 were the result of plotting by anti-industry lobbies. It is doubtful that even today the most efficient planning commission could devise a tariff structure that could result in positive effective protection for *all* industrial and rural activities.

---

valorem equivalent duties) legally applicable in Argentina was 151 percent. During 1967 steps were taken to lower duties and reform their structure simultaneously with a sharp devaluation of the peso.

6

Relative Prices, Industrialization, and Capital Formation

The evolution of relative prices of investment goods in Argentina since 1935 and its impact on real capital formation has attracted considerable attention.[1] During most of the period since World War II, gross fixed investment has represented around 20 percent of GNP, both variables measured at current prices. On the other hand, the annual growth rate of real GNP has been 3 percent during 1944–65, which seems small in relation to the investment coefficient, even after allowing for the fact that Argentine statistics have included in gross investment repairs not so included by most other countries.[2] It has been argued that the high gross investment coefficient, expressed in current prices, has not meant that *real* net capital formation was high, the difference being explained by the behavior of relative prices. If gross investment and total gross product are expressed in 1935–38 prices (using implicit price deflators) the gross investment coefficient drops to about 13 percent for the postwar period, a figure slightly above the 12 percent corresponding to 1935–41. If one assumes that 1935–38 relative prices were closer to the contemporary price pattern in semi-in-

1. See Rolf Hayn, "Capital Formation and Argentina's Price-Cost Structure," *Review of Economics and Statistics* 44 (Aug. 1962): 340–43; Hugh Schwartz, "Capital Formation and Argentina's Price-Cost Structure, 1935–1958: A Comment," *Review of Economics and Statistics* 46 (Aug. 1964): 320–21; and Rolf Hayn, "Capital Formation and Argentina's Price-Cost Structure: A Reply," *Review of Economics and Statistics* 46 (May 1964): 223. Several other authors have remarked on the apparently high capital-output ratios implied by the Argentine national accounts. Capital goods prices appear to have risen secularly more than those for consumer's goods in industrialized Western countries, but this increase in the relative prices of investment goods has been much less dramatic than in Argentina. See R. A. Gordon, "Price Changes: Consumers' and Capital Goods," *American Economic Review* 51 (Dec. 1961): 937–57.

2. The link between capital accumulation and growth rates need not be rigid. But even allowing for other influences on the marginal capital output ratio, the Argentine figures are out of line with the experience of other countries.

dustrialized countries than present Argentine relative prices, then the postwar real marginal capital-output ratio is not grossly out of line with those of other countries.[3] It also has been argued that the change in the price structure, combined with the postwar increase in the income share distributed as wages and salaries, inhibited private capital formation. Others have stressed additional factors that may have more than offset these negative influences on private investment, while pointing out data unreliability.

This essay will present new data on these issues and will explore the impact of post-1935 changes in relative prices of capital goods on the Argentine economy. First the data will be presented; then an attempt will be made to isolate the factors that explain, in an accounting sense, variations in relative prices. The basic causes and importance of these price changes on the level and allocation of investment and saving will be discussed later. The need to disaggregate the heterogeneous concepts of capital goods and investors will be stressed as a necessary step in understanding the impact of relative price changes.

The major conclusions of this essay may be stated as follows. Although data leave much to be desired, there is little doubt that capital goods prices rose substantially relative to the GNP deflator after 1935–38. They also rose relative to prices for other nonrural commodities. Prices for durable producers' equipment, especially transport equipment, were at the forefront of the rise. As a result, Argentine capital goods prices have reached levels much higher than those of most other countries. Although no single cause explains these price trends, the foreign exchange shortage and declines in labor productivity in construction taken together provide a satisfactory explanation. The apparently high marginal capital-output ratio in postwar Argentina can indeed be explained primarily by the evolution of relative prices. Real capital formation in the form of new producers' durable equipment during 1935–61 was determined mainly by supply conditions, which were heavily influenced by postwar public foreign trade policies. The extraordinary increases in capital goods' relative prices resulted first from the war and afterwards from those govern-

3. Although it is likely that in most semi-industrialized countries the relative prices of capital goods are higher than in fully industrialized countries, the pattern may have significant exceptions in countries where multiple exchange rates have operated so as to give importers of capital goods implicit subsidies, and where price controls have insured that these subsidies benefit the final users of these goods. Construction labor costs are also lower in less developed countries.

ment policies that also led to low rates of capital formation and technological change. The postwar high relative prices for capital goods
were a result of misguided public policies rather than an autonomous
cause of meager capital formation. Their high levels may be taken as
an index of the deterioration in the capacity to transform of the
Argentine economy, because they imply a situation where a given
amount of current savings bought less real investment. The saving effort of an economy should be defined in terms of how many units of
consumption goods must be given up to obtain one unit of investment
goods. So, while the real level of capital formation is best measured
using constant international relative prices, the saving effort should
be measured using current Argentine relative prices. Who made, or
was forced to make, the sacrifices in current consumption allowing for
the remarkably high Argentine postwar savings rates is not easy to
discover. This will be examined further in the next essay.

THE DATA: IMPLICIT PRICES

Most of the empirical analysis on this issue has to rely on implicit
prices obtained from the national accounts. True price indices (with
fixed weights) for capital goods going back to the 1930s are few.
In spite of the well-known difficulties of relying on implicit prices as
indicators of price movements, they will be used, supplemented whenever possible by true price indices. It will be argued that available
evidence indicates that broad tendencies suggested by implicit prices
reflect true price movements.

Table 6.1 presents relative implicit prices for major catagories in
total absorption. Relative prices for gross domestic investment showed
a sharp rise during the war years and continued to increase until a
peak was reached during 1949–51. Since then they have remained
between 40 and 60 percent above 1935–38 levels.

Table 6.2, using two different data sources, provides greater detail
on implicit prices for different types of investment goods. A major
subdivision of fixed capital formation (neglecting changes in inventories) exists between construction and durable producers' equipment.
The former has (in Argentina as well as in most semi-industrialized
countries) a substantially lower import content than the latter. The
rise of construction relative prices was much smaller than that for
producers' equipment during the war, but by 1949–51 both had
roughly doubled their 1935–38 level. Since then, construction relative

Table 6.1: Indices of Implicit Prices for Major Expenditure Categories
Divided by Implicit Prices for GNP at Market Prices
(1935–38 = 100, yearly averages)

	Private consumption	*Public consumption*	*Total gross domestic investment*
1935–38	100	100	100
1939–45	93	96	130
1946–48	93	90	156
1949–51	87	91	175
1952–55	89	95	148
1956–58	89	90	158
1959–61	90	89	145
1962–64	89	107	140

Sources: O.S. and BCRA. Data from these two sources were linked in 1950. It should be noted that the former used 1950 as the base year for constant price series, while the latter used 1960 for that purpose.

Table 6.2: Indices of Implicit Prices for Major Components of Gross Investment
Divided by Implicit Prices for GNP at Market Prices
(1935–38 = 100, yearly averages)

	1939– 45	*1946– 48*	*1949– 51*	*1952– 55*	*1956– 58*	*1959– 61*	*1962– 64*
BCRA							
Construction	127	172	197	181	172	154	159
All durable producers' equipment	160	149	180	161	187	196	172
Transport equipment	220	197	369	437	678	605	511
Machinery and other	162	159	150	125	141	160	141
Repairs	112	126	147	147	135	127	128
BCRA/CONADE							
Construction	127	172	197	186	176	155	–
All durable producers' equipment	161	150	202	198	243	244	–
Transport equipment	252	117	179	252	375	352	–
Machinery and other	162	159	165	153	187	188	–
Repairs	112	126	148	153	143	138	–

Note: For this series, the whole 1935–61 period used 1960 as the base for constant price data. Because of shifting base years and weights, total implicit price indices need not fall between those of subcategories of which they are made up. A dash means data not available.

Sources: As in Table 6.1, plus CONADE. The data on transport equipment of CONADE was kindly provided to me directly by Alberto Fracchia and Juan Sourrouille.

prices have tended to decline, while those for durable producers' equipment have followed a more erratic pattern from which no clear trend emerges. Relative prices for producers' equipment have remained substantially above those for 1935–38.

A clearer idea of fluctuations in relative prices, showing their total percentage changes between key years, may be obtained from Table 6.3. Even before the war, a tendency appeared for relative prices of

Table 6.3: Percentage Changes in Relative Prices of Construction and Durable Producers' Equipment between Selected Years (BCRA)

	Construction	*All durable producers' equipment*
1935–39	12	20
1939–45	27	70
1945–47	20	−31
1947–50	21	46
1950–55	−10	−18
1955–59	−15	35
1959–64	0	−27

Sources: BCRA, as in Tables 6.1 and 6.2.

both construction and equipment to rise. After the war, equipment and machinery relative prices fell sharply; their 1947 level was roughly the same as in 1940 (133, with 1935–38 = 100). Steep increases, however, came after 1947, to be followed by new fluctuations during the 1950s.

Durable producers' equipment may be subdivided into three components: new transport equipment, other new machinery and equipment, and repairs. The latter category has been made up primarily of repairs carried out in railroad and other workshops attached to transportation activities. Relative prices of these three types of goods have behaved differently. The two sources presented in Table 6.2 disagree on the extent of the rise in transport equipment relative prices; but both agree that they showed the largest increase since 1935–38.[4] Repairs, which have a small import component, show fast price increases until 1949–51 and a decline after 1952–55. For the whole period the relative price increase of repairs is modest. Explanations of

4. The smaller the category under examination, the greater the chance that changes in its composition will yield peculiar implicit prices. This may be the basic cause of the divergences shown for the relative prices of transport equipment. Transport equipment includes such dissimilar items as ships, trucks, locomotives, and freight wagons, which are purchased at irregular intervals.

capital goods relative price changes must take into account at least some of the variety hiding behind aggregate trends.

National accounts also provide time series at constant prices on gross capital formation, according to types of goods. From these quantum indices, the structure of apparent domestic absorption, expressed at prices for different years, may be calculated. Apparent domestic absorption is defined as the sum of private and public consumption, plus fixed gross capital formation. With the existence of relative price fluctuations, the structure of absorption for any given period changes drastically depending on what base year is used in the calculations. As an example, Table 6.4 presents estimates for 1950 and 1951

Table 6.4: Composition of Apparent Domestic Absorption during 1950–51
(Percentages of total)

	New BCRA current prices	Old series current prices	New BCRA 1960 prices	Estimates 1935 prices
Private consumption	70.4	65.6	73.6	74.5
Public consumption	9.9	12.1	9.4	13.4
Private construction	9.1	8.4	7.0	4.0
Public construction	4.5	5.5	3.3	3.1
Transport equipment	0.8	1.4	1.2	0.4
Other new machinery and equipment	4.6	4.9	4.8	3.3
Repairs	0.8	2.0	0.7	1.3
Total	*100.0*	*100.0*	*100.0*	*100.0*
All construction	13.6	13.9	10.3	7.1
All new machinery and equipment	5.4	6.3	6.0	3.7
All gross fixed capital formation	19.7	22.3	17.0	12.1

Note: It should be noted that the item "Repairs" was greatly reduced in recent revisions of the national accounts; for 1950, at current prices, the revised figures are only 41 percent of the old estimate. Minor changes were also made for other series.

Sources and method: BCRA, pp. 1, 10, 11, 50–52; O.S., pp. 122, 128, 129; and ECLA worksheets. "Estimates at 1935 Prices" were obtained by first making up quantum indices for each of the expenditures categories shown in the table (1935 = 100), on the basis of data from the sources already mentioned (linked at 1950), and then multiplying those indices by the figures for 1935 (at current prices)

according to old and revised national accounts at current prices, as well as estimates made using 1960 and 1935 prices. At one extreme, the old series showed fixed gross capital formation, measured at current 1950–51 prices, representing more than 22 percent of absorption;

for the same years, revised data measured at 1935 prices show that gross fixed capital formation was only 12 percent of total absorption! [5] Sharp differences also occur depending on whether revised BCRA time series are measured at current prices or at 1935 prices (20 percent vs. 12 percent).

The same type of calculation can be extended for 1935–64. This is done in Tables 116 and 117 of the Statistical Appendix, which estimate the structure of absorption at 1935 and 1960 prices, respectively. Calculations using 1950 prices (not shown) yield higher gross investment rates than those using 1960 prices, but it is already clear that a very misleading picture of real capital formation could be obtained just by looking at figures expressed in postwar prices. The gap between the two estimates is especially noteworthy for new machinery and equipment, goods through which a large share of foreign technological progress is transferred to Argentina, and which are more directly linked to commodity production than construction. [6]

OTHER PRICE AND RELATED DATA

A few other bits of evidence are available. The best are presented in Table 6.5. These price indices for a few rural capital goods show, on the whole, a pattern similar to that for durable producers' equipment, shown in Table 6.2. Wartime relative price increases were in some cases (rural tools and machinery, wire fencing) partially offset in later years, while for other goods (watering systems, automotive vehicles) further postwar increases took place. These and other data suggest that the postwar protective system buttressed the continuation of a price structure distorted by war, especially with regard to machinery, equipment, and vehicles. Table 6.5 confirms that transport equipment relative prices have risen the most, among the major capital goods categories (and also indicates that CONADE estimates for transport equipment, shown in Table 6.2, are more reliable than those in the upper part of the same table).

True price indices are also available, beginning in 1940, for con-

---

5. The recent revision of the national accounts increased consumption more than investment, as may be seen by comparing the first two columns of Table 6.4, so that not all of the gap between these two extreme estimates is explained by changes in relative prices. See notes to Table 6.4, especially with regard to "Repairs."

6. It has not been possible to subdivide construction into its housing and other components for the whole period.

Table 6.5: Price Indices for Capital Goods Used in the Rural Sector
Divided by Implicit Prices for the GNP, 1939–63
(1935–39 = 100)

	Rural machinery and tools	*Wire fencing*	*Watering systems*	*Automotive vehicles*
1935–39	100	100	100	100
1940–45	114	214	135	181
1946–48	106	199	174	186
1949–51	106	166	157	235
1952–55	105	170	160	257
1956–58	104	170	163	226
1959–61	117	191	182	205
1962–63	109	147	171	185

Sources: Asociación Argentina de Productores Agrícolas, *Precios de Paridad para Productos Agrícolas en la Argentina* (Buenos Aires, 1958), and from CONADE worksheets. The original data were presented in terms of 1935–39 = 100 (i.e. no yearly estimates were available for each of the 1935–39 years).

struction costs in the Federal District (Buenos Aires); these are shown in Table 118 of the Statistical Appendix. If one bears in mind that between 1935–38 and 1940 construction relative prices rose by about 15 percent (according to implicit prices), the Buenos Aires construction costs index comes close to construction implicit prices shown in Table 6.2.

Argentine wholesale price indices have grossly underrepresented machinery and equipment. A separate category for them was not established in the index until 1956; even then only domestically produced machinery and equipment were included. As a crude proxy, one may consider wholesale price indices for iron, steel, and other metals (and their manufacturers) for 1939–64.[7] These are presented in Table 119 of the Statistical Appendix, broken down into imported and domestically produced items. Once again, price indices concur in a general way with trends shown in Table 6.2. The war impact on prices is clearly shown, followed by a zigzagging pattern.

7. In defense of this proxy it may be noted that according to the industrial census for 1948, 23 percent of the gross value of output of vehicles and machinery (excluding electrical machinery), was made up of imported raw materials and intermediate products (excluding fuels and lubricants). Presumably, nearly all of these imported inputs were metals. For electrical machinery and appliances, the share of these imported inputs in gross value of output was 20 percent.

Postwar implicit prices for the *domestic* gross output of some capital goods and related items are available. These are also presented in Table 120 of the Statistical Appendix. Changes in these real prices are relatively minor, with the exception of automotive prices. This is consistent with the assertion that most relative price changes for durable producers' equipment took place during the war or shortly afterwards. Domestically produced machinery and motors show a declining price trend since 1949–51—years which, according to Table 6.2, also marked the high tide of relative prices for all durable producers' equipment.[8]

The recent decline in relative prices for domestically produced vehicles, machinery, and motors calls for further comment. The textbook discussion of import substitution points out that the beginning of domestic production of items previously imported is nearly always accompanied by an increase in the relative prices for these goods. The transition from importing to producing a given commodity is likely to be more complicated. Exchange difficulties often induce governments to ban or make prohibitive the importation of many commodities, especially durable goods for either consumption or capital formation, even when there are no immediate plans for producing them domestically. Therefore, between the time when those goods are imported (in substantial numbers) and the time when they begin being produced domestically (also in substantial numbers), many years may pass *during which their (free) relative prices reach the highest levels.* When domestic production begins after such a period of abstention, it is likely to be accompanied by a decline in the relative prices of these goods, although they will for a long time remain above the levels corresponding to open importation. For Argentina, automotive vehicles are a good example of this process; between 1939 and 1959 (substantial domestic production began in 1959) purchases of new autos, whether imported or produced domestically, was exiguous

---

8. Beginning in 1956 the wholesale price index includes domestically produced machinery and equipment (including prices for repairs). By deflating these wholesale prices by implicit prices for the GNP, the following relative prices are obtained (1956 = 100):

	1956–58	*1959–61*	*1962–64*	*1965*
Domestic nonelectrical machinery and vehicles	97	91	93	94
Domestic electrical motors	91	78	65	74

Data on wholesale prices were obtained as in Table 119 in the Statistical Appendix.

and negligible in contrast with those registered either before or after 1939–59.

All the information presented deals with relative price *trends*. By itself, it says nothing regarding the *level* of Argentine capital goods' relative prices compared with those in the rest of the world. The ECLA has provided data on comparative price structures permitting a further check on Table 6.2. In 1962 relative prices for new machinery and equipment were between 2.5 and 3.3 times higher in Buenos Aires than in two major United States cities.[9] This information on 1962 relative prices could be compatible with different trends during 1935–62. A rough check on the reasonableness of Table 6.2 data consists of considering what it implies for 1935–38 Argentine relative prices, compared with similar United States prices. The results are presented in the second column of Table 121 in the Statistical Appendix; the methods used are also outlined there. The estimates for 1935–38 indicate that even then relative prices for producers' durable equipment were higher in Argentina than in the United States, although construction prices were then relatively lower in Argentina. How reasonable are these results?

During 1935–38, about three-fourths of all new durable producers' equipment installed in Argentina was imported. Furthermore, the country was a net exporter of wage goods making up a large fraction of consumption expenditures. Thus, even in a world of free trade (but with positive transport costs) one could have expected a priori that relative prices for new producers' durable equipment would be higher in Argentina than in the United States. Impediments to international trade accentuate this tendency. For construction, a priori considerations are not as clear-cut; Argentina has been a net importer of such construction materials as lumber, sand, and metal products, but her relative abundance of labor and foodstuffs could be expected to lower labor costs.

Information bits on the prewar price structure do suggest that rela-

9. See Table 121 in the Statistical Appendix. Argentine prices were also found to be high compared to Latin American standards. The published version of this ECLA study points out for Argentina (in June 1960): "All types of Investment . . . were extremely expensive, Argentine prices exceeding the average for Latin America by about 50 percent for all three component groups [Construction, Transport Equipment and other Producers' equipment]. The 1962 situation showed little change." See "A Measurement of Price Levels and the Purchasing Power of Currencies in Latin America, 1960–62," *Economic Bulletin for Latin America* 8, no. 2 (Oct. 1963): 217.

tive prices of producers' durable equipment were then around 50 percent higher in Argentina than in the United States. A 1943 report had this to say on the basis of 1937 and 139 prices:

> There is a definite difference between the pattern of prices in Argentina and the patterns found in other advanced western nations. . . . Steel and copper are definitely, though not greatly, higher in Argentina. . . . Lumber is higher than in the United States but cheaper than in Europe, while cement prices do not differ much . . . comparable automobiles, radios and farm implements at Chicago are from 30 to 50 percent lower than in Buenos Aires.[10]

The following observation was made for the period around 1935:

> One company which imported a light car into Argentina in a semi-knocked-down condition estimated that a list-price difference of 7 to 8 percent in comparison to a Ford or Chevrolet in the United States increased to 22 percent when the cars were sold in Argentina.[11]

These comments presumably refer to direct price comparisons made at the going exchange rate. Similar comparisons showed foodstuffs, with high shares in total expenditure, to have lower prices in Argentina. Thus it may be concluded that relative prices of automotive vehicles, steel products, farm implements, etc., were somewhat higher than the percentages indicated in the quotes.

This evidence, although skimpy, also confirms the broad price movements indicated in Table 6.2. In addition, it implies that even the CONADE indices for transport equipment may slightly exaggerate the post-1935 rise of their relative prices.

There is no doubt, however, that relative prices for producers' durable equipment during recent years have been much higher in Argentina than in the rest of the world. A CONADE calculation of the Argentine GNP for 1960, *measured in current U.S. dollar prices,* shows gross domestic fixed capital formation of only 14 percent of GNP, in contrast with a share of 23 percent when all GNP components

10. See Armour Research Foundation, *Technological and Economic Survey of Argentine Industries with Industrial Research Recommendations* (Chicago, 1943), pp. 65–66.

11. Dudley M. Phelps, *Migration of Industry to South America* (New York: McGraw-Hill Book Co., 1936), p. 60.

are measured at 1960 Argentine prices.[12] CONADE also calculated exchange rates for some items equating Argentine and U.S. 1960 prices; at a time when the single exchange rate of 82.7 pesos to one U.S. dollar prevailed (with free convertibility), it was found that the parity exchange rates were 148 for tractors and other rural machinery and equipment and 227 for automotive vehicles.[13] David Felix, on the basis of a large sample of 1960–65 wholesale prices, found that for vehicles and machinery Argentine prices were on the average 2.2 times those of the United States. A comparison by Hugh Schwartz of prices for a selected group of metallurgical products showed that the exchange rates needed to equate Argentine and United States prices dur-

12. The contrast for all major items is as follows (expressed as percentages of GNP):

	1960 GNP at current peso prices	*1960 GNP at U.S. current dollar prices*
Private consumption	69	76
Public consumption	9	10
Gross fixed capital formation	23	14
Change in inventories	1	1
Exports of goods and services	11	7
Imports of goods and services	12	8

See *CONADE, Distribución del Ingreso y Cuentas Nacionales en la Argentina,* vol. 3 (Buenos Aires, 1966), p. 165.

Another source presents the following contrast in the structure of the 1960 Argentine GDP calculated first in dollars using the one prevailing exchange rate and then using purchasing power equivalents for each expenditure category:

	With prevailing exchange rate	*With purchasing power equivalents*
Private consumption	69.5	70.8
Public consumption	9.0	18.0
Gross fixed investment	21.7	11.0
Inventory change	1.0	1.0
Trade balance	−1.2	−0.8

See Stanley N. Braithwaite, "Real Income Levels in Latin America," *Review of Income and Wealth,* Series 14, no. 2 (June 1968), p. 135.

13. CONADE, *Distribución del Ingreso y Cuentas Nacionales,* p. 167. For 1962, when the average exchange rate was 113 pesos per dollar (by the end of that year it stood at 134 pesos), the parity rates were as follows, according to unpublished research of ECLA: gasoline engine, 290 pesos per dollar; diesel engine, 306 pesos per dollar; electric engine, 91 pesos per dollar; generating unit, 322 pesos per dollar; portable arc welder, 239 pesos per dollar; lathe, 90 pesos per dollar; drill, 108 pesos per dollar; ball bearings, 157 pesos per dollar; tractor, 186 pesos per dollar; disc plow, 202 pesos per dollar; lorries, 269 pesos per dollar; centrifugal pump, 134 pesos per dollar.

ing 1961, when the official rate was still 82 pesos per dollar, were distributed as follows:[14]

Pesos per dollar	*Number of products*
Less than 61	0
61–80	5
81–100	2
101–120	3
121–140	7
More than 140	2

In summary, it may be concluded that (1) capital goods prices in Argentina rose substantially relative to the GNP implicit deflator between 1935–38 and recent years and (2) they have reached levels considerably higher than in most countries.[15] The data also show that there are wide differences in the performance of individual prices within the category of capital goods.

EXPLANATION OF THE EVOLUTION OF RELATIVE PRICES: AN ACCOUNTING APPROACH

This section will look at the immediate causes for the rise in capital goods' relative prices. Discussion of more basic forces will come later.

Some readers may have become suspicious of the use of the GNP deflator as the denominator in most price ratios presented in earlier sections. If so, their suspicions are justified. Consider in Table 6.6 implicit prices for major activities divided by the GDP deflator. There is a striking diversity; in particular, the behavior of prices for such

14. David Felix, "Beyond Import Substitution: A Latin-American Dilemma" (mimeographed), p. 57, Table 8. These calculations were based on direct price comparisons using the going exchange rate. Hugh H. Schwartz, "The Argentine Experience with Industrial Credit and Protection Incentives, 1943–1958)," (Ph.D. diss., Yale University), Appendix P, p. 311. Recently an executive of an Argentine metallurgical grm asserted that the investment required to install an industrial plant in Argentina is 30 to 40 percent above corresponding costs abroad. See *Techint, Boletín Informativo,* Nov. 1966, p. 20.

15. One aspect of price movements whose exploration has not been possible is quality change that, it is often alleged, is underestimated by price indices for durable goods. Relative price movements between 1935–38 and recent years have been so violent that no realistic differential of unregistered changes in quality could offset them. Furthermore, it is not obvious that Argentine price indices for durable goods underestimate quality changes because secular quality improvements in these goods may be more than offset by decreases in quality arising from import substitution, also difficult to capture in price indices.

Table 6.6: Indices of Sectorial Implicit Prices
Divided by Implicit Prices for GDP at Factor Cost
(1935–38 = 100, yearly averages)

	1939– 45	1946– 48	1949– 51	1952– 55	1956– 58	1959– 61	1962– 64
Agriculture, livestock, fisheries	89	100	95	107	114	123	126
Mining	88	68	66	86	88	72	69
Manufacturing	122	127	132	127	126	130	127
Construction	127	187	225	211	215	197	203
Commerce	121	146	136	126	128	133	113
Transport	85	74	82	86	91	85	92
Communications	94	75	81	103	96	113	143
Other public utilities	76	55	44	35	33	39	43
Housing	94	62	45	42	41	27	—[a]
Financial services	102	85	104	103	101	85	–
Government services	89	72	76	79	76	74	93
Other services	91	85	96	106	97	90	90

[a] Dash indicates data not available.

Sources and method: Implicit prices were obtained by dividing indices of value added for each sector at current prices over indices of real output for each sector. Data for 1935–50 from O.S. and from ECLA worksheets. Data for 1950–64 from BCRA, p. 57, and CONADE, pp. 212–13. CONADE data were used only for Housing and Financial services; for these sectors implicit prices are not available during 1962–64. Data from different sources were linked using the overlapping indices for 1950. No changes were made in weights.

services as housing and public utilities is extraordinary. As a result of government controls barring increases in line with those of the general price level, their relative prices declined sharply, beginning during the war and continuing thereafter.[16] The figures also indicate that since 1935–38, prices for nonrural commodities, taken as a group, have increased more than those of all services, or at least more than prices for services as defined in the national accounts.[17] Table 6.6 indices for rural comodities also cast doubt on the use of GNP or GDP deflators, as it is unlikely that their real prices increased by 26 percent between 1935–38 and 1962–64.

16. Transport price data hide different trends for railroad and other activities. Data for just railroads, corresponding to those in Table 6.6, yield the following relative prices (1935–38 = 100): 1956–58 = 14; 1959–61 = 10.
17. In other words, neglecting quality changes, as well as the indirect tax imposed on the community by the inflationary finance used to cover up deficits in public enterprises caused by their low selling prices (as well as by their inefficiency).

A comparison of the wholesale price index for nonrural goods that includes only commodities, with the GDP and GNP deflators that give services a weight of about one-half, is presented in Table 6.7.

Table 6.7: Indices of Wholesale Prices for All Nonrural Commodities
Divided by Implicit Prices for GDP and GNP
(1935–38 = 100, yearly averages)

	Wholesale prices of all nonrural goods divided by GDP deflator	*Wholesale prices of nonrural goods divided by GNP deflator*
1935–38	100.0	100.0
1939–45	134.9	135.4
1946–48	109.4	118.1
1949–51	114.1	118.9
1952–55	131.5	133.0
1956–58	126.7	127.2
1959–61	139.0	140.2
1962–64	136.6	137.9

Sources: As in Table 6.1 and Table 119 of the Statistical Appendix.

The prices of all nonrural commodities (mainly manufactured consumer and intermediate goods) have risen faster than both the GDP and GNP deflators. This faster rise was sharp during the war; then the gap became smaller until 1955 when it widened once again.

Some of the increase in capital goods' relative prices shown in Tables 6.1 and 6.2 is, therefore, simply part of a general increase of nonrural goods prices relative to the GNP deflator, which has been biased downward by government policies freezing (or more exactly, melting) the prices of some services. But a comparison of Tables 6.2 and 6.7 also shows that most capital goods prices also show a significant rise relative to those of nonrural commodities.[18] The rise in capital goods' relative prices is *not* just a statistical mirage caused by the presence of services in consumption expenditures.

Further insight into the behavior of new producers' durable equipment prices may be obtained by looking at implicit prices for domestic

18. These relative prices are as follows (using BCRA data, 1935–38 = 100):

	1939–45	*1946–48*	*1949–51*	*1952–55*	*1956–58*	*1959–61*	*1962–64*
Construction	94	146	166	136	136	110	115
Durable producers' equipment	118	126	151	121	147	140	125

Table 6.8: Implicit Prices for Domestic and Imported
New Durable Producers' Equipment Divided by GNP Implicit Prices
and Factors Affecting the Relative Prices of Imported Capital Goods
(1935–38 = 100)

	Relative prices for domestic new durable producers' equipment	Relative prices for imported new durable producers' equipment	Foreign prices and exchange rate deflated by GNP implicit prices	Other factors (residual)
1935–38	100	100	100	100
1939–45	133	236	–	–
1946–48	146	161	85	190
1949–51	147	213	70	302
1952–55	134	138	65	212
1956–58	119	278	164	169
1959–61	117	341	149	229
1962–64	102	278	124	225

Sources and method: Domestic and imported implicit prices as in Tables 6.1 and 6.2.
Only BCRA data were used for the post-1950 period. No index of prices in foreign
currency is available for imported machinery and equipment for 1935–50. Price
indices of Canadian imports of iron, steel, nonferrous metals, and their products
were used as a proxy for those years; obtained from *Historical Statistics of Canada,*
ed. M. C. Urquhart (Cambridge University Press, 1965), p. 302. Canadian import
prices may underestimate those for Argentina during 1946–48, when the Perón
government ran into (politically inspired) difficulties in buying from industrialized
countries. For 1951–64, the index of dollar prices for machinery and equipment
imports of DNEC, *Boletín Mensual de Estadística,* was used. For 1935–50, the
average exchange rate applied to all imports was used to make up an index of the
exchange rate; this was linked in 1951 with the average exchange rate applied to
imports of machinery and equipment. The latter is obtained from the peso and
dollar data presented in DNEC *Comercio Exterior* Yearbooks. The indices for
foreign prices and exchange rates have been multiplied to obtain an index of their
combined effect, which has then been divided by the implicit GNP deflator to yield
the third column. The fourth column was obtained by dividing the domestic price
index for imported durable producers equipment (second column) by the third
column.

and imported items.[19] These data are presented in the first two columns of Table 6.8. The largest increase is registered in imported
goods; however, as the basket of domestically produced goods under-
went profound composition changes (e.g., for 1962–64 they include

19. The usual warning about implicit prices should here be redoubled, as
imported and domestic new producers' durable equipment are more unstable
categories in their composition than, say, transport equipment and other
machinery (each including both imported and domestic goods). As will be
seen below, the imported share of these goods changed considerably between
1935–38 and recent years.

items such as tractors and trucks not present in that category during 1935–38), the first column of Table 6.8 cannot be used for more than rough indications of price changes over *short* periods. An attempt has been made to decompose the relatively more stable category of imported goods by separating the influence of foreign prices and the exchange rate, on the one hand, and that of other factors, such as protection and commercialization margins. During 1946–55, the former influences (measured only crudely) cannot be blamed for the increase in capital goods' relative prices, as indicated by the third column of Table 6.8, especially after 1946–48.[20] Since 1955 frequent devaluations gave an upward push to imported goods prices. But relative to 1935–38 and with the heavy weight of services in the GNP deflator borne in mind, the push was modest.

"Other factors" bear most of the blame for the price rise. These include installation, transport, commercialization margins, import duties, exchange surcharges, harbor fees, costs of previous deposits, etc. No detailed data are available on these costs; a careful quantification of all the forces pushing up the relative prices of imported goods seems out of the question. Certain general tendencies, however, are reasonably clear. Exchange control became more strict after the war until 1955, first emphasizing protectionist ends and later its rationing features. Around 1949 import permits for new capital goods (especially those from dollar areas) first began to be considered as marginal recipients of exchange, to be granted only after imports of fuels, raw

20. A caveat is prompted by the possibility that Canadian import prices for iron, other metals, and their products may not give an accurate reflection of Argentine import prices for that period. During the war years, neutral Argentina certainly had a more difficult time obtaining capital goods in world markets than Allied Canada. The discrimination spilled into the immediate postwar period. Furthermore, it is well known that during 1946–48 Argentine buying agents launched an all-out effort to buy whatever machinery and equipment was available in world markets, without looking too closely at price tags, as they feared an outbreak of hostilities between the USA and the USSR. During those years the public sector through IAPI bulk-bought abroad many industrial intermediate products and raw materials, as well as capital goods. Argentine purchases were hampered by the fact that her ample reserves in pound sterling were of limited use in world markets at the time. It may also be noted that during these years Argentina purchased large amounts of rather special capital goods, such as ships and airplanes. As late as 1950, the *Memoria* of the BCRA for 1949 remarked (p. 38, Spanish ed.): "In the convulsed world in which we live, it is often preferable to obtain commodities without paying much attention to the conditions under which such [international] trade is carried out, rather than do without supplies waiting for a multilateral trade . . . which is still very far from being realized in the international field."

materials, and intermediate goods were satisfied. Permits for new machinery and equipment were often given only upon condition that the importer obtained medium-term foreign credits to finance the transaction. Motor vehicle imports were allowed only under special ad hoc arrangements.[21] As exchange earnings declined relative to GNP, the share of machinery and equipment in total imports declined from 30 percent in 1948, to 21 percent during 1949–51, and to 20 percent during 1952–55 (according to ECLA data).[22] New capital goods and even spare parts became very scarce, so that even when they were imported at favorable exchange rates, they could be (and were often) resold at astronomical prices.[23] Available evidence indicates that what can be called commercialization margins (for lack of a better name) on imported capital goods rose during 1946–55 relative to 1935–38, helping to explain in part the increase in the residual index of Table 6.8. Holders of import and exchange permits increased their margins relative to 1935–38, usually until 1955, but in some cases until 1959, when most quantitative import restrictions were removed.[24] Since

21. Some of these features of exchange control were maintained during 1956–58. See *Memoria* of the BCRA for 1955, esp. pp. 1, 10, 30–32. Reviewing earlier years, the 1955 *Memoria* states: "the value of imports of capital goods, even though limited to taking care of the most pressing needs, . . . in part had to be financed using commercial credit." These imports included parts required just for the maintenance of old capital goods. During 1949–55, some capital goods were imported under permits curiously labelled "for imports which do not use foreign exchange" (*autorizaciones para importaciones sin pago de divisas*). These permits represented a tacit acceptance by the regime of private dollar funds held abroad (illegally under exchange regulations).

22. For the whole period 1946–65 a regression expressing the logarithms of the percentage share of capital goods in the import bill (X_1) as a function of the logarithms of all imports as a percentage of GNP (X_2) and a time trend (X_3), yields the following result:

$$X_1 = 1.453 + 0.673\ X_2 + 0.018\ X_3$$
$$(0.778)\quad (0.286)\quad\ \ (0.010)\qquad R^2 = 0.26 \qquad\qquad (6.1)$$

23. The prevalence of black and grey markets for capital goods during these years (especially 1949–55), further complicates the research task as even available list prices cannot be taken as representative of actual transaction prices.

24. On the other hand, a greater percentage of investment goods, compared with prewar, were imported directly by their final users, especially public enterprises, thus avoiding commercialization margins. From worksheets of the National Accounts, found in the files of the ECLA, the following rough index for gross commercialization margins on all imported producers' durable equipment, expressed as a percentage of the c.i.f. value of imports, has been obtained up until 1955 (1935–38 = 100): 1946–48 = 106; 1949–51 = 146; 1952–55 = 115.

1955 the exchange rate, tariffs, and surcharges have been given a larger role in allocating exchange. The last column in Table 6.8 indicates, however, that on balance the new policy mix (excluding exchange rate policy) has exerted during 1959–64 the same pressure on imported goods prices that existed during 1952–55 under exchange control. Therefore, with the more flexible post-1955 exchange rate policy, these relative prices have undergone a further rise.

During 1959 average import duties (including exchange surcharges translated into duty-equivalents) on capital goods were between 78 and 130 percent ad valorem (depending on the weighting system used).[25] As 1935–38 duties fluctuated around 30 percent, an index (with 1935–38 = 100) for these import costs would reach at least 250 during 1959, thus helping explain the increase in the last column of Table 6.8.[26] But the picture is clouded by the fact that during recent years, to promote selected investments governments have granted ad hoc exemptions from surcharges and duties to many imports of capital goods and other commodities.[27] Nevertheless, in spite of ambiguities surrounding the exact incidence of tariffs and of additional costs implied by advanced deposits and changes in public administrative rulings, a large part of the postwar increase in the last column of Table 6.8 may be blamed on greater import restrictions of one type or another.

With the exception of import dollar prices, an important influence only during the immediate postwar and the Korean War periods, all of the factors explaining the increase in relative prices of imported capital goods have one thing in common: they arise from Argentine foreign exchange difficulties, especially since 1949. Whether this bottleneck led to devaluations, or tighter exchange control measures, or higher import taxes and exchange surcharges, the basic cause was the same. These pressures were often reflected in higher relative prices for similar goods produced domestically.[28]

25. See Santiago Macario, "Protectionism and Industrialization in Latin America," *Economic Bulletin for Latin America* 9, no. 1 (March 1964): 69, 70, 73. The figures for durable consumer goods range from 181 percent to 700 percent.

26. Heavy exchange surcharges, assimilated in the duty figures, were introduced during 1958 and 1959, as an offset to the removal of exchange and import controls. Some controls and regulations over imports of capital goods were reintroduced after October 1963.

27. Between 1959 and 1963, over half of Argentine imports entered free of surcharges.

28. But the nature of the protectionist system and/or the disruptions caused in international trade by war, often allowed wide divergencies to exist be-

Table 6.2 showed that prices for transport equipment have risen much more than those of machinery and other equipment. Even if one discounts part of the increase shown by implicit prices, this conclusion stands. The reason is that the restrictive system applied to imports bore more severely on transport equipment than on machinery, perhaps on grounds that requirements for longer lived equipment could be more easily postponed than those for machinery.[29] Domestic production of transport equipment also lagged behind that of machinery.

The immediate causes of the rise in the construction relative price may be explored with data already seen. A comparison of implicit prices for construction value added (Table 6.6) with those for finished construction (Table 6.2), indicates that real construction factor income per unit of output rose faster than prices for its intermediate inputs.[30] But this deduction is not borne out by Table 118 in the Statistical Appendix, which shows increases for construction materials not very different from those registered for labor costs in most years. At any rate, it is clear that during 1946–58, higher unit labor costs were a major cause behind the rise in construction costs relative not only to the GNP deflator but also to nonrural wholesale prices. A substantial drop took place in average labor productivity in construction between 1935–38 and 1946–55, with only a partial recovery since

---

tween the c.i.f. prices of imported goods, including taxes and surcharges, and the domestic prices of similar domestic goods. The reason lies in limitations placed on the supply of foreign goods either by war or quantitative restrictions.

29. As an indication of discrimination against transport equipment, the following table presents the average exchange rates applied to different types of imported capital and other durable goods during 1955–58 (in pesos per U.S. dollar):

	Machinery except electrical machinery	Electrical machinery, equipment, and utensils	Transport equipment
1955	8.6	8.7	10.7
1956	12.1	16.0	23.8
1957	26.4	31.0	36.6
1958	33.0	40.1	45.0

Imports in pesos and dollars obtained from DNEC *Boletín Mensual,* several issues. No comparable data are available for earlier years.

30. If the BCRA index of Table 6.2 is divided over the index of Table 6.6, the following residual index (presumably reflecting the real prices of intermediate inputs) is obtained: 1935–38 = 100; 1939–45 = 100; 1946–48 = 92; 1949–51 = 88; 1952–55 = 86; 1956–58 = 80; 1959–61 = 78; 1962–64 = 78. Differences between the GNP and GDP deflators are small, as may be seen in Table 6.7.

1955.[31] This drop resulted from some of the labor policies adopted by the Perón regime. While other sectors, such as new manufacturing branches, adjusted without much loss in productivity, labor-intensive construction was especially vulnerable to those policies. The productivity decline affected both public and private construction in a similar way. Furthermore, as construction has a higher than average wage component in gross value added (65 percent vs. 46 percent for the whole economy during 1950–61, according to CONADE), its relative price reflected post-1935 real wage rates changes (sharp rises during 1946–50 and mild declines thereafter).[32]

In view of conflicting evidence regarding other construction costs, little more can be said on immediate factors behind their rise. Lack of data also hinders exploration of changes in relative prices of repairs. But it is probable that, as with construction, labor productivity declines played an important role in raising their relative prices, especially during the Perón years. A large share of repairs is carried out in shops of nationalized enterprises, including the railroads, where productivity losses have been more spectacular than in construction, due to their employment and labor practices. These nationalized repair shops, unlike part of the construction industry, were sheltered from all competitive forces.

31. If rough data on employment in construction (from CONADE and ECLA) are used, the following indices for output per worker in construction are obtained and may be contrasted with corresponding indices for the economy as a whole (1935–38 = 100):

	Construction	All sectors	Years	Construction	All sectors
1939–42	99	103	1952–55	74	120
1943–45	90	103	1956–58	81	133
1946–48	79	115	1959–61	84	138
1949–51	74	116			

Writing late in 1955 Raúl Prebisch noted, referring to the construction industry during the Perón regime: "the number of man-hours required per square meter of construction seems to be nearly twice what it was before." See his report to the provisional Argentine government, entitled *Informe Preliminar Acerca de la Situación Económica*, published in the BCRA's *Memoria* for 1955, as Appendix I, p. xii.

32. The faster rise of wages in construction which appears to have taken place during the immediate postwar period may have been due to its greater average employment of unskilled workers, whose wage rates rose faster than those for skilled workers. Construction expanded so rapidly during 1946–50 that it also put pressure on wages for some skilled construction laborers. The growth pattern of construction has been jerky, as may be seen in the following annual percentage growth rates, obtained from BCRA construction value-added data: 1935–38 = 14.4; 1938–46 = 1.9; 1946–50 = 12.5; 1950–66 = 0.5.

ECONOMIC CAUSES AND CONSEQUENCES OF THE RISE
IN CAPITAL GOODS RELATIVE PRICES

No commodity group of comparable size has experienced during 1935–64 a faster price incréase than capital goods. Although no single immediate cause explains this behavior, pressures arising from an acute scarcity of foreign exchange account for a large part of a satisfactory explanation in the case of durable producers' equipment during 1949–64. The rise in relative construction costs during 1946–58 was associated with a decline in labor productivity, as well as with increases in input prices, some of which were imported.[33] Basic causes for this price behavior and its effects on investment and saving will now be discussed.

Little more need be said on the disparity between the investment coefficient (measured at postwar prices) and the growth rate of the economy. By now it should be clear that the apparently high marginal gross capital output ratio can be explained mainly by the evolution of relative prices, rather than by more complicated hypotheses. The observed marginal *gross* fixed capital output ratio for 1935–64 is 5.3 when data are measured at 1960 prices but declines to 3.8 when data are expressed at 1935 prices.[34] The latter figure implies a net marginal capital output ratio not very different from those of other countries, if one accepts the roughness of most of these estimates. These comments should not be interpreted as adherence to a growth theory solely based on the marginal capital output ratio; the point is simply that this ratio, when computed using a price structure reasonably close to the international average, does not by itself prove that realized Argentine investment has been allocated in a way much worse than in other countries.[35] In fact, preliminary CONADE estimates of the

33. Imports of construction materials represented 4 percent of the value of construction investment during 1955–64.

34. These estimates are obtained by dividing the average gross fixed investment coefficient in GDP during 1935–64 (16.5 percent and 11.7 percent, respectively), by the GDP growth rate between 1935/36 and 1964/65 (3.1 percent per annum). The contrast in capital output ratios would be greater if only postwar years are considered.

35. Both micro- and macro-misallocations of investment have taken place in Argentina, as it should be clear from previous essays. Periodic recessions caused by exchange crises also led to underutilization of installed capacity during several years; investment in construction of a social character was excessive during 1946–55; the "bunching" of investment in new durable producers' equipment may have resulted in faulty allocation, etc. But the most

net capital stock (excluding inventories) indicate that the growth rate of the economy has been slightly higher than that of the capital stock. For 1935–63, these unpublished estimates yield the following annual average growth rates (comparing end years):[36]

All net capital stock	*2.6 percent*
Construction	2.5 percent
Rural permanent improvements	3.8 percent
Transport equipment	2.7 percent
Machinery and other equipment	3.4 percent
Livestock	1.1 percent

Greater detail is given in Table 6.9; growth rates for aggregate output and population are included for the sake of comparison. In spite of massive imports during 1947–49, the 1950 net stock of machinery and equipment was lower, in per capita terms, than in 1935. Since 1950 the trend toward a greater construction share in the capital

---

important of these misallocations are not fully reflected in a capital-output ratio, as they have resulted in lower growth rates for both capital and output. Reliance on a single aggregate capital output ratio would be misguided for studying post-1930 Argentina, not so much because it neglects the contribution of other factors of production to growth (which in a period of severe foreign exchange difficulties may not be very important), but because it fails to differentiate between different types of capital goods (construction versus machinery) and different sectors of the economy and therefore fails to reveal possible effects of a given investment pattern on future rates of capital formation.

36. By comparing net changes in the capital stock (CONADE) with gross investment data (BCRA), both expressed at 1960 prices, estimates for depreciation can be obtained. The following data summarize these estimates, expressing depreciation of construction and producers' durable equipment as percentages of the net capital stock in the form of construction and machinery and equipment, respectively. Total depreciation is also presented as a percentage of the GDP, *at 1960 market prices:*

	Construction: depreciation as a percentage of its stock	*Producers' durable equipment: depreciation as a percentage of its stock*	*All depreciation as a percentage of GDP*
1936–38	3.5	8.3	11.7
1939–45	3.3	11.5	11.7
1946–48	3.6	7.5	8.2
1949–51	3.5	7.3	9.3
1952–55	3.4	8.5	10.5
1956–58	3.6	7.8	10.0
1959–61	3.3	8.1	10.5

Measuring both gross investment and depreciation at postwar prices still leaves net investment rates inflated relative to those in the rest of the world (unless net investment were zero).

Table 6.9: Preliminary Estimates of Growth and Structure
of the Net Capital Stock, 1935–62
(In percentages)

	Average annual growth rates			Structure		
	1935–50	1950–62	1935–62	1935	1950	1962
All net capital stock	1.8	3.7	2.6	100	100	100
Construction	2.2	3.0	2.5	53	56	52
Rural permanent improvements	3.0	4.7	3.8	5	6	7
Transport equipment	0.7	5.1	2.7	14	11	13
Machinery and other equipment	0.9	6.5	3.4	16	15	20
Livestock	1.7	0.3	1.1	12	12	8
GDP at factor cost	2.8	2.9	2.9	–	–	–
Population	1.8	1.9	1.8	–	–	–

Sources: Capital stock, expressed at 1960 prices, obtained from preliminary and unpublished CONADE estimates. GDP obtained from BCRA as in Table 6.1 (also in 1960 prices); GDP growth rates were estimated comparing three year averages centered around 1936, 1951, and 1963. Population from U.N., *Statistical Bulletin for Latin America* 3:5–6.

stock was reversed. These disparate trends suggest that it would be unwise, even if data were perfectly reliable, to estimate a residual for post-1930 Argentina on the basis of the growth rate for the aggregate capital stock (together with those for output, land, and the labor force). It is doubtful that during the period under study the value of the marginal social product of different types of capital goods was the same in all sectors of the economy, as a large share of capital was in the public sector and controls distorted prices and hampered market forces. An aggregate would neglect to take these divergences and their changing importance into account. A priori, one would also expect machinery and equipment investments (especially those involving imported equipment) to embody more technological change than most construction investments.[37]

Questions regarding the economic interpretation and impact of the observed price trends remain. The division of capital goods into (1) construction and repairs and (2) new producers' durable equipment will be maintained. It will be argued that it is a fruitful simplification to regard the level of *real* capital formation in the form of new pro-

37. Changes in capacity utilization, which were important especially during the war and postwar years, would also have to be taken into account in any fine calculation of the "residual." Data, however, are lacking.

ducers' durable equipment during 1935–61 *as depending solely on supply conditions*. (Construction and repairs do not lend themselves to such a simplification.)[38] Supply conditions, in turn, were greatly influenced by government policies on export capacity and import controls, especially since the war.

A brief review of the mechanism through which Argentina obtained practically all of its new machinery and equipment before 1930 is now relevant. The foreign exchange required to pay for these imports was generated by the rural sector producing exportables or by inflows of financial capital. One may visualize an increased Argentine desire to save and invest as freeing resources from consumption, which could be devoted to increasing exports by the amount required to finance higher imports of equipment. If the consumption cut took the form of a lower demand for importable consumer goods, so much the better. The transformation of saving decisions into tangible capital goods was facilitated by the fact that many consumption goods could be exported directly, and by the expanding and elastic foreign demand for Argentine exports. The rural sector, then, could have been called the major machinery and equipment industry of the country. After the onset of the Great Depression this situation changed. The rural sector still provided the foreign exchange needed for capital imports, but during 1930–45 world trade conditions were such that it was no longer obvious that domestic intentions to increase savings would lead to the larger exchange earnings required to import more machinery and equipment. After 1945, the rural sector's productive capacity dwindled as a result of official policies.

Gross capital formation during 1935–64 is presented in Tables 6.10 and 6.11. Table 6.10 shows data according to types of capital goods; fluctuations in the flow of producers' durable equipment are much larger than those for total construction and repairs. Fluctuations for new transport equipment have been especially severe. Total construction grew at an average annual rate of more than 6 percent during 1935–50, with cyclical variations thereafter around a slightly rising trend. The (synthetic) series for repairs (see notes to Table 6.4) rises steadily until 1962–64.

38. This approach is similar to those followed by Hollis Chenery (in his several well-known publications); Markos J. Mamalakis, "Forced Saving in Underdeveloped Countries: A Rediscovery or a Misapplication of a Concept," *Economía Internazionale* 17, no. 2 (May 1964): 1–31; and John Sheahan, "Imports, Investment and Growth: Colombian Experience since 1950" (mimeographed).

Table 6.10: Average Yearly Flow of Gross Fixed Capital Formation
According to Types of Capital Goods, 1935–64
(Billion pesos at 1960 prices; final demand values)

	New machinery and other equipment	New transport equipment	Total new producers' durable equipment	Private construc- tion	Public construc- tion	Total construc- tion	Repairs
1935–38	21.64	11.95	33.59	19.51	14.20	33.71	3.05
1939–42	15.35	6.70	22.05	25.23	12.45	37.68	3.87
1942–45	10.77	1.19	11.96	33.07	12.49	45.56	4.19
1946–48	34.95	24.87	59.82	42.56	14.41	56.97	4.35
1949–51	35.25	8.44	43.69	50.03	24.85	74.88	4.78
1952–55	37.95	8.90	46.85	49.85	22.79	72.64	7.43
1956–58	50.42	14.90	65.32	61.77	22.36	84.13	9.32
1959–61	71.12	33.26	104.38	51.79	32.15	83.94	9.61
1962–64	69.47	41.18	110.65	49.24	29.38	78.62	8.92

Sources and method: As in Table 6.11.

Table 6.11: Average Yearly Flow of New Machinery and Equipment,
Imported and Domestically Produced, 1935–64
(Billion pesos at 1960 prices: final demand values)

	Imported new transport equipment	Imported new machinery and other equipment	Total imported	Domestically produced new transport equipment	Domestically produced new machinery and other equipment	Total domestically produced
1935–38	12.88	15.03	21.20	0.89	6.17	7.06
1939–42	6.63	7.00	13.62	0.74	8.44	9.18
1943–45	0.17	1.72	1.89	0.54	9.45	9.98
1946–48	29.72	21.27	50.99	0.67	13.30	13.97
1949–51	7.96	19.58	27.55	0.81	15.59	16.40
1952–55	6.22	18.02	24.24	2.68	19.93	22.61
1956–58	10.03	17.64	27.67	4.87	32.79	37.66
1959–61	5.93	31.36	37.29	27.32	39.76	67.08
1962–64	7.54	33.23	40.77	33.63	36.24	69.88

Sources and method: For 1950–64, directly from BCRA, pp. 50–53. For earlier years, indices from sources listed in Table 6.4 were linked with BCRA data at 1950. For 1935–50 minor discrepancies appear between totals for machinery and transport equipment when they are computed using indices for imported and domestic components (as in this table), and when they are computed directly (as in Table 6.10). Also note that "imported" capital goods are valued at the point where they are installed (i.e. they include value added domestically in their internal transport, commercialization, processing, etc.).

Table 6.11 classifies new producers' equipment into imported and domestically produced. This division is somewhat arbitrary, as "imported" items include value added domestically (from the time the goods are landed to when they are installed), while those "domestically produced" embody imported intermediate products and raw materials. And what is called "new" equipment includes parts destined to keep old equipment in operation. In spite of these limitations, Table 6.11 gives a good overall view of the sources for machinery and equipment. The percentage share of imports in all new producers' equipment (measured at 1960 prices), evolved as follows:

1935–38 = 75	1956–58 = 42
1939–48 = 67	1959–61 = 36
1949–51 = 63	1962–64 = 37
1952–55 = 52	

tendencia ascendente

The flow of new imported equipment was interrupted by the war, but 1946–48 witnessed their massive importation, representing to a large extent pent-up replacement demand. During 1949–58 these imports settled down at levels only modestly above those of 1935–38 (when Argentina was still recovering from the depression). Machinery and equipment imports increased sharply again during 1959–64.

The flow of domestically produced equipment reveals less fluctuation. Although showing a persistent upward trend, its growth was not the same in all periods. After taking period-to-period changes, the following average annual growth rates are obtained for total domestically produced machinery and equipment (expressed in percentages):

1935–38/1939–42	=	6.8
1939–42/1943–45	=	2.4
1943–45/1946–48	=	11.9
(1939–42/1946–48)	=	(6.7)
1946–48/1949–51	=	5.5
1949–51/1952–55	=	9.8
1952–55/1956–58	=	16.0
1956–58/1959–61	=	21.0
1959–61/1962–64	=	1.4

The 1935–51 growth rate in the domestic production of machinery and equipment, although superior to that of the economy as a whole, was far from spectacular, especially taking into account that it began from a small base. Since 1952–55, its acceleration becomes noticeable, and very high rates of expansion were reached during 1956–61. But the severe 1962–63 recession practically halted growth. The tractor and automobile industries played a (key) role in accelerating growth of domestic capital goods production during the late 1950s, although other sectors, such as machine tools, also expanded vigorously.[39]

The thesis arguing that the quantum of machinery and equipment capital formation since 1930 depended solely on supply conditions for those goods may now be spelled out. For 1939–46 the argument is straightforward; on the whole, the Argentine market then took eagerly whatever few new machines could be imported or produced domestically. Before and after the war, the supply of machinery and equipment in any given year depended on exchange earnings and on the exchange left after financing consumer goods imports and those imported inputs used by activities producing consumer goods,[40] as well as on the installed capacity of domestic machinery and equipment industries. Argentine exchange earnings during the 1930s were on the whole determined exogenously; given world trade conditions at that time it could not have been expected to show much price elasticity. After the war, however, exchange earnings were very sensitive not only to exogenous factors, but also to domestic policies. The exchange not used to finance current imports could be used to purchase foreign machinery directly, or to import inputs going into domestic capital

---

39. Evaluated at international prices, some machine tool activities are probably the most efficient segments of the capital goods industries. During 1963, 1964, and 1965, Argentina exported an annual average of U.S. $1.8 million worth of simple machine tools. However, some observers have claimed that in foreign sales prices were lower than those for domestic sales. It should also be remembered that 1962–63 were years of depressed domestic economic activity. The skilled labor intensity of this industry, coupled with a relative abundance in Argentina of skilled and semiskilled labor, nevertheless suggest a bright export future for this activity, if appropriate policies are followed. The industry is made up of relatively small establishments, usually employing no more than 50 workers each. See ECLA, *La Fabricación de Maquinarias y Equipos Industriales en América Latina: IV: Las Máquinas-Herramientas en la Argentina* (Santiago, Chile, 1966), pp. 73–77. An idea of how far import substitution had advanced by 1962 for machinery and equipment is given by Table 122 in the Statistical Appendix. The share of domestic production in total demand for selected goods was as follows: tractors and agricultural machinery, 96 percent; electrical machinery, 69 percent; machine tools, 31 percent.

40. Without input-output tables it is difficult to classify imports of raw materials and intermediate products into those going to produce capital and consumer goods, especially when some of those imports go into domestic activities also producing intermediate products, going both into capital and consumer good industries.

goods industries. Although import requirements of most domestic activities decreased secularly, in any given year they were rather inflexible, usually lacking potential substitutes. The choice between importing finished investment goods or intermediate products to be transformed into capital goods was also limited in the short run by existing capacity. Decisions to enlarge that capacity often involved major government measures promising sustained and additional support to key activities. Although this capacity grew during 1935–61, it did so at different rates according to the policies followed by various governments. Given long gestation periods for investments in this field, in any one year capacity expansion came from completing projects begun in previous years, leaving little short-run flexibility for the maximum possible domestic output of machinery and equipment.

The argument for peacetime may be summarized as follows:

$$I_e \leqq F - M_c + (a - 1)M_{te} \qquad (6.1)$$

where

I_e = total investment in machinery and equipment at constant domestic prices.

F = total availability of foreign exchange (from exports, net capital inflow, exchange reserves, improvements in external terms of trade, etc.).

M_c = imports of consumer goods, and of intermediate products and raw materials going into the production of consumer goods, at constant prices.

M_{te} = imports of intermediate goods and raw materials going into the domestic production of machinery and equipment, at constant prices.

a = ratio of the value of domestically produced machinery and equipment to M_{te}. It is assumed $a > 1$.

This may be complemented with the following restriction:

$$M_{te} \leq \frac{[max.\ I_d]}{a} \qquad (6.2)$$

This inequality sets an upper limit to imports of intermediate products by domestic firms producing machinery and equipment, whose maximum capacity is given by $[max.\ I_d]$.

The variable M_c may be linked with the total consumption of the economy, (C):

$$M_c = bC \qquad (6.3)$$

Short-run flexibility of the coefficients a and b, and of [*max.* I_d] is limited, due to technological and policy reasons. Given F and a politically tolerable C, possible machinery and equipment investment in any one year was independent of the relative price of these goods, so long as it remained above a certain minimum. In other words, the (idealized) overall supply schedule for machinery and equipment is assumed to have had, because of either war or exchange limitations, a perfectly elastic range followed by a perfectly inelastic segment, as in the case of the simple Keynesian aggregate supply schedule. It is suggested that during practically the whole of 1935–61, Argentina was operating on the perfectly inelastic range.[41] Of all rigidities induced by the Great Depression, war, and postwar trade policies, this was perhaps the most damaging to growth.

Although short-run flexibility in machinery and equipment availability was limited, *with F given,* Argentine policies aimed at reducing coefficients a and b, while expanding [*max.* I_d]. Over a period of time, these trends shifted the supply schedule to the right. Favorable prices for import-substituting activities were one of the instruments employed to this end, but only in a very generalized and long-run sense can they be said to have caused the expansion of most activities producing machinery and equipment. As shown in Table 6.11, from 1935–38 until 1952–55 machinery and equipment production grew at an annual rate of about 7 percent, a rate insufficient to offset (in relative terms) the post-1948 decline in imports of these goods. Gross capital formation in new machinery and equipment, expressed at 1935 prices and as a percentage of domestic absorption, fell from 4.3 during 1935–38, to 3.6 in 1949–51 and to 3.8 during 1952–55.[42] Then, since around 1953, and under ad hoc arrangements, the automobile and tractor industries were established, new impulse was given to metalworking, and eventually (around 1961) significant amounts of steel began to be produced. The new policy involved a friendlier attitude toward foreign capital, whose technological know-how and funds flowed in large amounts into capital goods industries and into related intermediate goods industries. Domestic production of new machinery and equipment grew between 1952–55 and 1962–64 at an annual rate of

41. The perfectly elastic segment would be found at a level determined by foreign prices, the exchange rate and import duties. In other words, it would give the domestic price of machinery and equipment, if there had been no quantitative limitations on imports of these commodities.

42. See Table 116 in the Statistical Appendix. Table 117, expressed at 1960 prices, shows similar results.

about 13 percent. The share of all purchases of new machinery and equipment in domestic absorption, expressed at 1935 prices, rose to 4.4 percent during 1956–58 and to 6.2 percent during 1959–64 (surpassing by far the percentage obtained during the 1946–48 boom).

Postwar short-run price inelasticity in the domestic supply of machinery and equipment also resulted from the great uncertainty surrounding government regulations having a direct bearing on these prices and on expected rates of return in these activities. Changes in import regulations, exchange surcharges, public sector purchases, etc., could overnight spell doom or bonanza for investors; so naturally they looked toward government officials rather than ruling prices when embarking on a new venture.[43] But while the government thus reduced the effectiveness of the price system, it failed to provide a rational planning mechanism. Sharp cyclical fluctuations in the postwar Argentine economy also discouraged the domestic machinery industry.

Machinery and equipment not involving repair parts were treated usually as marginal in the import bill. New transport equipment, in particular, was given a precarious marginal role. During peacetime, machinery and equipment imports reflected, in a magnified fashion, fluctuations in the capacity to import. Their secular fall, however, was smaller than that for foreign exchange earnings (expressed in real terms), as light import substitution released a greater percentage of exchange earnings for capital goods imports.[44] Accumulated exchange

43. For several important capital goods the public sector is the main (or even the only) domestic customer under present institutional arrangements. Producers of ships, railroad equipment, electrical equipment, etc., must have a keen interest in public investment programs. Sudden reversals of these programs have often severely damaged private producers.

44. ECLA, Part I, pp. 30–31, shows a close correlation between the simple terms of trade and gross investment as a share of GDP for 1900–56. Using ECLA data on the "purchasing power of exports," the following comparison can be made of percentage changes from period to period of the dates shown:

	1946–48 to 1935–38	1949–51 to 1946–48	1952–55 to 1949–51	1956–58 to 1952–55	1959–61 to 1956–58
Purchasing power of exports	+13	−36	−24	+7	+17
Imports of new machinery and equipment (A)	+141	−46	−12	+15	+34
Imports of capital goods (B)	+53	−39	−22	+14	+49

Data on purchasing power of exports obtained from ECLA, "Inflation and Growth" (mimeographed Statistical Appendix), and the *Statistical Bulletin for Latin America* (vol. 1, no. 1) of the same institution. The second line, (A), was calculated from the third column in Table 6.11. The third line, (B),

reserves and capital inflows also influenced the margin available for these imports, the former especially during 1946–48, and the latter during 1959–61.

The supply of machinery and equipment has been treated as perfectly price inelastic, over the relevant range. For pre-1930 years this assumption is not warranted. In those days, beginning from equilibrium, an increase in demand for machinery would have led *ceteris paribus* to a payments deficit and devaluation, inducing (with a lag) a larger output of exportable rural goods as well as a reduction in their quantity demanded domestically, plus a reduction of the quantity demanded of nonmachinery importables. So, an increase in relative prices for imported capital goods, caused by devaluation, would have been accompanied by an expansion in the quantity supplied of machinery and equipment, financed by the exchange generated by larger exports and lower current imports. The relevant price elasticities may have not been high, but it would be difficult to argue that in the medium run they were zero.[45] Post-1930 exchange control and multiple rates altered this mechanism. Export exchange rates were on the whole divorced from those for imports; they were changed infrequently and responded to payments pressures usually with a long lag. The rural sector and exporters were not allowed to benefit from the exchange and machinery shortages, even though as indirect producers of capital goods they could have been expected to do so.[46] While these policies were justified during 1930–46 by world trade conditions, such an argument becomes weaker for postwar years. The supply inelasticity of machinery and equipment after the war was not only a result of

---

was obtained from ECLA (as cited in Abbreviations) and the *Statistical Bulletin for Latin America*. Construction materials have been excluded from the ECLA definition of capital goods imports.

45. The case when the Marshall-Lerner condition is not met may also be disregarded for those years of keen international competition and relatively free trade.

46. After 1955 this state of affairs began to be modified. The return to freer exchange rates redistributed quasi rents arising from exchange and machinery scarcity away from intermediaries and holders of exchange and import permits, toward exporters, and even toward actual or potential domestic producers of machinery and equipment. Previous to 1955 the domestic sector producing machinery and equipment did not always have the certainty that it could obtain for its output the ruling internal price for these goods, as such prices depended on government regulations regarding which exchange rates would be used for future capital goods imports, changes in commercialization margins due to price controls, tariffs, etc.

technology, but also of government policies, especially those toward foreign trade.[47]

For construction and repairs, which have a lower import component and are highly labor intensive, it could *not* be argued that supply is perfectly inelastic. Except during the peak of the postwar construction boom the supply of construction was highly price elastic. Changes in labor productivity and input costs, however, resulted in substantial shifts in this supply schedule.

The discussion of supply conditions for machinery and equipment implies that their domestic demand served only to determine their relative prices but had no influence on the *aggregate quantum* of real investment in these goods, as it has been supposed that during most of 1935–61 the schedules intersected somewhere in the vertical segment of the supply curve. Only in a few peacetime years excess exchange reserves and/or excess capacity in domestic machinery and equipment industries appeared. These circumstances imply that only during those few years the economy operated on the elastic segment of the supply schedule.[48]

Although short-run supply conditions for new machinery and equipment were difficult to modify by public or private efforts, the government had at its disposal a vast array of instruments for shifting domestic demand for producers' durable equipment and for altering its price elasticity. By manipulating credit, tax exemptions, import taxes and restrictions, etc., the public sector could generate a demand curve intersecting the vertical segment of the supply schedule. Until 1961 enough rates of return were made sufficiently high to induce private entrepreneurs to use all available domestic and imported supplies of producers' durable equipment, even at their inflated postwar relative prices. It is therefore mistaken to argue that high relative prices for machinery and equipment were the basic cause for

47. During the immediate postwar years Argentina also had difficulties in finding some specific capital goods, such as oil-drilling equipment. Supply difficulties in industrialized countries and the political isolation of the Perón regime account for these temporary bottlenecks. Note, however, that between 1945 and 1947 producers' equipment relative prices fell sharply.

48. After 1961, these circumstances did in fact occur frequently. During 1959 they also appeared briefly. It is significant that in Table 6.11 the columns for domestically produced goods show dips only during the war and after 1961. The perfectly elastic segment of the supply schedule shifted upward during and after the war as a result of the forces discussed regarding columns two, three, and four in Table 6.8.

low postwar rates of capital formation. Rather, both high relative prices and low capital formation in machinery and equipment resulted from unfavorable supply conditions.[49] A brief review of the main sources of demand for producers' durable equipment and of public sector instruments influencing them may clarify these points.

Demand for machinery and equipment, neglecting microscopic amounts of external demand, may be subdivided into public and private sectors. During 1950–61, public machinery and equipment investment represented 7 percent of all gross investment and 17 percent of gross investment in machinery and equipment.[50] The nature of that public demand depended on the attitude of authorities toward the budget for investment projects. The more carefully cost-benefit calculations were made, and the more concerned the authorities were to work within a budget once it had been prepared, the more stable and price-elastic one could have expected their demand schedule for capital goods to be. Most fiscal observers agree that such cares and concerns were not usually present in the budgetary process. Public investment behavior tended to be erratic on the aggregate, while individual projects were chosen and implemented often following noneconomic criteria. Relative price increases for machinery purchased by government were shifted to society, not through higher taxes and prices of public enterprises but mainly via inflation, as during most postwar years the public sector had substantial deficits financed largely by central bank credit.[51] Under these circumstances, it is

49. It would be misguided, for example, to argue that during 1939–45 high relative prices for machinery and equipment *caused* the observed decline in capital formation. It seems more correct to attribute both of these phenomena to a war-induced leftward shift in the supply schedule for producers' durable goods, which for all practical purposes may be taken as perfectly price inelastic beyond a short elastic range, which also shifted upwards during the war.

50. Data obtained from CONADE, pp. 176–77. Percentages calculated from yearly data in current prices were averaged. As repairs are included under machinery and equipment in this source, it is likely that the share of public investment in new machinery and equipment was smaller. During 1950–61 total public investment represented 25 percent of all gross investment. Both general government and public enterprises are included in the public sector.

51. After 1948 when the public sector purchased machinery and equipment abroad, it was more concerned with how much of it could be bought on credit, and with whether the purchase could lead to new markets for Argentine exports, than with prices or even repayment schedules (e.g., the purchase of Japanese rolling stock for the railroads during the early 1960s). Shifts in public sector demand for capital goods were strongly influenced by balance

doubtful that public demand was very price elastic, or that its shifts could have been predicted accurately on purely economic considerations.

Private demand for producers' durable equipment is more complex.[52] The forces influencing expected profits, desired private capital, and the rate of investment have been many—current and expected sales, current profits, domestic and foreign credit availability, the climate of labor relations and politics, the level and rate of change of direct foreign investment, the value of investment projects underway from previous years, changes in taxes and the system of protection, special promotional government policies, etc. The actual and expected prices for machinery and equipment also no doubt entered into these calculations, so that *if all the other factors were held constant,* it could be said that private demand for machinery and equipment had some nonzero price elasticity.[53] But historically more important than this price elasticity, were the shifts of the *ceteris paribus* demand schedule resulting from changes in public policy. By manipulating bank credit granted at negative real interest rates, the government could fairly quickly change the quantity of machinery and equipment demanded for any given relative price. Changes in protection, tax policy and its administration, etc., could achieve similar results in the full employment climate prevailing during most of 1935–61.

Different groups of entrepreneurs, however, were affected in unequal ways by the combination of high relative prices for machinery and equipment, and selective credit and protection policies. On the aggregate, enough entrepreneurs were always found to pick up avail-

---

of payments trends, the same key factor that brought about shifts in the supply schedule of producers' durable equipment.

52. During 1950–61 private gross investment in machinery and equipment represented 36 percent of all gross investment, and 83 percent of all gross investment in machinery and equipment.

53. Even under the *ceteris paribus* assumption, it could be argued that this elasticity is not likely to be high. The demand for machinery and equipment is derived demand, and as such tends toward price inelasticity. Shifts by consumers from very capital intensive final goods to others whose production use less capital are likely to be small. Secondly, the foreign exchange shortage that resulted in higher prices for producers' durable equipment at the same time raised the output prices not only for potential domestic producers of machinery and equipment but also for a large number of private entrepreneurs in the import-competing sector.

able supplies of producers' durables, but the composition of demand was altered. The rural sector, suffering from unfavorable output prices and labor scarcity during most of the period, had its investment incentives reduced by high prices for machinery and equipment.[54] Within manufacturing effective rates of protection, credit, and tax favors were unequal among different activities, so that sectorial investments reacted differently to the rise in machinery prices.

To domestic producers of investment goods the trend in relative prices was apparently beneficial, and one would expect that the higher capital goods prices, the greater will be the quantity of investment goods demanded by them. But in this field investment decisions are of such a nature that in many important cases, at least in Argentina, they have not been taken without ad hoc agreements involving government commitments on protection, tax concessions, industrial regulations, etc. Motor vehicles are perhaps the best example of an industry requiring this type of bargaining and arrangement. In the long run, rising machinery prices should serve at least to signal public authorities the need to take measures assuring stability and minimum profitability to these investors (or to exporters).[55] But in the short run, fluctuations in these relative prices have yielded quasi rents rather than significant changes in the quantity of capital goods demanded by producers of machinery.[56]

The following well-known identity can be used to illustrate the effect of protectionist policies on sectorial investment decisions:

54. Even for the rural sector, however, supply availability looms more important than relative prices in explaining observed investment in new machinery and equipment. Witness the fast growth during recent years in the stock of tractors and automotive vehicles in the rural sector, in spite of high prices of these goods.

55. These considerations are simply the same as those given to defend the assumption of a perfectly inelastic supply schedule (above a certain point) for producers' durable equipment. It should be remembered that such an assumption is an idealization; in practice, the supply of the simpler types of machinery and equipment may have a relatively elastic supply with respect to their relative prices. Furthermore, in countries with a laissez faire tradition stronger than that of Argentina, even the more complex types of machinery and equipment may show greater supply elasticity, even in the short run.

56. For entrepreneurs in construction, higher construction prices may or may not results in a greater demand on their part for capital goods. If the higher relative prices arise from cost-push sources, they will not induce them to expand their activities. When postwar demand pull forces were also at work, higher relative prices led to an expansion of construction capacity and a greater demand for construction equipment.

$$\frac{R}{P_k \cdot K} \equiv \frac{R}{P_y \cdot Y} \cdot \frac{P_y}{P_k} \cdot \frac{Y}{K} \tag{6.4}$$

where

R = profits.

K = capital quantum.

Y = output quantum.

P_k = price per unit of capital.

P_y = price per unit of output.

For a given *real* output-capital ratio and a given profit share in total sales (or value added, ignoring intermediate inputs), the profit rate will depend on the *ratio* of output prices to those for capital goods. For a given private activity, manipulating the former (say via protection) can offset changes in the latter. But because of aggregation problems, which become severe when government controls and lack of competition lead to disequilibria among and within sectors, the use of this identity for the total private Argentine economy is less meaningful. In that aggregation one would include housing, where the average rate of return on the existing stock (as well as the average output-capital ratio measured at current prices) is extremely low due to rent controls, together with other activities whose prices are relatively free. Furthermore, in many sectors, including housing, the average rate of return is a poor indication of rates of return on *new* investments (new housing is exempted from rent controls).[57] For the public sector, naturally, the aggregate calculation is even less meaningful.[58]

In summary, it may be said that the position and shape of the aggregate demand schedule for machinery and equipment helped to determine the relative prices of these goods, rather than their quantum purchased by public and private users. (Private investment in

57. Similarly, it is not sensible to deduce from changes in the wage share of national income changes in the rate of return on capital. Fluctuations in the wage share have had different effects on investment incentives for different sectors. The decrease in the wage share that tends to accompany a devaluation is associated with an increase in profits (and rents) in the rural sector, but with a decrease in the profits of manufacturing activities producing wage-goods. If the investment response of different sectors to changes in profits is not similar, it becomes difficult to generalize about the aggregate link between the wage share and capital formation.

58. Especially in sectors such as the railroads for which, due to price policy, the capital-output ratio measured at current prices is very high.

new machinery and equipment, in fact, reached during 1960–61 the highest levels observed since 1935, at a time when the relative prices of these goods also reached all-time highs.) In other words, while in economies with a high capacity to transform, gaps between desired and actual capital stock disappear mainly through an expansion of output in capital goods industries, in postwar Argentina the adjustment mechanism relied more heavily on changes in capital goods' relative prices and on rationing available investment goods, due in a great extent to public policies hampering supply flexibility. What normally would be only part of short-run adjustment, became a fixture of the postwar Argentine economy.

In contrast with the demand for producers' durable equipment, that for construction played an important role in the determination of *real* capital formation, and on its relative prices.[59] Even in this case, however, it is more fruitful to examine the sources of shifts in the demand schedule than its price elasticity. An example is provided by private demand for residential housing, accounting for about three-fourths of all private construction during 1950–61. Until 1959, new gross credits of the government-owned National Mortgage Bank and related public institutions represented between 40 and 60 percent of all private investment in housing.[60] These credits were usually given at interest rates of about 6 percent, with maturities often extending to thirty years. As the average postwar annual rate of inflation has been 20 percent, this situation could be maintained only by a steady injection of BCRA funds into mortgage institutions. For those able to obtain these credits, the increase in construction prices was not a very significant consideration in their investment decision. Balance of payments and stabilization objectives determined, as with public investment, whether an expansionary or restrictive attitude was to be followed in granting loans. Having decided to make available a certain amount of loans at negative real rates of interest, the government did not have to worry that enough borrowers could be found to accept them, regardless of the relative prices for construction goods.[61]

59. During 1950–61 private construction amounted to 38 percent of all gross investment, while public construction represented 17 percent of all gross investment.

60. These figures refer to 1953–59. Similar, or even higher percentages, probably existed during 1946–52. Data provided by CONADE.

61. The *real* level of construction that could be financed by such loans, however, depended on the relative prices for construction. If, beginning from equilibrium, the government decides to increase loans for housing, the real increase in houses built would be greater the larger the price elasticity of

The approach that has been presented suggests the following summary view of Peronist growth policies. From about 1943 until 1953 few efforts were made to expand exports, while the domestic machinery and equipment industry was not given special attention. An acute shortage of new machinery and equipment resulted, as import substitution in consumer and intermediate goods did not release enough exchange for the importation of either finished capital goods or intermediate products for domestic industries producing machinery and equipment. Capital formation in these goods fell as a percentage of GNP, and their relative prices increased. Economic growth suffered, as a result of both meager increases in physical capital and a slower rate of absorption of the technological change embodied in new machinery and equipment. The economy was left with a productive capacity oriented mainly to the production of consumer goods.

A return since 1955 to freer exchange rates further increased the relative prices of producers' durable equipment, but it is doubtful that this increase *by itself* was important in determining the quantum of capital formation. The switch in exchange policy was more important in redistributing quasi rents arising from the exchange and machinery scarcity. Ad hoc arrangements with foreign investors in key activities were the most important elements behind the post-1955 expansion in domestic machinery and equipment production.[62]

The Argentine experience illustrates how supply conditions, including capacity not only in the consumption and machinery industries but also in the sector producing exportables, can influence indirectly the structure of aggregate demand. To maintain existing capacity in consumer goods industries in full operation, imports of new machinery and equipment were squeezed out by public policy. Installed capacity in sectors producing directly or indirectly capital goods was not consistent with the growth and employment targets of policy makers, and in effect investment and growth targets were sacrificed for the sake of (short-run) employment and consumption goals.

---

the supply schedule. On the other hand, also beginning from equilibrium, the increase in loans required to maintain the volume of housing construction constant in the face of an upward shift in the supply schedule for construction (assumed for simplicity perfectly price elastic) would be greater the larger the price elasticity in the private demand for housing.

62. Of the increase of domestic production of new machinery and equipment between 1955 and 1961, 56 percent came from the automobile and truck industry, and 9 percent arose from the tractor industry. Data obtained from worksheets of CONADE.

The expansion taking place during recent years in Argentine capital goods industries reduces the future validity of the extreme assumptions made about supply rigidities for 1935–61. In terms of equations 6.1, 6.2, and 6.3, the more diversified and integrated industrial base will result in a greater flexibility and price responsiveness of coefficients a, b, and [$max\ I_d$]. Changes in capital goods prices arising from exchange rate movements will also have a greater likelihood than in the past of being followed by changes in the production of exportables, making exchange earnings more flexible.

UNRESOLVED ISSUES

In a sense, all of the issues discussed in this essay remain unresolved. But the time required to obtain more information on true price indices for capital goods and on microresponses to changes in these prices looms so large (given present availability of raw data), that one may be willing to take what has been presented as adequate to reconcile the observed growth rate with the postwar investment share. The explanations offered for the rise in capital goods prices and their effect on real investment, while not definitive, are plausible.

One issue that has been left totally unanswered is how the economy was able to expand its saving effort, *best measured as a coefficient of magnitudes in current prices*,[63] from 1935–38 to the postwar period. The (scanty) data available on savings are presented in Table 6.12.

These data do not suggest a good answer to the question of who made, or was forced to make, the efforts behind the remarkably high postwar savings rate, achieved while the price level was rising at an annual rate of about 25 percent. Of a savings rate averaging 20.2 percent during 1950–61, 15.4 percent corresponds to private savings, 3.6 percent to public savings (including public enterprises), and 1.3 percent to net foreign savings. As private savings were about equal to private gross capital formation, public investment exceeded its savings by an amount similar to net foreign savings. Within the private sector, about two-thirds of the savings came from family units (10.4 percent of GNP), the rest coming from retained earnings and

---

63. The real saving effort may be defined in terms of how many units of consumption goods must be given up to obtain one unit of investment goods. As the relative prices of capital goods rose, more units of consumption goods had to be given up per unit of investment goods.

depreciation allowances of corporations.[64] The distinction between family and corporate savings has limited usefulness, as there have been important changes in the degree of incorporation in the industrial and commercial sectors. Furthermore, practically all of rural savings

Table 6.12: Gross Saving in Argentina as Percentages of GNP (CONADE)

	Total gross savings	Net foreign savings	Total gross national savings	Gross private savings	Gross public savings
1935–38	13.0	−0.2	13.3	−[a]	–
1946–49	22.3	−2.2	24.5	–	–
1950–52	20.0	1.5	18.5	13.6	5.0
1953–55	18.9	−0.2	19.1	16.3	2.8
1956–58	20.1	2.1	18.0	14.8	3.2
1959–61	22.4	1.9	20.5	17.1	3.5

[a] Dash indicates data not available.

Sources and method: As in Table 6.2 (CONADE). Gross public savings combine the savings of the general government and those of public enterprises. The latter data have been obtained from CONADE worksheets. Totals may not add up due to rounding errors.

are included under family savings. These categories are too aggregated to cast much light on the issue at hand. The figures do not seem unreasonable when compared with the share of gross (pretax) returns to capital and entrepreneurship, also appearing in the national accounts, and representing half of GNP, during 1950–61. As inflation coupled with regulation of interest rates reduced the usefulness of financial markets, it may be supposed that a large proportion of private nonhousing investment was financed by direct reinvestment of gross profits and that a significant part of real financing was also provided indirectly by savings forced by inflationary credit creation. These issues will be further examined in the next essay.

Finally, the remarkable increase in the savings rate between 1935–38 and the postwar period indicates that in an economy such as Argentina's, savings rates are rather flexible, and constraints on growth from a scarcity of savings are easier to handle than those aris-

64. The source for this information on the structure of savings is the same given for Table 6.2. It has been assumed that all depreciation allowances come from the private sector. This probably yields a slight overestimation of these savings.

ing from a lack of foreign exchange.[65] Furthermore, it is likely that
a more relaxed situation in the foreign accounts, either because of a
faster growth of exports or a capital inflow, would reduce the relative prices of capital goods, leading to both a decrease in the rate of
savings (measured at current prices) and an increase in the real level
of capital formation.

65. On the other hand, this experience also implies that unless efforts are
made to relax the exchange bottleneck and to improve the economy's capacity
to transform, attempts to increase the rate of savings may lead not to higher
real capital formation, but simply to higher relative prices for capital goods.
These higher relative prices then become an index of the deterioration in the
capacity to transform, which may have been caused either by exogenous world
circumstances (as in Argentina during 1930–45), or by mistaken domestic
policies (as during the postwar period).

Stop-Go Cycles and Inflation
during the Postwar Period

Two outstanding features of recent Argentine economic history have been the jerky nature of growth and the persistent rise of the price level. Postwar stop-go cycles will be first examined in this essay, stressing their connection with fluctuations in merchandise trade and the exchange bottleneck. The record of inflation during the twentieth century will then be reviewed, followed by an exploration of the mechanics and other characteristics of postwar price rises. The relationship between inflation and the exchange bottleneck and that between recessions and stabilization plans will also be discussed briefly.

STOP-GO CYCLES: AN OVERALL VIEW

Table 7.1 presents year-to-year changes in real GDP during 1945–66, according to the two major sources of national accounts data. The dispersion of annual growth rates is remarkable, and may be summarized in the following tabulation showing the number of years having the indicated growth rates:

	BCRA	CONADE
Less than zero percent	6	5
Between zero and 2 percent	3	1
Between 2 and 4 percent	2	2
Between 4 and 6 percent	1	4
More than 6 percent	9	7

Of the twenty-one years shown, nine registered drops in *per capita* GDP (BCRA), while nine others witnessed growth rates above 6 percent. If 1945 and 1966 are compared, an average annual growth rate of 3.1 percent is obtained, but few years came close to that average.

It will be convenient, as shorthand, to refer to "good" and "bad" years. "Bad" years include 1949, 1950, 1952, 1956, 1959, 1962, 1963, and 1966. "Good" years include all others beginning with 1946. The categories are of course somewhat arbitrary. For example,

Table 7.1: Annual Growth Rates of Real GDP at Factor Costs, 1945–66
(Percentage changes from previous years)

Year	BCRA	CONADE	Year	BCRA	CONADE
1946	8.3	8.7	1956	1.7	2.2
1947	13.8	12.7	1957	5.5	5.1
1948	1.2	5.2	1958	7.2	5.0
1949	−4.6	−1.5	1959	−5.8	−4.6
1950	1.6	0.4	1960	8.0	6.2
1951	4.0	3.8	1961	7.0	6.0
1952	−6.3	−5.9	1962	−1.8	−2.9
1953	7.0	6.1	1963	−3.6	−4.6
1954	3.8	5.0	1964	8.1	8.5
1955	6.9	7.2	1965	8.6	−ᵃ
			1966	−0.5	−
		Average "good" years:		*6.9*	*6.6*
		Average "bad" years:		*−2.4*	*−2.4*

ᵃ Dash indicates data not available.

Sources: BCRA, p. 18; CONADE, and unpublished estimates; BCRA, *Boletín Estadístico.*

if rural and government value added are excluded from GDP at factor cost (on the grounds that weather and exogenous factors are their main determinants in the short run) the following annual percentage changes are obtained (using BCRA data):

1946	10.0	1953	1.8	1960	10.4
1947	15.3	1954	5.0	1961	9.4
1948	2.1	1955	8.4	1962	−2.7
1949	−4.1	1956	2.9	1963	−4.8
1950	1.5	1957	7.4	1964	9.1
1951	3.3	1958	8.5	1965	9.6
1952	−4.8	1959	−7.5	1966	−0.1

These percentage changes cast doubt as to whether 1956 should be considered a bad year or 1953 a good year. But these categories are convenient; for most years there is little ambiguity.

The exchange bottleneck braking Argentina's growth since 1949 has done so, not in a smooth and steady manner, but via a severe

exchange crisis occurring every three or four years.[1] Table 7.2 shows
that increases in exchange reserves since 1949 as a rule took place

Table 7.2: Changes in Net Exchange Reserves and Balance
of Merchandise Trade, 1949–66
(Million current U.S. dollars)

	Change in net foreign exchange reserves[a] *of BCRA*	*Balance of merchandise trade*[b]
1949	−269	−136
1950	+166	+213
1951	−333	−311
1952	−173	−492
1953	+279	+330
1954	−33	+48
1955	−175	−244
1956	−19	−184
1957	−60	−336
1958	−217	−239
1959	+113	+16
1960	+161	−170
1961	−57	−496
1962	−234	−141
1963	+202	+384
1964	−11	+333
1965	+139	+295
1966	+53	+469

[a] Gold plus foreign exchange held by BCRA minus BCRA foreign exchange liabilities.
[b] Merchandise exports f.o.b. minus merchandise imports c.i.f.

Sources: International Financial Statistics, several issues.

when GDP declined or during years immediately following such declines. On the other hand, good years, especially those following other years of expansion (e.g. 1951, 1954, 1955, 1957, 1958, 1961, and 1964) witnessed reserve losses. Positive trade balances have been associated with recessions and negative ones with expansion.[2]

1. Lack of reliable GDP quarterly data makes precise dating of the cycles difficult.
2. Lags combined with yearly data blur this relationship in Tables 7.1 and 7.2. In recent years, especially 1965 and 1966, the link between reserves, the trade balance, and domestic economic conditions has become less rigid. The growth of exports and large foreign debt obligations account for such a change.

On average, bad years have been also characterized by falling real wage rates, severe exchange rate devaluations, relatively slower credit expansion, and a drop in real cash balances. They also witnessed price rises which were on the average *higher* than those taking place during good years. Tables 123 and 124 of the Statistical Appendix present data supporting these assertions. The peculiar coexistence of sharp output declines with substantial price increases may also be seen in these tables; 1949, 1952, 1959, and 1962–63 are noteworthy in this respect. This phenomenon strongly suggests that inflationary pressures have arisen primarily from cost-push elements and/or sectorial imbalances, rather than demand-pull forces.

IMPORTS, EXPORTS, AND STOP-GO CYCLES

Because jerky postwar growth has been closely linked to periodic exchange crises, it is worthwhile to examine the short-run characteristics of imports and exports. Other balance of payments items have played important roles only on some occasions (i.e. an increase in capital inflows during 1960–61 and their reversal in more recent years) but it is difficult to provide general quantitative explanations

Table 7.3: Summary of the Balance of Payments of Argentina, 1951–66
(Yearly averages in millions of current U.S. dollars)

	1951–55	1956–58	1959–61	1962–64	1965–66
Merchandise exports	988	971	1017	1331	1541
Merchandise imports	−1121	−1224	−1234	−1138	−1160
Net profits and interests	−18	−20	−66	−81	−120
Net other services and transfers	19	42	23	−113	−43
Net private capital	53	82	229	−48	−182
Net long-term official capital	13	−49	68	−43	−21
Official short-term capital and					
monetary gold	65	207	−36	91	−11
Errors and omissions	0	−10	−2	1	−3

Note: A negative sign indicates a debit entry.

Sources: BCRA, *Boletín Estadístico*, several issues.

for their behavior covering the whole postwar period.[3] Table 7.3 provides an overall view of the balance of payments during 1951–66

3. Homogeneous data for most items in the capital account are not available for the whole period. Even if they were, probably their changes could be explained only by ad hoc policies and circumstances.

(for which period fairly comparable data exist); it may be seen that merchandise imports and exports dominate the picture.

General characteristics of imports and exports have been examined in earlier essays; here discussion will concentrate on attempts to explain statistically their short-run behavior and to relate these results to exchange crises and stop-go cycles.

Table 7.4 presents four multiple regressions explaining postwar

Table 7.4: Regressions Explaining Changes in the Real Level of All Imports, 1947–65

	(1)	(2)	(3)	(4)
Constant term	−5.60	−5.29	−3.33	−11.64
	(5.10)	(3.51)	(3.66)	(6.07)
Total absorption	0.29	—	—	—
	(0.07)			
Consumption	—	0.11	0.14	—
		(0.06)	(0.06)	
Gross domestic investment	—	0.15	—	—
		(0.09)		
Gross investment in machinery and equipment	—	—	0.29	—
			(0.13)	
Wage income	—	—	—	0.13
				(0.20)
Nonwage income	—	—	—	0.33
				(0.13)
Capacity in import-competing sector	−0.16	0.51	0.18	0.75
	(0.59)	(0.47)	(0.52)	(0.66)
Relative import prices	0.21	−0.00	−0.09	0.01
	(0.22)	(0.14)	(0.15)	(0.35)
Quantitative restrictions	0.03	0.39	0.39	0.02
	(0.04)	(0.08)	(0.08)	(0.06)
R^2	0.76	0.94	0.94	0.65
D	2.15	1.49	1.98	1.80

annual changes in the level of all imports of goods and services (expressed in billion pesos at 1960 prices) as a function of income, prices, and other variables.[4] A first striking result in regression 1 is the very

4. Data and their sources for these and following regressions are presented in the Statistical Appendix, Tables 125–27. Regressions used first differences of these data, because earlier attempts using untransformed data gave evidence of considerable serial correlation in the error terms. Standard errors are given in Table 7.4 in parentheses under the corresponding coefficients. The D at the bottom of each regression refers to the Durbin-Watson statistic. The use of the simple least squares method for the estimation of Argentine import functions seems at first easy to justify, as it is reasonable to suppose that the foreign supply of these imports is perfectly price-elastic. However, it is also

high coefficient for total absorption (consumption plus investment plus government exhaustive expenditures, also expressed in billion pesos at 1960 prices). As during 1947–65 the *average* import propensity (defined as the ratio of merchandise imports to absorption) was only 0.11, a marginal import propensity of 0.29 implies an income elasticity of demand for imports of 2.6. This characteristic of the import function is one of the main reasons why upswings in real income and expenditure quickly led to exchange crises.[5] When absorption is subdivided into consumption and gross investment, however, the marginal coefficients become smaller (and less significant). But when only gross investment in machinery and equipment, together with consumption, are included in the expenditure variables better results are obtained, showing a large coefficient for investment than for consumption. Yet, these results indicate that while direct imports of finished consumer goods are few, a considerable part of imports of raw materials and intermediate goods go into consumer goods production (especially durables). The higher marginal coefficient obtained for machinery and equipment reflects the emphasis of early stages of industrialization on light activities and explains why policy makers, concerned with reconciling payments equilibrium with high domestic economic activity, tended to discriminate against new machinery imports.[6]

Two other income variables were tried in regression 4 of Table 7.4: wage and nonwage income. The fit of this equation is the worst shown in Table 7.4; only the coefficient for nonwage income is more than twice its standard error. Nonwage earners appear to have a (direct and indirect) marginal propensity to import higher than that of wage earners, a result agreeing with casual observation.

An estimate of changes in existing productive capacity (expressed in billion pesos at 1960 prices) in the import-competing sector was

true that many imports represent critical inputs into several domestic industries. Under these circumstances, a simultaneous estimation of aggregate import and production functions is the proper procedure. Quality data for estimating production functions, however, are not available. Imports of goods and services (column 4 of Table 125 in the Statistical Appendix) were used as the dependent variable in the regressions shown in Table 7.4.

5. Introduction of absorption lagged one year (in addition to current absorption) did not improve the fit in regressions using untransformed data. The coefficient for lagged absorption is negligible and smaller than its standard error.

6. In regressions using untransformed data, the coefficients for gross investment, especially that in machinery and equipment, were higher.

included in all regressions.[7] A priori, one would expect a coefficient of −1.00 for this variable reflecting its long-run competitiveness with imports, and values close to that were obtained in equations using untransformed data. But with first differences the results are insignificant.

Changes in an index of the ratio of domestic wholesale prices for imported goods to domestic wholesale prices of nonrural, nonimported goods were also included in all regressions. In Table 7.4, all price coefficients are smaller than their standard errors. There are a priori reasons for expecting price inelasticity in the Argentine demand for imports (as it is mostly a derived demand); in fact most statistical results fail to turn up significant and high price coefficients.[8]

Because exchange controls, quantitative restrictions, and all sorts of nonprice administrative measures have been used to depress imports during the period under study, a proxy variable for changes in their intensity has been included in all regressions. The untransformed variable for a given year t (shown in Table 127 of the Statistical Appendix) is made up by BCRA *net* gold and foreign exchange reserves at the end of year $t − 1$ expressed as a percentage of average merchandise imports during years $t − 1$, $t − 2$, and $t − 3$ (both variables in dollars). The expected sign for the coefficient of changes in this proxy variable is positive, as increases in reserves relative to recent imports are supposed to lead to less strict quantitative restrictions, and vice versa for a lowering of reserves. In regressions 2 and 3 of Table 7.4 this variable performs well, with a positive coefficient several times its standard error.

For 1948–64 merchandise imports can be subdivided into capital goods and other goods (both expressed in billion pesos at 1960 prices). The best regressions using first differences for these categories are presented in Table 7.5. The first shows the short-run com-

7. The import-competing sector was defined to include the following activities—oil and mining, textiles, paper and cardboard, chemicals, petroleum refining, rubber, metals, vehicles and machinery, and electrical machinery and appliances. Capacity was estimated by taking for each sector in a given year the maximum value added (at 1960 pesos) produced in that sector up until and including that year. The import-competing sector is here defined more broadly than in earlier essays.

8. See my *Exchange Rate Devaluation in a Semi-Industrialized Country: The Experience of Argentina, 1955–61* (Cambridge: M.I.T. Press, 1965), chapter 3; Richard D. Mallon, "Balance of Payments Adjustment in a Semi-industrialized, Agricultural Export Economy: The Argentine Case" (mimeographed), pp. 14–18; and Jeffrey B. Nugent, "Country Study: Argentina" (mimeographed).

Table 7.5: Regressions Explaining Changes in the Real Level
of Merchandise Imports, 1948–64

	Noncapital goods		Capital goods
	(1)	(2)	
Constant term	−0.35	0.85	0.12
	(4.81)	(4.99)	(1.84)
Manufacturing value added	0.56	—	—
	(0.25)		
Consumption	—	0.18	—
		(0.09)	
Gross domestic investment	—	0.22	—
		(0.12)	
Gross investment in machinery and equipment	—	—	0.13
			(0.11)
Capacity in import-competing sector	−0.41	−0.63	—
	(0.63)	(0.66)	
Capacity in domestic production of new machinery and equipment	—	—	0.35
			(0.29)
Relative import prices	−0.04	−0.25	0.13
	(0.19)	(0.20)	(0.09)
Quantitative restrictions	0.21	0.15	0.20
	(0.11)	(0.11)	(0.06)
R^2	0.72	0.75	0.82
D	2.55	1.32	2.34

plementarity existing between imports and manufacturing activities; again a very high marginal coefficient is obtained. The coefficient for consumption in equation 2 of Table 7.5 confirms the importance of imported inputs for domestic consumer goods industries. Noteworthy is the greater significance of the index for quantitative restrictions for capital goods than for other imports, which even robs the coefficient for investment in machinery and equipment of its significance.[9] As before, price and capacity coefficients are insignificant.

On the whole, the regression fits shown are reasonably good, if one bears in mind data difficulties, which among other things do not allow investigation of the role of inventory changes on import demand. Although unrefined, these regressions show the tendency of upsurges in domestic economic activity to spill massively into imports, while giving little hope that changes in relative prices can in the short run

9. When untransformed variables are used, higher and more significant coefficients are obtained for all expenditure variables—especially for investment in machinery and equipment. Import data used in Table 7.5 appear less reliable than those of Table 7.4.

reduce imports (without reducing output). This, of course, makes it especially difficult to reconcile high levels of employment and output with balance of payments equilibrium. Even quantitative restrictions appear to be most effective (in the sense of reducing imports *without* depressing economic activity) in the field of capital goods, where the burden is placed on future growth. It is likely that before 1948 the larger presence of consumer goods in the import bill gave greater room for maneuver to both relative prices and quantitative restrictions.

While upswings in activity lead to a more than proportional expansion in import demand, they have *not* been accompanied by a cyclical export expansion. The *short-run* behavior of exports has been dominated by exogenous factors, such as weather (and its impact on pampean rural activities) and changes in foreign prices for exports. The former factor has been more important than the latter during 1947–66. A regression between year-to-year percentage changes in the dollar value of exports and corresponding changes in the real output of pampean exportable activities (including cereals, linseed, other oilseeds, wool, fodder crops, and livestock) during 1947–66 yields an R^2 of 0.67. In other words, short-run changes in the output of exportables (dominated by weather conditions) explain two-thirds of fluctuations in export dollar earnings. This result, incidentally, casts doubts as to the importance of the role played by fluctuations in the dollar prices of exports in causing instability in dollar earnings.[10]

To the extent that domestic activity influences exports, the influence is negative. Increases in domestic population and per capita income have resulted over the long run in an increase in the home demand for exportables, and therefore, for a given production of exportables, in a lower export quantum. In particular, as exportable goods are widely consumed by Argentine wage earners, increases in real wages could be expected to lead *ceteris paribus* to a lower export quantum (unless exportables become inferior goods). These forces may be expected to operate in the short run also.

Attempts to explain for 1947–65 year-to-year changes in the ex-

10. For 1947–66 the average annual percentage change in dollar export earnings was 3.8 percent, with a standard deviation of 22.0 percent. The average annual percentage change in the output of exportable goods was 1.2 percent, with a standard deviation of 12.3 percent. The instability of both variables has been, therefore, great. The high correlation between the current output of exportables and exports also implies a limited role for changes in inventories of exportable goods in determining exports. As most rural goods have a production period of about one year, changes in dollar prices in year *t* will not have much influence on production of exportables in the same year.

port *quantum* as a function not only of changes in the output of
exportables, but also of yearly changes in nonrural output (or real
wages) and of changes in the relative price of food, however, have
been only mildly successful. Both changes in output and real wages
have the expected negative sign, but only in the case of real wages
the coefficient is (slightly) higher than its standard error. The coefficient for changes in relative prices has a negative coefficient, only
a fraction of its standard error.[11] It is likely that more refined and
disaggregated data, not now available, could improve these results.

Since touching bottom during the 1951–52 droughts, but especially
since 1962, merchandise exports have expanded. Their current dollar
value has increased by 43 percent between 1951–55 and 1962–66.
Of the net increase in exports, 42 percent came from larger exports
of meat and live animals and 35 percent from expanded shipments
of cereals, linseed, wheat flour, and cereal by-products. Greater exports of other agricultural goods (including fruits, other oilseeds,
etc.) and of mining and manufactured products also contributed
significantly (13 percent and 20 percent of the increase of all exports,
respectively). However, exports of hides, wool, livestock by-products,
and forest products declined between 1951–55 and 1962–66. It is
noteworthy that while livestock played a very important role in
export expansion, between the same dates the increase in livestock
output contributed only 10 percent to the growth of all rural production. Although data difficulties and changes in dollar prices may
explain part of this contrast, it is also due to a post-1958 reduction
in the domestic absorption of meat.[12]

11. Curiously the simple R^2 between changes in the export quantum and
changes in the output of exportables is much smaller (0.30) than that obtained
above between changes in export dollar values and changes in exportable output. The opposite result could have been expected. Quality differences between
the two time series probably explain the difference (the series for export dollar
values being more reliable than that for the quantum index). All regressions,
however, yield an elasticity of exports (whether value or quantum) with
respect to exportable output that is greater than 1 (1.5 and 1.2, respectively),
for reasons indicated at the end of essay 3.

12. According to revised BCRA national accounts, rural value added at
constant prices rose by 18 percent between 1951–55 and 1962–66. Expansion
of agricultural activities (cereals, linseed, fodder, oilseeds, fruits and vegetables,
and industrial crops) accounted for 85 percent of that increase. Between
1954–55 and 1965–66, three countries have accounted for nearly two-thirds of
the increase of Argentine exports measured in current dollars. Italy leads with
35 percent, followed by the Netherlands (18 percent) and Spain (12 percent).
Between those two periods exports to three traditional customers, United
Kingdom, Brazil, and the United States, declined slightly. Lovell S. Jarvis has

The short-run characteristics of imports and exports indicate that cyclical upswings will lead to deficits in the merchandise trade balance. As a rule, the autonomous components of the balance of payments have not systematically compensated for these debits, so that trade deficits accompanying output expansion have usually led to a decline in BCRA net holdings of gold and foreign exchange.[13]

During the 1960s, the servicing of the foreign debt (both public and private) has become a major burden on the balance of payments and on policy makers searching for ways to refinance and spread out repayment schedules. Toward the end of 1964, for example, authorities had to look toward debt services (including interest) amounting to $520 million in 1965, $405 million in 1966, and $266 million in 1967. During the ten years following 1955, payments on the Argentine external debt have been renegotiated with major creditors three times.

When the exchange situation became desperate (as in 1955, 1958, and early 1962), stabilization plans were launched, usually involving devaluation and a less permissive monetary policy. As a rule, a burst of corrective inflation (mainly sparked by devaluation) and a fall in real output followed immediately. Before this link between exchange difficulties and inflation is discussed further, a review of Argentina's postwar inflation is required.

One may wonder whether, *given the same level of exchange availability actually realized during the postwar period,* smoother policies could have led to a higher growth rate. It is likely that such would have been the case. The burst of investments observed, especially during 1946–48 and 1960–61, could have been spread out more evenly, with a gain in their social rate of return. Often capacity was created during booms in activities that in later years faced declining or stagnant demand (e.g. textiles during 1946–48 and a host of activities during 1960–61). Competitive pressures generated by recessions were a painful and wasteful way of correcting inefficiencies in the private sector. But this suggests the academic nature of the question posed about the stop-go cycles: if the public sector had chosen to smooth out these cycles in all likelihood it would have also changed its policies accounting for the severe exchange shortage and the low

pointed out to me that his unpublished research indicates that official statistics seriously underestimate the growth of cattle herds during 1952–58.

13. During cyclical upswings, income effects clearly work for a larger deficit. But during most such upswings price effects also contributed in this direction, as the exchange rate typically increased by less than the general price level.

level of the growth rate. Given those policies it was inevitable that
stop-go measures would be taken, as political pressures during recessions and exchange pressures during booms were both irresistible
for weak governments unable to look ahead more than a short step
in the cycle.

INFLATION: A BRIEF HISTORY

Although inflation was a serious problem during the nineteenth century,[14] available indices for the first three decades of this century
indicate that Argentina followed broad movements in the world price
level but without superimposing on it an upward trend. Between
1914 and 1920 the Buenos Aires cost of living index rose by a total of
88 percent, declining by 30 percent between 1920 and 1929. During
the same periods, the United States consumer price index rose by
100 percent and declined by 14 percent, respectively. Between 1914
and 1929, the U.S. consumer price index rose by 71 percent and
that for Canada by 51 percent, while the Argentine increased only by
31 percent.[15] From these data the Argentine record for price stability
before 1929 appears superior to those of the United States and
Canada.

The Great Depression forced upon Argentina the need, if full employment was to be maintained, of reallocating resources toward the
import-competing sector. The change in world relative prices brought
about by the new circumstances was reinforced by domestic authorities
by such means as multiple exchange rates and higher import tariffs.
At first sight, it appears that the changes taking place in the Argentine
price structure during the 1930s were accomplished without generating
upward pressure on the price level. Between 1929 and 1939, the
wholesale price index rose by only 12 percent, while the Buenos
Aires cost of living declined by 7 percent. But during these years the
world price level showed larger declines or smaller increases than

14. See A. G. Ford, *The Gold Standard, 1880–1914, Britain and Argentina*
(Oxford: Clarendon Press, 1962), chapter 6, esp. pp. 90, 91. The Conversion
Law of 1899, bringing to an end an era of monetary instability, apparently
assured its balance of payment success by undervaluing the peso, an example
followed in the stabilization plan of 1967.

15. Data obtained from DNEC, *Costo del Nivel de Vida en la Capital
Federal* (Buenos Aires, Feb. 1963), p. 44; U.S. Bureau of the Census,
Historical Statistics of the United States, Colonial Times to 1957 (Washington,
D.C., 1960), pp. 125–26; and M. C. Urquhart, ed., *Historical Statistics of
Canada* (Toronto: Macmillan Company of Canada, 1965), p. 303.

those registered in Argentina. Table 7.6 compares price indices in Argentina and the United States; between 1926–29 and 1935–39

Table 7.6: Indices of Ratios of Argentine Price Indices
to Those of the United States
(1926–29 = 100, except where noted)

	Wholesale prices	Cost of living	Implicit deflators of GNP (1935–39 = 100)
1930–34	124	104	–ᵃ
1935–39	128	111	100
1940–44	158	110	99
1945–48	179	128	122
1949–51	274	228	214

ᵃ Dash indicates data not available.

Sources: Argentine price indices as in Table 124 of the Statistical Appendix. U.S. price indices obtained from U.S. Bureau of the Census, *Historical Statistics of the United States, Colonial Times to 1957* (Washington, D.C.: U.S. Government Printing Office, 1960), pp. 116–25, and Council of Economic Advisers, *Economic Report of the President* (Washington, D.C., 1965), p. 196.

Argentine prices rose significantly more than those of the United States. Indices of wholesale prices, where foodstuffs and services have a smaller participation, show this trend most clearly.

Thus, it may be said that the policies undertaken during the 1930s to relieve payments pressures in the context of full employment, involving changes in the price structure, generated mild inflationary pressures. This definition of inflation, i.e. Argentine price changes above and beyond those registered in the world price level (as represented by U.S. prices), seems appropriate for 1930–51 when periphery countries were heavily influenced by price trends generated in center countries via foreign trade.[16]

The war accentuated relative price trends appearing during the depression and forced further import substitution. Now, however, the world price level began to rise. Table 7.6 shows that while during 1940–44 the abundance of unexportable foodstuffs and price controls over some services kept the relative level of the Argentine GNP

16. Although by changing exchange rates periphery countries could offset world price trends, asymmetrical attitudes toward upward and downward exchange rate movements meant that in practice this defense was used only against world deflation. Even countries complaining most loudly about inflationary policies of other nations rarely choose to appreciate their exchange rates.

deflator and cost of living practically unchanged with respect to 1935–39, the Argentine wholesale price index rose again faster than that of the United States. Increases in Argentine prices began to reach alarming levels under the combined pressures of world inflation, war shortages and import-substitution efforts.

The Perón regime is often blamed for the reappearance of inflation in Argentina; indeed that regime followed during several years inflationary policies. During the 1946–48 boom massive use was made of BCRA credit to finance budget deficits, and substantial across-the-board wage increases were decreed throughout that government. The sudden increases in real wage rates generated higher prices, needed if the new money wages were to be compatible with full employment. But although during 1945–48 high annual percentage increases were registered in Argentine price indices (see Table 124 in the Statistical Appendix) they were not much above those for the United States, as indicated in Table 7.7. In fact, the index of the ratio of Argentine to

Table 7.7: Rural and Nonrural Wholesale Prices, 1926–65
(Average yearly levels with 1926 = 100; changes in percentages[a])

	Rural wholesale		Nonrural wholesale	
	Average level	Percentage change	Average level	Percentage change
1926–29[b]	102	—	96	—
1930–34	67	−34	97	1
1935–39	88	30	109	12
1940–44	89	1	183	68
1945–49	185	108	296	62
1950–54	476	157	867	193
1955–59	1,587	234	2,443	182
1960–64	6,804	329	9,339	282

[a] Percentage changes have been computed by comparing successive five-year averages.
[b] Four-year average.

Sources and method: As in Table 124 of the Statistical Appendix.

U.S. wholesale prices rose by less between 1940–44 and 1945–48 than it had risen between 1926–29 and 1930–34.[17] Beginning in

17. The large gold and foreign exchange reserves accumulated during the war and immediate postwar period were a key element in keeping down price increases until 1949. They were used to finance not only imports but also the purchase of foreign assets in Argentina, such as railroads and telephones. A very large share of the credit granted by the BCRA to the public sector during 1946–48 was simply a bookkeeping counterpart to the use by the government

1949, however, there was no doubt that Argentine prices were rising far above those in the United States and Western European countries.

There has not been any clear tendency for inflation to run away. By taking annual averages of the data presented in Table 124 of the Statistical Appendix, the following picture emerges for average annual increases in price indices (expressed as percentages):

	Buenos Aires cost of living	Overall wholesale prices	GNP implicit prices
1936–39	3.0	3.0	2.4
1940–44	2.3	12.0	4.5
1945–49	19.0	13.4	19.7
1950–54	21.7	23.1	19.8
1955–59	39.1	44.7	38.1
1960–64	23.0	21.9	21.8

The transition from mild pre-1949 inflation to the more virulent post-1949 inflation not only failed to lead to hyperinflation but also occurred in a far from smooth manner. Year-to-year changes in the rate of inflation have been marked until recently (1962–66) when the rate has settled down to a steady course of around 26 percent per annum (which happens to be the average for 1946–66). The spread in rates of inflation since 1942 may be seen in the following tabulation, giving the number of years having the indicated rates of price increase:

	Cost of living	Wholesale prices	GNP deflator
Less than 10 percent	5	6	4
10 to 20 percent	7	5	8
20 to 30 percent	6	8	9
30 to 40 percent	6	3	2
More than 40 percent	1	2	1

Tables 7.7 and 7.8 present a summary view of the evolution of the main components of the wholesale and cost of living price indices. The change in relative prices taking place during the 1930s and 1940s may be seen in Table 7.7. It may also be noted that until 1945–49 all of the upward pressure on the price level came from nonrural

---

of exchange reserves to pay for those assets. Thus, the *direct* impact of such deficit financing on the domestic price level was negligible, and price indices do not fully measure the result of the inflationary policies of 1946–48.

Table 7.8: Components of the Buenos Aires Cost of Living Index, 1935–65

	Food	Clothing	Rent and electricity	Fuel, housecleaning, etc.	General expenditures
A. *Level (1935–39 = 100)*					
1935–39	100	100	100	100	100
1940–44	113	126	103	116	107
1945–49	204	244	121	174	219
1950–54	623	848	134	438	743
1955–59	1,767	1,921	143	1,504	2,000
1960–64	7,385	7,801	342	5,219	8,689
B. *Percentage period-to-period changes*					
1940–44	13	26	3	16	7
1945–49	80	95	18	50	104
1950–54	206	247	10	152	239
1955–59	184	127	7	243	169
1960–64	318	306	139	247	334

Sources and method: As in Table 124 of the Statistical Appendix.

prices (of both domestic and imported products), as rural prices remained during 1930–44 below their 1926–29 levels. The first mild inflationary pressures arose from import-substituting efforts and from increases in the world prices for imported manufactured goods. In more recent years, however, especially since around the mid-1950s, rural prices have tended to rise faster than other prices. Table 7.8 shows the food component in the cost of living increasing by less than the clothing component through 1950–54, with a reversal of this pattern during 1955–64. Table 7.8 also shows the effect on relative prices of inflation combined with selective price controls; an index for rent and electricity relative to food was 100 during 1935–39 and 5 during 1960–64.

Several interpretations of the Argentine inflation have been suggested. Before proposing interpretations more explicitly, a look will be taken at other important features of this inflation.

THE DYNAMICS OF INFLATION

A way of obtaining more information regarding the mechanics of inflation is to try to explain statistically the rate of change of prices as a function of variables that may be considered direct or indirect causes of the inflation, such as the rates of change of the money supply and of wage rates. If inflation were perfectly homogeneous—i.e. if all prices, costs, and other money variables moved up at the same rate—this exercise would be hopeless. The Argentine inflation has been sufficiently irregular to encourage this effort, however, even though multicollinearity remains a problem.[18]

A first approach is to examine how well a naive quantity theory model explains price changes. The following variables will be used for this purpose:

X_1 = percentage change in the index of wholesale prices.

X_5 = percentage change in the cost of living index.

X_6 = percentage change in the quantity of money (defined as currency plus demand deposits in the hands of the public).

Data have been organized into periods of half a year; X_1, for example, represents the percentage change between the *average* wholesale price index for two successive semesters. Similarly, X_6 represents the percentage change in the *average* money supply between two consecutive six-month periods.[19]

Assuming a constant velocity of money, no lags nor expectation effects, one should obtain:

$$X_1 = X_6 - k \tag{7.1}$$

The letter k represents the exogenously given long-run rate of increase in real output. If lags were allowed, it would still be expected that the sum of all coefficients of the money terms would add up to one.

If we take 1950–65 (giving us 32 observations),[20] the following

18. This approach was first applied by Arnold C. Harberger in his "The Dynamics of Inflation in Chile," in *Measurement in Economics: Studies in Mathematical Economics and Econometrics in Memory of Yehuda Grunfeld,* ed. Carl Christ et al. (Stanford: Stanford University Press, 1963). Using annual data, I also used it in my *Exchange Rate Devaluation,* chapter 5. For the Argentine case it has also been applied by Adolfo C. Diz, "Money and Prices in Argentina, 1935–62" (Ph.D. diss. University of Chicago, 1966).

19. Sources and data used in the regressions are presented in the Statistical Appendix, Tables 127–30. It has not been possible to correct price indices for possible distortions caused by price controls.

20. The period 1950–65 has been chosen not only because data are more available than for earlier years, but also because during earlier years a large part of the price increases registered in Argentina could be said to have been induced by worldwide inflation. A broader definition of money supply, including quasi money, was also used, but yielded results inferior to those shown for the narrower definition of money. No attempt was made to subdivide 1950–65 into subperiods, a procedure yielding interesting results according to Richard Mallon.

explanations for the percentage rate of increase in the wholesale price index are obtained:

$$(X_1)_t = 2.13 + 1.30 \ (X_6)_t + 0.67 \ (X_6)_{t-1}$$
$$(6.19) \quad (0.33) \qquad\quad (0.30)$$
$$- 0.73 \ (X_6)_{t-2} - 0.21 \ (X_6)_{t-3} \quad (7.2)$$
$$(0.30) \qquad\qquad (0.33)$$
$$R^2 = 0.53$$
$$d = 1.17$$

The subscripts refer to time periods, i.e., t denotes a given half-year, $t - 1$ the preceding half-year, etc. The figures in parentheses under the estimated coefficients are the corresponding standard errors; d refers to the Durbin-Watson statistic, and R^2 to the squared correlation coefficient.

If we take as the dependent variable the percentage rates of change in the Buenos Aires cost of living index for the same period, the following results are obtained:

$$(X_5)_t = -0.29 + 0.89 \ (X_6)_t + 0.67 \ (X_6)_{t-1}$$
$$(5.67) \quad (0.30) \qquad\quad (0.28)$$
$$- 0.27 \ (X_6)_{t-2} - 0.11 \ (X_6)_{t-3} \quad (7.3)$$
$$(0.28) \qquad\qquad (0.30)$$
$$R^2 = 0.42$$
$$d = 1.03$$

It is surprising that increases in money explain only between 42 and 53 percent of the variance in the rate of increase in the price level. The pattern of lags emerging from these equations is also curious; while the sum of all coefficients is very close to 1.0 in equation 7.2, and around 1.2 in equation 7.3, it is made up of both positive and negative elements. However, only one of the negative coefficients, that for $(X_6)_{t-2}$ in equation 7.2, is more than twice the size of its standard error, while all the positive coefficients meet this test successfully. Even at this level of explanation, money rates of change do not provide a satisfactory explanation for price changes.[21] If a simple

21. Arguing ingeniously, Adolfo C. Diz has attached a theoretical explanation to negative coefficients that he also obtained in regressions similar to equations 7.2 and 7.3. He points out that an upward and sustained shift in the rate of monetary expansion would, *ceteris paribus*, bring about a similar increase in the rate of price changes after a while. At the higher rate of price increase, lower real cash balances would be desired. Therefore "some overshooting will occur in the path of the rate of change in prices during the

explanatory equation is desired, based on a single independent variable (with different lags), one using rates of changes in money hourly wage rates provides a better fit for the period under consideration, as may be seen below:

$$(X_1)_t = -0.91 + 0.77\ (X_{10})_t + 0.85\ (X_{10})_{t-1}$$
$$(4.71)\quad (0.19)\qquad\quad (0.19)$$
$$-\ 0.14\ (X_{10})_{t-2} - 0.36\ (X_{10})_{t-3}\quad (7.4)$$
$$(0.18)\qquad\qquad (0.18)$$
$$R^2 = 0.58$$
$$d = 1.59$$

$$(X_5)_t = -2.79 + 0.66\ (X_{10})_t + 0.82\ (X_{10})_{t-1}$$
$$(3.23)\quad (0.13)\qquad\quad (0.13)$$
$$+\ 0.01\ (X_{10})_{t-2} - 0.27\ (X_{10})_{t-3}\quad (7.5)$$
$$(0.12)\qquad\qquad (0.13)$$
$$R^2 = 0.71$$
$$d = 1.61$$

In these equations the notation is as before; X_{10} represents the percentage change in average hourly money wage rates (in urban occupations). Both equations 7.4 and 7.5 include two positive and one negative coefficient at least twice the size of their corresponding standard errors, while the sum of all coefficients is not very different from 1.0.[22]

A much worse performance is obtained when a pure "monetary-fiscalist" explanation of inflation is tested. Such an explanation blames public sector borrowing from the banking system as the major autonomous source of monetary expansion and inflation, considering

---

adjustment period, in order for real cash balances to decline to their lower desired level. Under these circumstances it may be possible to observe some partial sum of the . . . coefficients to be greater than unity and some of them to be negative, while the total sum approaches unity as the whole adjustment process comes to an end" (Diz, "Money and Prices," pp. 63–64). Some quarterly and semestral periods may include both an acceleration and deceleration of inflation; therefore their coefficients may not be significant. Note, however, that if the rate of monetary expansion fluctuates through time, say in a cyclical pattern, *no overshooting* is required to bring real cash balances to the desired levels. Simple lags will do the job. In fact, as may be seen in the Statistical Appendix, the rate of monetary expansion in Argentina has shown several ups and downs although they were often due to seasonal factors.

22. To the comment that there has never been a long lived inflation without increases in the money supply, one could add that neither has there been such an inflation without increases in money wages, exchange rates, etc.

banking credit to the private sector as induced by the level of economic activity, and changes in money arising from fluctuations in international reserves as unimportant in the long run. If one assumes further a constant money velocity, the rate of inflation depends only on one independent variable, the net public deficit financed by bank credit expressed as a percentage of GNP at current prices, and on several monetary parameters and long-run real growth. When this strict hypothesis is tested for Argentina, using annual data and both wholesale and cost-of-living price indices, the results are very poor.[23]

The relatively low R^2's obtained in equations 7.2 and 7.3 imply that either the income velocity of money was not a constant for the years under study or, if it was a constant, a given increase in the money supply was accompanied by different patterns of price and real output changes under different circumstances. Table 131 of the Statistical Appendix presents data on the income velocity of money, using GNP at current market prices as the income variable. On the whole, income velocity shows considerable instability both during 1950–65 and during earlier years. If one takes year-to-year percentage changes in the income velocity of money, and of money plus quasi money, the following averages are obtained for the *absolute* year-to-year percentage changes during different periods:

	Income velocity of money	Income velocity of money plus quasi money
1942–44	8.8	4.8
1945–49	7.5	7.3
1950–54	6.7	7.2
1955–59	11.2	11.9
1960–65	4.1	3.2

23. The term "monetary-fiscalist" has been coined by Roberto de Oliveira Campos. Arnold C. Harberger worked with a "monetarist-fiscalist" model similar to that outlined above in "Some Notes on Inflation," in *Inflation and Growth in Latin America,* eds., W. Baer and I. Kerstenetzky (Homewood, Illinois: Irwin, 1964). Regressions for 1949–66 expressing annual rates of inflation in year t as a function of net public borrowing from the banking system (as a percentage of GNP at current prices) in years t, $t-1$ and $t-2$ yielded R^2 of less than 0.2. The best coefficients were those for the deficit in the previous year, but the ratio of that coefficient to its standard error was never greater than 1.6. On the other hand, the R^2 between annual rates of inflation and contemporary changes in the average merchandise exchange rate was 0.46. During 1949–66, average annual net public borrowing from the banking system was 2.25 percent of current GNP, with a standard deviation of 1.76.

The six-year period 1960–65 shows the lowest year-to-year percentage changes in velocity, while the five years immediately preceding them witnessed their greatest instability. Between 1955 and 1959 the income velocity of money rose by 65 percent.[24] Between 1955 and 1965 the money supply grew at an average annual rate of "only" 25 percent while GNP at current prices grew at an average annual rate of 35 percent.

Even during the 1960s, when velocity has been relatively constant, it has not been a simple matter to go from increases in the money supply to a forecast of inflation. For example, during 1961 and 1963 the money supply grew at similar rates (18 percent in 1961 and 16 percent in 1963; money plus quasi money grew at 21 percent in 1961 and 20 percent in 1963). Yet during 1961 prices rose by about half the rate registered during 1963 (*wholesale prices:* 8 percent in 1961 and 29 percent in 1963; *cost of living:* 14 percent in 1961 and 24 percent in 1963; *GNP deflator:* 12 percent in 1961 and 26 percent in 1963). On the other hand, while real output rose by 7 percent during 1961, it *fell* by 4 percent during 1963. Similar contrasts could be obtained by comparing 1960 with 1966 (money growing about the same rate, but output and prices behaving differently in the two years), and by comparing 1962 and 1964 (prices growing at similar rates, but output and money rates of change being very different). Unless a systematic way can be found to predict real output and price changes separately, even a constant velocity does not provide very useful information for forecasting.

It is doubtful that a simple rule or equation will succeed in explaining short-run fluctuations in Argentine prices and real output. Frequent policy and institutional changes, the complexity of its semi-industrialized economy, sectorial imbalances and rigidities, suggest that nothing less than a comprehensive disaggregated model for the economy can hope to yield reasonably accurate predictions for the future and explanations for the past. It is beyond the scope of this essay to undertake this task; attention will be focused on obtaining more information regarding factors influencing the price level, without attempting

---

24. The fast growth of financial intermediaries outside the commercial banking system played an important role in this phenomenon. As a rule, these new financial intermediaries were allowed to pay and charge higher interest rates than commercial and official banks. The services provided by the banking system appear to have deteriorated as a result of the combination of inflation and government controls.

to build a complete short-run model of the economy.[25] The procedure will be the inductive methodology first applied by A. C. Harberger.

Besides variables already used in equations 7.2 through 7.5, the following will also be employed:

X_2 = percentage change in the index of rural wholesale prices (which form part of the index of wholesale prices).

X_3 = percentage change in the index of wholesale prices of non-rural domestically produced goods (also a part of the wholesale price index).

X_4 = percentage change in the index of wholesale peso prices of imported goods (also a part of the wholesale price index).

X_8 = percentage change in real supplies, defined as GDP plus imports (both in real terms).

X_9 = percentage change in the average exchange rate applied to *both* merchandise imports and exports. The exchange rate is defined in terms of pesos per one U.S. dollar.

Table 7.9 presents one of the best results explaining variations in the rate of change of prices as a function of percentage changes in money, real supplies, the exchange rate, and money wage rates. As before, semestral data were used covering 1950–65.

Consider first the regressions for the wholesale price index and the Buenos Aires cost of living.[26] Out of the 6 coefficients for the money variables, 4 are much smaller than twice their standard errors, while 1 meeting this criterion has a negative sign. In view of the scarcity of significant positive money coefficients, even a belief in overshooting is not sufficient to give a meaningful explanation to this negative coefficient. The coefficient for real supplies is much less than twice the size of its standard error for the cost-of-living regression, but not for wholesale prices.[27] The higher constant term in the cost-

25. A start in that direction was made in my *Exchange Rate Devaluation*. However, in that book the main interest was to explore the workings of the often neglected redistributive effect of devaluation, rather than to build a complete short-run model including all relevant variables. Planning commissions seem better suited for such a task.

26. For 1950–65 the average semestral increase in the wholesale price index was 13.6 percent. The high degree of irregularity in the inflation is indicated by the fact that the standard deviation corresponding to such average was 14.5 percent. The corresponding figures for the cost of living index are 12.9 percent for the mean semestral increase, and 12.0 percent for the standard deviation.

27. Semestral data for real output had to be estimated in a rough manner.

Table 7.9: Results of Multiple Regressions Explaining Changes
in the Price Level, 1950–65
(32 observations)

Independent variables	Wholesale price index	Rural prices	Nonrural domestic prices	Import prices	Cost of living
Constant	−2.66	1.62	−4.06	−7.08	−4.95
	(3.12)	(3.71)	(3.26)	(4.39)	(3.01)
$(X_6)_t$	0.49	0.60	0.42	0.70	0.06
	(0.25)	(0.30)	(0.26)	(0.36)	(0.24)
$(X_6)_{t-1}$	0.26	0.20	0.26	0.39	0.22
	(0.23)	(0.28)	(0.24)	(0.33)	(0.23)
$(X_6)_{t-2}$	−0.68	−1.14	−0.48	−0.50	−0.26
	(0.23)	(0.27)	(0.24)	(0.32)	(0.22)
$(X_8)_t$	−0.37	−0.45	−0.36	−0.45	−0.18
	(0.19)	(0.23)	(0.20)	(0.27)	(0.19)
$(X_9)_t$	0.25	0.34	0.19	0.60	0.17
	(0.06)	(0.07)	(0.06)	(0.08)	(0.06)
$(X_{10})_t$	0.37	0.24	0.45	0.13	0.50
	(0.15)	(0.18)	(0.16)	(0.21)	(0.15)
$(X_{10})_{t-1}$	0.41	0.45	0.42	0.16	0.53
	(0.15)	(0.17)	(0.15)	(0.20)	(0.14)
$(X_{10})_{t-2}$	0.18	0.24	0.14	0.21	0.17
	(0.15)	(0.18)	(0.15)	(0.21)	(0.14)
R^2	0.86	0.86	0.82	0.87	0.81
D	1.56	2.21	1.53	1.63	1.66

of-living equation appears partially to reflect the deflationary effect of secular increases in real supplies. The coefficients for $(X_9)_t$ and $(X_{10})_t$ and $(X_{10})_{t-1}$ are all significant, in the sense that they are more than twice their standard errors and of the expected sign.

What interpretation can be given to these results? While it would be foolish to say that money has not mattered in the Argentine inflation during 1950–65—after all, $(X_6)_t$ has several positive nearly significant coefficients in Table 7.9—these regressions imply that on the whole cost-push elements (wage increases and devaluations) have played an active role in the inflationary process, with monetary expansion taking a more passive role. Rather than attempting to offset price increases arising from devaluations and across-the-board wage increases by keeping the lid on money, the authorities preferred, *as a rule,* to validate higher money wages and prices with permissive (and at times overpermissive) increases in credit and money. Fears of recession no doubt motivated this attitude.[28] Similar considerations prevailed during the 1940s, when at least part of the monetary expansion was the result of an effort to accommodate price increases arising in the foreign sector of the economy, which had in turn received them from world prices. Throughout most of the postwar period, a relaxed attitude toward budget deficits in the public sector helped to convert price increases arising from devaluation and wage increases into further twists of the inflationary spiral.

We can only hope to obtain from these regressions an idea about the *mechanics* of the inflationary spiral. We certainly cannot say that wage increases and devaluations caused the inflation during 1950–65.[29] We *can* say that cost-push elements drove the price level upwards even when money was not expanding in proportion to the price increase.[30]

The regressions in Table 7.9 and others not shown imply that only in the case of the adjustment of the price level to changes in money wage rates, lags of more than one semester are significant. The price level seems to fully adjust within one semester to changes in the

28. An exception was the monetary policy followed during parts of 1962 and 1963. The assumption, implicit throughout this discussion, that downward price flexibility is very limited, seems realistic for the Argentine economy. Massive increases in money wages resulted, in the short run, in higher real wages. Subsequent expansions in money and prices may be interpreted as (unconscious) attempts to reconcile the new level of money wages with full employment, by reducing again real wages. Often wage boosts were quickly followed by extensions of bank credit to private entrepreneurs to finance those increases.

29. In fact, *real* wage rates tended to remain constant during this period, if any trend is meaningful when the data contain such erratic ups and downs. The wage share in national income showed a clearer tendency to fall.

30. The percentage increases in the money variables were less volatile than those for the other independent variables, as may be seen below (semestral data for 1950–65, in percentages):

	Mean	Standard deviation
X_6	11.2	6.8
X_7 (money plus quasi money)	11.0	5.9
X_8	1.7	6.4
X_9	14.7	24.6
X_{10}	13.1	10.8

Note in particular the erratic pattern in exchange rate devaluations and the growth in real supplies.

average exchange rate.[31] The coefficients for $(X_9)_t$, implying that a 10 percent devaluation will result, *ceteris paribus,* in an increase in the price level of between 1.7 and 2.5 percent, are near to what one would expect from a direct knowledge of the role played by importable and exportable goods in the economy.

Although the estimated lags are not as long as it is sometimes suggested, they are long enough in the case of wages to dash hopes of bringing about price stability within a semester, even when a shock treatment is followed in a stabilization plan. The coefficients for $(X_{10})_{t-1}$ are not only significant but also high.

The squared correlation coefficients for both the wholesale and the cost of living equations are satisfactory, especially when taking into account the shakiness of some of the data. They are substantially higher than those obtained in equations 7.2 and 7.3.

The regressions using components of the wholesale price index as dependent variables yield results similar to those already discussed, and confirm their reasonableness. As one would expect, the coefficient for the exchange rate variable $(X_9)_t$ is higher for imported and rural prices, even though it remains far from 1.0. For rural prices the coefficient for the wage variable $(X_{10})_{t-1}$ is more than twice its standard error. This result is reminiscent of that obtained by Harberger for Chilean import prices, which he suggested may have been due to the practice of authorities of devaluing (thus raising import prices) only after this bitter pill had been sugar-coated by a previous increase in money wage rates.[32] But Argentine import prices do not show a significant coefficient for $(X_{10})_{t-1}$, while it is likely that rural prices, as registered in the index, include substantial

31. This refers to the *direct* effects of such changes. Indirect effects can arise from the influence of devaluations on wage contracts, real supplies, etc. Furthermore, in practice, several frictions, not taken into account by the regressions, distort the direct link between the exchange rate and the domestic prices for exportable and importable goods. Such frictions include import and export taxes, changes in import restrictions and prior deposits, commercialization margins, and others. Export taxes have been used extensively to dampen the impact of devaluation on the domestic prices of exportable goods. Changes in these variables will also affect the price level. For a fuller discussion of these points see my *Exchange Rate Devaluation,* chapters 3–5. Other variables which have been left out although they could affect the price level, include dollar prices of exports and imports, droughts and transportation breakdowns (via their impact on rural prices), the level of indirect taxes, etc.

32. Harberger, "Some Notes on Inflation," pp. 242–43.

domestic commercialization margins, which would be affected by changes in wages. In contrast with the Harberger results, and as one would expect a priori, the coefficients for $(X_{10})_t$ and $(X_{10})_{t-1}$ are significant in the equation for nonrural domestic prices, and their sum is of larger size than that corresponding to rural and imported prices.

The money variables do relatively poorly; the only coefficient much larger than twice its standard error is that for $(X_6)_{t-2}$ in the regression for rural prices. Its sign, however, is negative. In the equation for nonrural domestic prices, in which one would expect money variables to do best, the positive coefficients are less than twice their standard errors.[33] The coefficients for the real supplies variable are less than twice their standard error in all regressions for components of wholesale prices.

33. The simple correlation coefficients among the independent variables are as follows:

	$(X_6)_t$	$(X_6)_{t-1}$	$(X_6)_{t-2}$	$(X_8)_t$	$(X_9)_t$	$(X_{10})_t$	$(X_{10})_{t-1}$
$(X_6)_t$	1.00						
$(X_6)_{t-1}$	0.10	1.00					
$(X_6)_{t-2}$	0.27	0.12	1.00				
$(X_8)_t$	0.08	0.01	0.02	1.00			
$(X_9)_t$	0.48	0.06	-0.11	-0.23	1.00		
$(X_{10})_t$	0.66	-0.13	0.30	-0.01	0.40	1.00	
$(X_{10})_{t-1}$	0.00	0.67	-0.11	-0.10	0.10	-0.22	1.00
$(X_{10})_{t-2}$	0.39	-0.01	0.65	-0.09	-0.00	0.44	-0.24

Surprisingly, *both* the simple correlation coefficient between $(X_6)_t$ and $(X_{10})_{t-1}$, as well as that between $(X_{10})_t$ and $(X_6)_{t-1}$ are extremely low (and the latter is negative!). But the correlation coefficient between $(X_6)_t$ and $(X_{10})_{t-2}$ is equal to 0.39.

The results presented in Diz, "Money and Prices," chapter 5, differ from those shown in Table 7.9. While the methodology is similar, the data are not. His exchange rate variable is based on the official rate applied to imports only. For example, from the fourth quarter of 1950 to the third quarter of 1955 he uses a rate of 7.5 pesos per dollar, and from the fourth quarter of 1955 to the fourth quarter of 1958 he uses a rate of 18.0 pesos per dollar. His (quarterly) wage data show erratic changes, because he uses quarterly rates of change of an index of nominal wages, rather than rates of change of quarterly *averages* of monthly indices of nominal wages. To avoid seasonality introduced by the end-of-the-year bonus, Diz took percentage changes between February, May, August, and November wage indices. In contrast, besides using semestral data, I have used average merchandise exchange rates and attempted to eliminate seasonality from the wage variable as discussed in the Statistical Appendix. I have also covered a shorter period than Diz. In his results the coefficients for the money variables are better and those for wages and exchange rates are worse than mine.

In regressions using money plus quasi money, instead of X_6, the coefficients for the money variables are worse than those shown in Table 7.9.

OTHER CHARACTERISTICS OF THE ARGENTINE INFLATION

The instability of postwar Argentine relative prices has been noted previously. Two gross measures of this instability are presented in Table 7.10, showing weighted sums of absolute percentage changes in two types of relative prices. The first were formed by implicit prices

Table 7.10: Average Annual Absolute Percentage Changes in Relative Prices, 1946–65

	Relative prices formed by implicit prices of components of the GDP	*Relative prices formed by components of wholesale price index*
1946	7.8	19.7
1947	10.6	7.9
1948	4.9	2.3
1949	7.2	5.4
1950	3.8	3.0
1951	6.6	3.5
1952	4.7	6.2
1953	5.5	4.6
1954	3.7	1.9
1955	3.5	2.0
1956	6.8	11.8
1957	4.3	2.0
1958	6.0	1.6
1959	11.7	7.3
1960	6.7	1.8
1961	7.0	3.1
1962	3.5	3.2
1963	5.0	3.3
1964	6.3	2.0
1965	5.1	7.4
Average 1946–65	*5.9*	*4.2*
Standard deviation 1946–65	*2.2*	*2.7*

Sources and method: Column 1 was obtained in the following way: First, the implicit prices of the twelve sectors (rural, mining, manufacturing, etc.) making up GDP at factor cost were deflated by the overall GDP deflator. Second, the year-to-year changes of such real implicit sectorial prices were computed. Third, for each year the *absolute* value of the yearly percentage changes were weighted according to the average contribution of each sector to GDP during 1937, 1950, and 1960, and summed. Basic data as in Table 7.1.

Column 2 was obtained following an analogous methodology applied to the three main components (rural, imported and nonrural nonimported) of the overall wholesale price index. Basic data as in Table 124 of the Statistical Appendix.

for different activities making up GDP, and the second by the different commodities making up the wholesale price index.

It is natural to inquire whether absolute changes in relative prices show any relationship with rates of inflation. Indeed, one expects a positive link between the rate of inflation and the size of absolute changes in relative prices. It was seen that a positive correlation exists between devaluation and the rate of inflation; the purpose of devaluation is precisely to twist relative prices in favor of importable and exportable goods. Furthermore, often certain prices were kept constant, or nearly constant, by official control (e.g. house rents, public utility rates, etc.) Under these circumstances, the greater inflation is, the larger the absolute percentage change will be in the *relative* prices of the goods or services whose nominal prices are frozen. Although in this latter case the change in relative prices was induced by inflation, in the former case (i.e. devaluation) inflation was accelerated by the attempt to change relative prices.[34]

The expected positive link is in fact found; about 40 percent of the variance of the relative price changes shown in Table 7.10 are explained either by a current inflation variable (in the case of the first column), or by current changes in the average merchandise exchange rate (for the second column), confirming the hypothesis that higher inflation is accompanied by greater changes in relative prices. In a textbook economy where *relative* prices are independent of the price level and are solely determined by real demand and supply, the corresponding R^2 would be zero.

Inflation has been accompanied not only by relative price instability, but also by declining trends in relative prices for several goods and services, which cannot be explained by faster than average productivity gains. Items whose prices were regulated directly or indirectly by public policy, generally lagged behind price level increases. A few examples are given in Table 132 of the Statistical Appendix, the most dramatic being housing rents. Beginning in 1956 the irregular declining trend in the real exchange rate was checked; since then a zigzagging but vigorous upward trend appears. Other examples of relative prices falling during part or all of the inflation include train

34. The thesis linking inflation with changes in relative prices was first put forth in Argentina by Julio H. G. Olivera in 1959, in his "El Caso de la Argentina," an unpublished paper prepared for ECLA. For an interesting running commentary on Argentine inflation (and stop-go cycles) see also the issues of *Panorama de la Economía Argentina,* edited by Carlos Moyano Llerena.

fares, the real interest rate, and rural prices (during the early phases of inflation).[35]

This question is related to who lost as a result of inflation. On the whole, it appears that only a few groups (with a relatively homogeneous composition) systematically lost real income throughout the inflation. Examples of steady losers include owners of houses under rent control; small savers trusting money as a store of value or having few choices of financial assets besides money; citizens living on social security pensions; and perhaps some categories of civil servants. Major groups such as urban workers, rural entrepreneurs, industrialists, etc., alternated between being ahead of and behind the inflation. The rural sector was a loser in the early stages of inflation, but it gained during years like 1959 when sharp devaluations accelerated the inflationary spiral. Similarly, urban workers were ahead when the main inflationary push came from massive wage increases decreed by government, but were behind when devaluation induced corrective inflation. Industrialists lucky enough to have access to banking credit granted at negative real rates of interest of course benefited from the price rise, but industrialists as a whole also suffered as a result of the damage done to financial markets by inflation. Before the war the Argentine capital market was, in spite of many shortcomings, relatively well developed, and showed a promising expansion.[36]

Some rough idea of income redistribution taking place since 1930 as a result not only of inflation but also of other public policies may be

35. In the United States several of these relative prices declined (secularly as a result of faster than average productivity gains and in the immediate postwar period as a result of price controls) but not by as much as in Argentina, as may be seen in the following comparison where the GNP deflator has been used to obtain real prices (1935–39 = 100):

| | Housing rents | | Public transportation | | Household electricity | |
	Argentina	USA	Argentina	USA	Argentina	USA
1947–49	47	70	39	76	45	50
1953–55	17	76	46	93	26	46
1959–61	6	73	41	96	24	42

The Argentine index for housing rents probably gives a larger weight to controlled rents than that of the USA. See Table 132 in the Statistical Appendix and Table 7.11 in this essay.

36. While stock markets are supposed to flourish under inflation at the expense of bond markets, the Argentine inflation demolished a thriving bond market without strengthening the stock market, which remains thin and which, except for a few years during the early 1960s, has not been an important source of finance to the industrial sector. Transactions in Argentine bourses, valued at constant prices, were lower during 1960–62 than in 1936–38.

obtained comparing GDP shares actually observed with those which could have been expected to obtain had Argentine relative prices followed world trends after 1926–29. Only value added by three groups are distinguished: rural activities, other squeezed sectors (including housing, railroads, mining, electricity, telephones, and other public utilities) and the rest of the economy, which covers major urban activities (manufacturing, construction, financial services, public and private services, and other communications). World price trends have been selected somewhat arbitrarily; using as a base Argentine wholesale prices for 1926–29, dollar price indices for exports and imports (shown in Tables 2.10 and 2.11) have been applied to observed quantum indices for rural and major urban activities, respectively. U.S. prices were used together with the observed Argentine quantum for other squeezed sectors. Clearly, these rough calculations are meant to provide only orders of magnitude. The results are shown in Table 7.11.

Table 7.11: GDP Shares of Three Major Groups, 1926–64
(In percentages of GDP at factor cost)

| | At current prices | | | At 1926–29 prices following world trends | | |
	Rural sector	Other squeezed sectors	Other sectors	Rural sector	Other squeezed sectors	Other sectors
1926–29	33	19	48	33	19	48
1935–39	26	19	55	28	19	53
1947–49	16	8	76	32	15	53
1950–52	15	8	77	25	16	59
1953–55	18	8	74	26	18	56
1956–58	17	7	76	19	18	63
1959–61	17	6	77	18	19	63
1962–64	17	7	76	18	20	62

Sources: As indicated in the text. U.S. implicit prices for "Other squeezed sectors" obtained from U.S. Department of Commerce, *The National Income and Product Accounts of the United States, 1929–1965; Statistical Tables* (Washington, D.C., 1966), pp. 162–63. Argentine accounts obtained from sources listed in the Statistical Appendix and unpublished tables.

Although the rural sector was heavily taxed during 1947–55, in more recent years its share has not been much different on the average than that resulting from weighing its actual quantum by world price trends. Other squeezed sectors, however, have seen their share at current prices dwindle relative to one obtained using U.S. price trends throughout the postwar period. Price and rent controls coupled with inflation explain this phenomenon.

Possible favorable effects of inflation on growth are hard to find in the Argentine case. Although between 1935–38 and 1946–61 the gross savings rate (expressed as a percentage of current GNP) rose by more than 50 percent, *real* capital formation (excluding repairs), measured at 1935–38 prices and expressed as a percentage of GNP, rose by about 10 percent. As shown in essay 6, increases in the relative prices of capital goods explain the divergence. The postwar investment rate benefited from accumulated reserves during 1946–48 and from capital inflows during 1959–61. Inflationary conditions were necessary to bring about the sharp increase in the rate of current savings, but they were unable to increase substantially the *real* flow of foreign and domestic capital goods, especially machinery and equipment. In fact, inflation contributed to make the exchange and machinery bottlenecks more intractable. Postwar public foreign trade policies perpetuated the price structure that had developed during the war; to maintain real capital formation at prewar levels given the new relative prices, sharp gains had to be made in the current savings rate. The sacrifices involved in this process were first borne mainly by accumulated reserves, the rural sector, and rentiers, but since 1949 the burden began to be diffused and shifted back and forth among the major social groups, accompanied by higher rates of inflation. On balance, however, and relative to 1935–39 the rural sector, rentiers, and some civil servants saw their postwar relative position suffer. But it should be noted that the postwar milking of rural producers was more the result of the creation of a state monopsony in the marketing of most exportables, and of exchange rate and export tax policies, then of inflation per se. The postwar change in the structure of nonwage income (away from rural producers and rentiers and toward urban entrepreneurs), may have helped to increase *current* saving rates, but a good part of the taxed rents and rural income benefited urban workers with low savings propensities. At any rate, the set of policies shifting nonwage income from rural to urban entrepreneurs also deteriorated the economy's capacity to transform current savings into machinery and equipment to such an extent, that on balance *real* capital formation was little helped.

As forced savings theories stress the role of urban real wages, it is of interest to view the behavior of this variable. Table 133 of the

Statistical Appendix presents indices of real wage rates as well as of
per capita GNP. If pre-1947 years are taken as the base, real wage
rates have increased by more than per capita GNP. But if one
begins the comparison using 1950–54 as the base, real wage rates
show smaller increases than per capita GNP. These figures, besides
stressing the exiguous and unstable nature of Argentine growth,[37]
also cast doubt on the effectiveness of inflation for systematically
generating forced saving out of wage income. As during different
phases of the inflation different variables (the exchange rate, wages,
etc.), accounted for most of the pressures on the price level, one
cannot expect to find a steady link between price increases and the
pattern of income redistribution.[38] The haphazard and arbitrary way
in which benefits from inflationary conditions were often distributed
at the microlevel (e.g., public projects, granting credit at negative
real interest rates and distributing, rather than auctioning, import
and exchange permits) assured neither that the most efficient entrepreneurs within the favored groups were the ones who obtained
most of the real gains, nor that those real gains were invested in high
priority activities.

In summary, while the growth-promoting effects of inflation have
been exceedingly small, its negative effects on the use of money as
a medium of exchange, on financial markets, on the financing of new
social overhead capital and on the structure and stability of relative
prices indicate that it has acted as a brake on growth.[39] Perhaps the
best that can be said of the inflationary process is that its most important negative effects were not so much due to the rise in prices

37. According to BCRA data, the per capita GNP reached in 1947 was not
surpassed until 1965, nearly twenty years later. The per capita GNP obtained
in 1937 was not surpassed until 1946. The real wage rates reached in 1949
were surpassed both in 1958 and 1965. The importance of the choice of a base
year is obvious from these figures. Even if five-year averages are taken, quite
different results may be obtained for the average annual rate of increase in per
capita GNP:

> 1940–44/1960–64 = 1.2 percent per annum
> 1945–49/1960–64 = 0.4 percent per annum

The performance of the economy looks a bit better if the per capita GDP
rather than GNP is used in the calculations. It will be recalled that during the
early phases of inflation the wage share in national income rose dramatically,
but, especially since 1955, it has tended to fall.

38. For more data on income distribution in Argentina during the postwar
period see my *Exchange Rate Devaluation,* pp. 109–15.

39. There is little evidence, however, that inflation *by itself* reduced net
long-term capital inflow.

per se, but to the fact that official policy chose a few prices for sporadic control, while leaving others to increase freely, thus distorting and destabilizing relative prices.

INFLATION AND THE EXCHANGE BOTTLENECK

After reviewing the main characteristics of the Argentine inflation, it may well be asked: to what extent is it related to the postwar exchange difficulties? Alternatively, one may ask whether inflation caused the exchange difficulties, or whether the latter led to inflation. These issues call for a general interpretation of what caused the inflation, and why it has been so difficult to stop it.

The inflationary pressures generated by import substitution during the 1930s and early 1940s were mild and could hardly be held responsible for the rates of price increases observed during the last twenty years. The roots of serious inflationary pressures are found in policies undertaken during the second half of the 1940s to redistribute income away from the rural sector producing exportable foodstuffs toward the urban sector, especially wage earners. Favorable external prices and exchange reserves accumulated during the war shielded Argentina from the unfavorable balance of payments effects of these policies, but only temporarily.[40] A wise investment of the real income captured from the rural sector in high priority import-substituting activities, or in the development of manufactured exports, could have ameliorated the payments effects of this income redistribution. But most went to finance a larger supply of urban wage-goods and wage-services. When the international terms of trade began to turn against Argentina around 1949, the economy was found with a weakened export sector and an import-substituting sector vitally depending on imported fuels, raw materials, intermediate products and capital goods. The resulting trade deficits quickly ran down exchange reserves, which had also been substantially reduced from their 1946 peak by the purchase of foreign-owned railroads and public utilities. A hostile attitude toward foreign capital during the first Perón presidential term shut off another possible way out of the exchange shortage.

40. It is said that during the euphoric years of 1946–48 General Perón advised a fellow Latin American chief of state that "the economy is the most flexible thing in the world." It is doubtful that he would have said the same thing later on in his presidency, not even during the short-lived Korean commodity boom.

Since around 1949 it became increasingly apparent to the authorities that a partial undoing of the redistributional policies followed earlier was a necessary step for the recovery of rural exportables. Several years of unfavorable weather conditions, culminating in the droughts of 1951–52, dramatized the plight of pampean rural activities and exports. It is doubtful that even austere monetary and wage policies could have achieved price stability in the midst of the new changes in exchange rates and relative prices. Furthermore, the urban trade unions, which together with the armed forces provided the main government support, could hardly have been expected to yield gracefully gains so recently obtained. Thus, the urban-rural struggle over income shares, taking place against a background of balance-of-payments weakness and a drop in per capita output, yielded an inflation during the four years 1949–52 averaging about 30 percent per annum, a rate never seen until then in Argentina, for such a long stretch of time, during the twentieth century. It is noteworthy that of the total increase in net banking credit (including the BCRA) between December 1949 and December 1952, only 13 percent went to the public sector, while 87 percent went to the private sector.[41] Public budget deficits could hardly be blamed as the main source of inflation during these years.

Depressed economic activity, a partial rural recovery and a change of attitude toward foreign capital led to a more relaxed payments situation during 1953 and 1954, inducing a truce in the urban-rural struggle, a lessening of inflationary pressure, and a gradual recovery of economic activity.[42] Efforts to relieve the rural sector, however, were half-hearted, and by 1955 economic recovery was again massively overflowing into imports while exports stagnated. The overthrow of Perón in September 1955 inaugurated a more vigorous policy of helping the rural sector, mainly by moving the exchange rate closer to what could be considered equilibrium levels.

The post-Perón realignment of the price structure, however, was

41. Of the total increase in banking credit between December 1948 and December 1952, only 21 percent went to the public sector and 79 percent was directed toward the private sector of the economy. Data obtained from BCRA, *Estadísticas Monetarias y Bancarias*, p. 3.

42. During 1953, 1954, and 1955 inflation averaged only 8 percent per annum. However, of the total net increase in banking credit between December 1952 and December 1955, only 57 percent went to the private sector and 43 percent went to finance public sector deficits. The increase in gross banking credit to the public sector during these years averaged 3.7 percent of the GNP at current prices.

dirccted by politically weak governments subject to great pressures not only from rural interests, trade unions, and urban entrepreneurs, but also from several factions within the heterogeneous armed forces. Economic ministers came and went with distressing speed, and few managed to get a simultaneous hold on exchange rate, budget, credit, and wage policies. Devaluations and other attempts to change relative prices in favor of exportable and true import-competing activities were carried out amid financial and political disorder. Each sector resisted bitterly attempts to reduce its real income and used political and economic weapons to avoid losses. The rural sector was slow in responding on the aggregate to the more favorable circumstances, no doubt concerned by erratic fluctuations in relative prices. The rigidity shown by rural output during 1955–62 contributed to pressures on exports, the exchange rate, and the price level. On the whole, however, relative prices were changed in the desired fashion, although with frequent detours and zigzags. The cost was an acceleration of inflation.[43]

Under better political and social conditions and with higher resource mobility the post-1955 realignment of relative prices would not have had the acute inflationary effect that it, in fact, had. Upward pressure on the price level could have been expected from corrective increases in the exchange rate and in other prices that had lagged behind the pre-1955 inflation. But the failure of post-Perón governments to keep under control public budget deficits and to convince Peronist trade unions of the wisdom of wage restraint, led to the spiraling of corrective price increases. The spiraling made necessary further exchange rate devaluations to preserve real rural income gains, leading to fresh wage demands and new twists in the spiral. Had governments managed to maintain relative prices in a steadier course, while pushing ahead in research and extension services, rural output would have shown faster growth.

Since 1955 the shares of wage income and of public expenditure in aggregate income and absorption were, on the whole, on the defensive. They had gained during the Perón inflation. But while

43. The average exchange rate for merchandise transactions, which was 7.7 pesos per dollar in 1955, rose to 113.0 pesos per dollar during 1962 and 166.5 pesos per dollar in 1965. In March 1967 the official exchange rate reached 350 pesos per dollar, or 45 times the 1955 rate. In 1966 the cost of living stood at a level 19 times that reached in 1955. During 1955–66 the average annual rate of inflation was 33 percent. It may be noted that a decline in the simple terms of trade between 1952–55 and 1956–64 contributed to exchange difficulties. But by itself this effect was small.

wage income accounted for 41.8 percent of GNP during 1950–55, it dropped to 39.6 percent in 1956–58 and to 35.8 percent during 1959–61.[44] Exhaustive public expenditure on consumption and gross-fixed investment fell from 14.0 percent of GDP during 1950–55, to 12.7 percent of GDP during 1956–63.[45] The partial disintegration of the public revenue machinery since 1955 appears as one of the main culprits for public deficits. Current revenues of the general government and the social security system declined from 21.7 percent of GNP during 1950–55, to 19.6 percent during 1956–63. Expressed at constant prices these revenues fell (slightly) between 1956–58 and 1959–61 and fell again (more sharply) between 1959–61 and 1962–63.[46] Between the last two periods both the deficit of public enterprises and social security payments rose as percentages of GNP.[47] The rise in social security payments reflected the growth in the number of persons benefiting from this system, which began only during the second half of the 1940s, rather than an extension of the nature of the benefits.[48] The increase in the net deficit of all public enterprises was due not only to their growing inefficiency, but also to a fall in their real receipts.

The weakness of the public revenue machinery (leading to the use of banking credit to finance deficits,[49] as it was not politically feasible

44. See my *Exchange Rate Devaluation,* p. 112.

45. CONADE, *Plan Nacional de Desarrollo* (Buenos Aires: 1965), p. 34, Table 9. This share averaged 12.3 percent for 1956–58; 13.2 percent during 1959–61; and 12.6 percent during 1962–63. Social security and other transfers are excluded. The importance of public enterprises also declined after 1955, at least measured by the proportion of the labor force they employ. Several (small) public enterprises were transferred to the private sector, and employment in the remaining public enterprises appears to have risen less than the labor force. By 1967, employment in state enterprises may be estimated at around 300,000, of which about 170,000 worked in the railroads.

46. CONADE, *Plan Nacional de Desarrollo,* p. 35, Table 10. As sales and income taxes are based on the transactions and revenues of the previous year, the acceleration of inflation during these years reduced the real value of tax receipts. Tax evasion also became a more serious problem after 1955, especially with the income tax and the social security contributions. During this period the government also granted generous tax exemptions to promote investment in selected activities and regions. On the other hand, after 1955, import and export taxes became important sources of revenues. See CONADE, *Plan Nacional de Desarrollo,* pp. 29–31.

47. CONADE, *Plan Nacional de Desarrollo,* p. 35, Table 10.

48. Until 1959 the current revenues of the social security system in fact exceeded its current outlays. Especially during the Perón years the system provided the public sector with a substantial source of funds.

49. As shown in Table 123 of the Statistical Appendix, increases in gross banking credit to the public sector during 1956–65 averaged to 3.3 percent of

to contract expenditures fast enough) and the failure to implement an incomes policy acceptable to the main social groups were consequences of the bitter social and political conflicts that plagued Argentina, threatening at times to erupt into open civil war.

It may be concluded that the sectorial and exchange disequilibria created by misguided policies during the latter half of the 1940s gave autonomous Argentine inflation its first potent push. The virulence of the spiral arising from efforts to correct such disequilibria, however, can only be explained by government weakness in handling fiscal, monetary, and wage policies. That weakness was caused in turn by the social and political instability of postwar Argentina, and by the stalemate politics of most of this period. While it is true that once inflation had started, its irregular and nonhomogeneous nature made the correction of the exchange shortage more difficult, it is not correct to argue that since 1949 inflation has *caused* the exchange shortage. The opposite is more nearly true.[50]

This interpretation, coupled with earlier discussion on the structure of foreign trade, suggests that in the long run stabilization efforts will fail unless exchange earnings are made to increase at yearly rates not far below the desired overall annual growth rate.[51] The strengthening of sectors producing exportable goods (whether rural or manufactured) is therefore necessary. A permanent elimination of inflation would also call for a coordinated handling of fiscal, monetary, and wage policies, to insure that their interactions and lag structures are taken into account. Failure to do this results in the imposition of severe

---

the GNP. The corresponding figure for the private sector was 4.1 percent of GNP.

50. One may wonder what would have happened if Perón had allowed the exchange rate to move freely while keeping a marketing mechanism for taxing the rural sector and following the other rural policies (or nonpolicies) that in fact were followed. The weakening of pampean rural activities would have sooner or later led to a weakening of the exchange rate, generating inflationary pressures. Depending on the reaction of nontraditional exports, such pressures could have been of different intensities. Whether the peso was overvalued during 1946–48 is not an easy question to answer; while data shown in Table 132 of the Statistical Appendix indicate that, according to a simple parity calculation, signs of overvaluation appeared in 1947, it should be remembered that during these years the terms of trade were very favorable to Argentina.

51. It seems unrealistic to expect that a long-run "solution" to the exchange and inflation problems could come from acceptance of a permanent stagnation of output. A policy of complete reliance on further import substitution to handle the exchange problem would not only lead to substantial economic inefficiencies, but it might not even be able to result in net savings of foreign exchange. It would also generate cost-push inflationary pressures.

hardships on some sectors of the economy, thus opening the possibility of future counterattacks jeopardizing the stabilization effort. At the end of the stabilization plan the economy should have set the basis for a steady growth in the output of exportable goods, but it should also have a fiscal policy permitting budget deficits only to the extent that they pose no serious demand-pull inflationary threats, plus an incomes policy acceptable to the major economic groups.

Even a coordinated stabilization plan is unlikely to succeed overnight in stopping price rises. Past stabilization attempts that hoped both to stop inflation and to correct exchange difficulties within a short period of time, by relying on just a few policy tools (such as devaluation and monetary stringency) resulted in severe contractions in real output (as during 1959 and 1962–63) without obtaining more than a temporary relief from price increases and exchange difficulties. Efforts carried out during 1953–58 to stop inflation did not meet with lasting success either, but their negative influence on real output was smaller. As any sensible stabilization plan is likely to call for a good dose of corrective inflation, involving the catching up of prices that had lagged behind the general price rise, and because of the lagged response of prices to cost increases that had occurred before the plan, it may as well be faced that a stabilization plan cannot result in an immediate end to inflation. Attempts to achieve that end will result in contractions of real output. A gradual and coordinated program is more likely to avoid a recession, while bringing down the rate of price increase over, say, a two- or three-year period.[52] A government lacking the will power to stick to a plan for two or three years is unlikely to suceed in stopping inflation using a shock treatment.

52. At the time of writing (1968), it is too early to judge the results of the stabilization efforts begun in Argentina in March 1967. It may be said, however, that the initial conditions for this plan were superior to those of the 1955, 1959, and 1962 stabilization plans. The distortions in the relative price structure are less now than they were, while the rural sector producing exportables has shown great strength during the last four years. Bottlenecks in electricity, oil, and transportation are also less pressing than what they were a few years ago. The foreign debt has been reduced substantially during the last three years. Finally, the new stabilization plan stresses the need for a coordinated and gradual attack on inflation, hoping to avoid both a fall in real output and putting too much of the stabilization burden on a few sectors of the economy. The fact that the plan is being implemented by a government controlled by the powerful armed forces represents a short-run advantage with doubtful long-run benefits.

DEVALUATIONS, RECESSIONS, AND STABILIZATION PLANS: MECHANICS

The mechanism through which several devaluations and stabilization plans resulted in contractions of real output remains to be discussed. At least two possible mechanisms have been suggested—one stressing the impact on real output of the monetary stringency that usually accompanies stabilization plans, and another giving special attention to the regressive redistribution of income arising from devaluation and its impact on aggregate demand.

Those stressing monetary tightness point out that during the early phases of stabilization plans the money supply has not increased by as much as the price level. The reduction in real cash balances is then supposed to induce liquidation of inventories and a reduction in real expenditure, leading to recession. A similar argument is sometimes presented, contrasting increases in banking credit to the private sector with increases in money wages; when the latter are larger than the former monetary tightness is supposed to follow.[53] A difficulty in this type of analysis in Argentina is the lack of reliable prices in the money and financial markets; most transactions take place at interest rates officially set, and the representativeness of other transactions undertaken in free markets is doubtful. As during recent years a large number of money substitutes have appeared, thanks to an expansion in financial intermediaries, aggregates such as money and quasi money, and their rates of change, may be compatible with different levels of liquidity in different years.[54]

Because banking credit has been granted as a rule at negative real rates of interest, there has been excess demand for it. Under these circumstances, it is not surprising that many business men will focus on banking credit as the key variable affecting their production plans. An increase in inventories due to a fall in demand, for example, for which normal banking credit is insufficient, may lead to a reduction in output that will be blamed on tight banking credit rather than on sluggish demand.[55]

53. This argument is elegantly presented by Geoffrey Maynard and Willy Van Rijckeghem in a mimeographed paper entitled "Stabilization Policy in an Inflationary Economy: An Analysis of the Argentine Case."
54. Reliance on foreign markets for secondary liquidity has also changed depending on official regulations and policies.
55. The gap between the interest cost at which banking credit can be obtained and that at which credit in the free market is forthcoming has been very large in most years.

The argument linking devaluation with recessions appears at first paradoxical. It is a well-known result of trade theory that a devaluation (in a small country) will result in *upward* pressure on real output, by first stimulating production of exportable and import-competing goods. But the argument stresses that with a wage lag, devaluation will also lead to a redistribution of income toward nonwage earners (mainly rural and urban entrepreneurs) who in the short run will have a lower propensity to spend, especially on domestic products. Unless supply responses of exportable and import-competing goods are very price-elastic, a drop in real output may result.[56] In an economy characterized by all sorts of rigidities and a lack of resource mobility, as in postwar Argentina, this short-run result becomes quite likely. The speed of contraction in sectors producing home or nontraded goods and services is likely to be greater than the speed of expansion in sectors favored by the new constellation of relative prices. Devaluation may also trigger a reduction in real cash balances.

The present state of knowledge regarding behavioral equations in the Argentine economy is insufficient to decide which of the two mechanisms is more potent in explaining recessions. Attempts to untangle their respective effects have until now met with little success. But it may be concluded that both monetary tightness and lack of demand arising from a fall in real wages have played a role in recent recessions. In some of them the latter force seems to have dominated (as in 1959), while in others the former played the major role (as during 1962–63). Furthermore, special circumstances have also on different occasions contributed to reinforce the mechanism of recession —the severe drought of 1951–52, the higher than average political and economic uncertainty of 1962–63, and a sudden increase in the peso value of private foreign debts as a result of devaluation (as in 1959 and 1962).

56. The redistributive effect of devaluation is discussed in greater detail in chapter 2 of my *Exchange Rate Devaluation*. This book also analyzes the 1959 stabilization plan. Contrary to the experience in other countries, in some recent years (such as 1958, 1959, and 1961) the wage share in output has increased when output expanded and has declined during recessions.

Statistical Appendix

The tables that follow present basic information regarding the Argentine economy; they do *not* present all available information on that economy. The data in these tables should be adequate for analysts interested in cross-country comparisons but are likely to be insufficient for the scholar who wishes to dig deep into Argentine reality. Such a scholar will have to go to the original sources listed in the tables of the main text as well as those listed in this appendix.

Argentine statistics have a long and checkered history. The enlightened liberals who came to power during the second half of the nineteenth century left us with statistical information which is on the whole superior to that of most less developed countries. Censuses exist for 1869, 1895, and 1914, and foreign trade data are ample. Curiously, the "populist" governments of the Radical Party (1916–30) provided no important new data sources, although during those years remarkable individuals like Alejandro E. Bunge began to publicize available data and to urge the need for developing better sources of statistical information. It was left to the conservative governments of the 1930s to undertake the second industrial census of the century, taken in 1935, which was followed every two years by fresh detailed industrial data. Indeed, the quality and quantity of industrial data reached a peak during 1935–48 which has not been reached again. The Perón regime continued for a while this service and also carried out the general census of 1947 and the industrial census of 1953. However, together with the Argentine economy, official statistical services began a decline around 1949. In spite of new data-gathering and data-processing efforts stimulated by the creation of new institutions such as the Consejo Nacional de Desarrollo (CONADE), very serious gaps have appeared even in areas for which data existed in the past. The most dramatic example is the lack of a reliable industrial census after 1953. Unfortunately, it appears that the industrial census undertaken during 1963 has not been a success.

In spite of the difficulties of the last twenty years, it may be said that Argentine data are far above average among those of semi-industrialized and less developed economies. In the field of national accounting Argentina has pioneered, not only because of the work of Alejandro Bunge, but also because of the post-World War II research of a distinguished school of national accountants and economists. An enlightened member of the Perón regime, Alfredo Gómez Morales, during the early 1950s promoted the research of a group of economists led by Manuel Balboa (now of ECLA), which led to the publication in 1955 of national accounts for 1935–54. This work built on previous estimates of national income by the Central Bank (for 1935–44), which were prepared during the last years of World War II. This early work on national accounts was encouraged by Raúl Prebisch, then a high official of the Central Bank (Banco Central de la República Argentina, or BCRA). After 1955, BCRA continued the preparation of yearly estimates based on this set of accounts.

After the overthrow of General Perón, the U.N. Economic Commission for Latin America (ECLA) prepared a detailed study of the Argentine economy during which estimates of national income were pushed back to 1900. Many economists who had participated in the preparation of the national accounts for 1935–54 also helped to prepare these new estimates (which produced data in constant prices only).

During the late 1950s it became increasingly apparent that the industrial data on which the continuing national accounts estimates of BCRA were based were seriously underestimating industrial growth. New branches of manufacturing were being neglected, and slowly growing branches had an excessive weight in the indices. After some delay, both BCRA and CONADE undertook a revision and extension of the national accounts. The chief economist in this project for CONADE was Alberto Fracchia, who as a disciple of Manuel Balboa had helped to prepare the first postwar national accounts.

In the tables relating to national accounts I have presented both CONADE and BCRA revised estimates. On the whole they yield similar results, although for some items discrepancies exist. Both sets of estimates rely on the same basic data; both lacked the help of an up-to-date industrial census. As I am quite convinced that I know much less about national accounting and Argentine data than Alberto Fracchia and his colleagues in CONADE and BCRA, I have not tinkered with their results, which are presented without adjustments. In fact, I doubt very much that there are in the world many people who know more about national accounts and Argentine data than Alberto Fracchia.

Both the revisions of the national accounts by CONADE and BCRA are expected to generate more data, which at the time this is written are not available in published form. As of now, the published CONADE figures present greater detail than those of BCRA, but the latter are both more up to date and go further back in time. The final results of the CONADE/ECLA project on national accounts and income distribution are scheduled to include a detailed discussion of the methodology used, as well as the sources of data.

An effort has been made to avoid presenting in the appendix tables information already presented in the main body of the book. For example, data on land tenure are discussed in some detail in essay 3, and therefore nothing on that topic appears in the appendix.

The appendix tends to neglect pre-1930 data; as a partial remedy, let me strongly recommend the following publications to the economic historian wishing to examine the golden years of Argentina:

Comité Nacional de Geografía, *Anuario Geográfico Argentino* (Buenos Aires, 1941). A veritable mine of data on all aspects of the Argentine economy. This volume was followed by a supplement: Comité Nacional de Geografía, *Anuario Geográfico Argentino, Suplemento 1942* (Buenos Aires, 1943).
Sociedad Rural Argentina, *Anuario de la Sociedad Rural Argentina*, No. 1 (Buenos Aires, 1928). A most useful compilation of statistics on the rural sector. Raúl Prebisch directed the research.
The *Revista de Economía Argentina* was directed by Alejandro E. Bunge from 1917 until the early 1940s. It contains data and commentary on Argentina between the wars. The commentary is not always objective, but it is seldom dull. Bunge also published several books and collections of essays, among which I have found the following two very useful: (1) *La Economía Argentina: Política Económica y Aduanera*, 4 vols. (Buenos Aires, 1928); (2) *Una Nueva Argentina* (Buenos Aires, 1940). Bunge was an ardent advocate of industrialization and left behind a large number of

disciples. A good essay should be written on the influence of Bunge on Argentine economic thought.

Ernesto Tornquist and Company, *The Economic Development of the Argentine Republic in the Last Fifty Years* (Buenos Aires, 1919). A thorough compilation of statistics on pre-World War I Argentina.

Adolfo Dorfman, *Evolución Industrial Argentina* (Buenos Aires: Editorial Losada, S.A., 1942). A useful review of early Argentine industrialization.

The General Censuses of 1869, 1895, 1914, and 1947 contain a wealth of information; the yearly *Anuario del Comercio Exterior* provide abundant foreign trade data. Other publications of the Dirección General de Estadística (which later became Dirección Nacional de Estadística), including partial censuses, contribute more detailed information on population, rural activities, labor, industry, etc.

Economic historians wishing to look deeper into the fascinating 1930–43 period should also see the following:

Banco de la Nación Argentina, Oficinas de Investigaciones Económicas, *Revista Económica*. This publication was continued after the creation of the Central Bank by Banco Central de la República Argentina, Oficina de Investigaciones Económicas, *Revista Económica.*

The yearly *Memorias* of the Central Bank. In both the *Memorias* and the *Revista Económica,* the pen and thought of Raúl Prebisch are quite evident.

The Statistical Appendices of the Ph.D thesis of Lucio Reca at the University of Chicago ("The Price and Production Duality within Argentine Agriculture, 1923–1965," December 1967) contain a wealth of rural statistics.

Table 1: Gross National Income and Product Account, 1950–64 (BCRA)
(Current prices; billion pesos)

Expenditures on GNP	1950	1951	1952	1953	1954	1955	1956	1957
A. Private consumption expenditures and changes in stocks	48	68	83	90	103	125	160	201
B. General government consumption expenditures	7	9	11	13	15	17	22	23
C. Gross fixed capital formation	12	21	21	25	26	31	39	54
D. Exports of goods and services	6	8	6	9	8	9	24	27
E. Less: imports of goods and services	6	10	9	6	8	11	26	34
F. GDP	68	96	112	129	145	171	218	271
G. Net factor income from abroad	–	−0.5	−0.1	−0.2	−0.2	−0.3	−0.6	−0.6
H. GNP	68	95	112	129	145	171	217	271

Expenditures on GNP	1958	1959	1960	1961	1962	1963	1964
A. Private consumption expenditures and changes in stocks	279	538	668	805	962	1,221	1,682
B. General government consumption expenditures	38	64	86	117	156	176	243
C. Gross fixed capital formation	77	135	218	265	315	295	419
D. Exports of goods and services	33	89	102	94	155	207	216
E. Less: imports of goods and services	40	85	114	132	177	165	197
F. GDP	387	741	961	1,148	1,412	1,734	2,363
G. Net factor income from abroad	−1.6	−3.2	−4.8	−8.4	−8.2	−9.5	−14.4
H. GNP	385	737	956	1,140	1,403	1,725	2,349

Source: BCRA, p. 1.

Table 2: Gross National Income and Product Account, 1950–61 (CONADE)
(Current prices; billion pesos)

	1950	1951	1952	1953	1954	1955	1956	1957	1958	1959	1960	1961
Expenditures on GNP												
A. Private consumption expenditures and some stock changes	48	71	84	90	102	124	157	206	284	534	678	838
B. General government consumption expenditures	7	9	12	13	15	18	22	25	38	64	86	112
C. Gross fixed capital formation	14	21	22	24	26	31	43	59	81	144	227	278
D. Change in selected stocks	−1	1	–	1	1	1	−2	−1	1	8	6	−5
E. Exports of goods and services	6	8	6	9	8	9	24	27	33	89	102	94
F. Less: imports of goods and services	6	10	9	6	8	11	26	34	40	85	114	132
G. GDP	70	100	115	130	145	173	218	282	397	754	985	1,184
H. Net factor income from abroad	–	−0.5	−0.1	−0.2	−0.2	−0.3	−0.6	−0.5	−1.6	−3.2	−4.7	−8.4
I. GNP	69	100	115	130	144	173	217	281	395	751	981	1,176
Distribution of Gross National Income												
J. Payments by producers to individuals	58	82	95	107	120	145	178	228	337	635	796	935
1. Wages and salaries	30	39	50	54	62	70	86	107	163	268	344	430
2. (*a*) Profits of nonincorporated enterprises	22	35	36	43	46	60	75	99	145	318	384	423
(*b*) Interests, rents, and dividends	6	8	9	10	12	14	17	21	29	49	68	81
K. Income retained by producers	4	5	6	7	9	10	13	19	23	47	65	84
1. Capital consumption allowances	3	4	5	5	6	8	10	13	17	26	38	49
2. Retained earnings of corporations and public enterprises	1	2	2	2	2	2	3	6	6	22	27	35

Table 2—Continued

	1950	1951	1952	1953	1954	1955	1956	1957	1958	1959	1960	1961
L. Payments by producers to government	10	16	16	20	23	26	32	42	48	90	141	182
1. Social security contributions	2	3	4	5	6	6	8	9	11	18	27	33
2. Direct taxes on corporations	1	1	1	1	1	2	2	3	3	6	12	15
3. Indirect taxes	7	12	11	14	16	17	21	30	33	65	101	131
4. Other revenues of the general government	—	—	—	—	—	1	1	1	1	1	2	2
M. Less: adjustments	2	3	3	5	7	8	6	8	12	22	22	25
1. Subsidies	2	3	2	4	7	7	5	7	12	20	20	23
2. Interest on the public debt	—	1	1	1	1	1	1	1	1	1	2	3
N. Gross national income at market prices	69	100	115	130	144	173	217	281	395	751	981	1,176

Source: CONADE, pp. 34–35.

Table 3: Gross National Income and Product Account, 1935–50 (O.S.)
(Current prices; billion pesos)

	1935	1936	1937	1938	1939	1940	1941	1942
Expenditures on GNP								
A. Private consumption expenditures and some changes in stocks	6.9	7.2	8.0	8.0	8.5	9.0	9.2	10.5
B. General government consumption expenditures	0.9	1.0	1.1	1.2	1.2	1.3	1.3	1.4
C. Gross fixed capital formation	0.8	1.0	1.4	1.5	1.4	1.4	1.5	1.7
D. Change in selected stocks	0.1	0.1	-0.1	0.4	–	–	0.4	0.1
E,F. Exports less imports of goods and services	0.5	0.6	0.9	-0.1	0.4	0.2	0.5	0.8
G. GDP	9.3	9.8	11.3	11.0	11.6	12.0	12.9	14.6
H. Net factor income from abroad	-0.5	-0.5	-0.5	-0.4	-0.5	-0.4	-0.4	-0.5
I. GNP	8.8	9.4	10.9	10.6	11.1	11.6	12.4	14.0
Distribution of Gross National Income								
Wages and salaries	3.4	3.7	4.0	4.2	4.3	4.4	4.7	5.1
Capital consumption allowances	0.7	0.7	0.8	0.8	0.9	0.9	1.0	1.1
Social security contributions by employers	0.1	0.1	0.1	0.1	0.1	0.1	0.1	0.1
Indirect taxes minus subsidies	1.1	1.1	1.3	1.1	1.3	1.4	1.4	1.3
Other income	3.5	3.8	4.7	4.4	4.6	4.8	5.3	6.4
Gross National Income at Market Prices	8.8	9.4	10.9	10.6	11.1	11.6	12.4	14.0

	1943	1944	1945	1946	1947	1948	1949	1950
Expenditures on GNP								
A. Private consumption expenditures and some change in stocks	10.2	11.9	12.9	16.7	22.4	25.8	34.9	40.6
B. General government consumption expenditures	1.6	2.1	2.4	2.9	3.9	5.7	6.8	7.7
C. Gross fixed capital formation	1.8	2.2	2.6	3.9	6.9	10.3	11.9	14.3

Table 3—*Continued*

	1943	1944	1945	1946	1947	1948	1949	1950
D. Change in selected stocks	0.1	-0.3	-0.3	0.4	1.5	1.6	-0.5	-0.7
E,F. Exports less imports of goods and services	1.6	1.7	1.7	2.2	1.2	0.3	-0.5	0.4
G. GDP	15.3	17.5	19.3	26.2	35.9	43.8	52.6	62.2
H. Net factor income from abroad	-0.4	-0.5	-0.4	-0.5	-0.3	–	-0.1	–
I. GNP	14.9	17.0	18.9	25.6	35.6	43.8	52.5	62.2
Distribution of Gross National Income								
Wages and salaries	5.5	6.4	7.2	9.8	13.8	18.7	24.9	29.5
Capital consumption allowances	1.2	1.4	1.4	1.5	1.7	2.0	2.4	2.8
Social security contributions by employers	0.1	0.1	0.3	0.4	0.8	1.2	1.6	2.2
Indirect taxes minus subsidies	1.3	1.4	1.6	2.0	3.0	2.3	3.0	3.7
Other income	6.7	7.6	8.4	11.9	16.4	19.7	20.7	24.1
Gross National Income at Market Prices	14.9	17.0	18.9	25.6	35.6	43.8	52.5	62.2

Sources: O.S., pp. 116–19, 122–23, and ECLA worksheets.

Table 4: Personal Income Account, 1950–61 (CONADE)
(Current prices; billion pesos)

	1950	1951	1952	1953	1954	1955	1956	1957	1958	1959	1960	1961
Receipts												
A. Payments by producers to individuals	58	82	95	107	120	145	178	228	337	635	796	935
1. Wages and salaries	30	39	50	54	62	70	86	107	163	268	344	430
2. (*a*) Profits of nonincorporated enterprises	22	35	36	43	46	60	75	99	145	318	384	423
(*b*) Interests, rents, and dividends	6	8	9	10	12	14	17	21	29	49	68	81
B. Transfer payments from government	2	3	3	4	6	7	9	10	16	29	40	57
C. Personal income	60	84	98	111	126	152	187	238	352	664	836	992
Outlays and Savings												
D. Private consumption expenditures	48	71	84	90	102	124	157	206	284	534	678	838
E. Payments to government	3	5	6	7	8	8	12	13	16	24	38	50
1. Social Security contributions	2	2	3	3	4	5	6	7	8	14	19	26
2. Direct taxes	2	2	3	3	3	3	5	6	7	11	19	23
3. Other	–	–	–	–	–	–	–	–	–	–	–	–
F. Personal saving	8	8	8	15	17	19	19	19	53	105	120	104

Source: CONADE, pp. 36–37.

Table 5: Government Revenue and Current Expenditure Account, 1950–61 (CONADE)
(Current prices; billion pesos)

	1950	1951	1952	1953	1954	1955	1956	1957	1958	1959	1960	1961
Current Receipts												
A. Payments by producers	10	16	16	20	23	26	32	42	48	90	141	182
1. Social security contributions	2	3	4	5	6	6	8	9	11	18	27	33
2. Direct taxes on corporations	1	1	1	1	1	2	2	3	3	6	12	15
3. Indirect taxes	7	12	11	14	16	17	21	30	33	65	101	131
4. Other revenues of the general government	–	–	–	–	–	1	1	1	1	1	2	2
B. Payments by individuals	3	5	6	7	8	8	12	13	16	24	38	50
1. Social security contributions	2	2	3	3	4	5	6	7	8	14	19	26
2. Direct taxes	2	2	3	3	3	3	5	6	7	11	19	23
C. Total receipts	13	21	22	27	31	34	43	56	64	115	179	232
Current Expenditures												
D. General government consumption expenditure	7	9	12	13	15	18	22	25	38	64	86	112
E. Subsidies	2	3	2	4	7	7	5	7	12	20	20	23
F. Interest on the public debt	0.4	0.6	0.7	0.6	0.6	0.7	0.9	0.6	0.6	1.4	2.2	2.8
G. Transfer payments to individuals	2	3	3	4	6	7	9	10	16	29	40	57
H. Surplus on current account	2	6	4	5	2	1	6	13	–2	–	32	37
I. Total current expenditure and surplus	13	21	22	27	31	34	43	56	64	115	179	232

Source: CONADE, pp. 38–39.

Table 6: External Transactions Account, 1950–61 (CONADE)
(Current prices; billion pesos)

	1950	1951	1952	1953	1954	1955	1956	1957	1958	1959	1960	1961
A. Exports of goods and services	6.4	8.2	6.2	8.6	8.3	9.5	23.6	27.0	33.3	89.2	102.5	93.6
B. Factor income from abroad	–	–0.5	–0.1	–0.2	–0.2	–0.3	–0.6	–0.5	–1.6	–3.2	–4.7	–8.4
C. Imports of goods and services	–5.7	–10.0	–9.5	–6.1	–7.7	–11.4	–26.0	–34.1	–40.1	–84.9	–114.1	–132.4
D. Surplus of nation on external account	0.6	–2.3	–3.4	2.3	0.3	–2.3	–3.0	–7.6	–8.4	1.1	–16.3	–47.3

Source: CONADE, pp. 40–41.

Table 7: Gross Domestic Capital Formation Account, 1950–61 (CONADE)
(Current prices; billion pesos)

	1950	1951	1952	1953	1954	1955	1956	1957	1958	1959	1960	1961
Gross Domestic Capital Formation												
A. Gross fixed capital formation	14	21	22	24	26	31	43	59	81	144	227	278
1. Public sector fixed capital formation	4	6	6	7	7	7	8	11	21	32	50	61
(a) Construction	3	4	5	5	5	5	5	8	14	22	33	44
(b) Equipment	1	2	2	2	2	2	3	3	7	9	17	16
2. Private sector fixed capital formation	10	15	16	16	18	24	35	49	60	112	177	217
(a) Construction	7	8	10	10	12	14	19	22	28	50	54	69
(b) Equipment	3	6	6	6	7	10	16	27	32	63	123	148
B. Change in selected stocks	−1	1	–	1	1	1	−2	−1	1	8	6	−5
C. Gross domestic capital formation	14	21	22	25	27	32	41	58	82	152	234	272
Gross Domestic Saving												
D. Income retained by producers	4	5	6	7	9	10	13	19	23	47	65	84
1. Capital consumption allowances	3	4	5	5	6	8	10	13	17	26	38	49
2. Retained earnings of corporations and public enterprises	1	2	2	2	2	2	3	6	6	22	27	35
E. Personal saving	8	8	8	15	17	19	19	19	53	105	120	104
F. Government surplus on current account	2	6	4	5	2	1	6	13	−2	–	32	37
G. Less: surplus of nation on external account	0.6	−2.3	−3.4	2.3	0.3	−2.3	−3.0	−7.6	−8.4	1.1	−16.3	−47.3

Source: CONADE, pp. 42–43, pp. 176–77.

Table 8: Industrial Origin of GDP at Factor Cost, 1950–64 (BCRA)
(Current prices; billion pesos)

	1950	1951	1952	1953	1954	1955	1956	1957	1958	1959	1960	1961	1962	1963	1964
Rural sector	9.0	14.2	15.5	23.4	24.0	26.4	33.4	42.7	59.3	138.1	153.7	149.8	198.2	273.7	425.8
Mining	0.5	0.7	0.9	0.9	1.2	1.4	1.8	2.3	3.0	6.6	9.7	13.6	21.4	26.1	26.9
Manufacturing	18.4	24.9	29.0	31.8	37.3	48.0	58.9	75.0	117.2	212.1	284.4	347.2	417.5	496.6	696.3
Construction	3.9	5.0	5.7	5.8	6.5	7.2	9.3	11.8	19.4	27.5	37.0	47.6	55.9	63.9	79.0
Electricity and other public services	0.7	0.8	0.9	1.1	1.3	1.6	2.1	2.1	3.8	7.0	11.2	15.9	22.3	31.2	37.7
Transport	4.0	5.6	7.2	8.0	8.8	9.8	13.5	18.0	23.8	43.9	57.9	67.9	82.7	113.8	155.5
Communications	0.6	0.8	1.2	1.3	1.4	1.7	2.2	2.1	3.3	7.0	8.8	12.0	16.3	21.7	24.2
Commerce	10.7	16.2	17.5	17.2	19.1	23.7	32.9	41.1	58.1	118.3	150.4	173.6	201.6	233.3	307.2
Banking, insurance, and ownership of dwellings	4.1	5.4	6.5	7.4	8.5	10.0	11.7	14.6	19.8	27.0	36.6	46.2	59.2	70.3	92.5
General government	5.6	7.4	9.3	11.1	13.1	14.8	17.7	19.7	33.0	51.9	65.2	91.9	127.6	145.9	206.6
Other services	5.0	7.3	9.9	11.0	11.9	13.2	15.9	20.1	27.0	56.7	67.5	77.2	99.4	120.6	155.4
Total	62.5	88.2	103.7	119.0	133.2	157.9	199.1	249.6	367.7	696.0	882.2	1,043.1	1,302.1	1,597.2	2,207.1

Source: BCRA, p. 2.

Table 9: Industrial Origin of GDP at Market Prices, 1950–61 (CONADE)
(Current prices; billion pesos)

	1950	1951	1952	1953	1954	1955	1956	1957	1958	1959	1960	1961
Rural sector (livestock and agriculture)	9.0	14.7	15.1	23.1	23.8	26.1	32.8	41.8	58.7	136.4	152.3	146.3
Fisheries	0.1	0.1	0.2	0.1	0.1	0.1	0.2	0.3	0.4	0.5	0.8	0.8
Mining	0.5	0.7	0.8	0.8	1.1	1.3	1.8	2.4	3.2	9.0	12.1	14.8
Manufacturing	22.0	30.4	36.0	39.1	45.9	59.5	70.6	92.2	135.5	240.6	336.9	412.9
Construction	4.4	5.7	6.4	6.5	7.2	8.1	10.0	12.7	18.1	31.2	37.1	48.4
Commerce	10.6	16.2	16.9	15.7	16.0	20.8	33.8	47.9	63.2	122.0	169.0	197.2
Transport and storing	4.1	5.2	7.3	7.6	8.1	8.8	12.2	15.8	19.1	37.4	52.5	62.2
Communications	0.4	0.7	0.9	1.0	1.0	1.3	1.7	1.6	2.0	4.4	5.3	9.2
Electricity and other public services	0.8	1.0	1.3	1.6	1.8	2.3	2.5	3.0	4.7	9.4	13.3	19.4
Banking, insurance, and other financial intermediaries	1.7	2.6	3.2	3.5	3.9	4.6	5.9	7.4	9.3	15.4	20.1	28.3
Ownership of dwellings	3.3	3.9	4.6	5.5	6.3	7.3	8.3	10.1	14.0	16.7	23.1	27.8
General government	5.8	7.6	9.6	11.4	13.4	15.2	17.8	20.1	33.0	51.8	65.1	89.1
Other services	6.6	9.3	12.3	13.4	15.0	17.5	21.1	24.5	35.0	69.4	82.3	98.9
Total	69.3	98.2	114.5	129.3	143.8	172.9	218.6	279.8	396.1	744.2	969.9	1,155.4

Source: CONADE, pp. 66–67.

Table 10: Industrial Origin of GDP at Factor Cost, 1935–50 (O.S.)
(Current prices; billion pesos)

	1935	1936	1937	1938	1939	1940	1941	1942	1943	1944	1945	1946	1947	1948	1949	1950
Agriculture (crop raising)	1.24	1.29	1.73	1.40	1.32	1.19	1.33	1.38	1.35	1.75	1.64	3.45	3.53	4.21	4.25	4.38
Livestock	0.86	0.95	1.12	0.99	1.08	1.27	1.42	1.71	1.69	1.83	1.94	2.13	2.74	2.98	3.55	4.68
Fisheries	0.01	0.01	0.01	0.01	0.01	0.01	0.01	0.01	0.02	0.02	0.02	0.03	0.04	0.06	0.07	0.09
Mining	0.10	0.11	0.13	0.13	0.16	0.17	0.18	0.21	0.21	0.22	0.24	0.25	0.30	0.36	0.47	0.57
Manufacturing	1.21	1.37	1.49	1.60	1.75	1.77	2.07	2.60	3.01	3.71	4.00	5.57	7.73	9.44	11.84	13.70
Construction	0.17	0.19	0.26	0.30	0.30	0.28	0.33	0.38	0.42	0.53	0.62	0.91	1.42	2.46	3.54	4.33
Commerce	1.09	1.15	1.41	1.39	1.45	1.58	1.69	2.07	2.16	2.60	2.72	3.92	7.08	8.66	8.41	10.01
Transport and communications	0.84	0.90	0.92	0.91	0.92	0.91	0.96	1.14	1.28	1.43	1.55	1.88	2.68	3.76	4.96	5.87
Other public services	0.18	0.18	0.19	0.20	0.21	0.21	0.21	0.21	0.22	0.23	0.25	0.33	0.39	0.46	0.57	0.67
Financial services and ownership of dwellings	1.06	1.07	1.15	1.29	1.37	1.41	1.47	1.54	1.54	1.37	2.02	2.17	2.42	2.77	3.35	4.19
Personal services	0.73	0.77	0.81	0.82	0.84	0.86	0.91	0.99	1.07	1.18	1.43	1.76	2.18	2.80	3.85	4.79
General government	0.67	0.73	0.78	0.86	0.91	0.94	0.96	1.02	1.08	1.20	1.34	1.73	2.48	3.53	4.71	5.33
Total	8.15	8.71	9.99	9.91	10.32	10.59	11.53	13.26	14.04	16.07	17.77	24.12	32.98	41.50	49.56	58.60

Source: O.S., pp. 112–13.

Table 11: Gross National Income and Product Account, 1935–65 (BCRA)
(1960 prices; billion pesos)

Expenditure on GNP

	1935	1936	1937	1938	1939	1940	1941	1942	1943	1944	1945
A,B,C,D. Total domestic absorption	422	441	495	534	509	505	508	529	506	562	533
E. Exports of goods and services	127	116	134	95	116	95	97	89	98	97	97
F. Less: imports of goods and services	96	99	134	127	105	91	70	58	40	41	42
G. GDP	453	458	495	502	520	509	534	559	563	618	588
H. Terms of trade effect	7	37	72	33	15	−3	−10	3	9	12	5
I. Gross domestic income	460	496	568	534	535	507	525	562	573	630	593
J. Net factor income from abroad	−22	−20	−18	−17	−20	−16	−17	−18	−13	−17	−12
K. Gross national income	438	475	549	517	514	491	508	544	559	613	582

Expenditures on GNP

	1946	1947	1948	1949	1950	1951	1952	1953	1954	1955
A,B,C,D. Total domestic absorption	602	772	800	743	713	773	717	724	766	844
E. Exports of goods and services	112	105	89	66	91	72	53	81	87	78
F. Less: imports of goods and services	76	152	155	109	94	105	78	64	83	100
G. GDP	637	725	733	700	710	739	692	741	769	822
H. Terms of trade effect	32	66	61	26	14	14	−2	8	3	5
I. Gross domestic income	669	790	794	725	724	753	690	749	772	827
J. Net factor income from abroad	−11	−6	−1	−1	–	−4	−1	−1	−1	−2
K. Gross national income	658	785	794	725	723	749	689	748	770	826

Addendum: Main Components of Absorption, 1950–65

	1950	1951	1952	1953	1954	1955
Private consumption	542	555	523	523	567	627
General government consumption expenditures	70	69	68	66	69	71
Gross fixed capital formation	114	140	125	123	120	140
1. Private construction	51	54	49	48	48	54
2. Public construction	24	26	23	26	23	20
3. Durable producers' equipment	39	60	53	50	49	66
Changes in selected stocks	−13	8	1	12	10	7

Table 11—Continued

	1956	1957	1958	1959	1960	1961	1962	1963	1964	1965
Expenditures on GNP										
A,B,C,D. Total domestic absorption	835	887	952	881	973	1,069	1,011	944	1,047	1,113
E. Exports of goods and services	90	95	97	102	102	95	128	131	122	132
F. Less: imports of goods and services	90	100	104	92	114	136	130	101	118	112
G. GDP	835	881	945	890	961	1,028	1,009	974	1,052	1,133
H. Terms of trade effect	-8	-15	-11	-5	-	1	-14	-4	7	2
I. Gross domestic income	827	867	934	885	961	1,030	995	970	1,059	1,135
J. Net factor income from abroad	-2	-2	-4	-4	-5	-8	-6	-5	-6	-5
K. Gross national income	825	864	930	882	956	1,022	989	965	1,052	1,130
Addendum: Main Components of Absorption, 1950–65										
Private consumption	619	660	711	653	668	740	710	695	765	807
General government consumption expenditures	79	76	78	79	86	88	85	82	82	82
Gross fixed capital formation	148	158	171	139	209	246	223	180	192	210
1. Private construction	58	61	66	47	53	55	51	45	51	58
2. Public construction	16	21	29	25	34	36	31	30	27	28
3. Durable producers' equipment	73	76	76	66	121	154	140	105	113	124
Changes in selected stocks	-10	-8	-7	10	10	-4	-6	-13	9	14

Source: BCRA, p. 14.

Table 12: Gross National Income and Product Account, 1950–61 (CONADE)
(1960 prices; billion pesos)

Expenditures on GNP	1950	1951	1952	1953	1954	1955	1956	1957	1958	1959	1960	1961
A. Private consumption expenditures	549	573	544	536	587	654	659	683	722	664	678	753
1. Meat	63	62	57	58	60	65	72	74	75	58	63	71
2. Other rural goods	42	44	41	47	50	50	49	45	46	39	42	48
3. Manufactured foodstuffs, beverages, and tobacco	119	117	117	121	120	135	138	134	153	145	145	146
4. Textiles, clothing, leather, and rubber products	135	138	135	125	131	143	145	154	156	149	155	152
5. Wood and metal products, vehicles and appliances	36	43	33	33	41	48	50	68	72	61	73	87
6. Other manufactured products	50	51	45	45	53	60	66	71	77	73	77	83
7. Housing services	23	23	24	24	25	26	26	27	28	28	28	28
8. Transport, communications, electricity, gas, and water	24	25	25	25	27	29	30	32	33	33	35	40
9. Financial and other services	59	61	63	65	67	69	71	72	72	73	77	79
10. Discrepancies and changes in stock	−1	+9	+5	−8	+12	+29	+11	+7	+10	+7	−16	+20
B. Government current expenditure	68	69	69	68	72	75	80	79	80	80	86	87
C. Gross fixed capital formation	138	150	134	139	133	148	156	178	183	166	227	248
1. Public construction	23	27	23	25	23	20	16	21	29	25	33	36
2. Private construction	53	54	50	49	50	55	60	62	59	56	54	57
3. Producers' durable equipment and repairs	62	70	61	64	61	73	80	94	94	85	139	154
D. Change in selected stocks	−15	6	1	8	10	9	−12	−8	−2	9	6	−4
E,F. Exports less imports of goods and services	−3	−33	−25	17	3	−22	–	−6	−7	9	−12	−41
G. GDP	739	767	724	769	805	864	884	926	976	930	985	1,044
H. Terms of trade effect	12	12	−3	7	2	5	−9	−15	−11	−6	–	1
I. Gross domestic income	751	779	722	776	807	869	875	911	965	924	985	1,045
J. Net factor income from abroad	–	−4	−1	−1	−1	−2	−3	−2	−3	−4	−5	−7
K. Gross national income	750	775	721	775	806	868	873	909	961	920	981	1,037

Source: CONADE, pp. 178–79, 182–83, 188–89.

Table 13: Gross National Income and Product Account, 1935–50 (O.S.)
(1950 prices; billion pesos)

Expenditures on GNP	*1935*	*1936*	*1937*	*1938*	*1939*	*1940*	*1941*	*1942*	*1943*	*1944*	*1945*	*1946*	*1947*	*1948*	*1949*	*1950*
A. Private consumption expenditures	23.9	24.9	26.3	25.9	27.5	29.7	29.7	31.1	29.3	32.9	31.3	32.4	35.4	38.1	42.1	40.6
B. Government current expenditures	3.2	3.4	4.0	4.1	4.0	4.0	4.1	4.3	4.7	5.9	6.7	6.5	6.9	8.3	7.6	7.7
C. Gross fixed capital formation	7.0	7.5	10.2	10.9	9.3	8.3	7.9	7.4	7.3	8.4	8.4	10.9	16.5	17.0	14.6	14.3
1. Private construction	2.0	1.7	2.4	2.6	2.7	2.4	2.9	3.2	3.4	3.8	3.8	4.4	4.6	5.1	5.0	5.7
2. Public construction	1.6	2.1	2.5	2.9	2.4	2.1	1.9	1.7	1.6	2.3	2.1	2.0	1.9	3.1	4.0	3.8
3. Durable producers' equipment and repairs	3.4	3.7	5.3	5.5	4.2	3.8	3.1	2.5	2.3	2.3	2.5	4.5	10.0	8.9	5.6	4.8
D. Changes in selected stocks	0.8	0.2	−0.7	1.0	0.1	0.1	1.4	0.7	0.2	−0.3	−1.2	0.7	2.3	2.1	−0.7	−0.7
E,F. Exports less imports of goods and services	2.6	3.2	4.5	−0.5	1.8	0.8	1.8	2.2	4.0	4.1	3.8	4.7	2.2	0.5	−0.7	0.4
G. Gross domestic product	37.5	39.3	44.2	41.4	42.7	42.9	44.9	45.7	45.6	50.9	49.0	55.2	63.3	66.0	62.8	62.3
H. Net factor income from abroad	−2.4	−2.4	−2.4	−2.0	−2.4	−1.6	−1.6	−1.5	−1.1	−1.3	−1.0	−1.1	−0.6	−0.1	−0.1	–
I. GNP	35.2	36.9	41.8	39.4	40.3	41.3	43.3	44.2	44.5	49.5	48.0	54.1	62.7	65.9	62.8	62.2

Source: O.S., pp. 135, 136–37.

Table 14: Gross Domestic Capital Formation Account, 1950–65 (BCRA)
(1960 prices; billion pesos)

	1950	1951	1952	1953	1954	1955	1956	1957
A. Gross fixed capital formation	114	140	125	123	120	140	148	158
1. Government construction	24	26	23	26	23	20	16	21
2. Private construction	51	54	49	48	48	54	58	61
3. Transport equipment	4	14	10	10	6	9	12	21
(a) Automotive vehicles	2	5	5	4	2	6	8	18
(b) Other	2	9	5	6	4	3	4	3
4. Other new producers' durable equipment	31	41	36	33	35	48	51	46
(a) Machinery and equipment	27	36	32	29	31	43	47	41
(b) Tools	1	1	2	1	1	1	1	1
(c) Furniture and others	4	4	3	3	4	4	4	4
5. Repairs	5	5	7	7	8	8	9	9
B. Changes in selected stocks	–13	8	1	12	10	7	–10	–8
C. Gross domestic capital formation	101	148	126	135	130	146	137	151
Addendum: Sources of Durable Producers' Goods								
Domestically produced	20	23	25	26	30	39	43	47
1. Transport equipment	1	1	2	2	2	4	3	6
2. Machinery and others	15	17	16	17	20	26	31	32
3. Repairs	5	5	7	7	8	8	9	9
Imported	19	36	27	23	19	27	30	29
1. Transport equipment	3	13	8	8	4	5	9	16
2. Machinery and others	16	23	20	16	15	22	21	13

Table 14—*Continued*

	1958	1959	1960	1961	1962	1963	1964	1965
A. Gross fixed capital formation	171	139	209	246	223	180	192	210
1. Government construction	29	25	34	36	31	30	27	28
2. Private construction	66	47	53	55	51	45	51	58
3. Transport equipment	12	12	39	49	46	33	44	51
(a) Automotive vehicles	8	8	36	44	39	26	41	49
(b) Other	4	4	3	5	8	7	3	2
4. Other new producers' durable equipment	54	46	73	95	85	63	61	62
(a) Machinery and equipment	49	41	67	89	80	58	55	56
(b) Tools	1	1	1	2	1	1	1	1
(c) Furniture and others	4	4	4	4	4	4	5	5
5. Repairs	9	9	10	10	9	8	9	10
B. Changes in selected stocks	−7	10	10	−4	−6	−13	9	14
C. Gross domestic capital formation	163	149	218	241	216	167	201	224
Addendum: Sources of Durable Producers' Goods								
Domestically produced	51	51	81	98	82	67	87	100
1. Transport equipment	6	8	32	42	35	26	41	48
2. Machinery and others	35	34	39	46	39	33	37	41
3. Repairs	9	9	10	10	9	8	9	10
Imported	24	15	41	56	58	38	26	24
1. Transport equipment	5	4	7	7	12	8	3	3
2. Machinery and others	19	12	33	49	46	30	24	21

Source: BCRA, pp. 50–53.

Table 15: Gross Domestic Capital Formation Account, 1950–61 (CONADE)
(1960 prices; billion pesos)

	1950	1951	1952	1953	1954	1955	1956	1957	1958	1959	1960	1961
A. Gross fixed capital formation	138	150	134	139	133	148	156	178	183	166	227	248
1. Government construction	23	27	23	25	23	20	16	21	29	25	33	36
2. Private construction	53	54	50	49	50	55	60	62	59	56	54	57
3. Transport equipment	11	23	15	17	13	16	19	31	20	17	45	51
4. Other new producers' durable equipment	40	36	35	36	36	45	47	50	60	54	80	88
5. Repairs	10	11	11	11	12	13	13	14	14	13	14	15
B. Changes in selected stocks	−15	6	1	8	10	9	−12	−8	−2	9	6	−4
C. Gross domestic capital formation	123	157	135	146	143	157	144	170	181	175	234	244

Source: CONADE, pp. 188–89.

Table 16: Gross Domestic Capital Formation Account, 1935–50 (O.S.)
(1950 prices; billion pesos)

	1935	1936	1937	1938	1939	1940	1941	1942	1943	1944	1945	1946	1947	1948	1949	1950
A. Gross fixed capital formation	7.0	7.5	10.2	10.9	9.3	8.3	7.9	7.4	7.3	8.4	8.4	10.9	16.5	17.0	14.6	14.3
1. Government construction	1.6	2.1	2.5	2.9	2.4	2.1	1.9	1.7	1.6	2.3	2.1	2.0	1.9	3.1	4.0	3.8
2. Private construction	2.0	1.7	2.4	2.6	2.7	2.4	2.9	3.2	3.4	3.8	3.8	4.4	4.6	5.1	5.0	5.7
3. Transport and communications equipment	1.1	1.2	1.9	2.1	1.3	1.1	0.7	0.5	0.2	0.2	0.2	1.5	5.2	3.0	1.1	0.6
4. Machinery and engines	0.7	0.7	1.1	1.2	0.7	0.6	0.5	0.3	0.3	0.4	0.4	0.8	1.9	2.8	1.8	1.7
5. Furniture, tools, and others	1.0	1.1	1.3	1.2	1.2	1.1	0.9	0.6	0.7	0.7	0.8	1.1	1.8	1.8	1.5	1.3
6. Repairs	0.6	0.8	0.9	1.0	1.0	1.0	1.0	1.0	1.1	1.1	1.1	1.1	1.2	1.2	1.2	1.2
B. Changes in selected stocks	0.8	0.2	−0.7	1.0	0.1	0.1	1.4	0.7	0.2	−0.3	−1.2	0.7	2.3	2.1	−0.7	−0.7
C. Gross domestic capital formation	7.9	7.7	9.5	11.9	9.4	8.4	9.3	8.1	7.5	8.0	7.2	11.6	18.7	19.2	13.9	13.6

Source: O.S., pp. 137, 140–41.

Table 17: Industrial Origin of GDP at Factor Cost, 1935–65 (BCRA)
(1960 prices; billion pesos)

	1935	1936	1937	1938	1939	1940	1941	1942	1943	1944	1945	1946	1947	1948	1949	1950
Rural sector	121	112	119	112	123	119	134	135	127	146	124	130	141	135	123	124
Mining	2	2	2	3	3	3	4	4	4	4	4	3	4	3	4	4
Manufacturing	107	114	121	128	133	130	135	150	157	172	164	179	208	202	188	192
Construction	12	13	16	18	16	15	16	16	18	20	19	21	22	29	31	33
Electricity and other public services	3	3	3	3	3	4	4	4	4	4	4	5	5	5	6	6
Transport	22	22	24	24	25	26	27	28	30	30	30	35	39	43	43	44
Communications	4	4	5	5	5	5	5	5	5	6	6	6	7	8	8	9
Commerce	80	83	95	95	93	89	86	89	87	93	89	103	128	128	113	111
Banking, insurance, and ownership of dwellings	16	16	16	17	17	18	18	19	19	20	21	23	23	25	27	28
General government	21	23	24	25	26	27	27	29	30	33	38	40	46	50	51	53
Other services	29	30	30	31	32	33	33	35	37	38	40	41	42	45	48	49
Total	416	421	455	461	477	468	490	513	517	567	540	585	665	673	642	652

Statistical Appendix

416

Table 17—Continued

	1951	1952	1953	1954	1955	1956	1957	1958	1959	1960	1961	1962	1963	1964	1965
Rural sector	133	114	149	148	154	147	146	153	151	154	152	155	156	167	173
Mining	4	4	5	5	5	5	6	6	7	10	13	14	14	14	15
Manufacturing	196	191	191	204	227	238	257	282	260	284	312	298	284	327	365
Construction	34	31	31	30	30	30	35	41	31	37	39	36	33	33	37
Electricity and other public services	6	7	7	8	8	9	10	10	11	11	13	15	15	17	19
Transport	47	44	45	47	50	50	53	56	55	58	62	59	57	63	69
Communications	8	8	8	8	8	8	8	9	8	9	9	9	8	9	9
Commerce	116	104	106	112	123	128	138	148	130	150	170	168	153	160	176
Banking, insurance, and ownership of dwellings	29	30	30	31	32	33	34	36	36	37	38	39	40	40	42
General government	55	54	55	58	58	62	64	65	65	65	66	65	65	65	66
Other services	50	49	52	54	56	55	58	61	64	67	70	69	67	69	71
Total	678	635	680	706	754	767	809	867	817	882	944	927	893	966	1,040

Source: BCRA, p. 18.

Table 18: Industrial Origin of GDP at Factor Cost, 1935–61 (CONADE)
(1960 prices; billion pesos)

	1935	1936	1937	1938	1939	1940	1941	1942	1943	1944	1945	1946	1947	1948
Rural sector (agriculture and livestock)	139	127	132	118	132	139	155	151	131	162	130	134	146	146
Fisheries	0.4	0.4	0.4	0.5	0.5	0.5	0.6	0.5	0.6	0.5	0.4	0.5	0.5	0.6
Mining	2	3	3	3	3	4	4	4	4	4	4	4	4	4
Manufacturing	97	103	110	116	120	119	125	130	136	151	148	163	185	194
Construction	13	13	17	19	16	16	17	17	18	21	21	23	23	29
All services	174	179	196	199	200	200	203	205	209	220	228	253	293	311
Total	426	426	458	454	472	477	504	508	498	559	532	578	651	685

	1949	1950	1951	1952	1953	1954	1955	1956	1957	1958	1959	1960	1961
Rural sector (agriculture and livestock)	134	125	134	114	148	148	153	146	145	152	150	150	148
Fisheries	0.6	0.5	0.7	0.7	0.7	0.7	0.7	0.7	0.7	0.7	0.8	0.8	0.8
Mining	4	4	5	5	6	6	6	7	7	7	9	12	16
Manufacturing	195	201	202	200	200	217	243	257	275	296	274	290	312
Construction	31	33	35	31	31	30	31	30	35	37	34	36	39
All services	309	314	327	314	319	338	359	372	388	402	386	414	442
Total	674	678	704	665	705	739	793	811	851	895	854	904	958

Source: CONADE worksheets.

Table 19: Industrial Origin of GDP at Factor Cost, 1900–35 (ECLA)
(1950 prices; billion pesos)

	1900	1901	1902	1903	1904	1905	1906	1907	1908	1909	1910	1911
Agriculture	1.25	1.39	1.21	1.92	2.24	2.13	2.29	1.83	2.58	2.58	2.40	1.76
Livestock	1.43	1.93	1.81	1.84	1.71	1.94	1.88	1.76	1.92	1.76	1.77	2.00
Fisheries	0.02	0.02	0.02	0.02	0.02	0.03	0.03	0.03	0.03	0.03	0.03	0.04
Mining	0.02	0.02	0.02	0.02	0.02	0.03	0.02	0.03	0.03	0.04	0.05	0.05
Manufacturing	1.27	1.27	1.34	1.48	1.62	1.89	1.99	2.21	2.34	2.32	2.83	3.04
Construction	0.66	0.64	0.58	0.60	0.88	1.58	1.48	1.74	1.72	2.32	2.59	2.65
Commerce	1.72	1.74	1.72	2.01	2.41	2.69	3.05	3.23	3.36	3.53	3.86	4.04
Transport	0.34	0.35	0.35	0.41	0.44	0.53	0.63	0.67	0.77	0.80	0.87	0.94
Other public services	0.02	0.02	0.02	0.02	0.02	0.03	0.03	0.03	0.03	0.04	0.04	0.06
Ownership of dwellings	0.65	0.67	0.69	0.71	0.72	0.74	0.76	0.80	0.85	0.89	0.94	1.00
Financial services	0.14	0.14	0.15	0.17	0.18	0.20	0.22	0.24	0.25	0.26	0.28	0.31
Personal services	0.84	0.88	0.92	0.97	1.01	1.05	1.10	1.14	1.19	1.24	1.29	1.34
Government services	0.50	0.53	0.56	0.58	0.61	0.64	0.68	0.72	0.77	0.82	0.88	0.93
Communications	0.02	0.03	0.03	0.03	0.04	0.04	0.05	0.05	0.06	0.07	0.08	0.08
Total	8.87	9.62	9.43	10.77	11.92	13.50	14.18	14.48	15.90	16.69	17.90	18.22

Table 19—*Continued*

	1912	1913	1914	1915	1916	1917	1918	1919	1920	1921	1922	1923
Agriculture	3.34	3.22	3.12	3.69	2.91	1.73	3.29	3.40	3.94	3.64	3.28	3.46
Livestock	2.14	1.82	1.82	2.24	2.38	2.62	2.81	2.66	2.37	2.72	3.31	3.26
Fisheries	0.04	0.04	0.04	0.04	0.04	0.04	0.04	0.04	0.04	0.04	0.04	0.05
Mining	0.06	0.08	0.06	0.05	0.05	0.06	0.05	0.05	0.06	0.04	0.06	0.07
Manufacturing	2.88	3.05	2.79	2.50	2.56	2.54	3.02	3.15	3.27	3.44	3.82	4.47
Construction	1.96	1.84	1.06	0.60	0.50	0.33	0.35	0.38	0.73	0.91	1.17	1.78
Commerce	4.27	4.50	3.66	3.41	3.35	3.08	3.47	3.85	4.28	4.28	4.76	5.50
Transport	1.10	1.25	1.09	1.10	1.17	1.07	1.20	1.20	1.36	1.29	1.43	1.61
Other public services	0.07	0.09	0.10	0.11	0.12	0.12	0.13	0.14	0.15	0.16	0.16	0.17
Ownership of dwellings	1.07	1.11	1.16	1.18	1.19	1.20	1.21	1.22	1.23	1.25	1.27	1.30
Financial	0.33	0.35	0.31	0.28	0.29	0.29	0.33	0.41	0.40	0.44	0.52	0.57
Personal services	1.38	1.42	1.47	1.53	1.64	1.66	1.73	1.79	1.84	1.91	1.98	2.05
Government services	0.98	1.05	1.09	1.13	1.17	1.20	1.24	1.27	1.31	1.36	1.41	1.47
Communications	0.09	0.10	0.09	0.08	0.09	0.08	0.09	0.10	0.11	0.12	0.14	0.16
Total	19.71	19.91	17.85	17.95	17.43	16.01	18.95	19.65	21.08	21.62	23.35	25.92

Table 19—Continued

	1924	1925	1926	1927	1928	1929	1930	1931	1932	1933	1934	1935
Agriculture	4.29	3.60	4.65	4.86	5.07	5.11	4.16	4.50	4.81	4.72	5.03	6.00
Livestock	3.41	3.28	3.35	3.35	3.28	3.22	3.28	3.13	3.23	3.36	3.47	3.70
Fisheries	0.05	0.05	0.05	0.06	0.07	0.06	0.08	0.06	0.06	0.06	0.05	0.06
Mining	0.10	0.11	0.13	0.14	0.14	0.16	0.15	0.18	0.20	0.22	0.22	0.26
Manufacturing	4.71	5.11	5.02	5.33	5.95	6.24	6.18	5.48	5.15	5.84	6.63	6.81
Construction	1.81	1.59	1.47	2.05	2.25	2.76	2.66	1.56	1.12	1.31	1.83	1.68
Commerce	5.73	5.98	6.12	6.63	7.11	7.39	6.85	5.94	5.37	5.87	6.34	6.22
Transport	1.88	1.93	1.97	2.21	2.45	2.65	2.57	2.58	2.35	2.19	2.29	2.42
Other public services	0.18	0.19	0.20	0.21	0.22	0.23	0.24	0.26	0.28	0.29	0.31	0.32
Ownership of dwellings	1.35	1.40	1.44	1.48	1.52	1.57	1.63	1.68	1.72	1.74	1.77	1.80
Financial	0.57	0.60	0.62	0.62	0.66	0.69	0.73	0.72	0.66	0.65	0.66	0.67
Personal services	2.17	2.20	2.27	2.35	2.43	2.51	2.58	2.64	2.70	2.76	2.83	2.91
Government services	1.54	1.60	1.65	1.71	1.77	1.83	1.89	1.95	1.99	2.04	2.08	2.13
Communications	0.17	0.19	0.21	0.23	0.25	0.26	0.27	0.29	0.30	0.31	0.32	0.33
Total	27.94	27.82	29.16	31.23	33.17	34.70	33.26	30.96	29.93	31.33	33.81	35.30

Source: ECLA, p. 4.

Table 20: Population, 1869–1965
(Thousands)

Year	Total	Year	Total
1869 (I census)	1,737	1939	13,948
1895 (II census)	3,955	1940	14,169
1914 (III census)	7,885	1941	14,401
1915	8,072	1942	14,637
1916	8,226	1943	14,877
1917	8,374	1944	15,130
1918	8,517	1945	15,390
1919	8,672	1946	15,654
1920	8,861	1947	15,928
1921	9,092	1948	16,269
1922	9,368	1949	16,656
1923	9,707	1950	17,070
1924	10,054	1951	17,481
1925	10,358	1952	17,858
1926	10,652	1953	18,202
1927	10,965	1954	18,544
1928	11,282	1955	18,893
1929	11,592	1956	19,250
1930	11,896	1957	19,614
1931	12,167	1958	19,979
1932	12,402	1959	20,325
1933	12,623	1960	20,669
1934	12,834	1961	21,011
1935	13,044	1962	21,350
1936	13,260	1963	21,688
1937	13,490	1964	22,019
1938	13,725	1965	22,352

Note: Figures for 1869, 1895, and 1914 come from population censuses. For 1914–65, data refer to estimates of population at midyear. Population censuses were also taken during 1947 and 1960; the estimates shown adjust census figures. The following estimates for pre-1869 population have been made: 311,000 in 1797; 406,000 in 1809; 527,000 in 1819; 675,000 in 1837; 1,210,000 in 1860. See Dirección Nacional de Estadística y Censos (hereafter, DNEC), *Censo Nacional de 1960, Población: Resultados Provisionales* (Buenos Aires, 1961), p. 7.

Sources: Dirección Nacional de Estadística y Censos (hereafter, DNEC), *Informe Demográfico de la República Argentina, 1944–1954* (Buenos Aires, 1956), p. 14; ECLA, *Statistical Bulletin for Latin America* 3:5–6.

Table 21: Provincial Distribution of Population
According to Census Data (Unadjusted)
(Thousands)

	1869	1895	1914	1947	1960
Total	1,737	3,955	7,885	15,897	20,009
Federal capital	187	663	1,576	2,981	2,967
Buenos Aires province	308	922	2,067	4,274	6,735
(a) Greater Buenos Aires zone	–	–	458	1,741	3,796
(b) Rest of province	–	–	1,609	2,533	2,939
Catamarca	80	90	101	147	172
Córdoba	211	351	735	1,498	1,760
Corrientes	129	240	347	525	543
Chaco	–	10	46	431	535
Chubut	–	4	23	92	142
Entre Ríos	134	292	425	787	804
Formosa	–	5	19	114	178
Jujuy	40	50	78	167	240
La Pampa	–	26	101	169	158
La Rioja	49	70	80	111	128
Mendoza	65	116	278	588	826
Misiones	–	33	54	246	391
Neuquén	–	15	29	87	111
Río Negro	–	9	42	134	193
Salta	89	118	142	291	413
San Juan	60	84	119	261	352
San Luis	53	81	116	166	174
Santa Cruz	–	1	10	43	53
Santa Fe	89	397	900	1,703	1,866
Santiago del Estero	133	162	262	479	477
Tucumán	109	216	333	593	780
Tierra del Fuego, Malvinas, Islas del Sur Atlántico	–	1	3	8	10

Note: Data for each province are those of the population censuses. Estimates for the population in the province of Buenos Aires living in the area around the federal capital and forming the metropolitan area of Greater Buenos Aires were obtained by adding the populations of the following districts: Almirante Brown, Avellaneda, E. Echeverría, F. Varela, G.S. Martín, G. Sarmiento, La Matanza, Lanús, Lomas de Zamora, Merlo, Moreno, Morón, Quilmes, S. Fernando, S. Isidro, Tigre, Tres de Febrero, and Vicente López. The 1960 census was taken on September 30 for most of the country; some southern provinces had the census taken on November 4. No final results from the census are yet available; data shown are preliminary.

Source: DNEC, *Censo Nacional de 1960, Población*, p. 12.

Table 22: Population by Age and Sex, According to Censuses
(Thousands)

	1869	1895	1914	1947	1960
Total population	*1,737*	*3,955*	*7,885*	*15,894*	*19,971*
0–9 years	530	1,142	2,169	3,359	4,214
10–19 years	397	836	1,699	3,095	3,610
20–29 years	312	696	1,584	2,776	3,040
30–39 years	221	563	1,039	2,386	3,009
40–49 years	138	363	659	1,897	2,386
50–59 years	74	192	412	1,277	1,877
60–69 years	39	92	209	696	
70–79 years	16	34	79	264	} 1,786
80+ years	9	15	29	79	
Unknown	–	22	6	65	50
Total, males	*892*	*2,089*	*4,227*	*8,145*	*9,982*
0–9 years	269	581	1,099	1,700	2,139
10–19 years	201	423	872	1,561	1,792
20–29 years	160	364	878	1,391	1,502
30–39 years	118	319	597	1,215	1,499
40–49 years	73	210	379	1,021	1,193
50–59 years	39	110	235	702	963
60–69 years	19	48	112	367	
70–79 years	8	16	40	128	} 873
80+ years	4	6	12	32	
Unknown	–	12	4	27	20
Total, females	*845*	*1,866*	*3,658*	*7,749*	*9,989*
0–9 years	261	561	1,070	1,659	2,075
10–19 years	197	413	827	1,534	1,818
20–29 years	152	332	706	1,385	1,537
30–39 years	103	244	442	1,171	1,510
40–49 years	65	153	280	876	1,192
50–59 years	35	82	177	574	915
60–69 years	20	44	96	329	
70–79 years	8	18	39	136	} 913
80+ years	5	9	17	46	
Unknown	–	10	2	38	29

Note: The 1960 figures are preliminary.

Sources: DNEC, *Informe Demográfico de la República Argentina, 1944–1954,* p. 34; DNEC, *Censo Nacional 1960, Población,* "Características principales de la población obtenidas por muestreo" (Buenos Aires, Nov. 1963).

Table 23: Population Distribution by Size of Community, According to Census

	Total population for communities of given size (thousands)			
Communities, by population	*1869*	*1895*	*1914*	*1947*
More than 100,000	187	663	2,025	5,905
50,000 to 99,999	–	93	332	786
20,000 to 49,999	52	202	450	990
10,000 to 19,999	61	116	350	695
5,000 to 9,999	85	197	491	664
2,000 to 4,999	111	209	509	892
Less than 2,000	1,240	2,475	3,728	5,962

Source: DNEC, *Informe Demográfico de la República Argentina 1944–1954*, pp. 56–57.

Table 24: Overseas Immigration and Emigration
(Second and third class foreign passengers only)
(Thousands)

	Immigration	*Emigration*	*Net balance*
1857–60	20	9	11
1861–70	160	83	77
1871–80	261	176	85
1881–90	841	203	638
1891–1900	648	328	320
1901–10	1,764	644	1,120
1911–20	1,205	936	269
1921–25	708	255	452
1926–30	690	286	404
1931–35	331	204	127
1936–40	135	58	77
1941–45	9	6	3
1946–50	452	69	383
1951–55	362	161	201

Sources: Comité Nacional de Geografía, *Anuario Geográfico Argentino* (Buenos Aires, 1941), p. 186; DNEC, *Anuario Estadístico de la República Argentina, 1957* (Buenos Aires, 1959), p. 129.

Table 25: Foreigners Entering and Leaving the Country, All (Legal) Routes
(Thousands)

	Entering	Leaving	Net balance
1941–45	1,081	1,051	30
1946–50	1,969	1,488	481
1951–55	1,444	1,118	326
1956–60	2,373	2,135	238
1961–65	2,394	2,188	206

Note: It is generally believed that considerable unregistered net immigration from Chile, Bolivia, and Paraguay has occurred during the last 30 years. The net balance between Argentine citizens entering and leaving the country has been as follows in recent years:

$$1946\text{–}50 = \quad 24 \text{ thousands (net inflow)}$$
$$1951\text{–}55 = \quad 2 \text{ thousands (net inflow)}$$
$$1956\text{–}60 = \quad 1 \text{ thousand (net inflow)}$$
$$1961\text{–}65 = \; -86 \text{ thousands (net } outflow)$$

Source: As in Table 24, plus DNEC, *Boletín de Estadística*, several issues.

Table 26: Literacy and Primary Education of Population
(Thousands)

	1869	1895	1914	1947	1960
Population of 14 years and older					
Total	1,008	2,452	5,027	11,319	14,199
Males	514	1,318	2,776	5,829	7,057
Females	494	1,133	2,251	5,490	7,143
Illiterates of 14 years and older					
Total	780	1,306	1,806	1,542	1,221
Males	374	637	891	705	529
Females	406	669	916	836	692
Population of 6 through 13 years					
Total	413	794	1,486	2,477	–[a]
Males	219	410	755	1,254	–
Females	194	384	731	1,223	–
Population of 6 through 13 years attending school					
Total	83	247	714	1,821	–
Males	45	128	371	954	–
Females	38	119	342	868	–

[a] Dash indicates data not available.

Sources: DNEC, *Informe Demográfico de la República Argentina 1944–1954*, p. 52; *Censo Nacional 1960, Población* (as in Table 22).

Table 27: Educational Systems
(Thousands)

	1914	1939	1953	1960
Preprimary				
Teachers	–ª	–	3.1	4.4
Pupils	–	–	65	85
Primary				
Teachers	26.7	74.3	107.9	135.7
Pupils	863	1,977	2,560	2,948
Secondary				
Teachers	–	17.6	60.2	88.0
Pupils	–	135	650	995
Superior and university				
Teachers	–	1.7	5.0	9.4
Pupils	–	29	163	300

ª Dash indicates data not available.

Sources: Anuario Geográfico, pp. 498–509, and DNEC, *Boletín de Estadística* 3 (1963): 18–22.

Table 28: Demographic Indices, 1915–55
(Rates per 1,000 inhabitants)

	Birth rate	Death rate	Marriage rate
1915	35.1	15.5	5.8
1920	31.5	14.7	6.8
1925	30.7	13.3	6.8
1930	28.7	12.2	6.9
1935	24.7	12.5	6.6
1940	24.0	10.7	6.5
1945	25.2	10.3	8.0
1950	25.5	9.0	8.3
1955	24.1	8.8	7.4

Sources: DNEC, *Informe Demográfico de la República Argentina, 1944–1954*, p. 14, and DNEC, *Anuario Estadístico de la República Argentina, 1957*, p. 36.

Table 29: Infant Mortality
(Deaths under one year per 1,000 live births)

	All country	*Federal capital*
1911	148	105
1915	124	98
1920	127	88
1925	121	85
1930	100	70
1935	107	52
1940	87	48
1945	82	41
1950	68	37
1955	62	31

Sources: Anuario Geográfico, p. 173; DNEC, *Anuario Estadístico de la República Argentina, 1957*, pp. 69, 95.

Table 30: Distribution of Active Population by Main Economic Sectors, 1900–49 (ECLA)
(Yearly averages; thousands)

	1900–04	1905–09	1910–14	1915–19	1920–24	1925–29	1930–34	1935–39	1940–44	1945–49
Total active population	1,996	2,463	3,069	3,283	3,739	4,288	4,634	5,016	5,517	6,261
Rural sector	783	891	1,051	1,179	1,346	1,539	1,674	1,784	1,838	1,829
Manufacturing	396	488	633	700	780	890	973	1,111	1,310	1,498
Mining	4	5	7	6	7	10	13	18	27	31
Construction	90	196	218	72	146	202	176	162	188	298
Transport	92	122	170	189	200	218	231	237	248	327
Electricity and other public services	8	12	16	18	21	25	28	33	42	49
Communications	7	9	11	15	21	27	33	39	43	60
Commerce and finance	256	315	426	488	528	594	638	674	747	849
Personal services	288	330	408	457	504	562	615	659	704	766
Government services	72	94	129	159	186	221	253	299	370	554

Source: ECLA, p. 400.

Table 31: Distribution of Working Population by Main Economic Sectors
(Thousands)

	1947	1948	1949	1950	1951	1952	1953	1954	1955	1956	1957	1958	1959	1960	1961
Total working population	6,855	7,033	7,185	7,330	7,461	7,474	7,371	7,483	7,616	7,753	7,936	8,057	8,139	8,111	8,067
Rural sector (agriculture and livestock)	2,023	2,017	2,011	2,005	1,999	1,994	1,965	1,936	1,906	1,877	1,848	1,818	1,789	1,759	1,734
Fisheries	5	6	6	6	8	7	8	8	8	8	8	8	8	9	9
Mining	33	34	34	34	35	40	41	42	44	45	45	47	45	45	47
Manufacturing	1,683	1,714	1,752	1,777	1,799	1,822	1,742	1,804	1,902	2,003	2,078	2,147	2,214	2,134	2,066
Construction	319	403	451	478	510	467	456	431	431	413	456	484	450	468	496
Commerce	897	887	887	937	968	953	935	976	995	985	1,008	1,001	1,032	1,044	1,031
Transport and storage	326	351	373	331	380	405	395	400	409	421	446	454	460	462	452
Communications	52	58	61	53	65	68	69	70	71	73	76	79	80	82	84
Electricity and other public utilities	45	47	49	51	55	55	54	54	59	61	63	61	66	68	69
Banks, insurance, and finance	54	62	66	59	71	74	75	78	82	85	86	90	92	94	100
Ownership of dwellings	15	15	15	15	16	16	17	18	19	20	20	21	22	23	23
General government	602	621	646	668	680	677	702	725	733	778	797	816	823	832	844
Other services	802	818	835	856	876	896	920	941	959	985	1,006	1,032	1,059	1,092	1,112

Source: Unpublished CONADE worksheets.

Table 32: Money Wage Rates

	Index of industrial wage rates (1943 = 100)	*Index of industrial wage rates (1952 = 100)*	*Index of hourly wage rates according to collective contracts (1960 = 100)*
1939	89	–	–
1940	88	–	–
1941	91	–	–
1942	96	–	–
1943	100	–	–
1944	110	–	–
1945	126	–	–
1946	157	–	–
1947	223	–	–
1948	312	–	–
1949	429	–	–
1950	515	–	–
1951	654	–	–
1952	805	–	–
1953	902	–	–
1954	1,001	–	–
1955	1,112	–	–
1956	1,268	157	–
1957	1,695	211	–
1958	–	290	–
1959	–	493	–
1960	–	648	100
1961	–	807	125
1962	–	1,014	157
1963	–	–	196
1964	–	–	256
1965	–	–	346

Table 32—*Continued*

	Rural (*monthly*)	Foodstuffs manufacturing (*hourly*)	Cotton textile manufacturing (*hourly*)	Clothing manufacturing (*hourly*)	Construction (*hourly*)
			Unskilled workers (*in pesos*)		
1939	–	–	–	–	–
1940	–	–	–	–	–
1941	–	–	–	–	–
1942	–	–	–	–	–
1943	–	–	–	–	–
1944	–	–	–	–	–
1945	–	–	–	–	–
1946	–	–	–	–	–
1947	–	–	–	–	–
1948	–	1.65	1.95	1.63	2.06
1949	–	1.98	1.95	2.15	2.69
1950	206	2.48	2.26	2.55	2.81
1951	285	2.98	2.58	3.08	3.19
1952	399	3.66	3.85	3.56	4.22
1953	505	3.77	4.10	3.66	4.43
1954	555	4.50	4.83	4.28	5.01
1955	583	4.65	4.90	4.41	5.13
1956	687	6.18	6.44	5.94	7.30
1957	749	6.32	6.58	6.08	7.50
1958	1,186	9.44	14.39	8.76	10.92
1959	2,001	16.87	16.42	14.96	17.69
1960	2,213	22.00	17.94	17.38	19.69
1961	2,481	25.93	27.79	20.92	24.15
1962	–	–	–	–	–
1963	–	–	–	–	–
1964	–	–	–	–	–
1965	–	–	–	–	–

Table 32—*Continued*

	Foodstuffs manufacturing (*hourly*)	Skilled and semiskilled workers (*in pesos*) Cotton textiles manufacturing (*hourly*)	Clothing manufacturing (*hourly*)	Construction (*hourly*)
1939	–	–	–	–
1940	–	–	–	–
1941	–	–	–	–
1942	–	–	–	–
1943	–	–	–	–
1944	–	–	–	–
1945	–	–	–	–
1946	–	–	–	–
1947	–	–	–	–
1948	1.88	2.59	2.69	2.63
1949	2.17	2.59	3.42	3.38
1950	2.71	2.93	3.95	3.53
1951	3.21	3.28	4.43	4.00
1952	3.90	4.85	5.30	5.31
1953	4.00	5.17	5.47	5.57
1954	4.73	5.90	6.05	6.24
1955	4.88	5.97	6.17	6.38
1956	6.50	7.79	8.32	9.70
1957	6.65	7.96	8.52	10.00
1958	9.89	11.84	12.28	14.62
1959	17.38	18.63	20.96	24.00
1960	22.63	20.35	22.22	26.25
1961	26.96	28.12	28.86	32.98
1962	–	–	–	–
1963	–	–	–	–
1964	–	–	–	–
1965	–	–	–	–

Sources: The first two columns have been obtained by dividing the index of all money wages paid in industry by the index for industrial labor force (1939–43) or by the index of man hours worked in industry (1943–62). All of these indices have been published by DNEC in *Anuario Estadístico de la República Argentina, 1957,* pp. 286–94, and DNEC, *Boletín de Estadística,* several issues. The index presented in the third column is also published regularly in *Boletín de Estadística* for skilled and unskilled workers; that shown in the table is a simple average of the two. The rest of the table was obtained from unpublished CONADE worksheets; wage rates refer to those of collective agreements. Earlier data on wage rates may be found in *Anuario Geográfico Argentino,* pp. 548–60.

Table 33: Indices of Rural Output, 1900–35
(1950 = 100)

	Total agriculture (crop raising)	Cereals and linseed	Industrial crops	Fruits and vegetables	Total livestock	Slaughter			Wool	Milk
						Beef products	Sheep products	Pork products		
1900	29	64	9	16	29	21	75	9	62	21
1901	32	73	11	16	39	21	73	9	134	21
1902	28	61	9	16	37	20	76	9	117	22
1903	44	109	12	17	37	22	78	9	114	22
1904	51	134	12	17	35	20	76	9	101	23
1905	49	125	12	18	39	25	77	10	113	23
1906	52	136	12	18	38	22	72	10	118	25
1907	42	105	13	15	36	24	73	11	94	25
1908	59	153	15	20	39	24	91	12	105	26
1909	59	152	15	21	41	29	81	13	107	27
1910	55	135	17	21	42	32	89	15	92	29
1911	40	85	18	22	46	43	97	15	82	29
1912	76	195	20	28	49	44	81	13	101	32
1913	74	179	26	29	43	39	65	15	76	32
1914	71	165	29	32	43	39	70	19	73	31
1915	84	216	21	30	43	38	62	26	80	32
1916	66	155	19	33	46	40	78	31	83	33
1917	40	61	18	37	52	45	81	26	94	38
1918	75	173	22	39	56	56	81	25	75	46
1919	78	173	31	39	52	42	88	32	93	48

Table 33—Continued

| | Total agriculture (crop raising) | Cereals and linseed | Industrial crops | Fruits and vegetables | Total livestock | Slaughter | | | Wool | Milk |
						Beef products	Sheep products	Pork products		
1920	90	210	28	43	46	35	105	41	64	51
1921	83	186	30	44	54	37	115	42	102	54
1922	75	164	27	42	66	55	109	42	121	55
1923	79	176	31	41	71	75	87	36	79	61
1924	98	242	32	39	74	85	79	34	69	59
1925	82	175	42	41	71	82	82	36	63	56
1926	106	250	43	44	73	77	82	42	91	58
1927	111	265	37	48	73	76	92	49	86	55
1928	116	279	43	46	71	71	96	57	90	57
1929	117	282	44	46	70	69	103	62	82	56
1930	95	208	41	49	71	67	119	61	90	61
1931	103	299	45	54	66	59	111	63	84	63
1932	110	261	32	51	68	58	114	67	95	65
1933	108	247	45	48	71	62	120	82	91	64
1934	115	258	49	55	73	66	112	90	93	62
1935	137	326	49	59	75	71	116	88	88	62

Source: ECLA, pp. 8, 10.

Table 34: Indices of Rural Output, 1935–65
(1960 = 100)

	All rural output	All agriculture (crop raising)	Cereals and linseed	Fodder crops	Oilseeds	Industrial crops	Fruits and flowers	Vegetables	All livestock	Livestock slaughter	Wool	Milk	Other livestock	Rural construction	Hunting, fishing, and other
1935	79	82	157	78	22	45	26	26	78	78	85	61	98	60	37
1936	73	70	117	81	21	52	30	22	80	81	78	65	102	56	38
1937	77	76	137	84	22	48	33	19	82	84	82	67	100	59	41
1938	73	67	97	84	29	59	31	28	83	84	87	69	96	55	44
1939	80	79	134	84	29	58	27	29	85	85	90	74	98	61	45
1940	78	73	116	64	40	61	41	32	88	85	102	79	100	59	46
1941	88	86	153	76	55	52	45	33	93	89	110	86	115	67	49
1942	88	85	130	101	65	55	44	43	95	90	114	86	125	67	50
1943	82	72	84	101	46	69	60	37	100	96	117	88	130	63	52
1944	95	94	139	111	102	68	48	37	100	96	117	95	126	73	63
1945	81	69	72	112	94	58	46	36	100	96	117	93	120	62	61
1946	85	74	77	113	86	66	47	45	102	99	116	99	115	65	65
1947	92	85	106	126	69	70	45	42	105	105	104	98	98	70	66
1948	88	84	105	102	85	77	47	41	97	97	98	92	101	67	71
1949	80	71	75	91	94	72	51	39	95	95	96	94	102	61	68
1950	81	72	60	65	66	88	84	80	95	95	100	93	98	62	67
1951	86	80	81	63	91	85	73	84	95	94	90	96	89	94	82
1952	74	63	40	52	73	90	70	75	89	86	98	104	88	67	89
1953	97	96	109	86	68	97	90	94	98	96	101	112	94	87	97
1954	96	91	94	91	55	90	77	105	106	107	96	108	100	83	91
1955	100	95	95	92	48	106	92	102	110	113	87	112	98	89	87
1956	96	90	81	96	91	95	92	92	102	104	91	113	106	117	88
1957	95	92	99	84	99	83	91	95	101	103	94	106	94	87	95
1958	99	99	99	95	100	111	98	87	101	103	95	102	92	86	92
1959	98	97	105	90	68	106	99	83	104	106	100	99	101	72	89
1960	100	100	100	100	100	100	100	100	100	100	100	100	100	100	100
1961	99	99	81	110	84	109	111	114	99	99	100	100	96	101	106
1962	101	107	95	117	126	114	114	99	96	95	94	101	98	78	99
1963	101	105	88	108	86	131	116	103	99	100	95	102	95	65	98
1964	108	112	117	106	88	123	115	97	106	106	100	111	108	88	113
1965	113	117	123	91	119	120	115	128	109	108	104	116	113	94	117

Source: BCRA, p. 36.

Table 35: Output of Selected Rural Products, 1891–1965
(Thousand metric tons)

	Wheat	Corn	Linseed (flax)	Beef	All meat
1891	845	–	–	–	–
1892	980	–	–	–	–
1893	1,593	–	–	–	–
1894	2,238	–	–	–	–
1895	1,670	–	–	–	–
1896	1,263	–	–	–	–
1897	860	–	–	–	–
1898	1,453	–	–	–	–
1899	2,857	–	–	–	–
1900	2,767	1,413	225	–	–
1901	2,034	2,511	390	–	–
1902	1,534	2,134	365	–	–
1903	2,824	3,783	711	–	–
1904	3,529	4,450	938	–	–
1905	4,103	3,574	740	–	–
1906	3,672	4,951	592	–	–
1907	4,245	1,823	826	–	–
1908	5,239	3,456	1,101	–	–
1909	4,250	4,500	1,049	–	–
1910	3,566	4,450	717	–	–
1911	3,975	703	595	–	–
1912	4,523	7,515	572	–	–
1913	5,100	4,995	1,130	–	–
1914	2,850	6,684	938	941	1,118
1915	4,604	8,260	1,144	938	1,104
1916	4,600	4,093	895	1,023	1,226
1917	2,289	1,495	102	1,087	1,291
1918	6,391	4,335	498	1,316	1,519
1919	4,904	5,696	782	1,011	1,233
1920	5,905	6,571	1,267	841	1,113
1921	4,249	5,853	1,524	895	1,186
1922	5,199	4,475	916	1,283	1,571
1923	5,330	4,473	1,209	1,661	1,884
1924	6,744	7,030	1,473	1,922	2,117
1925	5,202	4,732	1,145	1,830	2,034
1926	5,202	8,170	1,908	1,661	1,868
1927	6,262	8,150	2,052	1,709	1,944
1928	7,683	7,915	2,100	1,533	1,775
1929	9,500	6,412	1,991	1,481	1,747
1930	4,425	7,128	1,270	1,495	1,788
1931	6,322	10,660	1,990	1,359	1,638
1932	5,979	7,603	2,262	1,375	1,653
1933	6,556	6,802	1,575	1,435	1,741
1934	7,787	6,526	1,590	1,512	1,812

Table 35—*Continued*

	Wheat	Corn	Linseed (flax)	Beef	All meat
1935	6,550	11,480	2,025	1,532	1,839
1936	3,850	10,051	1,510	1,583	1,909
1937	6,802	8,640	1,978	1,725	2,068
1938	5,650	4,424	1,550	1,690	2,022
1939	10,319	4,864	1,448	1,806	2,135
1940	3,558	10,375	1,080	1,690	2,011
1941	8,150	10,238	1,720	1,854	2,247
1942	6,487	9,034	1,600	1,725	2,234
1943	6,400	1,943	1,348	1,603	2,248
1944	6,800	8,730	1,573	1,619	2,371
1945	4,085	2,966	787	1,456	2,113
1946	3,907	3,574	964	1,682	2,207
1947	5,615	5,815	1,034	2,024	2,459
1948	6,500	5,200	901	1,958	2,345
1949	5,200	3,450	433	2,003	2,387
1950	5,144	836	676	2,044	2,372
1951	5,796	2,670	559	1,879	2,171
1952	2,100	2,040	313	1,788	2,117
1953	7,386	3,550	584	1,766	2,113
1954	6,200	4,450	410	1,815	2,176
1955	7,690	2,546	405	2,147	2,501
1956	5,250	3,870	238	2,476	2,856
1957	7,100	2,698	620	2,459	2,827
1958	5,810	4,806	630	2,541	2,893
1959	6,720	4,932	620	1,944	2,271
1960	5,837	4,108	825	1,883	2,242
1961	3,960	4,850	562	2,145	2,498
1962	5,725	5,220	818	2,216	2,536
1963	5,700	4,360	839	–	–
1964	8,940	5,350	771	–	–
1965	10,100	5,140	815	–	–

Note: Weight of beef and meat refers to "peso playa de faena."

Sources: Sociedad Rural Argentina, *Anuario de la Sociedad Rural Argentina*, no. 1 (Buenos Aires, 1928), pp. 140, 174, 197; *Revista de Economía Argentina* 37 (Dec. 1938): 357–58; *Anuario Geográfico*, p. 212; DNEC, *Anuario Estadístico de la Argentina, 1957*, and *Boletín de Estadística*, several issues; Junta Nacional de Carnes, *Estadísticas Básicas* (Buenos Aires, 1963), p. 6.

Table 36: Price Indices and Prices for Selected Rural Products, 1926–65

	Overall wholesale rural price index (1939 = 100)	Wholesale prices for cereals and linseed (1939 = 100)	Wholesale prices for meat (1939 = 100)	Wholesale prices for wool (1939 = 100)	Wheat (pesos per 100 kilos)	Corn (pesos per 100 kilos)	Linseed (pesos per 100 kilos)	Beef (pesos for 100 kilos at Liniers market)
1926	120	129	106	96	–	–	–	24
1927	117	121	107	97	–	–	–	24
1928	130	133	121	120	–	–	–	27
1929	123	130	118	99	–	–	–	27
1930	103	106	116	64	–	–	–	28
1931	76	72	96	53	–	–	–	25
1932	71	77	74	43	–	–	–	17
1933	68	70	70	53	–	–	–	16
1934	85	88	84	81	–	–	–	16
1935	86	87	90	72	–	–	–	20
1936	104	106	97	104	–	–	–	22
1937	126	131	99	138	–	–	–	22
1938	108	117	100	89	–	–	–	21
1939	100	100	100	100	7.0	6.0	14.3	23
1940	97	91	105	121	7.2	4.4	12.6	25
1941	95	81	115	129	6.7	3.0	9.1	28
1942	106	82	147	127	6.6	3.6	8.9	35
1943	115	97	145	108	6.7	6.0	9.6	35
1944	119	98	155	106	8.1	5.9	11.7	38
1945	139	131	156	115	9.9	7.8	14.0	38
1946	221	259	177	146	18.0	16.8	31.5	38
1947	220	224	216	159	17.0	10.4	30.0	48
1948	246	243	228	255	20.0	13.2	30.0	53

Table 36—*Continued*

	Overall wholesale rural price index (1939 = 100)	*Wholesale prices for cereals and linseed (1939 = 100)*	*Wholesale prices for meat (1939 = 100)*	*Wholesale prices for wool (1939 = 100)*	*Wheat (pesos per 100 kilos)*	*Corn (pesos per 100 kilos)*	*Linseed (pesos per 100 kilos)*	*Beef (pesos per 100 kilos at Liniers market)*
1949	280	271	260	291	23.0	15.2	30.0	62
1950	327	287	324	599	24.1	15.8	34.0	72
1951	498	406	532	1,169	30.7	26.7	42.7	115
1952	590	522	706	513	36.2	37.3	52.0	162
1953	712	669	823	626	50.0	43.8	65.0	194
1954	718	669	833	637	50.0	45.0	66.0	200
1955	757	693	836	766	51.2	45.0	78.9	200
1956	1,076	962	991	1,519	70.4	63.1	205.1	228
1957	1,350	1,188	1,111	1,979	77.1	102.6	214.7	252
1958	1,803	1,581	1,676	1,989	112.5	106.7	235.1	404
1959	4,511	3,477	5 460	5,489	327.7	272.0	637.3	1,406
1960	5,102	4,663	5,961	6,038	343.4	315.6	623.6	1,515
1961	5,397	5,507	5,654	5,738	412.4	377.1	804.5	1,378
1962	7,393	7,769	7,304	7,930	547.4	538.4	970.5	1,608
1963	9,990	10,253	9,959	13,665	703.9	715.1	1,184.5	–
1964	12,809	10,662	16,329	15,126	841.7	664.3	1,245.1	–
1965	14,031	11,350	20,049	14,737	776.8	881.4	1,325.0	–

Note: Dates refer to the year when the crops were harvested.

Sources: Anuario Geográfico, p. 369; BCRA, *Boletín Estadístico* (Sept. 1962), 5, no. 9, pp. 51–62; DNEC, *Boletín de Estadística,* several issues; Junta Nacional de Carnes, *Estadísticas Básicas,* p. 13; and data supplied by ECLA and the Dirección General de Economía Agropecuaria, Secretaría de Estado de Agricultura y Ganadería de la Nación.

Table 37: Area Planted with Selected Crops, 1900–65
(Thousand hectares)

	Wheat	Corn	Linseed (flax)	Oats	Barley	Rye	Rice	Sunflower
1900	3,250	1,009	355	23	49	1	2	–
1901	3,380	1,255	607	33	52	1	2	–
1902	3,296	1,406	783	33	52	2	3	–
1903	3,695	1,802	1,307	56	13	1	2	–
1904	4,320	2,107	1,488	48	31	3	4	–
1905	4,903	2,287	1,083	51	48	4	4	–
1906	5,675	2,717	1,023	72	50	4	4	–
1907	5,692	2,851	1,191	146	50	6	4	–
1908	5,760	2,719	1,391	386	94	9	8	–
1909	6,063	2,974	1,534	633	61	10	8	–
1910	5,837	3,005	1,456	575	60	11	8	–
1911	6,253	3,215	1,504	801	60	23	8	–
1912	6,897	3,422	1,630	1,031	68	30	3	–
1913	6,918	3,830	1,900	1,192	108	40	3	–
1914	6,574	4,152	1,834	1,249	169	92	4	–
1915	6,261	4,203	1,723	1,161	161	93	3	–
1916	6,645	4,018	1,619	1,038	175	86	7	–
1917	6,511	2,630	1,298	1,022	157	73	5	–
1918	7,234	3,527	1,309	1,295	244	102	7	–
1919	6,870	3,340	1,384	1,206	249	111	7	–
1920	7,045	3,312	1,766	931	271	83	7	–
1921	6,076	3,274	1,930	834	250	88	11	–
1922	5,763	2,972	1,575	852	251	98	11	–
1923	6,578	3,177	1,747	1,059	242	148	6	–
1924	6,952	3,435	2,182	1,112	277	164	4	–
1925	7,201	3,708	2,559	1,071	334	157	5	–
1926	7,769	4,297	2,509	1,293	364	203	5	–
1927	7,800	4,289	2,950	1,283	396	220	4	–
1928	8,373	4,346	2,855	1,279	480	362	4	–
1929	9,219	4,788	2,810	1,487	543	516	3	–
1930	8,286	5,647	2,870	1,511	587	522	4	–
1931	8,613	5,575	3,940	1,593	576	535	4	–
1932	6,999	5,855	3,497	1,404	582	558	6	–
1933	8,009	5,884	2,995	1,478	629	657	13	–
1934	7,957	6,514	2,774	1,443	721	716	19	–
1935	7,613	7,029	3,279	1,428	815	864	15	84
1936	5,750	7,630	2,660	1,195	785	708	15	124
1937	7,793	6,091	3,499	1,619	679	1,269	17	207
1938	8,384	6,066	2,864	1,608	693	1,199	22	319
1939	8,621	5,300	2,707	1,401	835	975	33	333
1940	7,217	7,200	3,075	1,395	859	929	33	506
1941	7,085	6,098	2,875	1,596	868	1,346	31	574
1942	7,300	5,000	2,730	1,424	798	1,077	34	750

Table 37—*Continued*

	Wheat	Corn	Linseed (flax)	Oats	Barley	Rye	Rice	Sunflower
1943	6,873	4,139	2,474	1,935	589	1,767	42	674
1944	6,811	4,412	2,284	2,147	718	1,825	56	1,573
1945	6,233	4,017	1,956	2,011	761	1,615	52	1,492
1946	5,762	3,951	1,865	1,708	1,043	1,504	49	1,639
1947	6,674	3,612	1,905	1,570	1,371	1,944	46	1,609
1948	5,450	3,319	1,573	1,323	1,049	1,766	51	1,533
1949	5,806	2,691	1,305	1,394	942	1,835	50	1,806
1950	5,692	2,156	1,078	1,230	803	1,863	48	1,491
1951	6,554	2,439	1,087	1,311	896	2,191	54	1,628
1952	4,791	2,532	641	1,189	872	1,997	62	1,604
1953	6,066	3,354	1,020	1,702	1,108	2,483	71	820
1954	6,354	3,268	732	1,500	1,085	2,445	71	571
1955	5,937	3,002	739	1,376	1,090	2,493	65	559
1956	5,210	2,888	675	1,450	1,251	2,580	61	1,397
1957	5,947	2,740	1,285	1,888	1,394	2,807	62	1,201
1958	5,311	2,860	1,447	1,919	1,372	2,862	66	1,648
1959	5,708	2,894	1,202	1,796	1,366	2,835	67	1,339
1960	4,792	3,062	1,228	1,627	1,315	2,895	62	1,250
1961	4,275	3,222	1,129	1,589	1,211	2,660	53	1,122
1962	4,952	3,300	1,307	1,409	1,214	2,646	59	1,351
1963	4,847	3,420	1,503	1,141	1,118	2,469	57	983
1964	6,276	3,778	1,409	1,382	1,074	2,163	58	873
1965	6,207	3,693	1,172	1,134	901	2,131	79	1,173

Note: Dates refer to the year when crops were harvested.

Sources: Revista de Economía Argentina (June 1945), p. 212; *Revista de la Bolsa de Cereales,* Número Estadístico (1962), p. 138; DNEC, *Boletín de Estadística,* several issues.

Table 38: Area Devoted to Main Groups of Cultivation, 1929–62
(Thousand hectares)

	Grains	*Oilseeds*	*Vegetables*	*Industrial crops*	*Fodder cultivations*	*Fruits*
1929	16,574	2,865	320	323	5,841	235
1930	16,580	2,918	334	352	5,755	242
1931	16,930	3,092	349	351	5,711	246
1932	15,455	3,555	344	385	5,686	251
1933	16,735	3,105	310	402	5,507	254
1934	17,440	2,920	318	470	5,725	257
1935	17,838	3,443	358	585	5,452	259
1936	16,151	2,882	344	699	5,555	261
1937	17,561	3,833	202	735	5,381	239
1938	18,160	3,305	210	783	5,475	249
1939	17,330	3,122	235	778	5,307	269
1940	17,815	3,670	328	767	5,498	283
1941	17,148	3,524	391	745	5,741	294
1942	15,755	3,554	416	743	6,110	306
1943	15,477	3,272	389	789	6,159	319
1944	16,066	4,017	390	902	5,872	333
1945	14,803	3,665	401	893	6,596	348
1946	14,226	3,685	402	894	6,635	367
1947	15,563	3,660	388	902	6,726	380
1948	13,352	3,228	405	911	6,685	400
1949	12,921	3,222	422	992	7,102	414
1950	11,984	2,669	425	961	7,192	428
1951	13,748	2,836	446	1,010	7,570	447
1952	12,020	2,406	402	1,093	7,636	466
1953	15,280	2,022	447	1,066	7,878	512
1954	14,926	1,493	463	1,089	8,536	527
1955	14,188	1,455	444	1,094	8,725	541
1956	13,706	2,276	430	1,139	8,563	555
1957	15,115	2,713	449	1,186	8,752	579
1958	14,808	3,343	433	1,284	9,107	593
1959	15,052	2,825	465	1,246	9,004	607
1960	14,096	2,678	474	1,157	9,120	615
1961	13,352	2,452	481	1,219	9,232	626
1962	13,656	2,946	398	1,150	9,477	638

Note: "Grains" include wheat, oats, barley, rye, birdseed, corn, and millet. "Oil-seeds" include linseed (flax), sunflower, and peanuts. "Fodder cultivations" include alfalfa, sorghum, and "pasto romano."

Source: Revista de la Bolsa de Cereales, Número Estadístico (1963), p. 70.

Table 39: Indices of Industrial Output, 1935–66 (BCRA)
(1960 = 100)

	All mining	All manufacturing	Foodstuffs and beverages	Tobacco	Textiles	Clothing
1935	18	38	–	–	–	–
1936	21	40	–	–	–	–
1937	25	42	85	54	32	65
1938	28	45	–	–	–	–
1939	32	47	90	59	47	73
1940	36	46	–	–	–	–
1941	37	48	90	60	43	72
1942	39	53	–	–	–	–
1943	38	55	101	65	74	73
1944	39	61	108	67	80	74
1945	37	58	94	72	83	82
1946	34	63	95	76	88	92
1947	36	73	104	82	89	105
1948	36	71	91	86	97	130
1949	37	66	92	92	95	113
1950	37	67	91	90	94	99
1951	43	69	85	92	96	103
1952	46	67	85	90	96	91
1953	49	67	84	92	92	94
1954	52	72	85	90	96	94
1955	54	80	95	97	103	101
1956	56	84	106	99	110	104
1957	59	90	104	101	106	105
1958	64	99	114	113	111	104
1959	73	91	100	108	92	92
1960	100	100	100	100	100	100
1961	130	110	105	112	112	102
1962	146	105	112	116	89	87
1963	146	100	115	114	87	80
1964	148	115	108	125	109	97
1965	152	128	114	127	125	106
1966	160	127	117	127	122	103

Table 39—*Continued*

	Wood products	*Paper and cardboard*	*Printing and publishing*	*Chemicals*	*Petroleum refining*	*Rubber products*
1935	–	–	–	–	–	–
1936	–	–	–	–	–	–
1937	56	33	73	26	29	28
1938	–	–	–	–	–	–
1939	49	44	80	30	33	28
1940	–	–	–	–	–	–
1941	50	53	81	39	35	30
1942	–	–	–	–	–	–
1943	67	59	54	49	34	14
1944	84	60	65	58	33	15
1945	80	60	68	49	32	13
1946	85	62	79	49	38	29
1947	82	66	80	59	40	47
1948	88	70	79	57	47	51
1949	81	68	69	52	47	48
1950	82	78	77	58	58	46
1951	87	82	86	60	61	61
1952	84	75	59	59	63	65
1953	99	66	51	62	66	63
1954	107	83	59	67	70	76
1955	107	114	66	74	74	85
1956	119	121	63	73	77	86
1957	124	126	86	84	91	89
1958	119	141	108	91	99	90
1959	107	121	86	94	93	80
1960	100	100	100	100	100	100
1961	115	125	115	105	109	127
1962	107	121	100	100	125	120
1963	95	116	99	105	125	91
1964	113	136	102	131	132	116
1965	126	154	117	149	149	139
1966	133	165	122	150	158	132

Table 39—*Continued*

	Leather products	Stone, glass, and ceramics	Metals, excluding machinery	Vehicles and machinery, excluding electrical	Electrical machinery and appliances	Others, including handicrafts
1935	–	–	–	–	–	–
1936	–	–	–	–	–	–
1937	38	41	33	17	6	47
1938	–	–	–	–	–	–
1939	50	47	33	17	9	49
1940	–	–	–	–	–	–
1941	57	52	31	14	10	52
1942	–	–	–	–	–	–
1943	71	65	25	27	7	59
1944	81	66	35	30	7	65
1945	83	68	33	31	7	63
1946	88	71	41	39	9	69
1947	75	80	45	76	14	82
1948	80	79	50	59	19	80
1949	74	80	50	37	19	81
1950	74	83	54	35	23	81
1951	84	86	57	35	25	84
1952	83	81	52	35	30	85
1953	88	78	53	36	32	83
1954	77	93	70	40	36	85
1955	86	92	85	47	43	89
1956	85	99	83	53	40	92
1957	99	105	94	59	60	98
1958	110	112	109	68	73	100
1959	111	101	97	65	80	101
1960	100	100	100	100	100	100
1961	83	117	111	121	116	100
1962	67	114	102	117	97	93
1963	65	100	103	100	81	89
1964	73	112	141	131	99	95
1965	75	129	157	150	117	102
1966	77	138	143	137	114	101

Sources: BCRA, pp. 38–41, and *Boletín Estadístico* (Feb. 1967), p. 48.

Table 40: Indices of Industrial Output, 1935–63 (CONADE)
(1960 = 100)

	All mining	All manufacturing	Foodstuffs and beverages	Tobacco	Textiles	Clothing
1935	19	34	–	–	–	–
1936	22	36	–	–	–	–
1937	24	38	64	49	33	56
1938	25	40	–	–	–	–
1939	28	41	70	54	36	58
1940	31	41	–	–	–	–
1941	33	43	71	55	41	56
1942	35	45	–	–	–	–
1943	36	47	80	59	52	56
1944	36	52	85	62	59	66
1945	35	51	79	65	64	70
1946	32	56	84	70	70	73
1947	34	64	93	76	77	79
1948	34	67	88	83	87	90
1949	35	67	91	90	89	89
1950	36	69	89	88	94	95
1951	41	70	82	93	96	96
1952	44	69	82	102	91	87
1953	47	69	84	103	83	85
1954	50	75	86	99	88	88
1955	52	84	98	104	98	99
1956	53	89	112	102	98	100
1957	56	95	109	101	102	105
1958	61	102	118	104	104	104
1959	71	95	102	103	95	96
1960	100	100	100	100	100	100
1961	132	108	99	103	101	100
1962	151	101	103	104	82	84
1963	144	95	108	103	75	70

Table 40—*Continued*

	Wood products	Paper and cardboard	Printing and publishing	Chem- icals	Petroleum refining	Rubber products	Leather products
1935	–	–	–	–	–	–	–
1936	–	–	–	–	–	–	–
1937	51	32	77	20	27	36	36
1938	–	–	–	–	–	–	–
1939	49	41	84	25	31	35	49
1940	–	–	–	–	–	–	–
1941	49	49	86	32	33	39	56
1942	–	–	–	–	–	–	–
1943	63	54	64	36	32	9	71
1944	87	54	75	40	31	8	80
1945	84	55	76	38	30	8	83
1946	90	58	90	39	36	31	88
1947	96	66	95	44	38	52	95
1948	100	71	103	47	45	53	97
1949	99	68	104	50	46	49	90
1950	98	74	101	53	57	46	87
1951	97	80	93	55	56	63	91
1952	95	69	64	56	61	67	94
1953	92	62	62	57	64	61	90
1954	95	79	72	66	68	74	87
1955	99	92	82	75	73	84	86
1956	96	101	91	79	75	83	91
1957	104	105	96	87	90	87	103
1958	101	118	100	94	99	89	113
1959	100	117	91	96	92	81	114
1960	100	100	100	100	100	100	100
1961	101	123	111	104	108	134	87
1962	89	120	96	98	123	131	78
1963	75	115	87	95	121	99	69

Table 40—*Continued*

	Stone, glass, and ceramics	Metals, excluding machinery	Vehicles and machinery, excluding electrical	Electrical machinery and appliances	Other manu- facturing	Handi- crafts
1935	–	–	–	–	–	54
1936	–	–	–	–	–	58
1937	38	26	13	6	37	61
1938	–	–	–	–	–	64
1939	43	26	13	8	40	67
1940	–	–	–	–	–	67
1941	47	25	13	9	42	69
1942	–	–	–	–	–	72
1943	56	20	16	7	45	75
1944	57	27	18	6	50	84
1945	60	26	19	6	49	82
1946	62	32	22	9	54	91
1947	73	39	33	12	62	97
1948	76	43	33	15	65	96
1949	78	45	31	17	66	95
1950	84	49	33	20	68	95
1951	84	55	34	25	68	98
1952	80	50	37	29	67	99
1953	80	53	40	37	68	94
1954	86	72	45	45	74	94
1955	94	86	51	56	83	98
1956	99	86	55	62	88	98
1957	108	98	65	81	94	103
1958	112	114	74	90	102	102
1959	99	96	73	89	94	105
1960	100	100	100	100	100	100
1961	112	119	120	120	108	94
1962	106	108	105	94	101	89
1963	92	108	88	79	96	89

Source: CONADE worksheets soon to be published as part of the joint CONADE/ ECLA Study of Income Distribution in Argentina.

Table 41: Indices of Industrial Output 1900–35 (ECLA)
(1950 = 100)

	All min-ing	All manu-facturing	Food-stuffs and beverages	To-bacco	Tex-tiles	Cloth-ing	Wood prod-ucts	Paper and card-board	Printing and publish-ing
1900	3	9	17	23	3	21	27	7	7
1901	3	9	18	15	3	23	28	7	7
1902	3	10	17	18	3	24	27	7	5
1903	4	11	18	32	3	28	27	12	5
1904	4	12	18	33	4	31	29	16	7
1905	4	14	19	22	4	34	61	14	10
1906	4	15	19	26	4	29	44	17	16
1907	5	16	22	32	4	33	56	18	17
1908	5	17	24	44	4	35	56	16	17
1909	7	17	23	37	4	36	56	13	22
1910	9	21	28	37	5	36	67	26	27
1911	9	22	34	32	5	35	66	24	29
1912	10	21	31	44	5	40	56	20	32
1913	13	22	31	43	7	45	57	32	34
1914	11	20	32	39	7	39	39	23	25
1915	9	18	28	60	8	48	31	15	20
1916	9	19	30	49	3	43	30	44	28
1917	10	19	33	42	11	38	27	23	28
1918	9	22	39	72	14	43	30	37	26
1919	9	23	39	51	13	51	34	30	42
1920	10	24	37	51	10	52	46	52	42
1921	8	25	42	40	12	49	49	54	45
1922	10	28	45	56	12	50	57	67	55
1923	13	33	53	69	11	56	72	54	68
1924	17	34	56	41	15	58	72	74	70
1925	19	37	63	53	12	60	69	42	89
1926	23	37	59	51	15	64	64	45	88
1927	24	39	60	52	13	70	70	45	92
1928	25	43	58	71	17	75	78	68	108
1929	28	46	59	70	13	75	88	98	108
1930	27	45	59	68	22	70	82	70	109
1931	33	40	55	71	18	66	66	69	88
1932	35	38	53	63	17	74	56	73	84
1933	38	43	57	61	26	77	55	95	89
1934	39	48	59	85	33	80	64	96	101
1935	47	50	–	–	–	–	–	–	–

Table 41—*Continued*

	Chemicals	*Petroleum refining*	*Rubber products*	*Leather products*	*Stone, glass, and ceramics*	*Metals, excluding machinery*	*Vehicles and machinery, excluding electrical*	*Electrical machinery and appliances*
1900	9	–	–	16	22	3	1	–
1901	10	–	–	16	19	2	1	–
1902	10	–	–	18	30	3	1	–
1903	11	–	–	19	29	3	1	–
1904	11	–	–	21	38	4	1	–
1905	13	–	–	24	40	5	1	–
1906	19	–	–	24	56	6	1	–
1907	15	–	–	24	67	6	1	–
1908	17	–	–	29	61	6	2	–
1909	21	–	–	31	50	7	2	–
1910	20	–	–	30	89	10	3	–
1911	24	–	–	34	89	11	2	–
1912	22	–	–	36	77	11	3	–
1913	29	–	–	38	66	12	4	–
1914	25	–	–	38	64	10	5	–
1915	28	–	–	45	24	7	5	–
1916	31	–	–	44	31	8	3	–
1917	24	–	–	43	25	8	4	–
1918	30	–	1	53	26	6	2	–
1919	30	–	1	55	26	9	6	–
1920	29	–	1	48	37	12	10	–
1921	29	–	1	48	47	10	10	–
1922	32	2	1	54	41	12	14	–
1923	43	3	1	64	56	16	10	–
1924	37	4	1	68	62	23	15	–
1925	43	4	1	76	70	26	20	–
1926	46	10	1	75	52	29	18	1
1927	47	14	2	75	58	37	25	1
1928	49	17	3	76	75	42	33	1
1929	55	26	4	66	83	43	37	1
1930	48	29	4	65	84	35	44	3
1931	46	33	16	73	73	24	22	6
1932	50	36	15	77	56	14	16	8
1933	57	35	21	82	62	27	19	10
1934	64	37	31	88	72	31	30	13
1935	–	–	–	–	–	–	–	–

Source: ECLA, p. 11. The notes to this table (ECLA, pp. 18–19) point out that data for 1900–35 were weighted using output weights for 1950. It is suggested that the index shown overestimates the level of output for earlier years. These indices were considered to be preliminary; they should be taken only as rough approximations, especially for pre-1920 years.

Table 42: Availability of Selected Industrial Products, 1925–65

	Oil (thousand m.³)		Cement (thousand metric tons)		Cotton textiles (thousand metric tons)		Total electricity output (million kwh)	Raw steel output (thousand metric tons)	Output of pig iron (thousand metric tons)
	Domestic output	Imports	Domestic output	Imports	Domestic output	Imports			
1925	952	90	133	311	—	—	—	—	—
1926	1,248	174	169	358	—	—	—	—	—
1027	1,372	228	201	400	—	—	—	—	—
1928	1,442	374	228	441	—	—	—	—	—
1929	1,493	574	343	444	—	—	—	—	—
1930	1,431	645	412	343	—	—	—	—	—
1931	1,861	422	588	207	—	—	—	—	—
1932	2,089	263	502	86	—	—	—	—	—
1933	2,177	183	487	43	9	43	—	—	—
1934	2,230	200	566	46	12	41	—	—	—
1935	2,273	480	722	27	16	45	2,146	—	—
1936	2,458	515	869	20	21	35	2,360	—	—
1937	2,600	669	1,010	99	26	40	2,578	—	—
1938	2,715	781	1,179	75	25	38	2,768	5	—
1939	2,959	801	1,135	20	29	25	2,955	18	—
1940	3,277	602	1,049	1	33	25	3,089	24	—
1941	3,500	583	1,160	—	38	19	3,173	45	—
1942	3,769	339	1,145	—	48	23	3,326	55	—
1943	3,948	158	959	—	54	12	3,480	70	—
1944	3,852	159	1,080	—	62	13	3,675	130	—
1945	3,638	168	1,088	2	62	10	3,575	130	3
1946	3,307	1,072	1,141	1	64	7	3,845	133	12
1947	3,473	1,374	1,353	—	66	28	4,190	125	16

Table 42—Continued

	Oil (thousand m.³)		Cement (thousand metric tons)		Cotton textiles (thousand metric tons)		Total electricity output (million kwh)	Raw steel output (thousand metric tons)	Output of pig iron (thousand metric tons)
	Domestic output	Imports	Domestic output	Imports	Domestic output	Imports			
1948	3,693	2,049	1,252	244	70	18	4,580	122	17
1949	3,591	1,871	1,446	359	70	19	4,978	125	19
1950	3,630	3,559	1,558	454	76	11	5,176	130	18
1951	3,890	3,432	1,543	449	92	10	5,502	132	19
1952	3,946	3,865	1,509	539	80	11	5,538	126	32
1953	4,531	3,890	1,659	—	74	2	5,843	174	36
1954	4,702	4,354	1,709	275	83	—	6,616	186	40
1955	4,850	4,621	1,869	220	92	2	7,205	218	35
1956	4,931	4,753	2,029	45	101	1	7,895	202	29
1957	5,398	6,698	2,340	31	98	1	8,668	221	34
1958	5,669	7,555	2,443	—	100	2	9,374	244	29
1959	7,087	5,944	2,344	7	88	1	9,544	214	32
1960	10,153	3,685	2,614	4	96	1	10,146	277	181
1961	13,431	2,082	2,876	3	95	1	10,958	444	393
1962	15,614	—	2,920	4	76	1	—	643	397
1963	15,434	—	2,495	—	—	—	—	895	424
1964	15,943	—	2,878	3	—	—	—	1,250	589
1965	15,625	—	—	—	—	—	—	1,346	663

Sources: Oficina de Estudios para la Colaboración Económica Internacional (hereafter, OECEI), *Importaciones, Industrialización, Desarrollo Económico en la Argentina* (Buenos Aires, April 1963), 1:172, 186–88; 2:314; Junta Nacional del Algodón, "La Industrialización de Fibra de Algodón en la República Argentina, Año 1962," mimeographed (Buenos Aires, Nov. 1963), Table 1; *Techint*, Boletín Informativo 130 (Sept.–Oct. 1962), pp. 12–44; DNEC, *Boletín de Estadística*, several issues.

Table 43: Output Indices for Electricity and Transport, 1935–65
(1960 = 100)

	Electricity	*Air transport*	*Sea transport*	Railroads	Trucks	*Land passenger transport, excluding railroads*
1935	21	4	48	60	23	37
1936	23	5	48	63	24	38
1937	25	7	61	64	27	40
1938	26	8	52	63	29	41
1939	28	7	55	66	30	42
1940	29	7	52	68	31	42
1941	30	9	53	73	34	44
1942	31	10	54	82	29	49
1943	33	12	59	89	28	54
1944	35	13	64	92	26	56
1945	34	15	61	91	26	59
1946	38	18	70	89	40	64
1947	41	29	88	90	47	76
1948	45	28	86	97	53	85
1949	47	22	75	98	56	89
1950	54	26	73	101	58	93
1951	58	30	79	105	62	97
1952	62	25	75	98	57	92
1953	66	32	76	97	62	92
1954	72	34	74	98	69	96
1955	78	37	84	100	78	95
1956	85	44	77	98	81	94
1957	89	52	91	95	90	98
1958	95	59	96	93	100	98
1959	96	65	95	103	88	99
1960	100	100	100	100	100	100
1961	108	113	108	93	113	109
1962	109	79	111	73	114	111
1963	114	85	114	70	105	117
1964	127	99	119	82	117	124
1965	140	103	130	85	131	128

Source: BCRA, pp. 45, 46.

Table 44: Implicit Price Deflators for GDP at Factor Cost, 1935–50 (O.S.)
(1950 = 100)

	Agri-culture, livestock, and fisheries	Min-ing	Manufac-turing	Construc-tion	Com-merce	Trans-port	Communi-cations	Other public services	Ownership of dwellings	Financial services	General govern-ment	Other services	Total gross domestic product at factor cost
1935	22	38	18	10	18	30	31	56	50	24	32	25	23
1936	25	34	19	11	18	32	32	54	50	23	32	26	25
1937	31	35	19	11	20	29	33	52	52	25	33	26	26
1938	29	33	20	12	19	29	33	52	57	26	34	26	26
1939	26	36	21	13	20	28	34	52	60	27	35	26	26
1940	25	34	21	14	22	27	35	52	60	27	35	26	26
1941	25	36	24	15	24	27	36	49	60	30	35	27	27
1942	28	39	30	17	29	31	38	47	61	32	35	28	31
1943	32	38	33	18	30	33	39	46	58	33	36	29	33
1944	31	38	36	19	35	37	38	47	48	33	36	31	34
1945	39	44	38	23	37	39	39	51	74	33	35	36	39
1946	58	48	47	32	46	41	49	63	76	34	44	43	48
1947	60	55	57	49	70	52	54	69	75	51	54	52	59
1948	69	68	68	66	81	67	69	76	75	65	71	63	71
1949	81	83	89	85	84	87	92	90	83	82	92	82	86
1950	100	100	100	100	100	100	100	100	100	100	100	100	100

Note: Implicit prices have been estimated by dividing value-added measured in 1950 prices by value-added in current prices.

Source: O.S., pp. 112–13, 132–33.

Table 45: Implicit Price Deflators for GDP at Factor Cost, 1950–64 (BCRA)
(1960 = 100)

	Agriculture, livestock, and fisheries	Mining	Manufacturing	Construction	Electricity and other public services	Transport	Communications	Commerce	Financial services	General government	Other services	Total gross domestic product at factor cost
1950	7.2	14.3	9.6	11.8	11.1	9.1	6.9	9.6	14.7	10.6	10.3	9.6
1951	10.7	15.8	12.7	14.7	11.9	11.9	10.0	13.9	18.7	13.5	14.6	13.0
1952	13.6	19.8	15.2	18.2	13.7	16.5	15.3	16.9	21.8	17.1	20.5	16.3
1953	15.7	19.4	16.6	18.7	14.7	17.8	17.0	16.2	24.4	20.0	21.2	17.5
1954	16.2	24.2	18.3	21.8	16.8	18.6	17.8	17.1	27.4	22.6	22.1	18.9
1955	17.1	26.1	21.1	23.7	19.3	19.5	20.3	19.2	30.9	25.4	23.7	20.9
1956	22.7	32.7	24.7	31.5	22.7	26.9	25.4	25.7	35.3	28.4	28.8	26.0
1957	29.2	39.7	29.1	34.2	21.9	33.7	24.9	29.9	43.0	31.0	34.6	30.9
1958	38.9	49.4	41.5	47.0	37.0	42.6	37.3	39.4	55.5	50.8	44.0	42.4
1959	91.4	9.26	81.6	88.8	66.9	80.5	85.2	90.9	75.1	80.1	89.1	85.2
1960	100.0	100.0	100.0	100.0	100.0	100.0	100.0	100.0	100.0	100.0	100.0	100.0
1961	98.3	108.1	111.3	121.6	121.5	110.0	127.1	102.3	122.3	140.1	109.5	110.5
1962	127.7	151.6	140.2	155.6	152.3	140.4	181.9	119.9	152.6	197.5	143.1	140.5
1963	176.0	185.4	174.8	193.0	201.9	198.1	262.9	152.1	177.4	223.4	180.0	178.8
1964	255.7	187.2	212.8	237.5	221.9	245.5	277.4	191.6	229.9	315.8	224.5	228.6

Source: BCRA, p. 57.

Table 46: Implicit Prices for Main Components of Total Absorption, 1935–50 (O.S.)
(1950 = 100)

	Private consumption	Public consumption	Total gross domestic capital formation	Construction	Producers' durable equipment	New transport equipment	Other new machinery and equipment	Repair of capital goods	Gross national product
1935	29	28	12	12	12	6	15	16	25
1936	29	28	14	13	13	6	15	17	25
1937	31	29	13	13	14	6	17	18	26
1938	31	30	16	14	14	7	18	18	27
1939	31	31	16	15	16	8	20	19	28
1940	30	32	18	16	19	11	24	20	28
1941	31	32	21	18	22	10	27	21	29
1942	34	34	22	21	26	11	36	24	32
1943	35	35	26	22	31	22	38	26	34
1944	36	35	24	23	34	28	40	29	34
1945	41	36	32	27	39	31	46	32	39
1946	52	45	37	34	37	20	48	40	47
1947	63	56	45	47	39	24	56	49	57
1948	68	69	62	66	56	36	66	57	66
1949	83	89	82	85	77	63	79	81	84
1950	100	100	100	100	100	100	100	100	100

Source: O.S., pp. 156–57; ECLA worksheets.

Table 47: Implicit Prices for Main Components of Total Absorption, 1950–64 (BCRA)
(1960 = 100)

	Private consumption	Public consumption	Total gross domestic capital formation	Construction	Producers' durable equipment	New transport equipment	Other new machinery and equipment	Repair of capital goods	Gross national product
1950	8.8	10.0	12.2	12.8	9.4	6.6	9.5	10.9	9.3
1951	12.3	13.1	13.8	15.8	10.9	7.7	11.5	14.9	12.7
1952	15.9	16.9	16.8	19.8	13.3	10.1	13.2	18.9	16.3
1953	17.1	19.6	18.2	20.8	14.7	12.0	14.3	20.1	17.3
1954	18.2	21.9	19.9	23.4	16.0	12.9	15.3	21.4	18.8
1955	20.0	24.4	21.0	25.7	17.1	19.3	15.4	24.1	20.7
1956	25.8	27.3	28.2	32.3	21.8	25.7	20.0	27.2	26.3
1957	30.5	30.7	35.5	35.2	33.7	38.8	31.2	34.1	31.3
1958	39.3	48.7	46.9	47.9	41.9	49.2	39.9	44.4	41.4
1959	82.3	81.1	90.5	87.9	93.3	92.3	96.0	80.6	83.6
1960	100.0	100.0	100.0	100.0	100.0	100.0	100.0	100.0	100.0
1961	108.8	132.4	109.7	119.9	104.3	104.7	102.9	114.8	111.5
1962	135.5	183.8	145.9	155.9	136.8	130.7	138.9	147.8	141.9
1963	175.8	213.9	176.3	194.4	161.8	156.0	162.5	178.6	178.8
1964	220.0	297.5	208.8	234.5	182.2	173.3	183.3	218.0	223.2

Source: BCRA, p. 57.

Table 48: Wholesale Price Indices, 1926–40
(1926 = 100)

	Overall level	Rural goods	Nonrural goods
1926	100	100	100
1927	98	98	97
1928	99	109	94
1929	96	103	95
1930	92	86	94
1931	89	64	94
1932	90	59	98
1933	86	57	93
1934	98	71	106
1935	97	72	104
1936	99	87	103
1937	113	105	114
1938	106	91	109
1939	108	84	115
1940	123	80	135

Source: Anuario Geográfico, p. 369.

Table 49: Wholesale Price Indices, 1939–65
(1939 = 100)

	Overall level	*Rural goods*	*Overall nonrural goods*	*Domestic nonrural goods*	*Imported goods*
1939	100	100	100	100	100
1940	107	97	112	109	123
1941	117	95	128	122	155
1942	147	106	168	151	234
1943	161	115	185	160	285
1944	175	119	204	172	330
1945	190	139	217	183	353
1946	220	221	220	195	320
1947	228	220	232	220	282
1948	263	246	273	260	324
1949	324	280	347	336	391
1950	390	327	422	415	452
1951	581	498	624	598	728
1952	762	590	852	827	949
1953	851	712	923	906	987
1954	877	719	957	944	973
1955	956	757	1,054	1,039	1,087
1956	1,204	1,076	1,279	1,221	1,771
1957	1,495	1,350	1,580	1,520	1,959
1958	1,958	1,798	2,057	1,986	2,402
1959	4,573	4,510	4,672	4,449	6,724
1960	5,292	5,102	5,457	5,213	7,514
1961	5,729	5,397	5,962	5,740	7,275
1962	7,468	7,393	7,619	7,318	9,668
1963	9,614	9,990	9,605	9,244	11,788
1964	12,131	12,809	12,032	11,643	13,421
1965	15,031	14,031	15,697	15,193	17,459

Source and method: Basic indices from BCRA, *Boletín Estadístico* (Sept. 1962), Year 5, no. 9, pp. 51–62; and from DNEC, *Boletín de Estadística*, several issues. Indices were linked together using overlapping years. The original index using 1939 as the base gave the following weights: Rural goods, 34.1%; Domestic nonrural goods, 52.7%; Imported goods, 13.2%. The index using 1953 as the base gave weights of 23.6%, 69.8%, and 6.7% to these categories, respectively.

Table 50: Cost of Living Index, Federal Capital, 1934–65

	Overall level	Food-stuffs	Clothing	General expendi-tures	Cleaning, fuel, and others	Rent	Electricity
1934	2.2	1.6	1.9	1.8	2.8	34.2	12.9
1935	2.3	1.8	1.9	1.8	3.0	34.2	12.9
1936	2.5	2.1	1.9	1.8	3.3	34.2	12.9
1937	2.6	2.2	2.0	1.8	3.3	35.8	11.1
1938	2.5	2.0	2.1	1.8	3.3	38.5	9.9
1939	2.6	2.1	2.2	1.8	3.3	39.6	9.9
1940	2.6	2.1	2.4	1.8	3.5	39.6	9.9
1941	2.7	2.2	2.5	1.8	3.5	39.6	9.9
1942	2.9	2.4	2.6	1.8	3.6	39.6	10.4
1943	2.9	2.4	2.6	2.1	4.0	37.6	11.1
1944	2.9	2.5	2.5	2.2	4.1	31.7	12.2
1945	3.5	2.9	2.9	2.9	4.6	44.2	12.4
1946	4.1	3.5	3.7	3.5	4.8	44.2	11.7
1947	4.6	4.0	4.6	3.8	5.4	44.2	11.7
1948	5.2	4.5	5.5	4.2	5.9	44.2	13.0
1949	6.9	5.9	7.8	5.9	7.5	44.8	15.6
1950	8.6	7.6	9.5	8.1	9.1	48.1	15.6
1951	11.8	10.3	13.9	11.5	11.6	48.1	15.9
1952	16.3	15.0	18.8	15.5	16.2	48.1	20.4
1953	17.0	15.4	20.2	16.0	17.1	48.1	22.7
1954	17.6	15.3	22.5	17.4	17.2	48.1	22.9
1955	19.8	17.0	25.8	20.1	19.1	48.1	23.6
1956	22.4	19.3	28.0	23.4	27.2	48.1	24.1
1957	28.0	25.8	31.5	28.9	34.5	48.1	27.5
1958	36.8	33.5	38.6	37.9	44.9	48.1	37.5
1959	78.7	82.8	68.7	73.8	118.1	48.1	115.0
1960	100.2	101.7	98.3	95.4	123.4	100.0	100.8
1961	113.7	111.0	121.6	113.0	132.5	105.0	104.7
1962	145.7	142.8	150.1	152.3	171.4	110.3	135.7
1963	180.7	175.5	187.6	203.9	198.2	115.8	184.0
1964	220.7	222.6	224.6	235.7	220.4	121.5	184.0
1965	283.8	284.8	289.1	310.9	285.1	127.6	267.4

Note: For 1914–33, data are available for the overall level only, as follows:

1914	2.1	1919	3.4	1924	3.0	1929	2.8
1915	2.3	1920	4.0	1925	2.9	1930	2.8
1916	2.5	1921	3.5	1926	2.8	1931	2.4
1917	2.9	1922	3.0	1927	2.8	1932	2.2
1918	3.6	1923	2.9	1928	2.8	1933	2.5

The indices shown for 1934–65 result from linking indices with base 1943 = 100 and 1960 = 100. As January 1963 was taken as the link-up date, the averages for 1960 are not always equal to 100 (see p. 36 of *Costo del Nivel de Vida,* cited below). The new index (1960 = 100) gives the following weights to the main groups: Foodstuffs, 59.2%; Clothing, 18.7%; General expenditures, 13.1%; Cleaning, fuel, and others, 3.9%; Rent, 3.0%; Electricity, 2.1%. "Rent" refers to dwellings subject to rent control; "General expenditures" include medical expenses, tobacco, educational expenditures, transport, toiletries, etc. Foodstuffs consumed by the "average family" represented 11,399 calories, or 7% above what is considered the minimum requirements, but deficits were registered in some food categories.

Sources: DNEC, *Costo del Nivel de Vida en la Capital Federal* (Buenos Aires, Feb. 1963), pp. 44–51, and *Boletín de Estadística,* several issues.

Table 51: Value of Merchandise Imports in Million Current Paper Pesos,
and Main Suppliers, 1910–53

	Total merchandise imports	Imports from Brazil	Imports from the United States	Imports from Germany	Imports from France	Imports from Italy	Imports from the United Kingdom
1910	862	22	119	150	82	78	268
1911	921	21	131	165	95	74	273
1912	1,016	25	156	169	99	86	313
1913	1,128	25	166	191	102	93	350
1914	733	25	99	108	60	67	249
1915	694	32	172	17	41	65	207
1916	832	46	243	1	57	82	235
1917	864	86	314	1	51	60	189
1918	1,138	112	385	1	59	45	284
1919	1,490	108	529	3	59	49	351
1920	2,125	115	705	101	125	94	497
1921	1,704	102	457	162	97	98	395
1922	1,567	111	347	211	80	90	367
1923	1,974	105	412	269	133	154	470
1924	1,883	85	415	236	125	161	440
1925	1,993	83	469	229	136	180	436
1926	1,869	96	461	212	138	168	361
1927	1,947	99	495	220	135	156	378
1928	1,902	73	441	222	136	169	373
1929	1,959	74	516	225	120	172	345
1930	1,680	69	371	198	101	157	333
1931	1,174	72	185	136	78	108	247
1932	836	53	113	77	47	89	180
1933	897	58	107	90	48	96	210
1934	1,110	63	146	97	53	86	292
1935	1,175	69	160	100	50	56	291
1936	1,117	61	161	103	49	46	263
1937	1,558	79	251	166	65	73	323
1938	1,461	75	255	151	69	89	293
1939	1,338	93	220	123	82	37	297
1940	1,499	113	450	10	41	32	325
1941	1,277	140	450	6	3	—	269
1942	1,274	226	397	7	—	—	231
1943	942	202	179	—	—	—	195
1944	1,007	344	152	—	—	—	80
1945	1,154	334	159	—	2	—	116
1946	2,332	338	665	—	31	58	308
1947	5,349	439	2,431	2	158	274	446
1948	6,190	521	2,287	13	130	549	775
1949	4,642	357	689	11	465	742	722
1950	4,821	460	787	106	693	348	569
1951	10,492	956	2,199	571	1,022	387	788
1952	8,361	881	1,537	687	553	247	509
1953	5,667	643	965	821	147	258	355

Sources: DNEC, *Comercio Exterior*, and *Anuario del Comercio Exterior*, several issues.

Table 52: Value of Merchandise Imports in Paper Pesos at 1950 Prices, by Major Categories (ECLA), 1900–53
(Million pesos)

	All merchandise imports	Nondurable consumer goods	Durable consumer goods	Fuels and lubricants	Metallic intermediate goods	Other intermediate goods	Construction and public works materials	Rural machinery and equipment	Industrial machinery and equipment	Transport and communications equipment	Other imports
1900	2,360	964	52	63	136	611	153	26	305	11	39
1901	2,452	1,001	53	75	202	628	179	23	235	16	39
1902	2,115	772	32	84	166	580	138	44	254	7	39
1903	2,743	937	48	88	230	777	153	51	323	18	118
1904	4,361	1,334	120	118	341	1,095	303	83	628	62	275
1905	4,137	1,299	123	119	313	1,002	353	77	538	235	79
1906	4,748	1,540	192	185	301	967	414	240	620	133	157
1907	4,624	1,347	158	185	288	1,004	463	205	620	236	118
1908	4,272	1,393	147	218	274	852	393	176	555	144	118
1909	4,941	1,612	207	181	345	1,175	461	156	585	141	79
1910	5,700	1,869	253	261	420	1,271	597	128	673	166	63
1911	6,186	1,943	309	290	424	1,461	694	101	797	130	37
1912	6,015	1,780	329	294	389	1,283	544	103	1,137	136	20
1913	6,611	2,070	383	318	417	1,335	745	181	942	193	27
1914	4,084	1,238	150	264	324	778	499	144	544	114	28
1915	3,102	1,090	91	202	192	821	237	148	275	15	31
1916	3,728	1,644	286	164	126	816	183	288	173	6	43
1917	3,250	1,497	232	92	98	707	126	273	172	4	48
1918	2,969	1,479	117	91	86	753	81	179	140	8	34
1919	3,677	1,535	198	132	159	991	133	253	243	10	23
1920	4,942	1,711	370	204	249	1,223	297	308	493	59	29
1921	4,686	1,493	304	208	224	1,007	376	179	814	64	18
1922	4,745	1,625	367	251	281	1,090	452	101	518	56	4
1923	6,189	2,089	626	290	358	1,403	493	129	727	71	4
1924	6,411	1,800	674	356	411	1,381	671	105	922	73	19
1925	7,435	2,135	896	338	450	1,484	784	106	997	193	52
1926	7,753	2,044	885	343	425	1,579	862	292	1,087	195	43
1927	8,312	1,962	809	411	468	1,683	879	562	1,156	366	15

Table 52—*Continued*

	All merchandise imports	Nondurable consumer goods	Durable consumer goods	Fuels and lubricants	Metallic intermediate goods	Other intermediate goods	Construction and public works materials	Rural machinery and equipment	Industrial machinery and equipment	Transport and communications equipment	Other imports
1928	8,711	2,324	879	409	529	1,770	821	569	1,083	312	15
1929	8,857	2,181	1,072	441	529	1,763	827	532	1,148	349	15
1930	7,379	1,960	676	433	454	1,537	739	371	1,007	185	17
1931	4,809	1,575	313	324	279	1,233	375	28	579	99	5
1932	3,735	1,444	156	273	226	1,116	198	14	254	50	4
1933	4,388	1,709	190	266	314	1,322	217	18	302	46	4
1934	4,615	1,586	146	302	341	1,405	283	25	319	205	3
1935	5,347	1,775	187	310	432	1,464	307	77	545	248	1
1936	5,448	1,596	314	325	406	1,461	356	57	683	248	3
1937	6,957	1,910	358	370	589	1,839	474	120	829	464	4
1938	6,558	1,805	381	371	415	1,670	388	165	827	534	2
1939	5,111	1,315	277	375	451	1,588	310	88	430	276	1
1940	4,257	1,082	139	297	452	1,453	226	51	330	224	2
1941	3,476	816	97	215	342	1,445	167	14	242	138	1
1942	3,006	972	76	117	222	1,230	108	14	177	89	1
1943	2,034	596	48	82	108	1,035	59	9	75	20	1
1944	2,008	636	49	78	113	996	57	16	55	7	3
1945	2,205	513	190	99	171	1,046	77	12	76	17	3
1946	4,307	548	772	330	453	1,390	182	54	309	266	2
1947	7,901	1,357	735	403	809	1,879	352	193	925	1,245	2
1948	8,147	983	722	586	818	2,004	528	258	1,394	852	2
1949	5,468	584	290	475	641	1,826	434	93	865	258	1
1950	4,821	434	202	593	656	1,559	391	167	652	168	3
1951	6,123	435	608	661	925	2,116	336	181	625	233	
1952	4,106	253	221	680	500	1,228	225	200	480	319	—
1953	3,590	266	109	654	301	1,137	113	187	403	421	—

Source: ECLA, p. 109.

Table 53: Value of Merchandise Imports in Paper Pesos at Current Prices, by Main Categories, 1928–53

	Total merchandise imports	Food-stuffs	Tobacco and its products	Beverages	Textiles and its manufactures	Chemical and pharma-ceutical products	Paper and cardboard and its products	Wood and its products	Iron and its products	Machinery and vehicles	Metals, excluding iron, and their products	Stone, earth, and ceramics	Fuels and lubricants	Rubber and its products	Other imports
1928	1,902	196	32	24	514	88	52	94	181	283	60	72	167	24	115
1929	1,959	208	32	24	465	92	48	107	171	342	69	72	188	31	110
1930	1,680	197	29	23	363	82	50	91	144	270	65	71	173	28	93
1931	1,174	136	33	16	307	74	43	60	81	114	42	48	137	17	67
1932	836	99	13	8	278	59	38	49	49	36	28	26	95	12	45
1933	897	109	19	8	315	65	31	51	65	39	35	24	82	11	44
1934	1,110	98	17	7	407	76	39	61	97	65	43	28	110	10	52
1935	1,175	103	12	8	383	80	38	72	118	98	47	33	114	9	60
1936	1,117	104	10	7	307	73	42	52	124	116	60	31	120	10	61
1937	1,558	142	11	9	359	89	64	80	234	196	80	41	147	18	89
1938	1,461	105	14	10	340	75	54	68	170	250	61	43	175	13	84
1939	1,338	93	16	10	281	95	56	82	171	150	69	38	183	18	77
1940	1,499	92	15	11	307	102	84	69	208	120	97	41	240	21	91
1941	1,277	76	19	7	228	113	69	86	146	109	95	42	185	28	74
1942	1,274	75	14	7	320	140	98	107	88	95	80	45	110	11	83
1943	942	67	18	7	223	107	90	99	57	37	44	41	90	6	56
1944	1,007	110	22	6	262	87	94	129	56	30	41	37	82	7	44
1945	1,154	105	22	8	230	127	103	122	93	51	76	45	97	14	61
1946	2,332	147	34	13	284	163	166	187	279	325	110	62	283	80	199
1947	5,349	196	36	23	853	318	230	295	662	1,350	275	115	397	152	448
1948	6,190	260	44	12	688	357	205	315	840	1,807	315	175	693	50	431
1949	4,642	148	28	7	866	201	200	309	756	999	177	139	490	24	297
1950	4,821	277	24	17	567	320	179	373	737	967	280	134	593	64	290
1951	10,492	490	25	28	1,064	857	425	884	1,605	1,922	681	302	1,095	242	874
1952	8,361	545	2	5	826	445	480	711	1,127	1,461	429	311	1,267	169	582
1953	5,667	534	1	4	516	381	60	400	498	1,479	294	92	987	106	316

Sources: DNEC, *Comercio Exterior*, several issues; and *Anuario Estadístico de la Argentina, 1957*, pp. 377–78.

Table 54: Value of Imports in Million Current Dollars Distributed by Major Geographical Areas, and Main Suppliers, 1954–65

	Total imports	America	Europe, excluding USSR	Asia, excluding USSR	Africa and Oceania	USSR	Brazil	United States of America
1954	979	420	381	143	4	31	115	128
1955	1,173	461	503	165	5	39	110	154
1956	1,128	528	435	134	4	27	85	230
1957	1,310	670	481	143	12	5	123	307
1958	1,233	544	550	102	17	19	128	203
1959	993	450	436	72	12	23	58	191
1960	1,249	568	571	76	19	14	63	327
1961	1,460	636	729	70	13	13	78	383
1962	1,357	601	632	106	9	9	63	396
1963	981	420	469	81	7	4	58	242
1964	1,077	506	479	84	4	4	101	255
1965	1,198	602	451	111	15	19	162	273

Table 54—Continued

	West Germany	France	Italy	United Kingdom	Venezuela	Japan	All Latin American Free Trade Zone countries	European Common Market countries	European Free Trade Zone countries
1954	77	47	33	72	49	48	189	209	116
1955	70	68	66	76	55	75	188	265	139
1956	107	38	56	53	74	71	137	266	120
1957	90	32	53	101	111	8	173	267	190
1958	115	35	59	102	102	18	174	314	185
1959	112	34	49	90	108	18	106	254	143
1960	151	60	86	113	91	28	107	349	170
1961	211	79	101	140	66	33	126	445	227
1962	185	69	121	119	48	64	103	413	190
1963	106	39	128	78	21	47	100	296	135
1964	107	50	113	81	29	23	–	–	–
1965	110	46	80	73	32	44	–	–	–

Sources: DNEC, *Comercio Exterior* and *Boletín de Estadística*, several issues.

Table 55: Value of Merchandise Imports in Current Million Dollars,
by Main Categories, 1951–65

	Total merchandise imports	Foodstuffs, beverages, and tobacco	Textiles	Chemicals and pharmaceuticals	Paper and cardboard	Wood and its products
1951	1,480	70	137	115	63	124
1952	1,179	79	106	58	67	95
1953	795	67	68	50	8	53
1954	979	101	63	89	14	90
1955	1,173	87	48	91	29	137
1956	1,128	80	26	78	27	82
1957	1,310	71	49	95	35	101
1958	1,233	83	36	77	34	95
1959	993	35	40	72	25	55
1960	1,249	40	39	62	30	47
1961	1,460	47	34	90	46	72
1962	1,357	49	48	81	33	49
1963	981	38	35	77	32	46
1964	1,077	57	51	115	38	68
1965	1,198	70	52	135	50	88

	Stone, earth, and ceramics	Iron and its products	Machinery	Nonferrous metals and their products	Fuels and lubricants	Rubber and its products	Other imports
1951	40	220	218	96	220	32	145
1952	39	148	175	55	248	18	91
1953	12	64	185	39	194	14	41
1954	14	151	172	52	181	12	40
1955	21	186	238	78	203	29	26
1956	9	161	310	65	251	17	22
1957	13	162	335	79	318	27	25
1958	11	217	324	57	251	24	24
1959	8	194	260	51	211	21	21
1960	10	204	534	59	156	43	25
1961	14	216	661	81	130	37	32
1962	13	145	731	60	92	26	30
1963	11	101	481	56	57	20	23
1964	16	135	339	92	84	39	45
1965	20	190	277	109	115	41	52

Note: Several observers have remarked that after 1959 the amount of unregistered imports (smuggling) seems to have risen.

Sources: DNEC, *Comercio Exterior* and *Boletín de Estadística*, several issues. Detailed explanation of the methodology used may be found in *Comercio Exterior*, Informe C. 48 (April 1958).

Table 56: Quantum Indices of Merchandise Imports, by Main Categories, 1951–65
(1956 = 100)

	All merchandise imports	*Foodstuffs, beverages, and tobacco*	*Textiles*	*Chemicals and pharmaceuticals*	*Paper and cardboard*	*Wood and its products*
1951	118	83	336	115	188	139
1952	86	93	227	54	152	86
1953	68	72	188	58	31	67
1954	92	86	221	100	55	115
1955	109	90	182	112	111	152
1956	100	100	100	100	100	100
1957	113	87	190	124	136	131
1958	118	112	160	110	146	126
1959	102	65	186	108	115	86
1960	125	88	169	84	136	79
1961	150	108	150	116	204	119
1962	137	112	190	110	141	81
1963	102	85	129	109	139	76
1964	111	97	187	152	160	102
1965	122	120	188	170	212	124

	Iron and its products	*Machinery*	*Nonferrous metals and their products*	*Stone, earth, and ceramics*	*Fuels and lubricants*	*Rubber and its products*
1951	110	98	136	418	76	114
1952	66	74	79	337	79	85
1953	36	75	64	132	72	99
1954	113	75	102	167	77	106
1955	137	89	140	241	86	152
1956	100	100	100	100	100	100
1957	95	115	144	141	106	168
1958	150	106	133	121	107	168
1959	143	87	108	98	102	137
1960	144	184	122	123	79	274
1961	163	232	174	167	64	258
1962	109	260	127	146	46	182
1963	76	173	118	174	30	148
1964	95	130	176	248	44	287
1965	141	105	173	272	59	318

Sources: As in Table 55.

Table 57: Indices of Dollar Unit Values of Merchandise Imports
by Main Categories, 1951–65
(1956 = 100)

	All merchandise imports	*Foodstuffs, beverages, and tobacco*	*Textiles*	*Chemicals and pharmaceuticals*	*Paper and cardboard*	*Wood and its products*
1951	111	105	159	125	124	108
1952	121	107	183	130	162	134
1953	104	116	142	107	94	96
1954	95	146	111	108	94	95
1955	96	115	104	105	94	109
1956	100	100	100	100	100	100
1957	103	101	101	97	95	93
1958	92	93	89	91	86	91
1959	86	67	83	86	81	78
1960	89	57	89	93	82	71
1961	86	54	89	93	82	74
1962	88	54	98	89	85	73
1963	85	56	107	88	85	73
1964	86	73	107	96	86	80
1965	87	73	108	101	86	86

	Iron and its products	*Machinery*	*Nonferrous metals and their products*	*Stone, earth, and ceramics*	*Fuels and lubricants*	*Rubber and its products*
1951	124	85	109	105	115	164
1952	138	90	108	127	126	123
1953	112	94	93	100	107	79
1954	83	87	79	96	93	67
1955	84	92	86	98	95	109
1956	100	100	100	100	100	100
1957	106	103	85	103	120	93
1958	89	106	66	96	93	82
1959	84	103	73	90	82	90
1960	88	100	75	90	79	90
1961	82	97	71	92	82	83
1962	82	97	73	99	80	83
1963	83	93	73	68	77	78
1964	88	90	80	72	76	78
1965	83	90	97	82	78	73

Sources: As in Table 55.

Table 58: Merchandise Imports, in Dollars at 1955 Prices,
by Main Categories, 1948–64

	All merchandise imports	*Nondurable consumer goods*	*Durable consumer goods*	*Fuels and lubricants*	*Metallic intermediate products*
1948	1,906	144	144	191	177
1949	1,325	90	60	152	144
1950	1,203	69	47	176	157
1951	1,455	80	104	201	192
1952	1,100	55	56	201	109
1953	868	48	31	181	65
1954	1,006	58	22	191	160
1955	1,173	73	34	207	209
1956	1,123	74	52	250	158
1957	1,374	56	69	262	180
1958	1,309	75	64	263	243
1959	1,105	52	38	244	181
1960	1,392	79	92	189	190
1961	1,669	114	100	157	262
1962	1,521	97	61	116	162
1963	1,163	82	38	79	96
1964	1,274	80	49	109	149

	Other raw materials and intermediate products	*Construction materials*	*Rural machinery and equipment*	*Industrial machinery and equipment*	*Machinery and equipment for transport and communications*
1948	471	151	68	333	217
1949	413	125	30	214	91
1950	371	100	43	177	58
1951	461	81	42	195	90
1952	310	62	46	140	116
1953	246	34	46	98	116
1954	314	54	22	114	68
1955	376	49	43	111	66
1956	303	20	58	108	84
1957	419	20	33	93	137
1958	393	19	44	129	75
1959	325	51	34	114	62
1960	358	55	63	241	115
1961	473	46	46	262	193
1962	407	54	37	322	251
1963	383	62	16	232	161
1964	503	40	24	157	149

Sources: ECLA, *Statistical Bulletin for Latin America*, vol. 3, no. 1, pp. 110–18, and unpublished ECLA worksheets for 1948–54.

Table 59: Value of Imports, in Current Million Dollars, According to the Standard
International Trade Classification, 1955–62

	1955	1956	1957	1958	1959	1960	1961	1962
Foodstuffs	75	60	72	83	35	39	45	44
Beverages and tobacco	1	1	2	3	2	3	4	9
Nonedible raw materials	182	116	147	129	94	92	126	96
Fuels and lubricants	203	251	318	251	211	156	130	92
Animal and vegetable fats and oils	13	23	1	1	1	1	1	1
Chemical products	93	80	100	81	75	66	92	84
Manufactured articles	339	266	309	339	295	326	356	259
Transport machinery and equipment	249	319	342	332	271	548	676	747
Other manufactured goods	17	13	20	13	9	17	30	24
Other imports	1	–	–	–	–	1	1	1
Total imports	1,173	1,128	1,310	1,233	993	1,249	1,460	1,357

Source: DNEC, *Boletín de Estadística*, several issues.

Table 60: Quantum Indices of Merchandise Imports According to Categories Used in Industrial Censuses, 1935-61
(1935 = 100)

	Foodstuffs and beverages	Tobacco	Textiles	Clothing	Wood products	Paper and cardboard	Printing and publishing	Chemicals	Petroleum refining	Rubber products
1935	100	100	100	100	100	100	100	100	100	100
1936	116	85	91	90	85	110	91	112	95	107
1937	140	100	108	97	114	135	99	143	109	152
1938	116	113	106	78	98	109	117	138	128	123
1939	102	108	78	76	108	116	103	78	117	137
1940	87	97	71	75	68	107	80	69	119	128
1941	74	115	50	74	72	97	59	61	108	140
1942	55	90	56	65	68	102	75	58	56	43
1943	48	101	31	40	55	80	71	48	26	22
1944	82	101	34	31	63	87	72	30	20	19
1945	63	90	25	45	39	96	74	45	31	63
1946	69	105	26	57	78	147	76	65	176	481
1947	75	100	64	99	107	164	84	96	230	783
1948	94	110	54	158	112	132	55	91	293	188
1949	59	76	49	212	108	142	24	68	253	125
1950	50	41	34	80	102	133	18	60	219	218
1951	54	27	34	25	122	150	19	112	244	281
1952	70	2	23	15	69	116	13	50	273	218
1953	60	1	23	6	62	28	5	45	227	260
1954	61	1	25	16	84	87	8	81	225	268
1955	70	3	18	73	113	134	6	108	264	395
1956	83	1	11	6	77	98	46	88	365	304
1957	62	1	21	20	102	123	88	120	290	475
1958	88	4	18	11	102	120	107	91	241	454
1959	50	4	18	3	60	95	95	95	272	471
1960	70	19	18	11	105	95	46	99	221	582
1961	72	5	12	23	87	155	65	164	227	911

Table 60—*Continued*

	Leather products	Stone, earth, and ceramics	Metals, excluding machinery	Vehicles and machinery, excluding electrical	Electrical machinery and appliances	Other manufactured products	Solid mineral fuels	Metallic minerals	Raw oil	All merchandise imports
1935	100	100	100	100	100	100	100	100	100	100
1936	108	103	106	119	129	81	105	99	107	102
1937	147	143	144	194	173	123	113	45	139	133
1938	132	140	109	231	169	119	102	80	163	127
1939	115	99	103	127	136	99	107	57	167	99
1940	83	84	93	108	103	70	74	71	125	84
1941	62	66	63	62	89	63	39	966	122	65
1942	82	59	40	42	61	55	21	1,341	71	54
1943	57	46	23	11	27	37	23	1,174	33	35
1944	43	37	19	8	12	32	22	1,315	33	35
1945	45	36	30	14	41	36	30	1,177	35	36
1946	90	57	75	106	98	99	40	1,071	223	73
1947	138	94	175	395	229	149	45	701	286	147
1948	41	146	164	430	304	147	81	746	427	151
1949	41	98	119	217	154	73	50	746	390	104
1950	5	105	120	174	157	51	52	1,306	479	92
1951	37	143	155	243	222	85	79	1,769	691	120
1952	33	135	82	190	164	41	64	562	739	87
1953	2	17	52	183	92	38	44	226	883	72
1954	2	62	122	157	74	71	56	363	894	90
1955	26	76	148	179	156	87	48	392	911	107
1956	6	28	112	227	143	67	58	670	1,083	102
1957	26	34	146	260	110	87	50	505	1,509	121
1958	17	26	163	242	141	92	55	987	1,633	121
1959	4	22	153	269	52	93	51	2,238	1,340	112
1960	13	29	157	464	147	84	54	4,670	813	133
1961	33	51	181	477	212	127	46	3,835	442	145

Source: OECEI, *Importaciones*, 2:308–09.

Table 61: Quantities Exported of Major Commodities, 1875–1939
(Annual averages; thousand metric tons)

	Chilled beef	Frozen beef	Frozen lamb and mutton	Preserved meat	Other meat	Hides (bovine cattle)	Hides (sheep)	Other hides	Wool	Wheat	Corn	Linseed (flax)	Oats, barley, and rye	Wheat flour	Quebracho extract	Quebracho
1875–79	—	—	—	—	34	38	27	5	90	6	13	—	—	1	—	—
1880–84	—	—	—	—	23	33	25	6	109	34	56	18	1	2	—	—
1885–89	—	—	11	—	33	46	32	7	129	111	277	51	1	6	—	10
1890–94	—	1	26	3	44	65	29	7	139	762	266	53	2	23	1	46
1895–99	—	5	51	2	37	55	38	7	211	801	910	209	10	48	10	148
1900–04	1	65	73	3	20	54	40	6	176	1,493	1,518	475	20	68	10	227
1905–09	25	166	72	15	23	66	29	5	169	2,789	2,036	780	224	126	38	263
1910–14	14	304	67	100	26	94	26	5	137	2,118	3,194	679	632	111	71	347
1915–19	227	403	47	47	25	97	17	9	129	2,405	2,250	602	551	175	112	115
1920–24	402	270	74	66	43	128	24	5	146	3,724	3,505	1,150	577	123	135	94
1925–29	354	201	80	56	7	156	20	5	136	4,233	5,521	1,618	772	151	194	134
1930–34	354	56	49	56	78	123	21	4	135	3,603	6,397	1,569	990	91	190	98
1935–39	350	75	51	75	67	140	18	6	139	3,208	6,071	1,503	751	89	183	83

Source: Anuario Geográfico, p. 380.

Table 62: Value of Merchandise Exports in Million Current Paper Pesos, According to Main Destinations, 1910–53

	Total merchandise exports	"On orders"a	United Kingdom	United States of America	Germany	France	Belgium	Italy	Netherlands	Brazil
1910	884	236	192	60	107	89	72	25	10	41
1911	778	83	220	58	103	95	85	33	15	43
1912	1,140	261	288	77	128	85	88	50	38	54
1913	1,180	268	294	56	141	92	80	49	55	59
1914	916	188	268	112	81	52	46	22	29	41
1915	1,323	325	391	213	–	96	–	97	45	52
1916	1,302	172	383	272	–	155	–	65	66	59
1917	1,250	70	366	367	–	165	–	66	12	52
1918	1,822	126	695	375	–	257	–	91	2	76
1919	2,343	282	669	430	21	260	135	94	127	85
1920	2,373	605	636	350	54	161	120	78	81	51
1921	1,525	385	466	135	115	71	84	51	57	65
1922	1,536	453	341	181	120	90	105	54	47	61
1923	1,753	426	429	204	145	132	106	65	70	57
1924	2,299	615	532	163	230	156	162	91	124	73
1925	1,973	505	472	163	202	145	127	79	76	76
1926	1,800	410	452	164	186	104	136	77	66	68
1927	2,294	27	649	190	377	155	227	101	253	85
1928	2,397	7	687	198	329	141	220	209	266	92
1929	2,168	4	697	212	217	154	232	124	209	85
1930	1,396	3	510	135	123	93	129	61	130	65
1931	1,456	–	567	88	120	124	135	70	154	44
1932	1,288	–	465	44	112	119	141	69	161	21

Table 62—*Continued*

	Total merchandise exports	"On orders"[a]	United Kingdom	United States of America	Germany	France	Belgium	Italy	Netherlands	Brazil
1933	1,121	–	411	87	86	72	114	44	108	49
1934	1,438	–	553	79	120	78	141	60	164	61
1935	1,569	–	538	189	108	75	137	62	139	76
1936	1,656	–	582	202	96	89	129	41	141	104
1937	2,311	–	672	295	157	96	217	143	217	132
1938	1,400	–	459	119	164	75	104	36	103	98
1939	1,573	–	565	189	90	76	111	33	128	67
1940	1,428	–	545	253	–	84	36	49	54	76
1941	1,465	–	477	543	3	2	–	1	–	87
1942	1,789	–	601	511	–	–	–	–	–	106
1943	2,192	–	780	533	–	–	–	–	1	143
1944	2,360	–	942	536	–	–	–	–	1	220
1945	2,498	–	649	554	–	87	79	9	38	238
1946	3,973	–	877	596	2	420	228	90	118	150
1947	5,505	–	1,651	547	30	280	293	275	262	249
1948	5,542	–	1,535	537	133	236	322	477	220	260
1949	3,719	–	849	399	152	189	163	339	161	405
1950	5,427	–	973	1,109	264	357	112	359	265	430
1951	6,713	–	1,148	1,183	459	441	98	465	386	704
1952	4,392	–	619	1,115	227	357	90	82	180	326
1953	7,189	–	1,404	1,363	262	266	240	395	304	1,116

[a] Exports "on orders" were those whose final point of destination was unknown at the time of loading; the ships received instructions as to their final destination after leaving Argentine ports.

Sources: *Anuario Geográfico*, p. 385; DNEC, *Comercio Exterior*, several issues.

Table 63: Value of Exports According to Main Products in Million Paper Pesos at 1950 Prices, 1910–54
(Annual averages)

	All merchandise exports	All livestock exports	Meat	Hides	Wool	Dairy products	Livestock by-products	Other livestock exports	All agricultural exports	Cereals and linseed	Fruits and vegetables	Other agricultural exports	Forestry products	Other
1910–14	4,480	1,972	478	430	859	36	82	86	2,260	2,242	15	–	188	61
1915–19	4,601	2,236	676	420	835	144	93	67	2,122	2,091	25	–	166	77
1920–24	6,393	2,814	831	530	939	297	108	108	3,279	3,213	46	20	187	114
1925–29	7,914	3,075	1,080	618	868	256	113	140	4,444	4,305	64	75	269	126
1930–34	7,405	2,658	850	505	879	223	86	115	4,420	4,255	56	107	252	77
1935–39	7,397	2,824	943	552	968	128	102	131	4,177	3,922	113	142	242	154
1940–44	5,963	3,267	1,295	1,017	897	252	165	131	1,890	1,578	105	207	166	641
1945–49	5,900	3,285	1,002	570	1,232	243	126	103	2,014	1,652	155	297	208	393
1950–54	4,686	2,195	566	539	765	180	66	80	2,165	1,561	238	367	221	105

Source: ECLA, *El Desarrollo Económico de la Argentina* (Mexico, 1959), 1:115.

Table 64: Volume of Exports of Major Commodities, 1934–62
(Thousands of metric tons)

	Live animals	Meat	Wool	Wheat	Corn	Linseed (flax)	Linseed oil
1934	62	560	111	4,794	5,471	1,375	–
1935	58	560	137	3,860	7,052	1,778	–
1936	63	586	140	1,610	8,382	1,488	–
1937	65	648	116	3,887	9,087	1,802	–
1938	79	639	152	1,940	2,642	1,265	–
1939	79	661	149	4,746	3,196	1,183	2
1940	78	557	136	3,640	1,875	752	6
1941	83	637	169	2,390	553	665	10
1942	111	697	100	2,176	220	315	34
1943	138	658	89	1,955	190	647	35
1944	135	789	90	2,326	550	275	25
1945	201	514	159	2,358	572	135	46
1946	170	548	206	1,387	2,200	38	148
1947	168	687	172	2,284	2,366	–	214
1948	175	509	182	2,174	2,534	–	46
1949	53	497	96	1,847	1,063	–	69
1950	76	346	142	2,767	794	139	205
1951	75	294	60	2,455	298	181	1
1952	58	236	106	63	652	26	1
1953	39	269	155	2,527	1,083	10	1
1954	24	284	98	2,943	2,185	11	1
1955	22	392	109	3,617	362	–	–
1956	59	574	109	2,526	1,065	–	–
1957	56	601	88	2,660	789	–	1
1958	34	655	105	2,113	1,679	–	162
1959	49	538	141	2,399	2,686	–	218
1960	84	438	140	2,486	2,570	63	169
1961	97	436	140	1,066	1,730	99	204
1962	136	570	159	2,832	2,931	–	264

Sources: As in Tables 53–55.

Table 65: Value of Merchandise Exports by Main Categories in Million Current Paper Pesos, 1928–53

	Live animals	Meat	Hides	Wool	Dairy products	Other live-stock	All livestock exports	Cereals and linseed	Flour and wheat by-products	Oilseeds and their by-products	Fresh fruits	All agri-cultural exports	All forestry exports	All mineral exports	Hunting and fishing exports	Other exports	Total mer-chandise exports
1928	21	305	188	182	40	47	782	1,452	46	6	1	1,522	56	—	—	35	2,297
1929	20	304	119	158	35	44	681	1,354	34	5	1	1,417	42	1	1	28	2,168
1930	18	297	105	105	38	34	597	678	26	5	1	734	38	1	1	26	1,396
1931	7	271	83	89	33	29	512	836	23	6	1	882	38	—	1	22	1,456
1932	6	193	61	76	29	28	393	804	21	6	1	848	28	2	1	16	1,288
1933	4	182	81	94	21	36	417	603	22	5	1	647	33	6	3	14	1,121
1934	8	201	82	119	17	38	464	826	30	7	2	894	42	8	7	24	1,438
1935	8	250	98	115	15	49	536	873	28	13	3	954	44	8	7	20	1,559
1936	10	268	116	151	24	45	614	864	34	15	6	963	39	10	9	22	1,656
1937	12	312	153	171	20	59	728	1,411	41	13	6	1,489	46	17	8	24	2,311
1938	14	318	101	154	15	37	638	590	33	13	7	664	41	17	7	32	1,401
1939	15	332	114	163	20	46	689	692	26	15	11	767	48	19	6	45	1,573
1940	17	307	114	195	28	40	701	532	18	19	5	596	34	21	6	70	1,428
1941	17	387	148	239	67	51	910	255	7	18	6	347	41	33	14	120	1,465
1942	30	557	170	187	46	94	1,084	230	8	40	8	387	46	33	10	233	1,789
1943	43	594	181	167	64	110	1,157	343	12	116	9	497	46	43	24	425	2,192
1944	49	732	194	147	72	153	1,346	381	30	96	14	597	40	26	10	342	2,360
1945	75	480	173	271	71	178	1,246	489	28	125	26	808	70	19	19	337	2,498
1946	66	593	341	357	147	205	1,708	976	51	195	41	1,702	77	18	23	446	3,973
1947	85	767	358	326	171	283	1,990	2,030	88	516	52	3,158	120	9	11	217	5,505
1948	105	662	420	413	167	273	2,040	2,566	97	920	27	3,265	101	10	8	117	5,542
1949	60	749	482	349	75	163	1,877	1,235	42	524	61	1,673	87	4	5	72	3,719
1950	92	593	690	873	163	294	2,703	1,163	51	309	105	2,322	229	13	6	154	5,427
1951	103	1,012	562	912	167	288	3,044	1,538	66	825	279	3,089	320	19	7	235	6,713
1952	97	885	415	719	110	195	2,420	593	19	962	302	1,485	316	20	1	149	4,392
1953	62	1,286	404	1,140	292	232	3,417	1,917	106	487	339	3,149	396	38	4	186	7,190

Sources: As in Tables 53–55.

Table 66: Value of Merchandise Exports in Million Current Dollars by Main Categories, 1951–65

	All merchandise exports	All livestock exports	Meat	Leather	Wool	Other livestock products	All agricultural exports	Cereal and linseed	Oilseeds and by-products	Other agricultural exports	All forestry exports	Other exports[a]
1951	1,169	526	155	110	176	85	574	308	190	76	44	25
1952	688	382	122	82	120	58	252	119	80	53	38	16
1953	1,125	486	155	75	187	69	575	383	95	97	40	24
1954	1,027	407	156	62	121	68	573	420	84	69	30	17
1955	929	449	207	55	124	63	424	321	46	57	27	29
1956	944	504	244	66	124	70	385	281	61	43	26	29
1957	975	500	259	60	117	64	406	266	95	45	25	44
1958	994	509	298	59	99	53	441	265	126	50	19	25
1959	1,009	520	259	70	121	70	445	293	98	54	18	26
1960	1,079	520	219	70	145	86	509	324	125	60	15	35
1961	964	516	217	79	142	78	388	195	128	65	13	47
1962	1,216	541	229	92	145	75	607	345	167	95	12	56
1963	1,365	665	334	78	161	92	526	281	139	106	13	161
1964	1,410	590	329	58	129	74	695	500	121	74	16	109
1965	1,493	563	329	50	112	72	821	576	160	85	16	93

[a] Includes nontraditional manufactured exports (including sugar).

Sources: As in Table 55.

Table 67: Quantum Indices of Merchandise Exports by Main Categories, 1951–65 (1956 = 100)

	All merchandise exports	All livestock exports	Meat	Hides	Wool	Live animals	Dairy products	Livestock by-products	All agri-cultural exports	Cereals and linseed	Flour and wheat by-products	Oilseeds and by-products	Fresh fruits	Other agri-cultural exports	All forestry exports	Other exports
1951	86	64	61	62	63	64	53	81	107	77	94	231	114	210	199	73
1952	58	66	46	75	104	66	40	61	42	23	21	102	99	148	141	49
1953	97	82	50	78	146	82	107	64	116	99	149	156	91	325	149	69
1954	104	68	53	72	89	68	101	71	156	151	190	188	72	194	113	53
1955	92	81	73	81	99	81	98	75	105	105	156	105	96	75	102	83
1956	100	100	100	100	100	100	100	100	100	100	100	100	100	100	100	100
1957	108	98	107	98	81	83	96	106	116	100	91	186	156	108	104	164
1958	116	105	113	94	107	67	81	97	134	105	158	269	128	113	90	102
1959	119	105	89	100	137	84	134	84	140	122	204	202	201	121	84	100
1960	119	96	73	83	133	149	145	83	148	129	161	231	200	110	99	145
1961	109	99	77	95	135	167	110	94	115	78	219	241	174	144	102	215
1962	153	118	96	132	154	225	97	92	185	144	233	335	223	263	82	404
1963	160	133	133	118	140	272	94	137	145	106	222	256	290	213	78	909
1964	150	101	101	88	108	158	83	104	193	185	266	235	185	128	91	477
1965	163	96	88	81	128	94	74	90	239	224	215	322	299	137	84	389

Sources: As in Table 55.

Table 68: Indices of Dollar Unit Values of Merchandise Exports by Main Categories, 1951–65
(1956 = 100)

	All merchandise exports	All livestock exports	Meat	Hides	Wool	Live animals	Dairy products	Livestock by-products	All agri-cultural exports	Cereals and linseed	Flour and wheat by-products	Oilseeds and their by-products	Fresh fruits	Other agri-cultural products	Forestry products	Other exports
1951	144	161	105	268	225	131	146	147	140	141	126	135	104	197	83	125
1952	126	115	111	168	93	168	97	127	157	186	166	129	130	174	101	122
1953	123	117	128	146	103	160	93	122	130	137	128	100	160	148	101	129
1954	104	118	122	132	110	176	102	116	96	98	105	73	150	139	102	108
1955	108	110	118	103	101	170	105	107	105	109	114	71	140	126	101	120
1956	100	100	100	100	100	100	100	100	100	100	100	100	100	100	100	100
1957	96	101	99	92	117	109	89	92	91	94	84	84	77	95	91	93
1958	91	96	108	95	75	107	89	84	85	89	95	77	83	89	80	85
1959	90	98	120	106	71	112	91	85	82	85	98	80	52	81	82	88
1960	96	107	124	128	88	119	93	85	89	90	103	89	75	96	58	85
1961	94	104	117	126	85	120	84	96	88	89	93	87	70	101	49	76
1962	84	91	98	105	76	103	84	94	85	85	97	82	75	106	56	47
1963	90	99	103	100	93	101	96	88	94	95	105	89	85	119	63	61
1964	100	116	129	134	99	96	105	81	94	96	91	84	90	106	67	79
1965	97	116	213	154	94	71	114	90	89	92	108	81	74	105	73	82

Sources: As in Table 55.

Table 69: Value of Merchandise Exports in Million Dollars According to Destination and Main Buyers, 1954-65

	Total merchandise exports	Total Africa and Oceania	Total America	Total Asia, excluding USSR	Total Europe, excluding USSR	Total USSR	Brazil	United States of America	Japan	West Germany	Belgium	France	Italy	Netherlands	United Kingdom	All Countries in the Latin American Free Trade Zone	European Common Market	European Free Trade Association
1954	1,027	8	288	57	634	40	92	105	47	112	38	50	34	71	188	173	305	253
1955	929	7	325	24	543	30	129	118	19	54	27	34	71	37	201	190	221	242
1956	944	9	248	43	628	17	65	118	36	115	28	71	71	55	212	112	340	243
1957	975	10	263	18	669	14	75	112	10	99	32	49	78	99	237	134	356	274
1958	994	8	269	32	669	16	75	128	25	95	32	25	65	115	237	119	331	269
1959	1,009	6	262	32	688	21	89	107	26	92	32	36	98	118	235	138	376	261
1960	1,079	6	269	52	733	19	83	91	40	87	37	37	128	131	221	162	419	255
1961	964	8	204	68	670	14	27	84	52	76	41	35	106	142	174	100	400	200
1962	1,216	12	255	61	877	11	68	88	27	121	58	59	139	170	204	141	548	236
1963	1,365	11	364	55	919	16	78	150	39	94	59	59	212	146	200	185	570	236
1964	1,410	7	340	146	891	26	97	91	40	110	53	66	245	139	154	—	613	—
1965	1,493	13	355	135	903	87	107	93	32	99	49	55	239	161	153	—	603	—

Source: As in Table 54.

Table 70: Value of Merchandise Exports in Million Current Dollars, According
to the Standard International Trade Classification, 1955–62

	1955	1956	1957	1958	1959	1960	1961	1962
Foodstuffs	639	642	652	699	701	715	575	769
Beverages and tobacco	–	–	1	1	–	1	1	4
Nonedible raw materials	198	215	201	171	207	244	266	284
Fuels and lubricants	–	–	–	–	–	–	1	13
Animal and vegetable fats and oils	35	33	62	76	54	74	81	103
Chemical products	49	48	47	37	36	35	30	29
Manufactured articles	3	4	8	6	6	6	5	8
Transport machinery and equipment	–	–	2	3	2	2	3	3
Other manufactured goods	1	1	2	2	1	2	2	2
Other exports	2	1	1	1	1	1	1	1
Total exports	929	944	975	994	1,009	1,079	964	1,216

Source: As in Table 59.

Table 71: Exchange Rate Expressed as Paper Pesos
per One U.S. Dollar, 1910–30

1910	2.37
1911	2.37
1912	2.37
1913	2.37
1914	2.36
1915	2.39
1916	2.36
1917	2.28
1918	2.24
1919	2.30
1920	2.54
1921	3.14
1922	2.77
1923	2.90
1924	2.92
1925	2.49
1926	2.47
1927	2.36
1928	2.36
1929	2.39
1930	2.74

Note: During the years shown the gold mint parity rate between paper pesos and
the dollar was 2.36. For exchange rates during earlier years see *Anuario Geográfico
Argentino*, p. 423.

Source: Anuario Geográfico, p. 431.

Table 72: Average Exchange Rates Applied to Merchandise
Imports and Exports, 1935–65
(Paper pesos per one U.S. dollar)

	Average import rate	Average export rate
1935	3.64	3.15
1936	3.22	3.05
1937	3.23	3.01
1938	3.03	3.14
1939	3.67	3.38
1940	3.96	3.36
1941	3.95	3.24
1942	4.03	3.60
1943	3.96	3.64
1944	3.81	3.50
1945	3.84	3.43
1946	3.97	3.44
1947	3.99	3.44
1948	3.96	3.40
1949	3.93	3.56
1950	5.00	4.61
1951	7.09	5.74
1952	7.09	6.38
1953	7.13	6.39
1954	7.27	6.58
1955	7.59	7.86
1956	16.2	19.2
1957	23.6	22.3
1958	28.4	28.8
1959	73.0	77.7
1960	82.7	82.7
1961	82.8	82.6
1962	113.3	112.7
1963	138.1	137.6
1964	140.5	139.1
1965	168.8	164.7

Sources: Computations for 1948–65 are from data in pesos and dollars found in
International Monetary Fund, *International Financial Statistics*, Supplement to
1966/67 Issues, pp. 2–3. Computations for earlier years are from unpublished
ECLA worksheets.

Table 73: Central Bank Gold and Foreign
Exchange Assets (Gross), 1935–65
(Million U.S. dollars, at the end of each year)

	Gold	*Convertible foreign exchange*
1935	449	4
1936	553	61
1937	552	4
1938	440	5
1939	478	2
1940	426	14
1941	508	27
1942	608	15
1943	824	25
1944	975	29
1945	1,192	20
1946	1,090	28
1947	338	32
1948	143	115
1949	210	90
1950	210	206
1951	267	128
1952	287	55
1953	372	47
1954	372	67
1955	372	30
1956	224	13
1957	126	36
1958	60	38
1959	56	220
1960	104	422
1961	190	196
1962	61	54
1963	78	192
1964	71	82
1965	66	170

Note: During 1940–49 Argentina also accumulated large balances of nonconvertible or "blocked" foreign exchange balances, which may be estimated as follows (in million U.S. dollar equivalents):

1940	30	1945	430
1941	30	1946	570
1942	60	1947	730
1943	160	1948	320
1944	300	1949	70

Sources: International Financial Statistics, several issues, and unpublished ECLA worksheets.

Table 74: The Balance of Payments, 1956–65
(Million current dollars; a minus sign indicates a debit entry)

	1956	1957	1958	1959	1960	1961	1962	1963	1964	1965
A. *Current account*	−129	−301	−256	14	−197	−572	−268	234	36	195
Merchandise exports	944	975	994	1,009	1,079	964	1,216	1,366	1,411	1,488
Merchandise imports	−1,128	−1,310	−1,233	−993	−1,249	−1,460	−1,357	−981	−1,077	−1,195
Net tourist services	4	1	−6	−6	−15	−16	−32	−17	−49	−43
Net transport services	63	49	34	35	41	43	50	46	38	56
Net insurance services	−1	−1	−1	−1	−1	−2	—	−3	−7	1
Net payments on interests and profits	−17	−13	−31	−40	−57	−102	−72	−68	−103	−89
Net government services	−21	−25	−15	−12	−11	−6	−9	−15	−17	−1
Net other services	26	24	2	22	16	8	−64	−94	−160	−22
B. *Net unilateral transfers*	−2	−2	−3	−3	−7	−13	−5	—	−2	−12
C. *Capital account*	144	304	275	−10	207	587	279	−240	−36	−183
Private long term and short term capital	201	60	−13	78	325	284	−31	−83	−29	−161
Long term official and banking capital	−77	−119	49	−12	139	77	−75	−21	−32	17
Short term official and banking capital and monetary gold	20	362	239	−76	−257	226	386	−137	25	−39
D. *Errors and omissions*	−13	−1	−16	−1	−3	−2	−7	7	2	1

Source: BCRA, *Boletín Estadístico*, several issues.

Table 75: Money Supply and Its Major Components, 1940–65
(Billion current pesos, at end of each year)

	Currency and bills in the hands of the public	*Private demand deposits*	*Money supply*	*Bank deposits of low turnover (quasi money)*
1940	1.13	1.30	2.43	2.76
1941	1.33	1.77	3.10	2.88
1942	1.51	2.12	3.63	3.20
1943	1.77	2.58	4.35	3.56
1944	2.20	3.18	5.38	4.16
1945	2.64	3.83	6.47	4.69
1946	3.58	4.88	8.46	5.62
1947	4.77	5.48	10.25	6.24
1948	6.74	7.03	13.77	7.48
1949	9.07	8.51	17.58	9.42
1950	11.91	10.14	22.05	10.26
1951	15.36	11.38	26.74	10.91
1952	18.26	12.16	30.42	12.06
1953	22.07	15.67	37.73	14.37
1954	26.74	17.14	43.88	16.95
1955	31.83	19.79	51.61	19.30
1956	36.14	24.09	60.24	24.51
1957	41.81	25.77	67.58	29.45
1958	60.28	38.55	98.83	40.74
1959	84.41	57.74	142.16	44.88
1960	105.36	73.28	178.64	60.10
1961	121.68	83.76	205.44	74.81
1962	135.38	84.28	219.66	85.53
1963	167.06	115.81	282.87	123.50
1964	227.83	167.82	395.65	178.89
1965	296.54	200.94	497.48	233.72

Sources: BCRA, *Estadísticas Monetarias y Bancarias, Años 1940–1960* (Buenos Aires, June 1962), pp. 5–8; and *Boletín Estadístico*, several issues.

Table 76: Money and Quasi Money: Semestral Averages, 1948–65
(Billion current pesos; six months' averages)

Year and semester	Money supply	Money plus quasi money
1948/1	10.95	17.68
/2	12.46	19.70
1949/1	14.47	22.63
/2	15.96	25.24
1950/1	18.03	27.90
/2	20.02	30.15
1951/1	23.23	33.91
/2	25.01	35.99
1952/1	26.41	37.71
/2	27.86	39.61
1953/1	32.64	45.65
/2	35.03	48.94
1954/1	38.57	54.05
/2	40.60	57.01
1955/1	45.03	63.15
/2	47.07	65.83
1956/1	53.14	74.48
/2	55.61	78.96
1957/1	63.34	90.11
/2	64.03	92.53
1958/1	70.92	103.61
/2	83.49	121.12
1959/1	114.33	158.52
/2	126.29	170.77
1960/1	150.45	201.03
/2	164.91	221.73
1961/1	183.20	249.35
/2	189.79	261.89
1962/1	208.00	286.55
/2	210.30	294.04
1963/1	229.29	325.83
/2	256.89	372.78
1964/1	310.60	451.51
/2	356.91	527.11
1965/1	414.68	619.64
/2	451.51	687.52

Sources: As in Table 75. The figures were obtained by averaging end of the month figures for money and quasi money.

Table 77: Tax Revenues of the National Government,
and Customs Revenues, 1900–50
(Million paper pesos, at current prices)

Year	Total tax revenues	Customs revenues
1900	120	73
1901	133	72
1902	124	67
1903	152	91
1904	159	97
1905	166	105
1906	185	121
1907	199	129
1908	209	137
1909	231	150
1910	260	173
1911	268	177
1912	291	188
1913	307	199
1914	211	118
1915	199	95
1916	203	105
1917	200	97
1918	262	139
1919	326	180
1920	448	297
1921	361	203
1922	369	206
1923	453	268
1924	495	296
1925	577	350
1926	534	304
1927	552	313
1928	602	358
1929	613	356
1930	529	291
1931	495	258
1932	632	241
1933	630	257
1934	687	248
1935	851	272
1936	855	261
1937	1,117	342
1938	994	376
1939	994	322
1940	1,089	272
1941	1,043	217
1942	1,090	192
1943	1,107	127
1944	1,417	120
1945	1,530	139
1946	1,981	291
1947	3,250	580
1948	4,094	537
1949	⌈5,613	330
1950	7,578	346

Sources: Unpublished ECLA worksheets and DNEC *Anuario Estadístico de la Argentina, 1957*, p. 400.

Table 78: Current Revenues of the National Government, by Main Categories, 1950–61 (CONADE)
(Billion current pesos)

	1950	1951	1952	1953	1954	1955	1956	1957	1958	1959	1960	1961
Indirect taxes	4.73	9.19	8.22	10.50	12.01	12.44	16.34	23.98	25.34	52.46	84.24	109.17
Sales tax	1.57	2.25	2.48	2.54	2.88	3.03	3.35	4.10	6.08	8.38	16.88	23.34
Excise taxes	0.88	1.75	2.01	2.03	2.55	3.41	3.88	4.14	5.27	8.24	12.52	16.14
Customs revenues	0.34	0.71	0.48	0.30	0.46	0.61	6.35	4.24	4.75	24.01	32.58	41.40
Property taxes	0.39	0.38	0.40	0.47	0.50	0.49	0.50	0.31	0.66	0.87	0.98	1.47
Other	1.55	4.10	2.85	5.15	5.63	4.90	2.25	11.19	8.58	10.96	21.28	26.82
Direct taxes on corporations	0.72	1.05	1.20	1.06	1.17	1.85	2.27	2.67	3.21	6.05	12.05	15.02
Direct taxes on families	1.58	2.37	3.30	3.24	3.18	3.21	5.15	5.79	7.13	10.88	18.86	23.49
Employers' social security contributions	2.18	2.65	3.52	4.55	5.22	5.75	6.91	7.88	9.59	15.63	23.16	28.25
Employees' social security contributions	1.62	2.27	2.35	3.09	3.86	4.60	5.70	6.74	7.14	11.43	16.41	22.07
Other	0.17	0.22	0.25	0.29	0.33	0.49	0.48	0.54	0.32	0.35	0.60	0.66
Total current revenues	11.00	17.74	18.83	22.74	25.79	28.35	36.85	47.59	52.73	96.80	155.31	198.65

Note: Current revenues include taxes collected by the national government but which are in part distributed to local governments.

Source: Unpublished CONADE worksheets.

Table 79: Current Expenditures of the National Government, by Main Categories, 1950–61 (CONADE)
(Billion current pesos)

	1950	1951	1952	1953	1954	1955	1956	1957	1958	1959	1960	1961
Consumption expenditures	4.52	5.91	7.53	8.57	9.47	11.69	14.59	15.63	23.19	39.43	55.31	67.83
Subsidies	1.87	2.66	2.46	4.12	6.82	7.34	4.92	7.28	11.55	19.81	19.17	22.02
Transportation activities	0.95	1.35	1.14	1.30	1.87	2.73	3.43	4.87	8.64	15.17	14.23	18.68
Communication activities	0.20	0.21	0.34	0.30	0.39	0.40	0.48	0.58	1.44	2.64	3.66	3.27
Other	0.72	1.10	0.98	2.52	4.56	4.21	1.01	1.83	1.47	2.00	1.28	0.07
Interest on the public debt	0.27	0.37	0.47	0.34	0.26	0.29	0.46	0.33	0.32	1.16	2.08	2.56
Transfers to local governments	1.78	2.69	3.36	3.11	3.72	4.55	5.19	5.69	8.59	17.39	27.24	35.69
Transfers to families	1.34	1.99	2.56	3.05	4.79	6.16	7.92	8.59	12.89	24.67	34.12	47.89
Net savings	1.23	4.13	2.45	3.55	0.72	−1.67	3.77	10.06	−3.81	−5.67	17.40	22.66
Total current expenditures and savings	11.00	17.74	18.83	22.74	25.79	28.35	36.85	47.59	52.73	96.80	155.31	198.65

Source: As in Table 78.

Table 80: Consumption Expenditures of the National
Government by Main Categories, 1955–60
(Million pesos at current prices)

	1955	*1956*	*1957*	*1958*	*1959*	*1960*
General administration	1,672	1,969	1,972	2,517	4,641	5,648
Defense	4,961	6,597	7,475	8,643	16,682	23,262
Justice and public order	892	1,016	1,076	1,492	2,478	3,720
Roads and waterways	540	583	574	923	1,456	2,528
Sewerages and sanitary services	1	–	–	–	–	–
Education and culture	2,651	3,090	3,460	6,475	9,528	11,398
Public health	720	1,008	1,040	1,676	2,288	3,722
Social security	247	306	394	794	1,244	3,647
Agriculture and livestock	727	808	986	1,328	2,176	3,212
Fuels, energy, mining, and industry	93	182	143	418	864	773
Transport and communications	303	164	197	363	693	903
Other services	528	1,046	610	903	1,482	1,777
Subtotal: Wages and purchases of goods and services	13,335	16,769	17,926	25,534	43,531	60,587
Minus: Sale of goods and services	1,634	2,163	2,271	2,311	4,059	5,216
Consumption expenditures	11,701	14,606	15,655	23,223	39,473	55,371

Source: CONADE, pp. 164–67.

Table 81: Consumption Expenditures of Provincial
Governments, by Main Categories, 1955–59
(Million pesos at current prices)

	1955	1956	1957	1958	1959
General administration	866	798	988	1,441	2,773
Defense	–	–	–	–	–
Justice and public order	1,384	1,590	1,919	2,944	4,670
Roads and waterways	260	304	363	526	863
Sewerages and sanitary services	41	43	60	72	153
Education and culture	1,282	1,628	2,002	4,099	5,253
Public health	645	782	910	1,405	2,518
Social security	163	197	220	378	624
Agriculture and livestock	158	193	224	358	629
Fuels, energy, mining, and industry	60	65	104	168	309
Transport and communications	22	27	31	35	63
Other services	81	76	91	124	251
Subtotal: Wages and purchases of goods and services	4,962	5,704	6,912	11,500	18,106
Minus: Sale of goods and services	510	566	724	903	953
Consumption expenditures	4,452	5,138	6,188	10,647	17,154

Source: As in Table 80.

Table 82: Current Revenues and Expenditures of General Government, by Level of Government, 1950–61
(Billion pesos at current prices)

	1950	1951	1952	1953	1954	1955	1956	1957	1958	1959	1960	1961
Current expenditures	11.23	15.08	18.16	21.74	28.49	33.44	37.21	42.95	66.00	114.50	141.86	195.08
Net national	8.00	10.92	13.03	16.07	21.35	25.47	27.89	31.84	47.95	85.08	110.67	140.30
Provincial	2.25	2.98	3.64	3.97	5.06	5.51	6.56	7.85	13.11	21.25	21.18	38.37
Municipal	0.98	1.18	1.49	1.70	2.08	2.46	2.76	3.26	4.94	8.17	10.01	16.41
Current revenues	13.37	20.64	22.36	26.90	30.77	33.99	43.22	55.56	63.99	114.96	179.51	232.33
Net national	9.22	15.05	15.47	19.63	22.01	23.80	31.66	41.90	44.14	79.41	128.07	162.96
Provincial	2.79	3.98	4.88	5.01	6.13	7.31	8.26	9.42	14.19	25.71	37.89	50.31
Municipal	1.36	1.61	2.01	2.26	2.63	2.88	3.30	4.24	5.66	9.84	13.55	19.06
General government saving in current account	2.15	5.57	4.19	5.15	2.34	0.55	6.02	12.61	-2.01	-0.45	37.65	37.25

Note: Revenue of the national government excludes taxes transferred to local governments.

Source: As in Table 78.

Table 83: Current Revenues and Expenditures of the Public Sector, 1950–63
(Billion pesos at 1960 prices)

	1950	1951	1952	1953	1954	1955	1956	1957	1958	1959	1960	1961	1962	1963
General government excluding Social security														
Current revenues	117	125	122	127	131	133	156	149	128	120	155	179	143	139
Current expenditures	96	96	93	104	121	120	104	97	102	89	100	117	118	102
Savings in current account	21	30	29	23	10	13	52	52	26	31	55	62	25	37
Social security system														
Revenues	35	34	32	38	43	43	44	43	32	27	33	38	28	33
Outlays	12	12	13	17	23	28	31	27	29	28	32	41	36	36
Savings in current account	22	22	19	21	20	15	13	17	3	−1	–	−2	−8	−3
Public enterprises														
Enterprises with savings	14	10	13	11	12	9	18	22	15	24	17	16	13	10
Enterprises with deficits	11	14	15	14	16	15	21	26	34	27	18	19	21	17
Net savings of public enterprises	3	−4	−2	−3	−5	−6	−3	−4	−20	−4	−1	−3	−9	−7
Public sector savings	46	48	46	41	25	22	62	65	10	27	54	56	8	27
Expenditures on capital account	58	52	45	47	45	39	38	48	77	49	65	72	59	62
Financial deficit or surplus	−11	−4	1	−6	−20	−17	24	17	−66	−22	−11	−15	−51	−35

Source: CONADE, *Plan Nacional de Desarrollo, 1965–1969* (Buenos Aires, 1965), p. 35, Table 10.

Table 84: Debt of the Public Sector in the Hands of the Banking
System, Including the Central Bank, 1940–65
(Billion current pesos, at end of each year)

1940	1.69
1941	2.49
1942	3.00
1943	3.50
1944	3.92
1945	4.12
1946	6.03
1947	9.29
1948	13.57
1949	16.56
1950	17.52
1951	18.20
1952	19.35
1953	24.69
1954	30.09
1955	35.86
1956	38.39
1957	46.79
1958	74.60
1959	104.70
1960	121.46
1961	132.81
1962	162.09
1963	225.95
1964	346.82
1965	455.48

Sources: As in Table 75.

Table 85: Indicators of Economic Progress in Argentina, 1925–61
(Annual averages)

	1925–29	1935–39	1957–61	Rate of growth 1925–29/1957–61	Rate of growth 1935–39/1957–61
1. Apparent Consumption of Nondurable Goods (thousand metric tons, except as indicated)					
Wheat flour	1,087	1,331	2,111	2.1	2.1
Beef and veal	897	1,052	1,688	2.0	2.2
Mutton and lamb	76	131	125	1.6	–
Pork	61	106	163	3.1	2.0
Edible oils	58	80	213	4.2	4.6
Sugar	338	403	719	2.4	2.7
Wine (thousand kiloliters)	590	686	1,461	2.9	3.5
Rice	71	96	176	2.9	2.8
Beer (million liters)	201	138	265[c]	0.9	3.0
Coffee	23	24	31	0.9	1.2
Yerba mate	92	102	155[d]	1.6	1.9
Cotton textiles	49	54	87[e]	1.8	2.2
Shoes (million pairs)	–[a]	9.8	31.2	–	5.4
Paper for cigarettes (metric tons)	–	713[b]	1,294	–	2.7
Rayon textiles	–	5.38	12.63[e]	–	4.0
All tobacco	19.69	23.59	34.38	1.8	2.6
2. Stocks of Durable Goods (thousands)					
Telephones installed	230[f]	379	1,261	5.5	5.6
Tractors	10.3	21.7	110.8	7.7	7.7
Automobiles	239	295	552[g]	2.5	2.6
All motor vehicles	285	388	991[g]	3.7	4.0
Radio receivers	–	–	3,370	–	–
Automatic refrigerators	–	34	1,414	–	–
Television receivers	–	–	410	–	–

Table 85—*Continued*

3. Apparent Consumption of Intermediate Goods (thousand metric tons, except as indicated)

	1925–29	1935–39	1957–61	Rate of growth 1925–29/1957–61	Rate of growth 1935–39/1957–61
Crude petroleum (thousand m.³)	1,589	3,250	13,535	6.9	6.7
All fuels (thousand tons, petroleum equivalent)	7,354	9,033	18,322	2.9	3.3
Cement	606	1,031	2,523	4.6	4.2
Iron and steel (gross steel equivalent)	1,590	1,167	2,152	0.8	2.8
Newsprint	—ᵃ	152ᵇ	168	–	0.5
Cardboard	—	33.10ᵇ	81	–	4.2
Caustic soda	9.95	20.04	80	6.7	6.5
Solvay soda	24.11	27.04	100	4.5	6.1

Note: Growth rates are given only where their numerical values are meaningful.

[a] Dash indicates data not available.
[b] Refers to 1935, 1937, and 1939.
[c] Refers to 1958–61.
[d] Refers to 1957–60.
[e] Refers to 1955–59.
[f] Average of 1926 and 1930.
[g] Refers to 1959–63.

Sources: Revista de Economía Argentina (Jan. 1942), pp. 158–90; Junta Nacional de Carnes, *Estadísticas Básicas*, p. 6; OECEI, *Importaciones*, vols. 1 and 2; U.N., *Economic Survey of Latin America, 1949* (New York, 1951), pp. 142–89; Asociación de Fábricas de Automotores, *Informe Estadístico No. 191*, p. 2; Consejo Federal de Inversiones y Confederación General Económica, *Programa Conjunto para el Desarrollo Agropecuario e Industrial, Primer Informe,* 3:15; DNEC, *Boletín de Estadística,* several issues; *Review of the River Plate,* several issues; *Anuario Geográfico;* Techint, *Boletín Informativo,* no. 150 (Oct.–Dec. 1965), p. 15.

Table 86: Average Labor Productivity, Total and by Sectors, 1925–61
(1960–61 = 100)

	1925–29	1935–39	1940–44	1945–49	1947–49	1950–54	1955–59
Whole economy	72.9	74.8	77.9	83.5	83.3	79.9	90.0
Rural sector	73.1	71.7	78.6	78.2	75.7	77.1	92.9
Oil and mining	31.8	46.1	46.7	38.8	43.5	47.6	54.7
Manufacturing	61.9	68.3	71.6	79.1	81.8	76.7	86.1
Construction	71.4	94.5	91.3	84.0	88.2	85.9	94.6
Public utilities	41.6	54.7	53.4	57.9	63.7	71.2	87.4
Transport	73.7	79.8	91.5	93.4	90.8	66.0	92.2
Communications	115.9	124.0	128.4	124.2	123.8	111.3	101.6
Commerce, finance, and housing services	95.8	88.7	81.8	90.8	90.2	78.4	88.5
Government services	104.9	107.5	107.6	110.1	100.3	102.3	102.0
Other services	66.0	72.9	78.5	88.8	87.7	90.2	93.2

Sources and method: Value-added data as in Tables 1 and 2. Data on labor force (active population) from ECLA, p. 400 (1925–50), and from CONADE unpublished data (1947–61). Both series were linked using 1950–54 as their common point. This procedure limits comparability for data before and after 1945–49. Labor force data are crude.

Table 87: Average Labor Productivity in 1960–61, Total and by Sectors

| | At 1960 prices | | At 1937 prices | |
	Thousand pesos	Index	Pesos	Index
Whole economy	*112.9*	*100*	*2,481*	*100*
Rural sector	87.2	77	2,108	85
Oil and mining	241.1	214	12,749	514
Manufacturing	142.0	126	1,756	71
Construction	79.0	70	1,272	51
Public utilities	178.2	158	4,024	162
Transport	130.8	116	4,292	173
Communications	109.7	97	2,912	117
Commerce, finance, and housing services				
Government services	78.0	69	2,590	104
Other services	62.6	56	1,653	67
(Commerce, finance, housing, and other services)	(117.9)	(104)	(2,867)	(116)

Sources: As in Table 86.

Table 88: Comparison of Average Labor Productivities
in Argentina and the U.S.A., 1960–61

	Average labor productivity in the U.S.A., 1960–61[a]		*Productivity in Argentina as a percentage of that in the U.S.A.*	
	Current dollars	*Index*	*1937 prices*	*1960 prices*
Whole economy	*7,652*	*100*	*26.4*	*26.4*
Rural sector	3,936	51	43.7	39.7
Oil and mining	15,881	208	65.5	27.2
Manufacturing	8,272	108	17.3	30.8
Construction	6,708	88	15.5	21.1
Public utilities	21,497	281	15.3	14.9
Transport	8,938	117	39.2	26.2
Communications	12,756	167	18.6	15.4
All other private services	8,274	108	28.3	25.5
Government services	5,161	67	40.9	27.1

[a] Defined for each sector as the GNP it generates divided by persons engaged in production in that sector (including part-time employees).

Sources and method: U.S.A. data obtained from U.S. Department of Commerce, *Statistical Abstract of the United States, 1965* (Washington, D.C., U.S. Government Printing Office), pp. 220 and 327. Data in 1960 pesos were translated into dollars using a purchasing power parity of 55.8 pesos per dollar; see ECLA, "Medición del Nivel de Precios y el Poder Adquisitivo de la Moneda en América Latina, 1960–62," E/CN.12/653 (April 6, 1963, mimeographed), p. 79. Data in 1937 pesos were translated using a rate of 1.226 pesos per dollar. This rate was chosen so that average labor productivity for the whole economy would be the same (in dollars) for both sets of data.

Table 89: Real Wholesale Prices for Selected Commodities
in Argentina and Indices of Their Variations, 1945–55
(1939 = 100)

	1945–46	*1947–49*	*1950–52*	*1953–55*	*1945–55* *Standard deviation* *divided by mean*
Cereals and linseed	93	91	71	76	0.19
Industrial crops	88	102	87	74	0.15
Cattle	81	87	89	93	0.07
Wool	63	85	141	75	0.47
Dairy products	75	107	95	87	0.14
Manufactured foodstuff	83	77	101	110	0.16
Beverages	94	95	87	96	0.06
Textiles	103	134	128	109	0.12
Clothing	88	129	123	115	0.14
Wood and wood products	121	152	153	136	0.12
Paper and cardboard	131	151	149	165	0.12
Leather	95	115	105	87	0.14
Rubber	462	78	83	82	1.08
Chemical products	85	86	75	74	0.09
Fuels and lubricants	107	101	76	64	0.23
Glass, stone, and earth	91	116	110	103	0.12
Iron and steel	166	139	133	131	0.13
Other metals	114	119	152	159	0.18

Sources and method: Price data obtained from BCRA, *Boletín Estadístico* (Sept. 1962), pp. 49–63.

Table 90: Allocation of Industrial Workers According to Size
of the Establishment in Which They Work
(Percentages of total industrial workers)

	1935 census	1939 census	1946 census	1954 census
All industry	*100.0*	*100.0*	*100.0*	*100.0*
Establishments with 10 and fewer workers	19.5	18.2	17.9	19.6
Establishments with 11 to 25 workers	11.6	11.7	12.4	12.3
Establishments with 26 to 50 workers	9.9	10.2	10.8	10.1
Establishments with 51 to 100 workers	11.6	11.4	11.8	10.2
Establishments with 101 to 300 workers	$\left.\begin{matrix}26.1\end{matrix}\right\}$	$\left.\begin{matrix}26.5\end{matrix}\right\}$	18.0	15.5
Establishments with 301 to 500 workers			6.4	6.9
Establishments with 501 to 1,000 workers	8.4	8.6	8.2	9.7
Establishments with more than 1,000 workers	12.9	13.4	14.5	15.7
Establishments with 50 and fewer workers	41.0	40.1	41.1	42.0
Establishments with 51 to 500 workers	37.7	37.9	36.2	32.6
Establishments with more than 500 workers	21.3	22.0	22.7	25.4

Sources: Industrial censuses for 1935, 1939, 1946, and 1954 published by DNEC.

Table 91: Contribution to Total Value of Gross Output in Each Branch
of Manufacturing of the Largest Establishments,
According to 1954 Census

	Value of gross output from 50 to 100 million pesos		Value of gross output of more than 100 million pesos	
	Number of establish- ments	*Shares in total gross output of the sector*	*Number of establish- ments*	*Shares in total gross output of the sector*
Total manufacturing	*94*	*8.0*	*61*	*18.5*
Foodstuffs and beverages	35	11.2	20	25.1
Tobacco	2	7.5	6	81.6
Textiles	18	11.7	6	10.7
Clothing	3	4.0	1	3.3
Wood products	0	0	0	0
Paper and cardboard	3	15.2	1	7.7
Printing and publishing	2	7.1	1	7.0
Chemical products	5	5.0	4	18.0
Petroleum refining	4	7.9	5	85.1
Rubber products	3	18.3	3	42.7
Leather products	2	4.9	0	0
Stone, glass, and ceramics	2	4.0	3	12.5
Metals	9	8.3	5	9.6
Vehicles and machinery	5	5.3	3	5.8
Electrical machinery and appliances	1	3.0	3	31.4
Other manufacturing	0	0	0	0

Source: Industrial census for 1954, p. 37.

Table 92: Structure of Gross Output in Industry According to
Legal Organization of Establishments
(Percentages of total gross output of each activity)

	Corporations and cooperatives		Public sector	
	1946 census	*1954 census*	*1946 census*	*1954 census*
All industry	*61.0*	*65.0*	*4.9*	*10.5*
Mining	27.6	31.1	59.8	54.8
Gas and electricity	87.6	77.5	10.5	21.2
Manufacturing	60.6	65.3	3.6	9.5
Foodstuffs and beverages	69.5	72.6	0.6	6.0
Tobacco	95.6	95.2	0	0
Textiles	69.9	78.0	2.3	2.2
Clothing	38.4	48.9	0.8	5.1
Wood products	31.7	39.0	1.0	3.0
Paper and cardboard	72.6	81.2	0	0.3
Printing and publishing	51.7	67.3	3.2	2.4
Chemical products	77.1	86.1	2.5	4.5
Petroleum refining	40.3	23.4	56.3	75.8
Rubber products	86.4	87.2	0	0.2
Leather products	43.2	54.4	0.1	1.0
Stone, glass, and ceramics	60.7	67.6	0.2	0.7
Metals	54.4	61.0	4.9	10.0
Vehicles and machinery	47.0	36.6	11.2	31.3
Electrical machinery and appliances	70.0	79.7	2.6	4.3
Other manufacturing	42.3	54.4	0.1	1.8

Note: "Corporations" refers to "Sociedades Anónimas de responsabilidad limitada"; this category also includes a minor contribution of cooperatives. The difference between 100.0 and the participations of corporations and the public sector for each activity represents the share of output generated by family firms, and various forms of partnerships.

Sources: Basic data obtained from Industrial census of 1946 (p. 52) and Industrial census of 1954 (p. 40).

Table 93: Geographical Distribution of Industry
(Percentages)

	Industrial employment			Industrial wages and salaries		
	1935 census	1946 census	1954 census	1935 census	1946 census	1954 census
Federal Capital	47.0	40.2	32.9	49.9	46.4	37.2
Province of Buenos Aires:	*13.2*	*18.9*	*13.0*	*13.3*	*20.5*	*25.5*
Metropolitan	*13.2*	*18.9*	*23.0*	*13.2*	*20.5*	*25.5*
Subtotal: Greater Buenos Aires	*60.2*	*59.1*	*55.9*	*63.1*	*66.9*	*62.7*
Province of Buenos Aires: Other	12.0	10.6	10.3	11.2	8.9	9.3
Provinces of Santa Fe, Entre Ríos, and Córdoba	*15.6*	*15.6*	*16.9*	*13.3*	*11.6*	*14.2*
Subtotal	*27.6*	*26.2*	*27.2*	*24.5*	*20.5*	*23.5*
All others	*12.2*	*14.7*	*16.9*	*12.4*	*12.6*	*13.8*

Note: Departments of the Province of Buenos Aires included in the metropolitan zone of Greater Buenos Aires are A. Brown, Avellaneda, E. Echeverría, F. Varela, G. San Martín, G. Sarmiento, La Matanza, Lanús, L. de Zamora, Merlo, Morón, Quilmes, S. Fernando, S. Isidro, Tigre, Tres de Febrero, V. López and Caseros.

Sources: Industrial censuses of 1935, 1946, and 1954.

Table 94: Cash Wages and Salaries as Percentages of Final Value
of Gross Output in Each Sector of Manufacturing

	1935 census	1939 census	1946 census	1950 census	1954 census
All manufacturing	*20.3*	*20.2*	*16.6*	*16.9*	*17.7*
Food and beverages	13.4	{12.6}	11.4	12.0	11.8
Tobacco	19.8		7.2	9.4	7.6
Textiles	20.0	{22.4}	17.2	20.7	20.8
Clothing	23.1		18.0	14.3	16.8
Wood products	28.7	30.8	25.0	19.5	22.4
Paper and cardboard	24.5	20.7	14.2	{20.9}	15.1
Printing and publishing	33.3	31.9	27.9		25.8
Chemical products	16.6	16.5	13.2	14.7	14.9
Petroleum refining	6.5	5.9	4.6	5.0	5.0
Rubber products	20.3	18.5	14.5	16.8	16.4
Leather products	28.3	24.9	15.9	19.5	18.4
Stone, glass, and ceramics	25.1	28.8	23.1	23.4	23.0
Metals	27.0	24.6	21.7	19.2	22.0
Vehicles and machinery	39.1	{30.1}	31.3	34.2	32.2
Electrical machinery and appliances	25.5		24.4	19.3	18.6
Other manufacturing	39.2	50.0	24.4	23.6	21.9

Sources: Industrial censuses for years shown.

Table 95: Structure of the Gross Value of All
Manufacturing Output: Input Side
(Percentages of total)

	1935 census	1937 census	1939 census	1946 census	1954 census	1957 census
Total gross value of output	100.0	100.0	100.0	100.0	100.0	100.0
Wages and salaries: workers		15.6	16.3			
Wages and salaries: other employees	20.3	3.7	3.9	16.6	17.7	14.2
Fuels and lubricants	1.8	1.7	1.9	2.1	1.5	1.7
Purchased electricity	1.0	0.9	0.9	0.8	0.8	0.8
Other domestic intermediate inputs	62.3	47.1	45.7	41.9	41.1	38.2
Other imported intermediate inputs		18.8	18.6	8.0	6.9	10.3
Other (gross profits, taxes, etc.)	14.5	12.1	12.6	30.6	32.0	34.8

Sources: Industrial censuses for the years shown.

Table 96: Allocation of Gross Output of Branches of Manufacturing
in 1950 (CONADE), According to Demand Sources
(Percentages of total gross output of each branch)

	Investment	Consumption	Exports	Intermediate demand
Foodstuffs and beverages	0	72.2	18.4	9.4
Tobacco	0	99.1	0	0.9
Textiles	0.6	40.5	5.1	53.8
Wood products	3.3	40.8	0	55.8
Paper and cardboard	0	10.2	0	89.8
Printing and publishing	0	55.1	0	45.0
Chemicals	0	49.7	33.2	17.1
Petroleum refining	0	25.5	0	74.5
Rubber products	0	48.0	0	52.0
Stone, glass, and ceramics	0.9	9.5	0	89.6
Metals	6.9	30.1	0	63.0
Vehicles and machinery	44.7	12.4	0	43.0
Electrical machinery and appliances	18.6	49.8	0	31.4
Leather, clothing, and other	1.1	82.9	6.0	10.1
All manufacturing	*3.9*	*55.1*	*8.7*	*32.2*

Note: Basic data are expressed in 1960 prices.

Source: Unpublished CONADE worksheets.

Table 97: Allocation of Gross Output of Branches of Manufacturing
in 1961 (CONADE), According to Demand Sources
(As percentages of total gross output of each branch)

	Investment	Consumption	Exports	Intermediate demand
Foodstuffs and beverages	0	75.6	17.3	7.1
Tobacco	0	99.2	0	0.8
Textiles	0.6	40.5	5.3	53.6
Wood products	5.9	36.4	0	57.6
Paper and cardboard	0	9.9	0	90.1
Printing and publishing	0	54.7	0	45.3
Chemicals	0	49.8	14.5	35.7
Petroleum refining	0	25.5	0	74.5
Rubber products	0	47.3	0	52.7
Stone, glass, and ceramics	0.7	12.6	0	86.7
Metals	6.4	23.3	0	70.3
Vehicles and machinery	57.7	25.1	0	17.2
Electrical machinery and appliances	25.5	42.7	0	31.8
Leather, clothing, and other	2.2	84.8	7.8	5.2
All manufacturing	*11.1*	*49.0*	*5.9*	*33.9*

Note: Basic data is expressed in 1960 prices.

Source: Unpublished CONADE worksheets.

Table 98: Exports of Selected Manufactured Products, 1935–61
(Annual averages)

	1935–39	1940–47	1948–49	1950–54	1955–59	1960–61
Edible oils (thousand tons)	0.33	67.68	41.34	50.13	34.27	73.48
Tobacco products (tons)	81	1,329	1,162	1,032	1,394	2,730
Spun cotton (tons)	135	107	107	7	5	4
Cotton textiles (tons)	128	428	428	113	111	9
Spun wool (tons)	3	937	30	157	175	51
Printing and publishing products (tons)	53	707	247	34	246	202
Leather shoes (thousand pairs)	37	598	30	15	24	3

Source: OECEI, *Importaciones,* 1:86, 101, 108, 111, 136, 158.

Table 99: Manufacturing Plants of United States Companies Operating
in Argentina in 1964, Classified According to Date of Establishment

	Number established	Personnel in 1964 (thousands)
1900–09	4	11.9
1910–19	10	10.5[a]
1920–24	3	3.0
1925–29	8	6.8
1930–34	12	4.2[b]
1935–39	14	6.5[a]
1940–44	9	3.6
1945–49	6	1.2
1950–54	3	0.1[a]
1955–59	24	3.5[b]
1960–63	20	4.2[b]

[a] One of the plants did not report number of personnel.
[b] Three of the plants did not report number of personnel.

Source: Elaborated from data found in U.S. Chamber of Commerce in Argentina, *Comments on Argentine Trade*, April 1964 (special issue).

Table 100: Distribution of Assets of Commercial Banks
in Argentina, 1915–27
(Million paper pesos)

	1915–19	1920–24	1925–27
Assets of commercial banks	2,495	3,800	3,868
Banco de la Nación Argentina	1,125	1,638	1,673
Other domestic banks	717	1,338	1,422
Foreign banks	593	937	806

Source: Total assets have been obtained as in Table 1.20. Assets for each sub-category obtained from *Anuario de la Sociedad Rural Argentina*, pp. 82–84. There is a small unexplained discrepancy between the two sources.

Table 101: Monetary Statistics in Argentina during the Great Depression
(Million pesos; end of the year annual averages)

	A Currency in the hands of the public	B Demand deposits	C Savings and other deposits	D A plus B
1928–29	865	1,240	2,688	2,105
1930–31	771	1,080	2,657	1,851
1932–33	694	1,127	2,369	1,821
1934–35	790	1,088	2,304	1,878
1936–37	952	1,345	2,430	2,297
1938–39	998	1,397	2,455	2,395

Note: Column *B* includes official deposits; therefore, column *D* is larger than the standard definition of money supply by the amount of those government deposits.

Sources: BCRA, *Suplemento Estadístico de la Revista Económica*, several issues (Aug. 1937–Apr. 1947).

Table 102: Structure of the GDP at Factor Cost in Manufacturing, 1900–29
(Percentages of total)

	BCRA/ECLA			CONADE/ECLA		
	1900–04	*1910–14*	*1925–29*	*1900–04*	*1910–14*	*1925–29*
Total manufacturing	*100.0*	*100.0*	*100.0*	*100.0*	*100.0*	*100.0*
Foodstuffs and beverages	43.4	38.2	36.6	34.8	30.8	29.3
Tobacco	1.3	1.0	0.8	1.4	1.2	0.9
Textiles	2.7	2.4	2.9	3.3	3.1	3.7
Clothing	1.03	7.9	6.9	13.2	10.1	8.9
Wood products	4.8	5.0	3.2	11.2	11.5	7.4
Paper and cardboard	1.3	1.6	1.9	1.6	2.1	2.4
Printing and publishing	2.5	5.9	9.8	2.5	5.9	9.8
Chemical products	4.9	5.7	5.7	3.5	4.1	4.0
Petroleum refining	–	–	1.6	–	–	2.5
Rubber products	–	–	–	–	–	–
Leather products	6.4	6.2	6.5	4.0	3.9	4.0
Stone, glass, and ceramics	11.3	15.6	6.9	10.2	14.3	6.2
Metals	1.6	2.8	4.5	1.8	3.2	5.3
Vehicles and machinery	0.4	0.7	2.9	0.4	0.7	2.6
Electrical machinery and appliances	–	–	–	–	–	–
Other manufacturing and handicrafts	9.1	6.9	9.6	12.0	9.2	12.9

Sources and method: See Tables 4.8 and 4.9.

Table 103: Main Industries in Argentina According to the 1914 Census
(Thousands of employees)

Dairy products	28.6
Bread making	27.1
Making of suits and coats	21.4
Charcoal making, processing of quebracho extract, and other lumber works	19.6
Wine making	16.4
Sugar mills and refineries	14.7
Meat packing plants	14.7
Repair shops, blacksmith shops, and other metallurgical establishments; making of nails, spikes, and machines	14.6
Leather shoes	12.9
Printing and lithography	11.5
Brick making	10.5

Sources and method: Data obtained directly from Industrial census of 1914 (several pages). It may be noted that many of the classifications of this census include occupations that do not belong in manufacturing according to modern conventions. The 1914 census obtained data for the year 1913.

Table 104: Value of Gross Domestic Production Plus Imports, 1925–61
(Billion pesos at 1960 prices)

	1925–29	*1937–39*	*1946–49*	*1950–54*	*1955–59*	*1960–61*
Mining plus						
manufacturing	*318.6*	*394.7*	*578.7*	*611.7*	*799.7*	*914.7*
Mining	*7.0*	*10.2*	*11.3*	*16.1*	*23.3*	*26.8*
Manufacturing	*311.7*	*384.5*	*567.4*	*595.6*	*776.4*	*887.9*
Foodstuffs and						
beverages	{111.4}	131.0	168.7	159.6	203.1	188.1
Tobacco		7.4	10.9	12.6	13.2	13.1
Textiles	{55.3}	44.5	68.1	70.8	74.8	75.4
Clothing		21.9	31.9	34.1	38.0	37.7
Wood products	22.1	16.1	25.8	25.0	26.1	26.6
Paper and cardboard	8.6	8.1	12.7	12.5	17.4	18.4
Printing and						
publishing	14.3	11.4	13.8	11.0	13.0	14.9
Chemical products	20.9	20.8	31.4	37.5	56.1	67.5
Petroleum refining	7.5	15.8	24.4	33.5	45.9	53.1
Rubber products	1.5	5.1	7.5	8.9	12.5	18.0
Leather products	10.0	8.2	17.5	16.8	19.0	17.6
Stone, glass, and						
ceramics	15.7	10.7	17.1	19.3	22.7	23.6
Metals	30.6	34.2	45.5	53.7	87.7	101.0
Vehicles and						
machinery	26.1	26.7	53.9	53.9	83.7	150.3
Electrical machinery						
and appliances	2.5	5.3	8.3	13.2	27.8	40.6
Other	7.5	6.6	9.0	8.3	11.4	13.1

Sources and method: Data sources as in Table 4.14. The total value of output for manufacturing as a whole was obtained directly using the overall index. A discrepancy exists between this estimate and the sum of the sectorial estimates.

Table 105: Imports as a Percentage of Total Domestic Production
Plus Imports for Selected Commodities, 1925-61

	1925-29	1935-39	1946-49	1950-54	1955-59	1960-61
Crude oil	17	20	31	48	51	20
Edible oils	67	17	2	1	1	0
Yerba mate	82	33	19	10	22	27
Rice	88	47	0	0	0	0
Tobacco	60	35	27	4	0	3
Cotton textiles	92	61	20	5	1	1
Cement	65	5	10	18	3	0
Silk textiles	—[a]	59	24	13	3	32
Rayon	–	70	38	10	1	1
Cardboard	–	48	31	19	1	3
Writing paper (excludes newsprint)	–	56	48	39	18	18
Woodpulp and cellulose	–	75	56	72	64	58
Rolled flat steel sheets and products	–	98	75	57	45	46
Electrical batteries	–	83	16	3	2	–
Caustic soda	100	95	50	–	40	–

[a] Dash indicates data not available.

Sources and method: Computed from data (mainly in physical quantities) found in OECEI, *Importaciones*, 1:86, 92, 94, 101, 113, 115, 132, 172, 196, 225; 2:314. Additional data found in "La Industrialización de Fibra de Algodón en la República Argentina, Año 1962," p. 4; *Anuario Geográfico*, pp. 245, 333; and *Revista de Economía Argentina* 41 (Jan. 1942): 158-60, 188-90. In several cases estimates for two or three years have been taken as representative for the whole four- or five-year periods indicated in the table.

Table 106: Wages and Salaries as Percentages of the GDP of Each Branch
of Manufacturing, at Market Prices

	1950–52	*1953–55*	*1956–58*	*1959–61*
All manufacturing	*41.0*	*38.5*	*38.9*	*35.3*
Foodstuffs and beverages	45.6	43.8	39.2	27.0
Tobacco	7.8	8.5	5.5	4.9
Textiles	41.7	44.0	40.1	37.6
Clothing	43.2	40.8	50.4	47.0
Wood products	47.3	43.4	38.5	32.3
Paper and cardboard	24.6	31.4	27.2	32.7
Printing and publishing	42.5	41.4	36.7	29.3
Chemical products	37.0	32.7	33.0	36.3
Petroleum refining	6.2	5.8	7.2	5.8
Rubber products	30.8	30.5	28.0	23.2
Leather products	46.8	41.1	38.0	34.8
Stone, glass, and ceramics	45.5	38.9	37.9	31.8
Metals	40.8	39.9	36.1	32.8
Vehicles and machinery	67.6	59.3	66.2	60.7
Electrical machinery and appliances	34.1	38.9	49.0	56.8
Other manufacturing	40.1	37.1	37.1	33.1

Sources: Unpublished CONADE data, expressed at current prices.

Table 107: Allocation of Industrial Workers According to Date of
Founding of the Establishments in Which They Work
(Percentages of total industrial workers)

	1935 census	1939 census	1946 census	1954 census
Date of founding:				
Before 1900	17.6	17.2	14.4	11.4
1901–10	12.5	11.6	10.4	7.9
1911–20	18.7	17.5	12.2	8.1
1921–25	11.1	11.1	8.7	6.0
1926–30	12.6	12.8	9.8	6.7
1932–35	12.9	15.9	10.0	7.8
1936–39	–	7.1	–	–
1936–41	–	–	15.8	–
1942–46	–	–	16.0	–
1936–40	–	–	–	8.7
1941–45	–	–	–	10.1
1946–50	–	–	–	17.8
1951–53	–	–	–	7.8
1954	–	–	–	5.5
Unknown	14.6	6.9	2.6	2.4
Total	*100.0*	*100.0*	*100.0*	*100.0*

Sources: Industrial censuses for the years shown. The following are the dates and
the periods covered for these and other Industrial censuses:

1935 census: Taken October 31, 1935; covered July 1934 through June 1935.

Industrial statistics of 1937: Taken December 31, 1937; covered January
through December 1937.

Industrial statistics of 1939: Taken December 31, 1939; covered January
through December 1939.

1946 census (part of the IV General census): Taken December 31, 1946;
covered January through December 1946.

Industrial statistics of 1948: Taken December 31, 1948; covered January
through December 1948.

Industrial statistics of 1950: Taken December 31, 1950; covered January
through December 1950.

1954 census: Taken July 30, 1954; covered January through December 1953.

Industrial statistics of 1957: Taken December 31, 1957; covered January
through December 1957.

"Industrial statistics" did not use as thorough a coverage as that of the censuses;
generally data in those cases were obtained by mail.

Table 108: Structure of Merchandise Imports by Industrial Origin
(FIAT), 1935–61
(Percentages)

	1935–39	*1945–49*	*1950–54*	*1955–59*	*1960–61*
Total	*100.0*	*100.0*	*100.0*	*100.0*	*100.0*
Mining products	6.8	7.0	13.4	16.1	8.1
Foodstuffs and beverages	7.0	6.0	4.5	4.3	3.6
Tobacco	0.9	1.2	0.1	0.2	0.1
Textiles	23.6	12.6	8.3	4.2	3.1
Clothing	0.7	1.0	0.3	0.2	0.1
Wood and its products	5.4	5.6	5.6	4.8	4.2
Paper and cardboard	3.4	5.3	3.5	3.4	3.0
Printing and publishing	0.2	0.2	0.3	nil	0.1
Chemical products	9.8	7.9	7.2	8.7	9.3
Petroleum refining products	2.9	5.5	7.8	7.7	4.9
Rubber and its products	0.6	1.8	1.5	2.0	3.0
Leather and its products	0.3	0.2	nil	nil	nil
Stone, glass, and ceramics	2.1	1.8	2.0	0.7	0.6
Metals	16.3	17.3	18.2	21.0	20.2
Machinery and vehicles	14.1	19.9	21.8	21.7	34.0
Electrical machinery and appliances	3.1	3.8	3.8	2.7	3.3
Other	2.9	3.1	1.9	2.4	2.4

Source: OECEI, *Importaciones*, 2:310–11.

Table 109: Structure of Merchandise Imports, According to Uses,
1953-63 (CONADE)
(Percentages)

	1953–54	*1955–59*	*1960–63*
Total merchandise imports	*100.0*	*100.0*	*100.0*
Nondurable finished consumer goods	6.3	5.0	3.8
Durable finished consumer goods	2.0	0.9	0.8
Raw materials	9.0	6.7	5.0
Semi-elaborated intermediate products	22.9	27.2	21.1
Elaborated intermediate products	9.0	10.3	22.6
Construction materials	7.1	6.6	4.6
Capital goods	22.6	22.2	33.5
Fuels and lubricants	21.1	21.1	8.6

Source: Unpublished CONADE data, expressed in dollars at current prices. A similar classification is presented in CONADE, *Plan Nacional de Desarrollo 1965-1969*, p. 28.

Table 110: Size Distribution of Agricultural and Livestock Holdings
in the Pampean Provinces, 1914

	Number of holdings	Area covered (thousand hectares)	Area covered as percentage of all lands in rural holdings
Agricultural holdings	*113,609*	*15,885*	*25.1*
10 hectares and less	16,845	87	0.1
11 to 100 hectares	48,770	2,496	3.9
101 to 200 hectares	25,781	3,850	6.1
201 to 300 hectares	11,579	2,946	4.6
301 to 500 hectares	7,202	2,790	4.4
501 to 1,000 hectares	2,726	1,821	2.9
1,001 to 1,250 hectares	213	248	0.4
1,251 to 2,500 hectares	322	574	0.9
2,501 hectares and more	171	1,075	1.7
Livestock holdings	*53,498*	*47,528*	*74.9*
625 hectares and less	40,452	7,235	11.4
626 to 1,250 hectares	5,586	4,518	7.1
1,251 to 2,500 hectares	3,603	6,780	10.7
2,501 to 5,000 hectares	2,095	7,848	12.4
5,001 to 12,500 hectares	1,375	11,227	17.7
12,501 to 25,000 hectares	287	5,091	8.0
25,001 to 37,500 hectares	53	1,659	2.6
37,501 to 50,000 hectares	22	941	1.5
50,001 hectares and more	24	2,227	3.5
All rural holdings	*167,107*	*63,413*	*100.0*

Note: Totals for holdings and area covered exclude available plots ("parcelas disponibles"); Table 3.4 includes these plots.

Source: R. Argentina, *Tercer Censo Nacional* 5 (June 1, 1914): 691–726.

Table 111: Indices of Gross Rural Output: Traditional and New Activities
(1935–39 = 100)

	Mainly traditional exportables[a]	*Mainly "new" activities*[b]
1925–29	95.2	76.8
1930–34	94.6	84.3
1935–39	100.0	100.0
1940–44	107.0	135.1
1945–49	100.9	153.6
1950–54	89.6	206.0
1955–59	102.8	225.2
1960–64	103.2	252.0

[a] For 1925–39 these include cereals and linseed, cattle and wool; for 1935–64 they include, in addition, fodder.
[b] For 1925–39 these include industrial crops, garden vegetables, fruits and flowers, and milk; for 1935–64 they include, in addition, oilseeds.

Sources: As in Table 3.12 (see also the notes to this table).

Table 112: Output of Selected Rural Commodities, 1925–64
(Annual averages in thousand metric tons)

	1925–29	1930–34	1935–39	1940–44	1945–49	1950–54	1955–59	1960–64
Wheat	6,770	6,214	6,634	6,279	5,061	5,325	6,514	6,885
Corn	7,076	7,744	7,892	8,064	4,201	2,709	3,770	4,778
Linseed	1,839	1,738	1,702	1,464	824	509	503	763
Oats	922	956	748	659	828	794	920	784
Barley	321	504	503	571	799	712	1,098	811
Sunflower	1	12	154	619	916	640	561	634
Peanuts	57	75	79	105	123	136	237	311
Sugarcane	5,118	4,060	4,945	5,445	7,233	8,798	10,678	10,659
Cotton (gross)	75	123	214	269	243	386	386	358
Grapes	890	953	1,225	1,346	1,359	1,656	1,884	2,210
Rice	9	16	51	107	125	170	182	178
Tobacco	7	10	16	18	25	35	34	48
Yerba mate	19	46	80	78	107	116	107	—[a]
Potatoes	760	965	663	1,120	1,020	1,363	1,401	1,613
Tomatoes	20	21	42	132	165	251	311	314
Apples	76	88	92	99	149	243	357	418
Oranges	107	122	137	305	253	283	434	510
Tung	–	–	2	6	33	80	106	112
Beef and veal[b]	1,643	1,435	1,667	1,698	1,825	1,858	2,313	2,081
Mutton and lamb[b]	162	188	192	255	273	183	176	169

[a] Dash indicates data not available.
[b] Includes only weight of slaughtered animals. The column for 1960–64 includes data for only 1960–62.

Sources: OECEI, *Economía Agropecuaria Argentina* (Buenos Aires, 1964), 1:49–51; Junta Nacional de Carnes, *Estadísticas Básicas*, p. 6; ECLA, *El Desarrollo Económico de la Argentina*, 2:55–75, and mimeographed appendix, "Estadísticas Agrícolas Básicas"; DNEC, *Boletín de Estadística*, several (1963–65) issues, Junta Nacional de Carnes, *Reseña 1964*.

Table 113: Value of Production According to Size and Tenure
in Pampean Zone, 1960

	Value of production per hectare (1964 pesos)	Distribution of activities (percentage of total output of each product)		
		Wheat	Maize	Cattle
Size of farms (hectares)				
Up to 25	6,866	1	4	1
25 to 100	6,876	14	29	8
100 to 400	5,276	44	40	28
400 to 1,000	4,011	19	11	18
1,000 to 2,500	3,347	11	7	17
Over 2,500	2,843	11	8	27
Form of occupation				
By owners	4,091	48	46	55
By tenants and sharecroppers	4,965	27	25	18
By owners who are also tenants and sharecroppers	4,417	14	16	17
Other forms	4,002	10	13	10

Source: Review of the River Plate 138 (Nov. 19, 1965): 280–81. Original data source is CONADE, based on the 1960 census.

Table 114: Estimated Number of Persons per Automobile[a]
in Different Regions of Argentina, 1964

All Argentina	28
Greater city of Buenos Aires[b]	21
Other large urban centers, Province of Buenos Aires[c]	19
Other, Province of Buenos Aires	21
Province of Córdoba, capital	25
Province of Córdoba, other	21
Province of Santa Fe, capital and city of Rosario	30
Province of Santa Fe, other	20
Province of La Pampa	20
Province of Entre Ríos	34
Rest of the country	66

[a] Includes taxis and jeeps. Data on automobiles refer to registration.
[b] Includes the Federal Capital plus eighteen municipalities in the Province of Buenos Aires (listed in the 1960 census).
[c] Includes Bahía Blanca, Coronel de Marina L. Rosales, La Plata, and General Pueyrredón.

Source: Data from Asociación de Fábricas de Automotores, *Parque de Automotores en la República Argentina, 1963–1964* (Buenos Aires, 1966), pp. 9–38. Data on population obtained from the same source and extrapolations from the 1960 census.

Table 115: Structure of Argentine Exports by Main Customers, 1927–62
(Percentages of total)

	1927–29	1930–34	1935–39	1948–53	1954–58	1959–62
United Kingdom	30	37	33	20	22	19
Holland	11	11	9	5	8	13
Italy	6	5	4	6	7	11
Germany (and West Germany)	14	8	7	5	10	9
United States	9	7	12	17	12	9
Brasil	4	4	6	10	9	6
Belgium	10	10	8	3	3	4
France	7	7	5	6	5	4
Japan	a	a	1	2	3	3
Chile	1	1	1	3	3	3
Other	8	10	14	23	18	19

a Less than 0.5.

Source: Several DNEC publications on foreign trade statistics, mainly *Comercio Exterior*.

Table 116: Composition of Apparent Domestic Absorption at 1935 Prices, 1935–64
(Percentages of total)

	1935–38	1939–45	1946–48	1949–51	1952–55	1956–58	1959–61	1962–64
Private consumption	77.9	78.9	73.4	74.9	74.8	74.9	72.9	74.3
Public consumption	10.9	12.1	14.5	13.3	12.9	12.4	12.7	12.0
Private construction	2.5	3.1	3.7	3.8	3.7	3.9	3.1	2.9
Public construction	3.0	2.2	2.1	3.1	2.8	2.3	3.1	2.8
Transport equipment	0.9	0.3	1.2	0.4	0.4	0.5	1.1	1.3
Other new machinery and equipment	3.4	1.8	3.7	3.2	3.4	3.9	5.1	4.9
Repairs	1.4	1.6	1.4	1.3	2.0	2.1	2.0	1.8
Total	*100.0*	*100.0*	*100.0*	*100.0*	*100.0*	*100.0*	*100.0*	*100.0*
All construction	5.5	5.3	5.8	6.9	6.5	6.2	6.2	5.6
All new machinery and equipment	4.3	2.1	4.9	3.6	3.8	4.4	6.2	6.2
All gross fixed capital formation	11.2	9.0	12.1	11.8	12.3	12.7	14.4	13.6

Sources and method: As in Table 6.4.

Table 117: Composition of Apparent Domestic Absorption at 1960 Prices, 1935–64
(Percentages of total)

	1935–38	1939–45	1946–48	1949–51	1952–55	1956–58	1959–61	1962–64
Private consumption	76.4	79.1	71.6	74.1	74.2	73.7	70.9	72.0
Public consumption	7.6	8.6	10.0	9.3	9.0	8.6	8.7	8.3
Private construction	4.4	5.6	6.5	6.7	6.6	6.9	5.3	4.9
Public construction	3.2	2.4	2.2	3.3	3.0	2.5	3.3	2.9
Transport equipment	2.7	0.9	3.8	1.2	1.2	1.7	3.4	4.1
Other new machinery and equipment	4.9	2.6	5.3	4.7	5.0	5.6	7.3	6.9
Repairs	0.7	0.8	0.7	0.6	1.0	1.0	1.0	0.9
Total	*100.0*	*100.0*	*100.0*	*100.0*	*100.0*	*100.0*	*100.0*	*100.0*
All construction	7.6	8.0	8.7	10.0	9.6	9.4	8.7	7.8
All new machinery and equipment	7.6	3.5	9.1	5.9	6.2	7.3	10.8	11.0
All gross fixed capital formation	16.0	12.3	18.4	16.5	16.8	17.7	20.4	19.7

Sources and method: As in Table 6.4.

Table 118: Indices of Construction Costs in the Federal Capital
Divided by Implicit Prices for the Gross National Product, 1940–63
(1940 = 100)

	Overall index	*Index of construction materials*	*Index of labor costs*	*Index of other costs*
1940	100	100	100	100
1940–45	112	124	93	111
1946–48	148	154	134	159
1949–51	162	161	158	178
1952–55	146	145	143	161
1956–58	141	130	151	152
1959–61	125	125	121	137
1962–63	131	125	135	147

Sources and method: Indices of construction costs obtained from CONADE worksheets and from DNEC, *Boletín de Estadística*, several issues. It was not possible to obtain pre-1940 costs.

Table 119: Wholesale Price Indices for Iron, Steel, and Other Metals
and Their Products Divided by Implicit Prices for the GNP, 1939–64
(1939 = 100)

	Imported	*National*
1939	100	100
1939–45	230	194
1946–48	149	149
1949–51	140	146
1952–55	164	169
1956–58	157	153
1959–61	205	168
1962–64	178	152

Sources and method: Wholesale prices obtained from BCRA, *Boletín Estadístico* (Sept. 1962), and DNEC, *Boletín de Estadística.* The indices for iron and steel and other metals for pre-1956 years were combined using the relative weights shown for the indices with base 1953. It was not possible to get similar data for pre-1939 years.

Table 120: Indices of Implicit Prices for the Domestic Gross Output
of Capital Goods and Related Items Divided by
Implicit Prices for the GNP, 1946–63
(1959–61 = 100)

	1946–48	*1949–51*	*1952–55*	*1956–58*	*1959–61*	*1962–63*
Cement	79	88	85	85	100	99
Rural machinery[a]	87	103	103	94	100	110
Nonelectrical machinery and motors	124	128	111	103	100	102
Electrical motors	109	121	113	107	100	92
Tractors	–	–	86[b]	82	100	84
Automotive vehicles	–	160[c]	142	130	100	84

[a] A branch of the general category of nonelectrical machinery and motors.
[b] Refers only to 1953–55.
[c] Refers only to 1951.

Sources and method: CONADE worksheets. Data for tractors and automotive vehicles start in 1953 and 1951, respectively. Postwar domestic production of those goods started during these years.

Table 121: Prices of Capital Goods in Argentina Relative to Prices for All
Nongovernment Expenditures, June 1962 and 1935–38,
Compared with U.S. Prices (Houston and Los Angeles = 100 in June 1962)

	Buenos Aires June 1962	*Buenos Aires: estimate for 1935–38*
Construction	112	94
New transport equipment	326	109
New machinery and other equipment	254	176

Sources and method: Column 1 from ECLA, "Medición del Nivel de Precios y el
Poder Adquisitivo de la Moneda en América Latina, 1960–62," p. 223. Column 2
was obtained by first dividing the data in Column 1 by corresponding figures for
1962 in Table 6.2. The real prices for 1962 were as follows (1935–38 = 100): Construction, 162; New machinery and other equipment, 153; New transport equipment,
310. The first two relative prices were obtained from BCRA; the one for transport
was obtained by taking the CONADE estimate for 1961 and applying to it the BCRA
estimate for the change in the corresponding relative prices between 1961 and 1962.
Finally, the resulting figures were multiplied by the implicit relative prices for investment goods in the United States (1935–38 = 100). The latter data from the Council
of Economic Advisers, *Economic Report of the President* (Washington, D.C., 1965),
p. 196. The real implicit deflator for all producers' durable goods was applied to both
transport equipment and machinery. The U.S. figures are 136 for construction and
106 for producers' durable equipment.

Table 122: Share of Domestic Production in Total Demand
for Selected Machinery and Equipment in Argentina during 1962

	Percentages of total demand	*Total demand in billion pesos at 1960 prices*
Machine tools	31	3.43
Primary motors	49	1.17
Electrical machinery	69	5.04
Instruments for measurement and control	40	1.15
Pumps and compressors	50	1.34
Universal industrial equipment	96	1.32
Data processing equipment	16	1.16
Tractors and agricultural machinery	96	11.89
Railroad, shipping, and air transport equipment	20	8.82
Equipment for steel industry	0	1.48
Equipment for petroleum, chemical, and petrochemical industries	77	0.61
Equipment for other "dynamic" activities	22	1.65
Equipment for "traditional" industries	24	5.21
Total for goods shown	*52*	*44.27*

Note: According to BCRA, gross capital formation in the form of new machinery and equipment amounted to 131.19 billion pesos at 1960 prices. Of this amount, 38.63 billion pesos were accounted for by automotive vehicles.

Source: Data adapted from Table 2.9 in CONADE, *Plan Nacional de Desarrollo 1965–1969*, p. 243.

Table 123: Changes in Real Wages and the Exchange Rate,
and Increases in Bank Credit, 1946–65
(Percentages)

	Annual percentage change in real hourly wage rates	Annual percentage change in average exchange rate for merchandise trade	Annual percentage change in real average stock of money and quasi money	Increase in banking credit to the public sector as percentage of GNP at current prices	Increase in banking credit to the private sector as percentage of GNP at current prices
1946	5.6	2.0	1.0	6.9	8.4
1947	25.3	1.9	1.1	8.4	7.3
1948	23.5	0	5.7	9.0	7.4
1949	4.9	2.2	1.7	5.2	4.8
1950	−4.4	27.4	1.4	1.4	7.4
1951	−7.0	35.5	−11.8	0.7	7.7
1952	−11.3	5.2	−13.8	1.0	5.4
1953	7.8	−1.9	15.3	4.1	3.7
1954	6.9	3.3	8.1	3.7	5.4
1955	−1.1	11.4	5.5	3.4	5.5
1956	0.5	127.6	−6.3	1.2	6.3
1957	7.2	31.3	0	3.1	4.5
1958	4.7	23.9	−7.0	7.2	6.7
1959	−20.5	164.0	−27.4	4.1	3.1
1960	3.2	9.7	7.3	1.8	5.0
1961	9.7	0	8.5	1.0	4.9
1962	−1.9	36.6	−10.8	2.1	1.5
1963	0.7	22.0	−4.5	3.7	1.9
1964	7.0	1.3	12.2	5.1	3.7
1965	5.1	19.2	3.9	3.4	2.9
Average: "good years"	7.5	10.6	3.8	4.4	5.6
Average: "bad years"	−4.6	55.0	−8.5	2.7	4.3

Sources and method: Hourly money wage rates were obtained from DNEC, *Anuario Estadístico de la Argentina, 1957*, pp. 286–98, and *Boletín de Estadística*, several issues. For 1945–62, hourly wage rates were obtained by dividing the index of all industrial wages paid by the index of man hours worked in industry. For 1962–65, an average of the index of hourly wages for skilled and unskilled workers in the Federal Capital was used. Both series were deflated by the cost of living index to obtain real hourly wage rates. Average exchange rate for merchandise trade was obtained by dividing the peso value of imports plus exports by their dollar value. Data obtained from *International Financial Statistics*, several issues. Data on banking credit and money and quasi money from BCRA, *Boletín Estadístico*, and BCRA, *Estadísticas Monetarias y Bancarias, Años 1940–1960* (Buenos Aires, June 1962). Data on money and quasi money for a given year were obtained by averaging twelve months' figures.

Table 124: Annual Rates of Inflation, 1936–66
(Percentage changes from average of previous year)

Year	*Buenos Aires cost of living*	*Overall wholesale prices*	*Gross National Product implicit prices*
1936	8.5	2.3	1.6
1937	2.6	13.5	2.4
1938	−0.7	−6.3	3.5
1939	1.6	2.6	2.2
1940	2.2	6.6	1.8
1941	2.6	9.6	2.9
1942	5.7	25.5	10.4
1943	1.1	10.1	5.3
1944	−0.3	8.2	2.1
1945	19.7	9.0	14.9
1946	17.7	15.8	20.6
1947	13.5	3.5	20.0
1948	13.1	15.5	16.7
1949	31.1	23.0	26.1
1950	25.5	20.2	19.5
1951	36.7	49.1	36.6
1952	38.7	31.2	28.3
1953	4.0	11.6	6.1
1954	3.8	3.2	8.7
1955	12.3	8.9	10.1
1956	13.4	26.0	27.1
1957	24.7	24.1	19.0
1958	31.6	31.0	32.3
1959	113.7	133.5	101.9
1960	27.3	15.7	19.6
1961	13.5	8.3	11.5
1962	28.1	30.4	27.3
1963	24.1	28.7	26.0
1964	22.1	26.2	24.8
1965	28.6	23.9	28.5
1966	32.3	20.0	—[a]
Average: "good years"	19.1	18.2	19.6
Average: "bad years"	38.4	41.9	36.6
Average 1946–66	26.5	26.5	25.5

[a] Dash indicates data not available.

Sources and method: Year-to-year percentage changes obtained by comparing yearly averages for each index. Cost of living indices from DNEC, *Costo del Nivel de Vida en la Capital Federal*, pp. 44–51, and *Boletín de Estadística*. Wholesale prices obtained from BCRA, *Boletín Estadístico* (Sept. 1962), pp. 51–62; *Anuario Geográfico*, p. 369; and from DNEC, *Boletín de Estadística*. Implicit prices for the GNP obtained from O.S., pp. 156–57, and from BCRA, p. 57. It may be noted that both the cost of living and the GNP deflator include prices fixed by government fiat (rents, public utility rates, etc.).

Table 125: Argentine Merchandise Imports, 1947–66
(Billion pesos, at 1960 prices)

Year	All merchandise imports	Imports of capital goods	Other imports	All imports of goods and services
1947	138.05	–	–	152.37
1948	141.45	57.04	84.41	155.11
1949	98.32	34.14	64.18	109.49
1950	89.27	27.98	61.28	93.75
1951	97.87	30.31	77.66	105.38
1952	71.42	26.94	54.71	77.67
1953	55.96	21.75	42.63	63.64
1954	75.72	19.16	55.52	83.49
1955	89.94	19.95	67.07	100.37
1956	82.66	20.01	63.34	89.76
1957	93.41	20.99	80.93	100.14
1958	97.54	19.86	77.26	104.47
1959	84.32	19.27	62.74	92.50
1960	103.33	35.13	68.20	114.05
1961	124.00	40.49	83.39	135.61
1962	113.25	49.24	63.66	130.25
1963	84.32	35.01	51.26	101.39
1964	91.76	27.46	67.05	117.70
1965	100.85	–	–	116.40
1966	–	–	–	111.90

Sources and method: The total import quantum index published in DNEC, *Boletín de Estadística* (available for 1951–65), was linked (at 1951) with a similar index estimated by ECLA for 1947–51. Quantum indices for capital goods imports and other imports were also obtained from ECLA (*Statistical Bulletin for Latin America*, several issues, and mimeographed appendices to *El Desarrollo Económico de la Argentina*). It may be noted that the figures for imports of capital goods plus those for other imports often do not add up to total imports. The discrepancy, however, is substantial only for 1951–53. Rather than force series from different sources to become compatible, it was preferred to let these discrepancies remain. Quantum indices were converted to pesos using 1960 figures on imports. All imports of goods and services have been taken directly from BCRA (revised national accounts).

Table 126: Income and Expenditure Variables "Explaining" the Level of
All Merchandise Imports, 1947–66
(Billion pesos, at 1960 prices)

	Total absorption	Con- sumption	Gross investment	Gross investment in new machinery and equipment	Wage income	Gross nonwage income
1947	771.79	632.60	139.19	77.95	258.52	414.20
1948	799.78	657.36	142.42	70.23	301.73	417.54
1949	743.16	640.05	103.11	41.55	319.52	353.04
1950	712.89	611.92	100.97	34.88	319.89	344.73
1951	772.52	624.37	148.15	54.64	305.86	373.52
1952	716.87	590.72	126.15	45.84	312.89	324.84
1953	723.79	588.67	135.12	42.69	321.01	359.94
1954	765.77	635.69	130.09	41.40	345.20	372.91
1955	844.12	697.76	146.36	57.47	353.57	424.72
1956	835.50	698.31	137.18	63.22	344.62	423.25
1957	886.99	736.38	150.62	66.60	346.93	451.72
1958	951.90	788.57	163.33	66.16	395.82	478.81
1959	880.73	731.89	148.84	57.47	328.35	507.52
1960	972.80	754.46	218.33	111.70	343.81	517.54
1961	1069.42	828.21	241.21	143.96	379.92	519.38
1962	1011.44	795.33	216.11	131.19	360.39	507.47
1963	944.46	777.09	167.37	96.40	342.33	491.02
1964	1047.03	846.32	200.71	104.36	369.72	530.30
1965	1124.20	906.60	217.60	107.20	398.45	571.50
1966	1106.90	909.50	197.40	106.30	–	–

Sources and method: Data obtained from the standard sources for national accounts listed in Table 7.1. The first four columns are from BCRA, the last two from CONADE. Wage and nonwage income for 1962–65 are preliminary; the figures for 1947–49 were obtained by linking CONADE data with those of O.S.

Table 127: Other Variables "Explaining" the Level of
All Merchandise Imports, 1947–66

Year	Capacity in import competing sector (billion 1960 pesos)	Relative prices of imported goods (1939 = 100)	Index of quantitative restrictions
1947	88.24	121.3	421.4
1948	94.03	119.0	147.2
1949	94.29	112.9	51.6
1950	98.56	107.0	24.6
1951	101.53	116.7	40.6
1952	103.20	111.4	14.0
1953	105.08	107.0	−0.3
1954	111.63	101.8	23.9
1955	122.08	103.2	24.6
1956	124.85	138.5	6.8
1957	136.10	124.0	4.4
1958	150.28	116.8	−1.0
1959	153.23	143.9	−18.7
1960	174.87	137.7	−9.8
1961	194.05	122.0	3.9
1962	198.96	126.9	−1.0
1963	198.96	122.7	−18.2
1964	217.60	111.5	−3.5
1965	242.12	109.7	−4.8
1966	245.14	109.8	7.7

Sources and method: Column 1 was calculated as explained in essay 7. Basic data obtained from BCRA. Column 2 represents an index formed by the ratio of wholesale prices of all imported goods to wholesale prices of nonrural domestic goods; data as in Tables 124 and 129. Column 3 obtained as explained in essay 7.

Table 128: Other Variables "Explaining" the Level of Imports of Capital Goods
and Other Goods, 1948–66
(Billion pesos at 1960 prices)

Year	Capacity in domestic production of new machinery and equipment	Value added in manufacturing	Gross Domestic Product at factor cost
1948	15.24	201.99	673.00
1949	15.24	187.94	642.24
1950	15.89	191.69	652.26
1951	18.21	195.68	678.15
1952	18.41	191.08	635.30
1953	19.35	191.22	679.86
1954	22.30	204.26	705.56
1955	30.37	227.09	753.96
1956	33.35	238.35	766.75
1957	37.84	257.21	808.82
1958	41.79	282.43	987.08
1959	42.10	260.01	816.87
1960	70.96	284.42	882.19
1961	88.19	311.91	944.03
1962	88.19	297.80	926.57
1963	88.19	284.14	893.36
1964	88.19	327.15	965.52
1965	–	368.70	1048.20
1966	–	363.90	1042.70

Sources: As in Table 127.

Table 129: Semestral Percentage Changes in Selected Price Indices, 1948–65

Year and semester	All wholesale prices	Rural wholesale prices	Nonrural domestic wholesale prices	Imported wholesale prices	Buenos Aires cost of living
1948/2	10.9	5.6	14.3	10.6	10.6
1949/1	11.4	6.9	13.4	13.3	15.8
/2	10.2	7.8	13.8	2.6	15.5
1950/1	7.4	3.9	9.4	6.8	10.2
/2	13.4	16.2	12.0	13.2	12.6
1951/1	26.6	34.6	20.4	34.1	14.9
/2	21.7	10.6	26.8	26.3	24.7
1952/1	14.0	6.4	17.8	14.4	21.8
/2	9.6	12.0	10.2	4.0	5.2
1953/1	6.3	13.3	4.1	2.4	2.4
/2	1.8	2.2	1.9	0.4	−2.0
1954/1	−0.5	−1.7	.0	−1.6	0.1
/2	5.4	3.1	6.6	−0.1	9.6
1955/1	3.5	−0.2	4.5	5.7	5.5
/2	5.3	8.0	3.9	11.3	3.5
1956/1	16.2	25.4	10.4	46.4	6.8
/2	11.4	17.8	9.0	11.4	8.9
1957/1	9.1	5.9	11.0	1.0	10.7
/2	16.1	19.1	15.2	8.1	16.1
1958/1	5.4	1.2	7.4	3.1	8.0
/2	31.6	43.1	27.4	31.6	26.8
1959/1	81.0	86.6	76.7	113.4	65.1
/2	27.2	28.3	26.9	24.8	31.5
1960/1	2.6	−1.1	4.2	3.4	10.4
/2	1.0	2.6	0.5	−2.2	3.0
1961/1	2.7	−1.6	5.0	−2.3	5.8
/2	9.8	12.8	9.2	0.1	11.4
1962/1	10.4	7.6	11.4	13.9	10.7
/2	25.6	40.1	19.2	33.8	19.5
1963/1	9.5	7.4	10.9	5.1	8.2
/2	11.2	15.6	9.7	2.1	10.7
1964/1	14.7	16.1	14.5	8.0	12.1
/2	9.1	7.0	10.2	8.9	7.4
1965/1	10.2	−1.2	15.3	16.6	13.2
/2	15.4	14.5	15.9	13.4	19.4

Sources: Semestral price indices were constructed from data found in the sources listed in Table 124.

Table 130: Semestral Percentage Changes in Variables
"Explaining" Inflation, 1948–65

Year and semester	Money supply	Money plus quasi money	Real supplies	Average merchandise exchange rate	Hourly money wage rates
1948/2	13.7	11.4	−4.7	0	4.9
1949/1	16.1	14.8	−6.4	0	29.8
/2	10.3	11.6	−0.6	4.3	7.2
1950/1	12.9	10.5	−2.0	9.4	17.1
/2	11.0	8.1	3.4	31.0	5.4
1951/1	16.1	12.5	−0.5	8.5	17.2
/2	7.6	6.1	7.8	17.8	6.8
1952/1	5.6	4.8	−5.0	−4.4	15.5
/2	5.5	5.0	−15.0	4.0	9.0
1953/1	17.2	15.3	9.9	4.4	4.3
/2	7.3	7.2	7.1	−14.8	−1.6
1954/1	10.1	10.5	−3.5	11.3	5.7
/2	5.3	5.5	12.4	0	17.3
1955/1	10.9	10.8	4.0	1.2	3.5
/2	4.5	4.2	−3.4	20.3	−0.5
1956/1	12.9	13.1	5.5	88.8	12.5
/2	4.6	6.0	−6.6	20.3	2.0
1957/1	13.9	14.1	7.5	18.3	41.3
/2	1.1	2.7	4.3	3.7	−9.1
1958/1	10.8	12.0	3.2	4.4	29.1
/2	17.7	16.9	2.9	32.6	23.2
1959/1	36.9	30.9	−5.8	108.8	44.4
/2	10.5	7.7	−4.1	19.4	11.8
1960/1	19.1	17.7	7.0	2.1	19.5
/2	9.6	10.3	8.8	0	7.8
1961/1	11.1	12.5	0.8	0	14.8
/2	3.6	5.0	6.1	0.1	9.0
1962/1	9.6	9.4	0.7	13.7	17.9
/2	1.1	2.6	−1.1	40.4	8.4
1963/1	9.0	10.8	−5.0	2.9	14.1
/2	12.0	14.4	11.1	2.7	9.8
1964/1	20.9	21.1	1.2	−3.3	15.3
/2	14.9	16.7	4.3	6.8	14.9
1965/1	16.2	17.6	1.1	9.7	17.6
/2	8.9	11.0	6.4	10.2	15.2

Sources and method: Semestral series for money and quasi money were obtained by averaging end-of-the-month data found in the sources listed in Table 123. Semestral series for "real supplies," including real gross domestic product plus merchandise imports, were built up from BCRA data (GDP) and import series listed in Table 125. As semestral data are not available for GDP, they were estimated using the (now obsolete) index of industrial production as a guide. Semestral average merchandise

Table 130—*Continued*

exchange rates were computed for 1955–65 from data in the *International Financial Statistics* of the International Monetary Fund. For 1948–55 they were estimated on the basis of annual data (also found in the *I.F.S.*) and monthly trade returns of the Argentine government. The method of computation was to divide the sum of imports and exports valued in pesos over the same sum valued in dollars. Hourly money wage rates for 1948–62 were obtained from industrial data of DNEC, *Boletín de Estadística*. To avoid excessive seasonal fluctuations, in the computation of semestral indices, the months of December and January were left out (they often included end-of-year bonuses). For 1962–65, semestral indices for wage rates were based on data on collective agreements also published in *Boletín de Estadística*. No further efforts were made to "take out" seasonality in the money and wage variables, on the supposition that the remaining seasonality could be expected to be reflected also in price indices. When a seasonal "dummy variable" was introduced in equations similar to those shown in essay 7, its coefficient was found to be statistically insignificant in all equations. The introduction of such a "dummy variable," however, improved slightly the performance of the money variables $(X_6)_t$ and $(X_7)_t$ in the equations, although the coefficients for these variables remain less than twice the size of their standard errors.

Table 131: Income Velocity of Money and Quasi Money in Argentina, 1941–65

| | *Income velocity of money* | | *Income velocity of money plus quasi money* | |
	A	B	A	B
1941	4.61	–	2.25	–
1942	4.15	–	2.17	–
1943	3.83	–	2.04	–
1944	3.50	–	1.94	–
1945	3.27	–	1.85	–
1946	3.53	–	2.05	–
1947	3.91	–	2.35	–
1948	3.74	–	2.34	–
1949	3.45	–	2.20	–
1950	3.27	3.55	2.15	2.33
1951	–	3.96	–	2.73
1952	–	4.14	–	2.90
1953	–	3.82	–	2.73
1954	–	3.65	–	2.61
1955	–	3.71	–	2.65
1956	–	3.99	–	2.83
1957	–	4.25	–	2.96
1958	–	4.99	–	3.43
1959	–	6.13	–	4.48
1960	–	6.07	–	4.53
1961	–	6.11	–	4.46
1962	–	6.71	–	4.83
1963	–	7.10	–	4.94
1964	–	7.04	–	4.80
1965	–	7.49	–	4.96

Sources and method: "Income velocity" is defined as the ratio of the GNP at current market prices to the *average* money supply (or money plus quasi money) in a given year. The average money supply was obtained by averaging the money supply at the end of the twelve months of each year. Columns *A* were based on the old National Accounts (O.S.); columns *B* used the new BCRA estimates for the national accounts. Data on the money supply were obtained as in Table 123, above.

Table 132: Indices of Selected Real Prices, 1940–65
(1935–39 = 100)

	Real average merchandise exchange rate	*Real controlled housing rents*	*Real electricity rates to households*	*Real rates of public transportation*
1940	107	101	81	93
1941	109	99	79	91
1942	119	89	75	82
1943	122	81	77	78
1944	117	66	82	76
1945	103	81	73	67
1946	96	67	57	55
1947	90	56	48	46
1948	83	48	45	39
1949	67	38	43	32
1950	72	35	36	62
1951	77	25	27	45
1952	64	20	27	47
1953	60	19	28	50
1954	58	17	26	46
1955	59	16	25	41
1956	109	12	20	47
1957	125	10	19	46
1958	120	8	19	35
1959	159	4	30	34
1960	148	7	22	43
1961	134	6	20	46
1962	145	5	21	61
1963	143	4	22	—[a]
1964	119	4	18	–
1965	112	3	20	–

[a] Dash indicates data not available.

Sources and method: All nominal price indices were divided by the GNP deflator to obtain "real" prices. The index for the nominal average exchange rate (expressed as pesos per one U.S. dollar) was also *multiplied* by the deflator for the United States GNP to obtain the "real" exchange rate. Average exchange rate was obtained from CONADE worksheets for 1935–48 and from *International Financial Statistics*, for 1948–65. Nominal price indices for household rents and electricity were obtained from DNEC, *Costo del Nivel de Vida en la Capital Federal*, pp. 44–51, and *Boletín de Estadística*, several issues. Rates for public transportation are those which help to make up the cost of living index; they were obtained from CONADE.

Table 133: Indices of Average Urban Real Wage Rates and
Per Capita Real GNP, 1939–65
(1943 = 100)

Year	Real wage rates	Per capita GNP		Year	Real wage rates	Per capita GNP
1939	100	98		1953	154	109
1940	97	92		1954	165	111
1941	97	94		1955	163	116
1942	97	99		1956	164	114
1943	100	100		1957	176	117
1944	111	108		1958	184	124
1945	106	101		1959	146	115
1946	112	112		1960	151	123
1947	140	131		1961	166	129
1948	173	130		1962	163	123
1949	181	116		1963	164	118
1950	173	113		1964	175	127
1951	161	114		1965	184	135
1952	143	103				

Five year averages:	Real wage rates	Per capita GNP
1940–44	100	99
1945–49	142	118
1950–54	159	110
1955–59	166	117
1960–64	164	124

Sources and method: Wage rates for 1939–43 refer to wages per worker; for 1943–65 they refer to hourly wage rates. Data on wages and calculation of real wages as in Table 123. GNP obtained from the source listed in Table 7.1 (BCRA). It should be noted that GNP figures include a correction for changes in terms of trade. BCRA data show an increase in the real GDP of 107 percent between 1935–39 and 1960–64, and an increase of 100 percent for the real GNP for the same period. Population data obtained from ECLA, *Statistical Bulletin for Latin America*, 3:5–6. Between 1935–39 and 1960–64 population increased by 58 percent.

Table 134: Number of Workers and Other Employees Per Industrial Establishment

	1935 census	1939 census	1943 census	1946 census	1948 census	1950 census	1954 census	1957 census
All manufacturing	11.7	11.8	13.7	12.4	12.8	12.7	8.2	8.9
Foodstuffs and beverages	9.8	10.5	13.2	12.9	13.0	13.1	10.2	10.3
Tobacco	60.7	65.0	82.5	94.5	104.0	107.8	100.0	115.7
Textiles	67.4	65.8	77.7	61.7	61.3	57.8	27.6	27.8
Clothing	7.6	6.3	6.9	6.4	6.5	5.8	4.1	4.4
Wood products	8.1	9.1	12.5	10.6	9.1	8.3	5.4	4.9
Paper and cardboard	34.3	39.2	39.0	36.7	34.8	33.3	21.6	25.2
Printing and publishing	12.3	12.8	13.3	14.4	14.1	13.9	9.9	10.3
Chemical products	16.6	18.5	21.8	24.9	27.2	30.1	22.5	25.2
Petroleum refining	88.0	80.0	72.9	112.0	160.0	178.7	115.7	127.5
Rubber products	72.0	115.0	52.2	62.3	75.7	67.4	29.6	31.3
Leather products	18.0	16.7	16.8	11.8	10.5	9.6	5.2	5.3
Stone, glass, and ceramics	8.1	9.8	12.5	10.1	11.6	12.6	5.9	6.6
Metals	11.3	13.2	14.3	11.6	11.1	10.5	7.3	8.9
Vehicles and machinery	10.0	8.5	8.6	8.4	8.7	8.4	6.7	6.6
Electrical machinery and appliances	10.0	11.0	11.9	11.1	13.5	14.5	9.5	12.2
Other	9.1	9.7	11.5	8.8	7.8	7.7	4.7	4.6
Electricity and gas	18.3	21.1	22.9	23.8	26.8	28.3	22.7	—[a]
Extractive activities	65.0	56.8	61.9	50.0	52.1	38.1	13.7	—

[a] Dash indicates data not available.

Sources and method: Industrial censuses and industrial statistics of the DNEC. Data for 1939, 1943, 1948, and 1950 are not strictly speaking from comprehensive censuses; they were gathered on the basis of the industries covered in the 1935 and 1946 censuses. "Workers and employees" include members of the family of the owners working in the establishment. The figures for the 1957 census were obtained from CONADE elaborations of that census, which is of doubtful reliability.

Table 135: Number of Workers per Industrial Establishment
(Establishments classified according to date of founding)

Date of founding:	*1935* census	*1939* census	*1946* census	*1954* census
Before 1900	29.7	35.2	42.0	56.6
1901–10	18.2	18.9	24.3	33.0
1911–20	13.8	13.8	14.8	16.4
1921–25	9.3	9.9	12.1	13.1
1926–30	7.1	7.6	9.0	9.8
1931–35	5.9	8.0	9.6	11.2
1936–39	–	6.3	–	–
1936–41	–	–	8.2	–
1942–46	–	–	6.0	–
1936–40	–	–	–	8.0
1941–45	–	–	–	7.1
1946–50	–	–	–	4.8
1950–53	–	–	–	2.3
Unknown	17.9	15.8	20.1	11.5
All industry	*11.6*	*11.5*	*10.9*	*7.0*

Note: "Industrial establishments" include, besides manufacturing, gas and electricity plants and most mining activities. "Workers" include *only* "blue collar" workers.

Sources: DNEC, Industrial censuses of 1935, 1939, 1946, and 1954.

Table 136: Indices of Manufacturing Production in 1950
(1943 = 100)

	O.S.	New BCRA	New CONADE	Schwartz estimate
All manufacturing	*148*	*122*	*148*	*167*
Foodstuffs and drinks	112	90	111	114
Tobacco	139	139	148	135
Textiles	153	127	180	162
Clothing	137	136	170	138
Wood products	137	123	157	251
Paper and cardboard	136	132	137	140
Printing and publishing	165	141	158	151
Chemicals	165	119	148	159
Petroleum refining	172	172	178	186
Rubber products	497	330	523	593
Leather products	103	104	122	90
Stone, earth, and ceramics	139	129	148	147
Metals excluding machinery	216	215	253	290
Vehicles and machinery, excluding electrical	128	129	199	150
Electrical machinery and appliances	316	321	306	369
Others	180	$\left\{137\right\}$	150	185
Handicrafts	–		127	–

Sources: "Schwartz estimate" obtained from Appendix M of Hugh H. Schwartz, "The Argentine Experience with Industrial Credit and Protection Incentives, 1943–1958," Ph.D. thesis at Yale University, 1967. Other sources as explained in the introduction to this Statistical Appendix.

Index

Economic Growth Center Book Publications

*Werner Baer, *Industrialization and Economic Development in Brazil* (1965).

Werner Baer and Isaac Kerstenetzky, eds., *Inflation and Growth in Latin America* (1964).

*Bela A. Balassa, *Trade Prospects for Developing Countries* (1964).

Carlos F. Díaz Alejandro, *Essays on the Economic History of the Argentine Republic* (1970).

*John C. H. Fei and Gustav Ranis, *Development of Labor Surplus Economy: Theory and Policy* (1964).

*Gerald K. Helleiner, *Peasant Agriculture, Government, and Economic Growth in Nigeria* (1966).

*Lawrence R. Klein and Kazushi Ohkawa, eds., *Economic Growth: The Japanese Experience since the Meiji Era* (1968).

*A. Lamfalussy, *The United Kingdom and the Six* (1963).

*Markos J. Mamalakis and Clark W. Reynolds, *Essays on the Chilean Economy* (1965).

*Donald C. Mead, *Growth and Structural Change in the Egyptian Economy* (1967).

*Richard Moorsteen and Raymond P. Powell, *The Soviet Capital Stock* (1966).

*Frederic L. Pryor, *Public Expenditures in Communist and Capitalist Nations* (1968).

Clark W. Reynolds, *The Mexican Economy: Twentieth-Century Structure and Growth* (1970).

*Lloyd G. Reynolds and Peter Gregory, *Wages, Productivity, and Industrialization in Puerto Rico* (1965).

*Donald R. Snodgrass, *Ceylon: An Export Economy in Transition* (1966).

* Available from Richard D. Irwin, Inc., 1818 Ridge Rd., Homewood, Ill. 60430.